W9-BFP-090
USED

Family Science

WESLEY R. BURR
BRIGHAM YOUNG UNIVERSITY

RANDAL D. DAY
WASHINGTON STATE UNIVERSITY

KATHLEEN S. BAHR
BRIGHAM YOUNG UNIVERSITY

Brooks/Cole Publishing Company
Pacific Grove, California

Brooks/Cole Publishing Company
A Division of Wadsworth, Inc.

Printed in the United States of America
10 9 8 7 6 5 4 3 2 1

Library of Congress Cataloging-in-Publication Data
Burr, Wesley R., [date]
Family science / Wesley R. Burr, Randal D. Day, Kathleen S. Bahr.
p. cm.
Includes bibliographical references and index.
ISBN 0-534-14268-0
1. Family. 2. Family—Research. I. Day, Randal D., [date].
II. Bahr, Kathleen S., [date]. III. Title.
HQ518.B87 1993
306.85—dc20 92-29840
CIP

Sponsoring Editor: *Vicki Knight*
Marketing Representative: *Hester Winn*
Editorial Associate: *Heather L. Graeve*
Production Editors: *Kay Mikel and Kirk Bomont*
Manuscript Editor: *Judith Johnstone*
Permissions Editor: *Karen Wootten*
Cover and Interior Design: *Lisa Berman*
Art Coordinator: *Lisa Torri*
Interior Illustration: *Hierographics*
Photo Coordinator: *Larry Molmud*
Photo Researcher: *Sue C. Howard*
Typesetting: *Harrison Typesetting, Inc.*
Printing and Binding: *R. R. Donnelley & Sons, Crawfordsville, Indiana*
(Credits continue on page 526.)

Preface

When we study something as complicated as families, the perspective we begin with influences what we think, what we see, and what we do. For example, if we begin with a psychological perspective, we focus on the role of mental and emotional processes. If we begin with a historical, sociological, or economic perspective, we use different terms, ask different questions, emphasize different things, and think in different ways. Therefore, it is important to know which perspective is used in a book about families.

This book uses a family science perspective. Family science differs from other perspectives in that we start with familial processes rather than psychological, social, historical, or economic processes. We try to get inside the family realm and think first and primarily about what families are like and what is happening when they are enabling or disabling, healthy or unhealthy, successful or unsuccessful. When we begin with this approach we find ourselves thinking about a different set of concepts, including generational alliances, differentiation of self, emotional triangles, developmental tasks, analogic messages, boundaries, emotional distance, family paradigms, and experiential aspects of mothering.

The family science perspective is a relatively new field in academia. It began in the middle decades of the twentieth century when four groups of scholars began to concentrate on family processes. The four groups were family therapists, scholars in child development and family relations departments, family-oriented feminists, and home economists. Each of these groups began to develop ideas different from those of the older disciplines. Each group made important contributions to how we think about families, but at first they were fairly independent and autonomous, and had little contact with each other. In recent decades, however, scholars have been trying to integrate the main ideas in these different schools of thought, and they have called the integrated perspective *family science*. This book is part of the attempt to integrate these ideas, and it is the first text that uses this perspective and tries to integrate a large number of the ideas that have been developed in these four areas of scholarship.

The field of family science is so new that many of the ideas in it are tentative and evolving. This means we should view the ideas in this book as emerging knowledge that is still being refined and tested. The authors believe the ideas in this book add in important ways to the ideas that have been discovered in older fields, and we hope they will be useful to educators, counselors, policymakers, and family members. We found it an exhilarating educational experience to gather and integrate the ideas.

This book is a joint effort, in that the three of us have worked on it for several years. We believe you would appreciate knowing something about the values and goals we've brought to this book. First, how do we view the family realm? We think the family is an important part of everyone's life—that, in fact, it is much more important than most of us realize. We also believe that what happens in families has a much greater role in the social problems of our day than has been recognized. The drug abuse problem is fundamentally a problem in our homes. The crime problem is fundamentally a problem in our homes. The problems of war, political unrest, and even economics are intricately intertwined with our homes. As Barbara Bush has often said when she's asked about the 1990s, "What happens in your house makes more difference than what happens in the White House."

A second belief we bring to this book is, to paraphrase Dickens in *A Tale of Two Cities*, **the family realm is the best of human life and it is the worst of human life**. Regarding the best parts, it is in family life that we experience some of the deepest joys and greatest pleasures that are possible. The home is also a crucible that refines and tests and helps us grow and mature in ways that are noble and great and wonderful. If we are wise in the way we manage this precious part of our lives, it can provide satisfactions, fulfillments, love, security, sense of belonging, and other beauties and riches that cannot be attained outside the family realm.

As for the worst parts, it is in families that the ugliest side of humans also flourishes. More murders are committed in families than anyplace else. Physical abuse is all too common. The privacy that allows intimacy and the deepest love also allows sexual and emotional abuse. Family life is the source of some of the deepest frustration, the most intense misery, the cruelest abuse, and the most despicable exploitation that humans ever experience.

There are several reasons the negative side of family life is as devastating as the positive side is good. It is as though there is a "law of opposition." The greater good and beauty that is possible because of the unique nature of the family realm also allows greater evil and ugliness. Family processes have a *permanence* and an *emotionality* that allow, on the one hand, a unique and unparalleled depth in beautiful things like love, peace, and beauty and, on the other hand, unique and unparalleled opportunities for excess and abuse.

We are presenting the ideas in this book to help readers find ways to enhance the positive aspects of family life, avoid the undesirable aspects that can be avoided, and more effectively manage the challenges and obstacles that cannot be avoided. Some of the positive things that can come from family life are intimacy that is not stifling, bonds without bondage, meaning and purpose, growth and progress, maturation and beauty, and enough security and stability that we have a sense of being in a healthy home. We want to help avert violence, exploitation, dominance, abuses, tyranny, negligence, and other forms of excess that bring pain, hurt, disappointment, and inhumanity.

One of our goals is to help families—and those who help families—attain the positive parts of the family realm and avoid the undesirable parts. Thus, this book is written *to* and *for* helpers. It is written to and for people who want to help families be more enabling, healthy, and successful. Each of us can help in many ways. We can help our own families and our friends, and we can help in our professions and avocations.

ACKNOWLEDGMENTS

We are grateful for the contributions of our families, colleagues, students, and friends who have assisted us in our intellectual journey, and we look forward to additional growth because of our interaction with each of them. In particular, there are three groups of colleagues who have given us valuable direction and support. First are those upon whose shoulders we stand. This includes the many scholars whose work we use in this book, as well as colleagues Reuben Hill, Beatrice Paolucci, Gerhard Neubeck, and Murray Straus, who provided invaluable mentorship and guidance. The second group are those who have directly impacted this volume with ideas, support, encouragement, reactions, and suggestions. They include Howard Bahr, Ivan Beutler, Carlfred Broderick, Owen Cahoon, Larry Constantine, Tom Draper, Don Herrin, Tom Holman, David Klein, Geoffrey Leigh, Joel Moss, Marvin Prigmore, Sandra Smith, Elizabeth Snowden, Robert Snowden, and Barbara Vance. Third, we have been privileged to have a resourceful group of assistants who have helped with various parts of the project. They include graduate assistants Robert G. Burr, who is the senior author of the stress chapter, and Diane Fish, who helped in the development of the *Instructor's Guide* that accompanies this book. Others who assisted were Nancy Ahlander, John Harding, Paul Martin, Jacqueline de Gaston, Dynette Reynolds, and John Beal. Also, we appreciate the help of Vicki Knight at Brooks/Cole, and of Ruth Burr, Larri-Lea Day, Kyle Kimzey, Debbie Greco, Tiffanie Crowley, and Jill Slayden, who provided secretarial, editorial, and proofreading assistance.

Finally, we'd like to thank the reviewers who critiqued the manuscript: Douglas A. Abbott, University of Nebraska at Omaha; Scot M. Allgood, Auburn University; Debra L. Berke, University of Delaware; Margaret M. Bubolz, Michigan State University; Janet Hare, Oregon State University; Thomas Holman, Brigham Young University; and Sylvia Stalmaker, Southwest Texas State University.

Wesley R. Burr
Randal D. Day
Kathleen S. Bahr

Brief Contents

Contents

7 // *Family Development* 180

8 // *Rules* 206

Part I

The Context in Studying Families

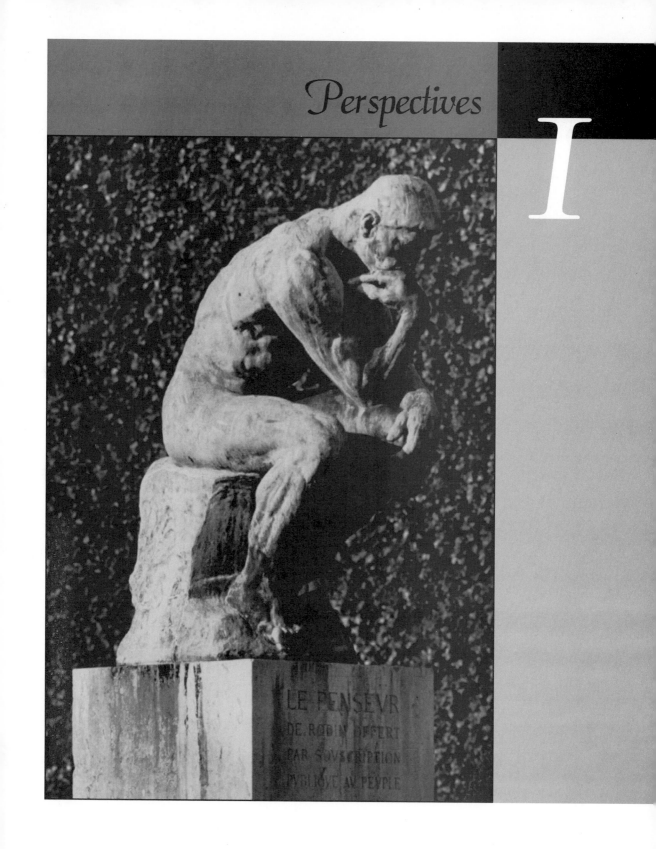

Perspectives

I

Main Ideas

1 // The perspective, or set of assumptions, from which scholars work influences how they get and use knowledge.

2 // Ancient ideas continue to influence modern perspectives.

3 // Economics, anthropology, psychology, and sociology are four major social science disciplines that have brought unique perspectives and significant contributions to knowledge about the family.

4 // The family science perspective is a new one created by the coalescence of several family-related specialties: family therapy, child development and family relations (CDFR), family resource management, and women's studies (feminism).

5 // The family science perspective represents a unique set of assumptions that emphasize the family as a whole and how its members perceive it and each other, as well as their family's place in society.

There is a delightful story about six blind men from Indostan who wanted to know what elephants are like (see Box 1.1). It helps us understand a principle that is important when we try to study something as complex as families:

Principle *The perspective from which scholars work influences how they get and use knowledge.*

For example, it influences the part of reality they think about, the questions they ask, the methods they use to try to answer their questions, and the way they try to apply their knowledge.

The term **perspective** refers to the way of thinking, or basic assumptions, people make about reality. In the elephant analogy, each individual used the

> "Man can fail to see what is in front of his eyes unless it fits into his theoretical frame of reference."
>
> —MURRAY BOWEN, 1978, P. 105

information he had to form a perspective about what elephants are like, and it became his way of thinking about that part of his reality. There are several synonyms for the term *perspective*. Scholars sometimes call it a "frame of reference." It also is sometimes called a "paradigm" or "paradigmatic view" (Kuhn, 1970).

Many different perspectives are used to study the family in our modern society. For example, some use a legal perspective, and others a theological perspective. The artistic community and the business community each have a unique perspective. In the academic community, some scholars study the family from the perspective of the humanities or history. Others have a philosophical perspective, and still others study the family from a scientific perspective.

All perspectives are distinctive ways of thinking, each has a limited point of

Box 1.1
The Blind Men and the Elephant
—J. G. Saxe

It was six men of Indostan
To learning much inclined,
Who went to see the elephant
(Though all of them were blind);
That each by observation
Might satisfy his mind.

The first approached the elephant,
And happening to fall
Against his broad and sturdy side,
At once began to bawl:
"God bless, me! But the elephant
Is very like a wall!"

The second, feeling of the tusk, cried
"Ho! What have we here,
So very round and smooth and sharp?
To me 'tis very clear
This wonder of an elephant
Is very like a spear!"

The third approached the animal
And, happening to take
The squirming trunk within his hands,
Then boldly up he spake:
"I see," quoth he, "the elephant
Is very like a snake."

The fourth reached out an eager hand
And felt about the knee.
"What most this wondrous beast is like,
Is oh so plain," quoth he,
"'Tis clear enough the elephant
Is very like a tree!"

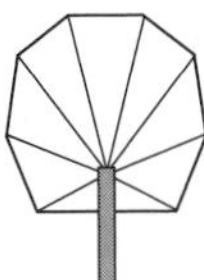

The fifth, who chanced to touch the ear,
Said, "E'en the blindest man
Can tell what this resembles most.
Deny the fact who can
This marvel of an elephant
Is very like a fan!"

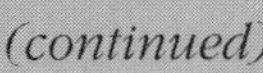
(continued)

Box 1.1
(continued)

The sixth no sooner had begun
About the beast to grope,
Than, seizing on the swinging tail
That fell within his scope,
"I see," quoth he, "The elephant
Is very like a rope!"

These six blind men of
Indostan
Disputed loud and long,
Each in his own opinion
Exceeding stiff and strong.
Though each was right in
how he thought,
They all were partly wrong.

And all who try to use their mind
On tasks both large and small,
Would best themselves and others too,
If they would but recall,
One view of things can help the mind,
But will not give it all.

view, and none are all-encompassing. Each perspective sees only the part of the elephant that its scholars care about. This is both an advantage and disadvantage. By focusing on a particular part of reality and thinking about it in a particular way, each perspective provides ideas we wouldn't otherwise have, but each perspective also limits what we know. Yet, because perspectives are unique ways of thinking, it is not possible to integrate them into one overarching approach or point of view. Sometimes one or two come together temporarily, but it is inconceivable to think about integrating all of them. In other words, it is impossible to think like a physicist, psychiatrist, medical doctor, theologian, historian, sociologist, and parent all at the same time!

One way to deal with the limitations of each perspective and our inability to integrate them is to learn several perspectives and then apply them as needed at different times and in different situations. This is rather like changing hats, or looking through varying kinds of glasses. For example, in a given situation you might think like an economist, then a psychologist, a consumer, and a parent. Each would enrich your experience and bring special knowledge to bear on it.

These ideas about the role of perspectives are important because the authors

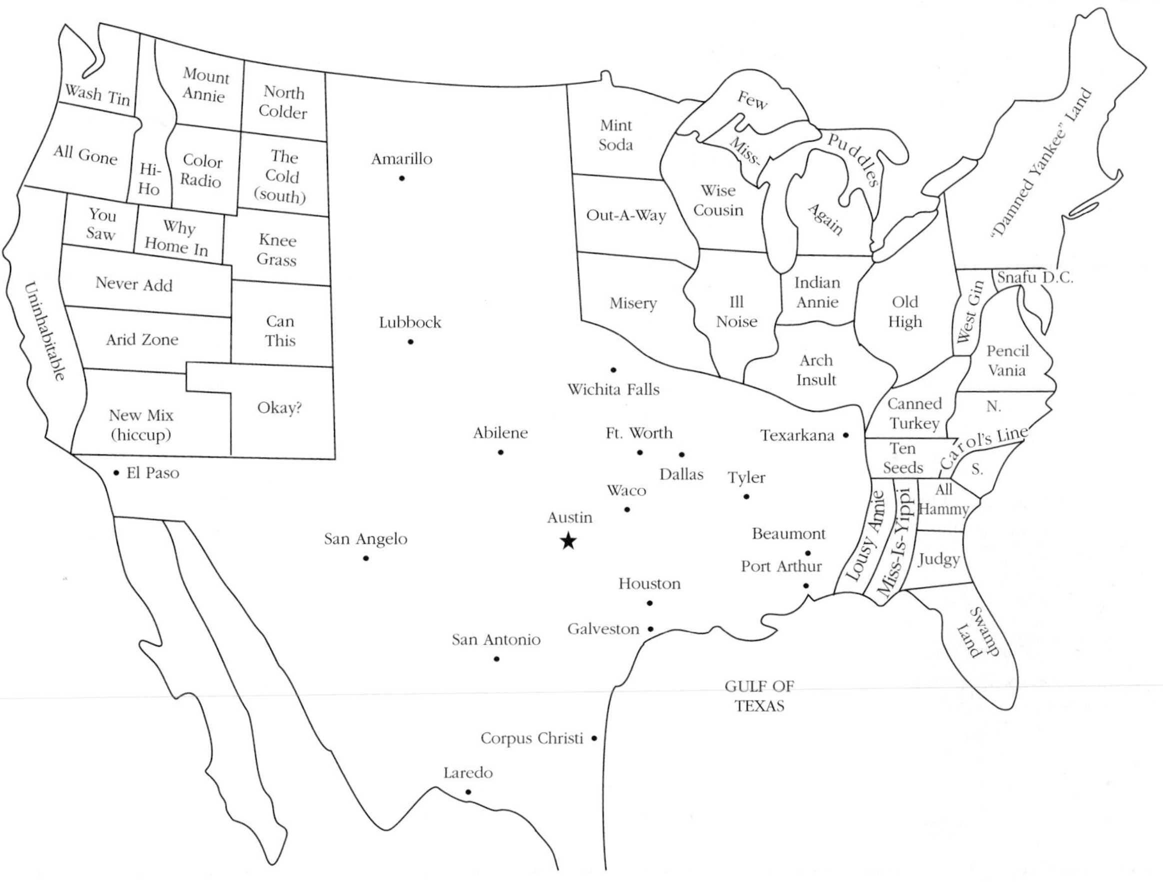

and readers of this book each have a perspective. The authors' perspective influenced how the book was written, and each reader's perspective influences how the book is understood and used.

The perspective used by the authors is fairly new in the academic community. It is known as a family science perspective. The goals of this chapter are to help readers appreciate the role of perspectives in scholarship, and to understand the family science perspective of this book. First we need to look at the ways in which ancient ideas continue to influence modern perspectives, and to review briefly some other perspectives that are used to study the family.

Influence of Ancient Ideas

Some aspects of modern perspectives date back to the intellectual traditions of ancient times. For example, Greek philosophers like Socrates (469?–399 B.C.) and Plato (427?–347 B.C.) assumed that reasoning is a good way to discover knowledge. Plato even argued that ideas determine our view of reality. He emphasized the power of reason over intuition, tradition, or mysticism.

This reliance on intellect and reason has become an important part of all modern scientific perspectives, including family science. For example, few family scientists turn to poetry, literature, intuition, or art to help them understand family life. They do not expect reliable knowledge from tradition, nor from mystical sources such as divination or spiritual revelation. Instead, they rely on their intellectual ability to develop logical, rationally defensible ideas.

A second attribute of modern scientific perspectives that may be traced back to the Greeks is a commitment to *empirical observation*, or gaining ideas from our observations and experience. Aristotle (384–322 B.C.) said the use of observation to gain knowledge is essential. Thus the scientific method is a marriage of Platonic rationality and Aristotelian empirical observation.

We are also indebted to the classical philosophers for some of the basic assumptions that are made in modern perspectives. In *The Republic*, Plato presented his view of an ideal society, and in the process asked some telling questions about relations between families and the state. The way to create an ideal society, he argued, was to educate just people and teach them to make wise decisions about their behavior. Such ideal citizens would also be courageous in confronting challenges and temperate in their desires and appetites. However, according to Plato, one could not produce such ideal citizens in families. Instead, children would have to be raised in large institutions where they would not have

ifferences in perspectives cannot be eliminated because some are right and others are wrong. These differences aren't a matter of accuracy or right or wrong. They are a matter of our frame of reference, our beginning assumptions, our way of seeing, or our way of thinking.

parents, a family heritage, or brothers or sisters. Moreover, when they reached adulthood, they would not marry.

Thus Plato asked a number of fundamental questions, such as:

- How essential is the family?
- What should the role of the family be in present and in future societies?
- What would an ideal society be like?
- Are there better ways to create healthy humans than by having families?

Plato's answers to these questions emphasized independence, rational thought, autonomy, and individuality, and these ideas have since become the intellectual bedrock of a philosophical perspective that is known as **individualism**. This perspective assumes that the individual is the main concern in life, and it emphasizes the importance of privacy, autonomy, individual concerns, personal processes, independence, and personal freedom. According to this perspective, the family is merely one part of an individual's life.

Presumably such questions were debated even before Plato's time; certainly they have been topics of controversy ever since. And, like Plato, some contemporary scholars have a perspective that emphasizes individuality so much that they believe the inefficient, old-fashioned family should be replaced with a more efficient, updated mode of socializing children, thus to create healthy humans and successful societies.

Plato's idea that the family is dispensable was not shared by all the classical philosophers. Some saw the family as a natural unit essential to the human species. Aristotle's ideas about how to create good citizens included an affirmation of the family. He suggested that family life was essential in helping people learn about duty, loyalty, responsibility, authority, obedience, and bonds between people.

Aristotle argued for a more integrated, connected view of humans, families, and their environment. He emphasized the connections people have to biological, intellectual, social, and environmental contexts. One of the modern perspectives that uses these assumptions is called an *ecosystemic* perspective (Paolucci, Hall & Axinn, 1977; Bateson, 1979; Capra, 1982). We will talk more about this in the section on family resource management on page 20.

Plato and Aristotle developed their views over 2000 years ago, but they remain two distinct perspectives (sets of assumptions) in our contemporary world. The differences between Plato's and Aristotle's views are worth noting and remembering because, in trying to understand today's families, many people begin with an individualistic (Platonic) perspective while others begin with an ecosystemic (Aristotelian) perspective, and these differences at the outset influence how we try to solve problems.

Four Social Science Perspectives

Before the family science perspective can be understood, it is necessary to understand some of the older perspectives that have been used to study the family. We will look at economics, anthropology, psychology, and sociology.

The Economic Perspective

Economics was the first of the social sciences to emerge as a separate academic discipline. It began with the writings of mercantilists like Thomas Mun (1571–1641), and it became a full-fledged academic discipline in the latter part of the 1700s. The publication in 1776 of Adam Smith's (1723–1790) classic book *The Wealth of Nations* clarified the main issues, questions, and methods in economics. In his work he clearly states that the economic perspective assumes that the resources we need, such as money, shelter, clothing, and food, are nearly always in short supply. He says that the basic challenge of every society and every individual is to distribute those resources fairly. They should be allocated to meet the wants and needs of as many people as possible (Fuchs, 1983, p. 7).

Another important assumption in the economic perspective is that people make choices on the basis of hedonistic motives. **Hedonism** is the idea that humans try to seek pleasure and avoid pain. Economics embraces hedonistic motives in its use of costs and benefits, or profits and losses. Underlying the analysis of the exchange of goods and services that translates into profits and losses is the notion that people are essentially profit-seeking creatures; that is, they try to maximize profits and minimize costs. There is a related assumption, often implicit but nonetheless part of the perspective, that people are basically selfish, in that they maximize their own profits by minimizing those of other people.

This is not to say that economists believe people are hedonistic in everything they do, or that people are hedonistic in every situation. Most economists recognize that the economic perspective is only one way to look at humans, and that there are many things in social life that are not explained very well from an economic perspective alone.

Another assumption of the economic perspective is that people are rational. This means in part that they tend to make choices on the basis of clear and logical thinking rather than in response to impulse or emotion. It also means it is appropriate for families to make decisions, including matters of time allocation, fertility, childrearing and mate selection, on the basis of self-interest and the maximization of family capital, both physical and human. In the economic model, it is assumed that families try to seek the highest level of living and well-being possible. Berk and Berk (1983) stated that the two primary barriers that keep families from well-being are lack of financial resources and time. Thus economic theory assumes that families make decisions "much as 'small factories' do when trying to maximize output in the least costly fashion" (p. 378).

The economic perspective encourages the study of how families use their resources—what their activities and consumption patterns cost, and how to maximize family benefits from a given outlay of time, energy, or money. The application of economic analysis to family life was the basis of home economics and home management as these fields evolved in the late 1800s and early 1900s. Educators and social workers, confronting poorly educated immigrant families crowded into urban tenements, as well as rural families burdened by poverty and overwork, attempted to improve matters by bringing the efficiencies of factory organization to home production. After all, the successes of modern industrial management were self-evident. They represented the application of rational economics, scientific management, and modern technology to industrial production. Clearly, that was what America's "inefficient" families needed (Gilbreth, 1913). Family life was to be modeled along the same principles of efficiency and maximization that were being applied to factories in the era of time-and-motion studies and efficiency experts.

It is noteworthy that the educators and social workers represented the middle and upper classes, while the families who needed to be taught "proper" principles of family economics tended to be poor or ethnic. Their poverty and their adherence to "foreign" or "primitive" values were evidence that they managed inefficiently. The possibility that they cherished values other than income maximization or economic advantage seems to have been entirely lost on the specialists grounded in the economic perspective who, over much of the twentieth century, devoted their professional lives to fostering family choices based on economic maximization.

More recently, economic models have been used to study fertility and child-rearing practices, mate selection, time allocation in households, household production, and investment in human capital to foster the development of skills, knowledge, and talents (Becker, 1981; Fuchs, 1983).

Few would deny that the economic perspective, as applied to families, has greatly enhanced our understanding of such family functions as production and consumption, resource allocation, and decision-making. The economic perspective is a valuable part of family science because it focuses our attention on the family economic processes. It has also provided a useful vocabulary and a set of technical concepts that enabled students of family life to understand economic processes, communicate about them, and do research about them. The economic perspective, applied to family production processes, has helped some families attain economic success. Among the useful concepts of family science derived from economics are production, consumption, exchange, goods, services, cost, profit, benefit, margin, utility, and scarcity.

There also are some negative consequences of the economic perspective as applied to family life. The emphasis it gives to hedonism, rationality, and the market certainly limits and sometimes distorts our view of family realities. Families do not live by bread alone, nor by capital maximization alone. As Berk and Berk (1983) have noted, "microeconomic approaches to the family possess a Jekyll–Hyde quality . . ." (p. 376). They help us to think about families in ways we might otherwise overlook, but at the same time their emphasis upon market behavior and profit have directed attention away from some of the more humanistic, idealistic, and holistic characteristics of family life. Helpful as it is, the economic perspective is limited, because people face problems other than scarcity. For instance, there is the problem of peace and public order, both in the community and in relations with other countries. There are problems of learning, of socialization, and of human relations. Finally, there are problems of meaning, ethics, and aesthetics. The diversity of human problems underscores the importance of multiple approaches to provide solutions.

The Anthropological Perspective

Anthropology is the study of the human physical structure as well as of human society and culture. It has two main divisions: physical and cultural. Physical anthropologists study how the human body has changed over time; their subject matter stretches from the prehistoric record to the contemporary varieties of humankind. Cultural anthropology encompasses archaeology, social anthropology, and linguistics; they differ in the kinds of culture studied. Archaeologists deal with the cultures of the past. They study ruins, artifacts, and other physical traces in an attempt to reconstruct the social life and cultures of former societies. Social anthropologists are more apt to study living societies, but historically they have tended to focus on societies less "advanced" or "modern" than our own, like the hunting-and-gathering societies still existing in remote parts of the world.

The anthropological emphasis on preliterate and, presumably, "simpler" societies has come in part from an interest in the origins of modern societies, under the assumption that contemporary preliterate societies are in many ways like the preliterate societies from which our own industrial societies have evolved. In studying preliterate and exotic contemporary societies, the social anthropologists have tended to use a method that is known as **participant observation**; that is, they have traveled to the subject societies and lived among the people, later returning to "civilization" to analyze their field notes and write their books.

Almost from its beginnings, cultural anthropology has stressed the important role of culture in determining the kinds of people a society produces. Because culture is transmitted through language, there has been increasing attention to the differences among the various languages, and to how language impacts social orientations and behavior. The science of linguistics has grown out of this anthropological concern with the role of language in making us human. Linguists are concerned with the origins and evolution of languages, the relationships among languages, and with how differentiation in language reflects differentiation in cultural practices and values.

In terms of numbers of practitioners, the social anthropologists are the most numerous. They represent the common stereotype of an anthropologist as one who does fieldwork, temporarily joining a "strange" society in the interests of science and professional curiosity. It is these social anthropologists, with their fascinating studies of the workings of societies unlike our own, who have explored the ramifications of family and kinship more thoroughly than anyone else.

One of the ideas anthropologists have developed is that in smaller, less differentiated societies, kinship plays a more important role in daily life, and in the maintenance of the solidarity of the society as a whole, than it does in more differentiated societies. In fact, kinship turns out to be *the* dominant organizing principle in some of these societies. Its preeminence has forced researchers to take it seriously, to develop complicated typologies, and to find new terms for relationships and kinship groups that do not exist or are less visible in Western societies. A result of the close attention paid by anthropologists to the organization of kinship in preliterate societies has been an increased sensitivity to kinship matters in their own culture. Many of the terms initially applied in the systematic description of kinship in preliterate societies—endogamy and exogamy, polygyny and polyandry, patriarchy and matriarchy, matri-, patri-, and bilineal, to name a few—have been borrowed by social anthropologists, sociologists, and others who study families in contemporary urban society.

Some anthropologists have offered an alternative familial perspective to the more typical, often implicit, economic assumptions routinely applied in ethnographic analysis. For instance, Dorothy Lee (1959) highlights the meaning of family work processes for valued social purposes other than the manifest product

In studying the family, cultural anthropologists examine role relationships, kinship structure, and rituals.

of the work, and points to powerful motivations other than the "obligations" of kinship that move the work along.

> I had been puzzled about the motivating forces in the life of the Tikopia. . . . Raymond Firth, the ethnographer, answering the unspoken questions of Western readers, spoke of obligations, duty, fear of adverse opinion, as motivations. I did not like his choice of words, because he spoke of the obligation to perform unpleasant tasks, for example, and yet the situations he described brimmed with joy. Now I saw that the Tikopia did not need external incentives. (p. 28)

The same emphasis upon process rather than product, upon the context of doing rather than what is done, also appears in anthropological descriptions of the Trobriand Islanders:

> It follows that the Trobriander performs acts because of the activity itself, not for its effects; that he values objects because they are good, not good for; in fact, objects and activities that are good for, are of no value to him. (Lee, 1959, p. 96)

Whatever the underlying assumptions, whether economic or familial, whether focused on ends or means, process or products, the anthropologists have thoroughly studied family groups in their quest for a science of mankind. Their efforts to make the realm of family and kinship intellectually manageable by creating systems of family concepts and testing their applicability to literally hundreds of societies across space and time have had a marked influence on scholars in other disciplines.

The Psychological Perspective

An interest in human mental processes was an integral part of the eighteenth-century intellectual movement we now call the Enlightenment. John Locke (1690), whom we remember primarily as a political theorist, tried to identify the "laws of association" that governed human learning. Others studied the mind and brain in the hope of understanding the origins of mental disorders, notable examples being von Haller (1708–1777), who advocated the post-mortem dissection of the brains of the insane, and Mesmer (1734–1815), who suggested that physical magnetism might somehow be linked to both physical and mental illnesses. His treatment procedures included a form of hypnosis, and his efforts are immortalized in the English verb *mesmerize.*

The origins of modern psychology are generally traced to late-nineteenth-century attempts to apply the methods of physical science to the study of human behavior. The pioneers were European students of physiological psychology, like Wilhelm Wundt, who in 1879 at the University of Leipzig established the first psychological laboratory. More than a decade earlier, Wundt (1864–1865) had argued that scientists could learn much about human behavior by appropriate studies of lower animals, a thesis that is the basis for the modern field of comparative psychology and much of the somewhat larger subdiscipline of experimental psychology. In Russia, Ivan Petrovich Pavlov's famous salivating dogs helped point the way to experimental psychology in general and, through John B. Watson and B. F. Skinner, to contemporary behaviorism. However, it is not an experimentalist or physiological psychologist, but rather a social psychologist, William James, who is remembered as the father of American psychology.

It was social psychology that came to have the most substantial influence on the study of the family, for unlike many of the other subdisciplines of psychology, its explicit focus was on the social influences that impact individual behavior. Preeminent among those influences, of course, was that of the family and its individual members. Social psychologists like George Herbert Mead and Charles H. Cooley explored the processes of socialization, showing how the "mind" and "self" depended upon communication by gesture and language, as well as the expectations and reactions of others.

Another impetus to the growth of social psychology and its emphasis on socialization, especially family socialization, was Freudian psychology. Sigmund Freud, like Mead and Cooley, was concerned with how the self developed. His theories about the components of the self and the personal pathologies that derive from stifling their "natural" evolution turned researchers toward the earliest years of childhood as the period when psychiatric pathologies were likely to have originated. Parents and siblings were key players in the dramas, both real and imaginary, that determined how the self evolved. Freud and his followers pointed to sexual competition and sexual envy within the family as "natural" stresses that had to be managed, and encouraged research on the ways children learn to manage their elemental drives in socialization processes such as weaning and toilet training.

> The psychoanalytic approach conceives of the socialization process as curbing and redirecting the infant's natural appetites, thereby producing an adult with a complex unconscious life, as well as with a conscience that operates to constrain subsequent behavior. (Lemert, 1968, p. 460)

The essential point here is that both the Freudians and the *symbolic interactionists,* as the Mead–Cooley school of thought came to be called, looked to socialization, most of which occurred in family settings, for the explanation of subsequent individual behavior patterns. Freudian analysts treated their patients by exploring with them their most personal memories, conscious and unconscious, of family and childhood. The therapy was generally individual, but the origin of pathologies tended to be social, and largely familial.

Despite their recognition that individuals are socialized in families and that individual problems usually have social, often family, origins, psychologists are more likely than other social scientists to focus their attention at the individual rather than the group level. This emphasis on the individual meant that research on family processes was relatively ignored for many years. However, in the last few decades psychology seems to have discovered the family.

Over the years, psychology has provided many ideas and concepts that proved very useful in the study of families generally and that have been borrowed by professionals in other disciplines and applied in their studies of family life. For example, psychology provided concepts about human learning such as conditioning, reinforcement, and extinction. Another widely used set of concepts deals with the development of the self, and embraces such terms as *self-concept, self-esteem,* and *self-actualization.* Developmental psychology has contributed some key concepts, including stages, readiness, complexity, trust, and identity, and psychologists studying cognitive processes have added terms and models of the processes of formal reasoning, stereotyping, and selective perception.

The Sociological Perspective

The kinds of social inquiry we now call sociology appeared in Western Europe in the 1830s with the publication of de Tocqueville's *Democracy in America* and the "moral statistics" of Adolphe Quetelet (1835) and Andre Guerry (1833). However, not until the latter part of the nineteenth century did people begin doing sociological research and calling themselves sociologists. Among the pioneers were Herbert Spencer in England (*Principles of Sociology,* 1876), Ferdinand Tonnies in Germany (*Gemeinschaft and Gesellschaft,* 1887), Albion Small in the United States (*An Introduction to the Science of Sociology,* 1890), and Emile Durkheim in France (*The Division of Labor in Society,* 1893). Today the boundaries of sociology are fluid and blurred, but there is a fair consensus about the thrust of the discipline as a whole. Rodney Stark's (1989) characterization of the field is apt:

> Sociologists differ from psychologists because we are not concerned so exclusively with the individual, with what goes on inside people's heads. We are more interested in what goes on *between* people. Sociologists differ from economists by being less

> exclusively interested in commercial exchanges—we are equally interested in the exchange of intangibles such as love and affection. We differ from anthropologists primarily because the latter specialize in the study of preliterate or primitive human groups, while we are primarily interested in modern industrial societies. (p. 8)

Sociology, like economics, originated in the study of nonfamily realms such as cities, markets, schools, religious institutions, and governments. This led to an emphasis on the public, institutionalized parts of social processes rather than the private and spontaneous aspects. There is a specific type of sociology known as *microsociology* that pays attention to patterns of social interaction in small groups, including families, but most sociologists are neither family sociologists nor analysts of micro settings.

Most sociology is broadly classifiable into the study of social structure and social integration in the major institutions of society, the latter generally defined to include the family, the school, the church, the military, the economy, and the government. Such *social institutions* (that is, patterns of repeated and organized behavior, essentially existing only in the process of social action) are the stable structures created by societies to accomplish important social functions. Societies exist only as long as their essential functions are performed.

The identification of the family as one of a handful of dominant social institutions has helped to insure that sociologists will continue to think and write about family matters. At the same time, however, it is one thing to assert that the family is "the most universal of social institutions and the source of the earliest and most powerful influences to which the normal individual in every society is exposed" (Caplow, 1971, p. 476), and quite another to illuminate just how those powerful influences work. The dominant sociological focus on the institutional perspective has meant that some aspects of family life that do not have readily apparent counterparts in the other institutions have been ignored or undervalued.

Many sociologists seem to view the family institution as infinitely malleable. This means they assume that there are innumerable ways of organizing society to manage the essential functions families serve, and that there is no particular benefit in any one way of organizing family life. Commitment to a particular pattern or set of family values is generally seen as ethnocentricity or personal bias, a violation of the social relativism that is the accepted professional orientation.

Sociologists have shown little interest in family processes that are not attributable to social causation. For example, they tend to discount family characteristics attributable to biological imperatives, physiological drives, genetic programming, or instincts. There is, however, a small but growing number of so-called sociobiologists who argue that at least some of human social behavior reflects our biological or evolutionary heritage and is not as socially conditioned as has been assumed (Wilson, 1975).

The sociological tradition encourages the study of the family in an objective, or value-free, manner. Therefore, when a sociological perspective is used, scholars avoid making value judgments about which family forms or styles are more or less healthy. Also, sociologists tend to be interested in acquiring knowledge about the family, but they usually leave the application of the knowledge to others. One implication of this is that the sociological perspective generally focuses on acquiring knowledge rather than on providing practical applications for practitioners such as family therapists or family-life educators.

Up to now we have referred to the *perspectives* of economics, anthropology, psychology and sociology, and we have defined *perspective* as a set of assumptions. When we look at these sets of assumptions it becomes apparent that in each field they discipline the scholars to think and study in a particular way, and that is what creates a *discipline.* The four disciplines just discussed have achieved over time the status of social or behavioral sciences. They are alike in that they attempt to apply the scientific method and in that they deal with interpersonal processes. They differ in the processes they emphasize, the research procedures they prefer, and the intellectual giants of the past whose works they seek to build upon.

The Family Science Perspective

While the older disciplines of economics, anthropology, psychology and sociology all provide information about families, there are some parts of the family "elephant" they overlook. As Paul Watzlawick (1967) observed:

> Family relations pertain to a plane where the ordinary rules of judgment and conduct do not apply. They are a labyrinth of tensions, quarrels and reconciliations, whose logic is self-contradictory, whose ethics stem from a cozy jungle, and whose values and criteria are distorted like the uncarved space of a self-contained universe. It is a universe saturated with memories—but memories from which no lessons are drawn; saturated with a past which provides no guidance to the future. For in this universe, after each crisis and reconciliation, time always starts afresh and history is always in the year zero. (p. 81)

Facing that labyrinth, several groups of scholars from different disciplinary backgrounds have developed a new way of looking at family processes. Beginning about mid-century, these groups of family professionals developed some new theories, new research questions and methods, and new ways of doing therapy. They created "familial" explanations that were different from the more traditional points of view.

By the 1970s theorists and researchers were beginning to pay attention to assumptions, variables, and research contexts that were not part of traditional family studies, and several groups began to claim a new discipline was emerging (Burr, 1973, p. viii; Kantor & Lehr, 1975; Burr & Leigh, 1982). This led to a series of debates about what to call the new discipline, and some of the terms that were suggested were: famology, familogy, family therapy, family studies, and family science. In this book we use the term family science.

Family science is the discipline devoted to the study of the unique realm of the family. Its primary concentration focuses on the inner workings of family behavior and centers on family processes such as emotion in families, love, boundaries, rituals, paradigms, rules, routines, decision making, and manage-

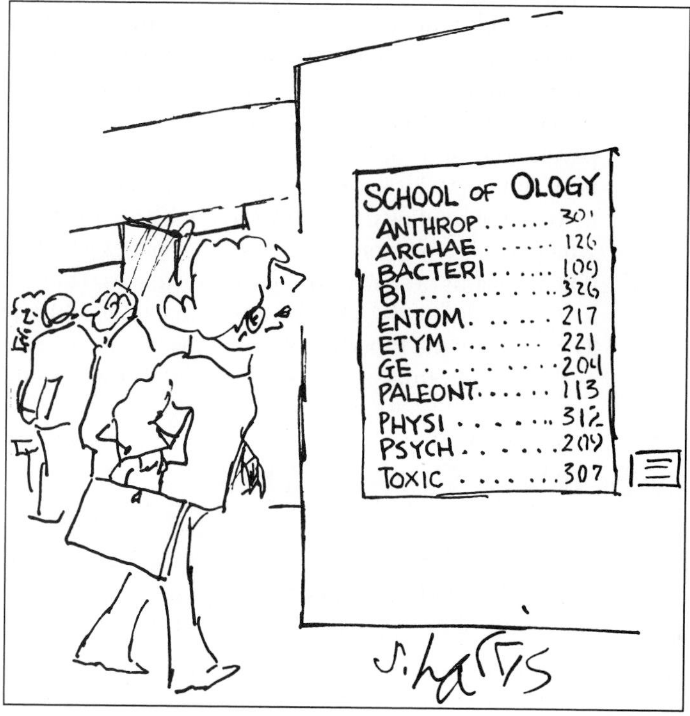

ment of resources. When the family is studied from a family science perspective, researchers, practitioners, and clinicians treat information from other related disciplines (i.e., sociology, psychology, and anthropology) as vital background information. The foreground emphasis, however, is on the family system and its intimate workings.

Contributing Disciplines

Four groups of scholars laid the groundwork for the new discipline. They were family therapists, academics in child development and family relations (CDFR), home economists who specialized in home management, and feminist scholars. It is helpful to understand how each of these groups contributed to the family science perspective.

Family therapy. The developers of family therapy were psychiatrists, counselors, and ministers who became dissatisfied with the individualistic ways of counseling in which they had been trained. They suspected family processes might be more important in both causing and curing mental and emotional illnesses than the traditions of their disciplines allowed.

These ideas led them to change the way they did therapy. In the 1940s and 1950s, rather than just treating the client who had symptomatic problems, some clinicians began having couples and even entire families attend therapy sessions together. Some therapists even had whole families live in hospital settings for a period of time, and a few involved members of extended families in the therapy (Bowen, 1966; Framo, 1976).

The most fundamental change was not merely in the number of people attending therapeutic sessions, but in the way problems were defined and treated. Therapists started asking familial questions, seeking familial explanations, gathering familial data, and experimenting with familial interventions. The focus of problem definition had moved from individual to family, and the locus of treatment followed.

These changes in problem definition produced dramatic changes in the nature of clinical practice and in the shape of the disciplines involved in therapy and counseling. There were new conceptual frameworks, new research methods, new intervention strategies, and a profession so large and dynamic that by 1987 there were a dozen new American journals and almost that many in other countries.

The therapists who started thinking with a familial perspective recognized that families have a number of emotional and communication processes not understood within older disciplines. They also realized families constructed their own definitions of reality—definitions that were to some degree unique to each family. These insights led to new familogical concepts such as redundancies, family paradigms, relationship messages, analog levels of communication, and levels of analysis in family systems. The therapists also discovered some generational processes not identified by the older disciplines, and developed new generational concepts such as triangulation, invisible loyalties, and balancing ledgers in families.

Child development and family relations. Another group contributing to the development of the new perspective were scholars in departments of child development and family relations (CDFR).[1] Usually these departments had grown up around, or in association with, university faculties of home economics, but they incorporated faculty members trained in a variety of disciplines. By 1990 there were about 60 of these departments offering graduate degrees in family science.

When the CDFR departments began, their primary emphasis was to teach "marriage and family living" to undergraduate students. This educational approach to the family was different from the clinical approach taken by family therapy groups. The educators were focusing on ideas that would help "normal" families, rather than concentrating solely on the most dysfunctional families. Like the clinicians, they were oriented to intervention—that is, to the application of research-based knowledge to practical improvements in real families—but they were applying their ideas with a different audience.

Initially, the primary emphasis in the CDFR departments was to help families through education, but in the course of seeking knowledge and refining propositions borrowed from other disciplines, these scholars began to use their familial perspective to build and test new theories. They created theories about how family processes contribute to mental health and deviance (Olson et al., 1983), how families cope with stress (Boss, 1975; McCubbin et al., 1980a), the nature and development of family strengths (Stinnett, 1979a, 1979b; Stinnett & Sauer, 1977; Stinnett, Sanders, DeFrain & Parkhurst, 1982), and the processes of family development (Duvall, 1955; Rollins & Cannon, 1974).

Family resource management. A third group that helped lay the groundwork for the family science perspective was the family resource specialists in home economics. Family resource management scholars do research and develop theories on the way families manage their resources. Resources are defined broadly to include anything that helps the family achieve its goals. Human resources like talents and interests are taken into account, along with real property, neighborhood and community facilities, and the time, money and energy of family members. A basic assumption of this perspective is that "things need not just happen in a family; they can be decided" (Paolucci et al., 1977, p. 1). Family members are seen as active agents. They have the capacity to choose new values, goals, and standards, or to affirm old ones, and to make choices about allocating family resources.

The history of family resource management provides a good illustration of conflicting perspectives within a single discipline and the organizational dominance of the economic orientation. Early in the field's development, around the turn of the century, many family resource specialists were impressed with the visible gains in industrial production associated with the application of "scientific" management. They urged that the same kind of systematic, efficiency-oriented analysis be applied to the home, to the end of releasing the burdens of household work and improving family life. They succeeded so well that the academic discipline they represented came to be popularly known as "home economics." The field came to be dominated by economic viewpoints and priorities, and aspects of family life that were not readily interpretable in economic terms tended to be overlooked. In the process, the more relational and developmental dimensions of family life, included in the discipline at the beginning of this century, were devalued. This deficiency prompted anthropologist Dorothy Lee to caution that the home management specialists had allowed the introduction of new knowledge and processes for managing homes to run ahead of the concern that family life be meaningful. Emphasis on efficiency and economy might ease the burdens of housework, but it could also disrupt relationships and interfere with the appropriate socialization of children.

After 1950, professionals in the field of family resource management began to be influenced by studies on family decision-making, values, goals, and standards. However, much of the innovation that this new subject area might have offered the field was lost because most family resource specialists continued to apply the same hedonistic, economic perspective they had used for half a century. As a consequence, the rational, maximizing model of economic decision making was adopted as *the* model for family decision making. Families were encouraged to identify values, goals, and standards to guide their choices, but with no provision other than that these standards be "their own" for evaluating the relative worth of goals and values.

A few family resource management scholars recognized all along that the economic perspective can only take them so far. Paolucci, Hall and Axinn (1977) and Beutler and Owen (1980) were among those who pointed out its inadequacies and urged their colleagues to apply other views and move beyond the limitations of earlier perspectives. Paolucci and her associates argued that family decision-making must be more "ecological" and reflect the interdependence of the family with its community and natural environments. They emphasized that the family was properly seen as an interdependent part of a physical and social ecosystem. Their approach to family analysis has been labeled the **ecosystems** approach.

In the ecosystems perspective, the family is viewed as a purposive system rather than as a mechanical or biological system. Ecosystems scholars pay attention to processes, rather than products; being and becoming, rather than having. They see the family as an active part of a wider, open system, rather than a closed, deterministic one. To the degree that the family science perspective reflects their orientation, it is holistic and indeterminate.

Feminist thinking. The feminist movements of the past century have contributed in several important ways to the shape and development of the family science perspective. In singling out a few social scientists whose writings have been influential, we do not mean to minimize the contributions of men and women in other realms—political, religious, economic, medical, journalistic, and others—whose efforts to increase women's rights, powers, and opportunities have made a difference in the way families, and those who enact family roles, are defined and treated. Betty Friedan is well known for *The Feminine Mystique* (1963), in which she dramatized feelings of meaninglessness, alienation, and frustration of middle- and upper-middle-class wives who, in the prevailing public economic point of view, were admired and envied for their "success." Jessie Bernard (1972), a sociologist, demonstrated that, from a variety of perspectives, a contemporary man and woman, legally married to each other, in fact "belong" to different marriages. The worlds they perceive, assess, and operate within are vastly different. The marriage from the man's perspective tends to be the marriage viewed as "real" by society. The marriage from the woman's perspective probably comes closer to the marriage as viewed in a family science orientation. Many of Bernard's insights were validated in the work of Carol Gilligan (1982), who identified strong gender biases in Kohlberg's (1976) presumably neutral theories of the moral development of children. In addition to the substantive findings of such efforts, their political thrust has helped make contemporary family scientists more sensitive to gender biases.

The feminist literature is not only aimed at expanding opportunities for women, but also at developing attitudes and intellectual frameworks that reflect "female" and "maternal" perspectives rather than the so-called value-free masculine perspectives that have long prevailed in the social sciences (Ruddick, 1984; Smith, 1987). For example, Rich (1976) suggests that the dominant view of motherhood as an "institution" misses much of the essential reality of motherhood as experienced by mothers. It is argued that using an experiential approach as a supplement to the more traditional institutional approach yields many new and valuable insights. A second example of this is in the work of Dorothy Smith (1987). When we apply the standard sociological categories of "work" and "leisure" to study the work women do in the home, "the kinds of responsibilities women take in relation to the home and to the children simply do not appear." If, rather than imposing those categories, a researcher were to begin from within a woman's experience, "the categories of 'work' and 'leisure' would never emerge" (1979).

Another useful insight contributed by feminists is Ruddick's (1989) analysis of the unique qualities of maternal thinking. She contrasts maternal thought with the dominant public modes of thinking, and asserts that "out of maternal practices distinctive ways of conceptualizing, ordering, and valuing arise" (p. 224). In the context of mothering, "interests," "demands," and "achievements" may be qualitatively different from the conceptions of interests, demands, and achievement in the world of business and politics. One set of maternal interests is aimed at fostering the healthy growth and development of her children; central to her conception of personal achievement is likely to be the development of attentive love, humility, and resilient, clear-sighted cheerfulness, as well as the ability to "change with change" in response to the progressing life of her children.

In short, many feminist writers have made a strong case that the worldview from inside the family, looking out, greatly differs from an orientation imposed on the family from the outside, using perspectives that originate in the male-dominated, economically oriented public spheres. In the last decades of the twentieth century, these feminist insights have had a profound influence on the thinking of family scientists.

Assumptions

When the ideas developed by these four groups are integrated, they form a perspective that differs in some ways from the other social sciences. One way the new perspective is different is that its unique set of assumptions deal with what the term *family* means and how we ought to study it. Five of these basic assumptions are:

1. We ought to seek knowledge that can help families be effective, and apply our knowledge in ways that improve the quality of family life.
2. It is helpful to think about the family differently than scholars have in the past.
3. Family processes are more important than most people realize.

4. There are indeterministic aspects of the family realm, such as values, goals, choice, agency, and freedom, and the study of the family realm must take this into account.
5. There are aspects of the family realm that have not been given enough attention in the older disciplines, and it is helpful to focus on them.

To understand these assumptions, we need to discuss each of them in more detail.

We ought to seek knowledge that can help families be effective, and apply our knowledge in ways that improve the quality of family life. This assumption means that family scientists are not a group of ivory-tower scholars who are interested in knowledge for its own sake. They are interested in creating ideas and doing research that can be used to help families cope with the challenges of life. For example, they want to help families avoid undesirable things such as lack of intimacy, alienation, abuse, exploitation, and violence. On the positive side, they are interested in finding ideas that can help families attain such goals as love and intimacy, nurturance and support, bonds without bondage, and healthy growth and development.

The family can reflect the extremes—the best and worst parts—of life. On the negative side, more murders are committed in families than anywhere else. More child abuse, abuse of the elderly, and other forms of violence occur in the family than in any other place. It is in families that incest occurs. On the positive side, families offer the greatest levels of intimacy, caring, nurturance, love, compassion, and security, along with a sense of home, belonging, peace, and meaning. The community of family science scholars and practitioners has evolved as a group of people who are primarily concerned with helping families attain as many of these positive elements as possible, eliminate as many negative and undesirable parts as possible, and cope as effectively as possible with the stresses, challenges, and difficulties that occur.

It is helpful to think about family differently than scholars have in the past. Most of the traditional ways of defining the family are fairly limited. Sociologists and anthropologists have viewed the family as "a cultural unit which contains a husband and wife who are the mother and father of their child or children" (Schneider, 1980, p. 33). Legal scholars view the family as a set of human relations that are protected by a group of laws. A demographic definition of the family emphasizes households or residences. Action groups such as the gay community want to broaden the definition of family to include those who commit themselves to living together for a meaningful period of time.

Many family scientists use a different definition of family, and Beutler et al. (1989) have suggested the term **family realm** be used to describe this view of what is familial. According to this view, the family is a part, arena, sphere, or aspect of the human experience that is different from the military, governmental, occupational, spiritual, and physical environment parts of the human experience. The family realm includes the birth process and the generational connections that are created with birth. The family realm also includes the deeply felt emotions that people have about procreating; the spatial relationships people have in their homes; the temporal, symbolic, emotional processes they experience in family rituals, traditions, and routines; and the experiential processes that come from sharing with other family members such things as births, growth, affection, struggles, successes, questioning, finding meaning, failures, love, and death. Such things as familial heritage, sense of familial identity, and lineage consciousness are also intangible parts of the family realm.

Thus, the family science view of family refers to shared relationships and experiences rather than to residential patterns, laws, or cultural conventions. This means that some parts of the life of a single person who lives alone or with friends are in the family realm. A single person has parents and grandparents and a wide range of familial emotions, definitions, memories, and aspirations; and single people have many other familial aspects to their lives. According to this view of family, those who live in nontraditional family forms are still in the family realm. For example, single parents, childless couples, or single grandparents living alone experience part of their life in the family realm.

It helps some people understand what the concept of family realm means when they realize that some relationships are "almost family." The "almost" in this way of thinking helps us understand that some things are "family," some things aren't "family," and some things are borderline. The term *family realm* refers to the parts of the human experience that *are* "family."

One of the advantages of the concept of family realm is that it helps us focus our attention on a number of family processes that are not given emphasis or attention in the older social science disciplines. Also, it is a broader, more flexible, and more inclusive term than we have had before. For example, it is more inclusive than the term *family institution* because the latter does not explicitly include relevant biological, emotional, experiential, communicative, developmental, creative, and ecosystemic processes.

In the concept of family realm, the family is viewed as more than just a social institution. Some aspects of the family realm are *natural* phenomena rather than cultural or social phenomena. This means that the idea of family, and much of what is done in families, was not invented or created by cultures, societies, technologies, governments, laws, or any historical period. Many family processes are similar to other natural or inherent aspects of being human. For example, humans did not decide to invent or create seeing, and they did not decide to invent hearing and thinking. These processes are inherent in the nature of the human species. Our prehistoric ancestors also did not *decide* that the way to reproduce their species was to form families in which men and women would copulate and then rear their children.

Some of the scholars in several of the older social science disciplines do not look at the family as a natural phenomenon. For example, some of them have tried to identify when families started appearing in prehistory (Westermark, 1891). If we look at the family realm as being a part of the nature of human experience, this type of scholarship is futile. Families have always been part of the human experience, and in some ways it is family life that makes us human.

Even though societies, cultures, historical events, and technologies did not create the family realm, they do modify and shape it. These changes are similar to the ways diet, climate, and social conventions change our physical bodies. For example, when the women in traditional China wrapped their feet, it temporarily changed the form and shape of their bodies, but it did not change the nature of human feet. The inherent genetic potential of the body is the same; what has changed is the opportunity for the natural potential to be more fully achieved through optimal environmental support. It is the same with the family realm. During some historical periods and in some cultures family life has changed so that some parts of the family realm diverge from the natural needs and tendencies of humans. Fortunately, these cultural patterns do not usually last very long as the natural tendencies reassert themselves.

When some people realize that parts of the family realm are natural, they assume that the "natural" parts are biological. However, family scientists are beginning to discover aspects of the family realm that seem to be part of human nature and are not merely biological. For example, Rich (1976) argues that the experience of mothering changes the mother, and this experiential part of the family realm is natural but not just biological. Bowen and Kerr (1988) argue that families have a family emotional system or climate that is an important natural process, and more than just biology.

The possibility that some parts of the family realm are natural rather than merely cultural or biological has a number of important implications. One implication is that some aspects of the family realm are probably permanent and inflexible, and to try to change them would disrupt natural processes and decrease the quality of life. A second implication is that, as with other parts of nature, when we learn the laws and processes that occur in the family realm, we can use this knowledge to make changes that will improve the quality of life.

Indeed, some aspects of the family realm may be more flexible and adaptable than most people believe. As we come to better understand which parts of the family realm can and cannot be changed, we increase our ability to eliminate undesirable things such as prejudice, inequality, abuse, and exploitation. We make it easier to let go of traditional ways of doing things that are outdated, unfair, unwise, and harmful. Presumably, greater understanding of the family realm will also make it easier to develop new ways of organizing families to adapt to the challenges and opportunities of our time.

Family scholars are still trying to learn which family processes are part of the inflexible and essential parts of the family realm and which parts are flexible and optional. One part of the family realm that seems to be a part of the inflexible core is the birth process. Davis has suggested that the birth process is the most fundamental, irreducible, or core aspect of everything that is familial. This makes it a central part of the family realm that probably cannot be changed without disrupting the quality of human life (Davis, 1984; Burr et al., 1987).

When we think about the process of birth we need to realize it entails much more than biological reproduction. Inherently it creates a number of connections and other processes (Davis, 1984). These connections are interpersonal, mental, emotional, temporal, spatial, hormonal, generational, sexual, and developmental. For example, a mother experiences dramatic changes in her hormones, body shape, thoughts, and feelings. She also experiences discomfort and pain, and she feels the movement inside her own body of the human being growing there. These *experiential* changes reflect many natural and inescapable influences, and they appear to be inflexible parts of the family realm.

Another aspect of the family realm that seems to be inflexible is the intense and nonrational feelings of caring, concern, and love that occur naturally in the family realm. Urie Bronfenbrenner (1979) has suggested that these feelings are both natural and essential to the parent-child processes, and that they are absolutely necessary for the optimal development of emotional and mental well-being in children and adults.

One of the areas where the family realm may be more flexible than most people realize is in the roles traditionally assigned to men and women. Many cultures throughout the world have developed patterns where males dominate and exploit females. In many of these societies, including the American, males have been in control of the political, military, and economic institutions for so long and so exclusively that they have developed traditions, laws, mores, and institutions that discriminate against females. This accumulation of traditional sexist culture has the net effect of reducing women's control over their lives and limiting their opportunities and achievements. These traditional patterns appear in the institutionalized parts of the family realm, where women are assigned the more demeaning, routine, and low-status work, as well as in the overarching language and belief systems that define the essential values and ways of perceiving things in the general culture (Thorne & Yalom, 1982).

Whatever the historical patterns in the past that created these abusive patterns, we believe there is no justification for them to continue. Much more flexibility is possible in the roles of men and women than was realized before, and family scientists have been in the forefront in documenting this reality and helping to create change. We believe that the application of the family science perspective and the exploration of the distinctive human features of the family realm will help to encourage equity and emancipation in family relations.

Family processes are more important than most people realize. Most of the scholars who have a family science perspective believe that as family life goes, so go the cities, nations, and the world. This is because they believe family processes have much more influence on humans than most people realize. They believe family processes are intricately involved in the main intellectual concerns and human problems of the contemporary world.

Even though scholars with a familogical perspective believe this, most of them are aware that this is not a widely shared belief in our society. There is lip service given to the idea that the family is the cornerstone of civilization, but most attempts to deal with societal problems use intellectual perspectives that minimize the role of family processes.

The perspectives currently dominant are political, economic, military, and psychological ways of thinking. These are so prominent in the public spheres that the uniqueness and the importance of private spheres like the family realm are largely ignored. Many efforts in our society to solve human problems apply public-sphere solutions to private-sphere problems, a process not unlike trying to put square pegs in round holes. As a society, we then wonder why our well-intentioned actions frequently create new and unanticipated problems. In the view of family scientists, many national and international problems—poverty, war, nuclear arms and disarmament, terrorism, drug abuse, inflation, unemployment, and famine—grow out of the family realm and might be ameliorated by the extension of family-realm thinking to the wider social sphere.

There are indeterministic aspects of the family realm, such as values, goals, choice, agency, and freedom, and the study of the family realm must take this into account. This assumption is a complicated idea, and before it can be understood it is necessary to understand the difference between determinism and indeterminism. **Determinism** is the belief that anything that happens has certain causes and that science can discover the laws of cause and effect. This view assumes that when scholars don't know the cause-and-effect patterns, it is merely because science has not yet progressed enough to identify the laws that are operating.

The Law of Gravity is an example of deterministic thinking. It states that the mass of an object influences the gravitational force exerted on other objects (Merrill et al., 1982, p. 18). This is deterministic because changes in the mass determine the force. The relationship is so predictable that there are no exceptions. Determinism also exists in the biological sciences. For example, changes in genes lead to differences in plants or animals. Nagel calls this type of determinism *genetic causality* (Nagel, 1961) because one thing (genes) determines or causes the other (kind of plant).

Many social sciences theories use a determinist way of reasoning. For example, *behaviorism* is a school of thought that employs deterministic thinking to try to discover laws about how people learn. When Pavlov conducted his experiments with dogs, he correctly assumed that ringing the bell would have a deterministic and linear effect on the dogs' salivation. The deterministic way of thinking is helpful when we are seeking genetic or mechanical explanations (Nagel, 1961), but many scholars believe it is not useful in understanding aspects of social systems like the family. This is because some parts of human systems operate according to indeterminism rather than determinism.

According to **indeterminism**, human thoughts and behavior are not completely determined. People are assumed to have at least some free will. Indeterminism holds that people have the ability to reason, evaluate, set priorities, and make choices in ways that are not caused by previous conditions. Even though physical objects may be subject to the laws of cause and effect, the human mind remains at least somewhat free of these laws.

The difference between determinism and indeterminism can be seen by comparing what happens when we kick a football and when we kick a member of our family. When we kick a football, it "causes" the football to react in a predictable way. If the football is kicked hard in an open football field, the kick will "cause" the ball to fly through the air for 50 or 60 yards and then bounce another 10 or 20 yards. If someone or something blocks the football at the time it is kicked, it will "cause" the ball to veer in a different direction. It is possible for scientists to identify quite precisely how the speed, direction, acceleration, and mass of the kicker's foot influences the direction, arc, and distance of the football's flight because all of these factors operate as cause and effect. It also is possible to identify the other factors, such as gravitational force and air density, that may cause changes in how the football responds. A football kicked on the moon will respond differently from a football kicked on earth because the gravitational force on the moon is only about one-sixth of the earth's, and there is no air to help slow the ball down.

If we kick a member of our family, it is not as easy to identify all the "factors" involved. It is true that speed and mass of the kicker's foot will have a certain physical impact that can be described with deterministic ideas about causation. In addition to the deterministic processes, however, there are a number of indeterministic processes also operating. The person who is kicked has a mind, values, objectives, and some degree of freedom to make choices. This person may decide to kick back! Or the person may decide to cry, run away, thank the kicker, hold a grudge, forgive, ask for an explanation, respond in a kind way, or find a way to get even. The "may or may not" part of this process is hard to explain with deterministic reasoning.

Family scientists have traditionally focused on the indeterministic processes that occur in the family realm. They pay a great deal of attention to family values and goals, and to the fact that people in families think, ponder, and choose in indeterministic ways. Some of the older social sciences have tried to be "objective" and "value free," but family science from its beginning has been just the opposite. The first family life texts that began to appear in the 1940s (for example, Hill and Duvall, 1946) emphasized the values, ideals, choices, and aspirations of people in families. Home management, one of the specialties out of which family science evolved, itself evolved from the premise that people make choices and manage, and this attention to the indeterministic aspects of family life is one of the distinguishing characteristics of the family science perspective.

That we should think about the indeterministic part of families is a complicated idea with far-reaching consequences; this idea is developed further in Chapter 2 and several of the later chapters.

There are aspects of the family realm that have not been given enough attention in the older disciplines, and it is helpful to focus on them. It is not possible for any discipline to emphasize everything. Therefore, all disciplines tend to focus on or emphasize a relatively small part of reality as they try to discover new knowledge. The topics that are given the most emphasis in family science include generational processes (Chapter 3), emotions (Chapter 5), ideologies (Chapter 6), and family development (Chapter 7). Focus on these kinds of ideas gives family science its unique set of insights.

Using the Five Perspectives

One way to clarify differences in perspective is to identify a problem and see how each discipline approaches it. Unfortunately we don't have a scarcity of problems in our society. We could look at arms control, AIDS, teenage pregnancy, inflation, substance abuse, famine, inadequate education, war, taxation, the cost of medical care, or poverty, to name just a few. We'll focus here on teenage pregnancy.

It is estimated that every year in the United States 1.2 million women under the age of 19 will get pregnant. Half of those will have a baby. The rest will have either a spontaneous or planned abortion. The social, psychological, and economic effects are enormous. The nation will spend at least $14 billion on this problem. Most of the funds will be in the form of welfare subsidies and health-related payments. Additionally, the children of teenage mothers are often born in poverty, and they usually have lower birth weights, more physical deformities, and a much lower chance of growing up in a two-parent home. The mother is much less likely to have good educational or work-related advantages, and is many times trapped in a situation of extended poverty and social dependence.

Imagine for a moment that every ten years in the United States we create a city the size of Los Angeles filled completely with children from disadvantaged teen mothers. (The city would be twice that size if the mothers were included.) Also imagine that we are scientists with a million dollars to spend on discovering ways to address this problem. How would the four disciplines differ in thinking about the problem? Let's start with economics.

Economics

Using an economic perspective to think about the problem of teenage pregnancy, we would describe the problem in terms of the costs to the individuals and society. We would try to figure out what the economic impact of having a baby would be on the county, state, or nation. We would also be interested in how the rewards of certain scarce resources might outweigh the costs of childbearing. There are monetary, social, and psychological benefits to having a child. We might conclude, from our assumption of rationality, that under current social conditions the risks and costs of childbearing must not be as severe as the rewards are attractive. If we wanted to try to solve the problem, we would try to think of ways to change things such as resources, rewards, and costs.

Anthropology

Using an anthropological perspective to study teenage pregnancy might be a more descriptive than prescriptive approach. We would think about the meaning of pregnancy and birth in the culture, how the culture responds to this type of pregnancy, and what the kinship connections and responsibilities are in various cultures. We could think about ways changes in technologies might contribute to pregnancy patterns and ways different cultures tend to respond to these changes. We might focus on the kind of rituals that are used to celebrate pregnancy and birth and how these differ when the pregnancy occurs in a marriage and when the mother is not married.

Psychology

Using a psychological perspective to study teenage pregnancy, we would think about things like the personality of the mother, the mental health of a pregnant teenager, the effects of teenage pregnancy on the intelligence and personality of the child, and the learning problems of infants born in adverse conditions. We would probably try to devise methods of psychotherapy that would help both mother and infant. To help us understand what is going on, we would concentrate on intrapersonal and intrapsychic processes.

Sociology

Using a sociological perspective to study teenage pregnancy, we might want to gather information about the social factors that tend to make pregnancy rates decrease or increase. We probably would pay attention to racial, ethnic, and class differences. We would note how the norms and mores about sexual behavior, pregnancy, and abortion have changed in the last several decades.

Family Science

Approaching teen pregnancy with a family science perspective, we would be interested in such things as how familial factors influence and are influenced by teen pregnancies. We would assume there are a number of deeply experienced emotions that would surround any pregnancy and especially a pregnancy that seems premature. We would think about whether the mother and her family are developmentally ready for a birth, and how not being ready may create problems in the future. We would probably think about how the family's ideology is involved. Each family's belief system gives it unique family paradigms, values, goals, and standards, and these influence how people feel and act. We could ask questions such as, how does this type of pregnancy affect the boundaries of existing relationships?

As family scientists, we would think about how the interaction with the environment makes a difference and how implicit family rules regulate the responses of the kin network. We would study how the integration of the teenage mother into her parental family is related to becoming pregnant. We would be interested in what would promote an altruistic and accepting view of the new infant, and how the family system would respond to the abrupt changes in the family structure.

All Disciplines Are Valuable

We have seen that the five disciplines are different ways of thinking. They are so different in their fundamental assumptions, methods, and worldviews that they cannot be integrated, and we need not try to integrate them. Trying to combine them would be like trying to look at both sides of a coin at the same time. It is also important that we do not make the mistake of the six blind men when they viewed the elephant. Each of them thought his view of the elephant was the true or most accurate or most valuable one. We need to realize that all the disciplines focus on important parts of the elephant, and they are all valuable and useful. *We would make a serious error if we were to believe that any one of these fields is* the *best or the ultimate solution to human needs and problems.* This book is about the family science way of thinking, and it is an important perspective, but to think family science will be able to solve all the problems not handled by older disciplines would be a serious error.

We need all the different ways of thinking available to us, choosing what will help us most in each situation. This means that sometimes thinking psychologically is the most helpful; at other times thinking economically, legally, or poetically is the most helpful. There are many options available as we approach our problems and strive to fulfill our human potential.

The family science perspective is a unique way of thinking, and it is much more helpful than most people in our society realize; but it should not be viewed as a panacea or cure-all. It is a new sibling in the academic family, but it is not the only kid on the block.

SUMMARY

We have looked at perspectives as sets of assumptions that allow us to pursue knowledge in a particular way. This means that each of them involves a unique way of thinking, asking questions, gathering information, applying ideas, and answering questions. Ancient perspectives, such as those of Plato and Aristotle, still profoundly influence the way we think today.

In this chapter we introduced some basic ideas of four contemporary perspectives—well-established social science disciplines—that have an interest in studying the family: economics, anthropology, psychology, and sociology. Then we introduced the family science perspective, a budding new discipline.

The family science perspective has benefited from the contributions of family therapists, academics in child development and family relations (CDFR), home economists who specialize in home management, and feminist scholars.

While we believe the family science perspective opens up an extremely useful way of looking at individual, family, and societal problems, we must be aware that it takes its place among many disciplines that contribute to our ongoing knowledge of the family and its members.

Key Terms

Perspective
Rationality
Empiricism
Individualism
Ecosystemic perspective
Economics
Hedonism
Anthropology
Sociology
Psychology
Family science
Assumptions
Discipline (academic)
Family realm
Natural
Experiential
Determinism
Indeterminism
Generations
Emotions
Development
Ideology
Communication
Gender

Study Questions

1. What is the significance of the elephant analogy in the chapter? How does it relate to the study of different disciplines?
2. What is meant by a *perspective?* What were the primary perspectives mentioned in the chapter? How does a perspective relate to a *discipline?*
3. Name several ways the family science perspective is different from the other social science perspectives mentioned in the text.
4. Describe three areas from which family science emerged. How did each contribute to the discipline of family science?
5. List the five assumptions family scientists make, as outlined in your chapter.
6. What is meant by the family realm?
7. Why are family processes more important than people realize?
8. Write two or three paragraphs describing how a social problem could be solved using a family-based approach.

NOTES

1. These departments have many different labels. Among them are: family development, family studies, family ecology, family living, family relations, family environment, and family science. Many of them are departments that have a child development or human development component, so they are called family studies and child development, human development and family relations, child and family studies, family science and child development, and so on.

Family Systems

2

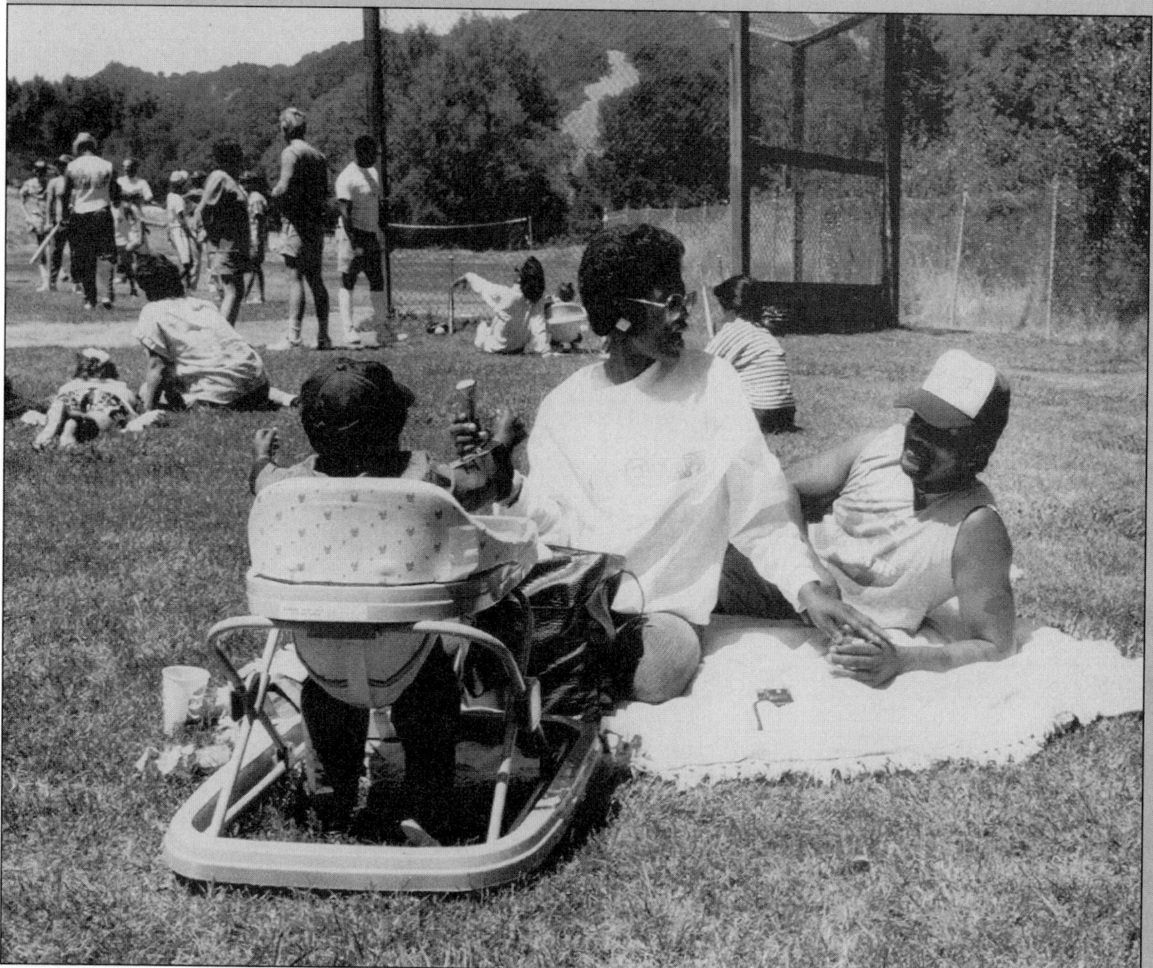

Main Ideas

1 // *General theories* are clusters of assumptions, concepts and principles (truth assertions) and are the main ideas or the intellectual "heart" of the disciplines.

2 // *General systems theory* is a broad, inclusive and multi-disciplinary theory that is used in a number of different disciplines.

3 // *Family systems theory* is a more specialized theory that includes a number of systemic ideas uniquely designed to help us understand process in the family realm.

4 // Several of the basic *concepts* in family systems theory are *systems, wholeness, interdependence, subsystems, inputs, outputs, boundaries, choice, information processing*, and *feedback*.

5 // The systemic approach is unique because of its emphasis on *indeterminism, equifinality, cycles*, and *emphasizing effects* rather than causes.

6 // One specific tool from the systems perspective is *punctuation*. The concept of punctuation helps us look beyond seeking "causes" of family problems.

Before we talk about family systems, we need to take a look at one of the basic building blocks used by all scholars. When scholars try to answer the question "What is going on here?" they are always building on the accumulated findings of others. In everyday life people refer to this phenomenon when they say there is "no need to reinvent the wheel." The process of using the work of others in scholarly investigation is made easier if the accumulation of ideas and observations has been collected and organized into theories. *Theories* are combinations of hunches, partially documented facts, and notions about which of the many characteristics of a situation deserve attention.

The theories we use in the social sciences are not the realities we are trying to understand; they are the mental models or intellectual diagrams we use to think with. A theory is like a map. It may be written down, and we may use it to orient ourselves, but it is only a representation of the external reality. A theory is also

> "Thus a systems approach asks: What circles are happening in this family? Are there behaviors that lead to other behaviors that lead back to themselves?"
>
> —Janet Bavelas and Lynn Segal, 1982

subject to change. As we use it, we may discover that it no longer fits the reality we observe. Just as maps must be revised to reflect changes in the physical environment, so theories are constantly being changed, or discarded entirely, as our "travels" reveal more about the processes that our theories are supposed to represent.

Some theories are more general, or abstract, than others. For example, a theory about how humans learn is more general than a theory about how humans learn mathematics. Theories that are so abstract and inclusive that they can be applied in many situations are called **general theories**, and theories that are more specific are called middle-range theories, limited theories, or specific theories. Each of the social sciences has developed a number of general theories that help to explain its subject matter.

One of the general theories that is widely used in the modern social sciences focuses on the patterns in systems and is called *systems theory*. **Systems theory** holds that the parts or elements of systems are interconnected and strive for balance as they define boundaries and achieve goals. General systems theory is so broad that it includes ideas about all systems, living and nonliving. It is so general that family specialists find only a few of its ideas helpful. Family systems are unique in a number of ways, so family scientists have developed a slightly more specialized version, which they call **family systems theory**. This theory has been very useful to family theorists, researchers, and practitioners, and is described in the remainder of this chapter.

Family Systems Theory

All scientific theories have specialized and technical terms, abstractions that stand for the categories of reality the theory treats. Such terms are called *concepts*. A set of concepts used in a particular theory or theoretical perspective is called a *conceptual framework*.

Learning a conceptual framework is a little like learning a new language. Like a new language, it increases our sensitivity to some aspects of reality. It helps us notice things we didn't notice before, or see things better than we did. Also, learning a conceptual framework may help us understand things better because we have distinct terms for things that formerly were ambiguous and ill-defined. That is, we not only can see more clearly, but we have new, ready-made categories for what we see. Seeing more, and having specific terms for what we see, we are better able to communicate about what is going on. Also, the framework increases the possibility of conceiving connections and consequences, possibilities and patterns, inherent in the situations we observe. Thus a good conceptual framework opens the door to fresh insights and may be a tool of discovery.

Systems

The most important concept in systems theory is the system. The term *system* refers to the regular and enduring patterns in an organized set of elements. At first we may be inclined to define a system as "a whole made up of interacting parts." But with this definition we are tempted to think a family system is made up of the individuals in the family. When we think this way, we are probably thinking *individualistically* rather than thinking *systemically*. The elements or parts that make up the family system are not the individuals. The key elements are the *patterns* in the processes as the individuals interact. For example, a family may have an implicit rule that "Father can criticize others, but others can't criticize Father." This rule creates a pattern in the processes of the family because it governs the interactions. Rules like this are the fundamental components of the system that are important in family systems theory. Individuals are needed to have a system, but there isn't a system until there is pattern in the processes, and it is the pattern in the processes that creates systemness.

Wholeness

"The whole is more than the sum of its parts" is a statement commonly used to describe a system. One of the significant ideas in family systems theory is the notion that the family has its own unique character, that it is something more than the sum of its individual members. This characteristic is sometimes described as wholeness; we refer to the *holistic* aspect of families.

When we think systemically, we focus our attention primarily on systemic processes rather than on the parts of the system. The parts have a secondary importance; they are the background rather than the primary concern. If we focus our attention on the nature of the parts of the system or on what the parts are doing, we are not thinking about the system. A rabbit helps to illustrate this in Box 2.1. Another example of thinking systemically (holistically) is an orchestra. An orchestra takes on a character of its own, over and above the sum of its individual players and instruments. Okun and Rappaport (1980) present still another look at the system—this time the *family* system:

> The system is an integrated, coherent entity that is more than the mere composite of independent elements. This wholeness transcends the sum of the system's component elements. A family consisting of Mother, Father, Sally, Johnny, and David Brown

Box 2.1 *Parts and systems*

Sometimes we assume the best way to study something is to divide it into its parts and study each of the separate parts. The process of dividing something into its parts rests upon a prior knowledge of what the parts are, and since parts may be subdivided into smaller parts, the way one "cuts it up" may determine what one learns. Also, there may be some characteristics of a system that derive from the ongoing operation of the system *as a whole*, or that emerge or evolve from the operation of the system generally but are not apparent when attention is focused on the parts of the system rather than the system as a whole.

An example of how researchers may be misled by concentrating on the individual parts of a system, rather than the system as a whole, is cited by Abraham Kaplan (1964) in his classic *The Conduct of Inquiry*. It applies directly to rabbit, rather than human, families, but makes the point nicely nonetheless.

> A famous set of experiments was once carried out to determine what produced ovulation in the rabbit. One after another a series of possible causative agents was eliminated—various hormones, nerve impulses, and so on—and still the rabbit ovulated, till at last it was recognized that when one source of stimulation is blocked others become effective. The rabbit, if I may say so, does not put all her eggs in one basket, and the experimenter would be well advised to follow her example. (p. 158)

> is viewed as a total interactional process that characterizes them as "the Browns"; it is not viewed as the sum of Mr. Brown, Mrs. Brown, Sally Brown, Johnny Brown and David Brown. If Sally is away at college and you are going to visit the family, you are still going to visit "the Browns," not "the Browns minus Sally."
>
> Despite this wholeness, a change in one part of the system may cause a change in many parts (subsystems) of the larger system and in the larger system itself. Suppose that Mr. Brown comes for treatment because he is having difficulties with alcoholism and that he is cured of alcoholism. This cure may have an impact on every subsystem within his family and on the total family system itself. For example, the subsystem of Mrs. Brown and her daughter Sally may be affected. Mrs. Brown may have to transfer her anger to Sally, since Mr. Brown will no longer be a feasible target. Sally, in turn, may act more aggressively toward her younger brothers, Johnny and David. David may begin to suck his thumb and whimper because of Sally's aggression, and Mr. Brown himself may express resentment that his family is not behaving appreciatively toward his giving up drinking. All members of the Brown family may change their characteristics, as well as their ways of relating, because of one person's change in behavior. And the *whole* family system may be changed in a way that is greater than the sum of its individual changes. Thus, the system cannot be fully comprehended or represented by *summing* its subsystems. (pp. 8–9)

Another way of saying this is *we cannot understand the Browns simply by understanding each individual member of the family.* We must also understand the relationships and interaction processes that have occurred and do occur when the family functions "as family."

The characteristic of wholeness is illustrated in Murray Bowen's conceptualization of the family as an emotional unit (Bowen, 1978; Kerr & Bowen, 1988). Bowen was a psychiatrist who worked extensively with schizophrenics. His observations of relationships between mothers and schizophrenic patients, and later, observations of entire families in "live-in" research, revealed a complex network of what he called "fusion of selfs" in an "undifferentiated family ego mass." The problems of a schizophrenic child, it turned out, were not "individual" problems, nor were they "mother-and-patient" problems, as had commonly been assumed.

> Instead, it was a fragment of a larger family emotional system in which fathers were as intimately involved as the mothers, which was fluid and shifting, and which could extend itself to involve the entire central family unit, and even non-relatives. (Bowen, 1978, pp. 104–105)

Even "normal" families are tied together in ways that make it impossible to understand each member without understanding the whole. Bowen's conceptualization of the family emotional system will be elaborated on in Chapter 5, Emotions. Here it is sufficient to cite his work as a pioneering effort in the discovery of the family as a holistic entity.

Interdependence

Okun and Rappaport's earlier reference to "the Browns" also illustrates the system characteristic of interdependence. The extent of interdependence of the parts in a system can be difficult to comprehend. The very definition of most family roles depends upon the existence of an other: One cannot be a mother without an offspring; a husband without a wife; a sibling without a brother or sister. How people in those system-defined positions behave is an ongoing net consequence of actions and reactions, perceptions, and interpretations of family members. The behavior of any one family member is related to and dependent upon past and current behaviors of the others.

> The family, because of its powerful and long-lasting effect on its members, represents a highly interdependent type of system. Traditionally this interdependence was viewed as the means of maintaining a delicate balance among the system's parts, or members. . . . As members respond to situations, certain other members may consciously or unconsciously shift to adjust to the quivering system. Current thinking suggests that families do not only seek balance, rather they move through evolutionary periods which affect all members. (Galvin & Brommel, 1982, p. 27)

Virginia Satir's (1972) comparison of the family to a mobile also illustrates the nature of interdependence. A touch to any part of the mobile creates change in other parts and temporarily alters the system as a whole. Similarly, "as events touch one member of the family, other family members reverberate in relationship to the change in the affected member" (Galvin & Brommel, 1982, p. 5).

Environment and Subsystems

When we think systemically we focus on one unit as the system. The systems that surround it are the environment and the systems inside it are subsystems. For example, when we are thinking about a mother, father, and children as a system, the conjugal system (the couple) and the sibling system are subsystems. Each of these subsystems could also be divided into subsystems. Alternatively, the family system interacts with many larger systems in its environment.

Systems can be analyzed at either a macro or micro level. We use a macrolevel analysis if we want to compare families across cultures or historical eras. It often involves large numbers of families (perhaps represented in trends or averages) in large, complicated systems. The micro level focuses on a smaller or lower level of analysis. For example, Bank and Kahn's *The Sibling Bond* (1982) is concerned primarily with the sibling system, which is their unit of focus. At that micro level of analysis, the parents are part of the environment and pairs or larger combinations of siblings are subsystems.

Inputs and Outputs

Inputs are anything that comes into a system, and outputs are anything that a system produces. Some of the inputs going into an automobile system are gas, oil, antifreeze, tune-ups, other maintenance, insurance payments, new tires, and the driver's actions (such as turning on the ignition). Among the outputs an automobile produces are transportation, convenience, pride in its cost or beauty or efficiency, wear upon the roads it travels, risk of injury in traffic, and many types of pollution.

Some of the inputs in family systems are time, energy, affection, communication, money, information, tenderness, understanding, teaching, nurturance, space, and support. Outputs that can come from family systems are acceptance, love, security, bonds, a home, understanding, a sense of meaning and purpose in life, affection, learning, and intimacy. (Unfortunately, there are also undesirable outputs such as hate, bitterness, abuse, exploitation, hurt feelings, resentment, and suspicion.)

Boundaries

System boundaries occur where two or more systems or subsystems interface, interact, or come together. They are the walls, borders, or limits of a system.

Some boundaries are physical. For example, city limits, county lines, and state lines are physical boundaries. Family systems also have physical boundaries, such as property lines between the family lot and the neighbor's. Inside homes there are many physical boundaries, ranging from private rooms to private drawers to private toothbrushes. Sometimes space is temporarily private, as indicated by locked bathroom or bedroom doors.

There are many subtle physical boundaries in family systems. There may be assigned or "traditional" places at the dinner table, or preferences for a favorite chair or position in front of the television. A physical boundary can also be the accepted degree of "personal space" shown in greetings, farewells, and expressions of intimacy or anger.

Some people think physical boundaries are the only ones that matter, but family scientists pay more attention to other kinds of boundaries. For example, emotional boundaries are critical to understanding the family realm. We use emotional boundaries to control how "close" we want other people to be to us emotionally. Most people have some superficial relationships, some close relationships, and a few intimate relationships. These differences become so natural to us that we manage them almost unconsciously. Generally we know who we have close relationships with and who we relate to more distantly, and we act in ways to maintain these relationships.

Boundaries in families are not static, and some are more changeable than others. They change at different times, at different rates, and sometimes vary drastically depending on contextual elements. For example, how "intimate" a greeting a wife bestows upon her returning husband may depend upon how tired she is, the number of observers present, how long he has been gone, and the probabilities that he would ever return. Changeable physical and psychological states affect boundary definition and maintenance. At one time a person may be tired, upset, or frustrated and send nonverbal or verbal messages to "Leave me alone, I need some space." At other times the same person may want closeness and fewer boundaries. Families develop elaborate rules and rituals in ongoing efforts to manage boundaries successfully.

Drawing by Teitelbaum; ©The New Yorker Magazine, Inc.

The variable of openness refers to the permeability of family boundaries, or how available the system is to inputs and outputs from the environment. The family system is an open system, influencing and influenced by its environment.

Choice and Information Processing

Information processing is an important process in family systems, and it is intimately associated with choice. Choice is the ability to make decisions based on information received and interpreted. Adaptation to an external environment is made possible by information processing: Options are not options until they are perceived and interpreted. Adaptive systems shape their own destinies by exercising choice, and the complexity and self-awareness of the processes of choice involved in social behavior are among the characteristics that seem to distinguish human systems from other biological systems (plants and animals, birds, fishes, insects). Human systems are sometimes described as *cybernetic*, meaning that they behave as if they can think, process information, make choices that influence their life course, and engage in purposive action.

Feedback. Feedback refers to the process of monitoring the transformation processes and assessing outputs to see if they are within acceptable standards. Family systems are constantly monitoring these processes. For example, parents may keep track of how much their school-age children argue, eat what they ought to, fight, do their homework, practice the piano, get enough rest, and stay clean enough. They may also monitor how effectively the family spends time together, uses money, welcomes visitors, carries on family traditions, shows interest in what others are doing, has enough consideration, and is responsible to neighbors.

Much of the feedback in family systems is routine and automatic: It demands little time and attention. A typical family has hundreds of transformation processes and outcomes going on in a typical day. As long as the operation of family life proceeds in typical or normal patterns—that is, within appropriate limits—the monitoring and evaluation processes demand little attention. Family feedback processes may be visualized as an enormous instrument panel having thousands of gauges, warning lights, and buzzers on it. When the family system is functioning "normally," family members go about their business and seem to ignore most of the panel. Only when a "warning light" flashes, dramatically pointing to an unacceptable input or output, does the panel compel interest and action of some kind. This feedback works very much like the warning lights on the dashboards of automobiles. Most of us drive without worrying about engine temperature until the temperature gauge signals that something is seriously wrong.

In a description of biological evolution, Kenneth Boulding (1981) depicts feedback processes in terms of "homeostatic mechanisms" and what he calls a carpenter function. His account fits feedback in family systems as well.

> If growth is to be orderly and fit into a pattern, there must be some kind of homeostatic mechanism at each point of growth. This is the "carpenter function." . . . A homeostatic or cybernetic mechanism involves some kind of knowledge structure that is capable of perceiving, presumably through some kind of structural changes in the knowledge structure itself, divergences between some actual state of affairs and some ideal state of affairs, and is capable of selecting and directing energy and matter toward diminishing this divergence. This is "deviation-diminishing feedback." If these processes do not exist, then what we have is a cancer or uncontrolled growth and chaotic cells. (p. 108)

When a part of a family system starts to deviate from the previously established patterns in the system, those responsible for the welfare of the system pay attention to that feedback, and try to determine if they need to intervene. They evaluate the feedback to see if it is desirable or undesirable, tending toward "cancer" or "chaos," or whether the deviation represents positive change, "growth," or "evolution."

When the feedback in a family system signals the occurrence of change, the family can respond in ways that suppress or facilitate continued change. Such action creates what is known as a *feedback loop,* because the evaluation of the feedback has led to attempts to alter the system in ways that will alter the feedback, and so on. If the responses are intended to maintain or increase the changes because they are perceived as desirable, the process is known as a *deviation amplifying feedback loop* (also sometimes called "positive feedback loops" or "variety feedback loops"). If the responses are attempts to decrease or eliminate the changes that have been signaled by the feedback, the process is called a *deviation dampening feedback loop* (also sometimes called "negative feedback loops" or "constancy feedback loops") (Constantine, 1986, pp. 58–61).

Figure 2.1 diagrams some of the characteristics of the systems we have discussed. This figure helps us appreciate the diversity of family inputs and the many types and effects of family outputs.

Some Contrasts and Comparisons

To show how family systems theory differs from other ways of looking at families, it is helpful to make some specific comparisons. First, some historical and theoretical context is provided by adding to our discussion of determinism and indeterminism in Chapter 1. Then the indeterminism of systems theory is compared to the deterministic view. Finally, family systems theory is compared to the institutional and market approaches of sociology and economics.

Determinism and Indeterminism

A major difference between family systems theory and most other social science theories is in the way the idea of cause and effect is interpreted. Most scientific theories take a deterministic view of cause and effect. According to the philosophy of determinism, everything can be explained in terms of a complex series of cause-and-effect relationships if only the relevant steps in that chain of events can be correctly identified. When an event happens it is because of previously determining events, and therefore the apparent options or choices in the immediate situation are, in fact, illusory.

In the deterministic perspective, application of the scientific method makes it possible to unravel the patterns of cause and effect. When they have been correctly mapped and catalogued, correct prediction of outcomes is possible, and if predicted outcomes do not appear, it is because the scientists do not yet understand all of the links in the chain of cause and effect. It follows that when science has progressed sufficiently, and all the determining factors are known, accurate prediction will be possible and notions of free will will be unnecessary to explain human interaction.

Historical development of determinism. Determinism is the dominant way of thinking in modern Western society, but it has not always been so. Other ways of thinking about how things happen have prevailed in other times and places. One of the other ways of thinking is that the gods (Divine Providence, fate, or predestination) control human history, both individually and collectively. Another is the voluntaristic or "free will" position, which is that, while many things seem to be determined, there is a component of individual choice in social life.

In the Middle Ages a "providential," or religious, paradigm prevailed. If things were predictable, it was because God was omniscient rather than because effect

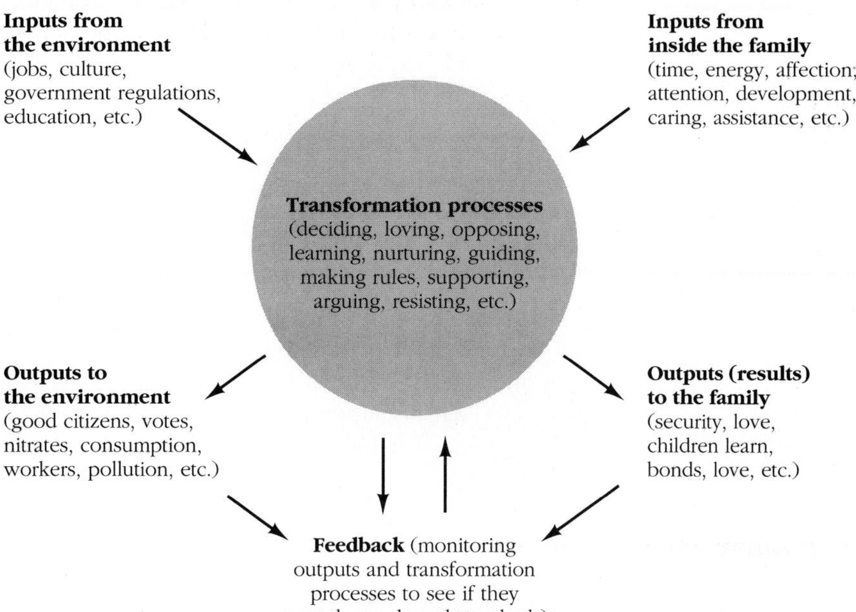

FIGURE 2.1 Diagram of the interrelationships of some of the parts of family systems

inexorably follows cause. Part of the intellectual awakening known as the Enlightenment was the growth of scientific reasoning and increasing confidence in natural rather than divine law. Many of the "natural" laws were cast in deterministic terms. Seventeenth-century scholars such as Thomas Hobbes (1588–1679) and Baruch Spinoza (1632–1677) developed elaborate arguments for determinism. Spinoza, for example, argued that men were born ignorant of the causes of the events that surround them. They have an unquenchable desire, however, to understand why things happen. When they believe they understand a cause, whether it is truly the cause or not, they think of themselves as a bit more free (Spinoza, *Ethics I*, Appendix):

> Thus the infant believes that it is by free will that it seeks the breast; the angry boy believes that by free will he wishes vengeance; the timid man thinks it is with free will that he seeks flight; the drunkard believes that by a free command of his mind he speaks the things which when sober he wishes he had left unsaid. Thus the madman, the chatterer, the boy, and others of the same kind, all believe they speak by a free command of the mind, whilst, in truth, they have no power to restrain the impulse which they have to speak, so that experience itself, no less than reason, clearly teaches that men believe themselves to be free simply because they are conscious of their own actions, knowing nothing of the causes by which they are determined: it teaches, too, that the decrees of the mind are nothing but the appetites themselves, which differ, therefore, according to the different temper of the body. (Spinoza, *Ethics III*, Prop. II, scholia; see Wild, 1930, p. 212)

Over the next two centuries determinism became the dominant view in science. Chemists sought chemical laws, and physicists, physical laws, and social scientists looked for the principles that would allow them to predict human behavior accurately. Many scientists were convinced that it was possible to achieve

> a complete integration of the various aspects of our experience in one great system of cause-and-effect relations. Meanwhile, philosophers became increasingly involved in the problem of causality, and they too had come to feel that "cause" is a central concept of human experience. Thus, by the end of the nineteenth century, the domain of determinism had attained almost universal extent. (Mead, 1953, p. 321)

The family systems approach is an attempt to break away from the deterministic way of thinking that dominates our society and our scientific perspectives. It is an attempt to focus on indeterministic aspects of family systems to try to understand what is happening and find ways to help people create more successful and effective families. The indeterminism in family systems theory can be better understood and the usefulness of these ideas can be better appreciated when we understand that, according to the systemic perspective, freedom varies.

Freedom varies. Many family scientists believe that freedom of choice is not an "all or nothing" thing. The amount of freedom families have depends on many things and it varies from one situation to another. One factor affecting freedom of choice is whether people *believe* they are free to choose. If they believe their choices matter and that they can help determine outcomes, they often do. If they are fatalistic, believing that God, nature, the government, or other forces outside themselves are the critical movers and that they themselves are merely acted upon, then that definition often becomes a self-fulfilling prophecy.

In the family systems perspective all people have some freedom to choose, but all are also subject to many constraints and imperatives that limit freedom. There are some factors that limit choice and others that expand our options. Examples of variables that influence choice include genetic makeup, physical and mental health, knowledge and talents, family history, geographic location, climate, laws, community facilities, governments, culture and family history. Clearly, the amount of freedom one has varies from one situation to another. For example, people have no choice about the genetic makeup that determines how tall they will grow. They have more choice regarding health habits that will influence whatever growth potential they possess.

Present and future choices are constrained by past choices. A couple beginning a relationship may have a great deal of freedom to choose whether they want to have children, whether one or both will pursue a career, and how much responsibility each will assume for household chores. Those early choices will influence the options available to them later in life. For example, once a baby is born, the options center about how best to care for that baby. The couple is no longer free to decide not to have children. Robert Frost's famous poem "The Road Not Taken" is a classic literary example of how present choices limit future options.

Equifinality

There are several concepts that have been created in systems theory that help us understand how systems analysts think about indeterminism and how systemic thinking is different from other theories. One of these unique concepts is equifinality. **Equifinality** is the idea that "many beginnings can lead to the same outcome, and the same beginning can lead to quite different outcomes" (Bavelas & Segal, 1982, p. 103). In other words, it is the notion that any "final" thing (some consequence or effect) can be brought about by multiple and hence, in our minds, fairly "equal" determinants or causes.

The concept of equifinality sensitizes us to the possible interchangeability of certain "causes," and alerts us to the possibility that there may be many "true" explanations of a given circumstance rather than a single "cause." At the least, it signals that family processes are potentially far more complicated than popular wisdom allows. For one thing, we know that many different processes occur simultaneously in family systems. Also, if many different antecedents appear related to the same outcome, perhaps the interaction processes that intervene between the supposed cause and the outcome should be studied. Thus the concept of equifinality forces us to consider the interaction of the parts of a system as well as the static characteristics of the parts. In the words of Okun and Rappaport (1980):

> These results may spring from different origins, but no matter where one begins, the same results are likely to occur. For example, a family who is scapegoating one of its members would probably blame that member for causing a family crisis regardless of who actually precipitated the crisis. Therefore, interactions are more significant than initial causal conditions, if such entities as causal conditions can be considered even to exist. Thus, to understand a family, one usually does not need to get a complete history of each member of the family, as the family pattern will be apparent from studying the current interactions of the family members. It is the nature of the organization of the system, the *interactional process*, that determines the *results* of the system. (p. 10)

A counterpart to the idea of equifinality is the notion that the same original condition, or cause, may produce different results. Friedman (1985) illustrates both perspectives in the following lists. Here are ways the same apparent cause can produce opposite effects:

- Parental investment can promote overachievement or underachievement.
- An overly strict father can produce an overly strict son (when he is a father) or one who is too permissive.
- Alcoholic parents can produce alcoholic offspring or offspring who marry alcoholics.
- Dependency can lead to helpless or controlling attitudes.
- Well-defined stands can lead to admiration or revulsion.
- Surrendering and taking over are both ways of adapting. (p. 58)

Here are examples of how the same effect could have come from opposite causes:

- Someone who sleeps a great deal could be depressed or content.
- A family problem could surface after a business failure or a business success.
- An extremely rigid offspring can be produced by an extremely rigid parent or an overly flexible parent.
- Lack of change can be a by-product of polarization or of too much togetherness.
- Ineffective leadership can result from stands that are too authoritarian or too concerned with consensus. (p. 59)

In view of the many possible causes of a given outcome, and the many possible outcomes of a given cause or set of causes, it seems appropriate to emphasize the system processes responsible for such alchemy rather than try to find "the" causes.

Cycles

Another aspect of systems theory that distinguishes it from other theories is in the emphasis systemic thinking places on cycles rather than linear thinking. A *cycle*, in the dictionary definition, is "a series of events or operations that recur regularly and usually lead back to the starting point." We are all familiar with cycles in the cosmos and in biological processes, from the diurnal cycles of sun and tides to the estral cycle of women. Most of the cycles in the family realm are less predictable and uniform than astronomical or biological cycles, but they are just as real. They consist of complex circular processes of behavior that lead to other behaviors and ultimately back to the starting point, or at least a situation very similar to the starting point.

> A systems approach asks: What circles are happening in this family? Are there behaviors that lead to other behaviors that lead back to themselves? For example, in Eugene O'Neill's play, Long Day's Journey Into Night, the family members watch the mother closely, which makes her visibly nervous, which makes them watch her closely . . . until the circle winds into a spiral leading to the return of her addiction, which they all fear. The above description could also have begun: the mother is visibly nervous, which makes the family watch her closely, etc. Our addiction, as analysts of human behavior, is to "beginnings" and "causes"; we cannot help thinking that it must start somewhere (Sluzki, 1981). And well it may, but it may not matter any more where it started—which is the principle of equifinality. (Bavelas & Segal, 1982, pp. 103–104)

Cycles are quite different from linear sequences. When we think in a linear way, we think of cause and effect to try to find what is "making" each individual act the way he or she does. When family scientists use some of the nonsystemic theories in the field, they look for "the" causes. Also, family members often think in linear, cause-and-effect terms, looking for someone or something to blame as "the" cause of an event or problem. O'Neill portrays a network of blaming, with each family member blaming one or more other family members for their individual and family problems. The blaming of each of them influences how they respond and they set up a vicious cycle that is repeated over and over again, gradually destroying the healthy aspects of their family system.

Daily life is sprinkled with routines and cycles, each person knowing what will come next.

Cycles also can be positive and healthy. For example, expressions of tenderness, sensitivity, and care tend to create their own constructive cycles in a family system. Also, many of these cycles are repeated so often they become as much of the structure of the family system as the people in the system. Family systems theory pays a great deal of attention to cycles. In fact, these cyclic processes are closer to the heart of family systems theory than the individuals or the roles people play.

Emphasis on Effects

When we understand the concept of equifinality, we recognize that in family systems it is impossible to find scientific laws that will provide causal explanations about the important aspects of family systems. This is a dramatic departure from the dominant ways of thinking in Western cultures, and it has enormous consequences.

One of the consequences is that when we use a systemic way of thinking we tend to ask *what* questions rather than *why* questions. We ask "what is going on" and "what can we do about it" questions rather than "why" and "what are the causes" questions. When families have problems, we find ourselves trying to identify future goals and ideals to strive toward rather than trying to find the causes (blame or responsibility) for the problems.

Family life is much like floating on a river, with stretches of smooth water, stretches of rough water, and unexpected twists and turns.

Of course, processes that precede (causes) and processes that follow (effects) are always connected, like the two sides of a coin. However, just as it is difficult to concentrate on both sides of a coin at the same time, it is hard to give equal emphasis to the exploration of causes and the identification of effects. Faced with this choice, the systems analyst usually chooses to think about probable effects rather than causes. A practical consequence of this emphasis in work with real families is that it helps us make beneficial interventions (by thinking about probable effects) even though the details of the causal processes are not clearly understood.

An analogy may clarify the point that effects, not causes, are the main concern. Define the family system as a family floating downriver on a raft. It is located in an environment of many other systems and subsystems, and bobs and spins according to many transitory forces and processes. The family, interested in safely navigating the river, is less concerned with the "whys" of each change in direction than with the probable effects of certain actions. Imagine that a family member sees a big rock looming ahead. There is immediate concern about the probable effect of the raft hitting the rock, but no one worries much about what caused the rock to be there. There may be a quick assessment of the probable effects of adding new forces to the unspecified forces already operating: Will rowing help? Which way? Shall we use a pole and try to push off? The focus on effects helps the family on the raft to concentrate on the critical outcome—

surviving the trip—and provides a rationale for choosing among the many possible responses to sighting the rock. Given limited time and resources, many of the causal systems operating are of no interest to the family. A focus on effects helps them to select those that, in their limited awareness of the various systems, seem most likely to produce the desired outcome.

Note that the systems perspective does not deny the operation of cause and effect. Instead, persons working from a systems perspective merely take the position that cause and effect is not a very *useful* way to look at family processes. In addition to the distortion inherent in defining reciprocal processes as linear, a focus on causes directs attention backward in time. The attention of the family on the raft is focused downstream, where the raft is headed. If there is too much backward looking, obstacles ahead may not be seen in time. Many family systems theorists have backgrounds in clinical work with problem families, and they tend to be oriented toward helping families in trouble. Like watchers on a family raft, many are willing to forgo a clear view of the scenery behind for a useful view of the rapids ahead.

Paul Watzlawick (1967) is among those who have urged the adoption of an effects-oriented systems approach in family science:

> Seen in this light, the possible or hypothetical causes of behavior assume a secondary importance, but the effect of the behavior emerges as a criterion of prime significance in the interaction of closely related individuals. . . . A rule of thumb can be stated in this connection: where the *why?* of a piece of behavior remains obscure, the question of *what for?* can still supply a valid answer. (Watzlawick et al., 1967, p. 45)

The idea of emphasizing effects rather than causes is very difficult to convey because the "natural" ways of thinking in Western societies link cause and effect in an inseparable and deterministic way. Systems thinking, equifinality, and the emphasis on effects all involve the use of a different worldview, a new paradigm that an enthusiastic minority of family scientists and other scholars offer as a better way to understand family life (Burr, 1973, pp. 26–28).

Other Theoretical Perspectives

Family institution theories. A comparison of the concepts *family system* and *family institution* highlights a further characteristic of family systems theory. If we take a family institution approach, we pay attention to the social and cultural definitions of family, and the ideals and expectations people bring to family life. Elements of the institutional approach include individuals, sets of roles (such as spouse, parent, and child), "scripts" or general expectations about how persons in those roles ought to behave, and sanctions that follow nonconformity. In contrast, a family systems approach focuses on family life as it is experienced, not on socially constructed expectations about it.

Consider motherhood as an illustration of the difference between a family institutions and a family systems approach. A feminist author has recently identified the ways the institution of motherhood constrains the experience of mothering. She makes an explicit distinction between institution and personal/familial enactment:

> Throughout this book I try to distinguish between two meanings of motherhood, one superimposed on the other: the *potential relationship* of any woman to her powers of reproduction and to children; and the *institution*, which aims at ensuring that potential—and all women—shall remain under male control. . . . At certain points in history, and in certain cultures, the idea of woman-as-mother has worked to endow all women with respect, even with awe, and to give women some say in the life of a people or a clan. But for most of what we know as the "mainstream" of recorded history, motherhood as institution has ghettoized and degraded female potentialities. . . . When I try to return [to my experience of mothering], I realize that I was effectively alienated from my real body and my real spirit by the institution—and not the fact—of motherhood. This institution—the foundation of human society as we know it—allowed me only certain views, certain expectations, whether embodied in the booklet in my obstetrician's waiting room, the novels I had read, my mother-in-law's approval, my memories of my own mother, the Sistine Madonna or she of the Michelangelo *Pieta*. (Rich, 1976, pp. 13, 38–39).

"Market" and "male" theories. A common criticism of the theories typically used to study the family, such as exchange theory and all its variants, is that they are based on hedonistic, marketplace, or masculine values (Glasser & Glasser, 1977; Ruddick, 1982; Gilligan, 1982). The market perspective has resulted in a predominance of theory that emphasizes individual needs and problems, and ways that families are like markets. In many so-called family theories, market-based values and attributes are elevated to a status that renders family values and attributes valueless and invisible.

Because historically men have been socialized for participation in the public sphere, and therefore trained more thoroughly in market values than in family values, critics argue there is a male bias in contemporary family studies (see, for example, Smith's *A Sociology for Women* [1979]). We take the view that the biases are not so much the result of male versus female orientation as of market versus family orientation. Thus, women socialized in market-oriented value systems may be expected to exhibit the so-called male perspectives on family life.

Theory that analyzes families from market-based perspectives helps us see ways families and markets are similar, but it obscures in particular the thinking and work mothers do in families (Smith, Ruddick, Gilligan). It reduces the complexities of nurturing (or "mothering") a family to "family management." Family systems theories have been useful in overcoming these particular biases.

Using Family Systems Theory

The payoff with family systems theory is that it gives us new and unique ideas we can use to help families cope more successfully with the challenges of life. Thus far in this chapter, a large number of systemic concepts and ways of thinking have been described, but there have not been examples of how to use these ideas to help families. In this last section, two examples of how to use these ideas are described.

Punctuation

The concept of punctuation encompasses many of the ideas introduced earlier in this chapter, and it is very useful in helping families. **Punctuation** refers to the process of simplifying cyclic and indeterministic patterns by dividing them into units with "beginnings" and "ends." People punctuate by dividing the ongoing processes into manageable sets or sequences of events and trying to isolate causes and effects within the brief sequences they have "marked."

The example from O'Neill's play on page 48 illustrates punctuation. Each character would punctuate the ongoing cycle of family interaction in his or her own way. Of course, such simplification (and abstraction) violated the complexity of the social processes in O'Neill's family, because each person was in reaction to many events, some of them complex and recurring processes reaching far back into the family's history or forward into the future.

In the construction of language, punctuation is used to break continuous streams of words into units of sentences, clauses, and paragraphs. It is a necessary and helpful process in reading and writing. In the analysis of family behavior, however, it usually is misleading and counterproductive. It creates artificial beginnings and endings in processes that are continuous, responsive, and reciprocal. The insistence on beginnings and endings, causes and effects, that characterizes such reasoning may even prevent analysts from seeing cycles and other long-lived, if not perpetual, patterns in family functioning.

Punctuation helps people think they have found "the" reasons for what is happening, but the pictures of family life it produces are artificial and unrealistic, and the "answers" it provides about family are generally biased and inaccurate. Interventions based on such artificial cause-and-effect linkages often make family situations worse. For example, after a husband has decided that his wife's behavior is the "cause" of a family problem, he tends to blame her. If a wife punctuates the same situation from her viewpoint, she is likely to find fault with the husband, and blames him. The result is that the original problem persists, and the couple now has the additional problem of mutual blame and the resentments that flow from it.

From the point of view of a family scientist, it might be acceptable to make a problem worse, if making it worse would have the "effect" of helping to solve it or encourage families to learn to deal with it effectively. Unfortunately, punctuation rarely helps families solve their problems. Instead, people select from the ongoing family process those "causes" and "effects" that fit their preconceived definitions of what is happening, and the distortions, inherent in conceiving circular processes as linear segments, make it even harder to see things from another's perspective or to take a holistic (systems) view of things. Thus the process of punctuation has the paradoxical and unintended effect of fueling another family cycle, namely an escalation of the complexity and seriousness of the problem.

It is possible to use the concept of punctuation to have constructive effects in the resolution of family problems. This is possible when family scientists or family members recognize that their attempts to punctuate are hypothetical and tentative. Viewing punctuation in this way, we say things like "*If* we punctuated this situation this way, we would see that . . ." or "*One way* to punctuate this situation would be . . ." When people think about punctuation in this way they do not think their punctuated version of family processes is "the" truth. They recognize that their punctuation is, at best, a static distortion of a more complicated process and that it represents only one of many reasonable views of what is going on. This type of reasoning is sometimes helpful in families because it opens up dialogue and discussion rather than closing it down. Also, it can help people see things in new and different ways.

Another positive outcome of thinking about punctuation in hypothetical and tentative ways is that an awareness of the processes of punctuation often moves discussions of problems to a discussion of ways of defining and "talking about" the problem. In other words, the focus of attention tends to move from events and who is to blame to the ways family members define and interpret events and what they can do about the situation.

The following situation illustrates how the systemic understanding of punctuation can be used to help families.

In this situation, Sue punctuated the situation by believing that Elmer's behavior was "the" cause of their problems. Elmer, on the other hand, would punctuate the situation by believing that it was Sue's behavior that was the "real" cause, and both of them could cite numerous examples to justify their conclusion. This kind of situation occurs frequently in families about many issues and with many different individuals, and frequently the result is the problems escalate or remain unsolved—contributing to resentments, recriminations, and so forth.

If we analyze this situation using a systemic perspective, we would focus on what was happening in the system rather than the behavior, responsibility, or

The Wiser Family

Sue Wiser enjoyed her career, and found herself devoting more and more of her time to it. She was successful, and the harder she worked the more successful she was. Besides, the family was able to do many things they couldn't do if she made less money. Also, Elmer was becoming so critical lately that the only peace and quiet or good feelings she could get were at the office.

Elmer was trying to take up the slack in the home. Somebody needed to, because Sue's career was taking her away so much that the children were being neglected. He didn't like what was happening. He felt Sue was not paying nearly as much attention to the family as she should, and it was interfering with his work.

Sue and Elmer had talked about their situation a number of times. Usually, though, it just led to a fight and things would get worse. Elmer would try to talk some sense into Sue, but she would just get mad and leave. Sue tried to talk him into being more pleasant and reasonable, but that just made him defensive and he'd make cutting remarks.

misbehavior of the individuals. We would look at the pattern in the cycle rather than try to determine what was "causing" the problem. We'd identify that the couple was caught in a vicious cycle neither of them wanted. The more he nagged her, the more she left the home for the office. And, the more she devoted her time and energy to the office, the more he'd nag. We'd observe that both individuals were trying to punctuate the situation in what they thought was a reasonable manner, but the punctuation was actually contributing to the problem.

In these situations it is very enabling to use systemic ideas to focus on the cycle; when the cycle is recognized the blaming tends to decrease and the defensiveness decreases. It is possible to *perturb* (intervene in) the system in a wide variety of ways. Sue can change her part of the cycle, or Elmer can change his. Even the mental process of thinking "cycle" rather than thinking individualistically can help change these systemic processes, so that the couple is better able to eliminate the problem and accomplish their goals.

Helping Six Filipino Families

Another situation that illustrates how systemic ideas can be used to help families was published by Auserwald (1987). It describes how a case worker thought systemically in working with six Filipino families.

In this situation, the mental health worker started out by assuming he would need to understand the ecological systems in the six children's lives if he were to understand their behavior. This helped him be sensitive to the ways the various systems were interrelated, and helped him keep looking for what else was happening even after four of the children responded. His assumption that he would not get a complete understanding if he ignored the ecological systems helped him to understand what was going on.

This case provides an opportunity to review the concepts introduced in this chapter. The worker assumed that although children live in a number of systems, their *family system* is the central and most vital in their lives. Therefore, when the children were referred by the school to the mental health worker, the first system the worker investigated was the family. When the worker focuses on the family system as the main system to be understood, then the school system is part of the *environment*, and the individual children are parts or *subsystems* within each family system. When the worker came to the home with news about the children's misbehavior, he provided a new *input* for the families.

After the worker understood the cultural heritage of the families, he recognized that the corporal punishment the children were receiving at school was incompatible with the *transformation processes* in the family systems. In the family systems, patterns were changed by having the children learn rules to live by. When the parents received *feedback* that the children were disobeying the rules, they responded to the disobedience by shaming the children rather than by corporal punishment. To the children, the corporal punishment in the school environment was a new input, and it apparently was so different that the children didn't know how to relate to it effectively; they responded by being disruptive.

Box 2.2
Six Filipino families

Six children from six immigrant Filipino families are referred by an elementary school to the Children's Team of a community mental health center over a span of two weeks. It is noticed that the six children come from one of two classrooms, fifth grade or sixth grade. It is also known that the decision to refer these children occurred at a single staff meeting at the school. In each referral the child is described as unwilling or unable to conform to classroom rules. Members of the Children's Team, who work within the community they serve and seldom in an office, are aware that the school is run by a principal of Portuguese heritage, a former marine who believes in strict discipline, and that the school is staffed by an unusual number of male teachers, also of Portuguese heritage.

The Children's Team worker, thinking ecologically, and beginning with the above information, suspects that an element in the children's ostensibly aberrant behavior might be some sort of cultural clash. He explores specific incidents in the classroom with each of the two teachers, both of whom turn out to be men of Portuguese heritage. He discovers that both teachers, with the support of the principal, use spanking as a means of discipline. The teachers are upset because the children do not respond to such disciplinary measures. They hit back or run out of the school. Afterward, the children do not seem to pay attention to what is going on in class. They are falling behind in their schoolwork, and when the teachers try to give them special, individual attention, they become even more inattentive.

The worker then visits the families of the children. He discovers that they all live in run-down houses in what had once been a sugar plantation village, now scheduled for demolition. Because the children speak fairly good English, he is surprised when he learns that all families had recently immigrated over a two-year span. He questions the families about how they discipline their children and discovers that once a child becomes old enough to understand rules clearly, no corporal punishment is used. Instead, children who disobey are taught to feel shame. The families report no disciplinary problems at home with the children in question.

The worker can now construct a story that contains the following event-shape that explains the children's behavior. The core events (the event-shape) in the story are:

- the disciplinary methods of the teachers in their local version of Portuguese culture
- the disciplinary experience of the children in their Filipino culture
- the immigration of the families from the Philippines to their new country
- the entry of the children into classes taught by Portuguese men
- the principal's support for and the teachers' use of corporal punishment
- the children's behavior

The Children's Team worker can now plan an intervention, an event or events that, when added to the event-shape, will achieve the desired outcome, which is the success of the children in school. He chooses to call a meeting of families, principal, and teachers, at which participants can discuss how the children's behavior in school can be controlled. The meeting is held, and it results in an agreement that the teachers will use the disciplinary method of the parents. They will not spank the children (who revealed on questioning at the meeting that they did not consider the spankings as outcomes of their behavior but, rather, as meanness on the part of the teachers, of whom they had become afraid). They will, instead, shame them.

When this agreement was carried out, the behavior of five of the children became exemplary. Two of them, however, one in each class, continued to have serious problems in learning, and one of these two, the sixth-grader, continued to engage in somewhat lessened but nevertheless troubling conflict with both the teacher and the other students.

The worker then assumed the event-shape he had uncovered was incomplete in these two cases and he continued his exploration. He discovered another event in the families of each child. He learned that [in] the family of the sixth-grader, the parents had been forced by their families to go through with an arranged marriage neither of them had wanted. Following the birth of their only child, they had turned away from each other and focused their lives on the child in a manner that created increasing pressure on the boy to be "perfect." In an effort to establish some sense of individual identity, the boy was rebelling in all situations outside his home. Thus, the additional event was the unwanted marriage. The worker visited this family for 10 weeks to work with the triadic bind. After the sixth week, the teacher reported that the boy's rebellious behavior had disappeared and that he was catching up in his class work.

The family of the fifth-grader, on the other hand, seemed to be functioning very well. The boy's two siblings were bright and successful in school, and there was much affection and clear organization in their family life. However, the family reported that the child in question had seemed to develop slowly following an accident in his fifth year. He had fallen from a tree and landed on his head, and he had been unconscious for nearly an hour and dazed for several days. The family had taken him to the emergency room of a Manila hospital. They had been told only that he would be all right. Based on this information, the worker arranged for the boy to be examined neurologically, and for a battery of psychological tests to be administered. The boy was found to have an abnormal EEG and other signs of brain damage. In this instance, the additional event was the sequelae of the fall from the tree. A remedial educator was assigned to work with the boy. A year later he had been promoted to sixth grade but continued to learn slowly, and transfer to a special class was being contemplated. (Auserwald, 1987)

Apparently, the *boundaries* between the family and school systems were so rigid that the families did not know about the transformation processes that were used by the school and the school did not know about the culturally different transformation processes that were used in the homes. If the boundaries between these two systems had been more permeable, the problem might never have occurred.

When the worker understood that the transformation processes in the family systems were in conflict with those in the school system, he devoted his attention to planning intervention strategies. He created more *openness* in the boundaries between the two systems so the differences could be discussed, and when the decision was made to change the transformation processes in the school, it helped to change the behavior of the children.

The technique of focusing primarily on effects is apparent in this situation. When the worker was confronted with problematic behavior, he did not start thinking about the law-like causes of problematic behavior. Instead, his strategy was to look at the ongoing processes and to see if he could find some events or processes that might be linked to the problem behavior. As soon as he understood what was happening in the systems his attention shifted from cultural differences to thinking about what would happen if various changes were made in the situation.

The idea of *equifinality* is also illustrated in this situation. The children's uncooperativeness was not caused by a set of conditions or factors that can be described with deterministic scientific laws. The children had considerable *freedom* to choose how to respond, and could have responded to the situation in many different ways. They might have become withdrawn, been sullen and quiet, overcompensated by being highly cooperative and compliant, or committed vandalism.

Summary

Family systems theory is a way of looking at families that places emphasis on the family as a whole rather than focusing on individuals. This theory attempts to understand how systems function, and to identify how the parts of systems interrelate. Systemic concepts help us see wholeness, interdependence, subsystems, inputs, outputs and boundaries. Other systemic concepts are transformation processes, choice, information processing, and feedback.

Family systems theory differs from many scientific theories in its view of cause and effect. It pays more attention to indeterministic processes than deterministic ones. The concepts of cycles and equifinality help us understand the family systems view of the complexity of cause-and-effect relationships. In contrast to theories that attempt to identify direct linear relationships between cause and effect, family systems theory emphasizes probable effects.

There are many ways that ideas from family systems theory can be used to improve the quality of life. An example of the application of systems theory titled "Six Filipino families" illustrates some of these ways.

Key Terms

Theory
General theory
General systems theory
Family systems theory
Conceptual framework
System
Patterns
Process
Choice
Thinking systemically vs. thinking individualistically
Wholeness (holistic)
Interdependence
Subsystems
Inputs and outputs
Boundaries
Structure
Information processing
Feedback
Deviation amplifying feedback loop (or positive feedback loops or variety feedback loops)
Deviation dampening feedback loop (or negative feedback loops or constancy feedback loops)
Determinism
Indeterminism
Freedom varies
Cycles
Linear causation (lineal causation)
Punctuation
Equifinality
Causal laws
Causes (that are unique to a particular situation)
Probable effects
Family institution
Market

Study Questions

1. What is meant by the statement that "general theories are the 'heart' of a discipline"?
2. Describe what is meant by the saying "the whole is greater than the sum of its parts." Why is this an important concept when studying the family?
3. Give examples of how you would describe the family from a microsystemic level and a macrosystemic level.
4. What is an example of an emotional boundary?
5. How do adaptive systems shape their own destiny?
6. Describe how thinking about "cause and effect" and "determinism and indeterminism" can alter one's approach to studying the family.
7. What is the difference between cyclic and linear thinking?

Part 2

Basic Processes in Family Systems

3 // *Generations*

4 // *Love*

5 // *Emotions*

6 // *Ideology*

7 // *Family Life Course*

8 // *Rules*

9 // *Communication*

Generations 3

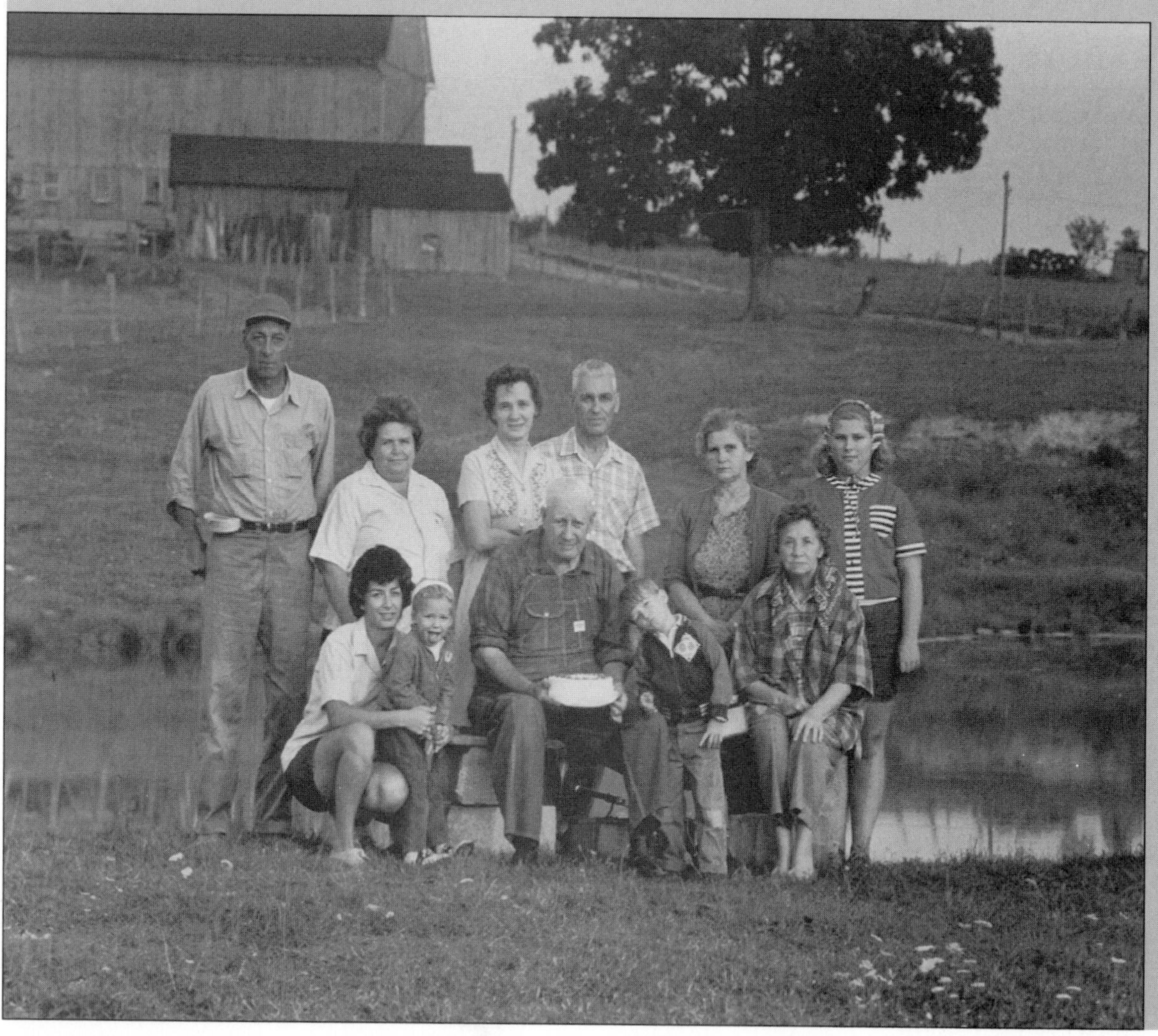

Main Ideas

1 // Generational transmission processes can be useful and healthy, but can also be problematic.

2 // Generational alliances usually are a sign of family dysfunction.

3 // Generational transmission refers to the idea that families tend to transmit their style of life to each new generation.

4 // Genograms are a tool that can help us understand generational processes.

5 // Ideas about generations can be used to liberate ourselves and others from undesirable generational processes by becoming transitional characters. Eight strategies that can help do this are: Deliberateness, having distinctive family rituals, maintaining emotional distance, marrying later than average, reading good books about family life, joining organizations that can help, getting an education, and developing a philosophy of life.

6 // We can conserve desirable generational processes by using generational ties and maintaining emotional closeness.

7 // Taking care of unfinished business can promote family wellness.

The birth of a person is a beautiful event because it creates the most valuable thing that exists. It creates a new person, a new human being. It also creates something else that is beautiful, important, and powerful. It creates generations, because a birth makes someone a child, someone a parent, someone a grandparent, and so on.

Generations is the word for our concept of the links that connect parents and children, but it includes much more. It includes the ties to others who are connected to the parents and children. For example, generations include ties with aunts, uncles, cousins, and siblings. **Generational processes** tend to include the connections people have to traditions, patterns, emotions, values, and ways of relating that become the heritage and determine the lifestyle of each family.

> *"Treat those younger than you as your child.*
> *Treat those older than you as your father.*
> *Treat those your own age as your brother."*
>
> —SULEYMAN

Generational processes are one of the basic parts of the family realm; they are part of the foundation, the bedrock, the core of what it means to be "family." Every aspect of family life grows out of and builds upon these processes. Generational processes are also unique to the family realm because they only exist in families. We don't have generations in schools or in neighborhoods. We don't have them in friendships. We don't have them in corporations or careers, and they don't occur in governments, laws, or social conventions.

Generational processes have an enormous influence on humans. They influence how we think, how we feel, what we believe, how we relate to others, what is important or unimportant to us, whether we think the world is a friendly or unfriendly place, and how we use our environment to help us learn and cope. They influence our aspirations, our values, our struggles, and our resourcefulness. They influence the attitudes we have toward other people, property,

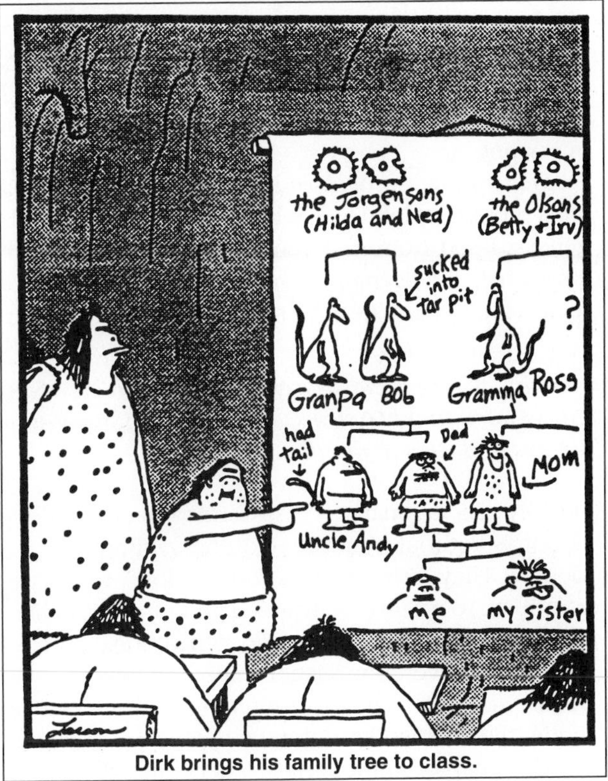

Dirk brings his family tree to class.

religion, and education, as well as the way we handle conflict, intimacy, anger, love, hate, and life in general.

There are many reasons generational processes influence us so much. One reason is that some parts of them are permanent. They are fixed and inalienable; we cannot annul, escape, or cancel them. For example, parents cannot decide to not be the biological parents of their child. Children cannot choose a different set of biological parents. We can make some changes in generational arrangements through legal processes such as adoption and custody, but these change only a few of the generational connections, notably the legal and social relationships. They don't change the intuitive, experiential parts; and they only partly alter the mental, interpersonal, and emotional expressions of heritage and lineage consciousness that are characteristic of generational connections.

A second reason generational processes are important is that, although some parts can be changed, it is very difficult to do so. Either we don't know how to change them, or it doesn't occur to us to try. Perhaps we don't have the resources or strength to change them, or we don't want to pay the emotional and interpersonal price. Most of us just live with them as they are.

A third reason generational processes are so influential is that they start making a difference at the earliest stages of our lives, when as infants and small children we are dependent on the older generation. They also involve our deepest feelings of who we are, what we are connected to, and what is important. Also, we don't choose them. As an old saying goes, "We can choose our friends but not our relatives," and our connections with our relatives are extremely important.

Generational processes influence us in many different ways. Perhaps the most prominent influence is biological, since physical traits are inherited through genes passed from one generation to the next. Other influences include the emotional, intellectual, developmental, interpersonal, and experiential. The focus of this chapter can be summed up by the *generational processes principle*:

Principle

Healthy generational processes tend to create many beautiful and enabling outcomes in family systems, and unhealthy generational processes tend to create serious problems in families.

Healthy generational processes tend to create enabling outcomes such as a sense of bonds without bondage, closeness without oppressiveness, and a sense of identity. They help create affection, love, and a sense of security, and they contribute to a sense of meaning and purpose in life.

On the other hand, unhealthy generational processes tend to be very destructive. They pervert our relationships, and many forms of abuse occur in generational processes. They can interfere with mental health, ruin marriages, and hinder the healthy development of children in many ways.

This chapter introduces two generational processes that can be healthy or unhealthy, and then describes several strategies we can use to help them be healthy. The two processes are generational alliances and generational transmissions.

Generational Alliances

Theodore Lidz (1957) was one of the pioneers in family science, and he made an important discovery in the 1950s. He discovered that it is helpful in family systems to have some of the alliances be within generations and not across generations.

The term **alliance** refers to the connections and the boundaries between subsystems in a family system. An alliance occurs when two or more individuals in a family become unusually close and align themselves as a unit in the family. In doing this, they change the boundaries in the family system. The **boundaries** in a

"f there is a fundamental rule of social organization, it is that an organization is in trouble when coalitions occur across levels of a hierarchy, particularly when these coalitions are secret." —Haley, 1976, p. 104

family system are the physical, mental or emotional barriers between parts of a system or between the system and its environment. What people do when they create an alliance is to reduce the boundaries (make them more permeable) between the individuals in the alliance, and increase the rigidity or strength of the boundaries between them and the others in the family.

One of the important and healthy alliances in families is to have a fairly clear **parental alliance** while the children are being raised. This means the parents form an alliance with each other in their relationships with their children. In ideal situations the parents are a cohesive, integrated, and coordinated team. They are supportive of each other and unified in the way they relate to their children, and the boundaries between the parents are few and permeable. At the same time, there are a number of more rigid or impermeable boundaries between the parental alliance and the children. For example, the parental alliance is "in charge" in the family, and the parents set limits and guidelines for the children. When this is done, the parental alliance becomes the **executive subsystem** in the family, and it is responsible for disciplining, correcting, and teaching the children.

There are many ways families can form unhealthy alliances. A fairly common one occurs where there is unresolved conflict or tension between the parents, and one of the parents forms an alliance with a child. For example, if one parent is an alcoholic, the other parent may turn to a child for help in running the home and disciplining the children, as well as for solace or companionship. A fairly frequent pattern of this is seen when a father can't keep a job, or is distant emotionally from the family, and the mother creates an alliance with one of the sons, making him a substitute husband.

These cross-generational or **intergenerational alliances** place the oldest child in an awkward position because the child becomes, in a sense, a member of two different generations. Intergenerational alliances often lead to emotional and interpersonal problems for the parents, the oldest child, and sometimes for the other children as well.

The principle that is involved here is the **generational alliance principle**[1]:

Principle

It is helpful in family systems to have clearcut generational boundaries about such things as leadership, responsibility, support, and emotional feelings. When the boundaries are relatively clear, it helps the adults and children develop in healthy ways, and when cross-generational alliances and coalitions occur it tends to lead to emotional and interpersonal difficulties for the adults and children.

"Previous research has demonstrated that a family with a substance abusing adolescent is often times rigidly organized, with mother and child closely aligned, and father distant (i.e., Klagsburn & Davis, 1977; Levine, 1985; Stanton et al., 1978). The close alliance between mother and child is then implicated as a problem factor in the substance abuse." —Bartle & Sabatelli, 1989, p. 264

The following two situations illustrate a healthy and an unhealthy pattern of generational alliances.

The Gardner Family

My parents were a great team. They'd get their heads together and think through what they wanted before they acted. They used to call their sessions the "meeting of the board of directors." They'd let us have a say in decisions, especially the ones that involved our friends and things like that, but they were together in their ideas enough that we didn't even try to play one of them against the other. I hope my wife and I are as good a team as they were.

Other patterns in family alliances are destructive and harmful.

The Tanner Family

My mother always wanted to be my friend. She was always saying, "I want to be your friend, I want to be your friend, I want to be your friend." And I used to tell her, "You're my mother. You're supposed to be my mother, not a friend." Maybe she just wanted to know what was going on in my life, but I wanted her to be my mother. Maybe it had something to do with her family as she grew up. Her mother got divorced when my mother was about 3, and they formed a really close alliance. Maybe it worked for them OK, but it was uncomfortable for me.

The following situation illustrates a family that had healthy generational alliances most of the time, but the boundaries between the generations became blurred temporarily to cope with a unique situation. In this situation, the unique demands and the temporary nature of the cross-generational alliance kept it from being unhealthy. This situation started to become an unhealthy pattern until the child pulled back.

The Clark Family

My parents and I have always been close, but there was a time when it almost got too close. When Mom had her last baby she became extremely ill with a chemical depression. She would often just sit and cry. Being the oldest daughter, I was relied on a lot to help. I loved helping because someone needed me. My father was under a lot of stress at this time, and he would come to me to vent his feelings. "What should I do? I just don't know what to do," he would say. I was his listening ear. I didn't mind because I knew the stress he was under. It only became a problem when he continued to come to me for advice after Mom was well and I began to doubt their relationship. Gradually I pulled back and didn't talk to them as much, and they relied on each other again.

In addition to the research on the generational alliance principle by Lidz and

his colleagues, James Framo (1970), Salvador Minuchin (1974, 1981), Jay Haley (1976, 1977), and Murray Bowen (Kerr & Bowen, 1988) have all studied the role of cross-generational alliances, and their data suggest that the principle is valid.

Many family therapists have found the generational alliance principle helpful. One example is presented by a team of therapists in Italy (Palazzoli et al., 1989). They work with families who have anorectic and psychotic problems, and the first part of their treatment program is to try to strengthen the parental alliance. They have developed a number of ingenious strategies to increase the cohesion between the parents and increase the status and influences of the parents in the home. Their strategies include having the parents keep secrets from the children, having the parents go on unannounced excursions, and excluding the "problem" child from the therapy sessions. They have found these kinds of strategies help the families cope with their challenges much more effectively.

The generational alliance principle is a good example of family science research, because it was not developed with a psychological, sociological, economic, or historical perspective. It was developed by thinking about generational processes that are unique to the family realm and how they make a difference in the healthy development of humans. While there is considerable evidence that it is valid and helpful, there is much more researchers still need to discover about this principle. For example, we don't know yet whether it is more helpful in some kinds of families than others. We suspect that it is more important when families are raising children and less important in the relationships between adult generations, but more research is needed on these kinds of issues.

Generational Transmission

The process of generational transmission has been researched in recent years by scholars from a number of different disciplines. **Generational transmission** is the process of transmitting from one generation to the next such things as ways of behaving, ways of feeling, ways of relating, ways of defining reality, and ways of coping with intimacy and distance. Researchers have developed the **generational transmission principle**:

Principle *Families tend to transmit their style of life to each new generation.*

The following situation illustrates this principle with a relatively simple part of life.

The Chosich Family

My father is 75 percent Yugoslavian and grew up eating a lot of sausage. His family would make their own sausage (kolbasa) quite a few times a year, and when it was made, everyone helped. Today we still do the same. It is something I am sure we will all keep passing down because we have enjoyed it so much.

The following situation illustrates how this principle operates with a desirable and wholesome aspect of family life.

The Garcia Family

One of my father's favorite pastimes is gardening. Each year he produces a beautiful, plentiful garden. My father grew up on a farm in Mississippi where he learned to love the soil and growing things. He has passed on his love of gardening to me. As a little girl I loved to watch my father work in the garden and to help him when I could. He put me in charge of a row of lettuce, carrots, and beets, which I learned to weed and care for. For my sixteenth birthday my father built me a greenhouse in which to start flower seeds in the spring. He made flower beds around the yard for me and I filled them with beautiful flowers. I love gardening just as my father does. I am thankful for the talent he has helped me develop. I hope to teach my children to love to grow things as well.

Generational transmission also occurs for less desirable traits, as in "The Smith Family" on page 71.

There are many conditions or qualifications that influence when and how this principle operates. For example, it seems to be more powerful for characteristics of the family realm than characteristics of the public realms. What this means is

The Smith Family

My great grandmother on Mom's side had a terrible temper. My grandfather was her oldest child and he was expected to take care of his siblings from the day they were born. If they even made one peep she beat him. As he grew up, he inherited his mother's temper. After he married, his wife finally forbade him to touch her children when he got mad because he could not control his temper. My mother also has a temper, and I've noticed some of my siblings have strong tempers. Apparently, it has decreased with each new generation, but I wonder how long this little bit of my great grandmother will last.

that there is more generational transmission with regard to ways of loving and maintaining intimate relationships than such things as political ideas, careers, leisure interests, and social class behavior (Troll & Bengston, 1979). Peter Steinglass and his colleagues (1987) also discovered another qualification: There is more generational transmission when behaviors are a part of family rituals.

One aspect of this principle is that it reinforces the idea that family life is "the best of times and the worst of times." For example, when families have patterns of relating in kind, loving, empathic, intimate, understanding, and facilitating ways, these patterns are passed on to new generations of children. When families interact harmoniously with each other and cope with life's challenges in helpful, creative, and humane ways, these patterns are passed from parents to children. It helps the children become well rounded, creative, constructive, resourceful people who can accomplish their goals and establish and maintain intimate, beautiful, peaceful, loving, harmonious relationships with others.

Unfortunately, the "worst of times" part of generational transmission is also very real, and it has so much effect in our society that we cannot escape it. When families have traditions of unwholesome, harmful, and abusive patterns, these too are passed from parents to children. The worst forms of human abuse, exploitation, discrimination, prejudice, hate, vengeance, and animosity occur in families, and frequently they too are passed from one generation to the next.

Ironically, the privacy that is so important for the positive and constructive dimensions of human growth, intimacy, and wholesome bonds also tends to allow, protect, hide, and preserve the heinous parts. The fact that most of what happens in families is behind closed doors—in the privacy of the home, the hidden part of the iceberg—means that the unfortunate parts of the human experience can be perpetuated in ways that are nearly invisible to outside observers.

Research about Generational Transmission

There has been a great deal of research about the generational transmission principle, and the research provides considerable evidence that it is a valid idea.

This chapter cannot summarize all of the research, but some of the research in three areas—the quality of marriage, abusive and nonabusive behaviors, and mental health—illustrate the evidence that has accumulated about this principle.

Quality of Marriage

One area where there is considerable evidence that generational transmission occurs is in the quality of marriage. Family scientists discovered in the 1930s that some families have a tradition of high-quality marriages, and others have a tradition of struggling with marriage (Burgess & Cottrell, 1939; Terman, 1938).

One way researchers have documented that generational processes influence the quality of marriage is by studying patterns in divorce. Judson Landis (1956) did one of the early studies in this area, where he analyzed the divorce patterns in the families of 1977 students at the University of California in the 1950s. He found a significantly greater proportion of divorces in families whose grandparents had divorced.

The data from Landis's study are shown in Figure 3.1, where only 14.6 percent of the parent generation had divorced when there was not a divorce in the grandparent generation. The percent of the parent generation that had divorced was 23.7 percent if one set of the grandparents had divorced, and it was 38 percent if both sets of grandparents had divorced. The conclusion Landis drew from his study was that

> People seem to be conditioned by their family background in ways that affect their marriage-ability. Those reared in happy homes have an advantage in that their parents were able to give them an example of successful family living. (Landis & Landis, 1963, p. 135)

Since 1956 many studies have tried to determine if Landis's conclusion is correct. The studies have become much more sophisticated. For example, several recent studies have tried to determine if the relationship is spurious. A relationship is **spurious** when there is a correlation that is eliminated when other factors are also considered. For example, it could be that people with certain personality traits tend to divorce more than the average and that these traits are genetically transmitted. If this were the case, differences in the personality traits would have influenced the correlation Landis found, suggesting that personality factors, not what people learn from their parents about successful marriage, are the real causes.

The most sophisticated study on this issue was a sociological study published by Norval Glenn and Kathryn Kramer (1987). They pooled data from 11 national surveys that had been conducted in the United States from 1973 to 1985, and then conducted a complicated analysis of the data, which were broken down by gender and race. Their study found additional evidence that the generational transmission principle is valid. They also discovered:

> The estimated total effect of parental divorce is stronger for white females than for any other sex-race category. The adjusted percentage ever divorced or legally separated is 59% greater for the children of divorce than for persons who lived with both parents

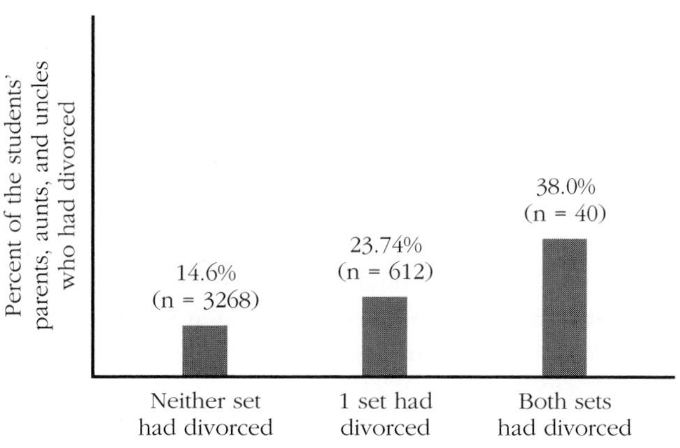

FIGURE 3.1 Percent of the students' parents, aunts, and uncles who had divorced, according to the divorce status of the students' grandparents (*Data from an analysis of the divorce patterns in the families of 1977 college students*) *Source*: Landis (1956)

> in the case of white females, compared with 32% greater for white males, 16% greater for black males, and 15% greater for black females. The differences for blacks can appropriately be termed modest, but Glenn and Shelton (1983) argued that differences for whites similar to those found by this study were substantial and important, and we agree. It would be especially difficult to sustain the argument that the difference for white females is so small that it is of little importance. (Glenn & Kramer, 1987, pp. 816–17)

In addition to the sociological research, there are also a large number of studies in developmental psychology that support the idea that marital disruption severe enough to lead to divorce creates the kind of conditions that tend to lead to divorce in later generations. Tuckman and Regan (1966), Heatherington (1972), Felner et al. (1975), Heatherington et al. (1979), and Zill (1978) all found important differences between children growing up in families in which the mother was widowed and those where the mother was divorced.

The amount of developmental difficulty in the children, whether in the cognitive, emotional, or social areas, was consistently greater when the mother was divorced. Families of widowed mothers, on the other hand, did not have the same level of problems. As Zill (1978) pointed out from the analysis of the data from the National Survey of Children, ". . . widowed mothers, who are not much better off in terms of either education or income, are surprisingly free from psychological distress" (p. 24).

Most of the research about how generational transmission influences the quality of marriage has focused on how problems such as divorce and pathology are transmitted. However, we should realize that the processes are the same for healthy, constructive, and desirable aspects of marriage. Thus, since we can assume the principle is valid, we can assume that patterns of effective communication, ways of coping with differences, and methods of handling anger are also transmitted. Patterns of loving, caring, being close, creating bonds, and meeting the challenges of life in a supportive and helpful way are also transmitted across generations.

Abusive and Nonabusive Behaviors

The presence or absence of abusive behavior is a second area where research has documented that human behavior tends to be repeated generation after generation in families. For example, the best predictor social scientists have been able to identify about whether someone will be physically abusive is whether abusive behaviors occurred in their parental home (Burgess et al., 1978; Milner & Wimberly, 1980; Pagelow, 1984). Also, the rates of sexual abuse in the general population are difficult to identify, but a number of research studies suggest that sexual abusers have been abused more than nonabusers (Pagelow, 1984). This suggests that generational transmission is probably an important factor in the perpetuation of physical and sexual abuse.

Substance abuse is a serious problem in our contemporary society, and it takes many forms. One form, the abuse of alcohol, has been studied extensively, and again the data suggest that the intergenerational factor is very important. Michael Elkin's (1984) experience illustrates this process.

> From 1973 to 1975 I was clinical director of Atlantis, a small community drug-treatment facility in Stoneham, Massachusetts. Because I was then studying family therapy at the Boston Family Institute in Brookline, Massachusetts, I was extremely interested in meeting the families of the young drug abusers referred to us. Of the more than one hundred families in whose treatment I participated, nearly all turned out to have at least one person who suffered from alcoholism. Some of these parents were out of the home and some were recovering, but the correlation between teenage drug abuse and parental alcoholism was almost invariable. (p. 10)

It is important that we also think about the positive side of this issue. Families apparently also help transmit the ability to have self-control and to cope with the stresses of life without abuse and excesses. Families who have traditions of moderation and of coping with extreme difficulties in humane ways help new generations learn these desirable ways of coping and adjusting.

Mental Health and Illness

A great deal of research has found that generational transmission influences mental health and illness. Most of the family science theories about how this happens involve the emotional processes in families (Kerr & Bowen, 1988).

There is a unique group of emotions that occur primarily inside the family realm, and some of them are extremely intense. The emotional parts of family life, especially the powerful and compelling ones, are mostly hidden. Thinking back to the iceberg analogy, we could say that they are in the submerged part that is difficult to see and understand. These emotions are largely invisible to the family members who experience them, and they aren't easily measured or detected with the questionnaires that social scientists use to study families. When families are interviewed or observed by social scientists, they have an uncanny way of putting their best foot forward while concealing the deeper, subtle parts (both more tender and more vicious) of what is happening emotionally inside the family.

Some family scientists, however, have begun to develop theories and to do research on the deeper emotional processes and languages that are used in families. One of these scholars is Murray Bowen (1978), and he has demonstrated that a great deal of the generational transmission of "the good, the bad, and the ugly," to recall a Clint Eastwood movie, is transmitted through the emotional parts of the intergenerational relationships.

According to what is now called "Bowen theory," some of the ways of regulating **emotional distance** and intensity in families are handed down from one generation to another, and they influence whether people become mentally healthy or develop mental and emotional illnesses. One way this is done is through what Bowen has called the **family projection process**. This is where parents are anxious or aware of one of their own inadequacies or abilities, and they "project" it (think they see it) in a child. They then act as if the child actually has the characteristic, and this tends to create the characteristic in the child.

> As an example, a mother who feels insecure about her abilities in interpersonal relationships may manifest this by focusing on any sign in the child that can be interpreted as a sign of a similar insecurity in the child. If the mother thinks she sees such a sign, it can quickly become a "fact" in her mind that the child is insecure. As a result, she increasingly relates to him as if he were insecure and the child is molded by the mother's anxious focus. The child begins acting more and more in a way that confirms the mother's original diagnosis. Once this process is established, both mother and child play equal roles in continuing it. The projection process, in other words, is a process in which parental emotionality defines what the child is like, a definition that originally may have little to do with the realities of the child, but that eventually does become a reality in the child. (Kerr, 1981, pp. 245–46)

The same processes can bring about healthy and unhealthy ways of living. For example, a parent may project or think they see a very valued way of behaving in a child and then focus on it and treat the child as if she had that trait. The following account from the life of one of the authors illustrates this process.

The Burr Family

My father was a skilled mechanic and carpenter, and when I was a child I used to watch him repair cars. One day, when I was about 7, he said at the dinner table something like, "I saw in Wes today the first signs that he has a mechanical aptitude." I didn't know what the word aptitude meant, but I had a number of feelings, and I liked what he said, the way he said it, and the way it made me feel. I could tell from the way he said it that he had seen something in me that made him think I might be good at working on cars too, and I knew that it was somehow important to him and to me. I remember working harder to not let wrenches slip and to memorize the names of all of the tools so I could be like my dad. I've realized since that his observation provided a great deal of motivation to develop that skill.

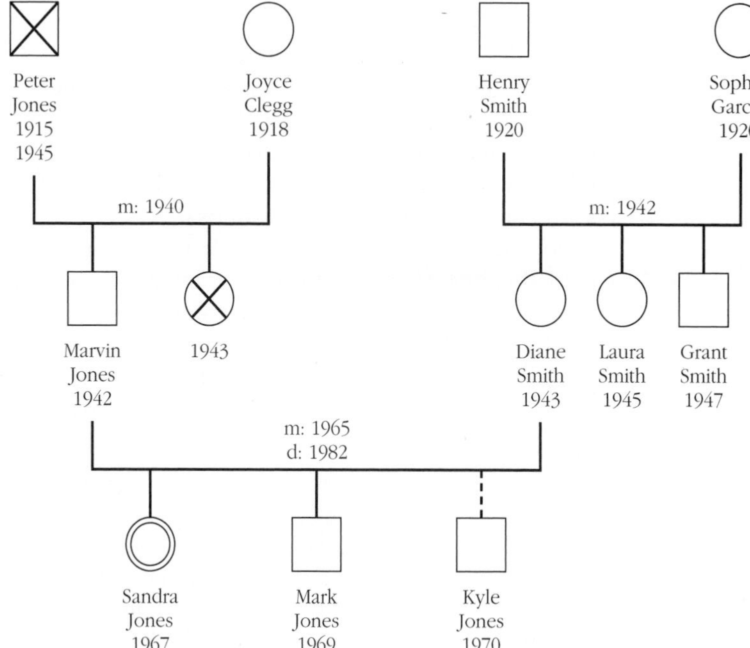

FIGURE 3.2
A simple genogram showing the family of Sandra Jones in 1980

THE GENOGRAM

A tool for understanding generational processes and helping families, a **genogram** diagrams the biological and interpersonal relationships of people across several generations. It provides information about significant characteristics, relationships, and events that can lead to insights and understanding of family problems. There are four parts to a genogram: the chart, the family chronology, a description of family relationships, and a description of the family processes.

Making a Genogram Chart

The first part of a genogram is the chart or diagram, and a simple one is shown in Figure 3.2. McGoldrick and Gerson (1985) developed a set of standardized symbols and methods for constructing these charts, and many of their conventions are used in this chapter. Figure 3.2 shows a fairly simple genogram for the family of a person we've named Sandra Jones; it illustrates how to diagram some of the basic parts of a genogram.

Each family member is represented by a box or circle; the boxes represent males and the circles, females. A genogram is usually created to understand a particular person, who becomes known as the **index person**. Double lines are used for that person, as shown for Sandra Jones. It is helpful to include names and

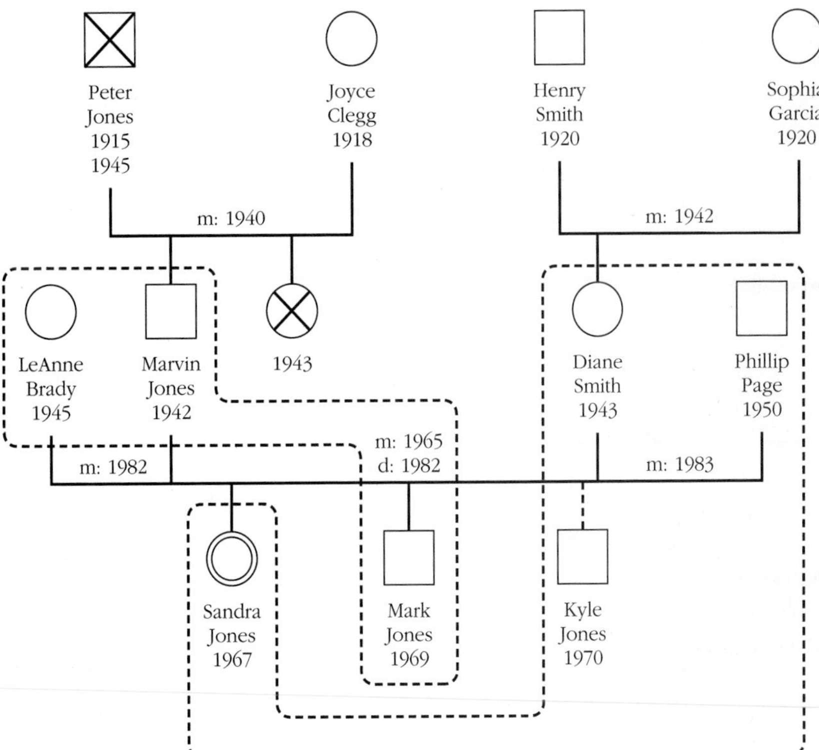

FIGURE 3.3
Sandra Jones's family in 1985

years of birth and death, and the best method the authors have seen is to put them just below the box or circle. If just one year is shown, it is the birth year and means the person was still living at the time the genogram was made.

The children are arranged with the oldest child on the left and youngest child on the right. Thus, in Sandra's family, she is the oldest child. Her younger brother Mark was born in 1969, and the youngest child, Kyle, was born in 1970. The dotted lines above Kyle show that he was adopted. Sandra's parents were married in 1965 and the marriage is shown with the horizontal line connecting them. Usually the male is placed on the left side and the female is placed on the right side when diagraming a marriage, but this arrangement is not always possible.

Sandra's father Marvin was born in 1942 to Peter and Joyce Jones, who were married in 1940. Peter Jones died in 1945, and Joyce did not remarry, so the genogram shows that Joyce raised her son as a single parent. The other aspect of their family that is shown is that they had an unnamed, stillborn child in 1943. The **X** inside a box or circle indicates a person died at an early age.

Figure 3.2 also shows that Sandra's mother was the oldest of three children. Her parents were the same age (both born in 1920), and they were married in 1942.

Families are seldom so simple as in Figure 3.2. They usually have a number of complications, and Figure 3.3 illustrates the methods of diagraming some of the

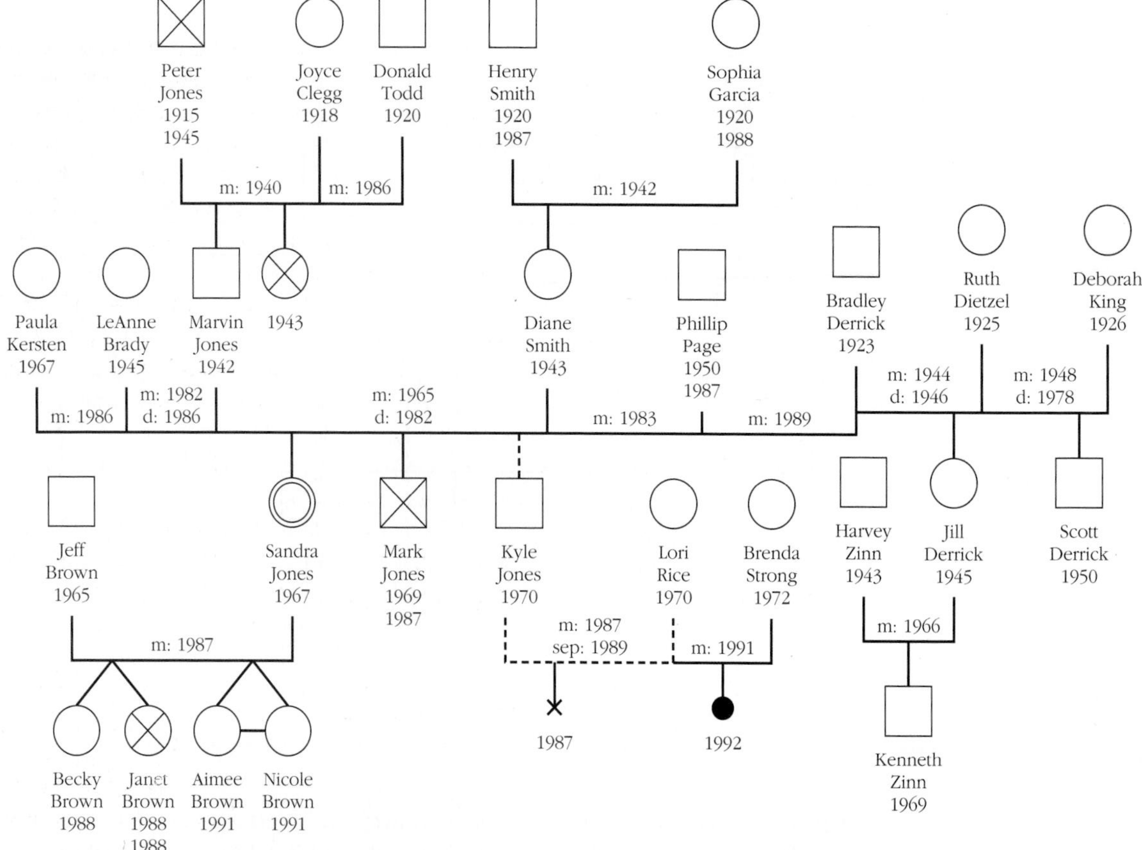

FIGURE 3.4 Sandra Jones's family in 1992

complications that can occur. This figure shows the same family five years later. Sandra's parents were divorced in 1982, and the year of their divorce is placed just below the year of their marriage. Marvin, Sandra's father, remarried quickly, to LeAnne Brady in 1982. Sandra's mother Diane was married in 1983 to Philip Page.

The dotted lines show a way to diagram the residential patterns of the stepfamilies. Sandra and her younger brother Kyle live with their mother and stepfather. Sandra's brother Mark lives with his father and stepmother.

Figure 3.4 shows how to diagram a number of additional complications that can occur in families. In this diagram, the stepfamily residential patterns are not shown because Sandra and her surviving brother are now married and have their own families. Sandra's brother Mark died in 1987, and since he was only 18 at the time an **X** is placed in the square.

Sandra was married to Jeff Brown in 1987, and they have given birth to two sets of twins. The older twins are fraternal twins, and one of them, Janet, died as an infant. The younger set of twins, Aimee and Nicole, are identical.

Figure 3.4 also shows how to diagram relationships where two individuals are a "couple" but they are not legally married. Sandra's youngest brother Kyle had a relationship with Lori Rice. They met in 1987 and separated in 1989. Lori had an abortion in 1987, and it is shown with a vertical line and small **x**. Kyle then married Brenda Strong in 1991, and Brenda experienced a miscarriage in 1992.

Figure 3.4 also shows that Sandra's stepfather Philip Page died in 1987, and her mother married Bradley Derrick, a man 20 years older, in 1989. This marriage was Bradley Derrick's third marriage. He was married to his first wife, Ruth Dietzel, for a very short time, and they had a daughter named Jill in 1945. Bradley's second marriage was to Deborah King in 1926, and they had a son named Scott. Thus, Jill and Scott are step-siblings, half-brother and -sister. Jill was married to Harvey Zinn in 1966 and they had a son in 1967. Thus, when Sandra's mother Diane married Bradley in 1989 it created some unusual family relationships. In addition to a stepfather, Bradley, the remarriage also gave Sandra a stepsister named Jill who is 20 years older than she, and a nephew, Kenneth Zinn, who is one year older than she. Another unique aspect of these relationships is that they did not begin until the year after Sandra was married.

On the other side of Sandra's family, Figure 3.4 shows that her father was divorced again in 1986 and married Paula Kersten, who was 19 at the time—the same age as Sandra. Thus Sandra acquired a stepmother her own age. Also, Sandra's paternal grandmother Joyce remarried at the age of 68. Her new husband, and Sandra's new stepgrandfather, was Donald Todd. The genogram also shows that Sandra's maternal grandparents died in 1987 and 1988.

There are many other situations that can occur in families, and genograms can be adapted to show them. For example, an increasing number of people are being born as the result of artificial reproduction methods. One method is artificial insemination, where the sperm comes from a donor rather than the husband. This method is sometimes called AID. It can be diagramed by adding a dotted line above the child to add another male not otherwise connected to the family. Another different situation is that some individuals have gay or lesbian relationships that are long-term, stable relationships, and they are so like family that some people find it useful to add them to their genogram. They can be added with the same dotted lines that are used for the living-together arrangement shown in Figure 3.4. Foster family situations are usually so different from one's biological family that it is best to add them off to the side or on a different sheet of paper.

Genogram charts can sometimes give us insights about what is happening in the lives of individuals and families, and potentially help us find ways to cope with and adjust to many of life's challenges. For example, we would expect that the period between 1986 and 1988 was a challenging time for Sandra and her family. During this time her 18-year-old brother, two grandparents, and stepfather died. Her youngest brother had a temporary relationship that included an abortion, and her father was divorced for the second time and remarried to a woman the same age as Sandra. Shortly after this marriage Sandra was married. With so many dramatic events, it is likely that Sandra and her new husband would have a number of emotional reactions to deal with. Many people find a genogram chart helpful in putting events in perspective, understanding their emotional reactions, and working through their many feelings.

Making a Family Chronology

The second part of a genogram is a **family chronology**. This is a chronological listing of major events experienced in a family. A family chronology should include both fortunate and unfortunate events. These could include events such as graduations, serious illnesses, moves, changes in careers, changes in family composition (a grandparent moving in), periods of drinking or other substance-abuse problems, runaways, special honors or awards, absence of a parent for an extended period of time, times of financial affluence or difficulty, accidents, and celebrations would all be important events if they were to occur in families, and they should be included.

Families may experience some very unfortunate events. These events have an important effect on individuals and families, and they should be identified. Care should be taken in describing them to be sure that confidences are not breached, and sometimes it is best to describe some of them in general terms. For example, saying something like "Paul and Sarah not close" could mean many things to the index person, and that is who is important.

Sometimes there is a tendency to focus on the tragic and traumatic in writing the chronology of family events, but this should be avoided. Unusual positive events also influence families and the individuals in them. Some examples of such events include a family member's being on a championship team, getting a special award or recognition, developing an unusually meaningful friendship, giving a special musical or artistic performance, taking a special trip, or being elected to a high office.

To show how a family chronology is written, the following family chronology for Sandra Jones lists some of the information from her family life:

1915 Peter Jones born.
1918 Joyce Clegg born.
1920 Henry Smith born.
Sophia Garcia born.
1939 Henry Smith moved to Mexico.
1940 Peter Jones and Joyce Clegg married.
1942 Marvin Jones born.
Henry Smith and Sophia Garcia married.
1943 Diane Smith born.
Child stillborn to Peter Jones and Joyce Clegg.

1944 Peter Jones had a severe stroke.
1945 Peter Jones died.
1952 Henry and Sophia Smith move from Mexico to South Carolina.
1965 Marvin Jones and Diane Smith married.
1967 Sandra Jones born.
1969 Mark Jones born.
1970 Kyle Jones born and adopted by Marvin and Diane Jones.
1982 Marvin Jones and Diane Smith divorced.
Marvin Jones and LeAnne Brady married.
1983 Diane Smith and Philip Page married.
1986 Marvin Jones and LeAnne Brady divorced.
Marvin Jones and Paula Kersten married.
1987 Sandra Jones and Jeff Brown married.
Mark Jones died at age 18.
Philip Page died.
Henry Smith died.
Kyle had affair with Lori Rice.
Lori Rice had an abortion.
1988 Diane Jones had a mental breakdown.
Sophia Garcia Smith died.
Twins, Becky and Janet Brown, born. Janet died.
1989 Kyle and Lori broke up.
1991 Twins, Aimee and Nicole Brown, born.
Kyle Jones and Brenda Strong married.
1992 Kyle and Brenda Jones had a miscarriage.

A thorough family chronology involves events from at least three different generations, and it usually has over 50 items. The above list has 35 items to illustrate how a family chronology is made, but it doesn't include many events that would be important in the family life of Sandra Jones.

Describing Family Relationships

The third part of a genogram is a description of the quality or character of the relationships between family members. These are usually fairly simple and straightforward, and some of them can be drawn on a genogram chart with the symbols shown in Figure 3.5. Usually it is not possible to diagram all of the important information about relationships because it becomes too complicated and confusing. Most of the time it is necessary to write the information about relationships on a few additional sheets of paper.

Another way to chart relationship information is to use a number of photocopies. For example, each photocopy could show the relationship information for a particular subgroup. Sometimes it is helpful to show the relationships at several periods in a family life cycle.

The following list of questions illustrates the kind of information that is usually included in the relationships part of a genogram.

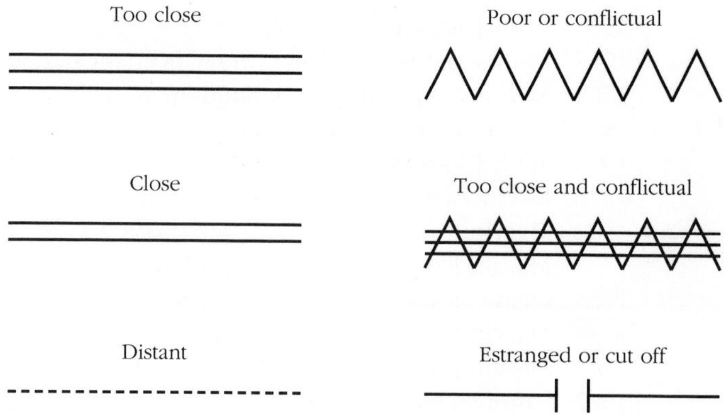

Too close

Poor or conflictual

Close

Too close and conflictual

Distant

Estranged or cut off

FIGURE 3.5
Symbols that can describe relationships in families

1. Who was close to whom?
2. Which individuals had conflictual relationships?
3. Which individuals were "left out"?
4. Who tended to be the family scapegoat if there was one?
5. If there was a "favorite" child of a parent or grandparent, who were they?
6. Who were the leaders, the followers?
7. Who was the family peacemaker? Troublemaker?
8. Who was distant from the family?
9. What were the alliances, cliques, or coalitions?
10. Who was "overfunctioning" or "underfunctioning"? (Overfunctioning individuals take upon themselves a lot of responsibility to make sure the right things get done. Underfunctioning individuals take little responsibility and initiative as they let others get things done.)

Describing Family Processes

The fourth part of a genogram is a description of circumstances, or processes, that can help us understand how generational relationships influence a family and the people in it. Examples of processes that can be significant are things such as cliques, alliances, and coalitions in families; ways children are treated differently by the parents; favorite relatives; conflicts that are not resolved; ways of solving problems; in-law pressures; and difficulties coping with life's challenges.

The following list of questions helps identify some of these processes:

1. How did the family react when a particular family member was born or died? Who took it the hardest? The easiest?
2. Have there been any job changes that influenced the family? How do people feel about their jobs?
3. How do people in the family get along with relatives? Are some relatives especially difficult, close, or helpful?

4. Have any members of the family had a drinking problem? What about trouble with medications or other substances?
5. Who is supportive or helpful of other family members? Who is unselfish, and who is selfish?
6. What does the family take pride in?
7. What are the leisure time and recreation patterns in the home, and how do the various members feel about them?
8. Were any individuals especially successful in school? Did any have problems?
9. What are the talents and special gifts that members of the family have?
10. Did the family have any special "program" or plans for a particular child?
11. Did sibling positions or relationships influence any of the children?
12. How involved was the family with churches, clubs, fraternities, or other organizations?
13. Were any life-cycle transitions (births, deaths, moving away from home, marriages, etc.) especially gratifying or difficult?
14. Did any members of the family have unusual ways of gaining recognition or success?
15. What were the successes, failures, traumas, satisfactions, and themes in the home?
16. Were there any coincidences of life events?
17. Did any economic or political events such as economic depressions or wars influence the family?
18. Were there any triangles inside or outside the family that had an effect on people?
19. Were there any "black sheep" or "family skeletons"?
20. Were there any resources such as inheritances or unusual brilliance or beauty that influenced the family?

Another helpful strategy in completing a genogram is to have the index persons tactfully do research about their own family history by interacting selectively with relatives. Many people find it easy to get more "involved" with their extended family when attending reunions, weddings, funerals, and other family gatherings; they can observe others and observe their own emotional reactions to what they experience. It is especially revealing to be around extended families at important emotional events such as a birth, a marriage, a death, a special achievement, a crisis, or an illness.

It usually is not very helpful to get involved with relatives to try to "straighten them out."

> A more suitable goal when approaching extended family is to attempt to learn about family processes, especially one's own role in them. One works to become more observant of oneself and others in the family. It is especially important to observe one's own emotional reactivity to other people. The task resembles a research project to determine one's own behavior which contributes to the reactive patterns of the family. The more a person can assume an observant, non-judgmental research posture, the greater the learning is likely to become. (Papero, 1983, p. 157)

Interpreting a Genogram

The payoff with a genogram is that it generally yields a lot of new information. Making a genogram of our own family often leads to better understanding of why we have some of the feelings we have, why we believe some of the things we do, why we have some of the attitudes we have, and why we relate to people the way we do. This may help us cope more effectively with life's challenges and difficulties. It can help us better attain the things that most of us desire in family life—such things as closeness, understanding, love, enrichment, fulfillment, commitment, healthy development, support, communication, empathy, and intimacy. As educators or therapists, we try to assist people in gaining insights about why they feel, act, relate, and think the way they do, and they can then use their new insights to better attain their goals.

Experience with genograms has identified several strategies for interpreting them. A good strategy to start with is to try to identify some positive things first. This can be done by looking for events, patterns, relationships, and processes that have helped create strengths or things that are valued and desired. All individuals and all families have some strengths and admirable characteristics. Identifying them at the outset builds morale and motivation. Even the most troubled and problem-ridden families have assets. In fact, sometimes the individuals and families that have had serious challenges have an unusual number of strengths.

Another strategy is to be tentative and hypothetical in trying to interpret a genogram. This means it is wise at first to state ideas as hypotheses or possibilities rather than revealed truths. You can say "It may be that . . ." "It's possible that . . ." "It could be that . . ." "Maybe . . ."

There are a few cautions that are helpful when as professionals we try to use a genogram to help someone else. Some people have very painful experiences in their families, and the strategies they have used to cope may be to avoid or forget them. These people may become extremely uncomfortable when they begin to think about those painful experiences, and forcing them to do so may do more

Box 3.1

We encourage readers to make a genogram for their own family. It provides an experiential type of learning that does not occur in any other way. We learn to better understand some of the interesting, informative, and subtle aspects of our own family situation. We also learn firsthand how our generational connections have an influence on us, and how we may influence our posterity. It takes several hours to make a good genogram, but the authors, their former students, and many colleagues who have made genograms for their own families have found it to be an interesting and useful learning experience. None of us should try to use a genogram to help someone else until we have made one for our own family first.

harm than good. People's feelings and wishes should be respected, and they should never be forced to face aspects of their family life they are not ready to deal with. Their personal desires need to determine what they do, and only when they are emotionally ready should they try to explore how their earlier family experiences have influenced them.

Using Generational Processes to Help People

Even though the study of generational processes is only a few decades old, family scientists have begun to discover ways some of the new ideas can help people attain their goals. We can use these ideas in our own family situations, and they can also be used by family therapists, family life educators, social workers, physicians, lawyers, and the clergy.

Liberating Families

Two approaches to social change have dominated the Western world for centuries. They go by the much-abused labels of *conservative* and *liberal.* **Conservatism** seeks to protect ideas and practices people think are valuable. It attempts to maintain traditional ways of doing things that people think are valuable. **Liberalism** takes the opposite stance, seeking to liberate people from conventions and practices that are oppressive and undesirable.

When we think of liberating people from political and economic oppression, we remember events such as the Magna Carta in 1215, the Declaration of Independence in 1776, the Bill of Rights in 1787, the French Revolution, the civil rights movement, the women's movement, and the fall of communism in the 1990s. We need to realize that the family realm can also be oppressive and dominating, and the liberal agenda ought to include liberating people from the undesirable bondage and oppression that can occur in families.

Many people inappropriately believe that we have to make a choice between being conservative or liberal. In practice we need to do both: to conserve what is valuable in established patterns and traditional ways, and to liberate ourselves by replacing patterns that are oppressive.

When undesirable patterns are being passed from one generation to another, there is a technique that can help liberate families from these patterns. It is to be a **transitional character**. The idea of a transitional character was developed by Carlfred Broderick (1988). As he explains:

> A transitional character is one who, in a single generation, changes the entire course of a lineage. The individuals who grow up in an abusive, emotionally destructive environment and who somehow find a way to metabolize the poison and refuse to pass it on to their children. They break the mold. They refute the observation that abused children become abusive parents, that the children of alcoholics become

> alcoholic adults, that "the sins of the fathers are visited upon the heads of the children to the third and fourth generation." Their contribution to humanity is to filter the destructiveness out of their own lineage so that the generations downstream will have a supportive foundation upon which to build productive lives. (p. 14)

There are many things people can do to help them be a transitional character. Eight strategies that seem helpful are: (1) deliberateness, (2) distinctive family rituals, (3) maintaining emotional distance, (4) marrying later than average, (5) reading good books about family life, (6) joining organizations that can help, (7) getting an education, and (8) developing a philosophy of life.

Deliberateness. A group of researchers at George Washington University have discovered that **deliberateness** can influence generational transmission (Bennett et al., 1987). They conducted a series of studies of the transmission of alcoholism in families, and one of the factors they found to be important is the degree to which people deliberately try to plan their own family identity, rituals, and ways of living.

In one of their studies they had 12 couples who had a high level of deliberateness, and 75 percent of them were able to be transitional couples by interrupting the transmission of alcohol problems. Of the 31 couples who were low on deliberateness, 77 percent of them transmitted from their parents the pattern of having alcohol problems (Bennett et al., 1987).

The following situation illustrates deliberateness in one family.

Distinctive family rituals. A second idea that was developed by the George Washington researchers has to do with family rituals, traditions, and routines. They discovered that families who do not allow a parent's alcohol abuse to disrupt important family rituals are less likely to pass their severe drinking problems to their offspring.

They found that when alcoholism becomes intertwined with family rituals and traditions such as birthday parties, dinners, family reunions, and holidays, the alcoholism tended to be transmitted to the next generation. However, when the alcohol problems were kept fairly separate from the family traditions and rituals, the alcoholism did not tend to be transmitted to the next generation. They called this process the **distinctiveness of rituals** because families that were

The Larson Family

My father has the tendency to be blunt in his communication. This makes him seem impatient or angry when he really isn't. I noticed as I got older that I often did the same thing, and I didn't like it. The past few years, especially after I was married, I have been able consciously to notice when I communicated that way, and I have been able to make a lot of progress toward eliminating that generational trait.

able to keep their family rituals and traditions distinctive from the problems they were having with alcohol were able to disrupt the transmission processes.

In one of their research projects, they studied the alcohol transmission in 25 families. They found five of the families were clearly distinctive and five were clearly not distinctive, and, even though the numbers in the study were small, the pattern was clear. In the five distinctive families none of them transmitted the alcoholism to the next generation, but in the five nondistinctive families, four of the five families had alcohol problems in the next generation (Wolin et al., 1980).

Maintaining emotional distance. Research about generational transmission has discovered that the emotional distance between people in families also tends to influence the transmission process. If the individuals in the children's generation of a family remain emotionally intertwined with their parents' generation, there tends to be more transmission, but if the children create a certain amount of emotional distance from their parents there is less transmission.

This idea is demonstrated in several of the studies in the George Washington research program (Steinglass et al., 1987; Bennett et al., 1987). The latter authors summarize in the following way:

> Couples with an alcoholic legacy are relatively more protected from transmission if they take certain measures regarding their family attachments. Ideally, contact with the child's alcoholic origin family is not high, although it may remain moderate with no strongly adverse effects. (Bennett et al., 1987, p. 128)

Thus, the best research evidence suggests it is not necessary to completely sever emotional attachments and visiting patterns with the parent generation. Apparently there can be a moderate amount of emotional attachment and interaction when someone is trying to become a transitional character, but if adult children are highly involved with their parents it is more difficult to disrupt the transmission of such things as values, traditions, rituals, attitudes, and behaviors from one generation to the next.

Murray Bowen has developed an additional concept that helps us recognize a destructive way of managing the emotional distance between the generations (Kerr & Bowen, 1988). His concept is emotional cutoff. **Emotional cutoff** occurs when a person tries to eliminate, deny, or avoid their emotional involvement with the parental family even though they actually have strong emotional reactivity with the family. Thus emotional cutoff is a pattern of trying to run away from the negative feelings, avoid the pain, and avoid having to deal with the emotional processes. Since it doesn't solve the problems, but leaves emotion seething beneath the surface, usually emotional cutoff makes the situation worse.

People who experience emotional cutoff may not see members of their family for years. Also, they may move to a different part of the country or even a different continent, but they are still emotionally involved with their parental family. Their personal responses to emotional ties with their parental family usually continue to influence how they act, respond, define situations, relate in their own marriage, and treat their children.

The process of decreasing emotional ties with one's parental family can help solve certain kinds of situations, but it also usually has some undesirable side effects. Reducing emotional involvement with parents usually involves pain, and it can leave deep scars in the psyche. It also creates a need to find substitute relationships that are deep and meaningful, not superficial, and this is not easy in contemporary society. Deeply binding relationships are created naturally as people grow up in families, even unhealthy families, and when people find it necessary to disrupt these natural relationships it leaves them in an emotional vacuum. We do not have in our society any well-established substitutes for the kind of relationships we experience in families. This leaves people who want to be transitional characters in a Catch-22 situation. They have difficulty if they create emotional closeness, and difficulty if they create distance.

There are certain stages of life when coping with these difficulties is more easily done. People who go through the process of distancing themselves from their parental family in their late teens and early twenties have an advantage over those who try to do it either at younger or older ages. In this optimal period people are generally looking toward marriage, and they can sometimes use their marital relationship and their own parenting relationships to create the deeper and meaningful emotional experiences they are reducing with their family of origin.

Creating new, deeply felt emotional relationships is in some ways like emigrating to a new land. It provides opportunities, but it usually means learning new language and new ways of relating to social and emotional environments, and new opportunities alternate with inevitable periods of loneliness and discomfort while we make the adjustments. Also, we need to recognize that we may always be somewhat divided emotionally between our new family and our old.

Marrying later than average. Another idea that can help disrupt generational transmission is for people to marry later than average. When people are in their late teens or early twenties, they usually have very limited experiences outside their parental family. If they will wait until they are in their middle twenties to marry, they can use these important years to learn new ways of interacting with others. They have access to a wider array of ideas, feelings, and ways of behaving. This broadening enables them to choose ways of living, loving, feeling, acting, and relating that are different from those learned in their parental home.

There are many reasons people who marry at young ages are more likely to repeat the patterns of their parental family. One reason is that they have less opportunity to learn alternative ways of relating. Many people who want to avoid patterns they grew up with don't understand that most of what happens in families is below the surface, and desire is sometimes not enough to effect change. Fortunately, some people find new models to copy, and they have enough experiences outside their family that they learn alternative ways of behaving.

Reading good books about family life. Sociologists have discovered that it is important to learn a lot about a role before we are in it. The technical term for this

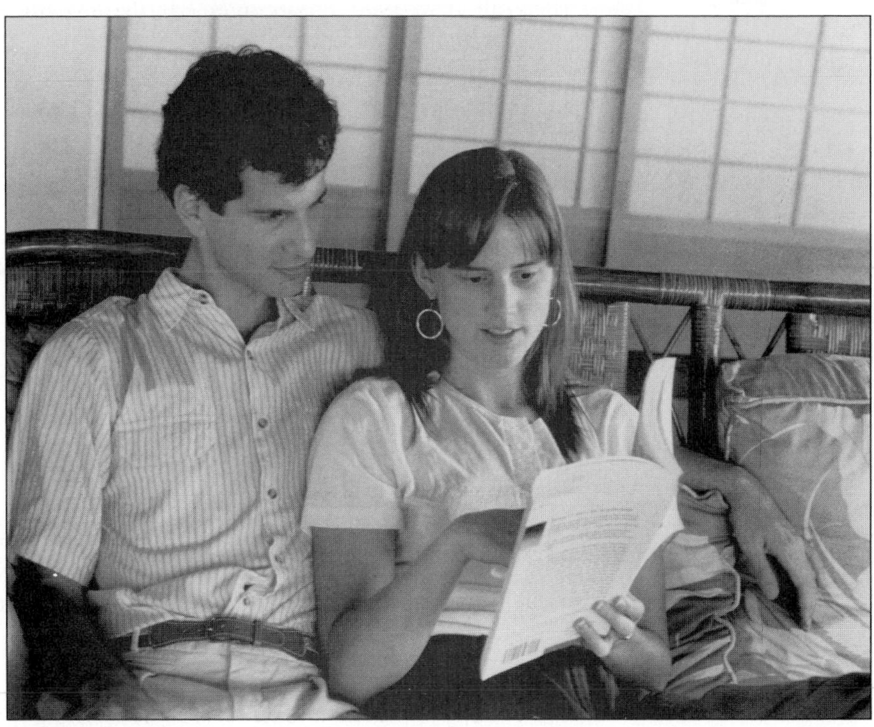

In building a relationship, positive emotions need to be nurtured as the new emotional system is created.

is **anticipatory socialization**, and reading books about healthy family life is one way to provide this preparation. There are many excellent books about how to create a good marriage and how to be effective parents. A few examples are:

Barlow, Brent, 1986, *Twelve Traps in Today's Marriage and How to Avoid Them*, Salt Lake City: Deseret Books.

Bellah, Robert N., Richard Madsen, William M. Sullivan, Ann Swidler, and Steven M. Tipton, 1985, *Habits of the Heart*, New York: Harper.

Broderick, Carlfred, 1979, *Couples: How to Confront Problems and Maintain Loving Relationships*, New York: Simon and Schuster.

Dobson, James C., 1991, *Straight Talk* (revised ed.), Dallas: Word Publishing.

Ginott, Haim G., 1969, *Between Parent & Teenager*, New York: Avon.

Isaacs, David, 1984, *Character Building: A Guide for Parents and Teachers*, Kill Lane, Blackrock, Dublin: Four Courts Press Limited.

Leman, Kevin, 1992, *Keeping Your Family Together When the World Is Falling Apart*, New York: Delacorte Press.

Napier, Augustus Y., and Carl A. Whitaker, 1978, *The Family Crucible*, New York: Bantam.

Pearsall, Paul, 1990, *Power of the Family: Tapping the Power of Family Life to Strengthen, Revitalize, and Heal,* New York: Bantam.

Satir, Virginia, 1972, *Peoplemaking,* Palo Alto: Science and Behavior.

Stinnett, Nick, and John DeFrain, 1985, *Secrets of Strong Families,* Boston: Little, Brown.

York, Phillis, David York, and Ted Wachtel, 1982, *Tough Love,* New York: Bantam.

Joining organizations. There are many organizations that can help individuals learn new ways of relating. Some possibilities include clubs, service groups, the military, the Peace Corps, fraternities, sororities, and so on. Some of these organizations may help more than others. Organizations that are "family-like" are probably more helpful than those that are formal, bureaucratic, and impersonal.

It is important to realize that different people find different groups as their ideals. For example, some people will want to associate with people in artistic communities because they want to be like them. Others will be more comfortable in intellectual or academic organizations. Others will find recreational or service organizations more suited to the style of life they want. Many people find churches or other religious organizations helpful in learning ways to live, believe, and interact.

Getting an education. A well-rounded education can broaden ideas, provide insights, and increase your ability to relate and make decisions. Classes on topics such as family science, parenting, and marriage preparation can be very helpful. A broad, general education is probably more beneficial to you in your family realm than technical or job-oriented training.

Developing a philosophy of life. Many people who grow up in troubled families do not have a philosophy of life with which they are comfortable. Inquiring into what gives life purpose and meaning can help clarify personal values, ideals, aspirations, purposes, and beliefs and enhance all aspects of life—both family and individual. Some people become involved in spiritual or religious activities as a way to develop their personal philosophy of life. Others find that becoming part of an intellectual or artistic close-knit community is satisfying. Still others look inward for answers. If people can find something they believe in deeply and then build their life around these beliefs, it can provide a foundation for learning how to relate to others in meaningful ways.

Conserving Desirable Generational Processes

Many of the things that are transmitted across generations are very desirable. For example, many people grow up in healthy families, and they learn the subtle values, goals, feelings, and attitudes that give meaning, purpose, and a sense of direction to their life. They learn ways of trusting, loving, being close, serving, supporting, and communicating at the deepest and most meaningful levels; they also learn to care for infants and the elderly in ways that give purpose and joy to their lives.

Many people acquire a set of bonds in their family that are multifaceted and strong, and that provide loving, intimate, close relationships of infinite value. They form lifelong connections with their siblings, parents and grandparents, and with their own children and grandchildren. These kinds of connections involve deep, complicated feelings that are fundamental to a healthy life and provide a richness and beauty that is difficult to describe. Even those who grow up in families where they vow to "do some things differently than their parents" learn many things from their parents that they want to continue in their own life. They also have bonds and feelings for their family that last all their lives.

One challenge for family scientists is to capitalize on the generational ties and transmissions that are desirable. There are a number of strategies for this. Some of the processes that help people disrupt unhealthy generational transmissions can also be used to help them conserve healthy generational processes. For example, the ideas about deliberateness and distinctiveness of rituals can be used to create healthy patterns. People who deliberately try to create healthy traditions, beliefs, rules, and patterns of relating will undoubtedly be more effective than people who never bother to think about it. Families who integrate their rituals, traditions, and routines with healthy and desirable ways of behaving are increasing the likelihood that the desirable patterns will be passed on to succeeding generations. In the same way, families who create emotional distance between the generations decrease transmission from one generation to the other, and families that create emotional closeness between the generations increase what is transmitted.

Creating Healthy Generational Alliances

A number of strategies can be used to create healthy generational alliances. Some of them are simple. For example, parents can help the parental subsystem become the executive subsystem in a family by conducting periodic planning sessions. The small children would not attend these sessions, and in them the parents could discuss the ways they are relating to the children, ways they are disciplining them, what's going well, and what needs to be changed. Sessions such as this can help them make plans together so they are a coordinated team. If they have disagreements about how to structure the family or relate to the children, they can use sessions such as these to try to find common ground and compromise. As the children mature, the family system can gradually change so the older children have an increasing access to the executive subsystem and influence it an increasing amount.

Another idea that can help families create healthy generational alliances is for the parents to have a social life as a couple in addition to the social activities of the family. This could include dates with each other, vacations as a couple, and joining social organizations together. These activities can help the bonds in the marital relationship, and can help everyone be aware that the couple subsystem is a unique and important unit in the family.

Unfinished Business

Another concept that can help families deal with generational processes in healthy ways is unfinished business. **Unfinished business** refers to the need to deal with unresolved issues, feelings, injustices, and conflicting loyalties in a family.

Invisible Loyalties, by Ivan Boszormenyi-Nagy and Geraldine Sparks (1973), helped the family science field begin to understand the role generational loyalties have in the healthy or unhealthy development of individuals and families. According to Boszormenyi-Nagy and Sparks, each generation has ethical obligations and loyalties to the generations that preceded it and to the generation that follows it. For example, parents have ethical obligations to their children to provide affection, care, and nurturance. They also owe their children a loving home, economic support, and security. These obligations create a complex web of invisible loyalties and obligations from parents to children. When parents fulfill their obligations to their children, it creates an obligation in the children's generation to appreciate the value of what they received. Children develop feelings of appreciation, respect, closeness, and admiration for their parents.

Boszormenyi-Nagy and his colleagues believe that network of intergenerational loyalties in family systems is not something created by cultures or societies. It is a "natural" part of the family realm that exists because the generations are so intricately intertwined emotionally, mentally, and experientially (Boszormenyi-Nagy & Krasner, 1986). Cultures and societies, however, influence and shape some of the ways these networks appear and whether they are healthy or unhealthy.

The network of invisible loyalties is about intangible things rather than material things; it is a system of invisible obligations, or what Boszormenyi-Nagy and his colleagues call:

> . . . *relational ethics.* Here "ethics" carries no implication of a specific set of moral priorities or criteria of right vs. wrong. It is concerned with the balance of equitable fairness between people. By "fairness" we mean neither the mechanistic rigidity of giving all three children bicycles for Christmas, nor a barter system in which each item is part of a trade-off, but rather the long term preservation of an oscillating balance among family members, whereby the basic interests of each are taken into account by the others. (Boszormenyi-Nagy & Ulrich, 1981, p. 160)

Sometimes the pattern of ethical obligations in family systems becomes unhealthy and disabling. A parent generation may not fulfill some of their obligations to the younger generation, or a younger generation may not fulfill some of their obligations to the older generation. One way of looking at these unbalanced situations is to view the family as having a ledger of ethical loyalties and obligations that can get out of balance. When this occurs, the parental generation may develop resentment, bitterness, or anger toward the children, or the children may develop animosity, enmity, or hostility toward their parents.

The research of Boszormenyi-Nagy and his colleagues helps us realize that these patterns of invisible loyalties in the family realm deal with deep feelings that are extremely important to most people. Therefore, when families have healthy patterns in their web of invisible loyalties across generations, it provides a reservoir of emotional stability for them. It also builds interpersonal bonds that help people deal effectively with the challenges of life, and it provides a deeply experienced sense of meaning, purpose, and lineage consciousness that extends across the generations.

Another aspect of these invisible loyalties is that they gradually evolve and change as the family members mature and move to new stages of life. For example, young adults gradually shift their primary family loyalties from their parental family toward their spouse and the children they want to have. As they make these shifts, they develop new loyalties and some of their old loyalties become less important. The old loyalties that diminish have to do with obedience, reverence, allegiance, and indebtedness, and the new loyalties deal with emotional dependence, connectedness, fidelity, nurturance, and creating together a sense of home, meaning, growth, and "rootedness."

There are some family situations where the disruption in the ledger of invisible loyalties becomes tragic. Serious misbehavior such as child abuse, incest, negligence, alcoholism, violence, manipulation, exploitation, or substance abuse can create severe disruptions in the invisible loyalties in a family system. It is extremely difficult for the members of such a family to find ways to balance the ledgers and free themselves from the hurts and fears and resentments they experienced. Amazingly, many of the people who have experienced these tragedies in their families are able to face their feelings and eventually work through their emotional responses in ways that are productive and enabling.

Virtually all of us find it necessary to deal with unfinished generational business at certain stages of life. For example, it is fairly typical for ledgers to become unbalanced during the launching stage of the family life cycle. It is natural for the younger generation to be striving to gain freedom and control over their life and for the older generation to be hesitant because of the perceived limitations in the young people's judgment and experience. Often there is considerable conflict during this period of the life cycle and the invisible loyalties twist and shift.

When this occurs, the family has unfinished business, and they would be wise to try to deal with it. They must work through the negative feelings and resolve the inequities so individuals can move on to new stages of life and new responsibilities.

There are many ways the younger and older generations can take care of unfinished generational business. Sometimes it helps to try to talk about feelings with parents, children, or siblings. In other situations it is neither possible nor wise to talk directly, because it would just make the situation worse. Then, perhaps, the younger generation can look at the unique circumstances that make it difficult for the parental generation to be as wise or fair as might be desired. Sometimes it is necessary to accept that parents are also frail and limited in their humanness and they may need acceptance, understanding, tolerance, or even pity. Sometimes it is possible to adopt a forgiving attitude, acknowledging that the parents probably had reasons for what they did and it will not help to continue feeling resentful. Sometimes it is helpful to get professional help to work through unfinished business.

SUMMARY

This chapter described how generational processes influence families and individuals. Two principles were introduced. The generational alliance principle states that there are some boundaries between parent and child generations that are natural and desirable, and when families maintain these boundaries it contributes to everyone's healthy development. Conversely, when these boundaries become blurred, it interferes with healthy development.

The generational transmission principle is that aspects of the family realm are transmitted from one generation to the next, and this includes both the desirable and undesirable. Three areas where there is considerable evidence that transmission occurs are: marital stability and instability, abusive and nonabusive behaviors, and mental health and illness.

The chapter described how to make and interpret a genogram, and then presented strategies that can be used to conserve desirable generational ties and transmissions and to liberate people from undesirable generational ties and transmissions.

KEY TERMS

Generations
Boundaries
Generational alliances
Generational coalitions
Generational transmission
Marital stability and instability
Spurious relationship
Mental health and illness
Abusive and nonabusive behaviors
Regulating emotional distance
Family projection process
Genogram
Conservative
Liberal
Transitional character
Deliberateness
Rituals
Distinctiveness of rituals
Emotional distance
Emotional cutoff
Unfinished business

Study Questions

1. What is meant by the term *inalienable?* How and why does this apply to the generational process?
2. Describe in detail three reasons why generational processes are unique to the family realm.
3. Define what is meant by a generational alliance. When could it be a positive occurrence?
4. Make a list of ten things that have the possibility of being transmitted from one generation to the next. By each one give it a rating ranging from 1 to 5 (a 1 means it is rare that this item would be transmitted to the next generation and a 5 means it is frequently transmitted).
5. Why is the family the "best and worst of times"?
6. Why, in your opinion, would someone who came from an abusive home be more likely to be abusive with his or her family of procreation?

Notes

1. Lidz did not give this principle a name, but we find it easier to communicate about principles when they have names. Therefore, we have called it the generational alliance principle.

Family Love

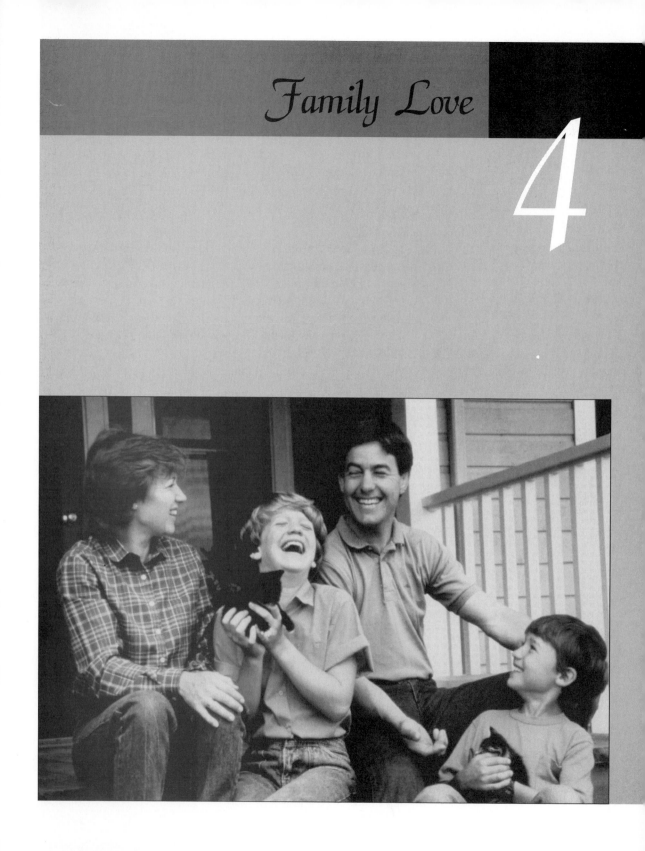

4

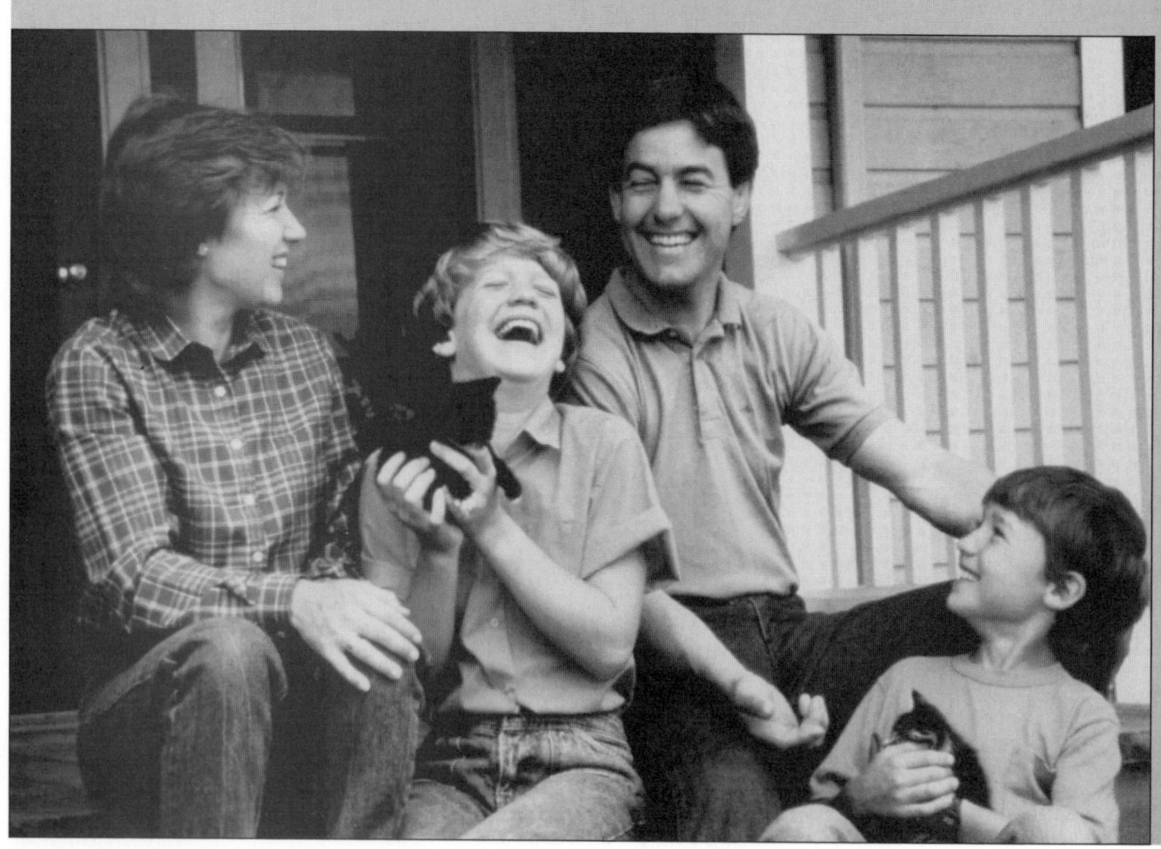

Main Ideas

1 // The practice of love—the giving and receiving of acts and gifts motivated by love—is one of the most basic processes of the family system. Love is normative in families; that is, we expect family members to love each other.

2 // The study of family love has been neglected by family scholars. There are at least four reasons for this neglect: (1) family theory has frequently been grounded in the study of disabled or problem families; (2) love is not easily defined, particularly within the parameters of "rational" science; (3) the dominant frameworks for studying the family have been individualist, economic, and hedonistic; and (4) male thought has predominated in social science.

3 // Five conceptual models that offer insights about family love are reviewed: a model of romantic love; a model of reciprocal altruism rooted primarily in anthropology; a "grants economy" model based in economics; a sociological model contrasting variants of individualism with altruistic commitment; and a feminist model of maternal love. All but the first involve variations of "altruistic love."

4 // Building on previous conceptualizations, we offer a definition of family love that identifies four attributes of love necessary for healthy individual and family life: it is other-oriented, it is action-oriented, it is unconditional, and it is enduring.

One of the ways families are different from other social groups is that love is "normative" in families. To say love is normative does not mean that love is "normal" or that loving behavior is typical in families. A **norm** is an expectation about what people ought to do, a standard of conduct that is expected to be followed. Therefore, to say love is normative in families is not to say that all families love, but that people think family members *should* love each other, and that families where love is absent tend to be regarded as unfortunate, deviant, or even pathological.

The Priority of Love

If you ask the average person in the street what is the essence of a family, or why family is important, love is always part of the answer. You get responses such as

> *"[Love is] one of the most talked-about and longed-for of human experiences in the Western world."*
>
> —Henslin, 1980, p. 3

"Family are those who love you no matter what," or "When you feel your family loves you, then you can handle the other disappointments in life." On the other hand, other experiences of love rarely can compensate for failures of family love. This is not to say the love of others is not a significant component of our lives. But in a real, day-to-day sense, love of family provides a sustenance that is difficult to replace. Antarctic explorer Richard E. Byrd, alone at the South Pole and fearing he might not survive, reflected on the priority of family love:

> At the end only two things really matter to a man, regardless of who he is; and they are the affection and understanding of his family. Anything and everything else he creates

> are insubstantial; they are ships given over to the mercy of the winds and tides of prejudice. But the family is an everlasting anchorage, a quiet harbor where a man's ships can be left to swing to the moorings of pride and loyalty. (Byrd, 1987, p. 179)

Some scholars say that in these modern times the family has lost some of its importance as a source of love. Others argue that the pressures of modern life have made family love even more important. One such view is articulated by Weitzman (1982):

> Despite the profound changes in the nature of the family that have come with the industrialization and urbanization of the past century, today's family remains the basic unit for the protection and rearing of young children, and the center of emotional life. Indeed, its role as the major source of psychological support for its members has, if anything, greatly increased. The family is a "haven in a heartless world," an oasis of stable, diffuse, and largely unquestioned love and support. (pp. 2–3)

The need for families—and parents, in particular—as a source of love is nowhere more evident than in the growth and development of children. Burton White, a noted expert on early childhood development, states that making an infant feel loved and cared for is the single most important factor in helping that child get a good start in life. It is impossible to overemphasize its importance (White, 1985, p. 26).

Each of the preceding statements emphasizes the importance of love, but the focus is one-sided: They all speak of the need to feel loved. Obviously, love is a reciprocal thing: We cannot be loved unless there are those who love us, persons who are loving. So perhaps the critical question is not "Do you feel loved?" but "Do you love?" From either standpoint, loving or being loved, the family is central. For most people, the family is the primary source both of being loved and of learning to love.

Strangely, although love has overarching importance in the hearts and minds of family members, the study of love in families has been neglected by family scholars.[1] Perhaps no characteristic of the research and writing on families by sociologists, economists, and psychologists so clearly demonstrates the need for a family-based paradigm as does the lack of attention to family love.

For some scholars, including the authors of this text, an interest in love as an essential aspect of family life is a distinguishing characteristic of family science. The conceptual framework we share views love as a basic, enabling family process, a core dimension of healthy families.

Why Social Scientists Avoided Love

The dearth of research and writing on family love is partly a result of the difficulties people have defining love. James Henslin (1980) comments:

> We all speak and act as though we know exactly what love is, but when one attempts to pin it down love turns out to be fantastically elusive. It is almost impossible to put into words. Although we all "know" what love is, our "knowing" fails when it comes to defining the specifics of love. (p. 3)

One way family scholars deal with the ambiguity of love is to pay attention to some of its more concrete aspects, and to substitute for "love" more limited and easily defined concepts such as affection, intimacy, and bonding. These are concepts that presumably overlap love in some way. In practice, love itself is rarely mentioned in the literature except in the study of romantic love or courtship.

Another way to simplify the problem of definition is to divide love into abstract types, such as romantic love, sexual love, mother love, or fraternal love, and to work from some operational definition of one or more of these types.

The challenge of defining love is not a sufficient explanation for the reluctance of social scientists to tackle the serious study of family love. The answer lies in how problems are defined. The way family scholars have looked at love in families (or, rather, *not* looked at it) is a result of at least four trends in the history of Western family sciences.

Love Is Not Rational

The first reason love has been somewhat ignored in scientific study has to do with the nature of science itself. Science by definition is rational, and throughout much of the present century, social science has been preeminently empirical. In part, this means that the dominant, most respectable ways of gaining knowledge have had to do with measurement. Concepts readily defined and measured have been preferred to more ambiguous variables.

"Love" was a feeling, a sentiment—mystical, philosophical, spiritual, visceral, moral, emotional, and immensely complicated. It was difficult to define, and even more difficult to measure. Therefore, the tendency was to substitute concepts like "adjustment," "intimacy," or "bonding" which, though still complex, were more easily converted into behaviors that could be measured.

Research Was Grounded in Pathology

Second, many of the theoretical perspectives that guide the study of the family had their origin in the study of disabled or problem families. Persons charged with helping problem families have been oriented to identifying and treating pathologies rather than understanding the workings of healthy, fully functioning families.

The aspect of family love that has been studied most thoroughly by family scientists is romantic love, specifically love as it relates to premarital relationships, courtship and the choice of a marriage partner. With marriage, scientific interest in "love," per se, seems to end. Attention shifts to the problems encountered in marriage, and to issues like satisfaction, adjustment, stress, expectations, role definitions and performance, interpersonal exchange, sexual activity and happiness, but not love.

Other Models Prevailed

A third reason love as a characteristic of family life has been ignored by researchers is that the dominant frameworks for studying family behavior have been individualistic and hedonistic.[2] These frameworks have highlighted the individual, his or her power and possessions, and personal gratification as the topics most worth studying. Consider, for example, Campbell's (1975) description of the hedonistic emphasis in psychology and the probable influence of this bias on the study of family love and the duties and sacrifices that flow from it.

> Psychology and psychiatry . . . not only describe man as selfishly motivated, but implicitly or explicitly teach that he ought to be so. They tend to see repression and inhibition of individual impulse as undesirable, and see all guilt as a dysfunctional neurotic blight created by cruel child rearing and a needlessly repressive society. They further recommend that we accept our biological and psychological impulses as good and seek pleasure rather than enchain ourselves with duty. (p. 1104)

The individualistic and hedonistic emphasis is illustrated in a review article summarizing psychological research on "women's emotional experience of mothering" and why some women choose to be mothers and others do not (Gerson, Alpert & Richardson, 1984, p. 435). The researchers looked at costs and benefits: "the perceived value of children . . . pitted against corresponding barriers (such as financial stress) and alternative sources of satisfaction (such as leisure time activities)" (p. 441); and at how "motherhood is, or is not, instrumental for women in realizing their personal goals" (p. 435). In place of love were concepts like "maternal feeling," "responsiveness to babies," and "maternal bonding." Nowhere in the article are "love" or "altruism" mentioned as possible reasons for having children or nurturing them, or as variables worth studying in connection with motherhood.

Masculine Thinking Prevailed

A fourth reason family love has not been a subject of serious research is the disproportionate influence of male thought in family theory. In the United States, at least, family love has everywhere been more the domain of women, while social science has been the domain of men. Historically, even those few women who achieved an opportunity to influence family theory were committed like their male teachers to the prevailing biases of positivism and economically oriented rationalism. Many of those women discounted their personal family-related experiences and feminine orientations in favor of the models of "male" science (Smith, 1987; Ruddick, 1989).

In view of the limited body of family science research on love, our sources for this chapter include philosophers, poets, novelists, and feminist scholars, as well as anthropologists, economists, historians, and social psychologists. After considering several distinctive ways of conceptualizing love and its relation to other family processes, we suggest a composite approach that combines insights from several disciplines in a single model for family love.

Theoretical Models

Conjugal Love and Romantic Love

One type of family love that has received some attention from family scholars is **conjugal love**, or the love between husbands and wives. Much of the writing on conjugal love has to do with the continuance of "romantic love," the "mutual affection based on personal attraction and compatibility" which is the major basis of mate selection in the United States and other Western nations (Giddens, 1991, p. 481).

Romantic love is love based on feelings, on "chemistry." It may be characterized as a "strongly felt emotion," a "fever" or an "obsession" (Rubin, 1973, p. 207). Even though the pragmatics of mate selection may include a degree of calculation as well as chemistry, in the popular ideal romantic feeling dominates. Unfortunately, feelings are inherently unstable, and because they are, the continuance of romantic love is always in doubt. There is need for continuing proof that the magic persists, the chemistry continues. Each of the partners continues to seek assurances that the other "really loves," or "still loves," and the relationship is threatened if one concludes that the other "has not met the test" of continuing attraction and no longer loves as before, or "really loves" as he or she should (Kilpatrick, 1975, p. 220). Then the chemistry is readily reversed, and feelings of love may change to bitterness and hate, the antitheses of love.

Where marriages are not arranged, romantic love is an important means for getting couples together. But it lacks the sustaining power of love conceived as duty, or of love as shared experience and mutual sacrifice. Many writers make a distinction between romantic love and "realistic love," by which they mean conjugal love or "love between settled, domestic people" (Goode, 1959; Knox, 1979, pp. 68–69). Madeleine L'Engle (1989), looking back on the immature images of future romance that contributed to the atmosphere of her New York City apartment, makes the same distinction: "As we settled into the apartment I had visions of work in the theater, of books published, of romantic love, *which had little to do with real love*" (p. 14; emphasis added).

From a familial perspective, the romantic ideal is important, but it is an inadequate conception of love in marriage. It tends to be egoistic, governed more by self-interest than an ethic of altruism. When love is viewed so narrowly it contributes to perceptions of inequity in the relationship (one wonders whether the other is "giving" the love she/he should, or whether one is "getting" all the other benefits deserved) and may encourage instability in the marriage.

Historically, the emphasis on romantic love in marriage is a relatively recent phenomenon. In preindustrial societies, marriage was primarily an economic and social institution. One did not marry for love as much as for economic cooperation, for procreation and child rearing, and to fill other socially-prescribed roles. Although family roles were quite sharply defined, with a clear distinction between men's and women's work, both men and women contributed to the same family enterprise. They worked together in the social sphere of the household, and each contributed a degree of personal service to the other and to their children (Cowan, 1983). As Berry (1981, p. 290; 1987, p. 119) has observed, particularly in hunting-and-gathering and in agricultural societies, men and women were literal helpmates. Both engaged in tasks of nurture.

The frequent result of this shared effort for provisioning and care of the household, including farm or shop, home and children, was love, action- and activity-based love, love anchored not so much in chemistry as in reciprocal sacrifices for the common good, in obligations to each other and to society. The duet "Do You Love Me?" in the musical *Fiddler on the Roof* illustrates such love. The Jewish father, Tevye, having confronted the influence of modern love in his daughter's arguments for her choice of a husband-to-be, asks Golda, his wife, about her feelings for him. He and Golda were married in the traditional way and in twenty years of marriage the issue has never come up. "Love" was not part of their courtship and marriage, and until now, the question has never occurred to Tevye. But there are things about this "new way" that Tevye likes, so he asks his wife, "Do you love me?" "Do I *what*?" Golda responds. They consider the many things they have shared over the years, and the things they have done for each other—tasks, gifts, problems and pains—and Golda concludes, "If that isn't love, what is?"

Another poignant illustration appears in Niethammer's (1977) history of Native American women. Describing ties between spouses in the typically arranged marriages of Indian couples, she comments that some couples loved each other from the beginning of their life together, while others "developed deep and abiding affection for each other after years of living and working together." Niethammer quotes a Papago woman, who described the love in her marriage this way: "I had grown fond of him. We had starved together so much" (p. 90).

The following models of family love differ from the romantic model in at least two ways. First, the emphasis in each is on love as a family process subject to individual will and action, not just feeling and emotion. Second, each is a conception of love applicable to all types of families and all family members, not just to romantic or sexual partners.

Each of the three models offers a perspective on what we call altruistic love. The Oxford English Dictionary's first definition of love is "that disposition or state of feeling with regard to a person which manifests itself in solicitude for the welfare of the object, and usually also in delight in his presence and desire for his approval; warm affection, attachment." Thus defined, love may be considered a synonym of altruism.

Reciprocal Altruism and the Rule of Amity

Altruism is the term used by social scientists to describe selfless concern for others and unselfish behaviors that foster the welfare of others. Thus altruism is the opposite of egoism. In many respects it is also the opposite of hedonism. In the hedonistic marketplace, one operates to maximize personal satisfactions. In the altruistic context, one places the welfare of others ahead of self.

Altruistic behavior is not limited to families, but we *expect* it there. In other settings, altruism merits attention and praise. In the family setting, it is the absence of altruism, not its appearance, that provokes comment. Differences in altruistic behavior between the family realm and the nonfamily realms are a matter of relative emphasis rather than absolute difference.

Motive in altruism. The difference between altruism and egoism is not observable in behavior but in motive. For conduct to be altruistic it must be motivated by love or generosity, by a willingness to go beyond the minimum prescribed by law. Sorokin ([1948] 1971) highlights this distinction in his comparison of "marginal altruism" and "real altruism." The essence of marginal altruism is embodied in the formula: "Exercise your legal rights and perform your legal duties when they do not harm anyone else and when they do not violate the rights and duties of others" (p. 58). Sorokin suggests such conduct is only minimally altruistic because

> it does not contain any elements of love or generosity. . . . Real altruism begins only when this [legal] minimum is transcended: when an individual freely sacrifices his rightful interests in favor of the well-being of another, refraining from harming him, even though his legal right entitles him to do so, and helping him in various ways, though no law demands of him such action. . . . In contrast to obligatory legal conduct, altruistic conduct is always free from any external compulsion. It is freely chosen and it is also the purest form of free conduct known. . . . *Genuine altruism is pure also in its motivation: altruistic actions are performed for their own sake, quite apart from any considerations of pleasure or utility.* (Sorokin, [1948] 1971, pp. 58–59)

The anthropologist Meyer Fortes (1969) argues that altruism may also include obligatory action or duty, and that "prescriptive altruism" is the basis of kinship morality. It is the "ethic of generosity" that governs social relations among kin. Fortes calls this kinship principle "the rule of amity." The term *amity* derives from two Latin words: *amare*, to love, and *amicus*, friend. The rule of amity as outlined by Fortes involves kindness, caring, and love. It assumes a morality of other-orientation. "Kinsfolk are expected to be loving, just, and generous to one another and not to demand strictly equivalent returns of one another" (Fortes, 1969, p. 237).

In practical application, this means that kinsfolk may have irresistible claims on one another for hospitality, support, consideration, and protection. Such norms characterize many American Indian tribes. Ideally, they are expected to share freely with their kin, no matter how distantly related, not because they are coerced or have contracted to do so, but simply because they are kin.

Reciprocity and altruism. The rule of amity incorporates a social norm of reciprocity—**reciprocal altruism**. All are expected to be givers as well as receivers. L. C. Becker (1986) identifies the following maxims as representing an ethic that one should reciprocate in altruistic ways:

> . . . that we should return good for good, in proportion to what we receive; that we should resist evil, but not do evil in return; that we should make reparation for the

> harm we do; and that we should be disposed to do those things as a matter of moral obligation. (p. 4)

From an ecological perspective, reciprocal altruism is an adaptive process that helps assure the survival of the family. Psychologist Donald Campbell (1975) suggests that altruistic behaviors not only help insure the survival of human societies, but also make life better for both groups and individuals:

> Indeed, much of the literature on altruism and group selection is devoted to explaining how specific group-advantageous traits . . . [e.g., altruism] are also individually advantageous. (p. 1111)

The question is sometimes raised, if altruism is an adaptive process necessary for group survival, does this mean to be altruistic is somehow "natural" or genetically predetermined? That the rule of amity is the ideal, and is universally applied as a "cornerstone of morality, rational action, and group life," (Brown, 1991, pp. 107–108), is not in itself evidence that it is "natural" or inherent in the human species. If it were biologically determined that we behave altruistically in family settings, there would be no need for the moral preachments of priests and parents.

History suggests that if anything can be called "natural," it is egoism—the "survival of the fittest" disposition to look after your own interests rather than an urge to protect the group at your expense. To correct this, it seems, almost all cultures have moral codes that encourage altruism and frown on certain selfish behaviors. These same moral codes, however, generally allow self-interest along with concern for others (Mansbridge, 1990). Clearly, egoism is also an adaptive process, one that is essential to survival. Individuals who totally ignored their own needs would soon be incapable of making positive contributions to the welfare of others.

Thus in the family system, as well as in society as a whole, altruism and egoism are interdependent. For optimum functioning of the system some balance is needed between them. By balance we do not mean equal amounts of each. The optimal balance between egoism and altruism varies by culture and system. In an integrative system like the family, it appears that more altruism than egoism is necessary to assure the stability of the family and the continuity of the culture.

Grants and Exchanges: The Economics of Love

A second social science model useful in exploring family love comes from the economist Kenneth Boulding. Boulding's interest is in "integrative systems," or aspects of society that involve "status, identity, community, legitimacy, loyalty, benevolence, and . . . the appropriate opposites." Boulding (1973, preface) considers how love may be created in family life, and how it can be sustained.

In systems terminology, grants and exchange are both processes involving transfer of resources from one person to another. A transfer may take the form of a grant or an exchange. Boulding applies the term **grants** to generous, altruistic actions that occur in the normal give-and-take of family interaction.[3] A grant is a one-way transfer of resources, a gift given without expectation of return. Grants in families may be economic (giving money or goods, providing food or shelter, giving gifts on special occasions), interpersonal (investing time, sharing information, giving support, showing affection), or both.

The term **exchange** describes a two-way transfer of resources. Exchange is an egoistic, self-interested behavior where the goal is to assure that the transfer is profitable, or that resources of approximately equal value are exchanged. In exchange relationships, one expects a fair return for what is given: a "good grade" for study efforts, pay for a day's work, praise and recognition for the favors done.

Exchange generally requires either an informal or formal contract to satisfy the self-interest claims of giver and receiver. An example of exchange in families is a formal "fair share" system for assigning household chores: "A" does the dishes on Monday, Wednesday, and Friday, "B" does them on Tuesday, Thursday, and Saturday, and on Sunday the family eats out. An informal exchange system is represented in statements like "I did dishes last night, so you owe me one."

Reciprocal grants. An important difference between grants and exchanges is in the expectations the giver brings to the relationship. With a grant there is no expectation of return, although sometimes there may be one. In contrast, an exchange always involves the expectation of a return. When an integrative system is operating as it should, all members are givers and all are also receivers. Boulding (1973) describes this phenomenon as reciprocity. It is the basis of the ethic of reciprocal altruism:

> Reciprocity can be defined as mutual grants or a pair of grants. That is, A gives something to B out of the sheer goodness of his heart and his benevolence for B, and B gives something to A out of the sheer goodness of his heart and his benevolence towards A, yet the two acts are not formally related since neither is a formal condition of the other. (p. 25)

An example of reciprocity in families is parental sacrifice for their children. The benefits may be reciprocated in later years as the grown children now care for their aged parents. However, parental sacrifices are not dependent upon the assurance of later care by the children. They are given unconditionally, with no contractual obligation that reciprocity will occur.

Often in systems based on grants the reciprocity is indirect, complex, and relatively open. That is, person A may give to B, who gives to C, who gives to D, who gives to A. The influence of grants multiplies and spreads like the proverbial ripple on the water. With benevolent grants there is no scorekeeping to assure the equivalence of resource transfers, to keep the transfers in a particular time frame, or even to assure that eventually the links of giving reconnect with an original granter.

In practice, it is not always easy to distinguish altruistic reciprocity from the more egoistic exchange. Motivations for grants are sometimes ambiguous. Attitudes of benevolence may be replaced by feelings of martyrdom or exploitation. Sometimes a competitive spirit develops, making it difficult to distinguish a grant

For Better or For Worse® **by Lynn Johnston**

from an exchange. The more conditional the grant, the more it resembles exchange.

Sacrifice and the integrative power of grants. According to Boulding (1973), the study of the difference between grants (which flow from altruism and caring) and contracts (which are oriented to exchange and the profit motive) reveals "how things come to hold together and how they fall apart." A key difference between grants and exchange, one essential to understanding the dynamics of resource transfers in families and how they may foster love and integration, is that grants require sacrifice while exchanges do not. Boulding says that sacrifice is the element with integrative power. A family or community characterized by sacrifice achieves solidarity through its sacrifices. Systems of exchange require little sacrifice, and therefore exchange "has no such power to create community, identity, and commitment" (p. 28).

In our culture we more often associate sacrifice with deprivation than with growth. We are much more aware of the pathologies than the positive consequences of sacrifice. As a result benevolent sacrifice is a much misunderstood and maligned concept.

In the benevolent grant, a "selfish" or strictly utilitarian alternative is sacrificed in favor of an alternative that benefits another. In practice, this kind of sacrifice can be beneficial for both the giver and the receiver. Consider the example of a young father who, rather than washing dishes using his own efficient method, agrees to wash them with his young daughter, at her pace, in the way she wants. Rather than feelings of deprivation, positive feelings tend to flow from such benevolent sacrifice.

Grants vary in their integrative power, depending on the motivation for the grant, the kind of grant, and the amount of sacrifice involved. Voluntary grants given with love generally carry greater integrative power than nonvoluntary grants given grudgingly, especially in the short term. Quite probably, children who clean the house to surprise their parents who have been away will have more loving and integrative feelings for their parents than children who clean the house because Mom or Dad has threatened severe punishment if the job is not done.

Bivens (1976) has suggested that interpersonal grants involving a giving of self—sacrifices of personal attention, time, and involvement—have greater integrative power than monetized grants (grants of money or purchased goods and services), particularly when the monetized grants are perceived as substitutes for grants of self. To illustrate, a parent who spends an afternoon working on a project with a child (a grant of personal time and attention) is more apt to feel increased bonding with and love for that child than is a parent who hires a caretaker or companion to work with the child. In the latter scenario, it is the one who invests the time, more than the one who pays the bill, who is likely to build solidarity with the child. (Why this is so will be explained in greater detail in Chapter 11, using Foa's model of interpersonal and economic resource exchange.)

Boulding suggests that grants create feelings of benevolence and identification partly because they create "an almost unconscious sense of obligation" in the recipient. However, it is the giver much more than the receiver who feels the integrative power of grants. "A gift helps to create the identity of the giver, and a gift . . . identifies the giver with the recipient" (Boulding, 1973, p. 27). This outcome is due largely to the sacrificial element in grants.

The power of sacrifice to bind the giver to the receiver is seen when sacrifice is excessively one-sided or misplaced (in what Boulding calls the "sacrifice trap," or "throwing good money after bad"). Examples include the seriously pathological attachments of abused wives to their abusive husbands, or the intense attachment to family of the exploited housewife who has sacrificed her adult life to an unappreciative husband and children.

Grants given with love increase the capacity for love in the giver. As the song says, "love isn't love 'til you give it away." Giving love generates the love of the giver for the receiver. Of course, grants work best when they are reciprocal; then love is also reciprocal. The mother gives life and love to her child, the child learns love in serving other family members. The father listens with love and respect to his child, and in return the child learns to listen to others in the same manner.

Carol Stack's *All Our Kin* (1974) is a revealing study of how a grants economy functions to build family (kinship) solidarity in a low-income black community. It also illustrates the blurring of grants and exchanges in "swapping" and trading among kin in "The Flats." The altruism exhibited in this community does more than create bonds, it also is necessary for survival.

> Black families living in The Flats need a steady source of cooperative effort to survive. They share with one another because of the urgency of their needs. Alliances between individuals are created around the clock as kin and friends exchange and give and obligate one another. They trade food stamps, rent money, a TV, hats, dice, a car, a nickel here, a cigarette there, food, milk, grits, and children. (Stack, 1974, p. 32)

It is expected that these resource transfers will be made with good will, out of love, yet "individuals who fail to reciprocate in swapping relationships are judged harshly" (p. 34).

Stack concludes that

> social relationships between kin who have consistently traded material and cultural support over the years reveal feelings of both generosity and martyrdom. Long-term social interactions, especially between female kin, sometimes become highly competitive and aggressive. . . . Everyone wants to create the impression that he is generous . . . but no one wants to admit how much he depends upon others. (p. 38)

It is apparent that grants contain the seeds of both increased love and increased animosity, of trust and distrust, of friendship and exploitation—depending, among other things, on the disposition of the giver. And typically the giver experiences the pushes and pulls between family and the self-interested drive for individual gain. However, family ties tend to buffer self-interest. Grants (even grants with limited reciprocity) seem to generate negative feelings less often among kindred than among acquaintances.

Altruistic Commitment and Individualism

In *Habits of the Heart* (1985), sociologist Robert Bellah and his associates trace the history and present influence of two dominant perspectives on the way people think about love, marriage and family life. The first is an altruistic perspective, with philosophical foundations in several parts of the Western heritage.[4] The second is an egoistic perspective called **individualism**. These contrasting perspectives are paradigmatic, or "taken-for-granted" ways of looking at things. They are

> central to the ways we define the meaning of our own lives in relation to the wider society. . . . For most of us, the bond to spouse and children is our most fundamental social tie. The habits and modes of thought that govern intimate relationships are thus one of the central places where we may come to understand the cultural legacy with which we face the challenges of contemporary social life. (Bellah et al., 1985, pp. 107–108)

Both altruism and individualism are rooted deep in the history of the United States. Each is an "American" outlook, and the incompatibility of these two "right" ways of looking at things may seem mystifying. Because these conflicting orientations both offer justification for commitment and love, love itself becomes a source of insecurity and confusion (Bellah et al., 1985, p. 108).

These classifications are philosophical abstractions. None of us fully fits the ideal type of the altruist or the individualist. It does appear, however, that the typical American adult is a more individualistic mix of the two perspectives than were his or her parents.

Individualism. Self-reliance is a pioneer virtue, and the right to the life and liberty necessary to pursue happiness is spelled out in our most sacred political documents. Many pioneers migrated in families and communities, and were bound by duties and responsibilities even as they pursued personal dreams of happiness, wealth, or power. We still admire the stereotype of rugged individualism that emphasizes the drive to explore and achieve regardless of the cost to others.

Historically, the individualistic pursuit of "liberty and justice for all" tended to mean more liberty and justice for the powerful, and less for the weak. Thus it often came down to a matter of self-love and self-indulgence versus love for others and self-sacrifice.

Individualism has taken two related forms in American society, utilitarian and expressive. According to utilitarian individualism, people have a right—even an obligation—to maximize their own interests. In this view, self-interest and the profit motive govern virtually all human interaction, and properly so. Success depends on individual initiative and self-reliance and is measured in materialistic terms.

Utilitarian individualism is the dominant philosophy of the competitive market economy. It is the capitalistic perspective that justifies social inequality. At the individual level, it tolerates putting others down and rewards personal effort aimed at getting ahead. The theoretical justification for the pursuit of individual gain was that "in a society where each vigorously pursued his own interest, the social good would automatically emerge" (Bellah et al., 1985, p. 33).

The irony in expecting that the accumulation, across society, of multiple acts of self-interest would somehow produce a system steeped in social benefit and outreach seems to have escaped the utilitarian individualists. So did the implications of individualism for that most social of institutions, the family. In the family, and in society, the multiplying of individual acts of self-interest produced inequity, strain, and suffering. In the families and in the society of the utilitarian individualists, the successes of the powerful were built upon the sacrifices, willing or not, of the weaker members. In both settings, love (or the altruism of "good citizenship") was defined, in part, as willingly helping someone else to get ahead.

Some of the strains produced by utilitarian individualism are responsible for the rise of expressive individualism. Bellah sees it as a reaction, mostly by women and priests, against the sacrifice of love, human feeling, and self-expression that often accompanied the "calculating pursuit" of material interest. Expressive individualism shares with utilitarian individualism the pursuit of self-interest. However, it is not as overtly materialistic. Instead, it assumes the freedom from external constraints that economic well-being allows. The emphasis in expressive individualism is on development, expression, and assertion of the self.

Expressive individualism celebrates experience, not possession, but it is individualism just the same. Noteworthy early advocates include Walt Whitman, who celebrated sensual experience and the affirmation of human feelings, and Henry David Thoreau, who asserted the morality of the nonconformist who responded to "his own drummer" rather than the crowd or the community.

Contemporary expressive individualism places priority on "getting what you want and enjoying it" (Bellah et al., 1985, p. 77). It builds upon freedom from the absolute values and moral constraints imposed by "duty" or traditional authority and belief systems. The self becomes the ultimate arbitrator of what is good or bad, right or wrong, and the claims of others are apt to be seen as impediments to freedom of choice rather than sources of wisdom and support. Only when you have "found yourself" or learned to "know yourself" are you able to love as a mature adult.

To Bellah, this is a "therapeutic attitude" that reinforces tendencies toward individualism already present in the culture.

> This therapeutic attitude . . . begins with the self, rather than with a set of external obligations. The individual must find and assert his or her true self because this self is the only source of genuine relationships to other people. External obligations, whether they come from religion, parents, or social conventions, can only interfere with the capacity for love and relatedness. Only by knowing and ultimately accepting one's self can one enter into valid relationships with other people. . . . Thus the therapeutic ideal posits an individual who is able to be the source of his own standards, to love himself before he asks for love from others, and to rely on his own judgment without deferring to others. Needing others in order to feel "O.K." about oneself is a fundamental malady that therapy seeks to cure. (pp. 98–99)

According to the therapeutic attitude, love for others is always conditional, varying with the extent to which the "relationship" fits the needs of self. If a partner feels the needs of self are not being satisfied, the option is to leave the relationship or lose something of self. We "love" those who exhibit qualities and characteristics that aid our own self-expression.

This notion of love as the temporary reward given to someone who fulfills you in some way reflects middle-class childrearing practices of the previous generation. Asked why people ought to be good and do things right, one of Bellah's respondents—a therapist by profession—replied, "Well, because people won't love you. . . . that was the implicit message. That if you weren't smart and nice and sort of did things properly, you wouldn't be loved" (p. 60).

The love of individualistic children for their parents is also conditional. They will lend a helping hand if it is convenient or it helps them maintain a favorable self-image. But self-interest takes priority over self-sacrifice. Under expressive individualism the old custom of employed children contributing their earnings to the aggregate family income was replaced by the definition that time and earnings were individual, not family resources (Zelizer, 1985, pp. 104, 110). This individualistic ethic conflicts with the norms of supportive parenting, and in many families the ambiguity has been resolved in favor of parental altruism and offspring individualism. Parents are expected to help support their children forever, but the children have no corresponding obligation.

In the therapeutic view, love is developed through discovering and sharing one's feelings. It is nourished through communication: Success in loving is predicated on success in communicating the deeply felt self to another.

> Thus sharing of feelings between similar, authentic, expressive selves—selves who to feel complete do not need others and do not rely on others to define their own standards or desires—becomes the basis for the therapeutic ideal of love. . . . Love then becomes the mutual exploration of infinitely rich, complex, and exciting selves. (Bellah et al., 1985, pp. 100, 108)

Couples whose love is grounded in communication of feelings often justify that priority by comparing their own relationships to their parents' marriages.

Generally the parents' marriages, less dependent upon the expression of feeling, fare badly by contrast. The elements of duty, commitment to community standards, and altruistic love—criteria by which the parental marriages might be judged as superior—are rarely mentioned or considered seriously.

If "love" in the therapeutic mode emphasizes communication and self-fulfillment, what does that emphasis replace? Among other things, it seems to crowd out self-sacrifice and unconditional commitment. Many of Bellah's respondents were uncomfortable even with the word **sacrifice** because of its connotations of open-ended obligation and putting the needs of the other before those of self. Love in the therapeutic view strictly limits the obligations of both parties.

It is one of the ironies of this approach that "a kind of selfishness is essential to love" (Bellah et al., 1985, p. 100). One is encouraged to assert the self, to assure that one's feelings and needs are expressed. This is not to say there is no give-and-take. There is the expectation that each partner will listen as well as talk, that when one is "down" the other will lift. However, these are not free commodities given unconditionally. The giving and taking are not "reciprocal grants" but exchange—each expects a return on an investment of time, caring, and concern. Time spent in "caring" listening generates a bill. This leads to the practice of "keeping score," which Lobsenz and Murstein argue (Box 4.1) is fine for football games but can be disastrous for a marriage.

Sacrifice, which involves real costs to the self, is incompatible with the therapeutic ideal of love. Sacrifices are motivated by commitment to moral ethics or purposes larger than (or at least beyond) the self. The therapeutic attitude rejects such "outside" commitments, and instead "liberates individuals by helping them get in touch with their own wants and interests, freed from the artificial constraints of social roles, the guilt-inducing demands of parents and other authorities, and the false promises of illusory ideals such as love" (Bellah et al., 1985, p. 102). It is another irony that the perception of such liberation is itself an illusion, since the self is a social product, inseparable from the confluence of outside social constraints it has experienced.

Ultimately, the rejection of sources of authority or meaning outside the self turns out to be an Achilles heel for love in the therapeutic mode. Love defined as full exchange of feelings in service of self, rather than as enduring commitment to another, turns out to lack the power to sustain stable family life. Feelings are fluid, emotions change. The "self" that is supposed to be actualized in a relationship is itself a very ambiguous entity, and whether activities or interactions do in fact enrich or unveil that self may not be clear until long after the fact. The term *relationship*, so widely applied as a euphemism for nonmarital, nontraditional associations, connotes impermanence. "Family" lasts; "relationships" are temporary.

Without the binding power of shared obligations, what holds individualistic relationships together, however imperfectly? Many relationships go beyond maximizing self-interest. As partners communicate over time, they share experiences, and shared history can transform a "relationship" into a family. Shared family culture—core values and ideals, affirmed in family ritual and communication—is another binding element.

Box 4.1

Keeping score vs. grants of commitment and love

Marital scorekeepers . . . keep track of every debit and credit in the emotional ledger of their respective marriages—and feel hurt, resentful or angry when the accounts do not balance evenly. . . .

Fearful lest a spouse "take advantage," a scorekeeper constantly seeks to make sure each partner comes out even. (By the same token, scorekeepers—in their own minds, at least—never take advantage themselves; their own psychological rules require that the marital scales must always be brought into balance.). . . How does a marital scorekeeper get that way? For one thing, our society is largely based on the principle of exchange. Business, of course, is built upon it. And though we're not always aware of it, so are many of our emotional relationships. Children quickly learn that exchange is a key tactic for dealing with parents. "If you eat your spinach," bargains Mummy, "you can ride the merry-go-round when we go to the park." Or Daddy offers a dollar for each A on a report card. When this kind of trading becomes routine, a youngster accepts the premise that whenever he does something to please his parents, he's entitled to receive something of equal value—material or emotional. The implicit lesson is that you don't do things because you're supposed to, or simply to please another out of love or concern, but because you'll get a reward in return. . . .

When similar attitudes are carried over into marriage, however, they lead to trouble because marital accounts can seldom be balanced out so exactly. To begin with, it's virtually impossible to keep score accurately. Most of us accept unthinkingly—or even as our due—the small but significant things spouses do for one another. . . . Scorekeeping also depends on subjective perception. While I know exactly what I do for you—and how much trouble it is to do it—it's unlikely that I will keep (or be able to keep) such accurate track of what you do for me. . . .

Moreover, there is the tricky question of motivation. . . . [I]t's possible that the basic motivation of both John and Mary is to get reciprocal proof of the other's love. Non-scorekeepers, who neither expect nor need an equal return for each favor or service they perform, derive emotional satisfaction from the image of themselves as caring and giving persons. But the exchange-oriented scorekeeper requires more than that. He or she must have reciprocal action as evidence of a spouse's love, so almost every incident is seen as a manifestation of love or the lack of it. . . .

Every couple realizes that an equal-exchange system is no realistic basis for happiness in marriage. Indeed, to reduce marriage to that level is to degrade its spirit and meaning. Furthermore, the signs of concern and love between partners are, by the very nature of marriage, bound to be *un*equal at any given time or even over the long run. . . . [T]he only kind of exchange that is truly meaningful to marriage . . . [is] the free exchange of commitment, dedication and love. Those are more rewarding scores to keep. (Lobsenz & Murstein, 1976, pp. 148, 150, 153)

But such bonds are fragile if their ultimate basis is a therapeutic model of reciprocal exchange with its central virtue of communication. Bellah et al. (1985, p. 85) conclude that "If love and marriage are seen primarily in terms of psychological gratification, they may fail to fulfill their older social function of providing people with stable, committed relationships that tie them into the larger society."

> In this sometimes somber utilitarianism, individuals may want lasting relationships, but such relationships are possible only so long as they meet the needs of the two people involved. All individuals can do is be clear about their own needs and avoid neurotic demands for such unrealizable goods as a lover who will give and ask nothing in return.
>
> [With] such a utilitarian attitude . . . love becomes no more than an exchange, with no binding rules except the obligation of full and open communication. A relationship should give each partner what he or she needs while it lasts, and if the relationship ends, at least both partners will have received a reasonable return on their investment. (Bellah et al., 1985, p. 108)

A decade before Bellah's *Habits of the Heart*, psychologist Donald Campbell (1975) expressed similar concern about the consequences for marriage and family of excessive individualism and the pursuit of pleasure. Expectations of "totally pleasurable experience samples" inevitably lead to disillusionment and dissatisfaction, because the experiences of real life—of people living together in real households—correspond more closely to the "ancient and well-documented principle" that life is "one-third pleasure, one-third pain, and one-third blah" (p. 1121).

Like Bellah, Campbell pointed to the positive features of other motives for action, especially those related to altruism, as alternatives to the self-defeating pursuit of pleasure.

> Psychologists and psychiatrists have thus joined forces with a popular ideology which united the two previously separate traditions of marriage and romantic love, producing the frustratingly high expectation levels that may be increasing the fragility of present-day marriages. A similar situation exists for the work experience. In both cases, a doctrine recommending duty rather than one promising pleasure might produce more overall pleasure. (pp. 1121–22)

The ethic of altruistic commitment. Opposed to individualism is the other dominant orientation to love and family life highlighted by Bellah and his colleagues, which we are calling *altruistic commitment.* It is the expectation that love in families will be other-oriented, unconditional and enduring. As with individualism, the altruistic tradition is a clearly visible part of the American landscape and has long played a key role in the binding together of family, friends, and community.

Altruistic commitment is at odds with expressive individualism in at least five ways. The first fundamental difference is a reliance on traditional moral principles or sacred writings rather than the self to determine what is right or wrong, good or bad. These principles are said to provide a larger purpose for loving than the pursuit of personal happiness.

A second difference relates to the individualistic principle that self-love and self-confidence precede love for others. In the altruistic perspective, positive feelings about the self are a possible outcome of treating others in loving ways, but they are not a *precondition* for loving. Whether you love yourself or have a positive self-image is, at best, beside the point, and at worst, self-defeating. Love is a duty and an obligation, or in the words of Madeleine L'Engle (Box 4.2), a policy; it is not an opportunity for self-enhancement.

The third distinction involves the relative priority given to duty and feeling, will and emotion. The "warm, comfortable feelings of love" are an important dimension of altruistic love, but where a choice must be made between the feelings of love and the obligations of love, "the tension is clearly resolved in favor of obligation" (Bellah et al., 1985, p. 95). It is assumed that emotions and

Box 4.2

Love is not a feeling

Cynthia, one of our Crosswicks family this summer, is thirteen. . . . We had been discussing, down by the brook, how nothing really important in life is in the realm of provable fact. Cynthia is pragmatic; she had her doubts.

"What about love?" I asked her as we were crossing the big meadow on the way home. "Can you prove anything about love?"

She held down an old strand of barbed wire for me. "I guess not."

"What is love?"

"A feeling."

"No," I said, "a feeling is something love is *not*." Cynthia didn't like this; neither do I, lots of the time.

"Why not?"

I asked her, "You love your parents, don't you?"

"Yes."

"Aren't there some days when all your feelings about them are bad? When you're furious with them, and all you *feel* is anger, or that they've been unfair?"

"Yes."

"But you still love them, don't you?"

"Yes."

We were silent for a while because we were picking daisies to make daisy wreaths for the babies. Cynthia was much more diligent about it than I was; I was thinking more about our conversation than about daisies, or even the babies.

Love can't be pinned down by a definition, and it certainly can't be proved, any more than anything else important in life can be proved. Love is people, is a person. A friend of ours, Hugh Bishop of Mirfield, says in one of his books: "Love is not an emotion. It is a policy." Those words have often helped me when all my feelings were unlovely. In a summer household as large as ours I often have to act on those words. I am slowly coming to understand with my heart as well as my head that love is not a feeling. It is a person.

It also has a lot to do with compassion, and with creation. (L'Engle, 1972, pp. 63–64)

feelings can be shaped and trained to follow the will. In a family context, the will to act on obligations rather than feelings can sustain a relationship through difficult times.

A fourth difference is the attitude towards sacrifice. While the therapeutic orientation rejects sacrifice as a loss of self and of personal freedom, in the model of altruistic commitment, the very essence of love is "a willingness to sacrifice oneself for others" (Bellah et al., 1985, pp. 95–96).

The fifth difference is the ideal that families—husbands, wives and children—should "become as one," an idea that runs counter to the individualist goal of the mature, loving adult as an independent self who needs no one. Altruistic commitment assumes that family members are "aspects of one whole," interdependent and interrelated social beings. "No man is an island" applies even more to families than to humanity as a whole.

In summary, the differences between individualistic and altruistic views of love center around the relationship between self and other, and on whether it is appropriate to sacrifice self-interest for the benefit of others.

A Model of Maternal Love

The last model we will present is one of "mother love," and is based primarily on the work of feminist Sara Ruddick (1982, 1989). Ruddick suggests that, as an ideal, the model of maternal love is appropriate for both fathers and mothers. In our view, it is an appropriate model for family love in general.

Before presenting Ruddick's model, it is useful to consider the popular stereotypes of mother love and father love. A widely held view holds that mother love is the ideal type of altruistic love. Contrasting mother love and father love highlights another important dimension of family love, its unconditionality.

Mother love and father love as "ideal types." In industrialized societies, the experience of mothering is more often associated with love and caring nurturance than the experience of fathering. This is not to say that fathers are necessarily less loving than mothers, only that the ultimate responsibility for protecting and nurturing a child is more often ascribed to the mother than the father. In other words, it is assumed that mother love is somehow stronger and deeper than father love.

There is also a cultural assumption that mothers will love their children unconditionally that is shown in the old saying about "a face only a mother could love." Again, the same assumption does not apply to fathers. Fromm (1956) highlights this distinction in his description of the ideal types of mother love and father love in American culture:

> Mother love by its very nature is unconditional. Mother loves the newborn infant because it is her child, not because the child has fulfilled any specific condition, or lived up to any specific expectation. (p. 35)

By contrast,

> Fatherly love is conditional love. Its principle is "I love you *because* you fulfill my expectations, because you do your duty, because you are like me." . . . In the nature

> of fatherly love lies the fact that obedience becomes the main virtue, that disobedience is the main sin—and its punishment the withdrawal of fatherly love. (p. 36)

Fromm heightens the mother-father contrast, emphasizing the essential difference between unconditional and conditional love:

> Unconditional love corresponds to one of the deepest longings, not only of the child, but of every human being; on the other hand, to be loved because of one's merit, because one deserves it, always leaves doubt; maybe I did not please the person whom I want to love me, maybe this, or that—there is always a fear that love could disappear. Furthermore, "deserved" love easily leaves a bitter feeling that one is not loved for oneself, that one is loved *only* because one pleases, that one is, in the last analysis, not loved at all but used. (p. 35)

Not only is mother love seen as deeper and more reliable than father love, but "mothering" as an activity is expected to play a much larger part in a woman's life than is "fathering" in a man's. Whether a woman has had a child is a dominant element of her identity, and she may be stigmatized by terms like "barren" or "childless" if she does not become a mother. In contrast, there is no explicit English term for "nonfather," and nonparental status is much less stigmatizing for males (Rich, 1976, p. 11).

Similarly, the verb *to father* denotes much less personal sacrifice, commitment, and responsibility than does its counterpart *to mother.*

> To "father" a child suggests above all to beget, to provide the sperm which fertilizes the ovum. To "mother" a child implies a continuing presence, lasting at least nine months, more often for years. Motherhood is earned, first through an intense physical and psychic rite of passage—pregnancy and childbirth—then through learning to nurture, which does not come by instinct. . . . A man may beget a child . . . and then disappear; he need never see or consider child or mother again. (p. 12)

Popular definitions of the nature of mothering and fathering sustain a pattern of visible paternal care and nurturance in public or on special occasions, but not on an everyday basis. Fathers may be considered good fathers even when they avoid minimal participation in day-to-day child care. Absentee mothers have much less leeway. This pattern is illustrated in Rich's (1976) comparison of fathers' and mothers' nurturing responsibilities:

> Most of us were raised by our mothers, or by women who for love, necessity, or money took the place of our biological mothers. Throughout history [and across cultures] women have helped birth and nurture each others' children. . . . Even those of us whose fathers played an important part in our early childhood rarely remember them for their patient attendance when we were ill, their doing the humble tasks of feeding and cleaning us; we remember scenes, expeditions, punishments, special occasions. (p. 12)

The social stereotypes of fathering have limited fathers' participation in some aspects of parenting. To the degree that the stereotypes have kept fathers from sacrificing for, serving, and interacting with their children, they have limited their ability to love their children, and the expressive and emotional richness of their own lives. In other words, the definition of fathering as more superficial and temporary than mothering has shortchanged men. We share with many the hope for a time when mother love defines the expectations and nurturant activities of both mothers and fathers, as well as all others who consider themselves family members.

Mother love is almost everywhere associated with enduring and unconditional love. As an ideal it connotes a supportive, continuing attention that enables all family members to feel secure and to thrive. We want to emphasize these growth-producing, security-facilitating aspects of love, and therefore offer "maternal love" as the appropriate model for family love generally.

Ruddick (1984, 1989) identifies two types of maternal love that we believe are essential building blocks in developing a model of family love. These basic, even rudimentary, forms of maternal love are called *preservative love* and *attentive love.*

Preservative love. Preservative love is a commitment to protect the life one has borne, or the life for whom one is responsible, and to behave in ways that improve its chances for survival. Preservative love has more to do with duty and commitment and a sense of visceral, cross-generational identity than with a mother's positive or negative feelings.

In American culture, at least, where the myths of motherhood define mother love in terms of feeling, it is essential to distinguish preservative love from the conscious feelings of liking, admiring, being satisfied with, or enjoying the company of a child. In reality, the feelings mothers have for their offspring are complex and often ambivalent. Mother love can be "intermixed with hate, sorrow, impatience, resentment, and despair; thought-provoking ambivalence is a hallmark of mothering" (Ruddick, 1989, p. 68).

Given the depth of personal commitment most societies require of mothers, it would be very unusual if preservative love were not sometimes accompanied by conflicting feelings and ambivalence. In other words, it is "natural" for mothers to feel love, anger, resentment, and fear so interconnected that analyzing each feeling is difficult. Mothers unprepared for these conflicting emotions may feel guilty about their "unnatural" feelings.

It is society's faith in motherhood that the *commitment* to preserve the child underlies all and will prevail. Preservative love can exist in the presence of ambivalence and even personal hostility toward the child because it has more to do with a commitment to assure the child's survival than with liking the child. This means acting in responsible, life-sustaining ways in spite of feelings that might make you want to do otherwise. Preservative love keeps a mother from harming her child even when fatigue and frustrations might bring her to think of doing so.

Attentive love. "Love, the love of children at any rate, is not only the most intense of attachments but it is also a detachment, a giving up, a letting grow." At the same time a mother is watchfully holding her child close to protect life, she must also distance herself enough "to see the child's reality with the patient loving eye of attention" (Ruddick, 1982, p. 87).

The terms *attentive love* and the *patient loving eye* describe this dimension of maternal love. Attentive love is a patient, empathetic love that seeks to understand what the child is experiencing and how to best help foster growth. The capacity for attention and the virtue of love are the attributes that "invigorate preservation and enable growth" (Ruddick, 1982, p. 86).

Attentive love requires looking closely, but not too close. It requires loving without "seizing and using" the child to satisfy selfish purposes. It requires exercising self-restraint when one would like to make things easier for the child, and permitting the child to experience the growth that comes from stretching and straining, exploring and risking.

The conflicting demands of preservative and attentive love. Mother love, as manifest in preservative and attentive love, is evident in maternal watchfulness, wakefulness, and wariness as children encounter the perils and opportunities of daily life. Children must be protected from moving cars, infectious germs, bullies, and a myriad of other potential threats to their health and well-being. At the same time, they need the freedom to learn and explore, to discover their world, and to develop their talents. Mother love tries to reconcile those conflicting demands. At its best, it seems to involve a balance between constraints and opportunities for experience that fosters a child's development. Mother love is always making judgments about whether to protect and control, or to risk.

This discerning process is limited by the mother's inability to control the child's will, to dominate the environment, or to predict outcomes. It is limited by the knowledge and technology of her culture, and by the myths and perceptions of causality and reality which it provides her. Given these limits, mother love requires humility as well as optimism. It requires a willingness to persist in maternal behavior despite impossible odds, historical fact, and manifest probabilities of failure. It is "a matter-of-fact willingness to accept having given birth, to start and start over again, to welcome a future despite conditions of one's self, one's children, one's society, and nature that may be reasons for despair" (Ruddick, 1989, p. 74).

Perhaps we should stress once more that we are speaking of ideals here. Mothers are *supposed* to be attentive and perseverent, full of faith in the future and in their own personal efficacy. In actual behavior, they often fall short. But to say that mother love is often impure does not diminish from its distinctiveness among human emotions nor its usefulness for sheer biological and cultural continuity.

The Components of Family Love

The foregoing discussion on models and conceptions of love in families provides a foundation for suggesting a model of family love. The risk in offering a model of love is that we may seem to make love the product of mere calculation. There does seem to be more to love than can be achieved by following a recipe or a set of steps. It is not at all clear that love follows quite as predictably from seeking it as does the skill of skiing from ski lessons. We explicitly allow for the holistic "more

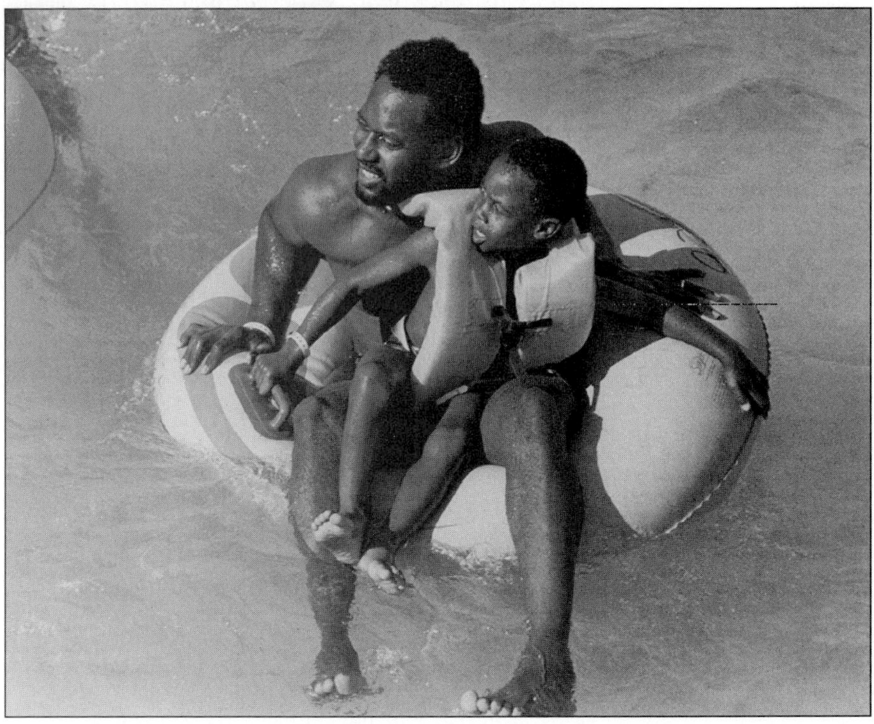

Our society seems to be moving toward a better understanding of the value of love in the family realm.

than the sum of its parts," the metaphysical or miraculous element in love. We suspect that, above and beyond what can be communicated in a model, love involves matters of heart and spirit that elude definition and that are not entirely predictable.

Drawing on the ideas presented in this chapter we can identify four assumptions about the kind of love necessary for healthy individual and family life: (1) it is other-oriented, in the sense that it aims to preserve the lives and foster the growth and development of others; (2) it is action-oriented, emphasizing the priority of doing over feeling, service over sentiment; (3) it is unconditional; and (4) it is enduring.

Family Love Is Other-Oriented

Other-orientation refers to the attentive and altruistic dimensions of love, and to its association with physical and psychological nurturance. The provision of support for members of one's family may range from behaviors that are mutually beneficial to all interacting parties to those that serve others at extreme cost to self.

Being other-oriented entails sacrifice, but not sacrifice as it is commonly understood in our culture. To understand the meaning of sacrifice in family love, it is important to distinguish between sacrifices made in the service of nurturance, and the sacrifice that leaves one feeling used, martyred, or deprived. Sacrifice is not the same as neglecting our own legitimate needs. Sacrifices are voluntary grants motivated by love. They do not necessarily impoverish the giver.

As Bellah's (1985) respondents observed, the sacrifice associated with family love generally does not feel like sacrifice. In fact, the sacrifice out of love enriches the giver. Fromm (1956) expresses this phenomenon this way: "Giving is more joyous than receiving, not because it is a deprivation, but because in the act of giving lies the expression of my aliveness" (p. 19).

The sacrifice that characterizes family love also requires humility—a humility that acknowledges a need for others. This is a recognition of interdependence and the desirability of mutual support. Such mature humility is seen in the father or mother, older brother or sister, who is free to learn from a child and does not have to say "I already know that." Here what is sacrificed is the need to appear all-knowing; what is gained is the opportunity to appreciate and encourage the expanding world of the child. Mature love is seen in the husband and wife who can appreciate, even celebrate, the strengths and weaknesses each brings to the relationship as opportunities for sharing and for growth. We see it in the busy adult patiently listening once again as an elderly grandparent struggles through the confused retelling of an oft-told story.

Developing the capacity for selfless love, while trying to teach other family members to do the same, is an extraordinary challenge. Michael Novak (1976),

Box 4.3

"These do not feel like bonds"

The quantity of sheer impenetrable selfishness in the human breast (in *my* breast) is a never-failing source of wonderment. I do not want to be disturbed, challenged, troubled. Huge regions of myself belong only to me. Getting used to thinking of life as bicentered, even multicentered, is a struggle of which I had no suspicion when I lived alone. Seeing myself through the unblinking eyes of an intimate, intelligent other, an honest spouse, is humiliating beyond anticipation. Maintaining a familial steadiness whatever the state of my own emotions is a standard by which I stand daily condemned. A rational man, acting as I act? Trying to act fairly to children, each of whom is temperamentally different from myself and from each other, each of whom is at a different stage of perception and aspiration, is far more baffling than anything Harvard prepared me for.

My dignity as a human being depends perhaps more on what sort of husband and parent I am, than on any professional work I am called upon to do. My bonds to them hold me back (and my wife even more) from many sorts of opportunities. *And yet these do not feel like bonds. They are, I know, my liberation.* They force me to be a different sort of human being, in a way in which I want and need to be forced. (Novak, 1976, p. 42; emphasis added)

journalist and philosopher, writes of his own efforts to learn family love, of the sacrifices and challenges he continues to face (see Box 4.3). As Novak's words suggest, the rewards of altruistic love are commensurate with the effort required. The mother loves her child not only because it is her child, but also because she has sacrificed to bear and rear it. The child loves her mother not only because her mother sacrificed for her (the love of gratitude) but also because she has helped her mother (the love of shared experience and of sacrifice).

Family Love Is Action-Oriented

Love as feeling is frail and useless beside love as action. In fact, confronted with love in action, whether love in feeling even exists may be irrelevant. Ray Bradbury (1969) forcefully makes this point in his story "I Sing the Body Electric!" It is another version of the "Do you love me?" theme. In this case, an "electric grandmother," a robot, serves a family *as if* she loves them. In the end, it is impossible to tell whether she actually *does*, for all the manifestations of love are there, and more. And to the children, now grown, it no longer matters. Neither biological connection nor common heritage is as important as the shared experience of loving acts. In Box 4.4 we have reprinted the grandmother's wise response to the father's "How can you love?" questions.

The acts of love include giving gifts of self, the works of one's own hands and heart. They involve humane and earthy acts essential to life and comfort, such as changing a baby's diaper, helping an elderly parent or grandparent dress, bathe, or walk, cooking meals, washing dishes. Among a parent's kindest acts of love are creating opportunities for children to learn love, by service and sacrifice, for example is an inadequate teacher of love. One learns to love by loving, not by being loved; and to serve by serving, not by being served. If children are always served, without the opportunity of serving in return, they learn to take, not to give.

Box 4.4

"If paying attention is love, if helping you is love, I am love"

Grandma . . . went on calmly addressing her remarks to the family. . . .

"Name the value you wish, tell me the Ideal you want and I can see and collect and remember the good that will benefit you all. Tell me how you would like to be: kind, loving, considerate, well-balanced, humane . . . and let me run ahead on the path to explore those ways to be just that. In the darkness ahead, turn me as a lamp in all directions. I *can* guide your feet. . . .

"I'll go on giving love, which means attention, which means knowing all about you, all, all, all about you, and you knowing that I know but that most of it I will never tell to anyone, it will stay a warm secret between us, so you will never fear my complete knowledge.". . .

"But," said Father, stopping her, looking her right in the face . . . "All this talk of love and attention and stuff. Good God, woman, you, you're not *in* there!"

He gestured to her head, her face, her eyes, the hidden sensory cells behind the eyes, the miniaturized storage vaults and minimal keeps.

"*You're* not *in* there!"

Grandmother waited one, two, three silent beats.

Then she replied: "No. But *you* are. You and Thomas and Timothy and Agatha.

"Everything you ever say, everything you ever do, I'll keep, put away, treasure. I shall be all the things a family forgets it is, but senses, half-remembers. Better than the old family albums you used to leaf through, saying here's this winter, there's that spring, I shall recall what you forget. And though the debate may run another hundred thousand years: What is Love? perhaps we may find that love is the ability of someone to give us back to us. Maybe love is someone seeing and remembering handing us back to ourselves just a trifle better than we had dared to hope or dream. . . .

"I am family memory and, one day perhaps, racial memory, too, but in the round, and at your call. . . . And my existence means the heightening of your chance to touch and taste and feel. Isn't love in there somewhere in such an exchange? . . . This, above all: the trouble with most families with many children is someone gets lost. There isn't time, it seems, for everyone. Well, I will give equally to all of you. I will share out my knowledge and attention with everyone. I wish to be a great warm pie fresh from the oven, with equal shares to be taken by all. No one will starve. Look! someone cries, and I'll look. Listen! someone cries, and I hear. Run with me on the river path! someone says, and I run. And at dusk I am not tired, nor irritable, so I do not scold out of some tired irritation. My eye stays clear, my voice strong, my hand firm, my attention constant."

"But," said Father, his voice fading, half convinced, but putting up a last faint argument, "you're not *there*. As for love—"

"If paying attention is love, I am love. If knowing is love, I am love. If helping you not to fall into error and to be good is love, I am love. . . . I will, if you please, and accept the strange word, 'love' you all." (Bradbury, 1969, pp. 180–82)

The acts of love also include recognizing and expressing gratitude for the gifts of others. Stinnett (1983) identified appreciation as one of the most important attributes shared by strong families. Recognition of the gifts offered by others seems to be essential to the integrating power of family love. Just as sacrifice is more apt to bond the giver than the receiver, so expressions of gratitude—verbal expressions acknowledging the services and gifts of others—bond the recipient to the giver. Expressions of gratitude form links consisting, not of equivalent exchange, but of mutual acknowledgement that the "exchange" was *not* equivalent.

Learning to respond sensitively to the gifts of others requires paying attention to differences in perceptions of what constitutes a gift, or what *feels* like a gift. Hochschild (1989, p. 506) found the happiest couples in her study were those who "shared a common understanding of what a gift would be," and who were both active givers and grateful receivers of gifts.

Family Love Is Unconditional

Unconditional love is love that is not "conditioned" (does not depend) on the degree to which the relationship satisfies your own self-interest. A person deserves and receives love simply because she or he *is*, and because she or he is *family*, and not because of admirable personal characteristics or accomplishments. To describe love as unconditional is not to say it is indulgent or permissive. Unconditional love must also encompass attentive love, alert to the needs for nurturance and growth in the other.

Unconditional love is evident in the everyday acts of love, and in the priority of duty over feeling. Family love cannot endure if it is conditioned primarily on feelings; that is, if family members love one another only when they feel like it or only when they feel another has "earned" or "deserves" their love. Feelings may not be within one's control, but duty is. As was indicated in the section on preservative love, mothers often feel astonished and guilty about negative feelings they have toward their children, feelings that seem beyond their control. Their actions, however, are more clearly within their control. In the spirit of unconditional love, feeling need not always dictate action.

Family Love Is Enduring

Family love is distinguished by the expectation that it will endure. The kinship and conjugal ties that bind family members to one another extend without apparent limit into the future, and so do their responsibilities to care for each other. Relationships in other spheres may fail us, but we expect that family ties, whether they be adoptive or "blood relations," will last. And of course, it is the links of family—parents to children, children to parents—that bind us to the past as well as the future. The continuity of humankind is, essentially, the continuity of family ties.

Berry (1987), writing of the longing for permanence in marital relations, writes that:

> Apparently, it is the nature of all human relationships to aspire to be permanent. To propose temporariness as a goal in such relationships is to bring them under the rule of aims and standards that prevent them from beginning. Neither marriage, nor kinship, nor friendship, nor neighborhood can exist with a life expectancy that is merely convenient. (p. 113)

SUMMARY

The study of family love has long been neglected by family scholars. Instead, family scholarship has paid attention to the romantic love that brings a couple together, and to aspects of love such as intimacy and affection. In this chapter we have highlighted four models, each a variation of altruistic love, that we consider approaches worth applying in the effort to understand processes of family love. Among the characteristics common to all four models is a recognition that sacrifice of "self-interest" is sometimes appropriate, ostensibly to promote the growth and well-being of the other, but often, in fact, to promote the vitality and solidarity of the family group and, with it, the well-being of the one who sacrifices.

Like other conceptualizations, the model of altruistic love is an ideal. It is much easier to talk about than to practice, more doable in the abstract than in the realities of everyday life. Theoretically and in fact, individual acts of sacrifice may well serve the welfare of the family as a whole. At the same time, the cost to the "sacrificer" may not be "repaid" in the short run, or in real time. In other words, in family life there may be times when one benefit can be achieved only at the expense of another. The legitimate demands of love may be in conflict, and loving relationships may sometimes amount to a zero-sum game, *in the short run.*

Another reason for real-life difficulty in practicing altruistic family love is that we don't know enough. Despite close attention, it may not be apparent what an appropriate loving response to a loved one's needs ought to be. However, in terms of family love, it is growth-inducing to the *giver* of love to struggle to learn, to be attentive, to try to understand, to develop the qualities that will aid the growth of another. Family love presents an ongoing challenge to discern what gifts or sacrifices are appropriate, and to decide how to foster the well-being of one person in ways that, over time, will not thwart the growth and development of another.

KEY TERMS

Normative Individualism

Hedonism

Conjugal love

Romantic love

Family love

Rule of amity
Altruism
Reciprocal altruism
Grants
Exchange
Interpersonal grants
Monetized grants
Reciprocal grants
Integrative systems
Sacrifice
Utilitarian individualism
Expressive individualism
Therapeutic attitude
Altruistic commitment
Preservative love
Attentive love
Conditional love
Unconditional love

Study Questions

1. Why has the study of family love been neglected by family scholars?
2. What has been the influence of "rational" science on the study of family love? Why has it had this effect?
3. How has the notion that women's place is in the home and men's in the work place influenced the study of family love?
4. What is family love? How does it differ from romantic love?
5. What are the defining characteristics of altruism? Of egoism?
6. Which tends to be more enduring, family love or romantic love? Why does this seem to be so?
7. Throughout history and across cultures, which type of love—altruistic or romantic—has received the greatest emphasis? What kinds of people have emphasized each of these kinds of love?
8. What is the rule of amity? In what sense is it a rule?
9. In their family, John washes the dishes and Mary cleans the living room. What would you need to know to determine if this is an example of reciprocal grants or exchange?
10. What characteristic of grants accounts for its power to create enduring integrative systems? Explain how this process works.
11. What is likely to happen to a family or society when the norms for altruism and self-interest are applied differently for males and females?
12. Contrast the ethic of individualism and that of altruistic commitment. Which tends to dominate contemporary society? Support your answer with real-life examples from the media or your personal knowledge.
13. How do conditional and unconditional love differ? What are the consequences of each for social responsibility and social bonding? Are permissiveness and indulgence characteristic of conditional or unconditional love? Defend your answer.
14. What are the objectives of sacrifices offered in the processes of preservative and attentive love? How do they differ from the sacrifices that leave one feeling "used," "deprived," or a "martyr"?
15. List four attributes of family love, and identify at least one essential characteristic of each.

NOTES

1. It is intriguing how much can be written about "quality" and "stability" of marriages without mentioning love. For example, the word *love* is virtually absent from the Lewis and Spanier (1979) comprehensive (25-page) review of research on marital quality and stability. Only one of their 87 propositions about marital quality and stability uses the word *love*; it reads, "The greater the love between spouses, the greater the marital quality."

   Recent reviews of research on marital quality (Glenn, 1990) and child care and children's socioemotional development (Belsky, 1990), reflecting the dominant emphases of a decade of scholarly work, each used the word *love* just once. It did not appear at all in the decade review of research on marital and family enrichment (Guerney and Maxson, 1990). Gaylin and Person (1988) say that their recent work on love and passionate attachment was "impelled by a certain shock at the curious neglect in the psychoanalytic literature of so fundamental a human experience [as love].
2. The reader is referred to Glasser and Glasser's (1977) review of the trends towards hedonism and individualism in the family and interpersonal practice literature.
3. Boulding identifies two types of grants: one, gifts, arises out of love and is at the heart of integrative systems; the other, tribute, arises out of fear and is at the heart of threat systems. Boulding also distinguishes between benevolent and malevolent grants, or grants given with the intent to bless and grants given with the intent to do harm. The discussion in this chapter focuses on benevolent grants arising out of love. The reader is referred to Boulding's excellent little book, *The Economy of Love and Fear*, for an elaboration of grants arising from other motives.
4. Bellah's study focuses on the comparison between traditional Christianity and individualism. However, it is important to remember that the altruistic ethic is not unique to Christianity but is a fundamental belief in many religions. Therefore in our review of Bellah's work we have chosen to substitute the more generic language of altruism.

   In most religions, both ancient and modern, the altruistic ethic is not only expected to govern in families but in other relationships as well. One example is found in the ancient Chinese traditions. According to the *Analects* of Confucius (551–479 B.C.), "the experience of love begins in the home among one's closest blood relatives," but, "when allowed to grow according to its natural inclination, will ultimately include the entire human race. . . . As such, *it is the norm for all human conduct*" (emphasis added). There are related concepts of love in both Hinduism (*dharma*) and in Buddhism (*dhamma*). (Long, 1987, p. 33)

Emotion

5

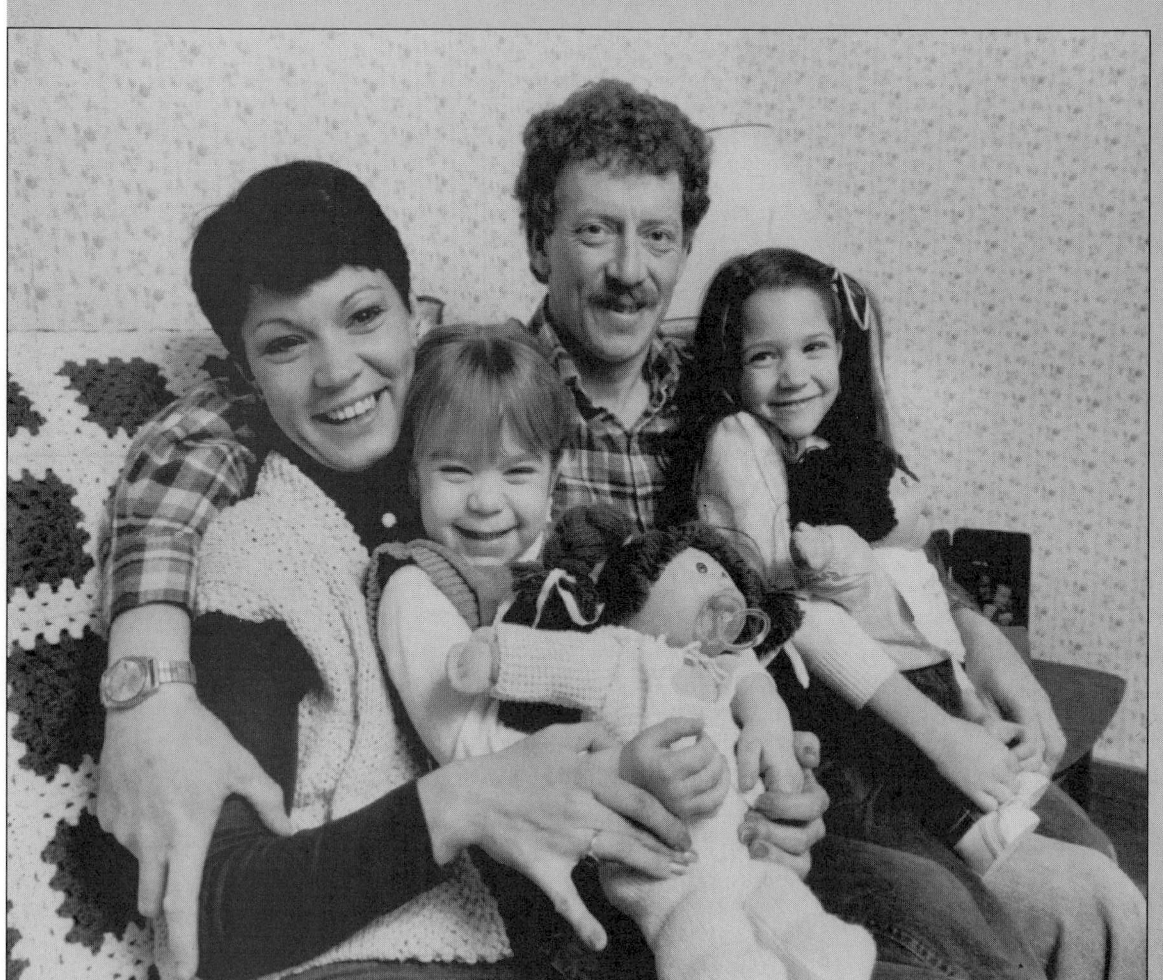

Main Ideas

1 // There are two areas of emotional processes in families where problems occur frequently: *fusion* and *chronic anxiety.*

2 // *Fusion* is when family members are overly connected to the family emotional system. When fusion occurs the emotional system dominates so much it interferes with the ability of family members to use their intellectual system.

3 // *Basic* fusion refers to the long-term level of fusion that is a part of the ongoing *structure* of a family system.

4 // *Emotional cutoff* is an unhealthy way to try to cope with high levels of basic fusion.

5 // *Functional* fusion refers to fusion that is temporary or situational.

6 // *Chronic anxiety* refers to long-term negative emotion in the family emotional system. All families encounter important negative emotions such as despair, futility, and serious disappointment. Family emotional systems can be wisely managed by dealing with these negative emotions so they do not become chronic.

7 // Two of the destructive processes that occur frequently are *emotional triangles* or *triangling.*

8 // The ideas about family emotional systems have several implications for families and those who try to help families.

The main principle in this and the preceding chapter is:

Principle *When the emotional part of family systems is managed effectively it tends to create a number of healthy outputs in family systems, and when it is managed ineffectively it tends to create a number of disabling and undesirable outputs.*

The previous chapter described the positive outputs that are created by the healthy management of emotion in family systems. This chapter focuses on two aspects of family emotional processes where problems seem to occur fairly frequently in modern families. The two areas are called *fusion* and *chronic negative emotion* (Kerr & Bowen, 1988). The goal of this chapter is to describe what family scientists think happens when these two areas are not managed wisely and what families and those who work with families can do to manage them wisely.

> "The more experience I have had, the more I am convinced that far more of life is governed by automatic emotional forces than man is willing to acknowledge."
>
> —Murray Bowen (1978)

Fusion

Fusion is a concept developed by Murray Bowen (1976) to describe what happens when family members are so connected to the family emotional system that it interferes with their ability to manage the other aspects of their lives. According to Bowen's theory, infants and young children are *fused* with an emotional "field," "atmosphere," or "climate" in their parental family. This means infants and children are naturally and involuntarily caught up in the emotional processes of their parents and siblings.

For example, when the emotional climate in a family has positive emotional processes such as trust, concern, confidence, and appreciation, the children sense these emotions and respond to them. On the negative side, when there are undesirable emotions such as tension, animosity, resentment, and bitterness, the children are caught up in these processes, and they respond to them and are influenced by them. The children participate in these emotions in an involuntary and symbiotic way because they don't have the capacity to choose not to.

Gradually, however, as children mature, they develop the ability to free themselves, at least somewhat, from responding to the emotional "field" in their family system. This emotional independence is the opposite of fusion, and Bowen's term for it is **differentiation**.

It is easy to misunderstand the meaning of these two terms because most people in our society think with an individualistic or psychological perspective. When we think with an individualistic perspective, we assume emotion is something that happens inside a person, but Bowen's theory does not view emotion this way. He views emotional processes as a part of family systems in that there is an emotional climate or atmosphere in families. It is an emotional "field" that is like a magnetic field. Therefore, fusion is being overly connected with a family's emotional field. Differentiation is "differentiation of a self from the extended family" (Bowen, 1976, p. 84). Bowen also used the term "emotional stuck-togetherness in families" to describe what it means to be fused.

Several other comments in the literature also illustrate how differentiation is a family science and systemic concept rather than a psychological and individual concept. Kerr refers to fusion as "emotional reactivity" (Kerr, 1981, p. 237), and Bowen calls it "emotional fusion" (1976, p. 79).

Thus, differentiation is not an intellectual process, and it is not the development of a unique identity or sense of selfhood. It is an emotional process that refers to how much people are able to differentiate from the emotional interdependence or emotional ping-pong reactions that occur in their family.

The twin concepts of fusion and differentiation are important because they are part of one of the main principles in family systems theory. The principle can be called the *fusion principle:*

Principle

When there is high fusion in a family system, the processes in the emotional system dominate what happens, and the ability to use the intellectual system is decreased. Conversely, as family members become differentiated from the emotional system, they acquire the ability to choose to use their intellectual system.

Papero described the main ideas in this principle as a fused state in which the emotional system tends to override the thinking system. He states that when there is less fusion of the thinking and emotional systems, the person is referred to as more differentiated. When people are more highly differentiated, they are able to maintain more objectivity and to think carefully for longer periods of time in spite of the emotional arousal (Papero, 1983, p. 140).

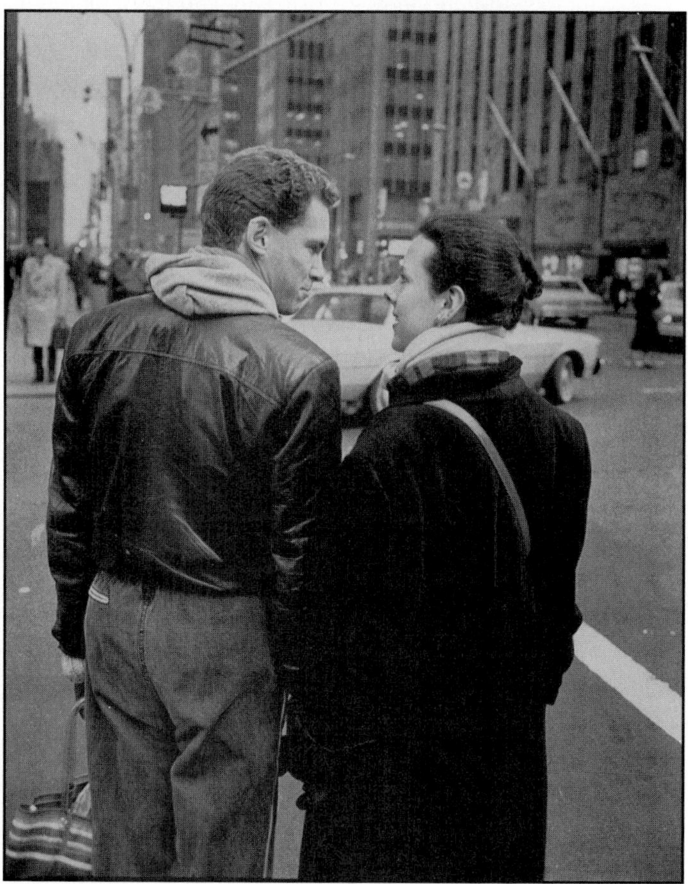

Even in close relationships, it is important to maintain differentiation.

Bowen described the involuntary nature of fusion and the freedom that comes with differentiation. In his opinion, "a poorly differentiated person is trapped within a feeling world. . . . A more differentiated person can participate freely in the emotional sphere without the fear of becoming too fused with others. He is also free to shift to calm, logical reasoning for decisions that govern his life" (Bowen, 1976, p. 67).

> "At the fusion end of the spectrum, the intellect is so flooded by emotionality that the total life course is determined by the emotional process and by what 'feels right' rather than by beliefs or opinions. The intellect exists as an appendage of the feeling system."
>
> —Bowen, 1976, p. 66

The following situation in a family illustrates how fusion can influence what happens in a family.

The Coleman Family

My family is a good example of a family with a lot of fusion. When we get upset with someone else in the family, all we do is yell. For example, this past summer I was out doing things with friends many nights in a row and until very late each night. After this had gone on for many weeks, my dad decided to set a curfew for us. He said 10 o'clock on week nights and 11 on weekends. I was so upset I immediately lost my appetite. He informed us of this at dinner, and I left the table and went to my room.

But before leaving the room I got very defensive and I said that I guessed my dad didn't want me to have any social life. None of the activities I was attending ended before 11 o'clock, and most of them were an hour's drive away. This just frustrated my dad more. His voice went up and so did mine. His patience went down and mine followed again.

My very first reaction was that he couldn't give me a curfew because I was no longer a child. I thought about staying out all night to prove my independence. I was so upset that I didn't realize until a little later that if I came in earlier for a while and then gradually stayed out late again, my dad wouldn't be as upset.

After I'd calmed down and talked with a friend and my mom, I realized the curfew was more for my sister than me, since I was leaving three weeks later to return to school.

Kerr (1981) gives us a glimpse into the insights that led to the development of the fusion principle. Bowen, he says, "developed the idea of intellectual and emotional centers in the brain based largely on clinical observation. Calm people can think fairly clearly and objectively. However, these same people, placed in an emotionally charged situation, can begin to operate more based on emotional reactivity. Seemingly well-thought-out principles are dropped in favor of expediency, retaining approval, placing blame on others, trying to dominate somebody and other such reactions" (Kerr, 1981, p. 237).

This principle could be called the "differentiation principle," and in the preliminary versions of this book we used that term. Unfortunately, however, we have discovered several disadvantages to focusing the attention on differentiation. One is that the word *differentiation* has several other connotations to it, and these connotations are often confusing. When students began to use the word *differentiation,* they would think mostly about nonemotional processes such as gaining their own identity as described by Erik Erikson in his theory of development. Or, they would think about leaving their parental family and going out on their own, or becoming independent economically or professionally. These connotations are reasonable, but they are quite different from the rather limited meaning of the term in Bowen's theory. Bowen uses *differentiation* to describe healthy disengaging from the emotional climate in the parental family. When we emphasize the *fusion* part of the process, it is easier to remember that these ideas refer only to an emotional fusion that is, in its extremes, disruptive.

A second disadvantage of highlighting the differentiation part of this idea is because the problems that occur in families are at the fusion end of the continuum, and it helps to focus the attention on the limiting and incapacitating aspects of fusion. When people are fused there is a similarity in what happens because their emotions tend to take over and control what they do. When people are differentiated there is great variability in what they do. Their intellect is used more, and they can choose to emphasize relationships, connectedness, and intimacy, or they can choose to emphasize independence, autonomy, impersonality, or other aspects of life.

Levels of Differentiation

Bowen makes a distinction between the *basic* level and the *functional* level of differentiation. The basic level refers to the long term, and it tends to stay with family members throughout their life. Bowen describes people with low levels of basic differentiation in the following way:

> Whatever intellect they have is dominated by the emotional system. These are the people who are less flexible, less adaptable, and more emotionally dependent on those about them. They are easily stressed into dysfunction, and it is difficult for them to recover from dysfunction. They inherit a high percentage of all human problems. (Bowen, 1976, p. 65)

The **basic level of differentiation** generally refers to level of fusion with the emotional field in the parental family, but it is also possible to develop basic or enduring fusion with other emotional processes. For example, it is possible to become fused with the emotional field in a spouse's family. In some situations it is even possible to become basically fused with nonfamilial things such as a religious movement, a sport, a social cause, or a hobby.

The **functional level of differentiation** refers to how differentiated family members are in specific situations. Even people who are usually calm, cool, and collected tend to "lose their cool" (become fused) when they get in intensely charged emotional situations. Probably every person reading these ideas has experienced some situations where they became fused. They became so angry, excited, depressed, jealous, or just plain carried away that their ability to control their behavior rationally decreased and their emotion tended to take over.

"An anxious family elevates a facet of a problem to the *cause* of the problem."

—Kerr & Bowen, 1988, p. 61

Sometimes these situations of fusion are memorable and beautiful. It happens frequently and enjoyably during sexual intercourse. It also is what is happening when tears are shed at weddings and other happy events. It also happens during the excitement of athletic contests and the intensely engaging moments of symphonies.

Unfortunately, in some situations functional or situational fusion doesn't work out well. When our emotions begin to dominate, we sometimes say and do things we later feel sorry or guilty about. In the sexual area, people sometimes do things they later regret or feel guilty about. At athletic contests, spectators sometimes get carried away in harmful, destructive, and abusive ways.

The concept of functional fusion is helpful because it helps us understand why emotions sometimes have little effect and at other times almost "take over" what is happening. The role of functional fusion is illustrated by the comments in Box 5.1, and in the following example.

The Taylor Family

One day about five years ago my parents were in their Radio Shack store. After having closed for the day, they started to argue as they had often done recently. After a short while both were becoming more upset, and my mom decided to just leave and go home. My father was so emotional that he locked the door and wouldn't let her leave. Then my mom lost all ability to use any reason and really went crazy. A screaming match nearly came to blows. My dad eventually let her out, but not until after the experience had scarred their relationship permanently. The inability to differentiate at a crucial time was detrimental to our family.

When families learn how basic levels of fusion and functional fusion influence what happens, it helps them understand processes not understood before and can improve the quality of their life. The following situations illustrate several ways people could have used these ideas.

The Kirk Family

One time when I was taking my girlfriend home after a date, we had a disagreement, and before long we were both quite upset and angry with each other. Instead of dealing with my emotions first, I said a lot of things that I didn't mean and that put our relationship in further jeopardy. Had I known of these ideas about fusion, I would have taken the time to count to ten, taking three deep breaths, or walk around the block before we discussed the problem any further.

The Loveless Family

One instance happened when my parents were away and only my little brother and I were home. My parents were due home that night and I wanted to clean the house so it would look nice for the folks. I tried to get my brother to do some work, but he started to run away to play with his friends. When I wouldn't let him go, he started smart-mouthing me. Usually I am patient, but my emotions got higher and higher, and I finally got so mad I hit him—which turned into a big fight. He never did help, so we got nowhere. If I had realized I was getting fused, and known what that meant, I could have let him go for then, taken a break to get back my control and then talked to him. This would have had much better results than hitting him.

Box 5.1

When I think of the fusion principle I think of my father. He tended to be a highly differentiated person who always seemed to have things in control when our family was confronting problems. My mother was more fused and tended to get emotional when we had problems. While mother panicked and frantically blurted out all the problems we may have been facing, my dad would calm her down and assure her that we could work things out.

An example that comes to mind occurred when we were living in Quebec. While my father was away on business, neighbors who were prejudiced against English people threatened my mother and our family. I did not know what was said, but my mother was very upset. When my dad came home she was in tears.

She expressed all her fears and was worried that one of us children would get hurt. She didn't want to leave the neighborhood, but she couldn't see any way but to leave. My dad calmed her down and assured her that we didn't have to move. He felt there were other alternatives, one of which was to talk with these neighbors.

My father, whose first language is French, confronted this man who had threatened us, and talked to him for about an hour. My brother and I eavesdropped to keep my mother informed, since she did not understand the language very well.

I remember being amazed at how calmly my dad settled the matter. That he was angry was clear to me by his firmness of speech (not by yelling). But, even though he was angry, he was not fused. He simply warned the man that he would take legal action if we were threatened again. The neighbor and his wife never threatened us again, and in fact became good friends eventually. This is a typical example of the unfused way my dad handled family problems.

Reprinted with special permission of King Features, Inc.

These situations illustrate several ideas that can help us all cope with emotionally charged situations. First, it is helpful to realize that emotions become very powerful when people are functionally (situationally) fused. They become so powerful that we sometimes let them take over, and do things we are sorry for later. Second, when we are aware of how functional fusion works, it helps us have more sensitivity to what is happening emotionally. Then we can recognize when we are becoming fused and that being fused will decrease our self-control.

A third idea that is helpful is to realize that when we are becoming fused it is often wise to *deal with the emotional aspects of the situation first.* Often this means we ought to stop, interrupt an argument, or get out of a situation until we can calm down. This may take a while, but sometimes it is enough to stop just long enough to count to ten, or ask to be excused for a minute, or just take a deep breath. What would have happened in the following situation if this individual had been aware of these three ideas?

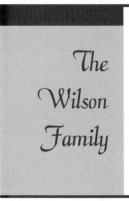

I have an example that I kind of hesitate to use because it makes me look really stupid, but I've matured a little since then. My dad and I got in a big argument one time. It started over something stupid, but as the emotions rose it got louder and louder. My father finally got mad and kicked me. By then I was out of control. I ran through the house, throwing chairs, kicking the dog. I hit my brother, and then ran out of the house. I didn't stop running for about ten minutes.

Emotions really got the best of me then and I lost control. It would have been a lot better to go outside and cool down before things got out of hand. Generally, I am a fairly passive guy, and I would never do any of that unless my emotions were so high that I started losing self-control.

Choice and Freedom

The fusion principle helps us better understand how one factor influences the amount of freedom, volition, or free agency people have. The principle states that differentiation influences the ability people have to choose how much to use their intellect, and this means they acquire the capacity, the ability, the freedom, or the agency to make the choice. When they are fused, they tend to have less ability or freedom to choose.

The role of choice is important because it means Bowen is not saying people ought to become unemotional robots that only experience intellect. They are not like Star Trek's Spock, with no emotional response possible. Instead, the theory is about selection and choice of response. Some people think Bowen has an aversion to emotion, or is saying that differentiated people are unemotional people. These ideas are not part of this principle. Bowen is saying that separating the emotions and intellect is a prerequisite to having choice about how much to be emotional.

In other words, people who differentiate acquire an increased capacity to choose, not a compulsion to use only their intellect. They still can experience the same range and intensity of affective states as those who are less differentiated. By using this principle the individual actually gains freedom—the freedom to use their intellect when they want to use it.

Differentiation in Literature

Poets, musicians, playwrights, and novelists deal with the processes Bowen's theory describes. They know there is a wide range of important emotions in family processes and some of these emotions influence people in powerful and unusual ways.

For example, in the ancient play *Medea* by Euripides, one of the strong themes is the tragedy coming from the sickness of fusion. In an early version of this play the family nurse sees the suffering Phaedra and proclaims:

> It is necessary that the mixture of affections that we mortals have in our common mixing bowl be kept in modest proportion and not let these affections reach the deepest parts of our marrow; but rather the ties of love must be loosable bonds that can be slackened or tightened. And that one soul must bear the labor pains for two is a difficult burden, as witnessed by the way I suffer so much on behalf of her. (Simon, 1988, p. 94)

The Greeks had a word for this type of strong love—*philtata* (the root *phil* connotes blood ties and obligations). In addition, the Greeks were very specific that philtata include the affectionate feelings accompanying the ties. It was sometimes referred to as undiluted wine in the bowl.

> We must always add enough water to prevent intoxication. Deep involvement leads to deep disappointment, anger, and frustration when the beloved one cannot or will not fulfill one's expectations, and from there it leads to the problems of conflict, jealousy, and the attendant desires for revenge. In a later play, the theme is again expressed in relation to childbearing—*The Suppliant Women* repeats the lament about how painful it is to have and to lose children—perhaps those without are after all much better off. (Simon, 1988, pp. 94–95)

The point of the example is to show that, even in antiquity, poets and writers understood the nature of the special emotional relationship within the family. From Shakespeare's *Macbeth* to O'Neill's *Long Day's Journey into Night,* the theme is often a struggle that involves fusion with the emotional system.

Fusion can create the illusion that other family members are extensions of one's self. The pathological grief comes in the refusal to acknowledge separation and growth.

Limitations of the Concept of Fusion

The concept of fusion has several limitations. First, Bowen's descriptions of fusion are sometimes gender biased. Feminist scholars have pointed out that Bowen overemphasized intellectual control and ignored many healthy forms of emotional attachment and priority to relationship maintenance (Goodrich, Rampage, Ellman & Halstead, 1988, p. 147).

We agree that many of Bowen's comments about the fusion principle were gender biased, but the principle that excessive fusion has harmful effects is not a gender-biased principle. Most of Bowen's writings occurred in the 1960s and early 1970s, when scholars were not as sensitive to gender issues as they could have been. For example, Bowen stated that fused people are "living in a feeling world." If we do not qualify that statement it is gender biased, because women traditionally have preferred a lifestyle oriented to feeling. The important issue is whether people live in a feeling world because they are fused or because they choose to. If they are living in a feeling world because they are fused, they are doing it in an involuntary way that traps them as a victim of their emotions. If they are differentiated (not fused), they can choose a lifestyle that is "living in a feeling world" because they think it is a desirable way to live.

The solution to these gender biases is not to conclude that Bowen's ideas about fusion are inherently gender biased and therefore indefensible. If we limit the meaning of emotional fusion so it only refers to being overly connected to the family emotional field it is a gender-free concept. When we define fusion in this way, it is a fairly narrow, clear, and limited concept, and it is equally appropriate for males and females.

A second limitation of the concept of fusion is that people sometimes think that if someone were differentiated they would live their life in a fairly intellectual, sterile, or unemotional way. Again, if we define fusion precisely and as described above, this is not true. Differentiated people can be as involved with the emotional aspect of their life as they want. Again, the key is that when people are differentiated they can do what they want rather than what the emotion dictates. Fused family members are not as free to choose what they want because the emotional part of their life controls them.

Coping with Fusion

Family scientists have discovered several strategies that decrease emotional fusion in families. These strategies can be used by friends, educators, or professionals who want to help families. They can also be used by individuals and families to increase their own differentiation. Two strategies are (1) to analyze a genogram and deal with insights it provides, and (2) to resolve invisible loyalties. A third strategy many people try is called *emotional cutoff*, but, as we have seen in an earlier chapter, it usually has undesirable side effects and most of the time is not effective.

Using a Genogram

Genograms can provide insights about the amount of differentiation occurring in families. One reason they are helpful is that patterns of fusion and differentiation are often carried from one generation to another. Usually in each generation there are some children who tend to have a little more differentiation, and there are some children who tend to have a little less, but many children repeat the patterns of the earlier generations.

"A common example of being overly focused on details in a relationship is people incessantly asking one another "why" they behave the way they do. In this example, the wife may get preoccupied with "why" her husband rejects her and the husband with "why" his wife is so needy and dependent. When one person asks the other, "Why do you do what you do?" *focus* on the *relationship process is immediately lost.* The focus is lost because the question assumes that the cause of the person's behavior exists *within* that person. The question shifts the "locus of control" from the relationship to one person. One person does not withdraw because the other pursues anymore than the other pursues because one withdraws. It is a process that transcends a "why" explanation that is contained within either individual." —Kerr & Bowen, 1988, p. 61

Chapter 3 described how to make a genogram chart. After the chart is completed, the first step in using it to help differentiation is to examine and evaluate the differentiation-fusion patterns that have existed over several generations in a family. This usually provides insights about how some people have been more fused than others, and it can provide clues about a particular individual's fusion. It also helps people think about their differentiation as part of a larger pattern.

Examining your own differentiation in the context of a genogram can make you become more aware of strategies you can use to become more differentiated. For example, it may help you realize you are an autonomous individual who needs to "stand on your own two feet." It also may help to realize that some feelings were appropriate when you were a child, but not as an adult. It also may help you realize how some of the family patterns which keep you "fused" to your family system were petty sibling rivalries you have now outgrown. It may help you be able to relate to your parents as individuals who also struggle with their limitations and circumstances.

Dealing with Invisible Loyalties

Ivan Boszormenyi-Nagy and his colleagues have developed a slightly different strategy for resolving undesirable emotional connections in family systems. Their first book was titled *Invisible Loyalties* (Boszormenyi-Nagy & Sparks, 1973), and in it they described how families accumulate multigenerational patterns of obligations and rights. Some of these patterns deal with things individuals receive from their family. Some examples of positive things received are existence, love, nurturance, identity, heritage, values, bonds, and understanding.

Part of these patterns are obligations that are deeply felt emotional ties. These include such things as indebtedness, basic duties, and a sense of ethical responsibility. Boszormenyi-Nagy calls these deeply felt connections *invisible loyalties*, and they involve such processes as giving and taking, helping and hindering, injustices and healing, teaching and receiving, and various combinations of hurting and acts of caring.

Boszormenyi-Nagy and Sparks suggested that it is helpful to use the concept of a *family ledger* to think about these family processes. The ledger is a balance sheet of obligations and rights, debts and credits, that accumulates over time. In healthy family systems, families tend to balance the ledger with justice in the exchange of debts and obligations. Sometimes, however, the justice comes too slowly, or it is insufficient and there is too great an accumulation of injustices. In other situations some individuals perceive the pattern has been unjust, and this is deeply troubling. When these inequities occur, it creates chronic anxiety, resentments, and animosities that are disruptive to family members individually and collectively.

One of Boszormenyi-Nagy and Sparks's examples of this process is a mother who is angry at being rejected by her mother, and she tries to correct this injustice by offering total devotion to her own daughter. However, in the language of balance of payments, the mother assumes the daughter should reestablish family justice by being appreciative and giving to her mother the acceptance and understanding her own mother did not give her. In this type of situation, the mother often is excessively devoted to her daughter, creating resentment rather than appreciation. This can lead to the daughter's having unexplained negative feelings toward the "loving" mother. Confusion and emotional disruption prevail between the mother and daughter. Improvement results when either the mother or daughter realize how the mother is trying to "balance the payments" or "make up" for her own deprivation. This can help the mother and the daughter understand what is going on and free them from the invisible emotional processes.

Fusion can be created because the emotionally based resentments are captivating and consuming. When this occurs the individuals are unable to differentiate from the emotional network. Then family members can examine the family ledger to see if patterns of emotional obligations, injustices, unresolved problems, misunderstandings, or debts are keeping some members of the family "fused" to the family emotional system. Often, according to Boszormenyi-Nagy and Sparks, the main difficulty is the invisibility of these patterns of "unfinished business." Therefore, when the patterns are discovered it is many times relatively easy to talk them through and resolve the emotional obligations.

Wamboldt and Reiss (1989) have proposed that this process of coping with generational connections involves two entwined developmental tasks. They suggest that when couples are in the formative stage of their family development:

> First, they must position themselves vis-à-vis their original family experience. They must resolve the questions "where have we come from and what do we think of those experiences." How they *define their heritage* assumes more importance than the legacy of their family per se. Second, they must define a new *relationship identity*, that is, chart their own course and decide who they, as a couple embarking on a new family voyage, are going to be. Accordingly, within the constructivist model several possibilities exist for dealing with one's background: it can be accepted in full and continued, it can be partially accepted and struggled with, or it can be repudiated and disengaged from. (Wamboldt & Reiss, 1989, p. 322)

Emotional Cutoff—An Undesirable Method

Emotional cutoff is a method of trying to deal with fusion that is generally ineffective. As we saw in Chapter 3, emotional cutoff refers to attempts to deny fusion rather than resolve it. The result is that people may stop interacting with their family, or they may move away from their family, but they are still emotionally fused. In these situations the fusion still has the same effects, even though the parental family may be thousands of miles away.

According to Bowen (1976), emotional cutoffs are determined by the way people handle their unresolved emotional attachments to their parents. He claims that all people have some degree of unresolved emotional attachment to their parents, and furthermore that the lower the level of differentiation, the more intense the unresolved attachment. How the individual approaches the idea of cutoff will greatly influence the way "people separate themselves from the past in order to start their lives in the present generation" (p. 83). Bowen put much thought into the selection of a term to best describe this process. For example, he considered using such terms as separation, isolation, withdrawal, running away, or denying the importance of the parental family. "However much *cutoff* may sound like informal slang, I could find no other term as accurate for describing the process" (p. 83).

He further states that "the degree of unresolved emotional attachment to the parents is equivalent to the degree of undifferentiation that must somehow be handled in the person's own life and in future generations. The unresolved attachment is handled by the intrapsychic process of denial and isolation of self while living close to the parents; or by physically running away; or by a combination of emotional isolation and physical distance" (p. 84). He is also convinced that the more intense cutoff is, the more likely individuals will exaggerate their version of family problems in their own marriages, ". . . and the more likely his own children to do a more intense cutoff with him in the next generation. There are many variations in the intensity of this basic process and in the way the cutoff is handled. The person who runs away from his family of origin is as emotionally dependent as the one who never leaves home. They both need emotional closeness, but they are allergic to it" (p. 84).

Thus, emotional cutoff is always a less desirable solution than working through or resolving the emotional problems in a way that will promote healthy differentiation. In some situations, however, it may not be possible to differentiate; then emotional cutoff becomes one of the options to be considered.

Chronic Family Anxiety

The second main idea in this chapter is also an idea that was first developed by Bowen.[1] This idea deals with a certain type of emotional tension or anxiety. *Anxiety* can be defined as a negative emotion that includes distress or uneasiness of mind caused by apprehension of danger or misfortune.

Acute anxiety is different from chronic anxiety. *Acute anxiety* is usually a short-term response to a stressful situation, and most of the time it is a rational response to a real (rather than imagined) problem. For example, when a couple is told by a doctor their child has a serious disease, the natural emotional response is to have acute anxiety or feelings of "distress or uneasiness of mind caused by apprehension of danger or misfortune." Acute anxiety tends to leave after a person learns to cope with the stressful situation or the danger leaves. For example, the anxiety leaves a couple when they learn how to cope with the illness or if the diagnosis is not accurate.

All individuals and families encounter situations that create acute anxiety. It occurs whenever there are serious problems to be dealt with and whenever negative emotions such as despair, futility, inadequacy, inferiority, lack of fulfillment, discouragement, emotional hurt, or serious disappointment occur. One of the challenges all families face is to find ways to deal with these problems and their negative emotions so that they do not lead to chronic anxiety.

Chronic anxiety is when uneasiness, distress, or apprehension endure for long periods of time. Usually the sources of chronic anxiety are difficult to identify, as are the original causes, and it is an underlying condition that persists and colors many different situations.

There are some types of chronic anxiety that usually are not important in family systems. For example, people can have psychic fears or apprehensions that are related to their work, their education, or their friendships, and these forms or types of chronic anxiety sometimes have little impact on family life. Also, people can have chronic anxiety about many other things that have little to do with family systems. They can have chronic anxiety about being in an elevator or being in dark places, and many of these chronic anxieties only occur outside the home and have little impact on family systems.

Bowen studied one type of chronic anxiety that is very important in family systems. It is long-term tension or resentment. This occurs when family members feel others in their family have been unjust to them in important ways. Emotional undercurrents can occur when family members love deeply, with close bonds, and then feel betrayed, abandoned, deceived, or ignored.

Box 5.2

There is an analogy that is helpful in understanding the role chronic anxiety plays in influencing family processes: Chronic anxiety operates in much the same way that termites operate in a building!

Termites tend to be invisible, and in many ways chronic anxiety tends to be hidden, unrecognized, and denied. Termites gradually eat away at the main structures in the system, and chronic anxiety undermines the love, bonds, and positive emotions that most families have in the beginning. Later, after there has been a long period of relatively invisible erosion, a minor event can disrupt the system enough that the main structures give way and the building collapses.

It is the same with the cumulative effect of long-term resentments and anger in families. They gradually undermine the basic structures, fairly invisibly, and eventually a relatively small event or series of events occur and the members of the family discover that the foundation and main structures they have built their family on have been eroded. At that point, it is usually not possible to go back and re-create the foundation or structures the family once had. The resentments almost always have led to serious misunderstanding, anger, conflict, suspicion, and mistrust, and the negative feelings of hurt, betrayal, and despair are so strong that the system is irreparable.

The solution is for families to find ways to deal with negative emotions such as resentment and disappointment so they do not lead to chronic ills in their system. The healing balm of such things as forgiveness, patience, and the willingness to let ourselves and others be frail and inadequate, are strategies that can help families keep chronic anxiety low enough that it doesn't invisibly erode the basic structures of the family system.

This type of chronic family anxiety is significant because it interferes with the healthy operation of a family's emotional "field" or "climate." More extreme emotional reactions such as animosity, malice, rancor, enmity, and hatred then appear. Emotions such as these create seriously disabling processes in most families because they interfere with the more positive emotions that people seek (such as love, compassion, care, and nurturance).

Another reason this type of chronic anxiety is usually disabling is because it keeps family members "on edge," and even minor problems can be enough to create intense emotional reactions of anger, aggression, violence, and abuse. It is similar to having a pot of water simmering, where a slight increase in temperature is enough to make it boil. When families do not have chronic anxiety in their emotional system they do not over-respond to minor problems, and they can marshall their resources to cope with the problems effectively. But, when they have ongoing tension, they have less ability to cope with even minor problems.

The principle that Bowen developed can be called the **chronic anxiety principle**:

Principle

The higher the level of chronic anxiety in a relationship system the greater the strain on people's adaptive capabilities. (Kerr & Bowen, 1988, p. 112)

One important aspect of this principle is that it does not assume chronic anxiety to be something that exists only in individuals. When it exists in a relationship system it is a part of the emotional field, climate, or atmosphere of the family, even if the individuals in the family are not aware of it.

Another aspect of this principle is that it refers to part of the family emotional system rather than to the behavior or activity level of the individuals. We might assume that if a person is unresponsive, detached, or uninvolved behaviorally in a family they have little anxiety. This may not be the case at all. Their inactivity may be their way of managing a high level of chronic anxiety.

Chronic anxiety tends to lead to many undesirable conditions in family systems. This chapter can focus on only two of these disabling and destructive processes: They are emotional triangles, and problems with mental and physical health. Readers looking for more detailed discussions of the harmful effects of chronic anxiety will find help in books by Boszormenyi-Nagy and Sparks (1974), and Kerr and Bowen (1988).

Emotional Triangles

Emotional triangles (or *triangling*) is a common result of chronic anxiety in families. **Triangling** occurs when two parts of a family system have an ongoing conflict and they focus on something else ("triangle in") as a way of gaining control over the situation or stabilizing their problem. There are many things that can be triangled in. Sometimes it is another member of the family or someone outside the family. (Often this is what is happening in unhealthy generational alliances, and it is often what happens when someone has an extramarital affair.) People can also triangle in other things—such as an issue, an organization, a hobby, or their career.

Emotional triangles have a number of rules that govern how they operate, and family scientists are beginning to isolate and describe these rules. Having a knowledge of these rules can help us understand the emotional processes that are always swirling around in triangles, and it also can help us keep from becoming fused ourselves or being triangled into situations in undesirable ways. This latter idea is reflected in an insightful observation made by Edwin Friedman (1988):

> It has been said, "What Peter says about Paul tells you more about Peter than it does about Paul." In the concept of an emotional triangle, "What Peter says to you about his relationship with Paul has to do with his relationship with you." (p. 36)

Another valuable reason to understand how triangling occurs is that it focuses on the processes that are involved rather than the particular content in a situation. When people are not aware of the rules of triangling they tend to focus on the specific issue and they fail to see the more abstract processes that govern what is occurring.

Friedman (1988) has developed seven "laws" about emotional triangles that help us understand what they are and how they operate in families (pp. 36–39). His laws, slightly edited for the purposes of this book, are:

> 1. The relationship of any two members of an emotional triangle is kept in balance by the way a third party relates to each of them or to their relationship. When a given relationship is stuck, therefore, there is probably a third person or issue that is part of the homeostasis.
>
> 2. If one is the third party in an emotional triangle it is generally not possible to bring change (for more than a week) to the relationship of the other two parts by trying to change their relationship directly. This includes anything from trying to make a child become more orderly, trying to make someone give up his or her "habit," or urging someone to come to church more frequently. It well may be that, in the history of our species, no family member, upon trying to correct the perception of another family member about a third, has ever received the response, "You're right honey. I don't know why I didn't see it that way myself."
>
> 3. Attempts to change the relationship of the other two sides of an emotional triangle not only are generally ineffective, but homeostatic forces also often convert these efforts to their opposite intent. Trying harder to bring two people closer (brother and sister, child and parent) or another party and his or her symptom together (anyone and his or her sense of responsibility) will generally maintain or increase the distance between them. On the other hand, repeated efforts to separate a person and his or her symptom or any two parties (a spouse and his or her paramour, a child and his or her peer group, an engaged daughter and her "horrible" fiancé), or anyone and his or her cherished beliefs (a congregation and its conservatism) increases the possibility that they will fall "blindly in love" with one another.
>
> For example, a mother became concerned when her 20-year-old son developed an imaginary girlfriend whom he used to bring home for dinner. She wanted him to see a therapist but he wouldn't go. She kept trying to "take her away" from him by forcing reality issues, but he only clung tighter. Then he said he was taking his "friend"

with him on a vacation. Mother was encouraged not only to stop fighting his fantasy but to detriangle by buying Ms. Phantom a gift for the trip. He left his friend in the Caribbean. Had mother continued to try to straighten her son out, upon his return he and his friend might have moved in permanently.

4. To the extent a third party to an emotional triangle tries unsuccessfully to change the relationship of the other two, the more likely it is that the third party will wind up with the stress for the other two. This helps explain why the dysfunctional member in many families is often not the weakest person in the system, but on the contrary, often the one taking responsibility for the entire system. The concept of an emotional triangle thus creates an interrelational rather than a merely quantitative view of stress. (All diseases are communicable.) On the other hand, the concept of triangulation permits a style of leadership that is healthier for both leader and follower. . . .

5. The various triangles in an emotional system interlock so that efforts to bring change to any one of them is often resisted by homeostatic forces in the others or in the system itself. . . .

Usually one triangle in an interlocking system is primary, so that change in that one is more likely to induce change in the others. The primary triangles tend to be those involving family of origin, even when the other interlocking triangle is in the work system. . . .

"The root of triangulation is ongoing, long-term anxiety (negative emotion) that is not resolved. The best alternative is to find ways to resolve the roots to the problem by finding ways to resolve the negative affect. The next best alternative is to find ways to manage the negative emotions so they do not disrupt healthy individual development, healthy family development, and attaining goals." —FRIEDMAN, 1988

---

6. One side of an emotional triangle tends to be more conflictual than the others. In healthier families, conflict will tend to swing round the compass, so to speak, showing up in different persons or different relationships at different times (even on the same day). In relationship systems that are not as healthy, the conflict tends to be located on one particular side of a triangle (the identified patient or relationship). It is often the distribution and fluidity of conflict in a family that is crucial to its health rather than the quantity or the kind of issues that arise. Systems in which the triangles are more fluid can tolerate more conflict (and therefore more creativity) because of that capacity for distribution. (This is also why other parts of a triangle, despite being upset by conflict elsewhere, often resist change, since that would result in redistribution.)

7. We can only change a relationship to which we belong. Therefore, the way to bring change to the relationship of two others (and no one said it is easy) is to try to maintain a well-defined relationship with each, and to avoid the responsibility for their relationship with one another. To the extent we can maintain a "nonanxious presence" in a triangle, such a stance has the potential to modify the anxiety in the others. The problem is to be both nonanxious and present. Anyone can keep his or her own anxiety down by distancing, but that usually preserves the triangle. . . .

> The most triangled position in any set of relationships is always the most vulnerable; when the laws of emotional triangles are understood, however, it tends to become the most powerful. (Friedman, 1988, pp. 36–39)

There are a number of practical implications of these ideas. One of the most obvious implications is that families can avoid emotional triangles or eliminate them if they can find ways to avoid long-term negative emotions such as resentment, tension, animosity, anger, fear, apprehension, and anxiety. Many families pay a great deal of attention to such overt and visible things as the behavior of members of the family, getting good grades in school, athletic accomplishments, efficiency in handling money, and the reputation of the family, but they ignore the emotional processes in the family. These families would be more effective if they were to also pay attention to what is happening in their emotional system and try to find ways to resolve the ongoing, long-term negative feelings.

Additionally, whenever we try to help families cope with family "problems" it is advisable to pay attention to the triangles in the system. Observing the triangles can provide useful clues about where there might be unresolved tension that may be interfering with the family's ability to cope with their problems.

A third implication is to try to be aware of how we might be part of triangles. Often when someone solicits advice or help for a relationship problem, it is an attempt to triangle us into the problem situation. Being aware of the triangulation processes can provide useful ideas about how to help and how to avoid making the problem worse.

In summary, some helpful guidelines whenever we try to deal with an emotional triangle are:

1. Avoid being fused when trying to think about a triangle. This means to wait until you can find a situation where your own functional level of fusion is within comfortable limits.
2. Try to align with *both* other corners. If this is not possible, be on guard about being triangled in.
3. Try to resolve the underlying negative emotion, because it is at the heart of the triangle. Questions that sometimes help are:
   - Is there some unfinished business in the past that needs to be taken care of?
   - Can the family rules be changed to help alleviate the chronic anxiety?
   - Does someone need to adapt to development that has been occurring?
   - Is it possible to reframe the situation so it can be seen in a different way?
4. If the underlying negative emotions can be eliminated, try to identify some ways to live with the situation so it is not disabling.

Chronic Anxiety and Health

There is growing evidence that chronic anxiety in families plays a bigger role in physical, mental, and emotional health than most people realize (Kerr & Bowen, 1988, Ch. 7). According to Bowen's theory, when anxiety is low, it provides a climate that is conducive to emotional, mental, and physical health. It allows the family members not to be "too reactive" when one family member becomes ill or is in a stressful situation, and

> the low level of reactivity allows the person who is feeling upset and unsettled to communicate his feelings and thoughts freely, unencumbered by a fear of unduly upsetting others, or by an apprehension that others will respond by sermonizing or withdrawing. Such circumstances provide maximum emotional support for people. (Kerr & Bowen, 1988, p. 123)

In these situations the family members are able to use their adaptive abilities effectively, and they tend to be resourceful in trying to deal with stressors and threats to their health. This helps in maintaining emotional and mental health, and it helps the physical body be able to resist problems or recover quickly from them.

When the chronic anxiety in a family's emotional system is high, it detracts from the ability of people to cope with stressors, and can contribute to a number of health problems. This can occur in a feedback loop, or escalating cycle, such as the following situation:

> The more anxious people become, the less constructive their responses to others tend to be. A common anxiety-driven cycle is emotional neediness in one person triggering distance in another, which triggers more neediness in the first, which triggers more distance in the other. Each person acts to alleviate his own distress and in the process adds to the distress of the other. Typically, one person achieves a more favorable position in this process than the other. The one who is chronically in the unfavorable position is vulnerable to developing a symptom. So while a specific event may upset one person, the way the person manages his upset, the way his management of it affects others, and the way others manage that effect become more important components of the anxiety spiral in a family than the "problem" itself. (Kerr & Bowen, 1988, p. 124)

In these situations we should not think of chronic anxiety in families as "the" cause of physical illnesses. Also, we should not view it as "the" cause of emotional and mental problems. The development of illness is usually a complex combination of many factors, and these processes may be more complex than most people currently believe. And, it may be that the chronic anxiety in family systems often has a more facilitating role than we have realized. Kerr and Bowen suggest:

> The patterns of emotional functioning in a nuclear family are a major influence on an individual's ability to adapt successfully to the presence of factors that can precipitate illness. For example, if the pattern of emotional functioning most active in a family fosters dysfunction in a spouse, that spouse is more vulnerable than other family members to becoming ill in response to such things as the exposure to allergens or toxins, the presence of a genetic predisposition to a disease, the exposure to infections agents such as viruses or bacteria, and the exposure to social attitudes that can foster various types of social irresponsibility." (p. 164)

This suggests that the emotional processes in families can have enabling or disabling effects. The key is in the management of these processes. If negative emotions and other stressors can be managed so the anxiety that is associated with them is acute rather than chronic, it is enabling and facilitating. On the other hand, when anxiety becomes intense and chronic in a family's emotional field, it tends to contribute to disabling and destructive processes.

The family scientists who have studied these processes suggest that the destructive aspects of chronic anxiety operate fairly slowly. Usually the onset of a particular illness occurs fairly quickly, but the family processes that have increased or decreased the *vulnerability* to the illness have usually been active for a long period of time before the onset of the illness (Kerr & Bowen, 1988, p. 169). This suggests that families generally have considerable time to deal with anxieties, but that it is wise to try to resolve negative emotional conflicts and resentments before they slowly erode the ability of the family to create and maintain health.

IMPLICATIONS FOR FAMILIES

The ideas presented in Chapter 4 and in this chapter have several important implications for families and those who try to help families. One of these implications is that *the emotional part of family life is much more important than most social scientists have realized, and we should emphasize it more than we usually do.* As Bowen (1976) has observed:

> Far more of life is governed by automatic emotional forces than man is willing to acknowledge. (p. 60)

This suggests that family scientists ought to give high priority to the emotional aspects of family systems whenever we try to understand family processes or try to help families. Ironically, though, most families and most social scientists tend to give much more emphasis to the rational parts of family processes than the emotional parts.

Family Decision Making

When we try to understand problem solving or decision making in families, we tend to judge the quality of the decision making by how rational, sensible, or efficient the people or the decisions are (Klein & Hill, 1979). Scholars, parents and spouses say things like:

"That wouldn't be smart."
"Calm down, and be reasonable."
"Let's think this through carefully."
"But that's not even logical."
"Let's be sensible about this."

If we were more sensitive to the emotional processes in the family realm, we would find ourselves making different kinds of statements. We'd say things like:

"How would it feel if . . ."
"I'm getting upset about . . ."
"It's not logical but it feels good."
"Down deep inside, it seems that . . ."
"I have a funny feeling that . . ."

Think about the decision making you have seen in your own family and in other families when you've been on the "inside." What is the ratio of the two kinds of statements? Do about half deal with what Bowen calls the intellectual system and half deal with the emotional system? We don't have any research about this, but our guess is that at least 90 percent of the attention in most American families is on the intellectual part. And, even when we use words like *feel*, most of the time we are referring to how we think rather than to an emotional state. We also suspect that an embarrassingly high percentage of the time when we family scientists think about decision making, we do the same thing.

These ideas have led the authors to advocate a rule of thumb for family decision making. It is that 99 percent of the time *the most important aspects of decision making in the family realm are, first, how do the individuals feel in the decision making process and, secondarily, how do they feel about the decision.* This means that the most important aspect is not how wise or effective a decision is. It is how the couple or family feels about what is going on.

Frequently in families the people who have the most power get their way, and this helps them feel good about the decision. Unfortunately, those who have less power don't feel quite as good about the process of decision making or the decision, and that matters a great deal. We suspect that the emotional aspect of decision making in families is so powerful that if it were truly considered, many of the most serious problems in our society would be reduced dramatically. Abuse, violence, divorce, and alienation would be reduced dramatically. We would never have needed to have a civil rights movement or a women's movement. Substance abuse would be a mere fraction of what it is, and on and on and on. In terms of the actual enhancement of life, our art and music would be different. Our complexions, life expectancy, and health would be better. We'd change the balance of time and energy we devote to professions and children, relatives and friends, disarmament and peace.

Many people believe that the important events that make a difference in the world happen in places like Washington, Moscow, and Geneva. But these public occasions are only the most visible flowering of a multitude of inner and private experiences. The roots of our problems are in the emotional aspects of the family realm.

On a more modest scale, these ideas help us understand why a "consensus-seeking"[2] method of decision making is so helpful in families. A **consensus-seeking method of decision making** is one in which a family keeps working until they find a decision that is emotionally acceptable to everyone. The issue is not whether it is acceptable intellectually. To be a satisfactory decision, it must be acceptable *emotionally.* The key to the process is for families to "shift gears" or change their method of making decisions so they can get solutions that everyone will feel good about. When this happens, it transforms the emotional atmosphere in most families in a way that is often almost magical. Things like morale, commitment to decisions, adaptability, listening, mercy, compassion, concern, and cooperation are sometimes dramatically increased. At the same time, negative behaviors such as resistance, rebellion, stubbornness, withdrawal, anger, and impatience tend to decrease.

The consensus-seeking method of decision making is different from using authority or power, and it is different from democratic methods where the majority wins. When decision making is based on authority, the powerful people in the family (usually the males or the parents) determine the decisions. Even when those who have the authority or the power are benevolent, and they consult with those who have less power, this authoritarian method has several limitations. It places the responsibility on those who have the power—rather than helping those who have less power, such as the children, to learn how to assume and manage responsibility. When those who have little power are mature adults, there is almost certain to be negative emotional response to the family members who have assumed control.

Power-based methods of making decisions are appropriate when some members of the family are incapable of responsibility. They are effective when children are small. However, as children gradually mature, it is necessary to begin to change the methods of decision making so they have a gradually increasing influence. **Authority-based decision making** is also useful when family members are seriously incapacitated. For example, when someone is gravely ill, or has become senile, it is effective to shift the decision-making methods to reflect the change. Only when family members are able to be responsible, and willing to function in an atmosphere of cooperation, is a consensus-seeking method of decision making feasible.

The democratic method of majority rule is an effective method in public realms. It is not realistic in the family, because the family realm is fundamentally an emotional one where relationships are permanent and intimacy is important. The voting method of making decisions tends to exploit minorities and is so inadequate in dealing with emotional and intimate processes that it is almost never used in family systems.

Family scientists have developed a number of marriage and family enrichment programs that help families learn the consensus-seeking method of decision making. Thomas Gordon (1970) developed the first of these programs, and it is called Parent Effectiveness Training (PET). Don Dinkmeyer and his colleagues also developed a series of programs that teach "win-win" decision making. Two of their programs are Systematic Training for Effective Parents (STEP) (1976) and Training in Marriage Enrichment (TIME) (1984).

It would be a mistake to think these ideas about decision making deal only with superficial feelings that don't really matter. We believe these processes are intricately intertwined with some of the most fundamental and important emotional states we humans experience. For example, when a family is able, even on rare occasions, to adopt a win-win style of decision making, it has implications for how the less powerful people feel about themselves and how they feel others feel about them.

When the ideas of a wife (or of a 10-year-old or 16-year-old) are ignored or trampled by members of their family, it communicates in some very real ways the idea that they are not valued. This has implications for very deeply experienced emotional responses about such things as who they are, how important they are, how respectable they are, how they feel about themselves, and how they feel about others. It influences their feelings about whether the world is a humane, pleasant, compassionate place or a hostile, aggressive, and attacking place. It influences whether and how much they reach out to others, how loved ones do and should treat each other, and what their place in the universe is.

Many of the emotional states that are involved in these processes are only experienced in the family. Others are experienced in many settings, but they are experienced more intensely and frequently in the family. For example, the desires to perpetuate the species, mate, reproduce, and create a home are emotional states that are experienced in the family. We get a sense of meaning and purpose, or futility and emptiness, more by what happens in our family than anyplace else. The emotional states we experience on the job, at school, at concerts, at athletic contests, with friends or alone with our hobbies are qualitatively very different.

These are not trivial matters. They are profound, and they are tied up, for good or ill, with the daily patterns of interaction in families. It is hoped that those of us who study families can use these ideas to:

- first, manage our own families wisely,
- second, use our insights to help other families, and
- third, try to influence the ecosystems that interact with families to help create an increasingly humane world.

The Role of Emotions in Family Abuse

The ideas we have been discussing have profound implications for another important area, that of abusive behaviors in families. When we think about physical abuse in families, we are likely to think of child abuse or wife abuse, but the problem is much broader. Research has discovered there is abuse of other members of families (Straus, Gelles & Steinmetz, 1980). For example, there is an unfortunate amount of abuse of the elderly, and it apparently leads to death more often than most people realize (Hotaling et al., 1988). To understand the implications these ideas about emotion have, it is helpful to briefly review the history of scholarly attempts to understand and influence physical abuse in families.

Amazingly, the scholarly study of physical abuse was almost ignored until the mid-1960s. At that time a series of papers was published that identified the "battered child syndrome" (Kempe et al., 1962). The first papers were written by and for the medical community, to help them become aware of abuse and learn how to recognize and treat parental abuse of children.

At about the same time the medical papers began appearing, Murray Straus, a sociologist, began to do research on the nature of violence in families. In 1970 Straus was elected program chair for the annual conference of the National Council on Family Relations (NCFR), and he decided to make violence in the family the theme for the 1970 meetings. To his and his colleagues' astonishment, they discovered that the area had been almost totally ignored by the social sciences that were studying the family: family science, sociology, psychology, home economics, communication, domestic law, economics, history, and so forth.

The result was that the 1970 NCFR meetings became a consciousness-raising occasion. This led immediately to a dramatic increase in the study of physical abuse in the family. But, in the early 1970s, Bowen's ideas about the importance of emotion had not become widely known, and the professionals who started to study violence paid little attention to the emotional processes. The result is that most of the theoretical and research literature about violence deals with objective, public-realm, easily quantified, social and psychological causes, and very little attention has been given to the role of the emotional domain in the family (Gelles & Straus, 1979).

Some of the nonemotional aspects of family processes *have* been dealt with in this literature. For example, Pagelow identifies ten "unique features of family life" (Pagelow, 1984, p. 5) that contribute to abuse, but she uses a sociological perspective and emotions are not even on the list. It is now possible to add some important insights by thinking about the role of the family emotional system. Some of the most intense emotional states that humans experience are tied up with their family processes. For example, feelings about what life is all about, intimate connections with others, reproducing, and what it means to be a man or woman are basically emotional and familial.

These emotional states provide the motivation for a great deal of healthy behavior, such as tenderness, attraction, love, nurturance and caring. Also, however, when frustrations, disappointments, and undesirable things are encountered (and most individuals and families encounter many of these), the intensity of the emotion prompts behaviors that do not occur in the more public realms. It leads people to behave in the most unhealthy, abusive, exploiting, hateful, and bitter ways imaginable.

It is useful to note where human abuse tends to occur. Most of it occurs when there is an intense emotional process that is threatened, frustrated, or stifled. Notice, for example, there is little student abuse in schools, little employee abuse on the job, little patron abuse at the concert, little customer abuse in the market, and little investor abuse in the stock market.

What conditions are needed for abuse to occur? David Finkelhor (1983, 1986) and his colleagues identify four factors they think are involved, but we suggest that privacy and intense emotion need to be added to their model, because these two conditions must exist for abuse to occur. Ironically, these two conditions are also essential for the deeper human connections that are positive and desirable. These include such things as love, deep caring and concern, nurturance, and enduring compassion. And we are not just thinking of the media-created feelings that occur spontaneously (and temporarily) when a child falls into a well. We're thinking of the enduring, lasting, deeply experienced dimensions of these conditions.

Thus there is a paradox about abuse: The very factors that make the best human relationships possible also allow the worst. In eliminating the conditions that create the worst, we might damage the ecology that allows the best.

Answers are very elusive in this area. We watch the media attention to the abuse problem, and the staggering statistics about the amount that occurs, and we watch our society trying to help. Some family science insights would probably be helpful if they were more widely understood. Hopefully, those of us who study the family will use these insights in creative, constructive, and effective ways.

SUMMARY

This chapter discussed two aspects of the family emotional system—fusion and chronic anxiety—where problems frequently occur, and suggested strategies for helping families deal effectively with them.

Fusion occurs when family members are excessively tied to the emotional system in their parental family. It is a condition where family members become victims of the emotionality in their lives, and when fusion occurs it interferes with the ability people have to use their intellect. Basis fusion refers to the average level of fusion a person has throughout their adult life. Functional fusion refers to fusion that occurs when someone becomes dominated by their emotions in a particular situation. Functional fusion can occur in an emotionally charged situation, and it can come and go in a matter of a few minutes. Sometimes functional fusion is desirable and wholesome. Examples of this are when people get "carried away emotionally" in athletic contests, symphonies, or during sexual intercourse. Many times, however, functional fusion leads to undesirable consequences, where people say and do things they are sorry for later.

Chronic anxiety comes about when feelings of resentment, apprehension, and rancor exist for long periods of time as part of the emotional climate (emotional field) in a family. Triangling and problems with health are two disabling processes in families that grow out of chronic anxiety. The chapter concludes with a discussion of several implications these ideas have for people who try to understand and help families.

Key Terms

Fusion
Differentiation
Basic level of fusion/differentiation
Functional (situational) level of fusion/differentiation
Genogram
Invisible loyalties
Emotional cutoff
Family ledger
Anxiety
Acute anxiety
Chronic anxiety
Emotional triangles (triangling)
Consensus-seeking decision making
Authority- or power-based decision making
Decision making based on preferences of the majority

Study Questions

1. In your own words, tell what is meant by the term *fusion.*
2. Describe how high levels of fusion create problems with differentiation.
3. Give a practical example of how a person's emotional world could override their thinking world.
4. What is meant by *basic fusion*?
5. Describe what is meant by *emotional cutoff.* Provide two examples of how a person could cut off family members. What results would you expect?
6. Define the term *invisible loyalties.*
7. Provide examples for each of the rules about triangulation.

Notes

1. This idea is similar to one that has had a long history in the social sciences. Bowen's contribution is that he changed the historical idea in several important ways. Scholars in many disciplines have discovered the impact of chronic anxiety. Psychiatrists for many years have argued that anxiety is a key element in the development of phobias, psychoses, and neurosis. For example, Adler (1929) suggested that people respond to feelings of inferiority, inadequacy, and powerlessness by developing their own unique "style of life." In recent times, Bowen helped us realize that chronic anxiety is a part of the family emotional system rather than just an individualistic or psychic phenomena. This is a different view of anxiety, and it led to several discoveries about how familial chronic anxiety influences human behavior.
2. This form of decision making is also known by several other labels. Gordon (1970) calls it *method III.* We are indebted to Gordon for developing these ideas, because they influenced what we presented in this text. (We would have used Gordon's terminology, but experience has taught us that people

remember the ideas better when they think in terms of consensus seeking and using power and authority.)

These ideas about decision making also are similar to the "win-win, win-lose, lose-win" terminology. We have not used this terminology because it tends to suggest competitiveness even when people are thinking about win-win situations; they seem to grasp the dynamics of the process better by thinking in terms of consensus seeking instead of power, authority, and winning.

Ideology

6

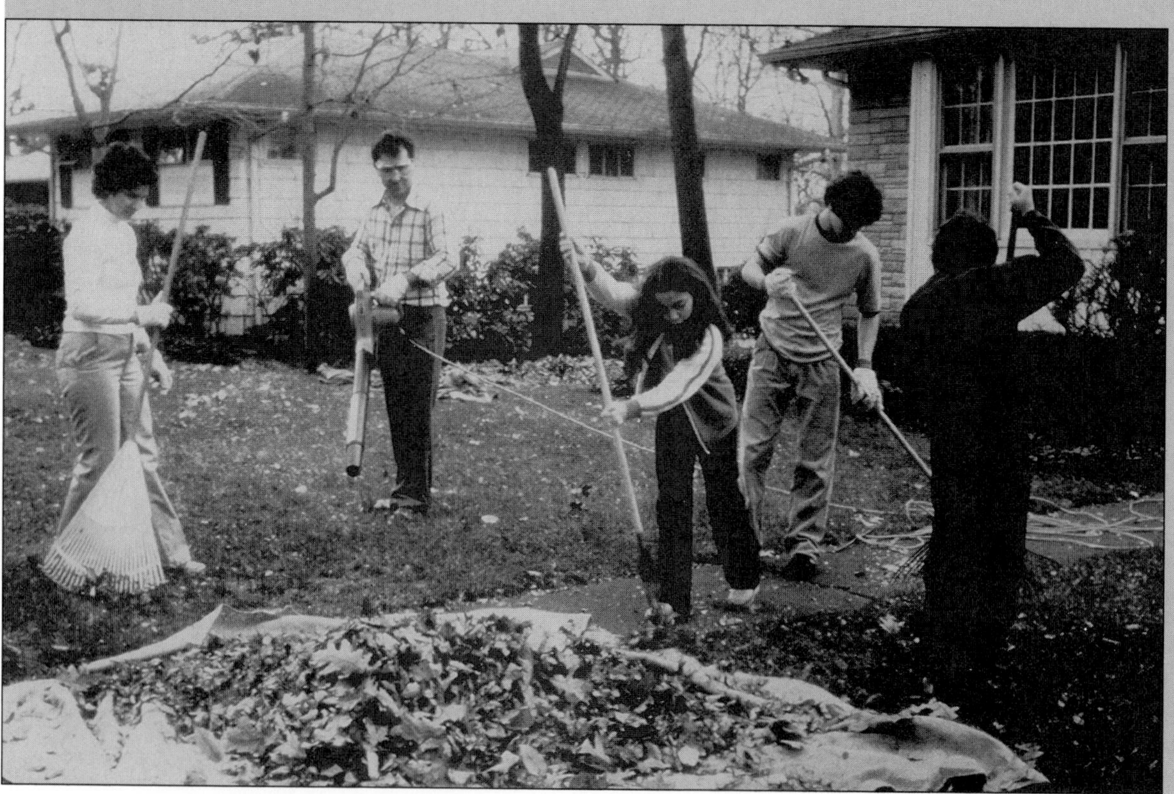

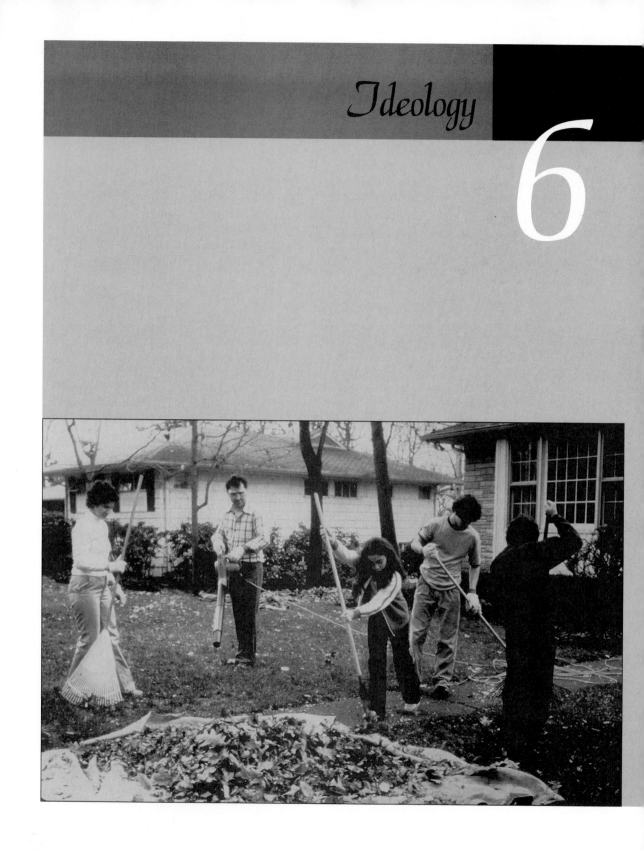

Main Ideas

1 // An ideology is a set of ideas or beliefs. The ideological part of family systems is different from the generational and emotional parts, and all three are important.

2 // Some aspects of family ideology are more abstract than others. Family scientists think about three levels of abstraction in family systems. Level I refers to specific or concrete processes; Level II refers to processes that are at an intermediate level of abstraction; and Level III refers to highly abstract processes.

3 // The constructivist belief is that families create or invent at least part of their ideology.

4 // Family paradigms are an important part of the Level III ideology in families, and families cannot be understood without paying attention to them. Family paradigms are the enduring, fundamental, shared, and general assumptions families develop about the nature and meaning of life, what is important, and how to cope with the world they live in.

- They are the basic templates or beliefs that form a family's philosophy of life, and they are the part of family systems that lead to goals, standards, and ways of relating.
- They are largely unconscious and general.
- They are formed in the early stages of family development; after they are formed they are very stable.
- They sometimes change when families face severe crises.

There are four family paradigms: open, closed, random, and synchronous.

5 // The exaggeration principle says that when families encounter stress they have a natural tendency toward exaggeration of the processes created by their paradigmatic beliefs.

6 // Values are a part of the Level III ideology in families.

7 // Some religious ideas are part of the Level III ideology in families.

Each of the last three chapters dealt with a fundamental part of family systems. Chapter 3 focused on generational processes, and Chapters 4 and 5 focused on emotional processes. This chapter deals with a third fundamental and important part of family systems—their ideology.

The root of the word *ideology* comes from the Greek term *ide*, which means "idea." Therefore, **ideology** refers to the body or group of ideas that exist in a group, society, or social movement. Thus when we focus on **family ideology** we are looking at the cognitive or intellectual aspect of family systems that is reflected in beliefs, thoughts, myths, symbols, ideals, aspirations, values, worldview, philosophy of life, or doctrines.

It is helpful to realize that the ideological aspect of family systems differs from the generational and emotional aspects. One difference is that the emotional part is experienced as sensations or emotions rather than as thoughts; it is an affective, emotional, or somatic process, not an intellectual one. Also, the generational processes are not part of the "idea" part of family systems. The connections, continuities, discontinuities, and other processes that occur between parents and children occur whether families are aware of them intellectually or not. When families develop ideas or beliefs about their emotions or their generational processes, the ideas are part of their ideology, but the emotions and generational processes themselves are not ideological.

> *"There is nothing either good or bad, but thinking makes it so."*
>
> —Shakespeare

Levels of Abstraction in Family Ideology

Some parts of family ideology are relatively abstract, and other parts are specific and concrete. These differences are important, because the abstract ideas play a different role in systems than the less abstract beliefs do.

To understand what this means, we need to first understand what the term **abstraction** means. Abstraction refers to the degrees of difference between things that are relatively specific, tangible, and concrete as opposed to those that are relatively general, intangible, obscure, and nonspecific. When we think of our own family life we are not thinking about families in general but of one particular family. However, when we think of "family life" as a way of organizing humans it is a more general—and abstract—idea. In a different analogy, shaking hands is one friendly act that is situation-specific, concrete, and not abstract. Friendliness, on the other hand, is more abstract and less situation-specific, so it is a more abstract concept.

To illustrate in a different way, thinking about apples, oranges, and lemons is less abstract than thinking about fruit. Fruit is a more general, or abstract, term. A law against child abuse is less abstract than the Bill of Rights in the Constitution, and that is less abstract than the basic form of our government (a republic). When we think about a family rule, it is less abstract thinking than when we think about how a family makes or changes its rules.

Abstraction is a continuum that varies between the two extremes of no abstraction (concrete, specific) and high abstraction (general, unspecific). This means it is like distance or height, varying without natural categories or units. However, with many continuous variables we find it useful to create measuring devices that divide the variables into units, and many of these measuring devices are widely understood. For example, we use inches or meters to divide distance into units or categories.

Family scientists in the 1970s developed a method of dividing the abstraction of family processes into two levels (Watzlawick, Beavin & Jackson, 1974). The lower level was called *first-order* or *Level I* processes. The higher level was called *second-order* or *Level II* processes. Then, in the 1980s, several family scientists identified some family processes that are even more abstract, and they are now known as *Level III* processes. Next we will look at how these levels are applied to the ideological part of family systems.

Level I Ideology

Level I ideas are very specific and concrete. Most of the "rules" families have fall in this category. For example, rules about calling to let others know when we will be late, or how to act at the table, are Level I rules. A typical family system has thousands of these specific ideas about how family systems ought to operate. For example, most families think they ought to put beds in bedrooms rather than in dining rooms, and they think it is OK to show appropriate physical affection to each other. (Of course, families differ in what they think is appropriate. Some families express affection a great deal and others express it less.) Most families have fairly specific ideas about where people should and should not eat, or how family members should dress. They also believe that lawn mowers and garden tools should not be left in driveways, electrical appliances should be kept safe, and toys should not be left on stairs.

Many Level I ideas in family systems are so obvious they are understood by small children. However, there are some Level I ideas that are more hidden or subtle. Because they are less obvious, families may not be aware of them. For example, a family may have the belief that "Dad can criticize other members of the family, but the other members cannot criticize Dad," but they may not be aware that their behavior reflects this belief. Or, some members of a family may think that "The baby is Mother's favorite child," but the mother may believe she has no favorite.

Level II Ideology

Level II ideas are more abstract than the specific ideas in Level I and less abstract than the highly abstract ideas in Level III. Thus, this level refers to ideas that are at an intermediate level of abstraction. Watzlawick and his colleagues (1974) were the first to describe this more abstract level of analysis. Two different ideas led them to discover the two levels.

One of the ideas they used is part of the theory of groups developed by French mathematician Évariste Galois (1832, cited in Watzlawick et al., 1974, ch. 1). The idea is that it is not logically possible for something to be a member of a group and also be the group itself. Thinking about a member of a group of things in a system is thinking at one level, and thinking about the group itself is thinking at a more abstract level (we say it is **meta** to the first level).

The second idea that helped Watzlawick and his colleagues develop the two levels in family systems came from the theory of logical types set forth by Whitehead and Russell (1910). This theory helped them realize that change in a whole group or a whole class of objects is a different "type" of change than change to just a part of the group or class. This seemingly simple idea provided the basis for realizing that changes *within* a group of things in family systems are qualitatively different from changes in a *whole* group of things. This extended their thinking, because with Galois's theory of groups they had thought only about the nature of groups and their members, but not about the nature of change or the ability of family members to control change.

Several examples help illustrate these ideas. Watzlawick, Weakland and Fisch (1974, p. 9) used the example of an automobile with a standard shift to illustrate shifts in levels. Within any given gear, a car has a range of speed and power, and changes within a gear are made by the appropriate use of the gas pedal. Changes with the gas pedal are Level I or first-order changes, because they occur within a particular gear. Shifting gears provides the driver with a new range of speed and power, and it is an intervention of a higher logical type than using the gas pedal.

Disciplining children can illustrate these differences in family systems. When parents want to change the behavior of a child, they may decide to use disciplinary behaviors. Reasoning, spanking, bribing, grounding, and encouraging are some of the members of a group (or class) known as disciplinary behaviors. As long as the parents are thinking about which method of discipline to use and they are using one or another of the members of the group, they are thinking at Level I. However, if the parents were to back off and think at a more abstract level, they might wonder whether they could accomplish their goal better by something other than discipline. When they start thinking about whether to discipline the child or do something else, they have shifted to a higher level of abstraction in their family system, and they are analyzing their system at Level II. Watzlawick and his colleagues summarize their ideas in the following way:

> To summarize what has been said so far: Group Theory gives us a framework for thinking about the kind of change that can occur within a system that itself stays invariant; the Theory of Logical Types is not concerned with what goes on inside a class, i.e., between its members, but gives us a frame for considering the relationships between member and class and the peculiar metamorphosis which is in the nature of shifts from one logical level to the next higher. If we accept this basic distinction between the two theories, it follows that there are two different types of change: one that occurs within a given system which itself remains unchanged, and one whose occurrence changes the system itself. To exemplify this distinction in more behavioral terms: a person having a nightmare can do many things *in* his dream—run, hide, fight, scream, jump off a cliff, etc.—but no change from any one of these behaviors to another would ever terminate the nightmare. *We shall henceforth refer to this kind of change as first-order change.* The one way *out of* a dream involves a change from dreaming to waking. Waking, obviously, is no longer a part of the dream, but a change to an altogether different state. This kind of change will from now on be referred to as second-order change. Second-order change is thus *change of change.* (Watzlawick et al., 1974, pp. 10–11)

Level III Ideology

The **Level III** parts of family ideology are at the opposite extreme of abstraction. They are the highly abstract or general beliefs. Some of these abstract beliefs deal with values such as the nature of reality and how to cope with it. For example, some families believe life is a fairly friendly experience and others view it as a hostile experience. Some think the world is basically simple and others believe it is complex. Some families believe they have considerable control over their destiny and others think they have little control over what happens to them.

Abstract ideas are difficult to define clearly because they are, by their very nature, general and diffused rather than specific and concrete. Nonetheless they are an important part of family systems, because they can be the basic assumptions that strongly influence the more specific beliefs and behaviors in families. People's abstract beliefs influence their major goals in life, the ways they try to attain their goals, and how they behave.

To summarize, it is helpful to think about three different levels of abstraction in family systems. Level I refers to specific and concrete things. Level II refers to things that are at an intermediate level of abstraction, and Level III refers to highly abstract things. These ideas about levels of abstraction are used in later chapters when we consider several aspects of family systems, but in this chapter they are applied to abstraction in family ideologies. However, before these ideas can be developed in more detail, it is important to describe another aspect of family ideology. At least some parts of family ideologies are *constructed*, rather than just copied, from the culture or society.

A Constructivist View of Ideology

That individuals "construct," or create, at least some of their perceptions of reality is an old philosophical idea. It is called **constructivism**, or the *constructivist* point of view (Watzlawick, 1976, 1984). The idea that families construct assumptions and perceptions is a different view of the family realm than many people have. As David Reiss (1981) says:

Box 6.1

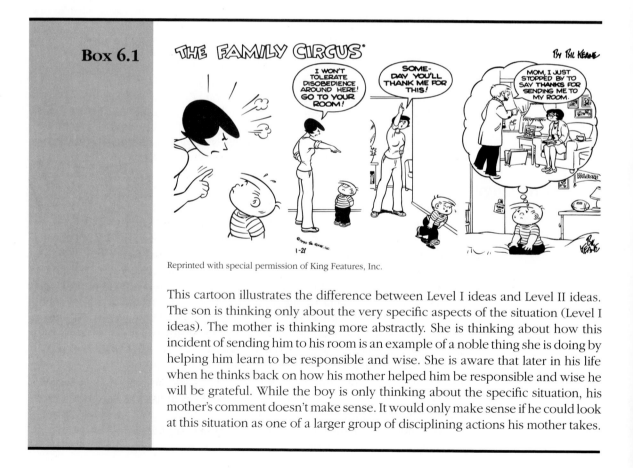

Reprinted with special permission of King Features, Inc.

This cartoon illustrates the difference between Level I ideas and Level II ideas. The son is thinking only about the very specific aspects of the situation (Level I ideas). The mother is thinking more abstractly. She is thinking about how this incident of sending him to his room is an example of a noble thing she is doing by helping him learn to be responsible and wise. She is aware that later in his life when he thinks back on how his mother helped him be responsible and wise he will be grateful. While the boy is only thinking about the specific situation, his mother's comment doesn't make sense. It would only make sense if he could look at this situation as one of a larger group of disciplining actions his mother takes.

> Our model rests on a picture of family which will come as a surprise to many readers. We are arguing, as we have said, that social evolution has placed the family in a position of strength, originality, and creativity. We are picturing the family as an active initiator: a historian of its past, an interpreter of its present, and a designer of its future. (p. 170)

The idea of constructing reality is an odd notion to most people in Western cultures because we usually think in a different way. We assume that "reality" exists independent of our perception of it, and what we do is discover, observe, and learn to understand the realities that are external to us. To help understand the constructivist point of view, it is helpful to review a contribution to our thinking that was made by a German philosopher about two centuries ago.

Immanuel Kant (1724–1804) made a number of important contributions to a branch of philosophy that is known as epistemology. **Epistemology** is the branch of philosophy that deals with how we acquire knowledge. The key question in epistemology is, how do we know what we think we know? This branch of philosophy has helped us understand that we have different methods of getting knowledge. For example, some of the different sources of the ideas we think we know are: tradition, reason, our five senses, spiritual or mystical experiences, and intuition (Thironx, 1985).

One of Kant's contributions was to show that the existence of a physical object and our knowledge about the physical object are not the same thing. For example, the planet Pluto existed before a group of astronomers discovered it existed. The contribution of the astronomers was to help us know that it exists. A rock in a forest that has never been seen by anyone exists even if no person knows about that particular rock. Therefore, things can exist independently of humans knowing about them.

The two concepts Kant used to describe the difference between the existence of something and the knowledge of its existence are **noumenon** and **phenomenon**. A *noumenon* is the unknown reality of something. A *phenomenon* is our perception, definition, or belief about something. Phenomena are *subjective* perceptions of things because the knowledge is inside the subject, or a matter of personal opinion. The noumenon of something is its *objective* existence.

It is helpful when there is correspondence between the noumena and phenomena (Speed, 1984), but all of us have experienced situations where there is a difference. For example, the air near the horizon of a hot highway or desert has waves that our eyes can discern. Under some circumstances the waves look like water on the surface, and it creates an illusion we call a mirage.

When we realize the noumena and phenomena are different, we can understand that our "knowledge" of objects may or may not be congruent with their physical aspect. It also helps us realize that the knowledge part of our human experience is not in the objects; it is entirely in our heads. It is just a short intellectual leap to thinking about nonphysical things that don't have a noumena. Truth, beauty, kindness, standards, aggression, resources, and harmony are examples. These are abstractions we use to think with, and they are entirely constructions in our heads (Watzlawick et al., 1974, 1976). We create words to

Box 6.2

The three levels of abstraction in family ideology: some examples

An example of Level I change is to change a family rule or norm. Another example is to change who is responsible for which family chores. A third example is to change the way a family ritual is celebrated. For example, a family may have one way of celebrating a child's birthday when the child is in elementary school, and they may decide to celebrate the birthday in different ways when the child becomes a teenager. These changes are changes *within* the family system and do not create change in a fundamental aspect of the system itself.

Level II change is at a higher level of abstraction in the system. It involves changing the system so it is fundamentally different. An example is to change metarules such as the rules about how rules are made and changed. A second example is to reframe the role of chores in a family. Assume, for example, that a family had a businesslike or economic orientation toward chores, and they believed that the important thing is to get the chores done efficiently. If the family were to reframe the nature of chores so they viewed them as a means for promoting closeness, sharing, interaction, and caring for each other, this would be a Level II or second-order change. A third example would be to make a major change in the way all of the rituals in a family are celebrated. Some research suggests that when alcohol has a central place in family rituals it tends to increase the likelihood that alcoholism will be passed from one generation to the next (Steinglass et al., 1987, ch. 10). If a family were to learn about this research and decide that alcohol will no longer be a part of their family rituals, this would be a Level II change.

Level III changes deal with the highly abstract parts of family ideology. For example, there are some parts of the Jewish community that are fairly conservative and orthodox and other parts that are fairly liberal and only slightly different from other religious or ethnic groups. If a family from a fairly liberal Jewish tradition were to change their basic beliefs and decide that they ought to live in a highly orthodox manner, this would be a change in their fundamental philosophy; and this would be a Level III change. Another example is that a family might assume that the world is basically a good and friendly place, but they may then be the victim of a tragedy where someone enters their home, robs them and kills one of the members of the family. This may lead to some dramatic changes in the family's assumptions. They may change their beliefs so they think that the world is an evil and unfriendly place. These would be changes in their basic philosophy of life, and they would be Level III changes that would lead to many other changes in the more specific parts of their ideology and behavior. In the last several decades a new development has been occurring in the constructivist way of thinking. It is that families also construct perceptions of reality. The first glimmerings of this idea appeared in a book by Robert Hess and Gerald Handel in 1959, and since then the idea has been developed and expanded by a number of other scholars.[1] The result is that the ideological part of family systems and the concept and constructivism are now central parts of family science.

describe these constructed ideas so we can communicate about them, think about them, study them, and use them.

Family Paradigms

In David Reiss's (1981) book *The Family's Construction of Reality*, he developed a concept that describes an important group of Level III ideas that are constructed in family systems. He coined the term *family paradigms* to refer to these abstract beliefs. **Family paradigms** are defined as the enduring, fundamental, shared, and general assumptions or beliefs that families develop about the nature and meaning of life, what is important, and how to cope with the world they live in (Reiss, 1981, Ch. 4).

One of the important aspects of family paradigms is that they tend to be shared by the members of a family.

> The assumptions are shared by all family members, despite the disagreements, conflicts, and differences that exist in the family. Indeed, the core of an individual's membership in his own family is his acceptance of, belief in, and creative elaboration of these abiding assumptions. When a member distances himself from these assumptions, when he can see no further possibility for creatively elaborating them, he is diluting his own membership and begins a process of alienation from his family. (Reiss, 1981, p. 1)

Awareness of Family Paradigms

Family paradigms are rarely explicit or conscious in families. They are usually implicit and unconscious. It is a bit paradoxical, but during the typical routines of life the paradigms that make normalcy possible are assumed and forgotten. Our attention is focused instead on managing daily routines, careers, recreation, education, politics, the arts, friendships, and so forth. The time when paradigms come the closest to being conscious is when families make major transitions and when they encounter crisis situations. During these periods, especially when the very existence of the family is threatened, they turn to their most basic shared beliefs to help them manage the crisis. When these periods of crisis are resolved, the basic beliefs recede into the assumed foundation of daily life, and attention can again be given to everyday matters.

Thus, to return to one of our favorite analogies, family paradigms tend to be part of the family "iceberg" that is beneath the surface, hidden from the view of outsiders and hidden (at least most of the time) from the families themselves. Observers of families, such as family therapists and family life educators, cannot directly see a family's paradigms. They have to infer what they are from repetitious patterns of overt behavior.

> They are manifest, more typically, in a mixture of fleeting experiences of the family and in its enduring patterns of action—action within its own boundaries, and between the family and the outside world. (Reiss, 1981, p. 1)

The invisibility of family paradigms is described by Constantine (1986) in the following way:

> The image or images comprising a family paradigm are not themselves visible to us, and may not even be in the conscious awareness of family members. What we see are particular patterns of behavior that, by their redundancy, become recognizable as characteristic of a particular family's way of dealing with life. The paradigm is the template for the patterns we see, but it is not the process itself. (p. 16)

How Do Families Construct Paradigms?

Family scientists are just beginning to understand how families create, modify, and maintain their constructs. Reiss (1981) recognized how limited our insights have been.

> We have lacked useful conceptual tools to understand how an individual family can elaborate and maintain its own shared construction of reality. We have not understood how the specific history of the family's own development can shape its idiosyncratic shared visions, understandings, and assumptions about the world in which it lives. (p. 170)

Apparently there are at least two stages in the construction of paradigms. The first stage occurs during the courtship and formative stage of the family life cycle, and the second stage occurs when families experience serious crises.

The formative period. When a man and woman begin thinking about getting married, one of their developmental tasks is to decide, consciously or unconsciously, what their new family will be like. In most situations the two individuals grew up in families that had been through a formative period and had constructed basic paradigms before they were even born. As they grew up the paradigmatic assumptions of their parental families were assumed to be the "normal" way of viewing the world.

However, as they start to form their own family, they have a series of choices. How will they be like her parents' family, and how will they be different? How will they be like his parents' family, and how will they be different? Also, how will they be like other families they have known?

Couples usually go through an interesting stage, and it can last many months. It is where they can talk with each other endlessly about what they want their relationship and family life to be like.

Since most people have never even heard of such things as family paradigms, and they are largely unconscious and implicit assumptions anyway, there aren't many books or checklists to help a couple decide what their family paradigms ought to be. Most couples experience this process of gradually identifying their family paradigms as a form of intriguing and beautiful uniqueness. They come to believe that they are going through a process different from what other couples go through. They are able to "understand each other better" and "communicate" and "empathize" with each other in ways they believe are more deep and rich than most others achieve. It is usually a very private way of looking at their relationship that is much more meaningful to them than reading about marriage in books, participating in marriage courses, hearing sermons at church, or discussing it with friends at the club, sorority, or fraternity.

This sense of richness and depth that is almost universally experienced probably is partly because each couple goes through a process of constructing their unique set of meaningful and basic assumptions about what the world "really is" like for them. This process is a combination of consciously and unconsciously selecting some aspects from the family each person grew up in, other families that are respected, and developing some entirely new assumptions and beliefs (Steinglass et al., 1987, p. 308).

In this process, the first paradigms of a new family are borrowed and invented. As various aspects of the relationship are identified, talked about, tested, and revised, they come and go in consciousness. They remain conscious as long as there is uncertainty, ambiguity, and conflict, and when they are resolved they slip into the implicit, implied, unconscious part of the gradually growing family paradigm.

Few couples realize what they are doing as they create their family paradigm. As far as they are concerned, they're just enjoying talking about and experiencing some things and working out areas of disagreement or things they are vaguely uncomfortable about. They don't realize they are gradually creating a jointly constructed worldview that is a complex set of assumptions about the nature of their relationship, the way they will relate to their environment, and how they will view the world.

Changing established paradigms. David Reiss devoted a sizable part of his book to the ways family crises influence paradigmatic beliefs. In his words:

> The remainder of this book will be an attempt to sketch out relationships of this kind. We will focus on periods of crisis in family history as a conceptual cornerstone. We will argue that the fundamental process by which a family recovers from crisis is the collaborative construction of reality—first of the crisis itself, and then by a process of generalization which we will describe in some detail, of a broad range of social and physical reality. (Reiss, 1981, pp. 170–71)

Thus Reiss argues that when family life is relatively uncomplicated and "normal" there is little change in family paradigms. The paradigms provide a sense of meaning and order, and they are used as the guiding beliefs in selecting goals, making decisions, and managing resources.

When families have to cope with stressful situations, they first try to use their established beliefs and transformation processes. If these work, the stressful situations are resolved without having to reorganize the underlying beliefs about ways of doing things. If the "standard operating procedures" do not work, the typical pattern is for families to begin to question old ways of thinking and doing things and to construct new ways of defining the stressful situation and new strategies for trying to cope with the stress.

Apparently, the usual pattern is that the longer a family experiences difficulty in coping with a stressful situation, the more the basic constructs are called into question, eliminated, or revised; and new definitions and perceptions emerge. If the new constructs are effective in coping with the stress, the general and abstract parts of the new beliefs are assimilated into the family paradigm.

> *The central idea in the entire model is that a construct that successfully deals with such a grave crisis in the life of the family stands out as an extraordinary achievement to all members of the family.* Its dramatic success means that the family will attempt to apply at least some aspects of its construction of severe crisis to more ordinary problematic events of daily life. This idea is the essence of what we are borrowing from Kuhn's concepts. Like Kuhn, we are arguing that a group cleaves to a particular mode of explaining its world because the essential elements of that mode of explanation were dramatically successful attempts to deal with a severe crisis. (Reiss, 1981, p. 175; italics original)

Reiss is describing a fairly creative and healthy pattern of dealing with stressful situations. This is the aspect of family life where it is the "best of times" because it is the part where families are able to creatively cope with the challenges they encounter. Apparently this pattern is used by millions of families on a regular basis.

Unfortunately, there is also a "worst of times" aspect to these processes. Some families are rigidly attached to some of their constructs, and they do not have the flexibility, creativity, or other resources to develop new constructs that can help them cope with some stressful situations. In these situations the families remain in chronic difficulty until they can get outside help.

The Role of Paradigmatic Beliefs

Family paradigms have a key role in the managing processes. They serve as the basic, underlying, enduring, central, and shared beliefs or assumptions that a family uses as they select, invent, and modify goals; create, modify, exchange, and use resources; make decisions; and evaluate how well they are doing and what needs to be given attention. In David Reiss's words, the family paradigms are the part of the system:

> which shapes and controls both the form and content of these situation-specific, representational images. They emerge in the life of a family in two ways. First, they operate as framing assumptions, specifying—with great generality—certain fundamental properties of the perceptual world, properties which are given, are not subject to dispute, and cannot be either verified or disproved with experience, analysis, or discussion. These **framing assumptions** specify how the perceptual world is to be investigated, what conclusions are permissible from those investigations, and how such conclusions are used to shape a full range of family action, especially further explorations of the perceptual world. (1981, p. 174; emphasis in original)

Several analogies illustrate the role of family paradigms in the system. The paradigms are similar to the north star in a family's attempts to navigate. They're like the constitution in a family's attempts to govern itself. They're the ideal bedrock that the rest of the managing processes rest on. (The term *ideal* here is not used in the sense of being best or most preferred. It is used in the Platonic sense of being an idea, a constructed perception.)

When we think about the visible and obvious parts of managing, we think about processes that are always in a state of flux and change. In fact they can change frequently, sometimes on a daily or even hourly basis. These are the processes that create and modify goals; create, exchange, and use resources to try to attain these goals; make decisions; and monitor what is happening to see how it compares with desirable standards.

Family paradigms are a less visible part of the managing processes. They provide the less flexible, more enduring, and more invisible perspective, beliefs, and assumptions that make the daily and hourly managing have meaning, purpose, and a sense of direction.

Reiss described this role by saying that family paradigms are the "central organizer" that do the "shaping," "fashioning," and "guiding" of what families do when they regulate, order and transact with their environment (Reiss, 1981, p. 2).

Types of Family Paradigms

The concept of family paradigms is so new that scholars have not had time to do much theorizing and research about what kinds of beliefs families construct and use as their basic assumptions. A few scholars, however, have begun this process, and their ideas are helpful. Kantor and Lehr (1975) and Constantine (1986) developed a way of looking at family paradigms that has four different orientations: They called them *closed, open, random,* and *synchronous* families.

A **closed family paradigm** exists when a family has a cluster of fundamental beliefs that emphasize continuity, steadiness, and conventional ways of doing things. They believe that security and belonging are very important. They prefer stability whenever possible and are concerned about deviations from what they believe are the "right" ways to do things. The motto in closed families could be described as "stability through tradition and loyalty" (Constantine, 1986, p. 20).

When families have a closed paradigm it leads them to establish well-defined boundaries. The parents are concerned about their children's friends, and there are

> locked doors, careful scrutiny of strangers in the neighborhood, parental control over the media, supervised excursions. (Kantor & Lehr, 1975, p. 121)

Families with this paradigm tend to organize their time so it is predictable and stable. They pay attention to the past and to the future, frequently seeking to preserve or restore something, or achieve something that has not been accomplished. They tend to have a well-understood pattern of using time, and the individuals tend to fit their schedules to the family pattern.

The method of making decisions in closed families tends to be relatively authoritarian. Tradition or aspirations are important, and what the parents think is important. These two qualities tend to create a more power-oriented system than exists in open and random families.

When families have an **open family paradigm** they have a different set of abstract beliefs. They believe in a style of life that emphasizes dialogue, communication, patience, and a willingness to change. These families believe in adaptability and innovation and are looking for new ways to do things. They believe in negotiation and collaboration as the fundamental ways to live and cope. Space in open families is more flexible than in the closed type, and the individuals have more freedom in what they can do.

> Individuals are allowed to regulate the direction and destination of their incoming and outgoing traffic as long as they do not cause discomfort to other members or violate the consensus of the group. Numerous guests, frequent visits with friends, unlocked doors, open windows, individual or group explorations of the community and its resources, and a freedom of informational exchange with only rare censorship of the media are all open bounding features. In general, open bounding fosters the desire for beneficial interchange with members of the community, since guests are not only welcome but made to feel important for the contributions they make to the family. (Kantor & Lehr, 1975, p. 127)

The method of governance that is more consistent with this style of life is less authoritarian than the closed type. Therefore, there is usually more discussion, sharing of ideas, democracy, and flexibility. The approach tends to be to try to find consensus rather than to try to find what is "right" or proper.

When families have a **random family paradigm** their cluster of abstract beliefs emphasize discontinuity and they maximize change in a radical focus on the present. In the random paradigm, the guiding images are novelty, creativity, and individuality. The motto of a random paradigm family might be "Variety through Innovation and Individuality" (Constantine, 1986, p. 20). Random families are flexible with regard to traditions and established ways of doing things, but they tend to be fairly rigid in emphasizing individuality, little restraint, and high levels of freedom.

These abstract beliefs are used to manage family resources in ways that are quite different from closed and open families. The use of space has some predictability, but less than with closed or open families. For example, eating and sleeping may occur in many places. Expressions of anger, affection, and joy may occur in the street as well as behind the closed doors of the home.

The method of making decisions and governing tends to emphasize individuality. The family interests are considered, but what is important to the family is that the individuals are free to fulfill their needs and goals. Therefore, the individuals are encouraged to "do their own thing," make their own connections, set their own goals, and arrange their own schedules.

Time is irregular, and can be used and viewed very differently at different times and by different individuals or groups in the family. The preference is for unstatic, evolving, and spontaneous patterns that emerge from and out of what happens rather than because it is part of a plan or structure.

Patterns of getting energy are fluctuating and changing. Family members may engage in fueling operations singly or in groups, and they have great freedom to seek the type of fueling they want. Foods tend to be prepared more individually. Music and entertainment is more spontaneous and varied.

The cluster of ideas that are emphasized in a **synchronous family paradigm** emphasize harmony, tranquility, and mutual identification. When families

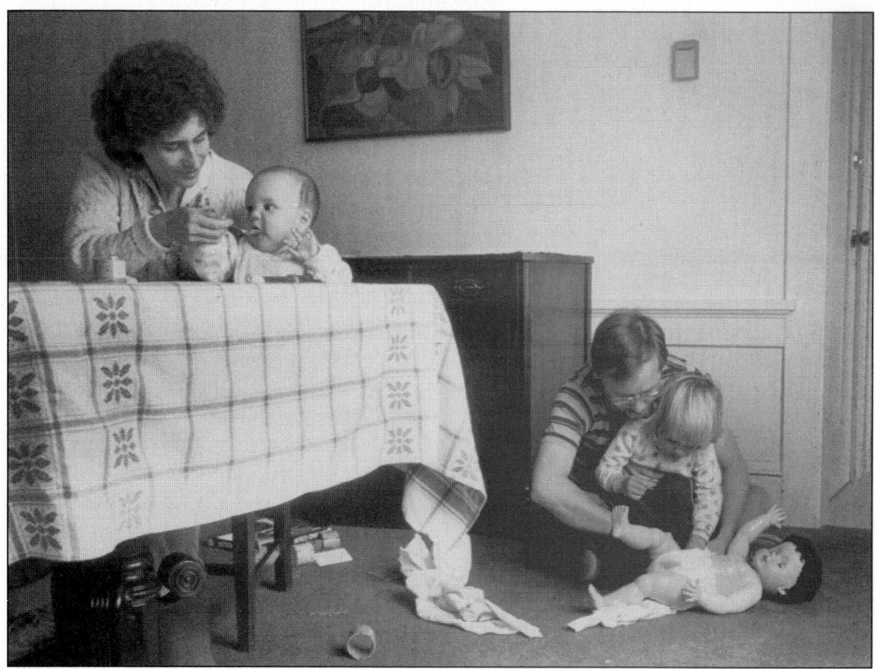

Family paradigms must be inferred; they can't be seen directly. What elements in the photo hint at the nature of this family paradigm?

have this paradigm they believe they will be able to move through life with little conflict and they will be able to easily resolve the conflict that does occur.

> The synchronous family depends on the extent to which its members "think alike" to avoid conflict and regulate its process. The synchronous regime may be said to be *coincidence-oriented*, depending on a coincidence of goals and world views among its members. To the extent to which such coincidence exists, there are no conflicts between the individual and the group; neither comes first. It is aptly described by certain little-used words: it is based on *consentience*, a nonintellectual sense of unity, functioning consentiently, that is, acting in harmonious agreement and unanimity of mind. . . . The synchronous paradigm in its various manifestations tends to have a distinctly utopian, mystical, or magical flavor; not surprisingly, families guided by it are not well understood. Though uncommon, synchronous families do exist and have been described by both clinicians and researchers, without their theoretical significance becoming recognized. The motto of synchrony might be "Harmony through Perfection and Identification." (Constantine, 1986, pp. 20–21)

The exaggeration principle. These four family paradigms are useful in a number of ways. For example, they helped Constantine develop a principle regarding some of the processes that lead to family disablement. The best name for this principle is the **exaggeration principle**, and Constantine's description of it is:

The basic principle behind the paradigmatic view of disablement is very simple, although its implications are myriad and complex. Confronted by problems, families do whatever they do best, each regime applying its own version of problem solving. When this doesn't work they try harder. "Trying harder" is itself defined paradigmatically: families try harder by doing more of the same. Thus, by using the resources of its regime and remaining true to its paradigm *each family under stress has a natural tendency toward exaggeration of its own special character.*

A family paradigm represents a commitment to certain priorities that incline a family in one direction or another as it seeks to overcome difficulties. For this reason, as families of different types become over-stressed, they are prone to basically distinct modes of failure. A family's methods of managing its resources consist of essentially stable structures maintaining coordinated family processes. The regime is resilient and not likely to change fundamentally in response to stress, especially as it is guided by the family's paradigm. Paradigms are regarded as even more invariant features of a family and are, therefore, quite unlikely to change under even severe stress.

The stability of paradigm can be appreciated if it is remembered that a family paradigm is the family's way of perceiving the world, including their problems, as well as their way of approaching and solving problems. Thus, the most likely response to any challenge from within or without is for a family to respond in a manner consistent with its paradigm and organization. The more difficult and intractable the situation, the more extreme are the measures that will be taken, extreme, that is, in a way consistent with the family paradigm. The longer an impasse is sustained, the greater the degree of exaggeration.

The closed family confronted by problems relies on tradition, authority, and loyalty to solve them. The more difficult the problem proves to be, the stronger are the attempts to control, to pull the family into line, and to maintain consistency against a threatening world. Thus closed families tend to become more isolated from the world, more strongly and intensely connected internally, and more rigid as they become increasingly disabled. The rallying cry is essentially "Fall in! Toe the line!"

The random family relies on spontaneity and creative individuality to find solutions to problems. As members work with increasing independence to find more creative solutions, family process becomes more chaotic, less coordinated. The random family tends toward greater separateness and chaos as it becomes more disabled. In the random family, the appeal is "Be more creative" or "Find something new" (which, it must be noted, does not imply a change of basic tactics; finding something new is what the random family does normally).

When initial attempts fail, the open family hangs in there, trying to hammer out a consensual solution. They gather more and more information and try harder to communicate. They become inundated with information and overwhelmed by hashing things through. As they question more and more of their basic rules, less and less is clearly known. They go around in circles. If problems remain insoluble they become more and more enmeshed in a process that generates chaos. Their rallying cry is "We've got to work this out. We'll talk it through again and consider it more thoroughly!"

The synchronous family relies on its essential agreement to enable it to solve problems in a coordinated way while acting independently. When this consentaneity breaks down, the family moves toward greater separateness. To remain coordinated and true to its paradigm, it narrows it scope and restricts its actions to those on which there is the closest agreement. Thus it becomes more rigid and stereotyped in its behavior while also becoming less connected. As synchronous families are based on similarity and do not deal as well with difference, which would contradict their

> synchrony, it becomes increasingly necessary to deny differences and problems, hiding these under a veneer of agreement and competence. As it becomes disabled, the synchronous family attempts to continue "business as usual" and insists, "There is no real problem. As always, we are really in agreement about this." Less and less happens as they become increasingly "dead" as a family or increasingly disconnected from their real problems. (Constantine, 1986, pp. 182–83; italics added to highlight the principle)

According to Constantine's ideas, most of the time when families become disabled it is not the family paradigms that are the root of the problem. The family paradigms are the abstract beliefs, and most families have defensible, coherent, and healthy basic assumptions. It is the less abstract processes, those that occur at Level I and Level II in the system, that become disabled. In other words, it tends to be the management that becomes disabled rather than the ideology that guides the system. It is families' strategies for clarifying goals, making effective decisions, and managing resources that become

> disabled or "dysfunctional," not the family paradigm. Although it is conceivable for a family to have a fundamentally defective and inadequate model of family and the world, the primary forms of paradigm are, in themselves, basically workable. (Constantine, 1986, p. 184)

Strategies for using the exaggeration principle. When families find themselves in trouble, they tend to seek help. Closed families are more cautious about who they turn to and how they do it, but closed, open, and random families all seek help in their own ways. They turn to books, friends, relatives, educators, therapists, ministers, Ann Landers, psychiatrists, or social workers.

The strategy for using the exaggeration principle to help families is to teach them how to "borrow" management strategies from another type. Constantine described this strategy in the following way:

> The most probable mode of failure for each management style is an exaggeration of its own paradigmatic commitments; to become less stereotyped, less tied up by its own guiding images, the family needs to reach outside the confines of its usual strategies. This does not mean a change of paradigms or an abandonment of basic values. The family is helped to "borrow" strategies from another style of managing, enhancing its basic flexibility without denying its paradigmatic commitment.
>
> Consider, for example, a random family chaotically disengaged, unable to resolve the crisis of a school-phobic child because everyone is too busy going off in every direction to hear the cry for help and too committed to radical independence even to consider her failure to attend school as possibly being a problem. They may need to borrow a strategy from either the closed or open paradigm to avoid escalating the situation into a more severe crisis. One person might be helped to take charge and act the part of a firm but caring parent with the child, listening to her fears and confidently supervising her going to school. This would represent one way an enabled closed type family might deal with the problem. Or the therapist might amplify the child's symptomatic statement to be dramatic enough to get all the members to sit down together and respond to the situation, drawing on an open type strategy.
>
> The above exemplifies a general principle for borrowing strategies from other types. As a rule, it is easier and more productive to borrow strategies from adjacent types. (Constantine, 1986, pp. 263–64)

For example, it is usually easier for a closed family to use open strategies than random strategies. And it is usually easier for random families to use open strategies than closed strategies.

VALUES

The term *values* is a central concept in family science (Nye, 1967) and in many other social sciences (Kluckhohn & Kluckhohn, 1951; Rokeach, 1969). It is a useful term, but it has so many different meanings that it has to be defined fairly carefully. For example, there is an important difference between value and *values*.

The term **value** refers to the relative worth, merit, or importance of an object or idea. For example, a car may have a value of $10,000, and a suit may have a value of $300. A family heirloom may have considerable value, and it may be difficult to put a dollar value on it. We may also value having a traffic light at a busy intersection because it helps traffic move efficiently. In each of these situations, however, the value is an appraisal of the worth of a specific object or idea. When we use the term *value* in this way, it is a modifier, an adjective.

The term *values* is different from appraising value because it is a noun rather than a modifier. **Values** are fundamental beliefs about abstract, general, and diffused ideas such as freedom, liberty, equality, beauty, and dignity. They are mental constructs that are partly intellectual but also involve emotions. They are basic beliefs that are the basis of attitudes, behavior, and choices (Rokeach, 1969). In Kluckhohn's words values are conceptions that are

> explicit or implicit, distinctive of an individual or characteristic of a group, of the desirable which influences the selection from available modes, means, and ends of action. (Kluckhohn & Kluckhohn, 1951, pp. 395–403)

Some values are created in families, and they are shared by the members of the family and are central parts of the family system. These familial values should be viewed as one aspect of family paradigms. The beliefs that form family paradigms have many functions, and one function is to help families define what is meaningful and valuable in life. David Reiss, for example, comments that family paradigms have the "capacity to provide explanations and meaning" (1981, p. 186). Watzlawick also observed that "meaning and value" are two key parts of the "reality" that framing constructs provide (1967, p. 96).

The familial values that are part of family paradigms are different from values that are part of a larger culture, because the larger culture's values may or may not be internalized in any particular family. Reiss and his colleagues have demonstrated that each family creates, invents, or constructs its particular paradigms, and they are unique to that family. Some of this construction process is very deliberate. In fact deliberateness has become an important concept in the later work of the Reiss group (Bennett et al., 1987). They have discovered that, when young couples are in the "forming stage" of their family system, they talk about how much they are going to have their family "identity" be the same as his family's, her family's, or some other family's. Each couple, in these picking, choosing, and constructing processes, literally creates their own family identity and paradigms. The values that are created in this process are very different from the values that are enduring parts of cultures.

Another aspect of values is that there can be differences between an individual's values and a family's values. Familial values are those that are shared and maintained by the individuals in a family and are central parts of the family system. It is these values that are part of family paradigms because they guide the Level I systemic transformation processes and the management processes in families.

Religious Ideas

Family scientists have not given attention to religious ideas as part of family paradigms, but it is likely that some religious ideas have a paradigmatic quality (Level III). Most of the scholarly study of religion has been to merely study differences in denominational affiliation and beliefs, and to see how various aspects of religion are correlated to such things as marital satisfaction, divorce, and other family behaviors. It is likely, however, that as the field matures more attention will be given to the role of religious ideas in the framing assumptions families have about reality and how to relate to their environment.

Many families have religiously based ideas that are paradigmatic. **Religious family paradigms** deal with such things as what people believe is sacred and not sacred, whether there is a life after death, how people ought to live, and the influence of spiritual forces on daily life. Some of these beliefs are paradigmatic in the sense that they influence the less abstract processes in family systems. They influence the goals and standards of families, their rules of transformation, and the way they use many of their resources.

Many families do not have religiously based family paradigms. As the American culture becomes increasingly secularized, it is likely that the number of families who have religiously based family paradigms is becoming smaller and smaller. We must pay attention to these paradigmatic differences and changes because they help us understand the roots of some of the more serious conflicts that occur in families, as well as some of the reasons for consensus and harmony in families.

Practical Implications

The idea that some parts of family ideologies are more abstract, central and fundamental than other parts of ideologies provides a number of useful insights. For example, it helps us realize there is great flexibility in the way families can organize themselves and be successful. Many family scholars have fallen into the trap of believing that families need to conform to one particular mold or style of life if they are to be successful, but there can be successful open families, successful closed families, successful random families, and successful synchronous families.

There can also be failure in any of these kinds of families. If any families get stuck in ways of doing things that are too narrow and restricted, their way of behaving can interfere with their ability to cope with new developmental, cultural, or technological changes.

This suggests that Leo Tolstoy's widely quoted comment that "Happy families are all alike; every unhappy family is unhappy in its own way" (1878) is more of a romantic and poetic comment than an accurate statement. More accurately, happy and unhappy families are all happy and unhappy in their own way. This isn't as dramatic as Tolstoy's sweeping comment, but it is more accurate, and it is an insight all family scholars and everyone who works with families should remember.

Constantine described some of the dangers of thinking there is one "best" style of family life:

> Families differ most dramatically in the setting of their priorities concerning certain fundamental human issues and in how they decide between competing goals. There are, in these choices, many ways in which families may fail, but there is also more than one way to succeed. For some families. . . . the past looms large, and the means by which they meet the demands of daily life and cope with change are tried and true, a basically unchanging repertoire of well-established approaches. For others . . . experimentation and exploration constitute a way of life. Any research that sums into one single column findings from such different families can mask important information about how families work. Similarly, therapy that recognizes only a single ideal for family living may try to push families into becoming what they are not, rather than becoming better at what they are. (Constantine, 1986, p. 15)

Another practical insight these ideas provide is that families who are extremely and exclusively open, random, or synchronous, tend to get along well (attain their goals) most of the time. They seem to get into trouble only when unusual events occur.

This also suggests that when families get into trouble, they usually do not need extensive therapy to get their life back in a workable and effective condition. They need to slightly broaden their repertoire of ways to respond to meet a particular situation, and sometimes this can be accomplished as easily as talking to a friend or reading a book.

Another practical implication of these ideas is that they help us understand why families do not change their basic way of life quickly, often, or easily. Sometimes when we try to help families we wish they would change easily and quickly. We naively want our therapy, advice, or educational programs to make big differences in families. However, when we realize how earlier generations are involved in family paradigms, how slowly and gradually they are initially formed in courtship and early marriage, how they are intricately tied up with deeply experienced feelings, and how they are probably changed only by severe crises, it helps us realize that these basic assumptions cannot change easily. They are the most fundamental rudders in the ship of life and, once they are formed, they change slowly and only under very unusual circumstances.

When we know the nature of family paradigms and the role they have in family life, we can better understand what families are going through when they are experiencing enough stress that they are changing their paradigms. Also, we can adapt our attempts to help them so we focus on the parts of their systems that can change.

Summary

This chapter described the three levels of abstraction that family scientists pay attention to in family systems. The three levels are called Level I, Level II, and Level III. Part of the Level III processes are what David Reiss has called family paradigms. Family paradigms are the fundamental, general, abstract, and guiding beliefs families construct about their world. These concepts help us better understand how family systems work and how we can help families.

Key Terms

Ideology
Abstraction
Level I (first-order)
Level II (second-order)
Level III
Constructivism
Family paradigms
Types of family paradigms: Open, Closed, Random, Synchronous, Religious, Nonreligious
Exaggeration principle
Values
Value

Study Questions

1. Give examples of each of the three levels explained in this chapter.
2. How is Level II different from Level III?
3. Suppose a family is an "open" family and in a time of stress the "exaggeration principle" happens to them. What could you expect it to be like?
4. Describe what we mean by the "constructivist" point of view.
5. Define epistemology.
6. What is the difference between phenomena and noumena?
7. How does a family go about the process of choosing a family paradigm?

Notes

1. A large number of scholars have made important contributions to constructivist thinking in family science. The work of Paul Watzlawick and his colleagues (1967; 1976; 1984) and the work of David Reiss (1981) have been the most creative and seminal. Developments in this area have continued since Reiss's book. For example, Sluzki's (1983) article integrates the constructivist's developments with the other branches of the family systems literature. Cronen, Johnson & Namann (1982), Speed (1984), Steinglass et al. (1987), Bennett et al. (1987), and others have also added important insights.

7

Family Development

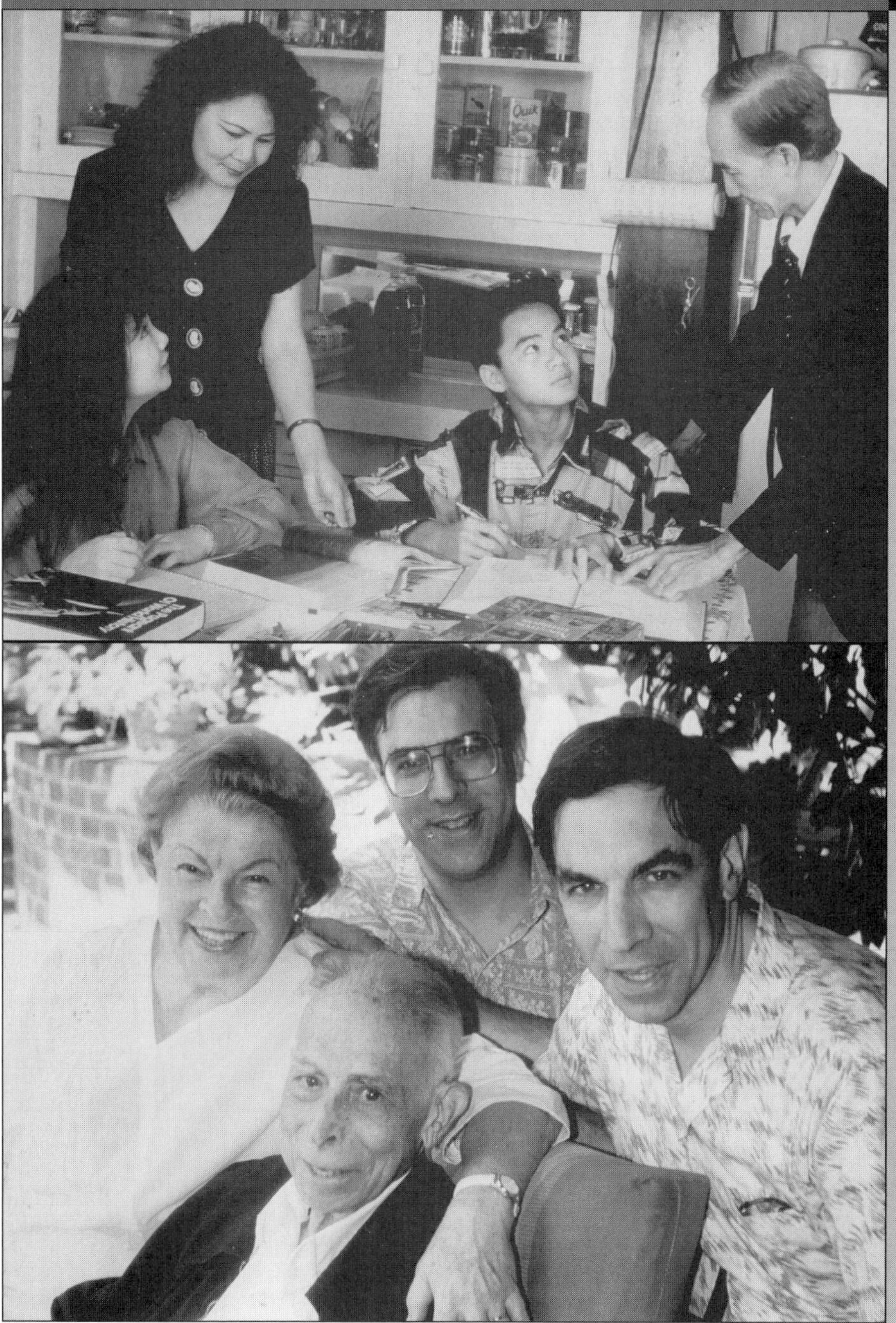

Main Ideas

1 // Family development is the process of family systems changing as a result of (a) events that help unfold the expected family life course, or (b) other events that trigger unpredictable developmental processes.

2 // Some events, such as births or weddings, trigger long-term and complex developmental processes. Other events, like illnesses or relatives moving in, create short-term and simple developmental processes.

3 // Divorce and remarriage are not developmental changes. Some of these nondevelopmental changes also create new developmental processes.

4 // Some elements of family development are predictable, but they can have great variability.

5 // The epigenesis principle states that what is done in the earlier stages of the family life cycle influences what can be done and what tends to be done in later stages.

6 // The concept of developmental tasks has to do with tasks that occur at certain developmental stages and must be successfully completed to assure the family's continuing health at later stages.

7 // Three ideas can help families accomplish developmental transitions. They are: anticipatory socialization (prior learning), managing role strain, and having clear transition procedures.

8 // Morphogenesis is change in the form or structure of family systems. The morphogenesis principle is that family systems are always changing. Families desire some morphogenesis, but they also try to avoid some of it.

9 // Morphostasis (sometimes called homeostasis) is the tendency in family systems to resist morphogenesis.

The term *development* is used in a number of disciplines, and its meaning differs slightly from field to field. In the field of music it refers to the process of unfolding the inherent possibilities of a theme. In mathematics it refers to the process of expressing a mathematical idea in a more extended form. In biology it has two different meanings. One meaning is the process of an organism's changing from an early to a more advanced stage in its life cycle. The second meaning refers to organisms' moving through the process of natural selection as a part of evolutionary change. In developmental psychology the term refers to the process of individuals becoming more differentiated and more complex in their physical, mental, and personality characteristics.

"You can never step in the same river twice."

—HERACLITUS

WHAT IS FAMILY DEVELOPMENT?

The concept of **family development** is an important part of family science. It is defined as the process of family systems changing as a result of (1) events that help unfold the fairly predictable and typical processes that make up the expected family life course, or (2) other events that trigger unpredictable developmental processes.

There are several aspects of this definition that need to be explained in more detail. First, the most important part of the definition is the word *change.* This is because development refers to processes that alter, convert, or modify what is happening in family systems. Development always involves transformations, evolution, instability, or an unfolding of developmental potentials.

A second important part of development is that it is a process rather than an event. Events create or trigger development, but the development occurs gradually over a period of time. Thus the developmental part of family science takes time into account, and it always involves a series of things or a sequence.

A third aspect of family development is that it includes some big changes in families, as well as some small ones. Big changes are major events such as births, marriages, and deaths. These changes have long-term and complex implications. They create major alterations in families because they begin new families, end families, and alter the life cycles of families.

There also are many aspects of family development that represent minor changes in the structure of family systems. For example, when children start going to school it creates minor adjustments that are part of family development. When a new sibling is born into a family, this event creates a series of minor developmental changes as the various family members adjust to and accommodate the new member. When the new sibling becomes a toddler, the family needs to "baby proof" the house by moving their fragile things out of reach. When a relative or friend comes to live with a family, it creates a different set of short-term developmental processes as the new member is assimilated into the family. When a family member starts to get senile, breaks a leg, or develops a serious illness, each of these events creates its own unique series of developmental processes.

Internal and External Events

There are many different events that trigger (create or initiate) future developmental processes in family systems. Some of these events occur inside the family system. For example, the birth of the first child is an event that occurs inside families, and it begins a complex series of predictable changes. It means that some adults need to take the responsibility to care, nurture, love, tend, teach, and be responsible for the child while it is an infant. It also begins a series of changes in the individual who is born, and they have an enormous impact on the family system. For example, when the child reaches teenage, it has an impact on everything from the noise level in the home to the budget for food, entertainment, and cars.

Many events that initiate developmental processes are inputs that come into a family system from the environment. For example, if a father or mother were to contract a serious illness such as cancer due to working around hazardous materials, this would be an external event that would trigger some developmental processes in the home. There is a developmental pattern to the illness itself, and the members of the family need to adapt their schedules and responsibilities (their family system) in predictable ways to care for the person who is ill. Retirement is another example of an input that comes from outside of a family system, and it creates a different set of developmental processes.

Contrasting Individual Development

The study of family development is different from human development. **Human development** refers to the systematic changes in individuals that occur between their conception and death (Shaffer, 1989, p. 6).[1]

The study of human development focuses on patterned changes that occur because of maturation and learning, and it also focuses on the cognitive, social, physical, and emotional development of individuals. It helps us understand that children and adults go through stages in their development. For example, most children go through a stage of negativism when they are about 2 years old. They say no frequently when they are asked to do something, and they are so negative that many parents, during this stage of their child's development, think that the child will never say yes. "No" doesn't mean the same thing to a 2-year-old as it means to an adult, because these toddlers say it about things they like to do, and often they say no about something and are still willing to do it. The negativism is a stage that is part of their cognitive and social development.

Later, when children are about 8 years old, they go through a moralistic stage where they are concerned with things being done according to the rules. If their parent is driving three miles over the speed limit, they're likely to point it out. During this stage, children pay a lot of attention to following the "right" rules of games and activities.

Family development is different in that it refers to the systematic or patterned changes that occur in family systems, rather than changes in individuals. Many processes illustrate how family development is different from individual development. For example, new families begin with a formative period. In some cultures this first stage begins with courtship. In other cultures it begins when the parents negotiate a marriage, and in other cultures it starts when couples begin to live together. During the formative stage, a family system becomes more complex, more differentiated, and increasingly competent. This initial stage is a creative period because many new family rules or "understandings" are constructed. Systems theorists call this the process of getting the *requisite variety* (required variety) of rules in the system. Also during the formative stage many routines, traditions, rituals, and family themes are created.

As families move into later stages of their development they pay less attention to creating family rules because they have the requisite variety they need to cope with most of the inputs they encounter. Emphasis in the system turns to other things such as providing economic necessities, rearing children, participating in

---

"The individual life cycle takes place within the family life cycle, which is the primary context of human development. We think this perspective is crucial to understanding the emotional problems that people develop as they move together through life."

—Carter & McGoldrick, 1989

The formative stage of family development begins before marriage, when a couple starts to create rules, traditions, and ways of relating to each other.

the community, and coping with developmental tasks. These changes transform and help unfold the family life course so they are a part of family development.

Kinds of Change

The changes that are created by development sometimes mean that people and families become more complex, more differentiated, and more able to cope with their life situation. This is especially the case when families are in the formative stage of the family life cycle. For example, when children start to arrive in a family, the system becomes much more complex and differentiated and a number of other predictable changes occur.

All developmental changes, however, do not lead to greater ability and complexity, and they are not all desirable. There are natural cycles for every living

"Families characteristically lack time perspective when they are having problems. They tend generally to magnify the present moment, overwhelmed and immobilized by their immediate feelings; or they become fixed on a moment in the future that they dread or long for. They lose the awareness that life means continual motion from the past and into the future with a continual transformation of familial relationships." —Carter & McGoldrick, 1989 thing, and these lifespans all have ends as well as beginnings. When an older person's body starts wearing out, this too is part of development. For example, most athletic skills "peak out" when the athletes are in their late twenties or, for the more durable ones, their early thirties. After that the legs, coordination, and endurance are just not the same. Athletes are not very thrilled about being "over the hill" when they are age 29, but it is a part of the natural development of the human body.

There are also undesirable aspects to family development. For example, every family system is eventually decreased in size by the death of family members. When death occurs it leads to painful changes in bonds, feelings of love, and closeness. Another difficult time for most families is when the needs of teenagers conflict with the needs of their middle-aged parents.

Many of the processes in family development have a bittersweet quality to them. Weddings, for example, are a time of joy but also a time of tears. The launching of children is a time of excitement and also loss. The coming of children is rewarding but also limiting and constraining. The natural movement away from the excitement and euphoria of new love during the early months of marriage is both a loss and a relief to most couples.

Many different types of change occur in development. For example, the cycles of life in human development include mental, physical, and emotional changes. People increase in their mental ability as they move from infancy to adulthood. Later, as they approach old age, their memory and other mental processes start to slip. Newborn infants do not see well, but their eyesight improves rapidly during the first month of life. Later, in their mid-forties, they'll need bifocals. Trifocals may come later, and for some, a magnifying glass as the years advance. Young people are fairly adaptable, but older people usually don't have the same level of adaptability, and all these changes are parts of normal development.

Family development also involves many different types of change. It involves changes in size, sex composition, complexity of interrelationships, expectations, help patterns, and the patterns of emotional distance and closeness. The generational alignments evolve in several predictable ways, and the ways the family system copes with the environment changes.

Changes That Are Not Developmental

Many changes that occur in family systems are not a part of family development. The difference is that developmental changes are part of the predictable and typical sequences that occur naturally, but nondevelopmental changes are unexpected and not part of the expected life course.

Having a family member who becomes handicapped is an example of a nondevelopmental change; it isn't a natural or expected part of the family life cycle. It is an event that creates unusual and unexpected changes in the family systems. A second example of a nondevelopmental change is when someone such as a relative, friend, or foster child becomes a new member of a family. This type of change is not a part of the typical unfolding of developmental processes in family systems.

Nondevelopmental changes are not a part of family development, but once they happen they often initiate or create a series of developmental processes as they set in motion a series of predictable changes. Some of the usual developmental changes it precipitates include discussions about the family rules and renegotiation of some of the rules. It also leads to realignments of the affection and authority patterns and adjustments in the household tasks and responsibilities.

Divorce is another example of a nondevelopmental change that creates its own set of subsequent family development. Divorce creates great changes in family systems, but it is not a part of the sequence of events that unfolds as a result of movement through the family life cycle. Divorce has become so common in the American culture "that about half of America's families will experience the disorganizing unscheduled transitions brought about by marital separation" (Ahrons & Rogers, 1987, p. vii). Thus divorce is fairly typical and it is a normal part of family life, but it is "unscheduled." It isn't a part of a developmental stage or transition. In fact most families try to avoid it, and they only resort to it as a last resort. However, when it does occur, it sets in motion a series of complex developmental processes in a family system. These developmental processes include coping with grief and loss, designing new ways of relating, and trying to cope with the loss of companionship that has become such a common part of each person's life. The developmental processes that are created by divorce are discussed in detail in Chapter 18.

Remarriage is another example of a nondevelopmental change. Remarriage occurs after a marriage has been terminated by death or divorce, but it isn't a part of the unfolding of the developmental pattern in family systems. It does, however, create a new series of developmental processes in family systems. It sets in motion developmental patterns of renegotiating family rituals and rules. It poses developmental tasks of creating new authority patterns, new loyalties, new patterns of affection, and new bonds and other connections. One of the unique developmental aspects of stepfamilies is that they need instantly to become an operational and complex family system, and this is very difficult. They do not have the luxury first marriages have of taking a long period of time to go through the process of creating unity and consensus in the marital relationship before they need to deal with children. They also need to deal with intense emotions about loss and grief and resentment, and these developmental challenges are different than the challenges faced by first marriages. The opportunities and challenges of stepfamilies are discussed in more detail in Chapter 19.

PREDICTABILITY AND VARIABILITY

When family scientists began to study family development in the 1950s (Duvall, 1955), they assumed most families moved through a very predictable series of stages. They developed the term **family life cycle** to describe this predictable pattern. One version of this cycle that has been widely used in recent years is the one suggested by Carter and McGoldrick (1989, p. 15). It has the following stages:

Stage 1 Leaving home: Single young adults.
Stage 2 The joining of families through marriage: The new couple.
Stage 3 Families with young children.
Stage 4 Families with adolescents.
Stage 5 Launching children and moving on.
Stage 6 Families in later life.

Gradually, however, family scientists discovered most families do not proceed in an orderly way through this series of stages. In fact, it is only a small minority of families who experience this cycle without any interruptions or without an unusual arrangement of the stages. This is because most families encounter nondevelopmental events that influence their life course.

When family scientists realized there was considerable unpredictability in family development, they began using the term **life course** rather than life cycle. The idea of a life course implies that development is like traveling along a highway that has many intersections, as shown with Figure 7.1. Each intersection is a transition where one route is taken and other routes are not taken, and each transition alters the life course. The following events illustrate the range of things that influence the sequence of events in a family life course.

- About 50% of American couples end their first marriage in divorce.
- About 20% of American people have more than one divorce.
- About 15% of couples do not have children.
- In how many families does one spouse die before reaching the typical age for retirement?
- How many children die before they reach the launching stage?
- How many children leave home or need alternative living arrangements before the usual launching age?
- After a spouse's death or a divorce, how many remain single?
- How many experience a remarriage?
- When there are blended families, how does it change the usual cycle?
- How many adult children return to live with their parents after they experience a divorce, or their spouse dies? (This is sometimes called the "boomerang" stage of family development.)
- How many children remain single, but do not leave home when they reach 18, 21, 30, or 50?
- How many families have several children almost reared, and then have one or two additional children that are almost a separate family?
- What about single people? (There are several ways in which they also are families. They are children, so they have parents and grandparents. Usually they also have brothers and sisters, and frequently they have nieces and nephews. They also often have aunts, uncles, and cousins, and some of them have children.) What are the cycles in their family life?

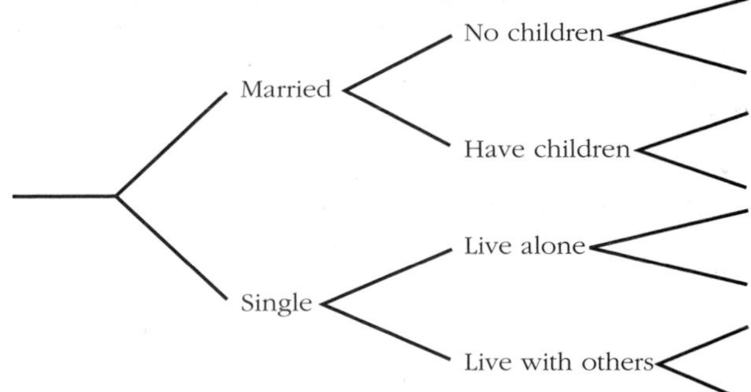

FIGURE 7.1 Possible life course transitions

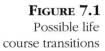

These questions lead to several important insights about family development. First they demonstrate there is great variability in the life cycles of families and individuals. Just as there are so many different types of families that we cannot talk about "the" American family or "the" English family or "the" Russian family, there are so many variations in family development that we cannot talk about "the" life cycle of individuals or of families.

A second idea is that, even though there are great variations in the cycles of family life, there also are some aspects of these cycles that are fairly predictable. Courtship usually precedes weddings, and births (or adoptions) usually precede childrearing. One's own aging tends to come late in the cycle of family life, but coping with the aging of parents and grandparents comes earlier. Mid-life crises don't usually happen to people in their twenties or in their eighties; they tend to come when people are in their forties and fifties. There are quite a number of rhythms and patterns in the ebb and flow of family life. The more we are aware of these patterns, the more we can help families prepare for and cope with their developmental experiences. Some of these rhythms are poetically captured in the lyrics of a song from the play *Fiddler on the Roof.*

Sunrise, Sunset

Is this the little girl I carried?
Is this the little boy at play?
I don't remember growing older, when did they?
When did she get to be a beauty?
When did he get to be so tall?
Wasn't it yesterday when they were small?
Sunrise, sunset. Sunrise, sunset.
Swiftly flow the days.
Seedlings turn overnight to sunflowers.
Blossoming even as we gaze.

Sunrise, sunset. Sunrise, sunset.
Swiftly fly the years.
One season following another,
Laden with happiness and tears.
Now is the little boy a groom.
Now is the little girl a bride.
Under the canopy I see them, side by side.
Place the gold ring around her finger.
Share the sweet wine & break the glass.
Soon the full circle will have come to pass.
(Repeat chorus)

EPIGENESIS

There is another general principle that helps us understand how developmental processes influence families. Lyman Wynne is the scholar who has developed this principle, and he called it the **epigenesis principle** (1984). This is a fairly effective name because the word *epigenesis* means after the beginning. The principle is:

Principle

What is done in earlier transitions and stages tends to influence what can be and tends to be done in later transitions and stages.[2]

This principle has three main ideas in it. One idea is that what is done during earlier stages of a life cycle sometimes limits future opportunities, and it can make

To everything there is a season:
A time to be born, and a time to die;
A time to weep and a time to laugh;
A time to mourn, and a time to dance;
A time to embrace and
A time to refrain from embracing;
A time to get and a time to lose.

—ECCLESIASTES 3:1–8

The Baird Family

The epigenesis principle was evident in our family even when I was very young. I had to play the role of mom. My mother was gone a lot and I really goofed things up. The only way I knew to keep control was to be violent. That violence has had a lasting impact on my brothers and sisters. I have never been able to develop really good, close relationships with any of them, although things are much better now than they were.

later challenges more difficult. A second idea is that what is done during earlier stages of a life cycle also can expand future opportunities, and this can make later challenges easier to cope with. The third idea is that what is done during earlier stages of a life cycle tends to create habits or tendencies in family systems and in individuals' behavior, and these tendencies are continued later even though the families or individuals have the capacity to do things differently. In other words, such things as rituals, patterns, traditions, routines, themes, and mannerisms tend to be continued once they are established.

There are also many situations that illustrate this principle. We know that what couples do in the formative stages of their family life cycle can influence their options later. For example, assume a couple is beginning to get serious and they develop a pattern of talking openly and honestly about their feelings. In the process of developing this pattern, they create a complex set of rules (understandings) about how they are going to act in their relationship (their system). Despite their pattern of discussion, many of these rules are established without their ever talking about them. They may develop rules such as agreeing to take the time to listen to each other when they are feeling strong emotions. They'll be understanding, and they'll avoid being demeaning or critical. They also will probably come to an understanding about how hard they ought to try, and what kinds of things, such as fatigue, can interfere without being a problem. In this example, we have only identified a half dozen of the understandings a couple could develop, but it would be possible to identify hundreds of these subtle rules

The Allred Family

Early in our family life my parents made the decision that religion would always be very important in their lives, and they taught this to us as children. Mary, Martha, and I have all gone through rebellious stages and caused some great strains in our family, but we've all stayed with our religious teachings. It has been a type of cornerstone or foundation in our lives.

about how a couple communicates about feelings. (Chapter 8, on Family Rules, covers this in more detail.)

The rules that are developed in the early stages of a relationship become the framework that is used to develop more elaborate understandings. They also influence what can be done in the future. If a couple creates a pattern of being candid about their feelings, their system will then demand certain behaviors of them, and they will get certain benefits from their system. These may include a certain degree of understanding, sense of belonging, closeness, and bondedness. In systems terminology, we call anything we put into the system an **input**, and the things we get out of a system—that the system produces—are called **outputs**.

A different couple may choose to create a different set of rules. For example, they may develop a set of understandings that they ought to have considerable independence and autonomy, and this may prompt them to ignore the emotional intricacies of each other's lives most of the time. This couple's system would have very different inputs and outputs. They would get more freedom to make their own choices, and they wouldn't need to take the time to deal with emotional complexities. They may have a great deal of love for each other, and have a very satisfying marriage, but it would be a very different one from that of the first couple.

The main point of these examples is that the rules created in the formative stages of a relationship influence what the couple can and cannot do and what they will tend to do in the later stages of their life. Anyone who thinks couples can go back and restructure the basic aspects of their relationship just does not understand the nature of family systems. A few parts of relationships can be changed later, but a large number of things cannot, and it usually takes a great deal of energy and effort to make even small changes.

There are many reasons for this. One reason is that the first understandings become the basis for very complex webs of interconnected bonds, beliefs, emotions, ties, aspirations, desires, hopes, expectations, experiences, memories, traditions, and rituals. Whenever there is an attempt to change part of this network there are implications for many other parts. Even little changes cause reverberations through the whole system and can become complicated.

A second reason what is done early in the system becomes so rigid is because most of what is done in family life is, using the iceberg analogy again, under the

The Connelly Family

After going over and over this principle I couldn't think of an example, so I went to my parents. My dad said, "Well, if you don't discipline kids when they're young, you won't be able to get them to do what they need to later." I realized that this is true. If they had not kept us in line when we were younger by disciplining and teaching us what was right and what was wrong we would have been much harder to deal with.

surface. The people who are experiencing the processes are generally not even aware of what is happening. Those outside the family are even less likely to know. When parts of our lives are managed unconsciously, it is very difficult to identify what is happening and make decisions about it. One result of this is that most families develop a "Don't rock the boat" or "If it ain't broke, don't fix it" attitude.

A third reason what is done early in family life becomes so rigid is because so much of it is a part of the basic, deeply experienced, fundamental affective (emotional) states. These affective states make a great deal of difference. They include desires for territory, belonging, leaders, a sense of meaning and purpose, maintaining the species by reproducing ourselves, sexual arousal, and being connected to each other in ways that are at least minimally secure. Most of these emotional processes are so deeply experienced that we are not very conscious of them. We don't have vocabularies to describe them well, and by and large they are imperceptible. This means that we don't have good enough access to these affective experiences to know how to deal with them, yet they are so powerful that they exert tremendous effect on our lives. When people establish the rules they are going to have in their family, they are dealing with many of the most fundamental emotional aspects that we humans experience, and when they get their system established, they find it deeply disruptive emotionally to go back and renegotiate or change fundamental parts of it.

The intensity of the affective aspects of these processes can be appreciated if we think about all of the elaborate human rituals, songs, dances, tokens, celebrations, covenants, and legal apparatus that are connected to the resolution of these affectively motivated experiences. An analogy is sometimes helpful in understanding the way this principle operates. Let's compare the malleability and rigidity of family processes with those of concrete. Concrete is initially a very malleable liquid that can be shaped into almost any form. When it sets up, however, it loses its flexibility and becomes rigid. Other things can then be built upon it, and people don't have to worry about the concrete changing its shape. But if they want to go back and change the shape, it takes jackhammers and explosives, and is very disruptive to the structures that are built on it. Also, all the explosives and jackhammers can do is destroy the concrete that was there. They cannot reshape it. It has to be replaced the same way it was before, with new liquid that will later become rigid.

Most of the discussion of this principle has focused on how it applies to the family system, but it also applies to developmental processes in individuals. What a person does in response to developmental changes and processes has important implications for what that person will tend to do later in life.

There are many examples of this process in individuals. If students do not apply themselves academically, they gradually eliminate future opportunities that demand educational excellence. If a person becomes proficient with a musical instrument, that person has choices that a person without the proficiency does not have. When people learn early in life how to express themselves orally and in writing, these skills open up many avenues that would otherwise be closed to them. When people learn social skills, or fail to develop social skills, these characteristics influence what they can and cannot do for the rest of their lives.

There is considerable research that indicates this principle is true. For example, Mirkin (1984) and her colleagues demonstrated that it is true with regard to teenage runaways, and Coleman et al. (1986) found it is a valid and helpful idea in understanding patterns of substance abuse.

The epigenesis principle is useful, but there are many aspects of it we do not yet understand, and more research needs to be done. For example, some of the rules that are created early in relationships seem to change easily at later times, while others are very resistant to change. We don't yet know very much about which operate which way and why. These are some of the unknowns that future analysis, theorizing, and research can help to answer.

Developmental Tasks

A group of family scientists and human development specialists at the University of Chicago developed a concept in the early 1940s that is helpful in understanding and using this principle. It is called **developmental tasks**.

> A developmental task is a task which arises at or about a certain period in the life of an individual, successful achievement of which leads to his happiness and to success with later tasks, while failure leads to unhappiness in the individual, disapproval by the society, and difficulty with later tasks. (Havinghurst, 1953, p. 2)

The term *task* is helpful because it implies that something needs to be done in response to a developmental situation. It does, however, have some limitations and disadvantages. It connotes a feeling that we "have to" do them rather than we "get to" do them, and this is not accurate in many situations. Some developmental tasks are onerous, but some are delightful and desirable opportunities.

For example, how many teens of age 16 view learning how to drive as a task to be avoided? How many young lovers view the processes of learning how to share and communicate intimately, grow together, and become a pair as work? More accurate terms for some of these would be rights, opportunities, adventures, and privileges that people are relieved and excited to be able to do. We therefore need to view the term *task* in a broad and flexible way, and not pay much attention to some of its connotations about difficulty.

Even though the concept of tasks has limitations, it is valuable. It describes a wide range of responses that need to be made to developmental changes. It also describes a part of developmental thinking that can be understood by the general public. Terms such as *epigenesis principle* are helpful, but confusing for those who are not professionals in family science.

It is not very useful to make long lists of developmental tasks, because they differ so much among subcultural groups, families, and individuals. However, Lewis (1986) has identified three developmental tasks that young couples face when they are beginning a relationship, and these three illustrate how we use the concept of developmental tasks. Young couples need to work out how much commitment they want in the relationship, how they are going to make decisions, and how much separateness and attachment they will have. According to Lewis, every couple entering a fairly permanent relationship must negotiate how this relationship fits into connections they make with all other humans. Commitment involves a shift of each spouse's primary commitment away from his or her family of origin to the new marital relationship.

The second developmental challenge, according to Lewis, is the allocation of power. "Who decides what?" and "How are conflicts resolved?" are critical questions each must answer. The third task of the early stage of a relationship is establishing the balance of separateness and attachment (Lewis, 1986, p. 236).

From a family science perspective, the main goal with developmental tasks is for families to work them out in a way that is affectively satisfactory. An intellectual satisfaction that they are worked out may be adequate in public-realm organizations, but it could be disruptive in the family realm. If tasks are not worked out at an affective level, many of them lead to resentments that create problems. When this happens in the family realm the situations need to be dealt with again and again. Like ghosts, they come back to haunt families. Unfortunately, the haunting usually occurs when the family is trying to cope with a stressful situation.

Many developmental tasks are never resolved in a final way. As later morphogenesis occurs, families find it necessary to adjust the solutions, understandings, or rules they have worked out in many areas. For example, when the first child is born and the last child leaves home, couples usually need to readjust the separateness and attachment in their marital relationship.

These three developmental tasks also illustrate some of the ways developmental processes can influence later stages of family life. Research as early as the 1930s found that when couples are able to resolve their decision-making system so it is satisfactory affectively, it influences their ability to cope with later events. In Komarovsky's (1940) study of how families responded to the Depression in the 1930s, she found that couples who had resolved their decision-making system satisfactorily coped with the Depression much better than those who had not resolved it.

TRANSITIONS

The concept of transitions was created when scholars realized that living systems usually do not have a constant rate of change. They tend to have periods of rapid change followed by periods of relative stability. In developmental terms, the periods of rapid or dramatic change are called **transitions** and the periods of stability are called **stages**.

The concept of transitions is important because new developmental tasks usually tend to appear during transitions rather than during stages. Many family transitions are fairly predictable and normal, and they can be anticipated when we think developmentally. Some of them, however, are part of the unpredictable and variable parts of family development. Some examples of transitions that

influence family systems are engagement, starting to live together, the wedding, the birth of the first child, children starting to go to school, children moving into adolescence, children leaving home, death of a parent, retirement, death of a spouse, and one's own death.

Not all transitions in family systems are brought about by developmental processes. Some of them are, but some of them are created by other factors. For example, becoming unemployed or employed, the onset of a serious and chronic disease such as cancer or a heart ailment, the recovery from a serious illness, sudden fame or fortune, and sudden defamation or misfortune can create important transitions in family systems, but they should not be thought of as a developmental process. These nondevelopmentally created transitions are discussed in several of the later chapters, especially Chapter 15 on Stress.

Developmental transitions can be brought about by many factors. They can be created by biological factors such as puberty, menopause, and senility. They can be created by experiences. For example, the process of experiencing pregnancy and birth creates many changes in the perspectives, insights, sensitivities, and concerns of the parents, and these experiential factors create part of the changes that occur in family transitions.

Some developmental changes are created by combinations of factors. For example, the changes created by adolescence or the mid-life crisis are not caused by one event. They are created by the complex interaction of physiological, social, mental, economic, spatial, and emotional changes, and they create sizeable transitions in the individuals and in the family system.

Social scientists have been studying developmental transitions since the beginning of the twentieth century. G. Stanley Hall, for example, published a book on the adolescent stage of development in 1904, and he gave the adolescent period a label that has been used ever since. He called it a period of *Sturm und Drang* (translation: storm and stress).

Some transitions tend to be relatively easy and problem-free, and others tend to be difficult. Also, some of them are easy for one family but difficult for another. For example, some families have a difficult time coping with children leaving home, but others find it an easy transition (Haley, 1981). Some families have a difficult time coping with retirement, but others find it easy. Some find the transition into parenthood easy, and others find it challenging. A small minority of parents find the transition into parenthood so difficult that they develop psychosis from it; psychiatrists have called it post-partum psychosis.

One important challenge for family scientists is to find ways to help families cope with transitions so they are growth-producing and healthy periods rather than excessively difficult. Fortunately, in the late 1930s sociologists such as Leonard Cottrell (1942) began to develop some ideas that help us understand why some transitions are easy and others are difficult. Their ideas include *anticipatory socialization*, *role strain*, and the nature of *transition procedures*.

Anticipatory Socialization

These two complex words refer to the process of helping people learn what will be expected of them in new roles and situations. The term **socialization** refers to the process of gradually learning the norms, scripts, attitudes, values, and subtle rules a person needs to know to be able to function effectively in society. Infants are in an unsocialized condition, but gradually they go through the process of being socialized by parents, teachers, siblings and others who teach them how to act and feel.

Anticipatory socialization refers to learning that is done before people are in a role where they actually use what they have learned. An example is the book-learning part of a driver training program. It prepares future drivers for the written exam. They haven't yet started driving, but they are learning information they will need when they do.

The idea of anticipatory socialization helps us realize that timing is important in trying to help people learn what they need to do. In developmental terms, there are moments of *readiness*, or teachable moments when people are eager and motivated and other times when they are less interested in learning (Guerney & Guerney, 1981). When, for example, is the best time to teach someone to drive? When they are 5, 15, or 50? When is the best time to teach people to care for infants? When they are 15, 50, or 5 months along in a pregnancy? What about how to cope with adolescents? What about preparing for retirement?

Role Strain

A second idea that helps people cope with transitions is known as role strain. **Role strain** refers to the difficulty that people experience when they try to conform to the demands of a role. Some roles, such as caring for infants, are so demanding that there can be considerable role strain. When the parents both try to work full-time and also try to keep up all of the other activities they were used to before the pregnancy, it can create one type of strain, an overload problem. To avoid this, couples need to learn when they are expecting their first child that it usually helps to cut back on some of their roles. Frequently at least one parent and sometimes both parents need to adjust the amount of time they spend on their career, leisure-time activities, educational pursuits, and other activities.

Role strain can be created by many things. For example, it can be introduced by ambiguity about what a person is supposed to do in a new situation, and by conflicting expectations about what should be done.

The concept of role strain also helps us understand why certain transitions out of roles are easy. For example, adolescence is usually a period of considerable role strain. The expectations for adolescence are ambiguous, and the important people in an adolescent's life do not agree on many of the expectations. The parents, teens, friends, and educators, for example, usually have different opinions. This makes the transition into adolescence difficult, but it usually makes the transition out of it much easier.

Transition Procedures

A third idea that helps us understand how to cope with transitions has to do with the nature of the transition procedures. When the social events that surround a transition are clear and important it seems to help families make the transitions.

Imagine, for example, how difficult it would be if someone's wedding were spread out over several months. They wouldn't know for sure when they were finally married. At what point would they have made the important commitments to each other, and when should their friends start thinking of them as a married couple. This type of ambiguity in the transition procedures would make the transition into marriage much more difficult than it usually is. Anthropological research has found some cultures that spread out some aspects of weddings (Van Gennep, 1960), but they are careful to make each part clear and important.

It would be the same for retirement. What would it be like if a person weren't sure when during a three-month period they no longer needed to come to work?

It would be ridiculous! Yet many things we do with the transitions in our society are just as ridiculous.

When, for example, do children reach the stage that their decisions ought to be considered in a family decision? When should children be able to decide if they get to do such things as wear high heels, get their ears pierced, wear nylons, choose their own friends, smoke and drink, and decide how long to stay out? When should they have the right to say to their parents, "I love you mom and dad, and I appreciate your advice, but I'm the one who now decides what I'm going to do, and I'm going to ______________ (fill in the blank with whatever you want)"?

Thus, anticipatory socialization, keeping role strain from being a problem, and having clear transition procedures help families manage the epigenesis process wisely. When they cope well with the developmental tasks that occur in transitions it becomes easier to cope with later challenges in the family life course.

Morphogenesis and Morphostasis

Morphogenesis and morphostasis are rather complicated words, but they can be understood easily if they are divided into their two root words. First, morphogenesis. The morpho part of this word comes from the Greek *morpho* and it refers to the form or shape of something. The genesis part comes from the Greek word *genesis*, which means beginning or creating, and in this word it also refers to changing or altering. Thus family **morphogenesis** refers to altering the form of a family system. It means more than just changing the number or the ages of the people in the family, as it includes other things like changes in family dynamics, traditions, routines, emotional responses, rules, rituals, and other processes.

The main idea that family scientists have developed about morphogenesis can be called the **morphogenesis principle**:

Principle *Family systems are always in the process of changing. They are never in a stable condition where change is not occurring.*

Some of the morphogenesis in families is developmental change and some of it is not. The difference is that development refers to changes that are part of the typical lifespan or life cycle of individuals or families. The morphogenesis that is not part of development can be created by many things. For example, a member of a family may be paralyzed by an automobile accident. A family may win a large lottery prize. Someone in a family may go through a religious conversion. These and many other random and unforeseen events can create changes in the form of the families involved, but family scientists do not think of them as developmental changes.

Many of the later chapters in this book discuss the morphogenesis that is created by nondevelopmental processes. Here we want to discuss the nature of developmental changes, the ways they influence families, and the many ways families can prepare for them and profit from them.

The concept of morphostasis[3] is the opposite of morphogenesis, and it is also easily understood when we break it into its two parts. *Morpho* refers to form, and *stasis* means stopped or static. Thus, family **morphostasis** is the process of maintaining the status quo or avoiding change in a family system.

Family scientists also sometimes use the term *homeostasis* rather than morphostasis. The two words are interchangeable, but we have chosen to use the word *morphostasis* here.

The **morphostasis principle** was one of the first to be identified after scholars began thinking with a family science perspective (Jackson, 1957). The idea in this principle is that:

Principle

When one part of a family system tries to change in response to new inputs, one of the reactions that usually occurs is that some of the other parts of the system try to preserve the status quo.

Jay Haley (1964) later called this principle the "first law of human relationships." He states that "people in on-going relationships function as 'governors.' The purpose of the 'governor' is to diminish change. *When one person indicates a change in relation to another, the other will act upon the first so as to diminish and modify that change*" (Haley, 1964, p. 189; italics added for emphasis).

When these systemic ideas were being developed, the scholars who were creating them paid most of their attention to morphostasis, and they ignored morphogenesis (Jackson, 1963). This meant that during the 1950s and 1960s, the systems-oriented scholars who were developing these ideas assumed that family systems are fairly stable and unchanging, and the primary tendency in them is to resist innovation and development.

In the early 1970s two papers were written that changed this emphasis. Lynn Hoffman (1971) introduced the idea that a morphostatic model of families is too biased and limiting. They convinced the systems-oriented scholars that family systems are also inherently morphogenetic. During the next two decades the developmental ideas and systems ideas were gradually integrated, and the result is that scholars now realize both processes are always operating in family systems (Keeney, 1983).

Thus the current view in the field is that, on the one hand, there are always pressures, events, and processes that tend to create change in family systems. At the same time, there are always pressures, events, and processes that tend to create stability and resist change. The two processes oppose each other and are incompatible, but both are inherent and unavoidable, and apparently they are natural and inevitable parts of family systems.

Why Does Morphostasis Occur?

There are many reasons morphostasis is an inevitable and fundamental part of family systems. Three of these reasons are:

BLOOM COUNTY **by Berke Breathed**

1. Rules that are created in the early stages of a relationship become the first part of a complicated web of rules. Later, if there are attempts to change the first rules, it has implications for many parts of the web. One result of this pattern is that it creates some tendency to resist change.

2. A great deal of what happens in families is unconscious; or, using the iceberg analogy, it is beneath the surface and fairly invisible. Also, people have enough of a desire to control their lives (Rollins & Thomas, 1979) that they like some degree of stability, security, and predictability. These tendencies lead to some resistance to change.

3. Family processes deal with many of the most fundamental and deeply experienced emotional processes that humans experience. For example, they deal with mating, reproduction, personal territory, intimacy, and belonging. People are highly motivated to arrange their life so these deeply experienced affective experiences are comfortable. One example of this is the unbelievable contortions humans, and many lower forms of life, go through to find a mate and settle down. When people get these parts of their life organized so the inner and core affective conditions are comfortable, they have very strong, affectively motivated, reasons to resist attempts to change things. This is one reason divorce and death are resisted so much, and why they are such tremendously disruptive experiences when they can't be avoided. They force us to reorganize some of the most fundamental parts of our lives.

Practical Implications

Presence of ambivalence. When we understand the twin processes of morphogenesis and morphostasis in family systems, it gives us ideas that have several implications. One implication is that it helps us be aware that families always experience ambivalence when they encounter significant change. Ambivalence is feeling two opposite affective states or desires at the same time. Even when families encounter desirable changes like weddings, births, and graduations, there is always ambivalence in the family about them.

The ambivalence is frequently uneven. This means that sometimes the feelings either for or against something are stronger than the opposing feelings. Usually when a change helps people attain important goals, the dominant feelings are in favor of the change. When a change interferes with important goals or is threatening in other ways, the dominant feelings are against the change.

Sometimes perceptions determine the nature of the feelings, but perceptions can be deceptive. Remembering the iceberg analogy, when a change has implications for the hidden parts of family life, people may not be aware of all of the pressures and processes. For example, a younger sibling may be relieved when an older sibling leaves home. He or she gets a new bedroom. There's less hassle about the bathroom. There's no more getting picked on. Yet the feelings of loss and emptiness may be very real, and may have an effect on the child, but the child may not be aware of what is happening.

Early intervention. Another implication of these two ideas is that, since systems tend to become increasingly rigid as time passes, generally speaking, the earlier in the life of an individual or family system we try to influence the system, the greater the impact we will usually have. The biblical admonition to "Train up a child in the way he should go: and when he is old, he will not depart from it" (Proverbs 22:6) is a good example of this idea.

In family science, there are many ways this can be applied. For example, we can make more difference in the way a couple relates by helping them early in their marriage rather than later. We can have more impact if we influence people early in their life than if we influence them later (Bronfenbrenner, 1979).

When we try to apply these insights, we also need to be aware of the readiness of individuals and families for change (Guerney & Guerney, 1981). People are ready at certain times and not ready at others. For example, we would probably have little impact on a life by trying to teach something about careers to a 3-year-old.

It has become widely believed in our society that the first years of a child's life are the most important, and the principle of morphostasis is consistent with this idea. Family scientists, therefore, ought to do what they can to help parents find the resources they need during this critical time.

Timing. Family scientists have discovered that periods of *transition* are good times to try to influence family systems. Often it is most effective to try to create a change just before a transition or just after it. Transitions are a good time to try to make changes because the morphogenetic processes are more powerful at transition points when systems are in a period of flux. After the transition, the family system tends to move into a new stage and the morphostatic processes take over; then systems tend to resist change and promote stability.

Just before the birth of the first child in a family is a good time for family scientists to help couples learn to care for infants. The parents are thinking about the birth, anticipating it, and are highly motivated by the emotions that surround birth and procreation. This is, therefore, a teachable moment for new ideas, skills, and ways of doing things. Attempts to help people learn how to cope with infants are not as effective before a couple is pregnant.

Similarly, it is not very effective to try to teach parents of infants how to deal with the transition into the teenage years. However, when the oldest child in a family is about 12, the parents are much more receptive to ideas about how to cope with teenagers.

This idea does not always work. Many other processes are at work simultaneously in family systems, and we need to consider as much of the total system as possible. This is sometimes called having a **holistic** orientation. For example, if we just paid attention to the morphostasis and morphogenesis principles, we would conclude that the best time to help young couples prepare for marriage is just before the marriage. Experience in trying to help engaged couples, however, has revealed that the period just prior to a wedding is not a very good time to try to influence couples. Research about the effects of educational and counseling programs has revealed that they have very little impact when they are in that transition (Druckman, Fournier, Robinson & Olson, 1979). Apparently the period just before weddings is such an intensely emotional time that couples are not receptive to new ideas. They are apparently so distracted by the relationship and the preparation for the wedding that intervention programs have little impact.

Studies have found that premarital programs that have a follow-up phase about six months after the wedding are much more helpful than programs that just work with couples premaritally (Druckman et al., 1979; Bader et al., 1980). Apparently after couples have had time to settle into their marital relationship, they move into a period when they are more ready to learn than they were earlier.

SUMMARY

This chapter discussed ways human development and family development influence what happens in families. There are some developmental processes that are predictable, and families can anticipate them and prepare for them. Most families tend to be fairly similar in these predictable developmental processes. There also are many developmental processes that are not predictable. These unpredictable processes create great variability in family development and individual development.

The chapter also discussed ways families can manage transitions so they are as manageable and growth-producing as possible. The processes of morphogenesis, morphostasis, and epigenesis were also discussed and illustrated, and we presented several strategies for using these concepts.

One of the main ideas in the chapter is that those of us who want to understand families should always be sensitive to developmental processes. We should never ignore them, even when we're concentrating on other parts of family processes or other things that are known in the field. This means that a developmental orientation[4] is an important part of a family science perspective. Another implication of this is that the developmental ideas should be integrated with the ideas about the family realm, generational dimensions, and affect to form an increasingly comprehensive and helpful set of ideas.

Key Terms

Development
Family development
Family life course
Requisite variety
Stages
Transitions
Epigenesis
Developmental tasks
Anticipatory socialization
Role strain
Transition procedures
Morphogenesis
Morphostasis
Ambivalence

Study Questions

1. What are the three primary aspects of family development?
2. Describe the difference between external and internal events.
3. How is family development different from individual development?
4. Give several examples of undesirable changes that might occur in a family.
5. What key factor tells us whether a change in a family is developmental or not?
6. List five events that occur in families that are fairly predictable.
7. Define what is meant by epigenesis.
8. What is the difference between morphostasis and morphogenesis?

Notes

1. For those interested in some of the more technical aspects of development, developmental psychologists have given considerable attention to how to define this term. Bronfenbrenner's (1979) definition of it is that it is "change that leads to differentiation and complexity." In our opinion, this view is too narrow because it focuses only on the developmental processes during childhood. The concept of development is more useful when it is broadened to include the development that occurs throughout the entire life cycle of individuals and family systems.
2. There is widespread agreement in the field about this principle, but there is a great deal that is not yet known about which behaviors, stages, sequences, transitions, etc., have which kinds of effects. There are so many different models and they are currently so poorly tested that we must think of this principle in fairly general terms and be cautious in concluding that any particular sequence

of stages is necessary. Erikson's (1950) model of individual development argues that some stages must be dealt with in certain sequences, but the necessity of the sequence with many of his stages can be debated. Doherty's (1987) paper suggested that the sequence of affiliation, power, and intimacy is important in systems. Wynne (1984) suggests a different sequence. His theory is that attachment/caregiving, communicating, joining, problem solving, and mutuality with psychological intimacy are necessary. Solomon (1973) has a different theory about developmental sequences. Others, such as Lewis (1986, p. 239), argue that there are changing patterns at different stages. There is, thus, a great deal to do in refining developmental thinking.

3. The word *homeostasis* is a synonym for morphostasis. Dell (1982) has suggested that the term *coherence* should be used to replace morphogenesis and morphostasis. We agree that many of the problems that Dell identified exist with these terms. Unfortunately, however, the term *coherence* is not helpful in understanding as many system processes. We are therefore trying to find a solution that is the best of both worlds. We're trying to use the two terms *morphogenesis* and *morphostasis* in ways that avoid problems such as inconsistencies in logical type and misplaced concreteness, while at the same time retaining the two concepts because they are so helpful in thinking about important system processes and in trying to intervene in family systems.
4. Unfortunately, many able family scholars fail to keep a developmental perspective in their work. For example, Thomas Gordon (1970), Michael Popkin (1983), and Don Dinkmeyer et al. (1976; 1984) have all made important contributions to the field; but their contributions would have been even greater if they had been sensitive to developmental issues. They all push for equality as a total condition, and they do not consider very well the developmental levels of the children. Popkin admits that children are not equal in experience and responsibility, but he and the others ignore the gradualness that is wise in the transfer of power to children (Bronfenbrenner, 1979).

Rules 8

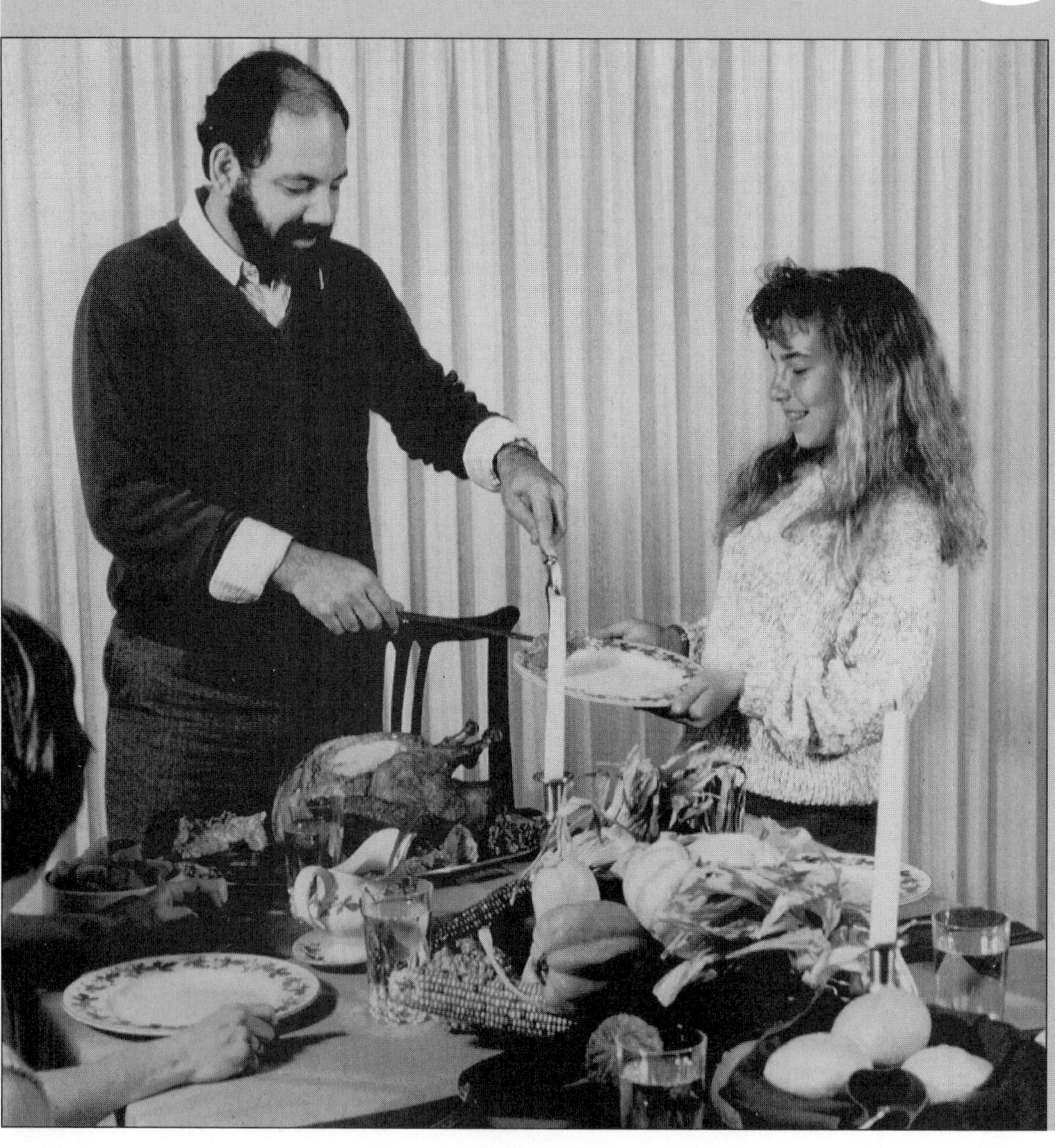

Main Ideas

1 // Some of the rules in family systems are social norms. Social norms are beliefs that prescribe or proscribe ways people should or should not behave in society. They are the normative part of social systems.

2 // Many normative rules are an important aspect of family heritage. They are learned by each new generation and are used or modified.

3 // Normative rules regulate the way resources are managed, clarify boundaries, regulate emotional distance, control the implementation of decisions, clarify how to deal with exceptions and violation of rules, and so forth.

4 // Some family rules are not social norms. The rules that are not a part of the normative ideology in families are called non-normative rules.

5 // Some family rules are simple and uncomplicated, but others form clusters called rule sequences.

6 // Rule sequences regulate patterned ways of behaving, though families are usually unaware of them. They can be healthy and enabling, and they can be disabling.

7 // There are several strategies that can be used to manage rule sequences effectively.

8 // Thinking about rule sequences is difficult, but helpful.

9 // Rules sometimes become developmentally inappropriate, excessively rigid, or disabling. When these problems occur, adaptability is needed.

10 // Usually the more implicit rules are, the better they serve the family.

11 // When conflicts about rules are not readily resolved, it can be helpful to concentrate on Level II or Level III parts of family systems.

Most families have thousands of formal and informal rules about their transformation processes. For example, think of the incoming mail. When it comes to the house, where is it placed? Is it sorted and delivered to each person's room? Can anyone open the junk mail? Can parents open the children's mail? Are there certain types of letters that do not have to be shared at all? Most of the rules that govern these processes emerge without much negotiation, but they have power to direct and dictate much of what we do. They influence where we sit when we watch TV or eat dinner. They direct which towels to use in the bathroom, where to store holiday decorations, and who should replace the empty toilet-paper roll.

Some of the rules in family systems are social norms. In addition, family systems create a number of rules that are not social norms. This chapter is about both kinds of rules. We will discuss what these two types of rules are and the impact they have on how we function in family life. We will also look at several

"In the complexity of the millions of messages exchanged by a married couple from moment to moment, there are multiple rules at multiple levels."

—Jay Haley, 1981, p. 170

ideas that have been developed by family scientists about how families, and those who work with families, can help the "rule" part of family systems be as enabling and healthy as possible.

Rules as Social Norms

Over the past one hundred years, the sociological perspective has been helpful in illuminating how certain social norms are created and influence people. **Social norms** are beliefs that exist in a culture that prescribe certain behaviors and proscribe others. Thus, they deal with "shoulds" and "oughts" in social groups.

Social norms can apply to minor acts, like what utensil one uses at the dinner table, or to more major occurrences like who should be chosen as a sexual partner. Sociologists have developed several concepts that help us tell the difference between norms that deal with serious matters and those that deal with less serious behavior. They refer to norms that deal with behaviors which a society considers especially important as **mores**, and behaviors that are preferred but more or less optional are called **folkways**. Also, when normative beliefs are thought important enough to be enacted by various governmental bodies into formal written rules, they are called *laws.*

Mores, folkways, and laws have a powerful influence with regard to how we manage family business. Laws tell us it is not acceptable to discipline children with abusive strategies. Mores and folkways pressure us to dress our children in certain ways, and speak to our spouses in particular ways. These mores and folkways are learned from the community, neighborhood, and families in which we live. By observation of what is "right" and appropriate, individuals assimilate the world around them and the rules that govern behavior.

Since social norms are an important part of family processes, it is important to consider how families teach, adopt, and change the norms they use. Additionally, understanding the nature of social norms helps us understand some of the sources of stress in families. This is because stress can occur when family members perceive rules differently. Stress may be introduced when certain age groups, such as teenagers in a family, learn new norms from their peers and try to introduce them into their family system. Also, husbands and wives can bring to a new family different ideas and strategies about how to manage the normative aspect of their family system.

How Normative Rules Emerge

There are many ways norms find their way into family systems. Some are copied from the family of origin by the husband or the wife. From the time of birth we assimilate and learn the rules we need to follow in order to live successfully within our families. People take many of their old, well-learned family rules with them into a new relationship. This can cause problems if there is a lack of consensus about the rules each member brings to a new family system. When two competing rule systems (one from each partner) come together, there is a fairly high degree of probability a clash will occur. One of the purposes of courtship is to begin the process of rule discovery, negotiation, and creation.

Families also acquire normative rules from the culture in which they live. They may adopt them by choice or simply assimilate beliefs and rules from external influences. The media is one cultural source from which we tend to build beliefs and expectations and therefore rules. Television often shows rather superficial and unrealistic families working through life's situations. We may adopt bits and pieces of how they act and assimilate them into our own family. We build rules on what we think "ought" to happen; sometimes the "ought" can come from those we admire.

A third way rules become a part of family systems is by negotiation. This process includes such mundane issues as who sleeps on which side of the bed, who sits where at the table, who puts their clothes in what closet, and whether to squeeze the toothpaste at the middle or the end of the tube. Negotiation also is used for rules about deeper issues like who controls the money, the distribution of other resources, and the division of labor.

Many rules also appear through a series of multiple interactions (Haley, 1963; Galvin & Brommel, 1982). Through the processes of trial, struggle, error, conflict, and resolution, family members adopt what seems to work for them. By "work for them" we mean the processes that families find helpful in keeping the system in balance, free from chaos, and working in harmony. Eventually most families learn, adapt, assimilate, and accommodate. However, not everything chosen is best for all members. Those within the system believe what they are doing is necessary to keep the system in working order. The process begins with the couple meeting for the first time, and continues on as a developmental process.

Most families have informal rules about each of these areas. Families construct hundreds of rules about how to manage their daily life. These rules emerge without fanfare or proclamation, but have a curious power to direct and dictate how we act toward one another, how we come and go, and what we say or do not say.

Purposes of Normative Rules

It is important to understand the purposes and functions of rules. In general, rules have the purpose of maintaining regularity, providing system accountability, and providing boundary maintenance. They also educate and regulate personal distance within the system. These vital functions make norms a critical force in helping systems avoid chaos.

Researchers (Cronen, Pearce & Harris, 1979) have noted that rules are an unavoidable and inescapable element of human interaction. Family systems need regularity to obtain goals, seek balance, and maintain cohesion. If the behavior of each member were random and impulsive, the system could not flourish.

Rules hold family members accountable for actions within and outside of the family system (Cronen et al., 1979). Since families have expectations, values, and goals, simple family rules advise members when they are not performing in ways that meet those generalized expectations or goals.

Norms also help family members know boundaries that exist between a family and its environment. Each family exists in a complex network of external systems, and must maintain its uniqueness and distance from the others. Therefore, norms define the boundaries between each family and other environmental systems.

The executive subsystem (see Chapter 2) is responsible for different tasks than the child subsystem. The boundary between those two systems is defined by simple rules about boundaries (Okun & Rappaport, 1980). For example, rules dictate the permeability of family and subsystem boundaries. If a mother is having a heated conversation with the father in the bedroom, family members may know it is not the time to interrupt.

When family rules begin to be questioned and challenged, often it is the rules about boundaries that are being questioned. A healthy family system has effectively created functional rule systems that tell system members where the system begins and ends, where they can and cannot go, and what they can and cannot do. This assumes, of course, that the system has created a flexible and nondestructive rule system.

One specific purpose of simple rules is that they regulate distance. Generally family researchers use the term *cohesion* (see Chapter 10) to refer to this aspect of family systems (Kantor & Lehr, 1975; Hess & Handel, 1959; Minuchin, 1981; and Olson & McCubbin, 1982). Cohesion means that each family establishes "a pattern of separateness and connectedness." Family rules tell us how and when we should be close and when we should be separate.

Another purpose of normative rules is to regulate how families allocate and exchange resources. These rules govern how any family resource is divided within the system. This includes how family money should be spent, rules about living space, and rules about intangibles like time and affection.

Rules of designated authority are rules about division of responsibility. Mother may be in charge of anyone who feels down. An older grandparent living with the family may be in charge of relieving tension when the pressure of an argument gets too intense. A father may be charged with the responsibility of the first reaction in times of emergency. At times of divorce or death, rule and role reallocation may occur to fill the void created by the absent family member.

Many of the rules we have in private life have to do with **implementation**. Rules of implementation exist for the purpose of implementing other rules and expectations. While a family may have a series of rules about a topic (how much schoolwork), they also have a series or rules that designate how they go about getting the work done. Rules of implementation are created to make sure larger rules are followed. The implementation rule might be: "If your younger sister is having trouble with math, you will help her."

Families may also have rules about **exceptions**. The exceptions allow the system to deal with the unexpected and regulate necessary behavior even when an important family rule cannot be followed. In the school work example, an exception might go like this: "José is very athletic and we believe personal talents should be enhanced. But we also believe everyone needs to get better grades." In José's case, both of these things are not going to happen. So the rule exception in these types of cases emerges as: "We will let José choose where he will put the emphasis of his time."

Another type of rules are those that deal with **violation**. What happens in a family when a member gets bad grades, thus violating a rule about good grades and achievement? What happens when someone talks about death or negative ideas when that has been proscribed by the family? These actions will trigger another type of rule that specifies what is to be done following violation.

Explicit and Implicit Rules

Some of the family rules are explicit and some are implicit (Satir, 1972). **Explicit rules** are the beliefs that are recognized, acknowledged, and known by a family, and usually they can be talked about. Explicit rules are usually more formalized because they are made visible. An example of an explicit family rule is one that is made by decree: "All children who go on dates have to be home by 12:30 P.M." or "Before a visit to your father, you must clean your room." Such rules are a little different from daily requests that require a specific (and perhaps a one-time) response. They take on the form of regulating behavior over time, as a generalized guideline meant to be in force forever or until altered.

Some rules are not recognized by the members of a family. **Implicit rules** remain hidden. They are not discussed, and have not been recognized or labelled by family members. Their invisibility makes implicit rules very powerful. They are the way things are. Because they are invisible, they are never questioned, and of course they are not changeable unless they are recognized.

An example of an implicit rule can be found in the way family members greet each other after a long absence. Do they hug, do they shake hands, or do they just smile? In this example, the norm reflects what the family has decided is appropriate about distance regulation: how close and affectionate family members should be.

Many families have implicit rules against sharing special feelings. They may go to great lengths to "help" family members learn ways to suppress how they feel. Suppose a family has an implicit rule that only good topics and feelings should be discussed. The belief may be that to talk about negative parts of life is a destructive process, so the negative feelings and experiences go unexpressed. Though the negative feelings remain unspoken, however, they are not unfelt. It could be very dangerous for a family to create a system where significant and important feelings cannot be discussed.

NON-NORMATIVE RULES

In the 1950s a group of family scientists led by Don Jackson and Gregory Bateson discovered that family systems have rules that are different from the normative rules families get from society or invent themselves (Jackson, 1957, 1965). These **non-normative** rules are patterns of behavior in family systems that are repeated so regularly that they are a governing or regulating part of the structure of the family systems.

The family scientists who have discovered these rules found that usually the rules "tend to be implicit and they are rarely, if ever, explicit or written down" (Ford, 1983, p. 135). Therefore, the only way to identify the non-normative family rules is to *infer* them from the repeated or redundant patterns in the behavior in a family. According to Jackson:

> Again, we must emphasize the rule is an inference, an abstraction—more precisely, a *metaphor* coined by the observer to cover the redundancy he observes. We say a rule is a "format of regularity imposed upon a complicated process by the investigator." (Jackson, 1965a, p. 11)

> Since we are always making *inferences* when we try to identify rules, it is usually helpful to precede each rule we think we see with the caution: "it seems as if . . ." (Jackson, 1965c, p. 592)

When we are thinking about games such as bridge, the rules are mostly explicit and mostly normative. In family life, however, there are many rules that are implicit and non-normative. For example, if we observed a family where they never demonstrated their feelings in an open way, we could infer that "it seems as if" they have a rule that they shall not demonstrate feelings overtly.

An example of non-normative rules is a rule that often exists about the way family members interrupt each other. Family scholars have discovered that, contrary to popular opinion, interrupting is actually a healthy sign in the family realm. This was found in a series of research studies that compared families—a group of families who were having serious problems with a group of families who were not in a clinical setting. The researchers found that the clinical sample was more careful in the way they communicated with each other, and they interrupted each other less. The more healthy families, on the other hand, were more spontaneous and careless in their communication patterns and there was more interrupting (Alexander, 1973).

This suggests there are some rules operating with regard to interrupting patterns in most family systems. These rules are not what we call social norms because they are in opposition to some normative beliefs. When most people are confronted with the finding that men interrupt more than women they usually respond by thinking this is an undesirable pattern because it illustrates another subtle way males dominate females, and they then try to develop social norms to reverse the pattern of male dominance. The non-normative rules in this situation are the rules that govern the interaction that is actually in opposition to the more consciously preferred agreements or understandings that are the social norms.

An interesting example of a non-normative family rule is in a book by Lynn Caine (1974) called *Widows*. Her husband is dying of cancer, and as the story unfolds he is dealing with the devastating feelings of knowing his life is about to end. Ms. Caine describes how this crisis debilitated their relationship. A source of major stress in her situation was a hidden rule that the subject of the husband's death could not be talked about.

No one in the Caine family said: "OK, rule number 23: if a member of our family gets a fatal disease, no one is to come right out and talk about it. In fact, we should pretend the dying person is going to live and continue as if nothing is happening." Ms. Caine's family, however, acted as if the rule were formal, written, and unchangeable.

A very poignant and depressing part of Caine's story is her lamenting about her feelings following his death. She reports how much she wished she would have changed the rule or suspended the rule and talked to him about the end of his life and the hundreds of issues that needed to be resolved. But the rule had prevailed and what was uppermost on their minds was never discussed.

This process was regulated by a series of non-normative and implicit rules about what could be talked about and what couldn't. The norms she wanted to live by were quite different from the implicit and hidden rules they had developed in their family system.

There are several aspects of non-normative family rules that are different from normative family rules. First, some non-normative rules create and maintain patterns of behavior that are different from the values, ideals, and goals of the families and the cultures they live in. The rules that operate in triangling illustrate this difference. Most societies, subcultures, and families have a normative system that believes family members should not "triangle in" lovers or children to escape from or stabilize unresolved emotional tensions in a marital relationship, but it occurs with unfortunate frequency. When triangling happens there are always a number of unwritten and undesirable rules that govern, regulate, and stabilize these processes. The patterns of triangling in family systems are so predictable, so repetitious, and so redundant, that they could not be operating randomly, and therefore they illustrate the operation of rules.

A second way non-normative rules are different from normative rules is that the non-normative rules are about Level I processes (see Chapter 6). We infer them by watching behavior patterns, and they describe fairly specific or concrete patterns in the behavior. Rules that are social norms, on the other hand, seem to deal with a wider range of levels of abstraction. They can be about specific (Level I) beliefs that define how to sit at the table, how close to be to someone, and how we should dress when we answer the doorbell. They also can deal with moderately abstract (Level II) beliefs such as rules that people should be kind, considerate, and compassionate.

A third way non-normative rules seem to be different from normative rules is that non-normative rules are usually hidden so well that it is almost impossible for most families to identify them or describe them. Usually it takes an outside observer to be able to see them initially.

A fourth aspect of non-normative rules is that, because they are not governed by the normative part of social systems, there can be great variability from one family to another. Box 8.1 illustrates that different families create different rules to deal with similar situations. The situation is that the mother arrives home from a trying day at work. She sees the kitchen in disarray, honey on the counter, and crusts of bread littering the table. The interaction that follows upon her arrival are predictable because of the non-normative rules, but these rules are unique to each family and they are not determined by normative beliefs, even though they may be influenced by family goals, values, and ideologies. For example, if neatness and personal responsibility are valued, one series of responses tends to emerge. If independence and autonomy are valued, a different script tends to emerge.

The idea that family systems have non-normative rules is a useful addition to the ways we think about family systems. This is because when we understand this idea it sensitizes us to aspects of family systems we don't have access to with other ideas. It also opens up a number of new ways to try to help families, but before the ways of using this concept are discussed, we need to understand what rule sequences are.

Box 8.1

Consider how different family rules govern the way people behave in the same situation.

Family 1

"Jason, come in here this minute!"
"Gee, Mom, keep your shirt on, no need to yell."
"I have told you a million times that when you get something out it is your responsibility to put it away. Why do you leave these messes? Do you think I am your maid, that I'll just keep on picking up after you like you're some type of prince?"
"Sorry, Mom, I . . ."
"Sorry isn't good enough, get in here and clean this mess up!"

Family rule: Make the child be responsible.

Family 2

"Jason, I'm home."
There is no reply from the bedroom.
"Jason, do you know anything about this mess? The ice cream is getting on the floor, Honey."
There is still no reply. She wipes up the mess, and begins to prepare dinner.

Family rule: Keep peace at any cost.

Family 3

"Jason, could you come out here for a minute?"
"Hi, Mom. What's up?"
"I'm not too happy about the ice cream mess. I need to take a shower and relax for a minute. When the kitchen is clean, I'll tackle dinner. Can you take care of it, please?"
"I am in the middle of a math problem."
"Well, I am hungry, but we won't start on dinner until the mess is gone."

Family rule: Insist on the logical consequences.

Rule Sequences

Jay Haley developed the idea that some family rules occur in what he called *sequences* (Haley, 1976, Ch. 4). A **rule sequence** is a connected series of rules that govern a complex pattern in the behavior of several individuals in a family system. These sequences tend to have a cyclic pattern to them, so they are sometimes called cycles. When they deal with negative or disabling patterns we often refer to them as **vicious cycles.** If the following situation were to occur regularly in a family, it would be an example of a fairly simple rule sequence:

1. When one parent has a bad day at the office, he or she comes home and is critical of the other parent.
2. The second parent takes the anger out on a child.
3. The child picks a fight with another sibling or kicks the dog.

Many rule sequences in families are healthy and enabling. For example, a family may have a pattern where the parents get up a few minutes early so they can visit with their child and express affection before beginning daily routines. When the parents conform to this rule it may begin a cycle of other rule-bound behaviors, such as the children and adults being more pleasant, listening to each other, and doing favors for each other. When the parents do not follow this pattern, a different cycle might be precipitated, with the children and adults being less patient, more irritable, more short-tempered, or more critical as they begin the day.

Most families probably have many healthy rule-bound sequences covering such activities as time management, allocation of scarce family resources (space, money, affection), interaction with those outside of the kin system, and every other aspect of family functioning. We suspect there are hundreds or even thousands of these repetitious patterns that an average family uses as they meet the problems of the day.

Some rule sequences are disabling and destructive. For example, the following situation illustrates an oversimplified situation where there is a father, mother, and child, and each of them is either competent or incompetent. Since these sequences tend to be cyclic, a series of steps eventually leads to the beginning of another, similar series. The description could start at any point in the cycle.

Step 1. *Father—incompetent.* The father behaves in an upset or depressed way, not functioning to his capacity.

Step 2. *Child—misbehaving.* The child begins to get out of control or express symptoms.

Step 3. *Mother—incompetent.* The mother ineffectually tries to deal with the child and cannot, and the father becomes involved.

Step 4. *Father—competent.* The father deals with the child effectively and recovers from his state of incompetency.

Step 5. *Child—behaving.* The child regains his composure and behaves properly or is defined as normal.

Step 6. *Mother—competent.* The mother becomes more capable and deals with the child and father in a more competent way, expecting more from them.

Step 7. *Father—incompetent.* The father behaves in an upset or depressed way, not functioning to his capacity, and the cycle begins again. (Haley, 1987, p. 113)

There are several elements of this sequence that illustrate how rule sequences usually operate. First, the steps seem to occur in a cyclic pattern, and the pattern repeats itself over and over. Second, it is quite arbitrary where the cycle begins because it can begin with several of the steps. Punctuation is an attempt to identify where complex patterns begin and end, but it usually distorts the cyclic reality of these patterns.

Third, the strategy the mother uses to "change" the husband and child by increasing her expectations actually has the opposite effect. The more she tries to get them to improve the more they go in the opposite direction. This points out how these repetitious rules may be painfully obscured from the vision of those who participate in them. A major element of family interaction patterns is that most of them are hidden from immediate view. Often only an outside observer or a person trained to focus on systemic processes can piece them together.

Fourth, the details of the behavior may change in different situations, but when the pattern in the cycle is rule-governed it will reappear over and over again in different forms. It is critical to remember that most of the time family members are unaware they are choosing behaviors that are rule-governed or pattern-like. Most people are surprised when such rules are brought to light in counseling sessions or by a skillful observer.

These rule sequences help us understand the way different perspectives influence how we try to help families. A common approach to problems in the family realm is to focus on the individuals rather than the family system. In the above situation, a therapist with an individualistic orientation might encourage the mother to be more assertive or let the child "own her own problems."

It is impossible to identify the beginning or the "causes" of the problems in these situations because they are ongoing cycles that have no beginning and no end. A systems theory perspective, however, suggests it is helpful to view these situations as rule-governed cycles. When we think of them this way it reduces defensiveness, helps us better understand the system characteristics that help maintain problems, and opens up several possibilities for improving the family system.

MANAGEMENT STRATEGIES

There are a number of important strategies that can help family members manage the rule parts of their family systems. Among them are developing a clear understanding of how and when to be adaptable, understanding developmentally appropriate rules, avoiding rule rigidity, and learning to avoid disabling rules.

When we focus on rule sequences as a strategy to understand family processes, it makes it easier to understand why Virginia Satir (1972) compared family life to an iceberg where the majority of what is happening is beneath the surface. Families are aware of some sequences, and most families try to deliberately manage a few of them. The totality of family life, however, is such a complex set of interlocking sequences that most of them occur out of the consciousness of the participants.

Even though most sequences are submerged, families can become aware of some of them, and they can learn skills that help manage at least some of them. In fact, our experience suggests that even families that are not well educated and not very resourceful find it relatively easy to modify vicious cycles when they become aware of them. Therefore, the key is recognizing vicious cycles.

Think "Sequences"

There are several skills that can help families become aware of rule sequences. One skill is to occasionally try to "think sequences" or "think cycles" rather than just "think individuals" when problems occur in a family. It is difficult for people in families to recognize cycles that are more complicated than three steps, but it is possible. Also, only identifying two or three steps in a cycle frequently is enough to be helpful. Often when families recognize two or three steps, these insights lead to the discovery of other steps that aren't readily apparent.

It may be necessary to enlist an outsider to spot these cycles. Others not caught up in the vicious cycles can sometimes recognize what is happening and make suggestions that can help those who are involved recognize what is going on. The following situation illustrates how an undesirable rule sequence was repeated in a family many times before it was recognized by a family member who was not involved.

Step 1. The father's emotional distress would occasionally increase. Many incidents could reactivate the cycle after a dormant period. For example, it could be activated by pressures at work, health frustrations, in-law troubles, or a personal disappointment.

Step 2. The father would behave in less patient and more critical or obnoxious ways. These first and second steps are a mini-cycle, called a positive feedback loop, that would increase both conditions with father getting more emotionally distressed, less patient, and more critical around the home. Eventually he would become angry or obnoxious enough that step 3 would occur.

Step 3. The teenage daughter's room was usually messy, and when the father wasn't upset he would usually ignore it. However, when he was upset and noticed the daughter's room was messy he would get after the daughter to clean her room.

Step 4. The daughter would clean her room according to her father's standards rather than her own.

Step 5. The father's pressure on the daughter would increase her emotional distress. Often this was because she would feel angry and resentful. (Sometimes the whole cycle would be reactivated with step 5.)

Step 6. The daughter's behavior in some area of her life would be less desirable. This could take many forms. It could be she became more irritable, did poorly at school, or misbehaved.

Step 1. The father's emotional distress would increase, and he would be less patient, etc.

The cycle would repeat again and again until something occurred to disrupt it. This particular cycle also had several variations. For example, sometimes the mother would get involved instead of the father, and sometimes both parents would get upset before pressuring the daughter. During one of the family "scenes" an older brother happened to notice the connection between steps 3 and 5. What he saw was 3 then 5 then 3 then 5, and so on. He described what he thought he saw, and it was enough for the family eventually to recognize they had created a vicious cycle. Once the cycle was in the consciousness of the family, they were able to see the other steps and devise several ways to disrupt it.

One strategy they devised was to work harder to find a compromise on the standards of cleanliness for the daughter's room. They realized that the ongoing negative tension (remember the chapter on emotions) could be contributing to the cycle, and, if the father and daughter were more comfortable about the standards for the room, it might help disrupt the sequence.

Being Adaptable

When family rules are too rigid, the family may break instead of bend when the winds of stress come their way (Haley, 1976). If families are willing to be adaptable in their rules and rule sequences it is very helpful. An example of the lack of adaptability is seen in what occurred after one mother died. Before her death the rules of family functioning were clear. Everyone knew the goals and knew how to achieve them. When she died suddenly, the system went into almost total shutdown. With no provision for flexibility, when she died there were great gaps left in the system's ability to function. Before her death, the mother had taken care of the bills, managed money matters, run the household, maintained connections with other relatives, and made many of the decisions about the growing children. It was months before this family could reorganize, change the rules, reallocate responsibilities, and begin functioning again.

The vitality of systems lies in a balance between the chaos of undefined competing rules and the rigidity of inflexible and unadaptable rules. **Rule rigidity** is another way to state the situation where families do not have enough flexibility or are resistant to change. Sometimes rule rigidity occurs when rules are appropriate in some situations but not in others. The story in Box 8.2 is an example of this type of rule rigidity.

The rule emerged, and it was necessary at one period of time. Later, it became obsolete, but it remained as an unexamined, submerged family rule. So are many of the rules families sustain. They have lost their purpose, but they continue on, as if breaking or changing them would be harmful. Sometimes families act as if changing a rule means destruction. In actual fact, to not change and adapt creates a better chance for destruction than holding to outdated and useless rules.

Rethinking Inappropriate Rules

Families sometimes create rules and rule sequences that are effective for a developmental stage, and they find it difficult to change as developmental changes occur. An example of this is a family that creates a group of rules around the notion that children must obey their parents. The rules could be appropriate when the children are young and immature, but as the children mature and increase in their ability to think for themselves, it is developmentally appropriate for the children to have increasing amounts of control over their life. As they mature, the rules about obedience become less useful and increasingly inappropriate.

For example, consider bedtime rules. An early-bedtime rule may emerge for several reasons when the children were young: Children need a lot of sleep when they are in grade school; parents need free time in the evening; having a set time allows for easy planning and makes the day orderly. However, if parents are still trying to make the child go to bed early when they are in high school, it can become unreasonable and developmentally inappropriate.

Another situation where it can be difficult for parents to change rules about obedience is when the rules are closely tied to family ideologies. When the parents in a family place a high value on obedience and conformity, they may be unwilling to let the system change so the children can become autonomous and independent.

It may also be difficult to change rules about obedience where parents have high standards for their children and they have a child who is not meeting their

Box 8.2

The story is told of the young newlywed who was preparing Sunday dinner. He was beginning to fix the roast when, to the surprise of his wife, he cut the end off the roast, wrapped it up, and put it in the refrigerator. His astounded wife asked him why. "I don't know," he replied. "That's the way my mom does it. I guess it's good to have a little left over." When the puzzled wife was visiting his mother, she asked her the same question, and got the same answer. Later, during a holiday, they all were at the grandmother's house eating roast, and to the wife's amazement the grandmother cut off the end of the roast, wrapped it, and continued with her preparations. "Could you tell me why you just did that?" asked the wife. "Well," the grandmother said, "I bought this roasting pan many years ago, and as you can see it is quite small. There is hardly a roast I buy that fits."

A sequence is a repetitive behavior pattern—of which participants are usually unaware.

standards. For example, if a child is rebellious or independent, or if the child gets into trouble often, the parents may be inclined to try to help the child by trying to enforce rules about obedience long after they are developmentally appropriate.

Developmental changes are continually occurring, so it is wise to expect that rules in family systems are always in a state of flux. Much of the time the rules change gradually without anyone paying attention to them, but in some situations it is helpful to make adjustments and modifications consciously.

Attacking Disabling Rules

Some family rules and sequences are disabling. This means that rules can cause family members to interact in unhealthy and damaging ways that interfere with their ability to accomplish family goals. **Disabling rules** are those that result in abuse to system members. Some families have a rule that legitimizes the hitting of family members by those who are bigger and stronger when someone violates a boundary. Another type of ineffective rule is one that labels individuals as having

"That was a most interesting and thought-provoking comment, Tommy. Now you will please leave the table and go to your room."

little value to the system. The rules may eliminate a person from important decisions and important conversation, as well as problem-solving processes. Unfortunately, many times other family members may not realize that they have established simple rules at the expense of one of the system members.

Some rule sequences limit expression and keep family members from disagreeing openly, without reprisal (Satir, 1972). Such sequences can limit freedom and quash individual growth and expression. They exclude individuals and make them feel like outsiders in their own family system.

Another type of destructive family sequence is one that communicates mistrust (Lidz, 1957; 1963). For example, sequences may exist that prohibit family members from testing ideas in the outside world. The realities of the world are distorted to meet the needs of family members. Consequently, the children may not learn to test reality, but be trained to accept the particular brand of irrationality constructed by the family as reality.

Some ineffective family rules and rule sequences may suggest two powerful, yet contradictory, behaviors. For example, a family may have consciously selected a democratic parenting style that encourages individual expression and growth but at the same time censures family members for seeking a life outside the family. They have constructed two competing messages: (1) We are an open and accepting family, and (2) we accept only certain types of choices about really important life decisions. In an extreme case, the family may have created a milieu of inconsistencies and contradictions. The usual result is that people act in inconsistent and unpredictable ways.

When families have rules that are disabling it is helpful to have enough adaptability and creativity that the old rules can be adjusted or new ones invented. In these situations honesty, openness, and willingness to compromise and try new ways of doing things can make the difference between a family's being an enabling and helpful place to live and a disabling and destructive place to live. When there is adaptability, the rule part of families can serve as a generative mechanism that is capable of creating regularity out of chaos (Yerby & Buerkel-Rothfuss, 1982, p. 2).

Maintaining Rule Implicitness

David Reiss (1981) developed an idea about what happens in families when they find attention is focused on the rules that are usually implicit. He suggested that:

> The first sign of a disorganizing family is the falling away of implicit regulation and coordination. In a smoothly running family, shared objectives, understandings, role allocations, and norms do not often have to be stated. . . . When a family finds it is engaged in laying out verbally explicit rules of itself, it is already in the midst of a stressful situation—although it may still be far from a full-blown crisis. (Reiss, 1981, pp. 179–80)

The disorganizing cycle occurs when greater attention is given to rules, more of them are made explicit, and the family becomes more disorganized. The disorganization apparently occurs for several reasons. As a family's attention is diverted to its rules, its concentration on coping with other aspects of life decreases. This results in chores not done, days of work missed, meals disrupted, and so on. Also, the family realm has such complicated and yet intimate systems that they bog down when attempts are made to explicate very many rules. In the public spheres, where relationships are more limited, rational, and efficiency oriented, it is helpful to bureaucratize and formalize laws, rules, and policies. But in the family realm, this strategy can be dysfunctional. Families can only operate when the majority of the beliefs they use to govern themselves are shared, implicit, and affectively comfortable.

This idea is helpful in understanding many disabling cycles in families. For example, many families have a difficult time adapting their implicit rule structure in a comfortable way during the teenage years. Many parents and teens try to deal with this by getting elaborate lists of explicit rules about what the teens can and cannot do, and the rules become part of the problem. Also, when one member of a family begins to deviate from the behaviors that have traditionally been acceptable in a family, a typical response is to lay down rules, but the rules seldom help. Whether the "deviant" behavior is alcoholism, drug abuse, or poor school performance, explicating rules tends to set up disabling cycles.

There are several stages of the family life cycle that may be exceptions to the generalization that families are functioning best when rules are implicit. One exception is during the formative stage of a family. When couples are engaged or newly married they find it enjoyable and helpful to focus a great deal of their attention on defining their rules and beliefs. At this stage of family life it is enabling to focus on their values and rules, as it helps to lay the foundations of the family system. Gradually, as they construct rules they can live with comfortably, the couple moves beyond this stage and the rule part of their system becomes implicit.

The same process may also occur when families encounter major transitions in the family life cycle. For example, when a new child is born, children reach adolescence, children start leaving home, retirement is near, or a death occurs, families seem to find it helpful to spend some time defining and redefining their rules. Usually, however, this occurs without the cycle escalating excessively, and the family is gradually able to let their new understandings recede into the realm of the implicit.

Using Levels of Abstraction

Some family rules mold the ideological part of family systems. Also, most rule sequences reflect fairly specific beliefs about how behavior should and should not occur, so they are at Level I (see Chapter 6 for a complete explanation of Levels I, II, and III). In fact, most of the time families manage the rule part of their life at a Level I focus.

Level I, the specific level of rules, is illustrated by what happens when a family decides one of its members is not behaving in accordance with the family standards. For example, if a husband believes his wife does not show enough respect for his ideas and opinions, he may be uncomfortable enough to tell her. He might say "You don't pay enough attention to my opinions" or "I'm uncomfortable with something. I don't think that my opinions are respected enough." This can lead to a discussion about when incidents occurred that didn't show enough respect, what the husband wants and feels, and what the wife wants and feels. She may realize that she is caught up in her own demands, and he has responded by feeling inadequate and isolated. They may then decide that she ought to pay more attention to his ideas and he ought to be less sensitive.

Some family situations are not resolvable by using only Level I processes. For example, when families begin to approach the adolescent stage of family development, the children often change some of their basic values more rapidly than their parents, and the conflicts that result from these changes often appear first as conflicts over family rules. The Level III changes in values are at the heart of the conflict, but it would be very unusual for the resolution to begin with the family members talking about their Level III value conflicts.

Suppose the teen wants more freedom and control. In these situations, parents often find themselves being concerned about how family rules are changed. The teen, on the other hand, is eager for autonomy and the freedom to explore new things, and pushes for major changes. Families who focus only on Level I processes could encounter considerable difficulty in this situation, and the conflict could easily escalate into pressure, arguments, defiance, attempts to enforce rules, and resistance.

When families find their usual ways of modifying and creating rules (staying at Level I) do not resolve their problems, a helpful strategy is to move to higher levels of abstraction and deal with values, paradigms, goals, and the basic structure of the way the family operates. Family scientists have discovered three fairly distinct ways of moving to the more abstract parts of family systems. They are:

1. Focus on differences and similarities in Level III things such as the family's worldview, values, family paradigms, and long-term goals.
2. Deal with Level II aspects of rules (meta-rules).
3. Deal with other Level II aspects of the family system, such as the methods of making decisions, the changing patterns of authority, or the changing power in the family system.

Focus on Level III. Family members tend to be fairly cautious and more rigid about family rules when the rule represents a more fundamental family value. What this means for managing family rules is that when a family is having difficulty managing their rules with their usual Level I procedures, it can be helpful to check out how similar the basic beliefs are. If there are fundamental differences or conflicts at the family paradigm level, these differences often make it impossible to come to consensus about Level I rules. If consensus can be reached at the philosophy-of-life level, this provides a foundation for dealing with the more specific and concrete level of family rules. Conversely, if agreements cannot be reached at Level III, this has important implications for what the family can and cannot do at the level of rules. When families have fundamental differences at Level III, the only way it is possible to have agreement at Level I is for the members to be flexible, adaptable, and tolerate considerable diversity in the family rules.

Focus on meta-rules. As noted earlier, the word *meta* means "about." **Meta-rules** are rules about rules. The meta-rules of interest here are those about how to create new rules, how to eliminate old rules, or how to change rules. Laing (1972) was referring to meta-rules in his comment that sometimes "there are rules against seeing the rules, and hence against seeing all the issues that arise from complying with or breaking them" (p. 106).

As the children in families mature, the meta-rules usually change. A meta-rule when children become teenagers might be that the ones who are the most upset by old rules, and make the biggest scene, determine the new rules. Effective families have a meta-rule structure that assists them when rules no longer work. This issue is closely tied to the idea of adaptability. As rules become obsolete, an adaptable family will have a viable meta-rule structure that allows them to replace, alter, or negotiate new rules that may be more appropriate for the situation. Some families do not have an adequate set of meta-rules about how to change their rules. When this occurs, families tend to become stuck in ways of doing things that were appropriate for earlier stages of development, and they have difficulty making the transitions into new stages of development.

SUMMARY

This chapter discussed two types of rules that operate in family systems. One of these types is social norms. These are beliefs that proscribe or prescribe behavior. Some norms are learned as part of the culture. Others are unique to a particular family, and they are passed from one generation to another. Still others are created by a particular family, and are unique to that family. Rules have many purposes. They regulate the way resources are managed, regulate emotional distance, clarify boundaries, control the implementation of decisions, clarify how to deal with exceptions and violation of rules, and many other things.

The second type of family rules is non-normative rules. Some non-normative rules govern and maintain behaviors that are inconsistent with the normative beliefs. These are usually not known by a family, but they can be inferred by watching the patterns in family behavior. Some non-normative rules in family systems are simple rules that govern the way individuals behave. Sometimes these rules are connected into rule sequences. These are patterned ways of behaving that involve sequences of behavior among several individuals. Rule sequences usually have a cyclic or feedback-loop aspect to them, and most families are not aware of them. These sequences can be healthy and enabling, or they can be disabling and help keep a family stuck in earlier developmental stages.

Problems sometimes occur in the rule part of family systems, and then families need to manage this part of their systems consciously. Family scientists have discovered several strategies for managing this part of family life. When rules become developmentally inappropriate, too rigid, or disabling, adaptability is helpful. Usually the more implicit rules are, the better. Therefore, when families find it necessary to deal explicitly with their rules, it is desirable to deal with them as little as possible and then let them slide out of awareness. Most of the time the rule aspect of families can be managed by focusing on Level I processes. However, when conflicts about rules are not readily resolved, it may be useful to move to Level II or Level III parts of family systems.

KEY TERMS

Rules
Social Norms
Normative
Non-normative
Mores
Folkways
Cohesion
Implementation
Implicit
Explicit
Rule sequences
Adaptability
Vicious cycles
Rule rigidity
Disabling rules
Meta-rules

Study Questions

1. List three ways normative rules emerge in a family.
2. List four reasons why normative rules are so important in families.
3. Define the words *explicit* and *implicit* and tell how each relates to the topic of family rules.
4. What is a non-normative rule? Give an example from your own experience.
5. List four ways normative and non-normative rules are different.
6. What is the definition of a rule sequence.
7. Why are certain rule sequences called vicious cycles?
8. How does one begin to "think sequences"?

Communication

9

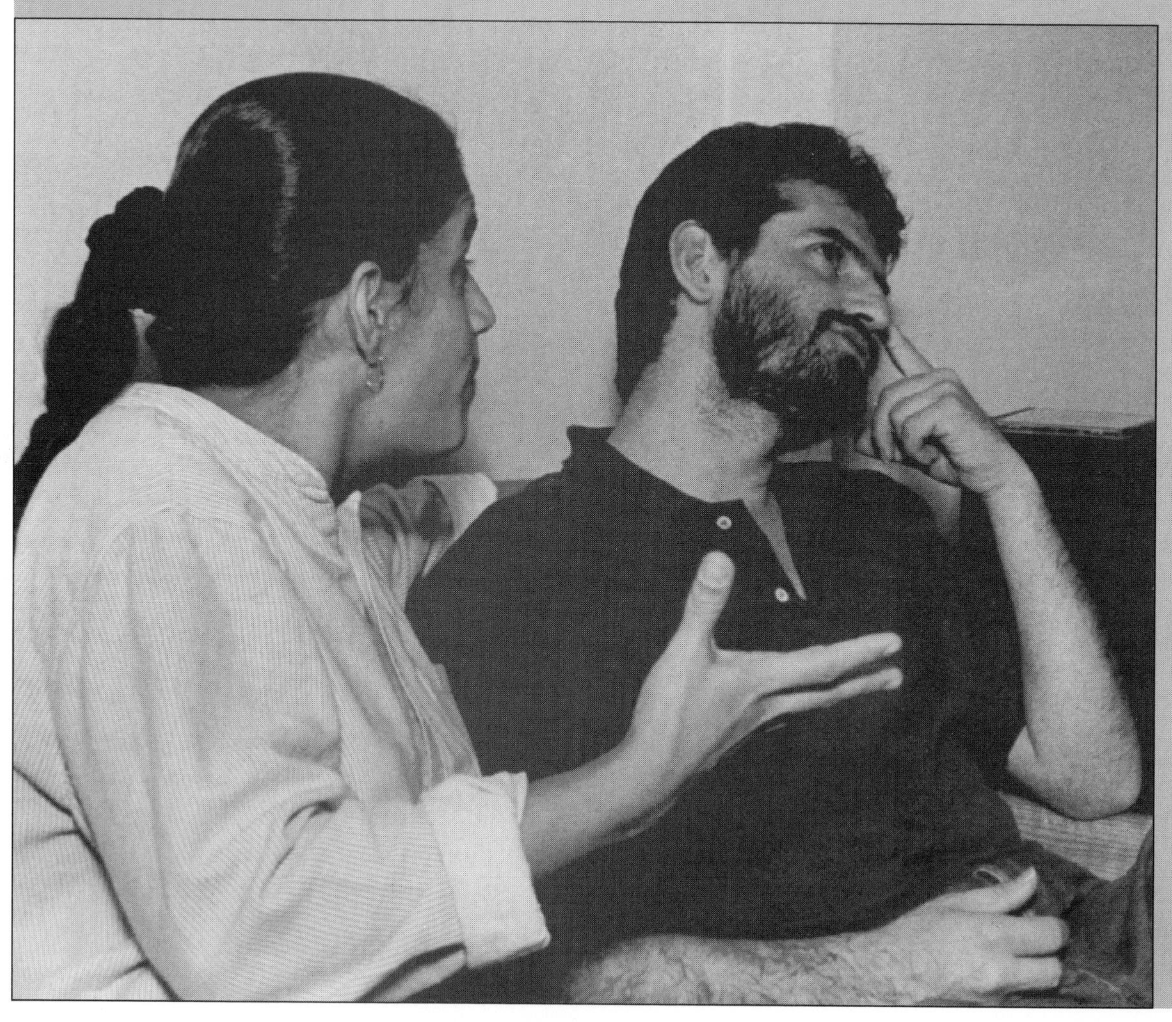

Main Ideas

1 // Communication can be defined as the exchange and sharing of messages, feelings, and intentions. It has two primary elements: digital and analogic messages.

2 // Being able to see context in analogic messages provides clues to understanding systemic processes in families.

3 // Competition and cooperation in families can be expressed through the communication styles they adopt.

4 // Sometimes families send paradoxical messages. These messages contain two different and competing messages at the analog and digital levels.

5 // A vicious cycle emerges when a strategy intended to achieve a certain goal actually produces the opposite result and triggers a repeat of the faulty strategy.

6 // Analogic messages often reveal information about non-normative rules that maintain gender inequality, oppression, and inappropriate uses of power and control.

7 // Some family ideologies promote appropriate levels of disclosure, while others promote either too little or too much. Appropriate level of disclosure is an important aspect of positive family functioning.

A capable Scoutmaster stood among his band of young, inexperienced Scouts. The forest before them was beautiful and inviting. As he began to talk with them, his goal was to help them see what they had not seen before, though it lay before them in full view. The tree nearest them was a Ponderosa pine. Its patchwork bark was bleached by years of sun. He asked them to not look at their compasses while guessing which direction was north. Arms pointed in a variety of directions. The Scoutmaster then asked the Scouts to look at the tall straight pine tree in front of them. On one side the bark was much darker than the other. He asked for suggestions as to why one side might have a different coloring. After a minute, the group guessed correctly that the sun had bleached one side. With well-placed questions, the Scoutmaster soon showed the group the arc of the sun, and how the south side of this type of pine tree is almost always lighter in color than the

"Once a human being has arrived on this earth, communication is the largest single factor determining what kinds of relationships he makes with others and what happens to him in the world about him."

—Virginia Satir, 1972

north side. He again asked the original question. All arms now pointed in the same direction, and their compasses soon confirmed the guesses.

Next, the Scoutmaster pointed to the ground cover underfoot. To the uninitiated, the leaves of the plants made a pleasant but rather uninteresting picture. The Scoutmaster picked out a small unobtrusive plant with three shiny dark-green leaves. He then reminded them of the painful itch of poison ivy. Where once they had seen only a mass of green, the Scouts now saw hundreds of small three-leaf plants with shiny leaves. They were surrounded!

An anonymous author once commented that seven-eighths of everything can't be seen. The purpose of this chapter is to help illuminate the subtle but critical world of family communication. Like the young Scouts in the story, most of us are usually unaware of the environment around us, particularly our family environment. But once something is pointed out our gaze becomes more discriminating and our analysis more accurate. This chapter is intended to reveal family communication in a new light. The family communication process, once understood, should turn family communication from a mass of green color into a field of individual plants—each with its own purposes, dangers, and uses.

The overall focus of this chapter is to examine the family communication process. First, we explore definitions and elements of family communication. Second, we examine several specific familial communication processes. And third, we look at the relationship between some important family processes and effective communication.

Understanding Family Communication

One way to begin to define the communication process is to look at some of the research about it. For many years it has been recognized that communication is a critical element in human interaction. It is commonly believed that the essence of fulfilling family relationships is the quality of their communication. While most family scientists would agree, they have struggled to define it precisely and to discover what makes it so important. They have also tried to learn how communication works between family members and which styles are more effective.

Early researchers focused primarily on the *amount* of communication. It was commonly believed that relationship satisfaction could be enhanced by sheer increases in communication; when family members shared more thoughts, feelings, and ideas, satisfaction was thought to be higher. When they shared less, satisfaction was lower. Advice peddlers, therefore, instructed couples to "tell all" (Broderick, 1984, p. 38).

The next approach to family communication enhancement came during the emergence of the electronic age. The process of sending and receiving electronic messages became a useful metaphor in describing communication. Instead of volume, family members were instructed to pay attention to the *clarity* of the message. Messages needed to be "encoded," "transmitted," and "decoded," without any "distortion." During this period most of the terms and metaphors used to describe communication came from how radio and television signals are sent and received. Anything causing message distortion was labeled *noise* (Broderick, 1984, p. 38). While this approach was useful and interesting, it soon became apparent there was more to family communication; family communication as a *process* became the key issue.

This chapter explores family communication as an integral element of the family's systemic process. The metaphor now being used to describe family communication is the *system*. The preceding chapters described family interaction as a unique and distinctive system of interacting parts. An accurate understanding of family communication, therefore, needs to focus on processes and dynamics relevant to the family system and how it functions. In particular, family communication is about how family members negotiate and transmit the rules and regulations of the system. Additionally, family communication is about emotional tone (Broderick, 1984); it is about when and how to share measured reactions with family members. The idea of measured emotional responses is critical because of the delicate nature of family systemic operation. Since messages sent to family members can have such diverse and unintended results, family members need to learn the subtle nature of appropriate response.

Defining Communication

In general, communication may be "viewed as a symbolic, transactional process, or to put it more simply, as the process of creating and sharing meanings" (Galvin & Brommel, 1991, p. 6). The communication process involves the exchange of symbols. We use a variety of both subtle and overt symbols in our messages. The communication of messages within a system is based upon certain assumptions. These assumptions set the stage for understanding how important and elusive our awareness of family communication can be. The "shared meanings" element of this process is an important idea upon which one should focus. The implication is that as we communicate with one another, the quality of that communication is dependent upon our ability to share common feelings, experience, desires, and goals. When communication is poorer and less effective, others are unsure of the intentions, feelings, and desires of others. And when there is confusion about those important aspects of familial experience, the richness of family experience is diminished.

Assumptions About Communication

One way to better understand how communication functions in families is to explore three specific assumptions describing family communication. Over the years, family scientists have considered several ideas about how systemic communication works. Many of these ideas come from observations of hundreds of families in counseling sessions. From these observations and subsequent research, theorists now suggest the following assumptions about family communication.

First, family communication is *not random.* Family communication consists of repetitive and relatively consistent patterns. Additionally, since these patterns are not random, they can be discovered and understood. Even if seven-eighths of every communication is initially hidden, some of the seven-eighths can still be discovered and clarified. We find that communication between family members is purposeful, meaningful, and critical to the understanding of human relationships.

Second, communication is *transactional.* Family members do not originate communication, but participate in it. The transactional nature of communication means that when people communicate, there is a reciprocal and mutual impact (Watzlawick et al., 1976). Therefore, it is rather unproductive to examine communication from the viewpoint of only one or two family members.

Since a system is a group of interacting parts, each interaction reflects the relationships of the system. Messages shape how each individual self-evaluates.

Communication is transactional. We don't originate it—we participate in it.

And, importantly, the message itself is shaped by both the content and the underlying intent, which may be the more important part of the message. It is that tone by which the individuals come to understand how they are perceived and valued.

Third, it is *impossible to not participate* in the communication process. Family therapists are fond of saying "you cannot *not* communicate" (Watzlawick et al., 1976). Even if the individual gets angry and storms out of the room, his silence still communicates; his refusal to talk it out is in fact a very powerful communication.

Even though a person may choose to limit severely the content of the message, not speaking is still a strong message that says "You really annoy me, and right now I demand that you and I will not exchange content information." A message is being sent, an unavoidable relationship message, clear and strong.

Elements of Family Communication

While family communication is about systemic processes, there are several structural elements that need explanation. The two primary elements of communication are digital and analogic. These two aspects of communication help describe and define how family communication works. Before we can understand how digital and analogic messages work together in a family to create communication, it is important to understand messages.

"I'm your wife, Arthur. You talk to me. You don't touch base with me."

Drawing by Joe Mirachi; © 1988, The New Yorker Magazine, Inc.

Messages

At the heart of understanding family communication are messages. **Messages** are the units of information sent between sender and receiver. In the seat of consciousness, the sender designs a message. This message can be about feelings, thoughts, ideas, or suggestions. Next the sender prepares, or encodes, the message. It may need to be disguised, censored, or otherwise made appropriate to the receiver (family member) and the situation. The message is transmitted to the receiver, who decodes and takes it in. At this point, he or she becomes aware of the message and its meaning.

Each message can have four general parts to it: (1) a subject telling us *who* the action of the message is about; (2) a predicate telling the receiver what is being *done*; (3) an object telling to *whom* the action is directed; and (4) the *context* of the action (Okun & Rappaport, 1980, p. 98).

In the example of family interaction found in Box 9.1, we see many of these elements present: Carolyn says "But I'm not like my mother at all. I don't think my mother has anything to do with this." Carolyn (the subject) is explaining clearly (the predicate) and plainly that she is not like her mother (the object). The context is a little more difficult. The context in this exchange is the intent of the message being sent to the counselor. Perhaps she is trying to send the message that she is feeling defensive and wants to change the direction of the counseling session. She may be defending her personal belief about what has gone on between her mother before, and her daughter now.

Box 9.1

Grand-mother's ghost

(from *The Family Crucible* by A. Napier and C. Whitaker)

The Family Crucible is a stirring account of two well-known family therapists dealing with a very troubled family. In the following segment, mother Carolyn and daughter Claudia have just had a very serious confrontation about who should be in control and how the father (David) tries to act as mediator between them. This segment reveals how much the daughter/mother relationship is like the mother/grandmother relationship, which greatly troubles the mother. The primary therapist in this book, Carl Whitaker, uses many principles from other therapists who highlight the importance of the family as a system and of family communication processes.

"Is all this [the confrontation between the mother and daughter] related to the battle between you and your mother? Was it like this in your own family?" Carl and I (the other therapist is Dr. Napier) had been down this road before, and I had a pretty good idea of what Carolyn would say.

The question startled and flustered her. "My mother and I?" Then she smiled a sort of crooked, private smile. "No, not quite like this."

"Can you say what it *was* like?"

"My mother was a very—well, how to say it—controversial woman in our home. Nobody really dared cross her, especially not my father. She had a temper, oh, did she ever have a temper! And she could be very critical." Then Carolyn paused and looked crossly at Carl, as if she were feeling betrayed by getting into this topic. "Why are we talking about my mother? She's not involved in this thing with Claudia!" She was irritated.

"Of course she is," Carl said firmly. "She is the only model you have for being a mother, and we're talking about your being a mother to your daughter."

Carolyn, still cross: "But I'm not like my mother at *all.* I don't think my mother has anything to do with this."

David stirred, as if trying to decide whether or not to say something. He dared. "Carolyn, you bristle if anybody says *anything* about your mother. I think after all these years you're *still* trying to please her."

Carl turned toward David, smiling broadly. "Listen, you psychiatrist you, I'll be the therapist here. You stay out of this!" He said it so genially that David couldn't help smiling, though he was a little embarrassed at being caught analyzing his wife again. It would indeed be a serious problem if David got into the middle of this dialogue. . . .

Carl was not to be deterred. "So your mother was critical of everybody? What was she so angry about?"

This was Carolyn's day to feel intimidated. If it wasn't her daughter, it was this damned therapist. But she acquiesced. "I don't really know. I know that my mother worked awfully hard all her life—she was a teacher and a very strong person. My father, on the other hand, had a 'back injury,' or so the story went, and he spent a lot of time reading and doing odd jobs and supposedly looking for work. And he did work for awhile from time to time. But Mother supported the family mostly, and she never let Dad forget it."

Carl: "So Mom was furious that Dad was sitting on his ass and mad at herself for letting him get away with it."

Carolyn, softly, as if to herself: "I suppose so. But she really took it out on him. He paid plenty. And so did the rest of us."

(continued)

Box 9.1

(continued)

"You too?" I asked.

"Me too." That devastated look again as she remembered . . .

"I have always been afraid of my mother, I suppose," Carolyn said, "and as my husband says, I probably still try to please her." A pause. "She can be very critical of me, just devastating at times, and it always tears me up."

I was startled to hear her use the word "devastating"—we obviously agreed about how she felt. As she talked more about her mother, her body tensed perceptibly. We were pushing her, true, but gently and slowly, and we were well aware of her pain.

"What does she criticize?" I asked.

"Oh, it doesn't really matter," Carolyn said angrily. "Everything I do displeases her—the way I handle the kids, where I live, the way I dress. When she's cross, it doesn't matter what she's mad at." Then she seemed to shift mood, smiling slightly. "But don't get the wrong idea. There are a lot of good things about her, too—and a lot of good things between us."

"Any sense of what's behind the attack on you?" Carl asked. "You aren't your father's favorite or something like that, are you?"

Carolyn blushed. "Well, yes I suppose I am. My father and I have always been quite close, though I'm not sure my mother would *know* that. I think she would say that she and I were quite close. And in some respects she would be right. It's really very confusing to me."

Carl: "So you're really pretty deeply connected with both your parents."

"More involved than either my brother or my sister, I think," Carolyn said matter-of-factly.

I asked if her siblings were both younger than she. They were. I had one more question, though I thought I knew the answer to it before I asked. "Did you ever fight with your mother? Ever push back when she pushed you?"

Carolyn shook her head slowly. "No. As I said, I think I've always been afraid of her."

"Still?" I asked, smiling. "Even at age . . . ?"

"She's sixty-eight." Carolyn thought for a minute. "Well, maybe I'm not still afraid of her anger. But I'd be afraid to fight with her now for fear of hurting her."

I wondered silently to myself about the mother, trying to visualize this older woman who had felt so powerful and so hurtful to her daughter, and about her being still older now and perhaps frail, and then about the father who was weak, yet who could make his wife so angry. These were hazy, unclear images, full of contradictions. My picture of where Carolyn fitted in their lives was blurred, too, though some patterns seemed very clear.

Carl, obviously thinking about some of the parallels: "Can I push you to take this a step further?"

Carolyn said yes rather tentatively, not knowing what Carl was up to.

Carl: "Does what happens between you and Claudia make any sense now, when you think about what has gone on with you and your mother?"

Carolyn: "No. It seems very, very different. I would *never* talk to my mother the way Claudia talks to me. Not in a thousand years!" She was indignant at the very idea of any parallels between the two relationships.

Carl smiled slightly. "That's what I mean. It's so different. It's as if you've become your mother in this dance, and Claudia's become like the part of you that wanted to stand up to Mother and didn't dare to." Carl was still smiling.

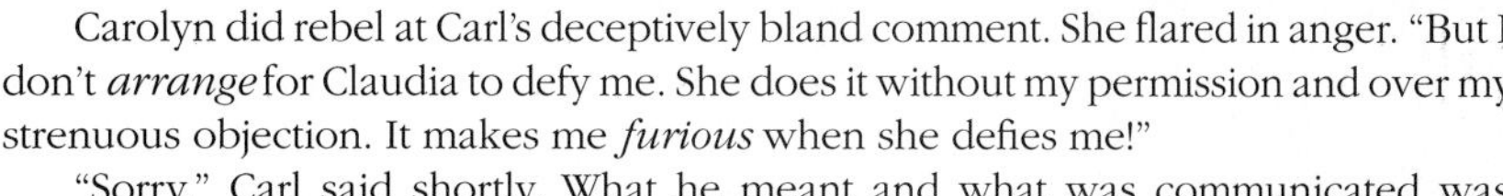

Carolyn did rebel at Carl's deceptively bland comment. She flared in anger. "But I don't *arrange* for Claudia to defy me. She does it without my permission and over my strenuous objection. It makes me *furious* when she defies me!"

"Sorry," Carl said shortly. What he meant and what was communicated was "You're wrong." Then, in a tough, even voice: "What you get credit for is what *happens*, not what you say you *want* to happen." Then he added, lightening his tone a bit and glancing at David: "Of course, your husband has to take a lot of the credit, too. I don't mean to scapegoat you." Another pause. "But it would be a mistake to avoid looking at your part in the way this thing goes."

Carolyn was still indignant. "I can't see it. I will not believe that any part of me would want my daughter to talk to me this way."

Carl, not relenting: "But it's what *happens*."

Carolyn: "But not what I *want* to happen!"

Digital messages. In addition to these primary elements of communication, there are other subtle ingredients. The idea of context involves two factors mentioned earlier: digital and analogic messages.

The **digital message** is the actual words and content; it is the raw statement. Consider the example in Box 9.1: "I don't think my mother has anything to do with this." Looked at digitally, it is a statement of fact. Only when we read it in context does it come alive, revealing a relationship element.

The **analogic message** defines the nature of the relationship between the sender and receiver. Analogic elements of messages can affirm or negate the content part of the message. One teen says to another: "You're so cute." While the digital element of this message is rather straightforward, the analogic part gives it life. In the context of the analogic element, the digital aspect of this message has many different possibilities: a statement of fact; a sarcasm; a put down; even a warning. Not until we know the analogic component of this message are we really sure of the intent.

Analogic messages. The analogic part of Carolyn's denying she is like her mother is probably a warning. She may be saying to the counselor "Let's not get into that. I don't want to bring up this topic. It is scary for me." In this way, the analogic component has that element of command to it. She is attempting to get the heat off.

Suppose a husband is lying on the couch watching the game of the week. He sees one of his children pass through the kitchen. "Please bring me a drink, Honey" he calls out. One family scientist states that "when one person communicates a message to the other, he is by that act making a maneuver to define the relationship" (Haley, 1963, p. 8). The analogic (command/relationship) element of the couch potato request cannot be avoided. The message clearly highlights the power difference between the sender and receiver. It defines one as "helper" and "caretaker" and the other as "helpee" (Okun & Rappaport, 1980, p. 9). When the child gets the drink, she is allowing her father to control her and she has contributed to defining the relationship by accepting the message. If she refuses, she also participates in relationship definition by refusing to be controlled.

As can be seen in Box 9.2, there are several types of analogic messages that can be sent. Some of those messages define relationships in positive, cooperative, supportive ways; other messages define the relationship as combative, competitive, and even abusive. The following section examines competitive and cooperative messages and how they affect the relationship process.

Familial Process

There are aspects of family communication that either are influenced by, or influence, family processes. Each of these fundamental processes are vital to family functioning. Most of them involve a clear understanding of the digital and analogic processes in communication. Each of the following are elements of ideology and the patterns maintained by a family system.

Competitive and Cooperative Communication

Box 9.2 shows a variety of analogic message types. Each is found under one of two general categories: **competitive** and **cooperative communication**. These two terms describe whether the messages sent in a family system produce feelings of competition and control or support and relationship enhancement. Box 9.2 also includes examples of cooperative and competitive messages: demanding change, specifying ownership, and so on.

Each competitive analogic message creates a situation where one family member is extracting or demanding something from others. Each cooperative message communicates feelings of security, acceptance, and trust. Competitive analogic messages say "I have a need to compete with you and make myself feel better by controlling you or changing you." Cooperative analogic messages convey noncompetitive messages that say "You are valuable, I trust you, and I want our relationship to continue."

When family members send primarily complementary analogic messages, the negative valence of those messages creates more competitive responses (Haley, 1976). It would be unlikely for a family member who is being punished or controlled to respond with cooperative analogic messages. Instead, when communication is about control and power, family members *maneuver* for power in order to stay in control. To respond in a noncontrolling, cooperative mode would probably be seen as a sign of weakness or defeat, not a sign of positive change. The same principle is true for families who respond to each other with primarily cooperative responses. In other words, kindness and gentleness beget more kindness and gentleness.

Box 9.2

Types of analogic messages

Cooperative Analogic Messages

Affirmation and Reward

These messages tell the receiver that what they are doing is pleasing and rewarding, and that the sender is happy and eager to be with the receiver. There is also the implication that the sender has some ability to reward the receiver. This means the receiver values the praise and admiration of the sender.

Digital statement:

"The things you say really make me laugh. I love the way I feel when we are together."

Analogic meaning:

Assuming this person is sincere and also one for whom there is great respect, the analogic message could be one of significant affirmation. "You are special, I like being around you, and I feel good when I am around you."

Building Trust

These analogic messages define the relationship as close and special. They can be transmitted by disclosing emotions, seeking understanding, or revealing the special, intimate parts of our past that we rarely share. Many times they communicate an intention of trust and sharing.

Digital statement:

(From Box 9.1) ". . . I know that my mother worked awfully hard all her life—she was a teacher and a very strong person. My father, on the other hand . . ."

Analogic meaning:

This paragraph contains the analogic message to the counselor that Carolyn is now ready to disclose some of her most special and important feelings. She feels safe and is willing to trust the counselor. This defines their relationship as more bonded and more trusting.

Competitive Analogic Messages

Creating or Maintaining Distance

The intent of these analogic messages is to set tight, rigid boundaries. It says there is limited information or feeling wanted from other family members.

Digital statement:

"I'm unsure about tonight. I've been very busy all week. Last week was such a bear for me. You know what I'm like when I don't get my rest."

(continued)

Box 9.2

(continued)

Analogic meaning:

One possible meaning of the above digital statement is "I am bored with our relationship and find it tedious. I am also trying to find a kind way of distancing myself from you without upsetting you too much."

Demanding Change

The purpose of this message is to force individual family members to change, and to alter family patterns of interaction. It is generally a control technique, and is usually a display or reaffirmation of relationship power.

Digital statement:

(From Box 9.1) "Everything I do displeases her—the way I handle the kids, where I live, the way I dress. When she's cross, it doesn't matter what she's mad at."

Analogic meaning:

In this example, Carolyn is describing how the analogic meaning of the messages she receives from her mother is demanding change from her. The messages from the mother define their relationship as one of control and submission.

Specification of Ownership

The function of this message is to assure the receiver that the sender perceives ownership with regard to the object of the message. This could be anything, including the receiver, or the feelings being expressed.

Digital statement:

Teen to mother: "This is my room, I will clean it when I want to. You do not have any right to tell me to take these posters off of my wall."

Analogic meaning:

Behind this exchange is a strong demand statement. It also has an intense competitive ring to it, which probably signals that the relationship between the parent and teen is competitive.

Punishment

Punishment messages define the relationships in particularly destructive ways. Messages about punishment are usually much more than just a parent teaching the child what is or is not expected. Instead, they interpret relationships in a severely competitive way. Messages of punishment may even include a relationship definition that says "If you do not allow me to punish you, our very relationship is in jeopardy."

Digital statement:

(Carolyn, in Box 9.1) "I have always been afraid of my mother, I suppose . . . and as my husband says, I probably still try to please her. She can be very critical of me, just devastating at times, and it always tears me up."

Analogic meaning:

The intent of Carolyn's mother in this dialogue is clear. She is using punishment and control to maintain and define their relationship as competitive.

Seeking Validation

Seeking approval and validation is a very competitive and debilitating communication theme. Typically, the analogic message says to the receiver "In addition to the digital information I am sending you, please, please, please, tell me I am a worthwhile individual, worthy of recognition."

Digital statement:

"I'm wondering dear, how do you like the job I did on the yard? You know I worked hard to make this look nice. What do you think?"

Analogic statement:

While the digital part of this message is asking for feedback, in this case the intent is to get the spouse to commend and reward the effort as part of a continuing strategy to seek approval and validation.

Surrendering and Declaring Martyrdom

Surrendering is also a competitive and manipulative strategy in family communication. The intent is to solicit and extract help, whine until rescued, and define the relationship in terms of helplessness and weakness.

Digital statement:

A couple has been arguing about the distribution of work around the home. She responds to his demand for change with the following: "I don't know why we can't resolve this. I just never seem to be able to please you. Every time I try to do better, you yell at me. I just feel like giving up."

Analogic meaning:

The woman in this dialogue is using a powerful analogic message to attempt to control the conversation. She probably feels it is her only defense against the strong, punishing male she is facing. The result is that both feel unsatisfied and demeaned by the process. She is saying, in essence, "since I can't stop you from pounding on me and controlling our relationship, I will retaliate by trying to get you to turn your attention to rescuing me. Please see me as a helpless child in need of your attention."

Paradoxical Messages

Communication has a direct and substantial impact upon the process of bonding within a family. How we bond with one another has a specific impact on the level of dysfunction or "normality" expressed by the individuals within a family

(Broderick & Pulliam-Krager, 1979). Sometimes family bonds can be too tight, other times too lax. According to current research findings, bonds that are too tight or too enmeshed contribute to mental illness and antisocial behavior of family members. Conversely, bonds that are too lax contribute to undersocialization.

As researchers began to uncover and scrutinize the relationship between mental illness in family members and the communication styles used by those families, some very interesting patterns were discovered. The first such pattern was described by Gregory Bateson (1954) and labelled the *double bind.* The double bind is a particularly destructive paradox that occurs in family communication.

The first element of the **double bind paradox** is that two conflicting imperatives are transmitted to a family member. An imperative is something that must be obeyed. To make the problem more confusing and intense, the conflicting imperatives occur at two different levels of communication, digital and analogic. That is, the spoken (digital) message is one thing, while the unspoken (analogic) message is the opposite. This is known as a **paradoxical message**.

In the classic example cited by Bateson and his colleagues, a mother goes to visit her son, who is a patient in the hospital. The son sees the mother coming, and impulsively puts his arm around her. As he embraces her, she stiffens (the analogic message being rejection and coolness). He responds to the coolness and backs off. She then says "What's the matter, don't you love me anymore?" He blushes, and she says "Dear, you must not be so easily embarrassed and afraid of your feelings." The therapist reported that the son was able to only stay with the mother for a short time, and then became so agitated that he assaulted an aide (Bateson et al., 1956, p. 259).

Another element of this double bind could be called a third imperative. It says "Our family paradigm is one of closeness and conformity. You cannot escape from the family emotional field." The trapped child in this case was literally driven crazy by the power of those imperatives.

These types of paradoxical communications are often used as a basis for humor in TV or movies. In the public realm, however, they are not tolerated for long. In business, if someone consistently sends two competing messages, customers soon go elsewhere. What makes this process so intense in the family realm is that emotional escape is quite difficult and costly. In the last 10 years new research has shown that mental illness such as schizophrenia may have at its root a strong chemical imbalance in the brain; however, it is clear that the patterns of interaction described here significantly contribute to the problem.

There are many types of double-bind messages that can be sent to family members. For example, at the digital level children may be told that independence and autonomy are valued or even preferred. But at the analogic level the parent could be sending a message that to leave and be independent is disloyal. At the digital level the husband could tell his wife that he supports her pursuing a career outside the home, while at the analogic level he displays his displeasure that she is not a full-time housewife. Families might say (digital) that they value honesty, while analogically condoning wide deviation from accepted community standards. What makes this paradox so devastating is the third imperative, which insists not only that you comply with two competing, contradictory messages but also that you cannot escape the situation.

Another double bind message that has been identified is described using the terms **pseudomutuality** and **pseudohostility**. There are commands at the verbal (noticeable) level to family members to maintain harmony, while at the analogic (unseen) level there is a pervasive and continuous tone of hostility. Similarly, some families maintain a surface hostility, when in fact the pervasive underlying tone is high bonding and closeness (Wynne, Ryckoff, Day & Hirsch, 1958).

It is important to remember that the problem of the double bind is exaggerated when the family system is closed. The family paradigm prescribes that no one can leave the field despite the conflict (Broderick & Pulliam-Krager, 1979). Some families may even generate a "crazy-making" digital message that says we are open and willing to have individuals come and go within the family, when in fact the analogic message communicates that the family is quite closed and rigid. One researcher referred to this type of double bind message as the "rubber fence" (Wynne, 1958). The imagery is clear: the boundary around the family appears to be permeable, the family says go ahead and leave, but the fence only stretches.

Even when the third imperative (the injunction that one cannot leave) is absent from the formula, double-message sending is destructive. Downgraded from the status of a true double bind, this message is labelled as message *inconsistency* (Kantor & Lehr, 1975; Broderick & Pulliam-Krager, 1979). The power of inconsistency is simple. Two conflicting messages are sent, and the receiver cannot choose either one without violating the other. Without the third imperative, the family member is more able to flee the crazy-making situation. Even so, fleeing the emotional family field is difficult and painful. In fact, it has been suggested that this fleeing behavior is strongly associated with deviant behavior in children (Broderick & Pulliam-Krager, 1979).

Vicious Cycles

The spider web is a place of death for those who are caught in its sticky, unyielding trap. The vicious cycle is like that sticky web. The more we struggle with the tacky glue in a vicious cycle, the more we become caught and confused. We first referred to vicious cycles in the Rule Sequences section of Chapter 8. When we use a given strategy to attain some goal in a relationship (make it stronger, change it, eliminate it), and that strategy takes us away from the very thing we are trying to achieve, we are said to be in a vicious cycle. The more the fly struggles, the more trapped he becomes; the very strategy he uses to get free is the thing that ensnares and binds him tighter.

A vicious cycle exists only when certain conditions are met (Broderick, 1984). First, a family member does something that breaks an implicit or explicit normative or non-normative rule. Imagine a 14-year-old who begins experimenting with smoking, much to the dismay of the parents. Second, in response to the rule

ROG BOLLEN reprinted by permission of NEA, Inc.

being broken, one or more family members designs a quick strategy intended to motivate the rule breaker to stop. The family grounds the 14-year-old, takes away privileges, or imposes some other sanction. In this situation, the analogic message is misread by the child. She probably does not understand the concern being expressed, misreading the intention as one of control and regulation. The occurrence of this discrepancy between intentions and behavior worsens the situation.

Third, once the analogic message is misread, the child does not abandon the target behavior, instead redoubling her effort to show she is independent and will not be controlled. This brings on the fourth stage of this fly-and-web drama, wherein the parents increase the power of the overt message of disapproval, and fail to take care of the unintentional analogic message that is still being received by the child. The parents turn up the volume of the chosen strategy, instead of trying a new strategy. Their fantasy is that if they do not do everything in their power to stop her, she will continue increasing the negative target behavior (smoking). They may ask themselves, if they cannot control this behavior what is next? So, they reason, we must gain control on this issue here and now. The very strategy they are using (to achieve a worthy goal) is the thing that makes the problem worse.

Many therapists have noted that families are very resistive to requests to re-examine their strategy of communication or to consider how analogic messages are being received. It is as if they fear a change in strategy would mean that gravity would cease, and the family would float off into space!

Again, the power of the analogic message is clear. When it is not understood and believed, the results can spell disaster.

Gender Inequality

There is a definite gender difference with regard to the analogic messages sent in relationships. It has been noted with some consistency that wives express more feelings and emotions in the covert/analogic parts of messages than do men (Notarius & Johnson, 1982). In this particular study, couples were videotaped as they discussed issues which they had rated particularly important to their relationship. Trained coders then watched the tapes and looked for incidence of positive (warm, tender, affectionate, cheerful) versus negative (cold, impatient, sarcastic, blaming, competitive) messages. Wives were much more likely to display both positive and negative analogic messages. Men are generally less expressive. They are much less likely to show love, happiness, or sadness (Balswick & Averett, 1977).

Men are, however, more likely to be dominating and forceful when they do show emotion (Kramarae, 1981). This research clearly shows that men and women use different types of analogic messages to achieve desired outcomes. Those desired outcomes are, in fact, different for men and women. Men seem to want facts, and have a need to solve problems, in their interactions. On the other hand, women seek empathy and understanding, and may want someone to "just talk" with them (Sherman & Haas, 1984). The tone or analogic intent of our messages demand different responses from the listener. If social support is desired, then the tone needs to be positive, tender, and affectionate. But if the goal of interaction is to solve problems, it would appear that the best strategy is to be more "businesslike."

In the family realm, the challenge for men especially is to learn how to shift from the tone of the nonprivate world to that of the patient, affectionate, and tender world of the family.

Disclosure in Families

The word *intimacy* is derived from two Latin words meaning "to make known" and "innermost." The intention of this word, therefore, leads people to equate disclosure with intimacy (Knapp, 1984). While it is true that, as individuals increase their affection for one another, as they join and become a family unit, they are more likely to increase the level of disclosure to one another. But an important question may be "Is more openness always better?" In other words, should families be encouraged to change or develop family rule structures based on the idea that the optimal situation is complete openness?

Definition of Self-disclosure

Self-disclosure occurs "when one person voluntarily tells another things about himself which the other is unlikely to discover from other sources" (Pearce & Sharp, 1973, p. 414). There is another aspect of self-disclosure that is important to family scientists. Self-disclosure is important in understanding trust and the development of relationship rules. For many years, family scientists taught that when family members were more open they would achieve greater levels of intimacy and bonding. For example, Jouard (1971, p. 46) stated: "The optimum in a marriage relationship . . . is a relationship between I and Thou, where each partner discloses himself without reserve." Lederer and Jackson (1968, p. 109) also supported this position by stating that "couples (high disclosing couples) who enjoy trust, who give trust to each other, probably are among the more fortunate people alive." To support this position, research on the topic revealed that couples having family rules that promoted high self-disclosure were more satisfied than those who did not (Levinger & Senn, 1967; Burke, Weir & Harrison, 1976).

Other family scientists, however, began to question this assumption. Gilbert (1976a) found some conflicting evidence for the idea that more disclosure created better relationships. She suggested that disclosure be considered in terms of content messages (the digital message), valence (whether the analogic element was positive or negative, competitive or cooperative), and message level (whether the message was digital or analogic). She also hypothesized that medium quantities of disclosure would result in higher family satisfaction.

Other authors have also suggested that "telling all" with blunt honesty is merely abusive. "The marriage relationship gives you no license to make childish confessions of past misdeeds, or to turn your mate into a dumping ground for your personal guilts" (O'Neill & O'Neill, 1972, p. 111).

The analogic tone of disclosure has much to do with the success of how much disclosure can be appropriate. While "higher self-disclosure levels are more characteristic of happily married couples, . . . unhappily married couples are higher in disclosure of a negative valence. Families characterized by pleasant, content self-disclosure will be able to experience intimacy at higher levels more easily than those trying to discuss painful, negative laden issues" (Galvin & Brommel, 1991, p. 94).

The emotional analogic tone set by disclosure messages, therefore, has a direct bearing on how family members feel about each other. When the tone is negative and critical (competitive), members are more likely to report dissatisfaction.

Based on a review of research about how self-disclosure affects family relationships, Gilbert (1976b) suggests a "curvilinear" relationship between disclosure and family member satisfaction (curvilinear means that the relationship is not linear). If the relationship were linear, then more disclosure would lead to more satisfaction. However, at a certain point too little disclosure can create dissatisfaction—just as can too much. Moderate levels of disclosure are the best.

Appropriate Self-disclosure

One way to apply the information on self-disclosure is to understand several general characteristics of how self-disclosure works best. These suggestions are taken from family scientists who work with family members as they enhance appropriate levels of intimacy (Pearce & Sharp, 1973, pp. 416–21).

1. Relatively few communication transactions need to involve high levels of self-disclosure. In the discussion of rules in Chapter 8, it was mentioned that we can know when problems are arising if families have to suspend their normal functioning and renegotiate the complex rules of functioning. Similarly, discussing intimate feelings occurs infrequently in established relationships like those found in a family. Only at special times and places is it advisable or even possible for family members to share deep personal feelings. Since disclosure requires special time and setting, feelings and unique moments can be inadvertently forgotten or ignored. The skillful family member recognizes when disclosure is timely and appropriate.

One exception to this general idea is the engaged or newlywed couple. The amount of time spent sharing intimate special feelings is probably quite high for most. One problem many couples report after several months (or possibly as long as a few years) of marriage is that the spark is gone out of their relationship, and it is not like it once was. One of the reasons for this is that as we know each other better it is simply neither as necessary nor appropriate to spend great amounts of time disclosing. In fact, as was mentioned, over-disclosing can bring much discontent.

Some couples who develop a relationship rule that specifies continual disclosure may find themselves in quicksand. To fulfill the rule of disclosure, they may have to search for new relationship issues to disclose, and find that the only things left are negative! From the beginning, therefore, younger couples can establish general communication rules like "Please monitor what is disclosed in our intimate conversations. If something negative needs to be discussed, do it gently and without competitive messages."

2. Self-disclosure is more effective in dyads. It is probably not as effective to share most intimate feelings with the whole family at once. Occasionally it may work to get the attention of all family members and tell about a special feeling or

experience. However, for the most part, research shows that disclosure is probably more effective one on one.

3. Self-disclosure is also more effective when it is noncompetitive. It is critical that it not be used in a manipulative way. One of the more unfortunate responses that can happen during disclosure is that the sender realizes the receiver now has power over the sender. Information about intimate and special feelings can carry great destructive force. One way this power may be neutralized is for each person to share, so that there is little imbalance between what family members know about each other.

4. More effective self-disclosure occurs in the context of positive relationships. It is critical for trust to be high before effective sharing can occur. This is particularly true as children reach adolescence. In addition, recall from Chapter 3 how generational alliances can be dysfunctional to family functioning. When a parent uses disclosure as a way to solicit the alliance of a child, a destructive triangle can occur. Appropriate disclosure occurs when the analogic tone is positive and there is no intent to form coalitions.

5. Appropriate self-disclosure occurs in increments. Family members cannot assume that just because a person is "family" they will automatically disclose. Even family members (*especially* family members!) must be convinced inch by inch that their feelings and special thoughts will not be squandered or exposed to public view at the pleasure of the receiver.

In summary, indiscriminate or overzealous disclosure can cause as much difficulty as a lack of significant family communication. Such indiscriminate self-disclosure drains "the force out of and cheapens people's feelings" (Knapp, 1984, p. 211). We went through an unfortunate period in American society where the advice peddlers counseled family members to spill all at any cost. By the 1970s, however, there was a backlash:

> An entire culture, just about, was involved in erasing a significant boundary line between public and private domains . . . taciturn children run the risk of seeing themselves as troubled. . . . But if there is a need to reveal, there is also a need to protect and withhold. (Cottle, 1975, p. 19)

Developing Effective Communication

By understanding the nature of analogic messages and developing an appropriate level of disclosure, family life can be enriched. In Box 9.3, there are several dos and don'ts of family communication. As can be seen, the first one is "Attend to the intent analogic messages." This is not an easy task; learning this skill takes practice. In the beginning of this chapter the story was told of the scouts who suddenly "saw" the poison ivy around them. The first step in learning to "see" (attend to the tone and intent level in a family's messages) is to understand the concept. The second step is to actively listen to and observe the pervasive tones being transmitted in a family. A most important element of this process is to make every effort to match the intent with the digital message. For some, that will mean seeking out a skilled counselor who can help identify discrepancies in analogic and digital messages.

It is also important to assume that your family members are decent people who for the most part share your desire to succeed. Many times there is confusion about the messages sent, and family members become confused about the overall goals. As was mentioned above, a key element in more effective communication is to decrease the competitive elements. This can be done by using a soft tone of voice, touching in a nondemanding way, and using direct eye contact. Also accepting responsibility for feelings is a critical skill. When feelings are denied, the beginnings of paradoxical messages are inevitable. Family members can easily read the feeling. If the digital message says "I do not have that feeling," confusion or distrust may be created.

What is assumed about our family members is critical. One of the most competitive aspects of relationships occurs when the assumption is made that family members are adversaries. When we treat them as competitors, we are

Box 9.3

Dos and don'ts of family communication

Dos

Do pay attention to the analogic messages of communication.

Do make sure that the intent (analogic) aspect of family messages matches the digital messages.

Do assume that family members are caring people who share your desire to work things out.

Do use a soft tone.

Do, if it seems appropriate, touch family members in a nondemanding way while talking.

Do, if it seems appropriate, use direct eye contact.

Do talk about your own feelings and accept responsibility for them.

Do say what you like and not just what you don't like.

Don'ts

Don't assume that family members are your enemies.

Don't use a whiny or insistent tone of voice.

Don't use a threatening tone.

Don't tell family members what you think they *really* think or feel.

Don't complain about things that cannot be changed, such as intelligence, physical appearance, or family history.

modeling our family-realm feelings on the less-intimate public realm, and the resulting interactions will tend to be void of the special feelings and emotions necessary to enhancement of the family realm.

Another important skill to develop is learning to not complain about things that cannot be changed. So much unnecessary emotion tends to be wasted in attempting to lay blame, figure out what went wrong, and identify attributes of those who cause us trouble. Instead of developing the skills of critiquing the past, more emphasis should be placed on sending positive analogic messages and solving the issues that are presently occurring.

SUMMARY

In this chapter we described the complex nature of communication within the family. One of the key elements in understanding this complexity is knowing how messages are sent and that they are composed of digital and analogic elements. We discussed the power of analogic elements and noted that several family processes are directly tied to analogic communication. Among those discussed were cooperative and competitive communication, paradoxical messages, vicious cycles, and gender inequality. It was also suggested that there is an appropriate level of disclosure associated with enhanced family functioning.

KEY TERMS

Communication processes
Message
Digital messages
Analogic messages
Cooperative communication
Competitive communication
Paradoxical messages
Vicious cycle
Gender inequality
Self-disclosure

STUDY QUESTIONS

1. Briefly describe how family researchers changed in their approach to communication over the years.
2. What is the definition of communication used in your text?
3. List the three assumptions about family communication found in your chapter.
4. Describe the difference between digital and analog messages.

5. Describe what analogic message is sent in a competitive communication.
6. What is meant by pseudo-mutuality?
7. Define what is meant by a "vicious" cycle and give an example of one, other than the one found in your text.

Part 3

APPLICATIC
AND ISSUES

Balance

10

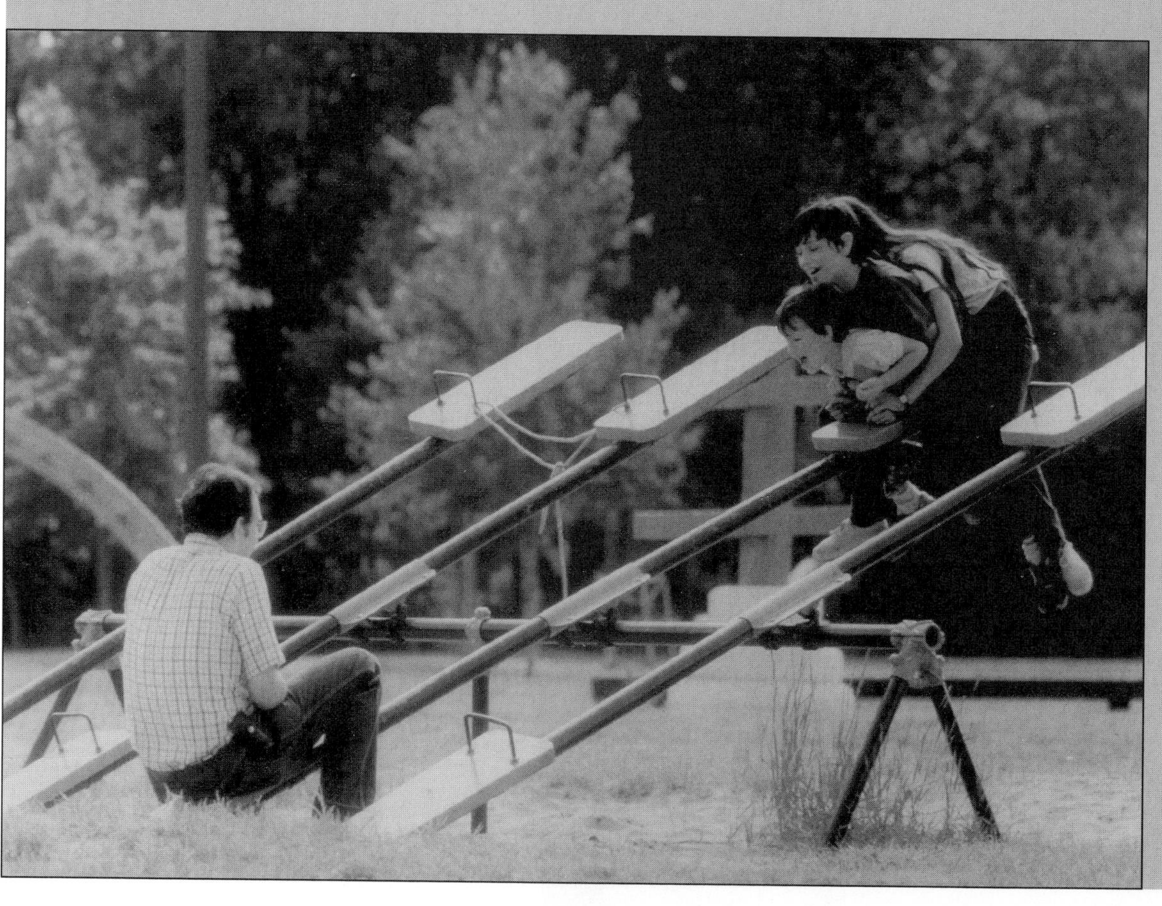

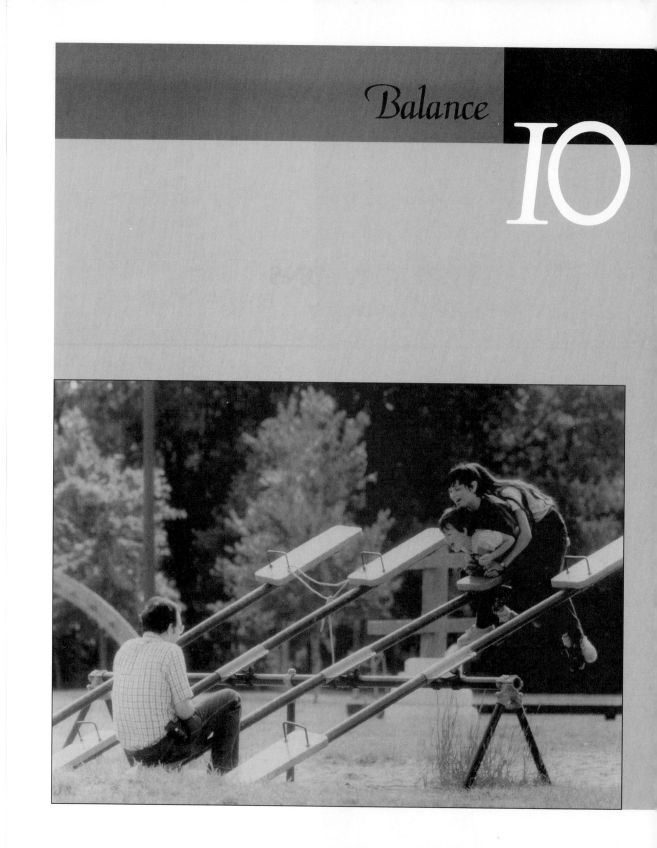

Main Ideas

1 // The golden mean is a term which means that finding the mean or moderation, by avoiding extremes, usually leads to the most desirable results.

2 // The golden mean applies to things that involve the allocation of time, effort, and energy. It cannot be strictly applied to issues of morality in an absolute sense.

3 // We must not think of the golden mean as a narrow point on a continuum. It is more useful to think about a relatively broad range of acceptable behaviors, and the ideal level is often closer to one of the extremes than to a midpoint.

4 // Even though the golden mean seems like an obvious, even simple idea, many people do not use this principle wisely.

5 // Olson's circumplex model is an example of using the golden mean in two areas: change and cohesion.

6 // When families have a balance of morphogenesis and morphostasis they tend to have fewer problems, but when there is excessive rigidity or chaos the probability of problems in higher.

7 // A moderate to high amount of cohesion tends to be associated with healthy family life; too little or too much cohesion is often associated with problems in families.

8 // The balancing of individual and group rights is a part of a larger issue in our modern world. The larger issue is that in Western cultures there has been a trend toward greater individualism for many centuries. This trend has been valuable in many ways, but excessive individualism can be undesirable.

The family realm presents some of the most controversial, complex, and emotional problems of our day. One example is the United States Supreme Court's decision on *Roe v. Wade* in 1973. The court ruled that women have a right to choose to have an abortion. This refueled a controversy that has become divisive and emotional, and the debate about the "right to choice" and the "right to life" continues into the 1990s.

Some of the other controversies centered in the family realm are: issues of the feminist movement, guidelines for test-tube babies, rights of surrogate mothers, ease or difficulty of divorce, legalization of homosexual marriages, federal government financing of day care, "parent divorce" by children, and guidelines for death with dignity. These issues are being debated in the media, churches, legislatures, and courts, and policies are gradually changing and evolving as new questions, new technologies, new information, and new issues are discovered.

> *"Marriage is that relationship between men and women in which the independence is equal, the dependence mutual, and the obligation reciprocal."*
>
> —Anspacher

Should the study of the family be isolated from these controversies? We think the study of the family should be right in the middle of them. We believe the careful study of the *familial* aspects of these controversies, from a perspective that emphasizes the unique characteristics of the family realm, can help all of the interested parties. It can provide insights that will help legislators, policymakers, judges, and lawyers. It can help the clergy, therapists, and educators. It can help individuals who are trying to make decisions about a wide range of important questions such as lifestyle, marriage, remarriage, divorce, abortion, artificial reproduction, and the custody of children.

The Golden Mean

A general principle developed over 2000 years ago is useful in dealing with these complicated issues. It was developed by the Greek philosopher Aristotle in his writings on ethics. Aristotle called his principle **the golden mean**, and it can be explained as follows:

Principle

Finding the mean or moderation, by avoiding extremes, usually leads to the most desirable results in aspects of life that deal with time, effort, energy, and emphasis.

Aristotle's principle has survived the test of time and considerable scientific scrutiny. Aristotle developed this principle by reasoning in the following way:

> The first point to have in view then is that in matters of conduct both excess and deficiency are essentially detrimental. It is the same here as in the case of bodily health and strength. Our strength is impaired by taking too much exercise, and also by taking too little; and similarly too much and too little food and drink injure our health, while the right amount produces health and increases it and preserves it. This also applies to self-control and courage and the other virtues. The man who runs away from every danger and never stands his ground becomes a coward, and the man who is afraid of nothing whatever and walks into everything becomes foolhardy; and similarly one who partakes of every pleasure and refrains from no gratification becomes self-indulgent, while one who shuns all pleasure becomes a boor and a dullard. It follows that self-control and courage are unimpaired by excess and by deficiency and are preserved by moderation. (Aristotle, 1943, p. 32)

Thus, the heart of his idea is that finding the mean or moderation, by avoiding extremes, usually leads to the most desirable results. Aristotle later refined this idea by adding two important qualifications.

The first qualification is that the golden mean does not apply to things that are either absolutely moral or immoral. For example, murder or theft are *not* best done in moderation! At the other extreme of ethics, the golden mean does not apply to honesty, loyalty, and fidelity. No one would hire a cashier who was *somewhat* honest and loyal. Nor is it wise to apply the golden mean to unethical behaviors such as abuse, deception, exploitation, or neglect of loved ones. Aristotle's reasoning about these absolutes is this:

> But not every action or every emotion admits of a middle state: The very names of some of them suggest wickedness—for instance spite, shamelessness, envy, and among actions, adultery, theft, murder; all of these similar emotions and actions are blamed as being wicked intrinsically and not merely when practiced to excess or insufficiently. (Aristotle, 1943, p. 38)

The areas of life where the golden mean does apply are those that involve an investment of time, effort, energy, or emphasis. For example, it applies to how much time it is wise to spend with one's career or friends. It is useful in making judgments about whether to have another child, how much to get involved in volunteer work, what to eat, and how much attention to give to one's spouse.

Aristotle's second qualification is that we should not think of the golden mean as a narrow point on a continuum. It is more useful to think about a relatively broad range of acceptable behaviors. Also, the mean or ideal level of something may often be closer to one of the extremes than to a midpoint. For example, Aristotle reasoned that:

> It is not easy to say precisely what is the right way to be angry and with whom and on what grounds and for how long. In fact we are inconsistent on this point, sometimes praising people who are deficient in the capacity for anger and calling them "gentle," sometimes praising the choleric and calling them "stout fellows." To be sure we are not hard on a man who goes off the straight path in the direction of too much or too little, if he goes off only a little way. We reserve our censure for the man who swerves widely from the course, because then we are bound to notice it. Yet it is not easy to find a formula by which we may determine how far and up to what point a man may go wrong before he incurs blame. But this difficulty of definition is inherent in every object of perception; such questions of degree are bound up with the circumstances of the individual case, where our only criterion is the perception.
>
> So much, then, has become clear. In all our conduct it is the mean state that is to be praised. But one should lean sometimes in the direction of the more, sometimes in that of the less, because that is the readiest way of attaining to goodness and the mean. (Aristotle, 1943, p. 44)

Using the Golden Mean Effectively

When we first encounter the golden mean, it seems a fairly simple, uncomplicated idea. It is not uncommon to react by thinking "Yes, that's pretty obvious and basic. So what? Let's get on to something important. Everybody knows that."

However, it is actually not that simple. Our experience, and our analysis of the family science literature, suggests that even though everybody "sort of" knows the principle:

1. We often do not think with it correctly or wisely.
2. Many times we forget or ignore it.
3. We often act and think in ways that are inconsistent with it.
4. When we do think with it, it sometimes leads us to insights that are different from our "common sense."

There are two areas of the family science literature that illustrate how easy it is to use the principle incorrectly and how valuable it is to use it correctly. A brief review of these two areas will help us all to use the principle more wisely.

Community Involvement

In the early years of the family science field, a large number of studies investigated the relationship between community involvement and the quality of family life. Community involvement refers to how much time and energy families spend in community activities such as the PTA, political activities, labor unions, city councils, library boards, church service, and so forth. In 1953 Burgess and Wallin summarized the research that had been conducted up to the early 1950s, and it showed that membership in organizations is positively related to marital success. For example, in their own surveys, they found church attendance of two to four times a month was associated with more success than less frequent attendance.

A number of early studies in the family field (Locke, 1951; Locke & Karlsson, 1952; Burgess & Wallin, 1953; Kirkpatrick, 1955) also found that high involvement with friends was associated with greater marital satisfaction. In addition, the early research on the relationship between employment and family life found a positive relationship between the amount of involvement in careers and the quality of family life (Hicks & Platt, 1970; Scanzoni, 1970).

When the previous research was reviewed by Lewis and Spanier in the middle 1970s, they summarized the prevailing view by concluding that there is a positive relationship between community involvement and the quality of marriage (Lewis & Spanier, 1979, p. 279). Some of the reasoning behind the pre-1980 conclusion was that people who are more competent and resourceful will become more involved in the community and also have the ability to succeed in their family life. People who are less resourceful tend to do less well in their family life and aren't as involved in community activities.

In the late 1970s, however, a number of scholars realized that the prevailing conclusion was inconsistent with the golden mean, and some of them suspected that the golden mean was more correct than the conclusions reached by previous researchers. The research of these scholars resulted in different findings. They found that a moderate amount of community involvement is associated with better family life and unusually low or high involvement was associated with lesser quality (Aldous, Osmond & Hicks, 1979; Holman, 1981).

The difference between these studies and the earlier research was that, apparently, the idea of the golden mean had been ignored by earlier researchers. They had merely compared low levels of community involvement with moderately high levels, and had not considered what would happen if there were high involvement in communities.

These findings have changed the conclusions that family scientists now make about the relationship between community involvement and family life. We now believe the golden mean is valid for this area, and undoubtedly for other areas (such as interaction with friends and involvement with religious organizations, social clubs, careers, children, relatives, hobbies, and social movements). The most interesting thing to us, however, is that the scientific community ignored the golden mean for several decades.

Alternatives in Marriage

A second area where it is easy to forget the golden mean has to do with the alternatives people have in marriage. A study that illustrates this was published by Joel Nelson (1966). Nelson was doing research on the way wives interact with part of their ecosystem, and he used a questionnaire to gather data from a sample of wives in New Haven, Connecticut. The questionnaire measured how much companionship they had in their marriage and how much they interacted with friends. He grouped the scores on these two variables into dichotomies. A **dichotomy** is a variable that has two categories or conditions. The dichotomies were high and low companionship in marriage and high and low cohesion with friends. When the two dichotomies are combined, it creates the 2 × 2 table shown in Figure 10.1.

Nelson was interested in how these two factors are related to the quality of marriage, so he also asked the wives how satisfied they were with their marriages. He found that a high percentage of the people in two of the cells were happy in their marriages, and a low percentage were happy in two of the cells.

Now, to see if Nelson's findings are consistent with our "common sense," here is a pre-test. Identify the two conditions where you think a high percentage of wives were satisfied with their marriage. Then identify the two conditions you think had the low percentage of satisfying marriages.

The two conditions that you think had the high percentage of satisfying marriages are:

Conditions ______________________ and ______________________

The two conditions that you think had the low percentage of satisfying marriages are:

Conditions ______________________ and ______________________

Write down these guesses before reading further. It will be interesting, and will help you understand the way the golden mean operates.

The findings in Nelson's study were that cells 1 and 4 had the higher percentage of people with satisfying marriages, and cells 2 and 3 had the lower percentage. The actual percentages who were satisfied with their marriages were 69 percent in cell 1, 35 percent in cell 2, 41 percent in cell 3, and 64 percent in cell 4 (Nelson, 1966, p. 670). Don't feel too badly if you did not guess right. In two decades of asking several thousand college students in four different universities to guess these cells, only about 20 percent have guessed correctly.

If you were one of the 20 percent who were able to see the golden mean at work in this study, give yourself an A. Most students guess that cells 2 and 4 have the high percentage of couples who are satisfied. They get a B. If you didn't guess or if you looked ahead to find the right answer, you get an E on the quiz. We hope the quiz will help everyone get an A on this part of the final examination!

How is the golden mean at work in this situation? Nelson's interpretation is that the people in condition 3 have the lowest total amount of sociability in their lives since they have low companionship in their marriage and low involvement with friends. This means they are at the low extreme of total social interaction—considering only these two variables. The people in condition 2 are at the other extreme. They have high marital companionship and high involvement with friends. The people in conditions 1 and 4 are both at a more "moderate" level of total social involvement. The people in condition 1 have their social interaction

Amount of marital companionship

Amount of involvement with friends	Low	High
High	Condition 1 Low marital companionship and High interaction with friends	Condition 2 High marital companionship and High interaction with friends
Low	Condition 3 Low marital companionship and Low interaction with friends	Condition 4 High marital companionship and Low interaction with friends

FIGURE 10.1 Four conditions of marital companionship and involvement with friends (Nelson, 1966)

with friends and the people in condition 4 have their interaction with their spouse, but they are both at what Aristotle would call a "mean" (moderate) level of total interaction.

The people in condition 3 tend be less satisfied with their marriage because, theoretically, they are too lonely and isolated. The people in condition 2 may be less satisfied with their marriage because they have too many demands. They are "stretched too thin," and cannot keep up with their social obligations.

One of the interesting aspects of Nelson's study is that most of us let our preference for a highly companionate marriage interfere with our ability to "think with" the golden mean. This prompts us to select cells 2 and 4 when we guess which conditions have the higher percentage of satisfied wives.

It is one thing for family scientists from the 1930s to the 1970s to "ignore" the golden mean. That was a long time ago, and the field was young and still developing. It is more sobering for 80 percent of us to be reading a chapter about the golden mean and then let our preferences for a companionate marriage interfere with our ability to "think with" this principle. When we look at the earlier trend in the field, and the guessing about Nelson's data, it reminds us how easy and how unwise it is to ignore the golden mean.

The rest of this chapter discusses ways to apply the golden mean in three areas of the family realm. Two of these areas comprise the main ideas in Olson's circumplex model, and they deal with balancing change (morphogenesis and morphostasis) and cohesion in families. The third area is balancing individualism.

The Lockhorns by William Hoest
2-16
Hoest
"IF YOU INTEND TO STAY TOGETHER, YOU'LL
HAVE TO BE APART MORE."

Reprinted by special permission of King Features, Inc.

Olson's Circumplex Model

In the mid-1970s David Olson (1991) reviewed the research about cohesion and about the balance of morphogenesis and morphostasis and developed a model that helps us think about these two variables in an integrated way. Olson's circumplex model (1991)[1] has since become one of the most widely known models in family science. To develop his model, Olson divided the two variables (cohesion and adaptability) into four categories. The categories for the amount of change in families are *chaotic*, *flexible*, *structured*, and *rigid*. When families are chaotic, they are so flexible they have little predictability, organization, or pattern.

"A viable family system is conceptualized as one that balances morphostatic (low adaptability) and morphogenic (high adaptability) processes so that there is a balance of stability and change." —Cameron Lee, 1988, p. 73

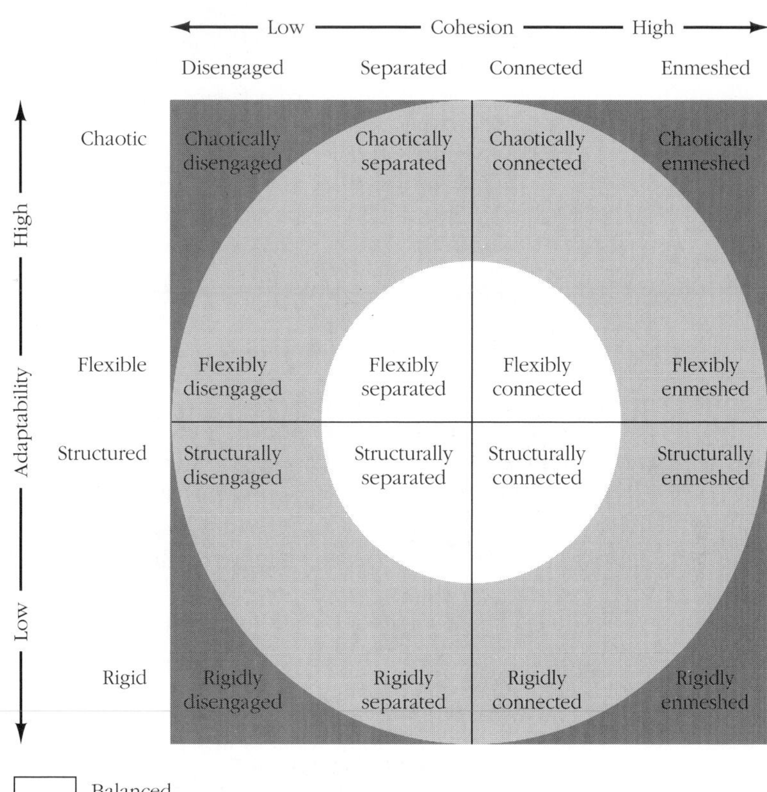

FIGURE 10.2 Olson's circumplex model (Olson, 1989)

At the rigid extreme, they resist change, cling to established ways of doing things, and oppose innovation. The four levels of cohesion are *disengaged, separated, connected,* and *enmeshed.*

Olson suggested the best way to think about these two variables is to view them as two different and independent dimensions in family systems. When these two variables are combined into a two-dimensional figure, it results in 16 different conditions, as shown in Figure 10.2. The four conditions in the corners of the chart are families who are chaotically disengaged, chaotically enmeshed, rigidly disengaged, and rigidly enmeshed.

Olson then made several circles to show how families who were at moderate levels of cohesion and change are in the middle of the model and families who are at the extremes are in the corners. When these ideas about the relationships between the variables are combined in the two-dimensional drawing in Figure 10.2, it leads to the conclusion that families in the inner four conditions of the diagram tend to "generally function more adequately across the family life cycle than those at the extreme of these dimensions" (Olson, 1989, p. 20).

> An important issue in the Circumplex Model relates to the concept of balance. Even though a balanced family system is placed at the two central levels of the model, it should not be assumed that these families always operate in a "moderate" manner. Being balanced means that a family system can experience the extremes on the dimension when appropriate but that they do not typically function at these extremes for long periods of time.
>
> Families in the balanced area of the cohesion dimension allow family members to experience being both independent from and connected to their family. Both extremes are tolerated and expected, but the family does not continually function at the extreme. Conversely, extreme family types tend to function only at the extreme and are not encouraged to change the way they function as a family. (Olson, 1989, pp. 20–21)

There have been a large number of research studies about Olson's circumplex model, and when the clinical and survey research is considered together it provides considerable support for the model.

We should also recognize that developmental processes, cultural factors, and some unique family situations influence how these variables are related to family problems. With regard to the developmental issues, families tend to float around on the circumplex model as they move through the family life cycle. Olson's study of 1000 families (Olson et al., 1983) found families tended to be relatively flexible when they were first married, and they moved toward less change during the childrearing stage of the family life cycle. When the children approach adolescence and the launching stage of life, families become more flexible.

Olson explained the ways cultural factors and personal family tastes are involved as follows:

> Families in our culture still vary greatly in the extent to which they encourage family closeness and individual development. Although most parents would prefer their children to develop values and ideas similar to theirs, most parents also want their children to become somewhat autonomous and differentiated from the family system.
>
> A sizeable minority of families, however, have normative expectations that strongly emphasize family togetherness in both the nuclear and extended families. Their family norms emphasize emotional and physical togetherness, and they strive for high levels of consensus and loyalty. Some ethnic groups in this country such as Slovak-American, Puerto Rican, and Italian families, and religious groups such as the Amish and Mormons, have high expectations regarding family togetherness.
>
> These expectations are also common, but less predominant, in many other American families regardless of ethnic or religious orientation. Many of these families could be described as extreme on the cohesion dimension (i.e., enmeshed), and they function well as long as all family members are willing to go along with those expectations. Problems occur when a family member, often an adolescent or mother, becomes frustrated with these extreme family systems (i.e., rigidly enmeshed). It is, therefore, important to assess not only the type of family system but how satisfied each family member is with that type of family. (Olson, 1989, pp. 21–22)

Balancing Cohesion

The concepts of morphogenesis and morphostasis were defined and discussed in Chapter 7, so it is not necessary to elaborate further here to understand and be able to use Olson's model. However, the concept of cohesion has not been defined before, and it needs to be defined and discussed before it can be understood.

Cohesion refers to the amount of togetherness, integration, or connectedness between people. It is an abstract or general concept that can be applied to any social category. For example, it can be applied to churches, neighborhoods, clubs, or society. Cohesion is not something that individuals have, as it refers to a characteristic of a social unit.

In family science it refers to "the emotional bonding that family members have toward one another" (Olson et al., 1983, p. 70). Families that have high cohesion have a sense of loyalty to the family, a sense of we-ness, a feeling that the welfare of the group is important, and that the rights of the individuals should be compromised in some situations for the rights of the whole. In families that have low cohesion, there is more individualism, and the interests of the individuals come first.

It is important to realize that a number of other concepts have been used in the family field to describe what is being labeled as cohesion here. Examples of these different terms may help clarify our meaning.

The very first research project that studied cohesion was in the 1930s, and it was done by Robert Angell (1936). Angell was interested in why some families were able to cope with the Depression and some were not. He observed that their financial status didn't seem to make a difference. Some families who had lost a lot of assets were doing well and some were not, and some families that were economically well off were doing well and some were not.

Angell's reading led him to believe that how well families were integrated might make a difference. His reasoning was that if families were well organized, close to each other, and had a sense of oneness, this resource would help them cope with the difficulties and demoralization of the Depression. He used the term *integration* to conceptualize this part of family systems, and his research supported the conclusion that families who had high integration did better than families exhibiting low integration.

Hess and Handel (1959) conceptualized this part of family systems in a

---

"One aspect of managing family emotional systems is to create a "balance" in the contradictory emotional desires for *togetherness* and *individuality*. When these two parts of the family emotional system are in balance neither of them dominates so much it is disabling and destructive. When there is balance it facilitates the intellectual system in families and the feeling system."

—Kerr & Bowen, 1988

---

different way. They described it as "the effort to achieve a satisfactory pattern of *separateness and connectedness*" (1959, pp. 12–13). Then, in 1975, Hess and Handel developed a third way to describe what seems to be the same aspect of family systems. They called it *distance regulation* in families (1975, p. 21).

In Bowen's (1978) model of family systems he used a fourth set of terms to describe these same processes. He said that family systems have two counterbalancing life forces. One is the desire for *individuality* and the other is a desire for *togetherness*, and families are continually balancing these tendencies.

All of these attempts to describe the process of family systems managing their closeness seem to be describing the same process, and we could have used any of

But let there be spaces in your togetherness,
And let the winds of the heavens dance
between you.
Love one another, but make not a bond of love:
Let it rather be a moving sea between
the shores of your souls.
Fill each other's cup but drink not from
the same cup.
Give one another of your bread but eat
not from the same loaf.
Sing and dance together and be joyous,
but let each one of you be alone,
Even as the strings of a lute are alone
though they quiver with the same music.
Give your hearts, but not into each
other's keeping.
For only the hand of Life can contain
your hearts.
And stand together yet not too near
together:
For the pillars of the temple stand apart,
And the oak tree and the cypress grow
not in each other's shadow.

—Khalil Gibran (1923)

Each family finds its own balance between togetherness and separateness.

these different sets of terms. In this chapter we have followed Olson's suggestion, and we are referring to these processes as *balancing the cohesion* in families.

With regard to cohesion, the golden mean is the principle that seems to apply. When families have excessive or inadequate cohesion, the probability increases that they will experience undesirable problems either individually or collectively. When families are in the broad range of "moderate" levels of cohesion, their probability of experiencing problems decreases.

Apparently, this moderate level of cohesion allows for considerable variation in the amount of cohesion and the way families maintain it. Some families find that relatively little closeness works well for them, and other families prefer lots of closeness. Also, families seem to be able to be closer at certain times or certain stages of their life cycle and more distant at other times. For example, when a death occurs in a family, many families will have a period of time when they are closer to each other. This closeness helps them adjust to the new circumstances and their feelings of loss. Later, after a period of healing, they may move to a less close pattern.

Thus the management of cohesion is a matter of each family's discovering how much closeness helps them accomplish their objectives, and of finding their own ways to maintain the balance of togetherness and separateness. It also is a "dance" that changes with the rhythms of daily, weekly, monthly, and seasonal routines. Families may find they enjoy being less close during the week and coming together on weekends. Or, they may find that they enjoy having more cohesion at certain holidays or vacation periods.

There are many ways problems can occur in the management of cohesion. For example, as young adults get ready to leave their parental home and go out on their own, they may begin to be more "distant" from the family months or years before they actually leave, and this may be uncomfortable for one or both parents. If the parents respond by trying to have too much cohesion or the youth responds by trying to have too little, these excesses can be disruptive.

Another example is that some young adults and some parents find it very difficult to "cut the apron strings" when the young adult marries or moves away. These difficulties in adjusting the cohesion so it is consistent with the new stage of life can be seriously disruptive.

Balancing Individualism

This chapter began by identifying a number of important controversies that are raging in our society, some of which are generating a great deal of emotion, anger, and frustration. The controversies mentioned include such issues as abortion, homosexuality, artificial reproduction, ease of divorce, and so on.

There is a common issue in many of these controversies, and the golden mean can help us identify and deal with it. This common aspect has been a central issue in Western civilization for many centuries. For example, it was one of the main issues in:

- The signing of the Magna Carta in 1215
- Adding the Bill of Rights to the U.S. Constitution in 1787
- Creating the Social Security system in the 1930s
- Modern questions such as the right to die, abortion, whether homosexual marriage should be legalized, and even the use of seatbelts

What is the issue? It is to try to determine what the wise or desirable balance should be between the rights of individuals and the rights of collectivities such as families, communities, states, and nations.

This issue is extremely important for students of the family, for three reasons. First, the family realm is in the middle of the controversy. Second, the family science perspective provides some unique insights about this issue and how to deal with it, and third, anyone who wants to work with families as a marriage and family therapist, social worker, psychologist, educator, or consultant, should be aware of the issue, the different points of view, the role of the family in the issue, and likely reactions in the many situations where this issue is involved.

The Trend Toward Individualism

It is not possible to find the original reasons for the trend toward individualism because the process has been under way for many centuries. However, one place to start is with the roles of the family and the individual in ancient societies. As one scholar pointed out over a century ago:

> [Society] in primitive times was not what it is assumed to be at present, a collection of individuals. In fact, and in the view of the men who composed it, it was an aggregation of families. The contrast may be most forcibly expressed by saying that the unit of an ancient society was the family, of a modern society the individual. (Maine, 1870, p. 163)

In pre-modern times, the father was the legal representative of the family; he was the one who owned property, sued and could be sued in the courts, and voted. The identity and rights of all of the individuals in a household, including the father, mother, children, and servants were therefore subordinated to those of the family.

Many of these patterns have persisted until modern times. For example, women did not get the right to vote in the United States until the 1920s. Only recently did they obtain the right to own property, to sue and be sued as individuals, and to get credit.

The limited rights of individuals in traditional society is illustrated by the relationship people had with government. In medieval times, royalty had almost total power. The dominant belief that kings had a "divine right" to rule meant that the power of the royalty was almost unchecked.

This pattern of absolute power has gradually been eroding, as we see the long-term trend of decreasing rights of governments and increasing rights of individuals. The Magna Carta was one of the early steps in this direction. When King John of England was forced to sign it in 1215, he was agreeing to limit the power of the monarchy by making himself subject to the laws of the land. In the process, the barons and church were assured certain rights.

The Magna Carta did not give very many rights to individuals, but it helped create a trend based on ideas that had been fairly dormant since the fall of the Roman Empire. The trend was toward individualism. Individualism is a point of view that holds the individual to be the important unit and asserts that individuals should have as many rights and freedoms as possible.

Individualism grew slowly during the late medieval period. Later, however, during the Renaissance, Reformation, and Counter-Reformation of the fifteenth and sixteenth centuries, it accelerated considerably. Notice, for example, how many of Shakespeare's characters wrestle with the rights of unjust kings versus the rights of subjects. Also, notice how often Shakespeare came down on the side of the unjust king. The issue was debated openly and with intensity in the first decades of the seventeenth century, and was the central issue in the English revolution of the 1640s and the American and French revolutions in the late eighteenth century. By then, individualism was a dominant force in all forms of human thought—legal, religious, scientific, and philosophical.

The trend toward individualism moved a substantial step further when the Bill of Rights was added to the U.S. Constitution in 1787. The Bill of Rights dramatically limited the power of the government by assigning a number of important rights to individuals.

The trend toward individualism has been a dominating point of view in the twentieth-century world, and it has improved the quality of human life in many ways. It helped eliminate the domination that religious organizations had over people in medieval society by creating separation of church and state. It was the impetus for the abolition of slavery in the nineteenth century. It provided the rationale for the women's suffrage movement in the late nineteenth and early twentieth century, the resurgence of the women's movement in the 1950s, and the civil rights movement in the 1960s. It decreased government's abuse, constraint, and control of individuals. It helped create extensive educational opportunities for ordinary people, and in many other ways gave individuals the freedom to make decisions about their own lives.

Reasons to Balance Individualism

Even though individualism has been of enormous value, it is important to realize that this is another area where *it would be unwise to ignore the golden mean* because it is possible to go too far in any direction. Just as it would be unwise to give all of the power and rights to groups such as nations, states, communities, churches, or schools, it would also be unwise to give all rights to individuals. Wisdom lies in avoiding extremes and finding a desirable balance between the rights of individuals and the rights of groups.

There are many reasons that it is wise to find a moderate condition in balancing individualism. One reason is that sometimes the rights of more than one individual are in conflict. For example, if a person is angry with someone and wants to hit the other person, who should have the right to get what they want? Should the angry person have the right to hit? Should the other person have the right not to be hit? There is a time-honored belief in our society that we have the right to be free from assault. This belief establishes at least one basis for asserting that individuals should have limits. It is easy to expand this reasoning to identify other beliefs that limit the rights of individuals.

A second reason to limit individual rights has to do with the care of dependent children. Human infants have a long period of dependency before they are mature enough to take care of themselves. Also, as a great deal of research by scholars such as Urie Bronfenbrenner (1974; 1979) has discovered, children need a certain type of care if they are to grow up to be healthy individuals who can relate intimately and effectively with others.

One of the things children need is stability in the individuals who care for them. They also need to have intense emotional bonds and affection for these individuals if they are to learn how to relate in intimate, enduring, affectionate, caring, and loving ways. If they do not have the emotional attachment and stability, they grow up impaired in their ability to relate, develop, and nurture the next generation.

These human needs mean that it is essential that some adults take the responsibility to rear the next generation. How does that affect the individual rights of these adults? It means that after these adults exercise their right to choose to begin rearing children, they lose their right to abandon the children.

A third reason has to do with marriage. When people exercise one of their rights by choosing to marry someone, they create a unique relationship that has commitments, obligations, and responsibilities. This limits their right to behave in ways that are not consistent with their commitments and obligations.

A fourth reason to limit individualism is more abstract and complicated than the other three, but it is very important. It is also paradoxical. It is that the greatest freedom does not come to humans when they are totally free from obligations, duty, connections to others, and responsibilities. The greatest total freedom exists when individuals have, in Aristotle's terms, a mean rather than an extreme level of rights.

The way extreme forms of individualism would limit rights can be illustrated with several examples. If everyone had the right to do whatever they wished, it would eliminate the expectation that relationships such as marriage, parenthood, and childhood are continuous, long-term, or permanent, because any individual involved could terminate the relationships whenever they wished. If this were to happen, people would lose their ability, their right, their freedom, to participate in relationships they expect to continue indefinitely.

The absence of expected permanence in human relationships would mean that people would not invest themselves deeply, completely, or totally in their relationships. They would not commit their heart and soul, because the possibility would always exist that the others in the relationship could withdraw. Thus no relationships would have the level of intimacy, understanding, connection, security, belonging, and closeness that is only possible with expected permanence. In other words, all relationships would tend to be relatively superficial, free of bonds, and limited in emotional commitment. This would eliminate the "right" people have to create the deeper, more enduring, more intimate, and more loving ways of relating possible only with less extreme forms of individualism.

The paradox that exists in getting rights by giving up rights is illustrated with the following anonymous letter written to the editor of *The New Yorker* magazine.[2]

> The spirit of emancipation has . . . touched deep nerves of truth [but it also reflects] the blind side of our age and the cost of the blindness; [and] a perhaps fatal stupidity intertwined with our enlightenment. The idea of emancipation, after all, has to do with an escape from bonds, not a strengthening of bonds. Emancipation has to do with power, not love. . . . I don't think it's a coincidence . . . that more and more people are living alone these days. . . . [There is a] general sense of the transformation of our society from one that is, at best, indifferent to them; a sense of an inevitable fraying of the net of connections between people at many critical intersections, of which the marital one is only one. . . . If one examines these points of disintegration separately, one finds they have a common cause—the overriding value placed on the idea of individual emancipation and fulfillment, in the light of which, more and more, the old bonds are seen not as enriching but as confining. We are coming to look upon life as a lone adventure, a great personal odyssey, and there is much in this view that is exhilarating and strengthening, but we seem to be carrying it to such an extreme that if each of us is an Odysseus, he is an Odysseus with no Telemachus to pursue him, with no Ithaca to long for, and with no Penelope to return to—an Odysseus on a journey that has been rendered pointless by becoming limitless. (*The New Yorker*, 1976, pp. 21–22)

Balancing Individualism in Families

Lois and Paul Glasser (1977) have pointed out that whenever we try to help families, it is important that we avoid the extremes of too much or too little individualism. Professionals (family life educators, therapists, physicians, lawyers, and social workers) need to be aware of this and so do lay people who try to help families. Box 10.1 reproduces some of the ideas in the Glassers' paper, and it illustrates that those of us who try to help families sometimes get caught up in the trend toward individualism, which may taint the advice we give to families.

Balancing Individualism in Daily Living

The process of balancing individual and group rights is an inescapable part of the everyday life of most families. For example, when one member of a family wants to do something like take gymnastic or music lessons and the family's resources of time and money are limited, the family is in the process of balancing rights. How much does the individual have the right to do what he or she wants, and how much does the family have the right to limit what the individual does? How much should some members of a family sacrifice for others? How much should the welfare (or rights) of the total family prevail?

Even minor decisions, such as whether family members should eat dinner with the rest and where they should sit at the table, involve balancing rights. These decisions have broader implications than just eating and sitting. They have implications for how important people are and how important they feel they are. Major decisions, such as whether to have another child or whether to change careers, have much broader, deeper, and more fundamental implications for the quality of family life.

Differences between males and females are also involved in balancing our daily lives. Traditionally in our society, men have had more rights than women. This has meant that men tended to get their way more, and the women had to give in more. These gender differences have been challenged in recent years, and many people in our society are trying to create greater equity. Usually this means finding ways for women to have the same degree of individual rights that men have, but these changes are slow and difficult.

The gender issues are also intricately intertwined with ideas about what it means to be a man. Like most privileged classes, many men give up their privileged condition very reluctantly. However, there is beginning to be some evidence that the traditional pattern of male dominance is gradually being changed, but unfortunately "the change is proceeding at a pace that is very slow, much too slow" (Scanzoni, 1987). In the meantime, a large number of women are being deprived of rights that wisdom, reason, and justice say they should have. We hope that those of us who study the family can allocate a substantial portion of our resources to influencing these patterns and helping to accelerate this process.

Box 10.1

The following illuminates how Lois and Paul Glasser struggled with rising individualism as it impacted the counseling profession during the 1970s and 1980s.

The consequences of such an imbalance in practice [referring to marriage and family therapy] and education can lead not only to negative effects for the society as a whole, but also much personal unhappiness as spouses and children are sacrificed in the effort to help the student or client find individual satisfaction.

We cannot provide the answers but at least we can raise some of the questions.

Are the T groups and encounter groups run in ways intended to turn clients on (and give them pleasure), provide them with greater comfort and understanding of themselves, or increase their sense of responsibility to others, particularly spouses and children? Are these goals always mutually compatible, and if not, how can this be handled?

Has the issue of fertility control been considered in the context of interpersonal and social responsibility? Should professionals involved in delivering contraceptive services require counseling for all unmarried minors requesting "the pill" or other forms of birth control? Where do counselors stand on the question of sterilization or abortion for a married person without the spouse's knowledge or consent? Is fertility control a matter of *family* planning or *individual* freedom?

In marital and family counseling, do professionals consider with their clients the consequences of separation and divorce for all of those involved—both spouses, the children, even grandparents? Many practitioners state goals in terms of increasing comfort for the individuals whom they see. In situations of potential divorce, this often includes helping spouses feel better about the idea of divorce by enabling them to handle their feelings of guilt, failure, and the consequences for their children. In a recent case presentation, the worker reported that the father stated, "He wanted a divorce because he hates kids five to fifteen." He had three of them in this age range, and the noise they made and their demands for time and energy were intolerable to him. Although the wife had very mixed feelings about dissolving the marriage, this experienced therapist felt that the husband's attitude made the marriage incompatible. Her response was one of empathy and understanding with both spouses. Her goals included helping this husband to achieve a full and rewarding life away from his family, and helping the wife to cope with her three children with a greatly diminished income. Maybe the wife could develop better job skills. There was no exploration of ways in which the husband's tolerance for noise could be increased, or ways in which the children's demands could be better organized so that he could find pleasure in his interactions with them. There was no attempt to help the wife lower the noise level in the house or present a united front with her husband concerning appropriate demands by the children. There was little effort to search out the underlying reasons for the husband's discontent, which may well have included radically different views by each spouse of the meaning of family life, and to use this knowledge to come to a creative solution which not only would keep the family together but also provide greater satisfaction to each member of the group.

A recent national study by the University of Michigan Institute for Social Research reveals that the single, most important cause for low family income is separation and divorce (Hampton, 1975). Should practitioners encourage clients to "do their own thing," no matter what the consequences, or should they invoke in clients a sense

(continued)

Box 10.1

(continued)

of responsibility to others which goes beyond present pleasure and personal happiness now?

Another case involved the forty-two-year-old wife of a professional man, who walked away from her husband and three minor children one day to make a new life for herself on our campus. Her professional counselor was successful in making her feel very comfortable with her new-found freedom and independence. The very fact that the client sought help was an indication that she was not fully content with the decision she had made and that she still felt strong attachments to her family. But the possibility of her returning to them was never discussed. The comfort of the client's husband and children, who lived in a distant city, was of no concern to the therapist, and by the end of treatment, of no concern to the client either. Is this a successful outcome, and if so, for whom?

Is sexual counseling seen as a means to achieve individual sexual satisfaction—an end in itself—or as a means to achieve greater interpersonal commitment and family cohesion? Do educators and counselors emphasize the biological organismic reaction to tactile stimulation or the meaning of the climax as a part of a "giving" relationship in which sex is one of many ways two people can express their strong positive feelings for each other? (Glasser & Glasser, 1977, pp. 15–16, italics in original)

Balancing Individualism in Laws

The idea that it is wise to balance individual and group rights also has implications for the way the family realm should be viewed in our legal and political system. Hafen (1986) has demonstrated that ideals such as liberty and freedom are intertwined with the need to balance individual and collective rights. Some of his ideas are reproduced in Box 10.2, and he helps us realize this issue has implications for the very fabric of our familial, legal, and political systems.

Summary

This chapter began with a discussion of Aristotle's golden mean. The golden mean is the idea that finding the mean or moderation, by avoiding extremes, usually leads to the most desirable results in aspects of life that deal with time, effort, energy, and emphasis. We demonstrated that this principle is deceptive. It appears obvious and easy to use, but the best scholars in the field tend to ignore it and not think accurately with it. This was illustrated by reviewing research about community involvement and alternatives in marriage.

We applied the golden mean to the two processes of balancing change and cohesion in family systems. After describing these two concepts, we introduced Olson's circumplex model to help us think about these two variables in an integrated way.

Box 10.2

The most serious future challenge to the protected place of marriage and kinship in American law is likely to come from the ongoing momentum of the movement to individual rights. Legal scholar Roscoe Pound believed years ago that "when the legal system recognizes certain individual rights, it does so because it has been decided that society as a whole will benefit by satisfying the individual claims in question" (Auerback, 1971). In this sense, individual and social interests were seen as mutually reinforcing. In recent years, however, individual interests, carried on a tidal wave of public discourse and constitutional overtones, have taken on such overpowering significance that it is difficult for the contemporary mind to see any interests other than individual ones. The passion for individual, unfettered choice has become strong enough that the risk or harm to long-term social stability is thought by some to be a price worth paying, in the interest of maximizing more immediate gains for the cause of personal liberty.

For example, some lawyers and social scientists advocate the elimination of all legal distinctions between minors and adults, including the repeal of all laws that require age limits—whether to vote, marry, enter into contracts, or drive a vehicle. . . .

Reflecting a similar underlying philosophy, Harvard legal scholar Laurence Tribe (1978) is disturbed that the Supreme Court has not yet extended the constitutional protection provided for marriage to the realm of intimate associations between unmarried persons. Professor Tribe believes that future legal developments will lead to a "liberation by the state" of "the child—and the adult—from the shackles of such intermediate groups as family." In other words, no person would "belong" to any other person in the name of such bonds as kinship and marriage. At the same time, he believes that being "liberated from domination by those closest to them" raises an urgent need for legal recognition of "alternative" relationships that "meet the human need for closeness, trust, and love" in the midst of "cultural disintegration and social transformation" (Tribe, 1978, pp. 988–89).

Those expressing such concerns are disappointed that the Supreme Court has not yet recognized the idea of individual autonomy as the core value of the Constitution. The Court has in fact recognized many expanding constitutional rights in the name of individual liberty; however, most of the nine judges who comprise the Supreme Court continue to believe that a strong family tradition, based on kinship and marriage, contributes ultimately to a productive individual tradition and to the social stability necessary to sustain individual liberty in the long run. Whether the momentum of today's incessant individualism will overpower this traditional view remains to be seen.

In the meantime, we should resist the naive belief that we could be liberated from the bondage of family ties and still somehow be assured of the personal security and support found only in long-term commitments. The search for personal autonomy alone, divorced as it now is in the public mind from attitudes of commitment and duty, is more likely to compound our sense of alienation than it is to eliminate it. In the early years of the American democratic experiment, the celebrated French writer Alexis de Tocqueville observed a potentially major flaw in the emphasis on self-interest he saw in our attitudes toward democracy: "not only does [the self interest of] democracy make every man forget his ancestors, but it hides his descendants and separates its contemporaries from him; it throws him back forever upon himself alone, and

(continued)

Box 10.2
(continued)

threatens in the end to confine him entirely within the solitude of his own heart" (Heffner, 1956, p. 233).

To divorce liberty from duty is to impair the search for freedom, no matter which extreme we pursue. The totalitarian state has divorced the two, as duty to the collective has become everything. The anarchistic libertarian would divorce the two, as the unrestrained and self-fulfilling pursuit of personal liberty becomes everything.

The reality is that liberty and duty are two poles on a single construct. Neither is meaningful without the other. When the link between them is severed, alienation is the only result, whether through the oppression of the State or of existential despair. One of the most productive sources of maintaining the dynamic link between liberty and duty in our own culture has been our understanding of mutual reciprocity between the family tradition and the individual tradition, between Status and Contract. In the long run, the maintenance of that reciprocal link is a critical need for those who seek to "establish Justice, insure domestic Tranquility, . . . and secure the Blessings of Liberty" not only "to ourselves," but also to "our Posterity" (Hafen, 1986, pp. 7–8).

The golden mean was applied to the trend toward individualism, and the principle suggests that the greatest wisdom is to find moderation, a mean, or a balance in individual rights and social rights. We then discussed the implications of these ideas for a number of areas, including family professionals' behavior, legal and political implications, gender discrimination, and other family processes.

One of the advantages of these ideas is that they give us a vocabulary to think with in trying to deal with family issues. For example, if we think of the abortion controversy in terms of balancing rights, it gives us a number of valuable ideas and insights. It helps us realize that a woman ought to have certain rights to control her own body and destiny. However, the woman does not live in isolation from others. If she has a husband and other children, they also are involved. If she does not have a husband and other children, she has parents who are inextricably connected to her, and her child is also their grandchild. Also, at some point after conception, the infant starts to get rights and they need to be considered. In thinking of all these complicated and important aspects of a situation, the golden mean is a helpful principle.

Key Terms

Balance
The golden mean
Community involvement
Olson's circumplex model
Balancing the amount of change: Morphostasis, Morphogenesis

Developmentally stuck (or arrested)
Levels of change: Rigid, Structured, Flexible, Chaotic
Cohesion: Integration, Individuality, Separateness vs. Togetherness, Distance regulation
Levels of cohesion: Disengaged, Separated, Connected, Enmeshed
Positive relationship
Curvilinear relationship
Individualism
Individual rights
Social rights

Study Questions

1. Who was the philosopher who gave us the concept of the golden mean?
2. What are some situations in which it is not good to have a balance?
3. Describe what is meant by the idea that the golden mean is not a single point on a continuum.
4. According to this chapter, what is the relationship between community involvement and marital satisfaction?
5. Which four of Olson's family types tend to function better over the life cycle?
6. Why is it a poor idea to build a family paradigm that emphasizes togetherness at all costs?
7. Name three ways that the trend toward individualism could influence family balance.

Notes

1. Olson's model has been revised several times and there have been several controversial aspects of this research. For example, much of the data that has been gathered, including Olson and McCubbin's (1983) study of 1000 families suggests the relationship between change and family problems is linear rather than curvilinear. Many of these problems stem from limitations in our ability to measure change in family systems. Lee (1987) also has suggested Olson confuses Level I and Level II processes in the way he operationalizes adaptability. The authors believe that when Lee's (1987) and Burr and Lowe's (1987) suggestions are taken into account, these controversies tend to be resolved. The discussion in this chapter differentiates between change and adapt*ability* in the way Beavers and Voeller (1983) do, and this chapter does not include a discussion of the Level I–Level II controversy because it is a fairly complicated set of ideas.
2. We greatly appreciate the ideas of the many scholars represented in this chapter, but we are especially indebted to the writings of Bruce C. Hafen. His ideas have substantially influenced us, and we appreciate his permission to use them. This quotation, for example, was located by his research.

Resources

II

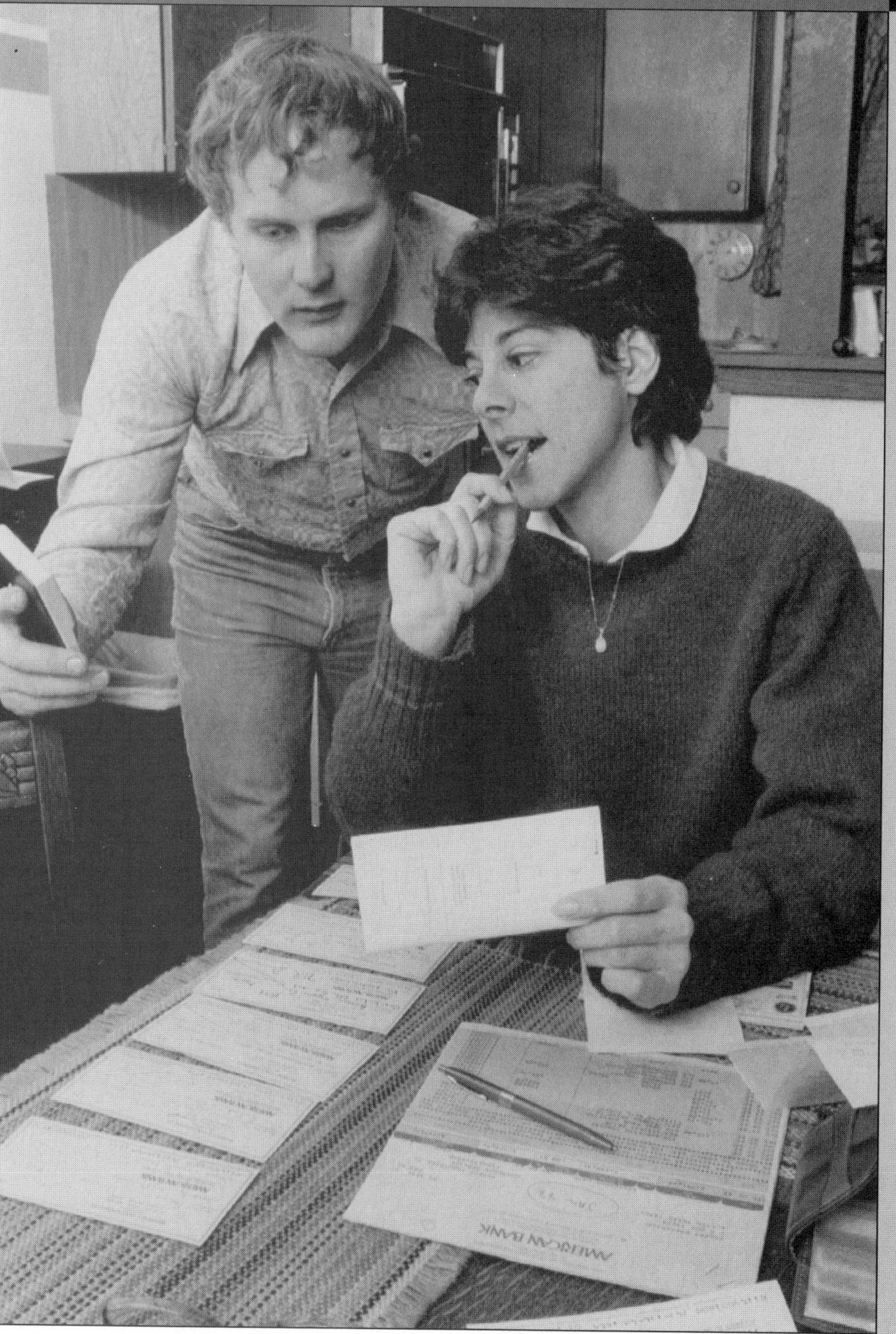

Main Ideas

1 // Resources are the means (methods, materials, etc.) that can be used to attain goals.

2 // Resources can be exchanged to acquire other resources or allocated to attain goals.

3 // Kantor and Lehr's distance-regulation model helps us understand how three kinds of resources (time, space, and energy) are used to attain three types of goals (affect, power, and meaning).

4 // Foa's theory helps us understand why it is not wise to mix economic and interpersonal resources. If they are kept separate, they can be exchanged or allocated effectively, but when they are mixed, both of them are less effective.

5 // Resources cannot be mixed because economic resources operate with a different set of "rules" than interpersonal resources. Six of these rules are described in this chapter.

There are many different kinds of resources. There are human and nonhuman, economic and noneconomic, tangible and intangible, personal and interpersonal. Human resources are such things as intelligence, ingenuity, creativity, sensitivity, delicacy, optimism, decisiveness, perseverance, and dedication. Nonhuman resources are things like time, sunlight, food, space, electricity, and tools.

Some human resources are individual characteristics, and others are interpersonal, family, or group characteristics. For example, intelligence, knowledge, awareness, and the ability to be decisive are personal resources. Things like agreement, cooperation, closeness, bonds, intimacy, interdependence, altruism, service, consideration, and trust are interpersonal resources because they all deal with things between people. The family realm has some interpersonal resources that do not exist in other realms. For example, parental love, family ties, sibling closeness, generational obligations, and marital intimacy are unique to the family realm.

"The heart of family therapy and family life education is helping families learn new ways to cultivate and use resources to attain their goals more effectively."

Economic resources are things that can be used for exchange or barter. Examples include money, land, labor, stocks, and capital. Noneconomic resources are means that are not readily exchanged in a marketplace. They

"The concept of family *resources* can be defined in the following way. Resources are . . . what the family has or can create to get what it wants. They are means to ends."

—Paolucci et al., 1977, p. 136

include items designed for consumption rather than exchange, material goods with historical or sentimental value, and such personal things as devotion, love, loyalty, and pride.

Tangible resources are things that have a physical existence and presence. We can touch, see, and easily identify them. They include things like money in hand (rather than money we expect to have), property, automobiles, books, and clothing. Intangible resources are more abstract and elusive. They usually exist in connection with something else, like a person's reputation, the good name of a family, and good intentions. Status, prestige, attention, influence, beauty, and commitments are intangible resources that can sometimes help families attain their goals.

The Role of Resources

Success in family life was defined in an earlier chapter as the extent to which the outputs in a family result in the attainment of family and individual goals. When success is defined this way, it makes the management of resources extremely important. This is because it is the management of resources that is the means of making changes and doing whatever else is needed to reach family and individual goals.

Resources can be used two different ways, through allocation or exchange.

Allocating Resources

Allocation is the process of assigning resources to various places, situations, or processes in order to attain goals. For example, if a family has a goal to have the table set in a particularly nice way for special company, they may turn to the family member they think is the most artistic and ask that person to decide what centerpieces, dishes, and arrangements should be used. This is allocating a fairly intangible, personal, noneconomic resource: artistic ability. This is the kind of resource that is used but not consumed or used up, because the individual who has the artistic ability has just as much—and perhaps even more—after setting the table.

Another example of resource allocation is a family dealing with a situation where one member of the family is discouraged or depressed. The family paradigm determines the goals. In some families this situation would not be defined as a problem, and it might be ignored. Other paradigms would define it as a problem that needs attention. These families would have the goal of taking the time to help and might marshal other family resources as well. In these situations, resources such as tenderness, patience, understanding, compassion, and nurturance would be called upon.

Sometimes allocation is a process of carefully dividing resources among alternative goals. Other times, allocation is done almost unconsciously. Time and money are limited resources for most families, so they are usually portioned carefully among the many desirable things a family wants to accomplish. Few families, on the other hand, have thought about dividing up the drinking water from the kitchen faucet. They generally assume there is more than enough to meet everyone's needs. However, if the family car broke down in the middle of Death Valley and there was only one quart of water in a canteen, the allocation of the drinking water would probably get quite a bit of attention.

Exchanging Resources

Exchanging resources is the process of transferring or trading one resource for another resource. Usually exchange does not in itself accomplish a goal, but we do it because we think that the exchange will help both parties better attain their goals. For example, when we apply for a job, we are offering to exchange our resources of time, energy, and expertise in return for an hourly wage or a monthly salary. We do this because it is an efficient way to accomplish goals like getting food, clothing, and shelter. If we tried to allocate our time, energy, and training directly toward getting food, shelter, and clothing, most of us would find ourselves hungry, cold, or poorly clothed, and maybe all three!

> Resources can be exchanged through two- or one-way transfers. A two-way transfer refers to those exchanges in which there is a contractual reciprocal arrangement; for example, exchanges of a specific amount of money for a particular item or of a given number of hours of work for certain sums of money or services. These transfers usually utilize market mechanisms. In two-way transfers there is immediate reciprocity; a resource is given and a resource is received simultaneously.
>
> One-way transfers usually occur outside the marketplace. Boulding (1973, p. 1) has referred to these one-way transfers as the grants economy. Grants are used to connote the idea that one-way transfers do not involve immediate or contractual reciprocity. They can occur between family members, from one family to another, from business to a family or individual, from government to individual, or from governments to governments. The basic idea is that the exchange does not have immediate reciprocity nor is it contractual in nature.
>
> A grant, however, may in fact involve reciprocity over time. Boulding (1973, p. 26) identifies this as serial reciprocity. For example, parents may provide a child with money for education and the child may then provide parents with housing at some future time or may provide education for another family member. Such arrangements are separate parts of the same transaction, but the reciprocity is implicit rather than explicit; it is not contractual and, in fact, may not be expected.
>
> One-way transfers can be made for either benevolent or malevolent reasons; out of love or fear. Hence, their effects can be either positive or negative. Positive effects of one-way transfers are feelings of goodwill, trust, and affection; negative effects can create the opposite or malevolent effects. One-way transfers within the family can help build trust and serve as an important integrating function for the family and between families and the rest of society. (Paolucci et al., 1977, pp. 137–38)

FAMILY PROCESSES THAT MANAGE RESOURCES

Kantor and Lehr's (1975) distance-regulation model helps us understand some of the mechanisms families use to allocate and exchange resources to attain goals.

Three Types of Goals

Kantor and Lehr focused on three kinds of goals in family systems. The three are affect, power, and meaning. Their term for these goals is *target dimensions*, a term that means about the same as goals. To maintain consistency in this book, and because the term *goal* is used more widely in the field, we will use *goal* here.

Affect goals. Kantor and Lehr (1975) define **affect** as "intimacy and nurturance—that sense of loving and being loved by someone in our world" (1975, p. 37). They have written that ". . . affirmative intimacy and nurturance are the primary targets of the affect dimension of family life. The specifics of what constitutes nurturance and intimacy vary, no doubt, from family to family and from individual to individual within families, but nearly all families claim that they seek to provide those two emotional qualities" (Kantor & Lehr, 1975, p. 48).

According to these authors, intimacy is a condition of mutual emotional closeness—often intense closeness—among peers. On the other hand nurturance is more of a mutual exchange. In this exchange, family members receive emotional support and encouragement from one another. They conclude by theorizing that intimacy involves two elements of this process. First, it implies that emotions and affect flow primarily in one direction. Second, as exchanges of the heart are regulated, a family determines how its members join and separate from one another. Further, how close family members are to one another is not a substitute for how much love or hate they have for each other. In fact, ". . . although members' joinings may be based on affection, they may also be based on hate and result in serious emotional conflict. Similarly, separations need not signify dislike. Rather, they may suggest an absence or sparsity of emotional exchange" (Kantor & Lehr, p. 48, 1975).

This process of joining together is labelled by them as emotional **distance regulation**. As they say,

> the ideal of the family is to satisfy its members' needs for intimacy and nurturance. Realization of this ideal is complicated, however, for the emotional distance which affirms one member may violate another and leave a third feeling relatively unaffected. For example, when a father closes the door to his study or flinches when it is opened, he is signaling his family that he considers it neither the appropriate time nor place for joining together. Similarly, if he should embrace his wife and child before dinner, he may be communicating his desire for emotional joining to begin. A child's grimace at his forcefully exuberant hug may, in turn, mean that the father is exerting too much energy for the child to feel comfortable joining him. In this way, family members are forever learning from one another how and when joinings and separations are tolerable, optimal, or intolerable. (Kantor & Lehr, 1975, p. 48)

Thus, families have an ongoing dance where we move closer together and further apart to regulate emotional distance. Sometimes family members join and separate many times a day.

Power goals. The concept of power is important in the family field. It has had a tremendous amount of attention in the last 30 years. This attention has been directed at defining it as a concept, theorizing about it, doing research about it, and trying to apply our ideas. Unfortunately, most of the work on power has been confusing, contradictory, and inconclusive. Our opinion of the reason for these problems is that most of the scholars who have developed theories about power and researched it have approached it from a public realm perspective rather than a family realm perspective. Others, such as Kranchfeld (1987), have expressed this same opinion.

When scholars approach power from a political, sociological, or economic perspective rather than a family science perspective, they usually view it as a confrontive, exchange-oriented, political, and/or coercive process where people are in adversarial or confrontive relationships. These kinds of relationships are the dominant pattern in some families most of the time and in most families some of the time, but they are the exception rather than the rule in the family realm.

As Kranchfeld (1987) points out, if we want to understand power in the family realm we need to approach it differently than if we were in the public realms. The family realm perspective focuses attention on power as a process that is intricately tied with generational bonds, developmental processes, emotion, and nurturance, and thus power operates very differently in family relationships. Still, in the words of Kantor and Lehr, it deals with many of the same things that are dealt with in nonfamily realms, including:

> issues of dominance, submission, and mediation, hindrance and furtherance, opposition and cooperation, competition and association, option and necessity, and superiority and inferiority. (Kantor & Lehr, 1975, p. 48)

However, these issues are dealt with in the family realm in a "different" way.

> Power relations focus on the aspects of freedom and restraint within family organization, and it is to these aspects that we apply the distance-regulation concept. In any given situation, then, one can measure a family's social traffic by quantifying the degree of freedom or restraint in members' movements. Many families formalize their vertical relations in such a way that a power hierarchy, both official and unofficial, is created. Such formalizations are used by families to determine situational distance-regulation issues. For instance, if Daddy is "boss" he probably has the right to tell Junior what to do. Situational distance regulations may be, and often are, at variance with official formulations, however. Situationally, a young child may be allowed to interrupt the movements of others, demand nurturance and affection, or be exempted from the restraint of family chores even though his formal status as "baby" relegates him to a low place in the power hierarchy. In short, a family's power regulations determine who and what will move freely, and who and what will be restrained.
>
> By means of its power relations, then, a family demands, rewards, protects, punishes, and tries generally to shape the social traffic of its members. Conflicts over

> the extent to which the family should be allowed to control individual lives invariably arise. But if family traffic is marked by either extreme freedom or extreme restraint, other potential problems arise. Thus if members feel totally free to do whatever they wish, anarchy can result, the movements of each subsystem disrupting and/or violating previously agreed upon family goals; at the other extreme, traffic that is totally restrained can produce conditions of tyranny, in which members are not allowed to do what they want, choose what they want, say what they think, or, for that matter, even dare to dwell on what they start to think. (Kantor & Lehr, 1975, pp. 49–50)

Thus, in the Kantor and Lehr model, some of the primary goals in the family realm are to find desirable levels of *freedom* and *restraint.*

Meaning goals. The goals in this area deal with mental things like ideas, aspirations, credos, beliefs, ideologies, worldviews, and a sense of what is right and wrong or good and bad.

> Purposeful identity is the primary target of the family's meaning dimension. . . . For an individual, to have an identity means to have an integrated sense of direction and destination, an awareness of who one is and what one would like to become. It is the antithesis of uncertainty, confusion, or disorientation. Like individuals, families strive to develop identities, usually by emphasizing the unity and solidarity of members in a common cause or purpose, and the existence of a meaningful "we," even if the "we" is a collection of individuals who agree never to interfere with the individual freedoms of one another. . . .
>
> It is almost impossible to overstate the importance of family meaning regulation in a society that is intellectually concerned with the meaning or meaninglessness of existence. A world as complex as ours puts extra strain on both individual and family identities. Like the caterpillar in *Alice in Wonderland*, it is forever asking, "Who are you?" If a family fails to offer itself and its members a model, or variety of models, on which the individual can base a purposeful identity that enables him to answer this basic existential question, or if it offers a model that is inappropriate for prevailing reality, it fails to fulfill one of its most important functions. (Kantor & Lehr, 1975, pp. 52–53)

Three Types of Resources

Kantor and Lehr (1975) also developed a topology (an organizing idea) of three resources that families use to attain their goals. The three resources are space, time, and energy. Kantor and Lehr call these three the *access dimensions*, a term that is very similar to "resources," because both terms view these processes as the means or media that are used to reach goals. Again, to maintain consistency, and because the term *resources* is more widely used in the field, we will use it here.

> The access dimensions—space, time, and energy—are the spheres of activity in which family process takes place. Without space there can be no place for an event; without time, no sequence; without energy, no vitality. These three, then, are the media in and through which families move. . . . When one system or subsystem approaches another, it immediately encounters the spatial, temporal, and energetic rhythms of the other system, rhythms which must be taken into account in regulating

> access. Mother and baby learn to anticipate each other's rhythms very early in their life together as nursing takes place to meet the hunger needs of the newborn child. Also, fathers and children, brothers and sisters, husbands and wives, siblings and friends, families and communities all learn to anticipate each other's rhythms, for unless people manage to occupy the same social field, spend time together, and combine energies to the same activities, they cannot hope to develop suitable conjoint affect, power, and meaning targets. (Kantor & Lehr, 1975, pp. 40–41)

Space. Space is managed by creating and maintaining boundaries outside and inside the family. Some boundaries, such as gates, doorways, rooms, and fences, are physical boundaries. Others, such as privacy, secrets, family councils, plans, and strategies are personal, interpersonal, mental, and emotional boundaries. Most of these boundaries are flexible and semi-permeable.

Families develop elaborate mechanisms for managing space to help them attain their goals. They develop methods of screening, buffering, channeling, locating, gathering, designing, arranging, and spreading. They develop "maps" of how areas are to be used. They also develop elaborate languages that help them communicate about how close they should be, when it is OK to be close and when it isn't, when to approach each other and when to retreat, when to conceal or reveal, when to invite others into the home and when not to, which parts of the physical space and emotional space of the family can be shared with others, and so forth.

Time. Time is a finite resource that gets a lot of attention in most families. They develop schedules of who uses bathrooms at which times, when meals are served, and when the many different kinds of family activities are carried out. Some activities are carefully scheduled, and others are very flexible.

As our society has become more complex and technologically controlled, the clock has become a more important part of our lives. School buses come at certain times, and families need to adjust. Work schedules are dictated by the company, and the family has to adjust. Churches, clubs, athletic leagues, and other organizations set their schedules, and the family adapts, adjusts, and chooses what it will do. The process of synchronizing the activities gets complicated when families are very large and during the stage of the life cycle when people are actively involved outside the family.

Energy. Energy provides the fuel that families need to get things done.

> [It] is both static and kinetic in families—static in that family members have supplies of stored energy available to them, and kinetic in that members actually expend these supplies. Though each family's use, deployment, and restoration of its energies will vary somewhat, a general pattern of charging and discharging energy operations is common to all families. By charging, we mean the accumulation of energy and, by discharging, the expending of it. If either activity alone—charging or discharging—repeatedly takes place at the expense of the other, a family can find itself in serious difficulty. (Kantor & Lehr, 1975, p. 44)

Many Other Resources

Larry Constantine (1986) extended the Kantor and Lehr topology by adding a fourth type of resource families use to attain their goals. He called it *material resources.*

> People give, receive, accept, reject, and exchange many material objects every day. Some of these are significant primarily for what they are physically (a sweater, a pencil), and others (money, a set of car keys, for example) are significant as tokens representing or giving access to other objects. (Constantine, 1986, p. 152)

Home economists have focused considerable attention on the kinds of resources families use, and they have developed additional topologies. For example, Gross, Crandall & Knoll (1980) point out some resources are tangible and others are intangible. Some are economic and some are noneconomic. Some are human and some are nonhuman. Human resources are such things as intelligence, ingenuity, creativity, sensitivity, delicacy, optimism, decisiveness, perseverance, and dedication. Nonhuman resources are things like minerals, time, sunlight, food, space, electricity, and tools.

Some human resources exist inside individuals and others are group resources. For example, knowledge and the ability to be decisive are personal resources, and cooperation, closeness, intimacy, consideration, and trust are interpersonal resources, because they all deal with things that are between people. The family realm has some interpersonal resources that do not exist in other realms. Some examples of resources that are uniquely familial are generational ties, family heritage, parental love, and family bonds.

Paradigmatic Differences

It is helpful to think on several levels of abstraction when we try to understand the role of resources in family management. Three levels were introduced in an earlier chapter: Level I (transformation processes), Level II (meta-processes), and family paradigms. Most of the processes that have been discussed in this chapter are Level I processes. As families manage their time, space, energy, material possessions, and other resources to attain goals such as affection, power, and meaning, these are relatively obvious, simple, and observable transformation processes—all Level I.

Many times when families are having trouble attaining their goals it is because they are trying to use Level I management processes that do not fit their family paradigms. When this is the case, they need to determine which beliefs are basic and paradigmatic, and which are specific and concrete. Then they can change or rearrange their Level I processes fairly easily and with little emotional disruption, but it is much harder and more emotionally intense to try to change the paradigmatic beliefs.

Looking at levels of abstraction can sometimes help us understand why families are not able to resolve conflicts that go on and on. Sometimes it is because the conflict centers on the Level I processes, and the family gets hung up there because they don't understand the role of the more abstract parts of the system—the Level II ideas, or family paradigms. It is useful to know if the conflict about Level I processes is because of family paradigm differences, and when we need to resolve the more basic issues. The conflict over Level I processes can become humorous and be resolved easily when the ambiguity in the underlying ideas is resolved. The shift to a Level II perspective expands insights about the range of possibilities that could be considered and helps resolve ambiguities and conflicts.

An example of moving to a higher level of abstraction to solve a management problem arises when families are struggling with conflict between parents and teenagers. When parents are focusing on how they can find ways (resources) to get teens to behave the way they want them to (goals), this is Level I thinking. When the teens are trying to find ways (resources) to get the parents to let them have the freedom they want (goals), they are also thinking at Level I. If either parents or teenagers were to back off and move to a higher level, they would be able to consider a broader range of possibilities. For example, parents could reexamine their role as disciplinarians; perhaps the family has reached a developmental stage where they could turn certain responsibilities over to the teens. They could go on to explore what would be necessary to help the teens willingly accept responsibility for certain areas of their own lives. Sometimes, when parents and teens focus their attention on these more abstract (Level II) issues, it helps them escape the cycle of parents trying to "clamp down" and teens trying to "assert themselves."

Managing Economic and Interpersonal Resources

A theory developed by Uriel Foa (1971) has become an important part of family science (Paolucci et al., 1977; Gross et al., 1980). Foa's theory helps us understand why some families are successful in managing their resources and others have failure after failure. It also presents us with several strategies that can be used by families to manage their resources and attain their goals more effectively.

The Two Dimensions in Foa's Theory

Foa's theory puts forth two dimensions that deal with the ways resources can be classified: concrete-symbolic and particularistic-universalistic.

Concrete-symbolic. The **concrete-symbolic dimension** refers to whether a resource is a tangible, specific, or physical object, or something that is abstract, symbolic, and intangible. Concrete resources are tangible things that we can touch, feel, and see. Examples are possessions like houses, cars, stocks, bonds, and contracts. Symbolic resources are abstract things that we can't touch, feel, or see. They include such things as information, status, ideas, creativity, ingenuity, power, and respect.

Foa thinks of this concept as a continuum with concrete at one extreme and symbolic at the other, as shown.

We should not think of concreteness as a dichotomy or trichotomy. It is a continuous variable that has many degrees. For example, a textbook is a fairly concrete resource; there is very little symbolic value to texts. Having a car, on the other hand, could fall on various places on the continuum, depending on the car. If it is a 10-year-old Volkswagen, it is a fairly concrete resource. If it is a brand new Porsche, it also has some symbolism, so it would be closer to the middle of the continuum.

Foa argues that money and love also have an intermediate level of concreteness, because neither of them are totally concrete or symbolic. Money is tangible, but it also has a great deal of symbolism. Love is fairly symbolic, but it also has some tangible aspects. Knowledge and status, on the other hand, would be fairly high on the symbolic end of the continuum.

Particularistic-universalistic. The second variable in Foa's model is the **particularistic-universalistic dimension**. It also is a continuous variable that ranges between two extremes.[1] Something that is universal is not tied to a particular person, object, or situation. It doesn't matter who gives or receives the resource in an exchange. As Foa points out:

> Changing the bank teller will not make much of a difference for the client wishing to cash a check. A change of doctor or lawyer is less likely to be accepted with indifference. One is even more particularistic with regard to a friend, a spouse, or a mother. Harlow (1970) showed that when the facial features of a surrogate mother are altered, the baby monkey reacts with fear, refusing to accept the change. In some animal species, certain communications are more target specific than others. Mating calls are more particularistic than status signals and the latter are less general than distress or alarm signals (Johnsgard, 1967). (Foa, 1971, p. 346)

Particularistic, therefore, refers to resources where people are concerned about the person who is involved. For instance, we tend to be particular about who we will accept as a spouse, mother, father, and siblings. We're particular about who to accept affection from, who we want as friends, and what we wear. After we become parents, we are very particular about who we regard as our children.

Combining the two dimensions. Foa arranges these two variables as shown in Figure 11.1. The concrete-symbolic continuum is the horizontal axis shown on the bottom of the figure; it varies between the extreme of symbolic on the left and concrete on the right. The particularistic-universalistic dimension is the vertical axis shown on the left side. When the two dimensions are combined in this way, it

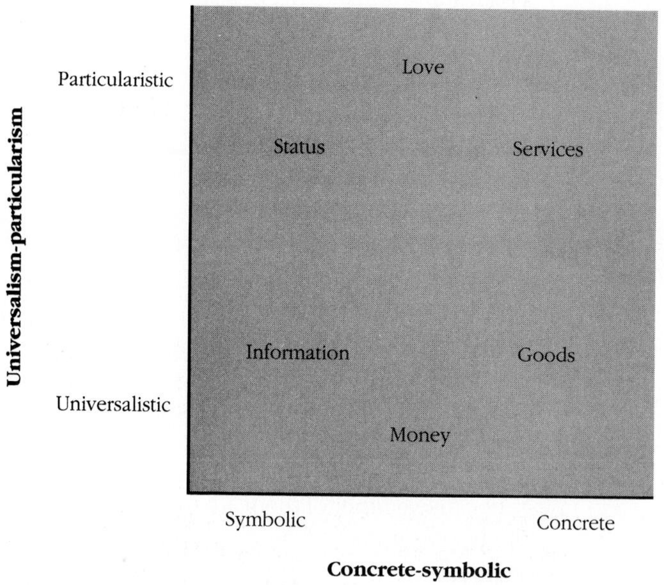

FIGURE 11.1 Foa's two-dimensional figure that classifies resources (Foa, 1971)

allows us to classify resources according to both dimensions at once. Money, for example, is very universalistic, but intermediate in concreteness. This means people are not particular about which quarter they have. One quarter is as good as another. It is intermediate in concreteness because it is fairly tangible, but the meaning and what it can do for us are fairly symbolic and abstract. Money is therefore placed at the bottom of the particularism dimension and in the middle of concreteness on Foa's chart.

Love is just the opposite of money. People are very particularistic about it, but it is intermediate in concreteness because people can see behavioral examples of it. It is also a vague, diffused, symbolic process, and therefore at the top of particularism and intermediate in concreteness.

Status is fairly particularistic and quite abstract or symbolic, so it goes in the upper left corner of the figure. Services, such as those of a doctor, lawyer, or teacher, are also fairly particularistic, but they are more concrete than status. Therefore, they are in the upper righthand corner.

Information is fairly universalistic and symbolic, so it is in the lower lefthand corner of the figure. Goods, such as cars, books, and houses, are fairly universalistic and concrete. Therefore, they are in the lower righthand corner of the Foa chart.

These six resources illustrate six different places on the chart, but they are not exhaustive. There are many subtle differences among them, and many other resources can be classified with the chart. Where would you put the following resources?

- A credit card
- A get-well card
- A telephone call from a loved one

- A kiss
- A job promotion
- A college education

For our judgment about where these resources would go on Foa's chart, see the notes at the end of the chapter.[2]

Foa's Theory

A principle about exchanging resources. The concepts and the two-dimensional arrangement in Figure 11.1 are the building blocks for Foa's theory. When we understand this conceptual framework, we are ready for his theoretical ideas. One of the principles in Foa's theory can be called the **exchange principle**:

Principle

The closer two resources are on Foa's model, the more easily they can be exchanged and the more likely the exchange will be effective. (Conversely, the more distant they are the more difficult it is to exchange them, and the more likely it is that attempts to exchange them will not work.)

With this principle, Foa gives us some insights about two-way exchanges of resources. The principle tells us that if people want to exchange their money for another resource, it will be easier to exchange it for things like information and goods than for resources that are highly particularistic, like love, affection, understanding, and concern.

We can use this idea to understand what is happening with many other attempts to exchange resources. For example, if we want to exchange services for resources we can exchange fairly universalistic services, such as professional services, for fairly universalistic resources, such as money and goods. However, if we were to try to exchange universalistic services for particularistic resources, we would have more difficulty, and the chances of the exchange breaking down would be higher. For example, it is not easy to exchange professional services for compassion, consideration, or an enduring relationship. On the other hand, if services are fairly particularistic, and parenting is a good example of a particularistic service, it is easier to exchange them for other particularistic resources and harder to exchange them for universalistic resources.

Allocating resources. In our reading of Foa's theory, we came up with an extension of his ideas that we think logically follows from the rest of his theory. It seems such an obvious idea that he may have simply assumed it, or it may be there and we have not seen it. It is a second principle that deals with the allocation of resources to try to attain goals.

It seems to us that we can place *goals* on Foa's two-dimensional chart. We would put a goal like buying a new car in the lower righthand side because it is fairly concrete and universalistic—unless we wanted to buy a car that is a status symbol, which would move the goal to the left on the concrete-symbolic dimension. Buying an engagement ring would be a goal more symbolic, and quite a bit more particularistic.

A goal of having children get good grades would be intermediate on the concrete-symbolic dimension and fairly particularistic on the other dimension. This goal would be particularistic because of the particularistic nature of children in the family realm, not because grades are particularistic. Having a goal of our children's getting a good education would be in the same place in particularism, but it would be more symbolic.

The principle we think can be derived from Foa's theory can be called the **allocation principle**:

Principle

The closer are resources and goals on Foa's model, the greater the likelihood that the resources can be used to attain the goals. (Conversely, the farther apart the resources and goals, the greater the likelihood that attempts to use the resources to attain the goals will be unsuccessful.)

This principle has many practical implications in the family realm. One of the most obvious is that it helps us understand why some resources are effective and some are ineffective in attaining particularistic goals such as love, understanding, concern, and tenderness. Particularistic resources are effective in attaining particularistic goals, whereas universalistic resources are not.

As obvious as this insight is, parents often try to win the admiration, love, or allegiance of their children by the things they provide for them. Many of these parents watch their teenage children choose a different style of life from that which the parents have and want for their children, and they lament "We did everything for them" or "We gave them so much." Often, what they gave them were things: lessons, cars, clothes, and expensive vacations. Had they given them more of themselves in a particularistic way, it is likely they would have less reason to lament.

As our society has become more materialistic, and as the central concerns become more with the GNP and the Dow, it is very easy to be seduced by the Madison Avenue mentality that having things is what is important in life. When people adopt that type of a family paradigm, it leads to goals that are consistent with it, and the particularistic dimensions of life are less relevant. Families who adopt those paradigms and goals will probably allocate their resources in ways that will bring financial success, but at the price of less involvement with the more particularistic dimensions of life. Consistent with this reasoning, families who adopt a paradigm that gives more emphasis to particularistic constructs and goals, are unlikely to have the same degree of success in the universalistic realms.

Operating rules. Foa developed a third principle as well. He reasoned that there is an important difference between economic and interpersonal resources. He noticed that these two different "classes" of resources are so dissimilar that there are fundamental differences in the way they are exchanged and allocated.

Foa seems to view all particularistic resources as interpersonal. In addition, he sees resources that are moderately universalistic as interpersonal if they are

"I can't swim! Would ten dollars help?"

Drawing by Handelsman, © 1971, The New Yorker Magazine, Inc.

symbolic. He also seems to view all universalistic resources as economic resources. Those that are moderately particularistic are also economic if they are fairly concrete. Thus he views services that are particularistic as interpersonal resources, but when they are moderately universalistic they become economic resources. Information that is universalistic is an economic resource, but when it is moderately particularistic it becomes an interpersonal resource. Figure 11.2 shows our understanding of which resources he classifies as economic and which he classifies as interpersonal resources.

The principle Foa developed about these ideas does not have a name, but we are calling it the **Foa principle**:

Principle

"The closer two resource classes are . . . the more similar will be their rules. Thus rules for economic exchange are only one set of rules, covering one subset of resources. Different rules . . . exist for the exchange of other resources." (Foa, 1971, p. 348)

After developing this generalization, Foa identified six differences that he called "rules of allocating and using economic and interpersonal resources." These rules mold his idea into a useful tool for helping families improve their ability to manage. The rules deal with: time, relationship, optimum group size, delay of reward, giving and receiving, and complexity.

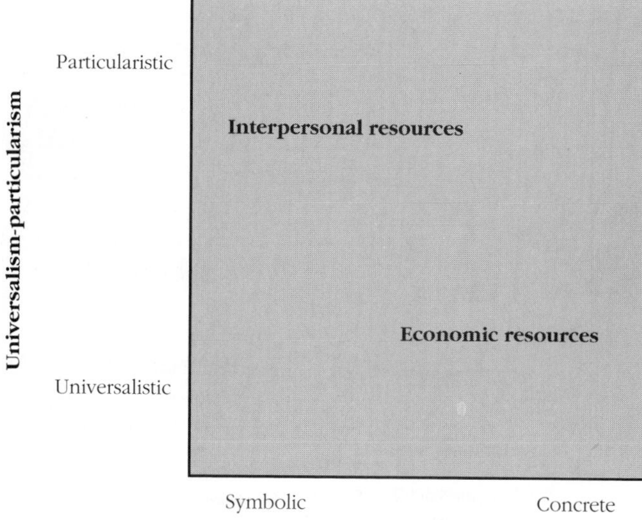

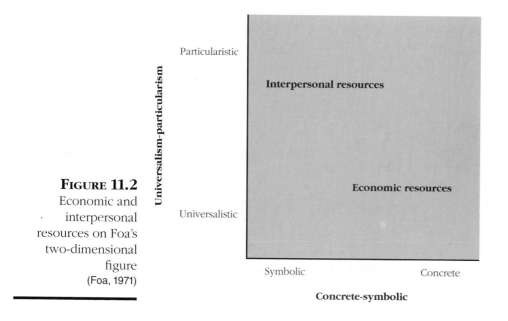

FIGURE 11.2 Economic and interpersonal resources on Foa's two-dimensional figure (Foa, 1971)

1. Time. It takes different amounts of time to process economic and interpersonal resource inputs. Economic resources can be exchanged or used in a short period of time, but exchanging interpersonal resources takes more time.

2. Relationship. The exchange of interpersonal resources needs a personal relationship, but the exchange of economic resources does not.

> Money does not require an interpersonal relationship in order to be transmitted or kept for future exchanges, and it can conveniently be sent through a third person. Love, on the other hand, can hardly be separated from the interpersonal situation, kept for a long time in the absence of actual exchange, or transmitted by an intermediary without incurring loss. (Foa, 1971, p. 348)

3. Optimum group size. Economic resources can be exchanged in very large groups. The more intimate the interpersonal resources that are exchanged, however, the smaller the group needs to be.

4. Delay of reward. Exchanges with interpersonal resources can tolerate considerable delay, and many of them *must* have a delay.

> Love is a relatively long-term investment, with rewards being reaped only after several encounters; a friendship needs to be "cultivated." (Foa, 1971, p. 348)

Economic exchanges, on the other hand, can be completed in a single encounter, and delays in identifying and agreeing on the benefits to both parties is disruptive. The contractual arrangements can be spread over a long period of time if there are adequate safeguards about the benefits (such as written contracts or sales agreements).

5. Giving and receiving. Exchanges of economic resources usually mean that giving decreases what the giver has. For example, when money, time, or energy are given, the giver has less. With interpersonal resources, the giving and decreasing is less clear and they are not inherently connected. When people give an interpersonal resource, they may not decrease their supply of it. In fact, in some situations they may actually increase their supply.

Consider, for example, what happens when one person gives another person affection. This does not decrease their supply, and the giving may help them even become more resourceful in their ability to give it. Also, giving another person respect, admiration, status, affection, and love in ways that increase these qualities in the other person does not detract from these qualities in the giver.

6. Complexity. Economic exchanges tend to be simple and uncomplicated, and most of the time the exchange is clear and straightforward. There usually is little ambivalence, little confusion, and the exchange is not complicated by things such as intensity, emotional attachment, or personal feelings.

The exchange of interpersonal resources is inherently more complicated. There is frequently ambivalence and the feeling of wanting to hold back what is being given. For example, when love is given, the complexity of the overall situation means there are likely to be such feelings as disappointment, confusion, hostility—and sometimes even hate. When status and respect are given, there are often second thoughts, wonderings, and ambiguity that need to be dealt with.

Applying Foa's Theory

There are many ways family scientists can apply Foa's theory. One of the more obvious implications is that it is inconsistent with Foa's ideas to try to love (a goal) with money or material possessions (resources). Money and love are at opposite extremes on the model, and possessions are almost opposite love.

Yet, how often do husbands think they are showing love by providing a good living, a house, and the economic necessities for their family (rather than giving their time and attention)? How often do grandparents try to get close to their grandchildren by giving them candy or gum and taking them to amusement parks? Imagine parents who have spent years saving for a son's education. In their mind, it is an act of love that has great meaning. But suppose that acceptance and caring were something these parents had a difficult time providing. The child's needs may go unmet, and the parents may not recognize why the problems have arisen.

"Managing interpersonal resources requires different processes than managing economic resources. Families need both, but it is wise to keep them separate. Trying to mix them usually creates problems that are neither expected nor understood by most families."

—THE AUTHORS

One of the most important aspects of Foa's model is that it helps us understand why attempts to use resources that are not consistent with the goals are destined to fail.

Societal problems. Another way we can use Foa's model is to help us think more realistically about how to cope with the serious problems our society faces. The economic perspective is the way of approaching problems that dominate in our society, yet Foa's model shows that we should only use the economic model with things that are fundamentally economic.

Most of the time we only think with half of Foa's model. The result is that we try to solve our personal, private, and interpersonal problems with economic solutions. Foa's model helps us realize that because of the "interplay of economic and noneconomic resources in the conduct of human affairs, it appears unrealistic to expect that social problems will be solved by material means alone" (Foa, 1971, p. 345).

Even though Foa's model was developed almost two decades ago, it has had little impact on problem-solving in our society. When the improvement of public education became a national goal in the early 1980s, how much attention was given to the "interplay of economic and non-economic resources"? How much attention was given to interpersonal resources in trying to attain our goals of improving education? There were a few voices who tried to advocate a number of noneconomic models, but they were voices crying in the wilderness. All of the proposals and programs seriously considered by the legislatures, the school boards, and the Department of Education were fundamentally economic models.

Research has shown that what happens in a child's family makes more difference than any other factor in the quality of school performance. Yet the role of the family was almost totally ignored in favor of career ladders, financial incentives, and economically oriented training of teachers. Another example of this type of misguided thinking occurred when the drug problem became a national priority in the middle 1980s. Did we examine any noneconomic ways of thinking about the causes and possible solutions? They were hardly mentioned. Drug abuse became an important issue in the 1988 presidential campaign, but the interpersonal dimensions didn't even make it into the political rhetoric. The federal government and all others involved have forged blindly ahead with our society's standard operating procedure: money for policing and enforcement agencies, money for medical research, money for rehabilitation, and money for the media to sensationalize the problem. We have failed to realize that the taproot of the problem, and the only factors that will substantially improve it, are in the interpersonal realm, and using interpersonal resources to improve the situation demands very different efforts.

Urban families. Foa's discussion of the implications of his theory helps us understand why we experience problems in urban areas. By adding some family science insights, we can begin to understand how to cope more effectively with urban problems. According to Foa, ". . . the aspects of resource theory developed in this article may be useful in understanding the effects of urbanization upon human behavior. Three properties of resources—time required for processing inputs, delay of reward, and optimal group size—converge in making the urban environment more suitable to the exchange of universalistic resources than of particularistic ones" (Foa, 1971, p. 349).

Milgram (1970) suggested that reducing the time allocated to the complexities of life is one way family members adapt to overload of pressures of living in larger urban centers. This means that, when we have to spend so much time reading signs, watching the traffic, obeying rules, and coping with other complexities, love will be curtailed. According to Foa, "in an urban setting many interpersonal contacts occur only once, while love, unlike money, requires at least several encounters to be exchanged." Finally, if optimum group size is smaller for love than for money, the large metropolitan crowds will again favor universalistic exchanges over personalistic ones (Turner, 1970; Zimbardo, 1969). A consequence of the selective influence of urban society on exchange is that it fosters antisocial (or asocial) behavior. Particularistic resources, especially status, are powerful instruments for social control; a person who misbehaves is likely to lose status in the community long before he runs into conflict with the law and meets its less particularistic forms of punishment. The relative scarcity of particularistic exchanges in the city deprives society of informal means for social control, so that individuals tend to behave less responsibly in the metropolis (Zimbardo, 1969). The difficulties for particularistic exchanges posed by an urban environment will also result in isolation and alienation, since the feeling of belonging is provided by love, the resource with the highest positive relationship between self and other.

These difficulties are further compounded in modern American society by the tendency of its social institutions to specialize in a narrow range of resources, thus excluding the exchange of particularistic resources from several institutions, even when environmental conditions are favorable" (Foa, 1971, p. 349).

These ideas are fairly complicated, but they can be said more simply. Foa is saying that an urban environment is very good at exchanging universalistic resources, and it is not very good at exchanging particularistic resources. Three results of this are that urban areas have high rates of isolation, alienation, and deviant behavior such as crime and substance abuse. Foa's model suggests that these problems would be less severe if we were able to exchange particularistic resources. This is because the particularistic exchanges help us attain the more human goals of status, meaning, love, acceptance, intimacy, affection, and purpose.

However, Foa is a psychologist, and his psychological thinking did not lead him to extend his ideas a step further. To do that, we need insights from family science. For example, where in the human condition can we find realms that are inherently particularistic and ideally suited to provide the exchange of particularistic resources in an urban environment? Can we find them in the schools, corporations, governmental bureaucracies, research centers, country clubs, and service clubs? Are they in the search for success in a career or profession? Are they in the electronic or written media? Are they in the social services, welfare agencies, or mental health clinics?

There are a few realms in urban societies where particularistic resources can be exchanged. But, if Foa's model is right, it will only be done where there are long-term relationships, delayed rewards, small groupings of people, and meaningful relationships. The obvious answer is that the family realm is the most ideally suited, natural place to provide these exchanges.

Fortunately, as Bronfenbrenner (1974; 1979) and his colleagues have pointed out, there are a few other institutions that could be managed so they would provide support. These include our neighborhoods, day-care facilities, local schools, and churches. However, when we think about the nature of these supportive institutions, it is readily apparent that they are second-best—frail substitutes for the naturally provided family realm.

Unfortunately, though, the family realm in our society is so buffeted by the dominant economic and materialistic values that it is taking a terrible beating. It is consistently low on the list of the conditions we take into account in making decisions about what to emphasize, where to build factories, how to zone, what to give our national resources to, where to allocate our time and money, and what to protect.

Why is the family so low in our actual priorities? Some of the reasons can be understood when we look at the nature of the family realm. It is like an iceberg. We can't see most of what the family does for us. What happens in the home is behind closed doors and invisible. Family goals are qualitative rather than quantitative. It also is fundamentally an affective area rather than a rational one. The result is that in the debates, discussions, allocations, and management of our society it is an invisible and forgotten area. We give lip service to the cliche that it is the "cornerstone of civilization," and then it is ignored. The result is that the effective outputs of our post-industrial society are such things as a growing GDP, elaborate freeways, sophisticated computers, microwave stations, arms races, space platforms, inflation, alienation, divorce, physical abuse, and substance abuse.

Our society is experiencing some of the greatest governmental achievements humans have ever known. We have the highest standard of living, high production, great technological advances, a global economy, a United Nations, and commercial travel at several times the speed of sound. At the same time we have the tragedies at the personal level of meaningless relationships, unachieved interpersonal goals, emptiness, single-parent homes struggling to survive, all kinds of disharmony within and among people, and extremely high rates of interpersonal abuse.

How do we solve these problems? Do we use Foa's model? Or do we stick to the economic approach—thinking of the profit and loss, the bottom line, creating a new agency, allocate more funds—as though funds will make the difference.

Summary

In this chapter we discussed the nature of family resources, defined as anything that can help families reach a goal. Several different types of resources were identified and contrasted, including human vs. nonhuman, economic vs. noneconomic, tangible vs. intangible, and personal vs. interpersonal. We then discussed the processes of allocating, exchanging, and granting resources. Kantor and Lehr's distance-regulation model was presented, along with several ways to apply it. A key idea is that families can adapt their goals, standards, and resources relatively easily because these are usually Level I changes. However, changes in the family paradigms that guide these processes are slow and difficult because they are more fundamental.

Next we presented a detailed review of Uriel Foa's theory of economic and interpersonal resources. His theory uses particularism-universalism and concrete-symbolic as two continuous variables. These factors are combined in a two-dimensional chart that allows us to classify resources and goals. Foa developed three principles that help us understand how various resources can be effectively, or ineffectively, used to attain goals. The principles are the exchange principle, the allocation principle, and the Foa principle.

Foa laid down six rules about the exchange of economic and interpersonal resources that help us understand why it is difficult to exchange economic with interpersonal resources, or use one of these to attain goals in the other. His six rules dealt with the time exchanges take, relationships that are involved, optimal size of groups, delays in rewards, involvement of both giving and receiving, and the complexity of the processes. Finally, we discussed a number of implications of these principles, especially for how we manage family resources and for how we manage societal resources.

Key Terms

Resources: Human vs. nonhuman; Economic vs. noneconomic; Tangible vs. intangible; Personal vs. interpersonal
Allocation
Exchange (two-way transfers)
Grants (one-way transfers)
Exchange economy
Grants economy
Goals (target dimensions): Affect (intimacy, nurturance, joining, separating); Power (freedom, restraint); Meaning (purposeful identity)
Distance regulation
Resources (access dimensions): Space, Time, Energy
Concrete-symbolic
Dichotomy
Trichotomy
Continuous variable
Particularistic-universalistic
Interpersonal
Economic
Rules of allocation and exchange: Time, Relationship, Optimum group size, Delay of reward, Giving and receiving, Complexity

STUDY QUESTIONS

1. What are "tangible" resources?
2. Define "allocation of resources" and "exchange of resources." How are these two different and similar?
3. What is meant by a grant economy?
4. Name the three types of goals in family systems. Explain each.
5. What are the types of resources in a family?
6. Explain what is meant by material resources.
7. Explain the difference between particularistic and universalistic resources.
8. Draw Foa's resource diagram and give five specific resources, showing where they fit on the diagram.

NOTES

1. This variable has been used in a number of different disciplines. Malinowski (1929) used it in anthropology, and Talcott Parsons (1951) used it in sociology. There are some important differences, however, in the way it is used by Foa. Foa uses the concepts as building blocks in developing some useful general principles. The term was used only for ethnography by Malinowski, and Parsons' use of it was merely as a part of a large and complicated conceptual taxonomy. After Black (1961) translated Parsons' complicated conceptualization, it was realized that his models were not theories that had principles or propositions. Sociology began to realize Parsons' models had little scientific or practical utility.
2. Here are some ideas about classifying six resources in Foa's diagram.

- A credit card. Credit cards are fairly concrete. We can touch them and they are low in symbolic value. Looked at from the viewpoint of a family, it is fairly particularistic, since only one or two members can usually use it. This puts them in the upper right corner of the model. However, if we look at credit cards from a company's point of view, as a way to increase sales, they are a universalistic resource.
- A get-well card. Pretty particularistic. It is tangible, but its value is mostly symbolic. We'd put it between love and status in the upper left corner.
- A telephone call from a loved one. Pretty particularistic and symbolic. We'd put it in the upper left corner. However, if the person wants to talk about the money we owe her, the call would move toward the concrete end.
- A kiss. Kisses are usually fairly particularistic, and they have both concreteness and symbolism, so they'd usually be in the upper middle, pretty close to love. The kind you buy at a fair would be more universalistic and concrete. They'd be toward the lower left a bit. How much? Well, that depends . . .
- A job promotion. Viewed from the person's point of view, it is particularistic. It is also fairly symbolic, so it goes in the upper left corner. However, if a promotion carries a big raise with it, the raise would move it somewhat toward the concrete end.
- A college education. Mostly symbolic, and when we look at it from an individual's or family's perspective, it is fairly particularistic,

so it goes in the upper left corner. If we think of college graduates as a societal resource, that would be a more universalistic resource, and it would move toward the lower left corner.

Cooperation 12

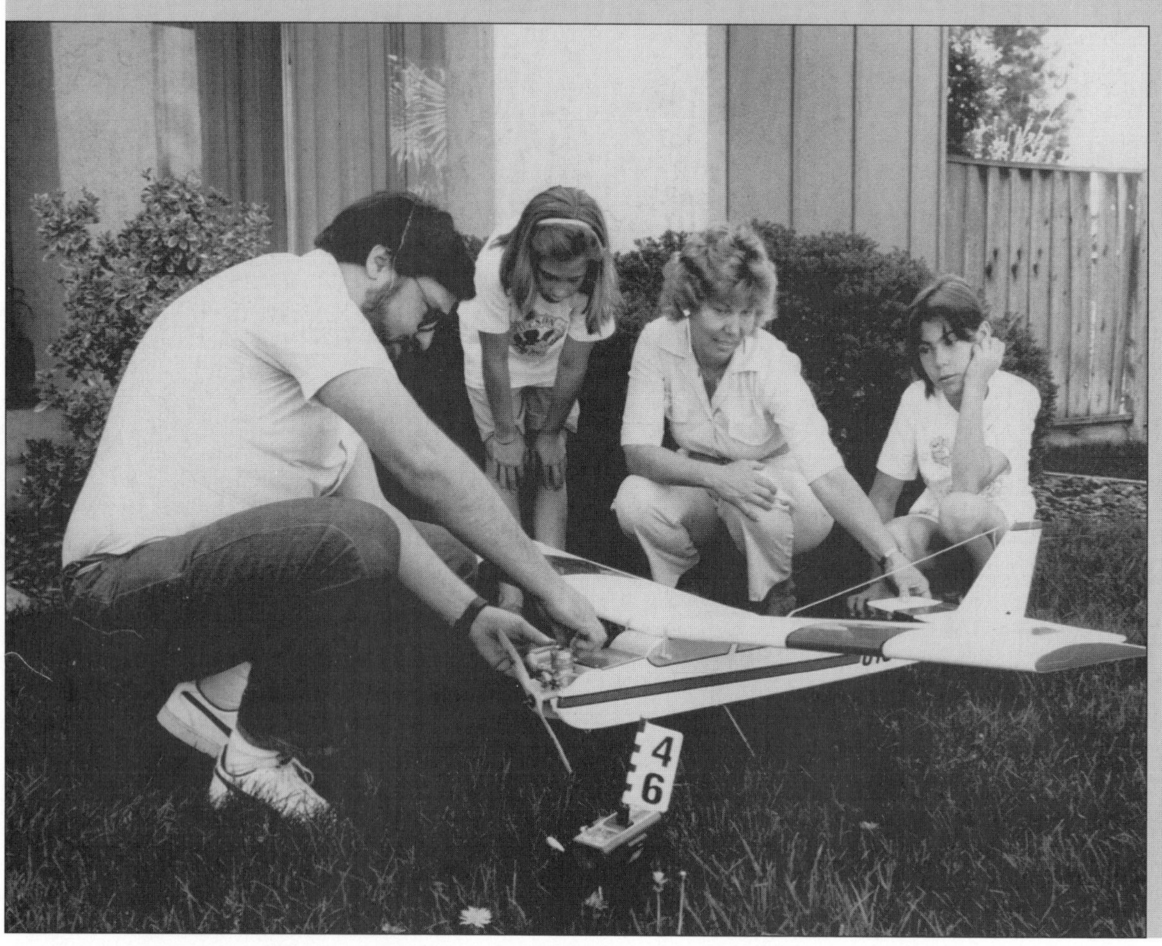

Main Ideas

1 // The cooperation principle states that cooperative patterns of relating in families tend to facilitate the attainment of many of the most fundamental goals in the family realm, and competitive patterns tend to disrupt the attainment of many of these goals.

2 // Cooperation and competition tend to influence at least five different parts of family systems: communication, perceptions, attitudes, methods of coping with conflict, and productivity.

3 // In cooperative relationships communication tends to be more open, honest, and relevant.

4 // In cooperative relationships people tend to focus on similarities and become more similar in their perceptions over time, but in competition people tend to focus on differences and become more different over time. In cooperative relationships people are more inclined to accept neutral or conciliatory gestures and they are more willing to "forgive and forget."

5 // Cooperation tends to facilitate attitudes of trust, friendship, comraderie, and helpfulness.

6 // Cooperation tends to lead to problem solving being viewed as a mutual and collaborative concern rather than a confrontation.

7 // Competition tends to increase effort and productivity.

8 // There is evidence that competition has more destructive effects in the family realm than it has in many of the nonfamily realms.

The dictionary defines **cooperation** as willingly working or acting together for a common purpose or benefit. **Competition**, on the other hand, is contending or striving with others for supremacy. A central aspect of competition is that one person or group betters or defeats another person or group. Synonyms for cooperation include "coordination" and "joint action." Synonyms for competition are "struggle," "contend," "outdo," "contest," and "prevail over."

Many disciplines use these two concepts. For example, historians have used these concepts to help explain the rise and fall of nations (Roberts, 1976). Psychologists use them to understand differences in group dynamics (Sherif et al., 1961; Blake & Mouton, 1961). Anthropologists and sociologists use them to describe differences in cultures (Park & Burgess, 1921), and psychiatrists use them to explain and cure mental illness (Adler, 1954).

Family scientists have also found these concepts to be very useful in under-

"Cooperative patterns within families tend to facilitate goal attainment"

standing and helping families (Dreikurs & Stolz, 1964; Gordon, 1970; Mace, 1983a). There are two reasons for this. First, they both occur a great deal in families, and they occur with an unusual flavor and intensity in the family realm. Second, they seem to have different effects in the family realm than they have in the more public realms that are studied in most other disciplines.

This chapter first describes the cooperation principle. It then summarizes what has been learned in previous research about how cooperation and competition influence five aspects of social systems. Then it shows how a family science perspective helps us understand why competition and cooperation have different effects in the family realm. This chapter demonstrates that competition tends to have both constructive and destructive effects in the public realms, but almost entirely destructive effects in the family realm. Cooperation, on the other hand, tends to have desirable effects in both the family and nonfamily realms. The chapter concludes with a discussion of ways to promote cooperation in families.

The Cooperation Principle

The main idea in this chapter can be stated as the **cooperation principle**:

Principle

Cooperative patterns of relating in families tend to facilitate the attainment of many of the most fundamental goals in the family realm and competitive patterns tend to disrupt the attainment of many of these goals.

There is a great deal of controversy about this principle. Some scholars believe competition is only undesirable when it is excessive. Others believe competition is inherently undesirable. For example, Kohn comments:

> The more closely I have examined the topic, the more firmly I have become convinced that competition is an inherently undesirable arrangement, that the phrase *healthy competition* is actually a contradiction in terms. (Kohn, 1986, p. 9)

The authors believe that the principle stated here is the most defensible position. It suggests that competition and cooperation operate in slightly different ways in the family realm than in most public realms. Public realms tend to be more rational and less emotional. Also, they tend to include temporary rather than permanent relationships. Many of the public realms deal primarily with tangible matters, but the processes in the family realm tend to be intangible—not material things and not part of market economies—and these differences are profoundly important.

A lot of evidence has accumulated in support of this cooperation principle, and it is an impressive array. The evidence comes from the social sciences, literature, and the arts.

Evidence of the Cooperation Principle

Research has found that when people act in cooperative ways it has a number of predictable effects on the behavior of individuals and the processes in social systems. When people interact in competitive ways it tends to have a very different set of predictable effects.

For example, Sanders and Suls (1982) found that married couples tend to avoid competition, but in an experimental competitive situation the competition adversely influences their communication and feelings. They also found that wives were affected more than husbands, and speculated that it was because the wives' identities were tied more exclusively to their marriage. They reasoned that the "husbands' identities tend to be based on nonmarital relationships and particularly in their professional careers" (Sanders & Suls, 1982, p. 728).

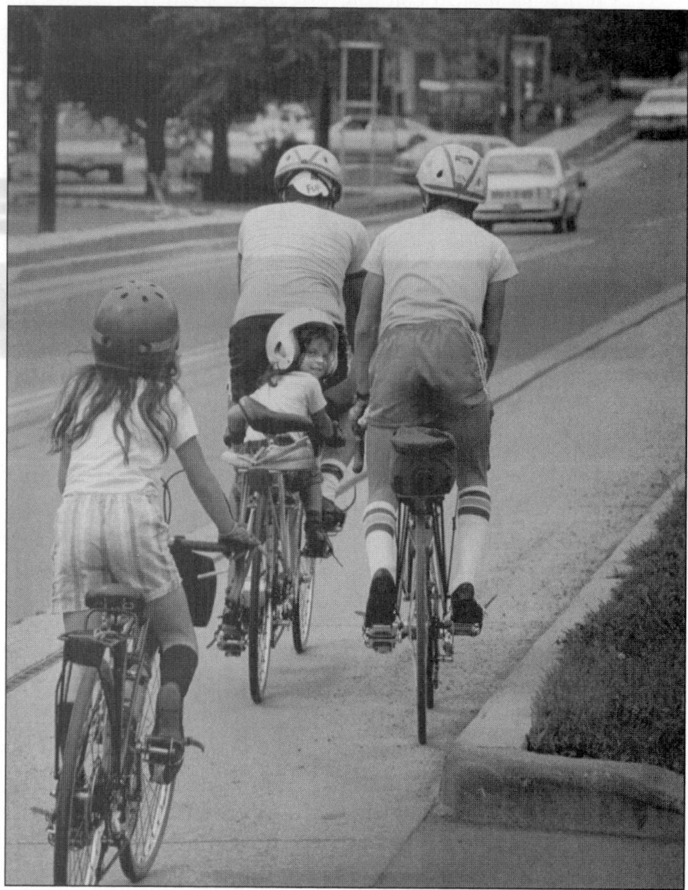

Increased cooperation can be very beneficial to family strength.

Harbin and Madden (1983) found that families who had assaultive adolescents tended to use more confronting styles of decision making, and families with fewer of these problems had styles of decision making that were consensus seeking rather than confrontive. Several studies have found that families naturally sense the disadvantages of competition and try to minimize it (Holmstrom, 1973; Brickman & Bulman, 1977).

Much of the research about cooperation and competition has been with small groups in work settings or recreational settings, and the methodology has been both imaginative and effective. This is illustrated by a classical study that has come to be known as the "robber's cave" study (Sherif et al., 1961). The experimenters used a summer camp to observe groups of boys in competitive and cooperative situations.

They began the camp by having two different groups of boys spend a week developing a feeling of "we-ness" within their group and a feeling of competition toward the other group. They created a number of situations where each group could achieve its goal only at the expense of the other group. For example, they had the groups compete in a number of tournaments and contests that had prizes. During this week the camp counselors carefully observed the methods the boys used to solve their problems and the ways they acted toward the others in their own group and the other group.

After they had created a spirit of rather intense competition between the groups, they then created a number of situations designed to promote a cooperative attitude between the two groups. These included having to work together to get an essential truck out of mud and needing each other to repair the camp's water supply. During this second phase, the counselors continued to observe the boys' problem-solving methods and ways of relating to each other.

The "robber's cave" and other studies on competition and cooperation have been analyzed by a number of scholars to find patterns in the effects of cooperation and competition (Deutsch, 1973; Allred, 1976; Kohn, 1986). Reviews of the research suggest cooperation and competition systematically influence five aspects of social systems: (1) communication, (2) perceptions, (3) attitudes, (4) methods of coping with conflict, and (5) productivity.

Effects on Communication

Openness. Research has repeatedly found that when relationships between people are cooperative their communication tends to be more open. In contrast when relationships are competitive the communication is less open.

This does not mean that people are completely closed when they are in competitive situations, but they are more cautious, careful, or selective in what they say. For example, children conceal information they do not want their siblings or parents to know when they have competitive relationships. They are careful to not reveal ideas, feelings, or information that the others could use to hurt them or get ahead of them.

The openness in cooperative relationships is shown by more spontaneity, a

---

"From the Little League ballplayer who bursts into tears after his team loses, to the college students in the football stadium chanting "We're number one!"; from Lyndon Johnson, whose judgment was almost certainly distorted by his oft-stated desire not to be the first American President to lose a war, to the third grader who despises his classmate for a superior performance on an arithmetic test; we manifest a staggering cultural obsession with victory." —Aronson, 1976, pp. 153–54

---

greater inclination to share ideas you're not sure of, and a greater tendency to share feelings. A wider range of thoughts and feelings are shared, and they are shared more frequently.

Honesty. A second pattern in the research was that in cooperative relationships the communication tends to have more honesty. The decrease in honesty in competitive relationships is sometimes quite subtle. For example, when a relationship is competitive and there are misunderstandings, the people may think about whether it is to their advantage to correct a misunderstanding or let it go.

In other situations, however, the dishonesty is deliberate and overt. For example, it is not unusual for spouses and children to tell lies or get others to lie for them when they are in adversarial or competitive relationships. People also sometimes deliberately try to create false impressions or create situations that will appear more favorable to them than they really are.

When people feel their relationships are more cooperative, it creates feelings of safety and security, and they do not have the same motivation to manipulate information to their own advantage. They are more inclined to correct misunderstandings, and to share with others what is really going on, rather than what would make them appear in the best light.

Relevance. When people are in cooperative relationships, their communication also tends to have more relevance. They try to share information that is helpful and pertinent rather than just convenient or mandatory. In competitive relationships they frequently give information that may be technically honest, but is designed to "throw the others off," divert their attention from what is important, get off on a tangent, or confuse rather than help the situation.

In Deutsch's summary of the effects of competitive relationships on communication, he comments:

> A competitive process is characterized by either lack of communication or misleading communication. It also gives rise to espionage or other techniques of obtaining information about the other that the other is unwilling to communicate. In addition to obtaining such information, each party is interested in providing discouraging or misleading information to the other. (Deutsch, 1973, p. 29)

Effects on Perception

Deutsch found several clear patterns in the research about the way people perceived things. Perceptions are the way we define or interpret things. For example, Figure 12.1 can be perceived several different ways. Some people see a fairly old, haggard woman who is facing left. Others see a younger woman who is

FIGURE 12.1 Perceptions differ. Do you see a young woman, an old woman, or both?

facing away from the viewer. Both are there, and seeing them is just a matter of selective perception.

Sensitivity to differences and similarities. Deutsch's review found that there are three ways cooperation and competition influence perceptions other than visual ones. First, they influence whether we focus on our similarities or our differences with others. In Deutsch's words,

> [a] cooperative process tends to increase sensitivity to similarities and common interests while minimizing the salience of differences. . . .
>
> A competitive process tends to increase sensitivity to differences and threats while minimizing the awareness of similarities. It stimulates the sense of complete oppositeness: "You are bad; I am good." It seems likely that competition produces a stronger bias toward misperceiving the other's neutral or conciliatory actions as malevolently motivated than the bias induced by cooperation to see the other's actions as benevolently intended. (Deutsch, 1973, p. 30)

This difference in perception usually occurs as romantic relationships are formed and dissolve. When a couple is in the process of falling in love they usually have a cooperative relationship, focusing on their similarities and minimizing their differences. They feel sure that they are alike in most ways, and even if they have some differences they are minor and won't be difficult to work out.

"Look, I didn't come down here to work on our relationship.
I came here to work on my backhand."

Drawing by Lorenz, © 1986, The New Yorker Magazine, Inc.

When couples go through the process of falling out of love, they often find themselves in a relatively competitive pattern, and their perceptions tend to match. They focus so much on their differences (and how impossible the other person is) that they find it hard to believe they have many similarities.

These two processes are both part of circular causation. A little change in either direction toward a competitive or cooperative relationship influences the perception. The new perceptions influence the relationship, which influences the perceptions, and so on.

Convergence and divergence. A second way cooperation vs. competition influences our perceptions is in how much our opinions become more and less similar over time. When we are in a cooperative relationship, we gradually become more and more alike. We tend to see things the same way more as time passes. In a competitive relationship, it is just the opposite. As time passes, we tend to become more and more different. We see things differently, and become suspicious of the way our "adversaries" see things.

This can be positive if divergent creativity is important. Divergent creativity is the kind of creativity that helps us think of new ways to do things—new designs and new approaches to problems. In industry and commerce divergent creativity can bring about new inventions, approaches to management, products, procedures, patents, and sales techniques that can make a company more competitive.

Motives. A third way competition vs. cooperation influences perception is in the area of other people's motives. If we are in a cooperative relationship and someone makes a neutral or conciliatory remark, we usually take it at face value. On the other hand, when we are in a competitive relationship and someone makes a neutral or conciliatory comment, we tend to be suspicious. We think they may have a hidden agenda. We may ask ourself, or even ask them, "What do you want now?"

This difference in our perception of motives influences how easy it is to solve conflicts, make decisions, or make up after an argument. The more competitive the relationship, the harder it is to make up, because everyone is suspicious and hesitant. The more cooperative the relationship, the more people are willing to forgive and forget, and assume that the others will too.

Attitudes

Deutsch also found that several attitudes are related to cooperation–competition. One of these is that cooperation tends to create a sense of trust, but competition tends to create a sense of suspicion. Cooperation also tends to create feelings of friendship or comraderie in the orientation toward others. Competition, on the other hand, tends to create feelings of hostility toward the adversary. He also found that in cooperative relationships people tend to have helpful and supportive attitudes toward each other. In competitive situations they tend to be more selfish, serving their own interests rather than those of their competitors.

Methods of Dealing with Conflict

Deutsch found that cooperation and competition influence the way we define, approach, and try to handle differences of opinion.

> A cooperative process enables the participants to approach the mutually acknowledged problem in a way that utilizes their special talents and enables them to substitute for one another in their joint work, so that duplication of effort is reduced. The enhancement of mutual power and resources becomes an objective. It leads to the defining of conflicting interests as a mutual problem to be solved by collaborative effort. It facilitates the recognition of the legitimacy of each other's interests and of the

necessity of searching for a solution that is responsive to the needs of all. It tends to limit rather than expand the scope of conflicting interests. Attempts to influence the other tend to be limited to processes of persuasion.

A competitive process stimulates the view that the solution of a conflict can only be one that is imposed by one side on the other. The enhancement of one's own power and minimizing of the legitimacy of the other side's interests in the situation become objectives. It fosters the expansion of the scope of the issues in conflict so that the conflict becomes a matter of general principle and is no longer confined to a particular issue at a given time and place. The escalation of the conflict increases its motivational significance to the participants and intensifies their emotional involvement in it; these factors, in turn, may make a limited defeat less acceptable or more humiliating than mutual disaster might be. Duplication of effort, so that the competitors become mirror-images of one another, is more likely than division of effort. Coercive processes tend to be employed in the attempt to influence the other. (Deutsch, 1973, p. 30)

Effects on Productivity

There is another idea about how cooperation and competition influence humans. This idea has not been as carefully researched, but it is widely believed in the Western world (Roberts, 1976). It is that competition tends to increase effort and productivity.

For example, many economists believe competition is a very important ingredient in modern economic systems (Fuchs, 1983). In fact, competition is so important to our current economic system that we have elaborate anti-trust laws and agencies to make sure that it is not undermined by such techniques as monopolies and price fixing.

The positive effect of competition is so widely believed in our society that we assume that when competition is eliminated it leads to a decrease in effort and productivity. There is considerable evidence that this is a correct conclusion. Think for example, about the efficiency of the federal postal system, the military, utility companies, socialized medicine programs, and public school systems. Are any of them pillars of effort, productivity, and efficiency? Even the trend toward socialization that was sweeping the European continent several decades ago has now been replaced by a trend toward privatization and competition. It is believed that when the competitive element was decreased there was an adverse effect on economic productivity.

Artistic and Historical Examples

Art and history reveal many examples of the effects of cooperation and competition, which provide additional evidence that the cooperation principle is true. Let's look at the effects of sibling rivalry in ancient families in the Middle East. The biblical accounts of the competitive relationships between Isaac and Ishmael and between Esau and Jacob showed they were very destructive. The cooperation in the family relationships in Homer's stories of ancient Greece illustrate healthy lifestyles.

Two contemporary films that illustrate these processes are *The Great Santini* and *Ordinary People. The Great Santini* is an account of a military man who needs to be better than others in everything he does. He is very successful in his career, and his competitiveness is not disruptive in that realm. However, as his son matures, the father feels threatened. The result is a devastating period of competitiveness between father and teenage son. The competition gradually crowds out the more delicate, sensitive, and tender aspects of the family realm that both father and son need (and inwardly wish they could attain).

Ordinary People illustrates a different type of devastation that can happen when relationships are competitive. The mother in this film does not respect the individuality of her two sons, and cannot bring herself to have a cooperative relationship with her younger son. These processes play a central role in the eventual destruction of the family.

Differences in the Family and Public Realms

As demonstrated repeatedly in the earlier chapters, the family realm is different in many ways from public realms such as government, sports, industry, commerce, and education. This idea is further reinforced in this chapter, because competition and cooperation seem to have different effects in the family realm.

Communication in Families

The effects of cooperation vs. competition on communication are well understood and accepted in nonfamily realms such as commerce, industry, international relations, and labor relations. Competitiveness in these realms puts a positive value on deception, secretiveness, selectivity in giving information, and suspicion—and these methods of communication are viewed as the normal way of doing things. What this means is that when competitiveness decreases the openness and honesty in communication it does not interfere with everyday operations in the public spheres. Why does interaction in these spheres go relatively well with closed and dishonest communication?

The dominant values in the public realms tend to be rationality, self-interest, efficiency, and productivity. Goals and methods of organization are consistent with these values. The primary goals are the production of goods and services, and they tend to involve temporary and voluntary relationships that are role-specific rather than involving people as a whole. These spheres also tend to have a **monochronic** (one thing at a time) **time orientation**, emphasize the pleasure-seeking part of humans, and approach relationships from a controlling rather than a nurturing stance.

With these values and methods of organization, it is valuable to have as much effort and productivity as possible, and a competitive way of relating accomplishes this. The negative effects of the competitive system on communication—decreasing openness, honesty, and relevance—are tolerable.

If we could find a system for our public spheres that would maintain a desirable level of effort and productivity while encouraging openness and honesty, most of us would consider it more desirable; but our society has not been able to develop that type of a system. The competitive way of relating in the public spheres seems to be the best system we know how to create, given the values of the Western world. It helps satisfy our economic, materialistic, and technological goals, and they are (whether we like it or not) the most valued goals in the contemporary Western world.

The family realm is very different. In the family realm, dominant values tend to be less materialistic, less technological, less quantitative. They include love, intimacy, affection, closeness, nurturing, caring, and helping people grow and mature with dignity. People are valued for what they are rather than for what they do. These values lead us to organize the family realm very differently from the public spheres. We create permanent relationships, relate to each other as total individuals, share emotions that are intense and personal, and care for each other as best we can.

In the relationship-oriented family realm, openness and honesty in communication are highly valued. Competition tends to be disruptive and destructive in the family realm, and cooperation is facilitating and constructive. What this means is that values and goals in the family realm tend to be inconsistent with competitive ways of relating. The family realm fosters such things as growth, intimacy, bonds, relatedness, and tenderness, and competitiveness (and the effects it has on communication) is inconsistent with these values.

It is possible for cultures, subcultures, or individual families to learn to devalue the more intimate and tender aspects of the family realm. Some segments of our modern society do. They've learned the values of the public realms that are consistent with competitive relationships, and it has changed the dominant values in these family systems to such things as achievement, production, superiority, rationality, dominance, and efficiency.

If our analysis of these ideas is correct, these cultures, groups, or individuals will find the processes in their family life are different from those who have values more consistent with the "nature" of the family realm. They will exhibit more efficiency and productivity, and this may lead some to success in the public spheres. There will be less openness in their communication, and this will influence other family characteristics such as intimacy, closeness, and trust. These families will be frustrated if they also had a goal of honest communication, because their values and style of relating will be fairly incompatible with the goal.

We're not sure how many subcultural groups or families have incorporated these public-realm phenomena into their family life, but we suspect it is a fairly sizeable group. The ideas presented in this chapter can provide considerable insight into the nature of the challenges, opportunities, ways of relating, frustrations, and sources of satisfaction for these public-realm families.

Perception in Families

The effects of competition vs. cooperation on our perceptions are important in family life because families always have differences of opinion. Two sources of differences in families illustrate this inevitability of conflict.

First, all family members are continually moving through developmental stages. Movement from one stage to another creates uneven changes in the ideas, opinions, feelings, desires, and aspirations of the members of families, and thereby differences arise. Second, families always involve several different generations, and generational differences are a fact of life. Parents look at things differently than children do, and grandparents have still different opinions. There are many other sources of differences in families. Males look at things differently from females, and people who spend most of their time in a career or profession look at things differently than those who spend most of their time in the home.

The inevitability and pervasiveness of differences in families underscores the finding that a competitive relationship tends to emphasize and increase differences, and a cooperative relationship tends to minimize difference and create convergence. One thing this means for families is that competition will increase conflict in the home and make it even more difficult to manage. (This is not as serious in the public realm because there relationships are more superficial, temporary, and role-specific, making it relatively easy to avoid or to manage the conflict.) It is a serious problem for the involved, long-term, intimate, affectionate relationships that occur in families.

Families who choose to have a relatively competitive style of life can, however, compensate. They need to adopt family goals that are consistent with the competitive style of relating. This might include more formality, emotional distance, and role-specific relationships.

The effects of competition on divergence probably have very different consequences in the family realm. Divergent creativity is valuable when the emphasis is on developing new products and maximizing efficiency. In the family realm, however, divergent creativity is less important. Divergent creativity can help when a family encounters new and stressful situations, but in the routine of daily living long-term relationships are built and maintained primarily on predictability and similarity rather than on creating novel ways of doing things.

Applying the Cooperation Principle

We need more research to determine when cooperation and competition have adverse effects on families. We also need more research to determine if other aspects of the family realm are influenced by these processes. In the meantime, we must do the best we can to use the cooperation principle wisely. Fortunately, a number of scholars have developed ways of using these ideas to help families move toward cooperative ways of relating.

In Family Life Education

Family scholars have developed a number of educational and enrichment programs to teach cooperative processes in families. One example is the Parent Effectiveness workshops developed by Thomas Gordon and his associates. Gordon published a book in 1970 called *Parent Effectiveness Training (PET)*. It became a bestseller and Gordon eventually developed an enrichment-oriented workshop to teach his ideas. There are now trained leaders in many countries who lead PET workshops.

One of the ways the PET program teaches cooperation is what Gordon calls "Method III" decision making. Gordon's "Method I" is a win-lose method where the parents, the powerful ones in the parent-child relationship, get their way in decisions. Method II is a lose-win approach where the weak one in the relationship, usually the child but sometimes one of the adults, wins and the strong person loses. Methods I and II are both competitive ways of making decisions.

An example of Gordon's methods I and II occurs when a parent tells a child she cannot play with a particular friend. This is Method I, because the strong one in the relationship wins and the weak one loses. However, if the child finds a way to continue associating with the forbidden friend against the wishes of the parent, the decision becomes a Method II decision.

Method III in Gordon's program is a cooperative method. The parents and children try to work out a decision everyone can feel good about. Trying to reach consensus and paying attention to feelings are the two most important elements of this method.

Don Dinkmeyer and his associates have also developed a group of educational programs that teach cooperation rather than competition in family interaction. Two of their programs are *Systematic Training for Effective Parenting (STEP)* (Dinkmeyer & McKay, 1989) and *Training in Marital Enrichment* (Dinkmeyer & Carlson, 1984). Albert and Einstein (1986) also developed a program for stepfamilies that uses many of the same ideas. These programs are helpful, but they are designed primarily for middle-class, white audiences.

In Therapy

There are a number of ways the ideas in this chapter are relevant for marriage and family therapy. One is that therapists need to examine therapeutic programs with care to determine how consistent they are with the family realm and the cooperative patterns that are important in this realm.

Leadbeater and Farber (1983) have pointed out that this was a problem in one school of therapy. In what is known as Behavioral Marital Therapy (BMT), the therapists developed techniques of having couples identify very precisely what kinds of desirable behaviors they wanted in their mate, count these behaviors, and make "deals" with each other about what they would do for one another (Jacobson & Margolin, 1979). Many of these techniques were based on assumptions that marriages are (and ought to be) basically hedonistic relationships where negotiation and exchange can be conducted in a way found to be successful in labor–management disputes and international negotiations.

After these bargaining strategies were tried for a few years, it became apparent that the therapeutic interventions were aggravating the problems in many of the marriages. This led the developers of the programs to rethink their basic assumptions about the nature of the family realm. Gradually strategies based on individualistic and hedonistic assumptions were replaced with strategies based on altruistic and systemic assumptions.

Another way these ideas are relevant for therapy is that some people lose their ability to shift gears between the family realm and the public realms, and they need professional assistance to reacquire this ability. Most people follow a relatively predictable developmental sequence in learning how to shift between the family realm and the public realms. This sequence begins in infancy when children develop deeply felt attachments to their parents.

During these early years of life children learn to relate, trust, interact, and function in the safety of a family setting. During the preschool years children begin to learn how to interact in nonfamily settings. They start attending nurseries, preschools, day-care centers, and shopping centers for short periods of time. These settings gradually introduce the children to the values and methods of the nonfamily realms. When children start school, they dramatically expand their ability to interact in nonfamily realms, but they are still primarily home-centered. The family realm is still the basic source of relationships, care, values, beliefs, emotions, bonds, and interaction.

Gradually the nonfamily realms take on more importance as people move toward adulthood, and some people become so involved in the public spheres that they lose their ability to relate effectively in the family realm. They lose their ability to function in a nurturing, caring, intimate, and bonded setting that has a polychronic time orientation because they are so enmeshed in careers and other public spheres.

Traditionally, this has been a greater problem for males than females because our society structured the male and female roles such that the male was primarily outside the home (as the provider) and the female was primarily inside the home (as the homemaker). Recently, as more women are becoming highly involved in careers, this is becoming a challenge for many of them.

This pattern is one of the causes of what has come to be known in the last decade as the "mid-life crisis." The mid-life crisis usually occurs with people who are in their forties or fifties who have been highly involved in the nonfamily realms. They have attained a certain degree of "success," as defined by the public spheres, and the success is hard-earned because it has demanded the majority of their energies, loyalties, concern, and time. Many now find these nonfamily successes relatively empty and unsatisfactory. This leads them to then reevaluate their priorities and (frequently) to change their lives so they can have more of what is inherent to the family realm: intimacy, bondedness, meaningful relationships, closeness, nurturing, concern, and care.

People who retain their ability to move comfortably between family and nonfamily worlds can adjust their values, goals, and behavior. But those who have become enmeshed in the public realms can experience considerable stress and personal disorganization. One of the goals of therapists who work with people who are trying to cope with these challenges is to help them learn how to shift gears between realms.

In Our Personal Lives

Another way to use the cooperation principle is to apply it in our personal lives. Those of us who value the family realm, and discover that we have considerable cooperation and little competition there, can consider ourselves fortunate and continue as before.

Those of us who value the family realm, but notice competitive patterns in our families, may want to examine whether the competitiveness is having negative effects, as the principle suggests. We need to examine the effects it has on our communication, perceptions of the family members, attitudes, and methods we use to resolve conflict. If it is having an adverse effect, we can try to find strategies to help us move to a more cooperative style of life.

There are many strategies we can use to help ourselves and others increase cooperation. One method is to become conscious of shifting gears as we move between the public realms and the family realm. It is inevitable that when we are on the job or at school life is basically competitive. The competitiveness is so embedded in our society that there is little we can do to change it. However, when we are in our own home, it is possible to view the family as Christopher Lasch (1977) has described it, a "haven in a heartless world." The privacy, the uniqueness, and the individuality of family life allow us to do things differently.

We have all learned that we need to change clothes and act in ways that our roles demand when we are away from home. We shave, comb our hair, put on business clothes and shift to "office manners" when we go to the office. We need to know that the competitiveness that is unavoidable in the public spheres can be shed as easily as the three-piece suit when we come home.

Attempts to shift gears consciously as we move from one realm to another can help focus the competition on other companies, the clock, and the people who are after our jobs. Then we can choose not to compete with our husbands, wives, children, and parents.

A second strategy that can increase the cooperation in families is to read literature that promotes it. Hugh Allred's books *How to Strengthen Your Marriage and Family* (1976), and *Teenager: A Survival Guide for Mom and Dad* (1986) can be helpful. Ann Morrow Lindeberg's *Gift from the Sea* (1932) is a more poetic approach, and Christopher Lasch's *Haven in a Heartless World* (1977) is a scholarly analysis.

A third strategy is to discuss the ideas of this chapter with members of our family. When people understand that competitiveness in families tends to destroy some of the things they want, they may find themselves talking about ways they can gradually increase cooperation and decrease competitiveness in their family life. The resulting conversations can create dramatic changes!

A fourth strategy is to try to change family rules. As discussed in earlier chapters, all families have rules, and they can be modified to promote cooperation and discourage competition. Some examples of rules that families have found helpful include:

1. Think in terms of "our" and "we" rather than "I," "you," "me," and "mine."
2. Help children have successes in their own areas by encouraging them to discover their own aptitudes and interests.
3. Support the activities of other members of the family. Go to their concerts, ball games, and so on.
4. Avoid wanting to do better than your spouse on such things as salary, humor, intelligence, kids' love, hardest day, best lover, and handling finances.
5. Allow your spouse some freedom to express individuality.
6. Allow family members to be different and unique, rather than expecting everyone to be like everyone else.
7. Call attention often to the good things people do, so they get the attention and recognition they need to feel important.
8. Interact with a child on a one-to-one basis often enough they are not hungry for it.
9. Compare progress to a person's own past and potential, not to others in the family. This means that parents avoid comparing children to each other.

SUMMARY

This chapter discussed the effects of competitive and cooperative relationships. A review of social-psychological research revealed that competitive and cooperative processes

> tend to be self-confirming, so that the experience of cooperation will induce a benign spiral of increasing cooperation, while competition will induce a vicious spiral of intensifying competition. This is true to some extent, but there are restraints that usually operate to limit the spiraling of both processes. Not the least of these restraints arises from the fact that a person or group is usually involved in many situations and relationships simultaneously, and his other involvements and relationships usually prevent or contain what might be termed an obsessive intensification of any particular relationship. (Deutsch, 1973, p. 30)

Research has found that competitive relationships tend to influence communication patterns so they are less open, honest, and relevant. They negatively influence perceptions of attitudes and motives, so differences increase over time and malevolent motives are emphasized. They influence attitudes in the direction of suspicion and hostility. They influence methods of coping with differences by making us more inclined to confront, be inflexible, coerce when we can, and expand the scope of problems.

Cooperative relationships have just the opposite effect. They prompt openness and honesty in communication. They influence perceptions so we minimize differences, tend to attribute benevolent motives, and become more similar. They promote more trusting, friendly, and helpful attitudes toward our associates, and we try to deal with differences by limiting their scope, increasing empathy, and increasing willingness to adapt and to search for mutually satisfying solutions.

The effects of competition may not be disruptive in many of the public-oriented spheres of life, but they are devastating in the family realm. They interfere with the natural inclinations in the family realm to be supportive, nurturing, affectionate, and helpful. The cooperative processes, on the other hand, are consistent with the needs of the family realm.

These ideas served as the basis for stating the cooperation principle: *Cooperative* patterns of relating in families tend to facilitate the attainment of many of the most fundamental goals in the family realm and *competition* in families tends to disrupt the attainment of many of these goals.

Key Terms

Cooperation
Competition
Communication: Openness in communication, Honesty in communication, Relevance of communication
Perception: Sensitivity to similarities, Convergence of perceptions, Perceptions of motives, Benevolent/malevolent
Attitudes: Trust vs. suspicion, Friendly vs. hostile, Helpful vs. not helpful
Methods of coping with conflict: Inclined to confrontation, Flexibility, Coercion, Expanding scope of conflict
Cooperation principle

Study Questions

1. Define competition.
2. According to the text, is there ever a time when competition is appropriate? If so, when?
3. What are two effects competition has on communication?
4. Explain what is meant by the idea that competition emphasizes difference.

5. Explain the difference between convergence and divergence and how competition effects each.
6. Tell how competition can influence our perceptions of family members.

Rituals

13

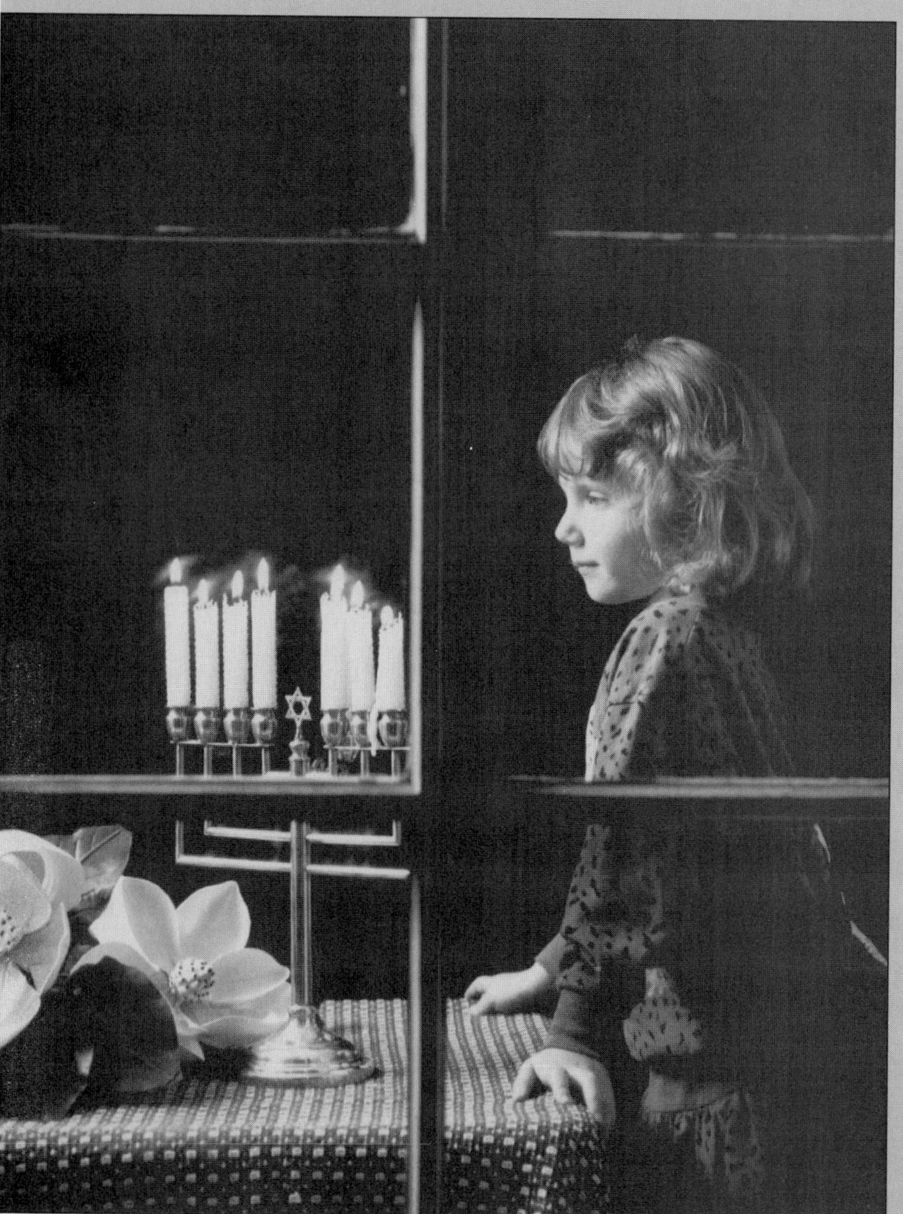

Main Ideas

1 // Family rituals and routines are similar in that they always involve more than one member of a family, involve overt or visible behavior or action, are repetitive in form and content, and have both morphostasis and morphogenesis in all of them.

2 // Rituals are distinct from routines in that they tend to carry more emotion, display more symbolism, be expressed by "staged" or unusual behavior, and are more elaborate in form.

3 // Family rituals and routines, when wisely managed, can help families to attain important goals.

4 // Sometimes old rituals need to be reevaluated, and families can be creative in adapting them or making new rituals to suit the evolving needs of all the family members.

5 // When creating new rituals, families are dealing with issues of form, content, and symbolism.

We are all familiar with family rituals. Some of them occur on holidays such as Thanksgiving, the Fourth of July, Christmas, Passover, or Three Kings Day. On these special days families do things slightly different from the ordinary. They roast turkeys, watch fireworks, conduct religious ceremonies, trim trees, go to parades, watch football games, and so on.

Some family rituals do not occur on holidays. They are more ordinary, and some of them are even repeated daily. For example, we kiss and hug in special ways and wave goodbye as we leave home for work and school. We tuck small children in bed, tell bedtime stories, eat certain meals at certain times and in certain ways, and have special places to sit and read.

Even though we're all familiar with family rituals, when we study this part of the family realm we find the terms we use vague and elusive. For example, are rituals the same as routines, traditions, customs and habits? Are they the same as family rules, or are they different? And, if they are different, what are the differences? Thus we begin this chapter by defining terms.

> *"We have concluded that family rituals are vital to the life of the healthy family."*
>
> —Wolin & Bennett, 1984, p. 407

What Are Rituals and Routines?

The term *ritual* is "an elusive concept, on the one hand transparent and conspicuous in its enactment, on the other, subtle and mysterious in its boundaries and effects on participants" (Wolin & Bennett, 1984, p. 401). Also, rituals and routines are studied by scholars in many fields. For example, anthropology, sociology, psychology, and family science all have accumulated a body of literature. Since the scholars in each of these disciplines have slightly different perspectives, they study different aspects of rituals, and they do not agree on how to define the terms.

To illustrate these differences, Boyce and others (1983) say it is not useful to try to distinguish between rituals, celebrations, and traditions, and they suggest we use the term *routines* for all of them. Curran (1983) and Meredith (1985) argue that all of the routine and ritualized parts of family life should be called *family traditions.* Wise (1986) prefers to divide them into routines and rituals, and a recent group of scholars suggest we use the term *ritual* to refer to all of these events because "while these terms—rituals, celebrations, and traditions—may have subtle differences, they all appear to refer to the same general collection of family-oriented activities" (Meredith et al., 1989, p. 76).

We think a useful solution to this confusion about terms is to use two terms, **rituals** and **routines**. These two terms can be defined by describing how they are similar in some ways and different in other ways. They are similar in the following four ways:

1. Both rituals and routines always involve more than one member of a family.
2. Both have overt behavior or action. (Thus, just thinking about something is not ritual or routine.)
3. There is repetition in the form and in the content of what is done. The *form* refers to how something is done and the *content* refers to what is done. Some rituals are repeated many times by the same family members, and some are just experienced once in the lifetime of a family member, but they are repeated by other individuals.
4. There is morphostasis and morphogenesis in all of them. This means they all have some continuity over time, but they also evolve and change as individuals and families develop and as the external environment changes.

In addition to these common characteristics, rituals are different from routines in at least four ways.

1. They differ in the amount of emotion that is involved. There is a great deal of emotion around weddings, births, funerals, children leaving home, a Bar Mitzvah, and celebrations of important holidays such as Christmas and Thanksgiving. We think that when these traditions involve important emotionality they become ritualized, and the best term for them is *family rituals.* There is relatively little emotion in the more ordinary events such as kissing each other hello when returning home each day, talking about the events of the day, vacuuming the carpet once a week, doing dishes, and helping children with their homework. There is routine in these traditions, but there is little ritualization, so they are called *family routines.*

2. A second way rituals and routines are different is in the amount of symbolism. Some traditions tend to have a large number of symbols. Weddings, for example, symbolize leaving home, achieving maturity, establishing a new household and a new family, making an adult commitment, and much more. Many other events—funerals, wakes, religious holiday celebrations—have several levels of symbolic meaning, and the symbolism in these events makes them

rituals. When family events have less symbolism and are repeated frequently, they become more ordinary and are called family routines.

Some family scholars in recent years have used the term *metaphor* (Imber-Black et al., 1988) to try to describe the symbolic aspect of family rituals. A **metaphor** in this context refers to an abstract set of ideas or beliefs that is understood and shared but difficult to put into words. Rituals provide a tangible representation of the more abstract idea in the metaphor. They have a symbolism that provides meaning, purpose, and a sense of completeness and integration that is difficult to acquire if limited solely to rational ways of behaving or conversing.

The symbolism in the Thanksgiving holiday illustrates its metaphorical aspects. The unity of the family gathered together to feast is a metaphor for the unity of the family wherever they are in the world.

Some metaphors in family rituals are less healthy. One family celebrated most holidays by drinking. Harsh words would inevitably be spoken, tempers would flare, and the celebration would turn into a living hell. This reoccurring ritual mirrored their entire life. The family was chaotic, having unresolved conflicts that had gone on for several generations, but were never brought into the open. The family retreated into distance, anger, and hostility, and dependency on the alcohol was an escape. All attempts to end the alcohol problem ended in disappointment. It was not until one of the sons insisted on abstinence of alcohol at holiday celebrations (even if it meant the absence of his drinking father) that the family was able to enjoy the healing effects of peaceful holidays, and greater harmony and peace in general.

3. A third way rituals and routines are different is in how ordinary or extraordinary their behaviors are. When traditions are part of the usual ways of behaving, they are not special and the term *routine* is a good way to describe them. Rituals tend to include behavior that is relatively unusual or extraordinary.

For example, when family members bow their heads, are quiet, and say a prayer in a reverent manner before eating a meal, these are special behaviors. Even if these special behaviors occur fairly frequently in the family they still have a certain "uniqueness" or lack of routineness in them. When families get dressed up and have a special meal to celebrate the new year, these are fairly unusual ways of behaving and are therefore rituals. Routines involve more ordinary ways of doing things. For example, English families tend to use a knife and fork to eat vegetables, and American families just use a fork; these patterns are part of the routines for family life. Getting up early in the morning, eating three sizeable meals rather than ten small meals, and turning the lights out before going to bed are routines.

Some rituals are so unusual and out-of-the-ordinary, being either highly dramatic or sacred, that it is easy to tell them from routines. Other rituals are just barely unusual. For example, using the special china for certain meals, cleaning the house extra well when company is coming, or getting ready for a special date may be unusual enough that they become family rituals. Even events such as reading the daily newspaper or watching certain television programs can evolve from routine to ritual if they become unusual enough. For example, if family members come to prefer a certain combination of refreshments, lighting, seating, and emotional involvement while watching certain television programs, these become family rituals.

4. The fourth way rituals and routines are different is in the preparation for the event and the follow-up activities. "Ritual is not just the ceremony or actual performance, but the whole process of preparing for it, experiencing it, and reintegration back into everyday life" (Roberts, 1988, p. 8). Even rituals that are fairly frequent have a preparation phase and a back-to-normal phase, and these phases are important parts of the ritual. Routines do not have the same three phases because they are such a normal part of everyday life.

An example of these phases is the preparation for the ritual of Thanksgiving dinner. Many American families put a great deal of time into inviting relatives and preparing the food and the home. Many schedules take a temporary change as miles are traveled in preparation for the Thanksgiving feast. If someone does not think these processes are important, witness the lack of students on college campuses during such holidays. When some students can't go to their own homes, it is painful to stay alone, and hence other students "adopt" them into their own family rituals.

Wolin and Bennett (1984) describe the preparation phase of rituals as a **transformation**. In their words:

> The phenomenon of *transformation* begins as the family readies the house and its participants for the subsequent performance. Children and guests may arrive from out of town and take up temporary quarters in unused bedrooms. Food is purchased and often prepared several days in advance. Special clothing comes from the closets or the cleaners. The house is at the same time organized and chaotic, with a general air of anticipatory excitement. On Thanksgiving morning, children may crowd around the television set for the Macy's parade or take some regular outing to occupy their time. Cooking begins in earnest.
>
> These important preparatory events constitute a transitional period, a passage from nonritual to ritual. (Wolin & Bennett, 1984, p. 408)

In summary, even though rituals tend to be quite different from routines, it is important to realize that there are some situations where they overlap and the differences are not clear. Figure 13.1 illustrates this blending. Some of the situations in the middle area are rituals with strong emotion but little symbolism or staged behavior, or routines that are ordinary but involve important emotions.

Rituals and routines are different from family rules because rules are the understandings about how all kinds of things are done. Rules deal with such things as using dishes and utensils when we eat rather than putting the food on a table and eating with our hands. Rules define how we should do millions of daily things such as closing a door when it is cold or ringing a doorbell rather than walking directly into a family's house. Rules are not rituals because they don't have the components of rituals. They have little if any symbolic meaning, and they aren't emotional (even though emotion occurs when some rules are broken). Rituals and routines are *events*, and rules are the *beliefs* that govern how these events are to be carried out in a family.

Rituals	Events not clearly rituals or routines	Routines
Strong emotion and considerable symbolism. Unusual or staged behavior. Three stages.	Various mixtures of the four characteristics (e.g., little symbolism but strong emotions).	Little emotion or symbolism. Ordinary behavior. Little preparation and few follow-up activities.

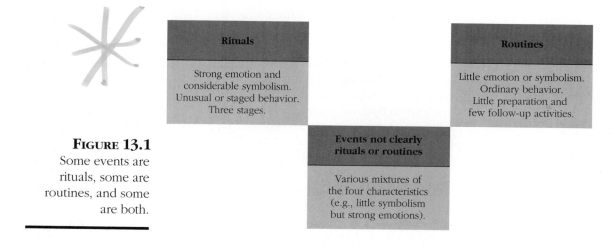

FIGURE 13.1 Some events are rituals, some are routines, and some are both.

HOW ARE RITUALS AND ROUTINES CREATED?

Bossard and Boll (1950) discovered that rituals originate in two ways in families. Some rituals are part of cultural traditions, and they are handed down from one generation to the next. Many of these "traditional" rituals involve holiday celebrations and religious activities such as having a Thanksgiving dinner, attending church, and sending Christmas cards.

The second way family rituals originate is for families to create or invent their own. These rituals arise

> out of immediate family interaction in a specific situation, such as going to bed, getting up, eating meals, doing household chores, relaxing over weekends, and vacationing in summertime. Whereas the traditional rites were usually rich pageants, the spontaneous ones were relatively simple. They were, however, more numerous, more frequently practiced, and were related to a stricter utilitarian purpose. For this reason, they were often more quickly subject to change. (Bossard & Boll, 1950, p. 61)

Bossard and Boll described a family situation that illustrates how these rituals can appear and evolve into fairly complicated and engaging patterns.

> One day when the children were small, Father brought home from work on Saturday afternoon a package of gift foods from a food specialty shop near his office. His wife and two children were at home when he arrived and together they opened the package, sampling the food from each little box. The children were delighted, and Mother, too, was pleased with the treat. Father enjoyed it most of all. The next Saturday, he went again to the same store and brought back a package. This time he happened to include a pound of his wife's favorite chocolates. This thoughtful act was especially pleasureful, and the children noted it as an extra token of affection for Mother from Daddy. The following week, Father added two small boxes of hard candies for each of the youngsters. This was extreme delight. And by that time the mold was formed. Subsequent Saturday afternoons found Mother and the children in the same room with a pair of scissors on the table awaiting the arrival of Daddy with "the Reading Terminal package." Always there was the chocolate for Mother and hard

Box 13.1

PEANUTS reprinted by permission of UFS, Inc.

This cartoon illustrates several aspects of rituals:

- Rituals are basically emotional and symbolic rather than rational.
- Rituals and routines are transmitted from generation to generation.
- Family rituals don't make a lot of sense to outsiders. Charlie is still an "outsider" to this family tradition.
- A wide variety of things can become helpful family rituals.

candies for the children. But, since the procedure started as a surprise, the surprise element had to be continued. So the rest of the contents of the bundle varied each week, and these small packages had to be guessed about, exclaimed over and sampled. Until the death of the father, this Saturday afternoon rite could not be abandoned thereafter. Part of its pattern, however, spread into other occasions for present-giving in that household. It seemed satisfactory to be able to depend on getting what one really expected at dependable times. It was also nice to maintain the element of surprise. This resulted, in that family, in the following customs: Breakfast was the time when all wants were made known. Father made his purchases when he could but, aside from the Saturday presentation, did not give the gifts directly: instead he hid them in the living room closet. After dinner, whenever a package had been hidden, the children's cue was Father's question, "Has anyone looked in the closet lately?" and the children would jump for it. Although they always remembered their last request and knew dependably that this was it, they regularly went through a guessing game, guessing everything they could think of that was less attractive than

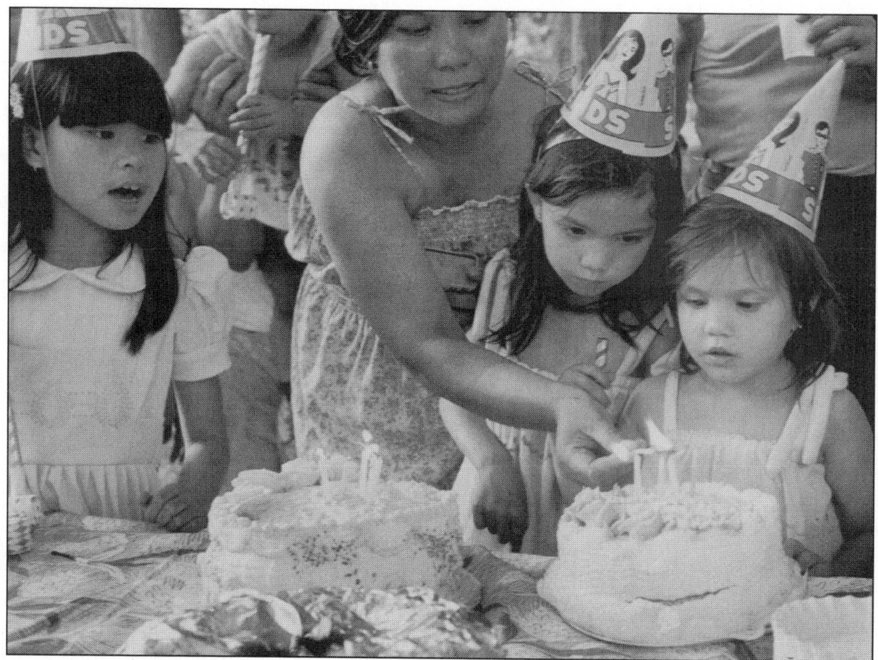

Family rituals serve as windows on our underlying, shared identity.

> the actual gift, and showing delighted surprise when the present was revealed. To have failed in any part of these rites would have been completely upsetting to all members of that family. Even after those children had grown and made their own homes, they still preserved the habits, with their mother, of giving gifts at stated times, gifts that had been asked for and were expected, but which had to be guessed about, without ever guessing right. (Bossard & Boll, 1950, pp. 61–62)

There are developmental processes in the way rituals are created and evolve over time in families. When a new family begins with the union of two or more people, they pull from their past to develop unique family rituals. Also, during the formative stage of the family life cycle there tends to be a searching for events that can be ritualized. For example, when a man and women start going together, they usually create rituals around events that would otherwise be minor things. For example, they may pick out a song that is "their song," and whenever they hear it they enact their own special ritual of hugging, smiling, and commenting on its being something special to them. Or they may have anniversary celebrations of things such as the day they met, their first date, the day they got engaged, or the

---

"In fact, the longer our studies of the inside of family life have continued, the more we have come to wonder if ritual may not be the best one starting point for the study of family life . . ."

—Bossard & Boll, 1950, p. 11

"As clinical researchers, we have also found family rituals to serve as a window into a family's underlying shared identity, providing special access to the behavioral and emotional tenor characterizing each family." —WOLIN & BENNETT, 1984, P. 401

day they decided to live together. They may develop rituals about certain places that had unusual importance to them, such as the place where they decided to get married.

As families continue to acquire new rituals, some of the rituals they created in the formative stage of family development fade away and are not remembered. Also, the way rituals are emphasized changes at different stages of the family life cycle. When families have children between 2 and 12 years old, they find themselves creating and experiencing bathing rituals, bedtime rituals, eating rituals, and rituals as they visit certain friends and relatives. During this childrearing stage of family development many families find they emphasize the traditional holidays in elaborate ways that center around the children.

As families move into the stages where they have teenage children and are launching children, their rituals usually evolve. Young adults prefer lively rituals that involve friends, music, and action, and parents often find themselves preferring more sedentary and symbolic rituals.

Rituals and routines continue to evolve and change as families move into the post-childrearing stages of the family cycle. Grandparenting brings rituals such as taking small children to parks and zoos, and telling stories about how things "used to be." The younger generations patiently, and sometimes not so patiently, listen over and over again to stories that become parts of the family folklore. The routines and rituals of aging couples become even less energetic, but they remain an important part of the emotional and symbolic fabric of the family life of the elderly.

HOW FAMILIES CAN USE RITUALS AND ROUTINES

Family rituals and routines help transform a house into a home and a group of people into a family. In many ways our modern society has become more like John Locke's version of what society should be: rational, contract-based, and individualistic. Yet there are strivings in the inner reaches of the human soul that

"Ritual is a statement in metaphoric terms about the paradoxes of human existence."
—CROCKER, 1973, P. 47

deal with emotional, nonrational, subjective, paradoxical, and ambiguous aspects, and rituals help us deal with these parts of the human experience.

The *rituals and routines principle* can be summarized in the following way:

Principle

Family rituals and routines are valuable resources, and when they are wisely used they can help families attain important goals such as unity, closeness, intimacy, and meaning.

Rituals tend to deal with the more cheerful and optimistic aspects of life, and this provides positive emotional bonds. Rituals also provide a reservoir of such things as goodwill, confidence, unity, and trust; this helps families cope with the tragic and challenging aspects of life. Rituals can also help provide a sense of "home" and a feeling that the world is, at least in some ways, a good and comfortable place. Also, since they tend to help families deal with paradoxes and ambiguities and have guiding metaphors, they can help family members acquire meaning and purpose, explanation and coherence, and a sense of being in some control of life, or having life be somewhat predictable. Rituals also provide the memories that lead to often-told stories and create a mythology that can undergird the sense of family. They help with life-cycle transitions by providing rites of passage. They may include many tender and affectionate moments, thereby helping family members learn that emotionality is appropriate and desirable.

Family scientists have identified seven specific goals of rituals and routines. They are (1) creating healthy emotional ties, (2) membership changes, (3) healing, (4) identity definition and redefinition, (5) belief expression and negotiation, (6) celebration, and (7) ability to deal with paradoxes and ambiguities.

Creating Healthy Emotional Ties

Several studies of family processes have found that rituals tend to help families create continuity, solidarity, integration, and bonds (Schvaneveldt & Lee, 1983; Meredith, 1985; Meredith et al., 1989). There are many reasons rituals help

Box 13.2

Why do we stay up on the roof if it's so dangerous. That I can tell you in one word . . . TRADITION! Because of our traditions we've kept our bonds for many years. Here we have traditions for everything—how to sleep, how to eat, how to work, how to wear our clothes. For instance we always keep our heads covered and always wear little prayer shawls. This shows our constant devotion to God.

You may ask, How did this tradition get started? I'll tell you (pause) I don't know, but it's a tradition, and because of our traditions everyone of us knows who he is and what God expects of him.

—Tevye, in *Fiddler on the Roof*

families accomplish these goals. Meredith and colleagues summarize some of these in the following way:

> Family rituals, first and foremost, encourage contact between family members, usually in a relaxed, enjoyable setting. Family conflicts and problems are temporarily set aside. This may lead to increased communication and cohesiveness. Rituals may help to bridge the intergenerational gaps that separate family members by providing activity between parents and children and extended family members. A major theme of most family rituals is appreciation of one another and the enjoyment of life together; therefore commitment to the family may be renewed by the regular observance of family rituals. Family values and beliefs may be learned and perpetuated through rituals fostering a sense of unity and oneness. In sum, rituals may be family strengthening for many reasons. (Meredith et al., 1989, p. 77)

Acknowledging Membership Changes

Families deal with membership changes in many ways. Some changes are major events such as births, deaths, marriages, and divorces; most cultures have rather elaborate rituals that help families deal with these major transitions. For example, weddings help individuals, families, and friends make the adjustment to the creation of a new family unit. Announcements, christenings, and other baby naming rituals help new members be assimilated, and funerals and wakes help families cope with death. Bar Mitzvah and Bat Mitzvah redefine membership in families and in the Jewish community, and graduation ceremonies help families redefine the relationship of parents and children.

There are some major changes in membership where families lack the rituals that help them make the necessary symbolic and emotional adjustments. For example, few rituals are associated with divorce and adoption. There are none when couples begin living together or stop living together, and there are none for beginning or ending homosexual relationships. Even though the number of stepfamilies has increased dramatically in recent years, there are few ways to ritualize the formation of a stepfamily. Weddings are used to create the marital part of stepfamilies, but the children have a peripheral role in the wedding, and sometimes they are even excluded. One consequence is that often the marital part of the new stepfamily is formed symbolically and emotionally, but the family system isn't usually formed as gracefully and effectively.

> An extreme example of this may be seen in a stepfamily who came for therapy due to stepparent–stepchild conflict that was rapidly leading to the extrusion of a child. This couple's wedding was celebrated with extended family and friends, but their five children from their prior marriage, ages six to twelve, were barred from attending. The wedding ritual had publicly affirmed the new couple, but not the new stepfamily. (Imber-Black, 1988, p. 52)

Healing

All individuals and families encounter situations where healing is needed. Healing is needed after periods of conflict, when there is pain and grief, when there is reconciliation, when there is death, and when major changes occur (retirement, disabilities, and mid-life crises). Rituals provide a vehicle that can help healing.

> Many religious and cultural groups have specific rituals for remembering and honoring a member who has died. For instance, in Catholicism, survivors may request that a mass be said to commemorate the anniversary of a loved one's death. In Judaism, a special ceremony is held to place the headstone on a grave a year following a death, and family members recite the Kaddish prayer both on anniversaries of the death and on certain holidays. Such rituals are time-bounded and space-bounded, allowing for the expression of grief and loss in a manner that simultaneously facilitates ongoing life. (Imber-Black, 1988, p. 54)

Defining and Redefining Identity

Rituals and routines can help individuals and families create, maintain, and change identities. Weddings, for example, do more than just redefine memberships. They transform identities, as a member of each family becomes a spouse and others become in-laws. Rituals such as birthday celebrations, daily goodbyes and greetings, and goodnight kisses reaffirm who the individuals are and that they are important members of a family, and they cement the emotional connections that maintain identity and create enduring intimacy.

Many of the religious, ethnic, and cultural rituals that families participate in have important implications for identity creation, change, and maintenance. In them

> specific foods, dress and ceremonies may serve to symbolize the identity theme. Such celebrations define an individual's identity as part of a larger cultural group. In the multi-ethnic society of the United States, participation in such rituals as the Chinese New Year or Greek Orthodox Easter allow even highly assimilated persons to stay connected to their ethnic and religious identity.
>
> Cultural rituals, such as Veteran's Day, Mother's Day, and Father's Day, all involve the identity theme, as these mark and celebrate particular aspects of people's identities. (Imber-Black, 1988, p. 64)

Rites of Passage

Some rituals provide the vehicle for rites of passage that facilitate growth and change. There are few rites of passage during adolescence in the American culture, but some cultural groups—Jews and Native Americans, for example—have a number of rituals that help families and individuals mark the transitions from childhood to adulthood.

Rituals have the power to be therapeutic. For example, the funeral ritual helps the participants move from one stage of life, through grief, and on to another stage of life. Doty (1986) explains that rituals have the power to transform. This is part of the wonderment and power of rituals. When transitions, catastrophes, or unexpected events occur in a family, rituals have a healing power that allows, encourages, and facilitates change.

Finding Meaning and Purpose

Farmer (1986) has suggested that rituals help families deal with the deepest levels of shared meanings and values, not only of the present, but also how things ought to be and can be. There are many abstract and ultimate concerns that are important to people that are difficult to understand. They are challenging intellectually and emotionally, and clear answers are elusive. These challenging concerns include questions about the origins of life, the meaning of existence, the nature of reality, the role of birth and death, the role of the sacred, and the possibility of life after death. Rituals provide a vehicle that helps families find and maintain solutions to these complicated and ultimate concerns.

Rituals also help with another aspect of meaning and purpose. Life presents us with many forms of injustice and inequity. There also are many times in life where we have little sense of control, and there are many contradictions and paradoxes. Rituals can help families deal with these complexities. As Roberts (1988) has observed:

> Ritual can hold both sides of a contradiction at the same time. We all live with the ultimate paradoxes of life/death, connection/distance, ideal/real, good/evil. Ritual can incorporate both sides of contradictions so that they can be managed simultaneously. For instance, a wedding ceremony has within it both loss and mourning and joy and celebration. People say, "You're not losing a daughter, you're gaining a son-in-law." Parents give their child away at the same time as they welcome a new member to their extended family.
>
> In Kumasi, Ghana, I once danced in an Ashanti dance funeral where we were all facing the same direction in a large circle and moving clockwise to the rhythms of a drum orchestra. Each person individually bent down and curled over, as if to feel the pain and loss of the person who had died. But this motion was done within the context of the whole group, everyone feeling the hurt and then coming up into the circle to see the others, to move with their energy, and celebrate our own bodies and life. The movement itself held both sides of life and death. (p. 16)

Creating Order and Predictability

Families can also use rituals and routines to help create a sense of order and predictability in life—a sense of "home." For example, routines such as preparing and eating meals, leaving and returning home, dressing and undressing, and relaxing in a favorite chair at the end of a day provide a sense of continuity, comfort, and peace that is an important part of life.

It is likely that rituals and routines contribute in different ways to this goal. Rituals probably provide a sense of order and predictability about the more important issues, questions, and paradoxes of life, and routines help provide a sense of order in the daily rhythms and cycles, contributing to a sense of comfort. Our daily routines make home a haven where we can let our hair down, be "offstage," and escape from the competitiveness and aggression of the marketplace or school.

Wisdom in Managing Rituals

Rituals and routines are not inherently healthy and facilitating. They can be unhealthy and destructive if families are not wise in the way they create them and carry them out. Research and clinical experience have identified five ideas that can help families be wise and effective. These ideas are: (1) it is enabling to have an adequate amount of ritualization—not too little or too much, (2) it is helpful to have distinctiveness in the rituals when there are problems that could be passed on to future generations, (3) families need to have developmentally appropriate morphostasis and morphogenesis, and (4) they need to avoid the inappropriate use of rituals and routines.

Moderate Ritualization

Research suggests a moderate amount of ritualization is helpful to families, and it is disruptive to have too much or too little emphasis on them (Bossard & Boll, 1950; Meredith et al., 1989). There is considerable variability in how many rituals families have and in the type of rituals they have, but being involved in rituals and being committed to them is helpful (Wolin & Bennett, 1984, p. 406).

This idea is consistent with the golden mean principle. The golden mean suggests that moderation is wise in all types of family processes that involve time, effort, and energy, and that includes rituals and routines. Family scientists refer to the extremes in this area as underritualization or overritualization.

Underritualization occurs when families have few or no rituals. Our fast-paced society emphasizes the economic, occupational, and materialistic parts of life, creating a hustle-bustle attitude in which many families spend little time with each other. Also, the reliance of many families on passive entertainment, such as watching television or listening to music with headphones, detracts attention from family rituals. The result of this is a loss of family and individual identity, loss of structure and stability, and little cohesiveness. Inudin (1967) found most of the disadvantaged families of the slums were disorganized, lacking set patterns of behavior, schedules, and norms, and making few claims to particular spaces and possessions. Apparently, the families had become prey to discrimination and oppression, lack of opportunity, and the hopelessness of poverty; the disorganization of the family, with few rituals and the loss of family identity, resulted. An example is a family with an alcoholic father who stopped all holiday ritualization so that drinking would not be there to pull him back down.

We do not have adequate ritualization, but there are many important events where rituals could help families cope. For example, there are few or no rituals to help families deal with such events as miscarriages, stillbirths, rape, transitions from childhood to adolescence and adolescence to adulthood, divorce, early retirement, and old age (Gordon & Gordon, 1984). Rituals could help unite people, provide support, provide containment of emotions, and move participants on to acceptance and positive growth in these situations, but there tends to be an underritualization (Quinn et al., 1985; Laird & Hartman, 1988). For example:

> The end of a nonmarried relationship not only has no healing ritual, but also often is not acknowledged as a loss by family and friends, or is considered "less serious" than a divorce. This very lack of confirmation of loss makes healing more difficult, as there is no context for the expression of pain and sadness. (Imber-Black, 1988, p. 58)

Another example of how underritualization can be disabling is what happened when there was a stillborn birth in a family known to the authors. The family had an unwritten rule that no one was to talk about the death. The body of the baby was taken from the mother soon after the cesarian section, placed in a casket, and shipped by air while the family drove a car to a distant state for burial. The casket was taken by an uncle from the airport to the cemetery in the back of a station wagon, while the parents rode in a separate car. The father declined to carry the casket from the car to the graveside, where there was a very short memorial service. Few visits were made to the cemetery and talk about the little child was almost nonexistent.

What a change could have taken place if rituals had been used. If only the family had been aware of the importance of touching and looking at the dead baby to help work through feelings of loss. If only they had realized the importance of talking about the grief and their crushed expectations. There are many rituals that can help families work through the paradoxes, complexities, and ambiguities in these situations. For example, if an honored person were selected to accompany the casket and baby, it could help. If the funeral or graveside ceremony allowed several people to express consolation, support, and understanding, it would help. It would help if the funeral were followed by a luncheon, dinner, or time to visit, where family and friends could gather to help express emotions and move in a forward direction. Rituals are one of the few ways we humans have to incorporate both sides of the contradictions involving living and dying. They not only allow the participants to see both sides, but also to understand, experience, and cope with both sides.

Many difficult and tragic events are not well ritualized in our modern society. Health changes that make it necessary to retire early, divorce, rape, and coping with physical abuse or incest are cases where rituals could be used. Rituals could acknowledge the destructive aspects of these experiences and help create new structures for the future. They could celebrate the survival of the participants, rather than leave them as victims, and this could open up communication about the events, use more of the family and community resources, and create cohesion rather than fragmentation in the families.

Overritualization can occur when families try to incorporate too many inputs from people or organizations outside the family. It can be too overwhelming if young couples try to incorporate all of the rituals from both parental families, and also try to include the rituals that are encouraged by various cultural, civic, religious, and fraternal groups. Couples need to be selective in adopting rituals for their new family.

Overritualization also can occur when families fail to give up rituals that have lost their usefulness. For example, many families who have young children find it meaningful to have a large number of rituals around Christmas. Later, as the children mature, some of the rituals are less relevant, and if members of the family try to continue them it can lead to being overwhelmed.

People and families also differ in the amount of ritualization that is desirable. Some families like to have a relatively large number of rituals and others want to invest less time and energy in rituals. There is some evidence that the parent and grandparent generations like more family rituals than teenagers and young adults (Meredith & Abbott, 1989). It is possible that teenagers and young adults have so many other demands, challenges, activities, and developmental tasks to manage that it is less effective for them to be involved in family rituals. Being less involved in family rituals may actually help young adults disengage from their parental family. Then, as they create their own new family, they may find it enabling to get reinvolved in some of the rituals of their larger family system and create their own for their new family.

Distinctiveness of Rituals

A group of researchers at George Washington University has discovered an idea that can help families be wise in the way they manage their rituals. The idea has to do with the **distinctiveness of family rituals**. They have found that when families have an undesirable characteristic such as alcoholism it is helpful to keep the rituals distinctive from (separated from) the problem. Apparently, if family rituals can be separated from family problems, there tends to be less generational transmission of the problems. For example, if families are able to keep the alcohol problems separated from their holiday celebrations it decreases the likelihood the alcoholism will be passed on to future generations.

This idea probably works with other kinds of family problems too. For example, if families have problems such as physical abuse, fighting, closeness avoidance, aggressiveness, excessive competitiveness, or lack of intimacy, it is probably true that the more they can separate these problems from their family rituals the greater the likelihood the problems will not be passed on to future generations.

A practical implication of this is to try to agree to "not fight," "not drink," "be nice," or "be home" during family rituals—such as Thanksgiving.

Balance in Stability and Change

One of the paradoxes of rituals is that they are stable and change at the same time. They need to have some stability (be repeated over and over again) to be rituals, but individuals and families are continually developing and changing, and rituals need to adapt to these changes.

> Flexibility is required of a family if its rituals are to remain relevant and effective. For example, as children reach an age at which their opinion carried increasing weight in

> the home, can the family accommodate their ritual life to the children's evolving views? Similarly, as the family adds or loses members through marriage, divorce, remarriage, death, etc., will the sense of obligation for ritual maintenance shift accordingly? The ability to adapt and modify ritual observance—ranging from the important holidays celebrated to the rules for routine family dinnertime—applies to both the type of rituals as well as their level of practice. (Wolin & Bennett, 1984, p. 416)

Healthy flexibility occurs when the type of birthday parties given to children change as they grow older. Young children enjoy small family parties with games, cake, and singing, but teens are different. They want to invite friends over, or go out somewhere for a movie, activity, or video arcade. Rituals must be flexible enough to change over time so they are meaningful to the participants and carry the power that is potentially available in them. It is wise to include members of the family in rituals to promote the shared aspect, but this too should not be overdone.

Too much stability occurs when families get stuck in certain developmental stages and try to maintain rituals after they have outlived their usefulness. Some families maintain rituals in rigid, repressive, and degrading ways to preserve the status quo. These rigid patterns appear sometimes when families experience serious problems such as incestuous behavior, and they use rigid rituals to keep their secrets from getting out.

Inappropriate Use of Rituals

There are many ways rituals can be abused. For example, parents can use rituals to try to control children long after the children should be in control of their own lives. Rituals can also be used to perpetuate pseudomutuality, hide skeletons, promote cross-generational alliances, or avoid letting children go. They are enormously powerful because they tap into a set of dimensions that are hard to identify, define, articulate, and understand. They deal with deep emotions that are implicit and symbolical rather than with simple, overt, cognitive processes, and attempts to defy the rituals can be defined as disloyalty.

Another way rituals can be abused is to adapt them to certain family members while ignoring others. For example, one wife emphasized her own traditions and demanded that the husband's traditions be eliminated. They visited her extended family to the exclusion of the husband's, and her past family's rituals became the present family's rituals. Not only was the husband's wealth of experiences and memories lost, but a number of new problems were created by the lack of balance.

Guidelines for Creating or Changing Rituals

Family scientists have discovered that deliberately trying to create new rituals can help families accomplish their developmental tasks and cope with difficulties.

One couple, for example, was struggling with past incidents of anger, mistrust, hurt, and lack of understanding. Extramarital affairs were present, as well as verbal declarations of wanting something different from what they had. A second wedding and honeymoon and a burning and burying of symbolic items from the dark past helped them create a new start. They ritualized the end of the past ways of doing things and creatively used new rituals to make things better and different, and the couple was able to change. It was a powerful way of getting "permission" to start over, while cutting off the old way.

Family scientists began in the 1970s to try to help families create new rituals as a strategy for dealing with problems and difficulties. The description of the Torres family in Box 13.3 illustrates how therapists or others can creatively help families design new rituals to help them cope with challenges that are introduced by cultural changes or other external events.

This approach to helping families began when a group of Italian scholars started to prescribe rituals as a part of their family therapy (Palazzoli et al., 1974; 1978). Gradually, as more and more family therapists and family life educators gained experience in helping families with rituals, a few guidelines have been developed that are helpful in trying to create or modify rituals (Van der Hart, 1983; Whiting, 1988). The guidelines have mostly to do with how to design rituals as a part of family therapy or psychotherapy. However, we think that by generalizing the guidelines a little bit they can be adapted so other family professionals can use them. We also believe that families can use them without any professional assistance to find new ways to create and modify their family rituals.

There are at least three concerns when deliberately trying to create or modify rituals. These concerns are with: (1) the goals, which are the purposes or objectives, (2) the form, which refers to how the rituals are carried out, and (3) the content, which refers to what is symbolized and what the behaviors are.

Goals

When we want to design or modify a family ritual, we need to have at least a vague idea about what we want to accomplish. Imber-Black (1988) and others refer to this part of rituals as the *theme*. A large number of scholars refer to this part of rituals as the *functions* of the rituals (Doty, 1986). In ecosystems theory, the term that describes this part of rituals is *goal*. Seven goals were described earlier in this chapter, but that list of goals is illustrative rather than exhaustive. There can be many other goals. Some additional examples are celebration, adventure, dealing with paradoxes and ambiguities, and preserving memories.

Most of the time when people want to design or change rituals they are dealing with more than one goal. Usually some of the goals are difficult to describe precisely, so it is helpful to not worry too much about getting a clear statement of the goals or how they will be quantified or measured. Rituals are so right-brain oriented that vague impressions, images, metaphors, and similes are sometimes enough.

Box 13.3

The Torres Family

A family consisting of a single mother, Ms. Torres, and two adolescent children—a boy Manuel (15) and a girl Maria (13)—were referred for therapy due to the son's problems in school. In recent weeks he had begun cutting school and hanging out on the streets. The family was from El Salvador, which they had fled four years earlier following the imprisonment and subsequent death of the father for political activities. The children spoke English, while the mother spoke primarily Spanish. They were living in The Bronx.

In the first session, the mother said that they had been very close, both in El Salvador and during the first two years in The Bronx, but that now they were distant. She said she could not understand her children anymore, and that she was very afraid of losing them, especially her son. The children both stated that they could no longer understand their mother. They said they wanted to be American and that she wanted them to be Salvadoran. They were angry that she had not learned more English, and the son said "My mother lives in the past!" While the children spoke, the mother cried. When they finished, she said that they refused to listen to her when she wanted to talk about home. The son immediately said "Home is in The Bronx now!"

They described a daily pattern in which the mother would try to speak about El Salvador, and both children would leave. When the children tried to talk about what was happening to them every day, the mother would get upset. Mother and children were becoming more and more separate. At the same time, the children's care and concern for their mother became evident when the conversation shifted to their dead father, as both children moved swiftly to protect their mother—changing the subject to issues that would upset her in more manageable ways! Thus the children's seeming refusal to affirm their connection to El Salvador not only expressed fairly typical adolescent rebellion in situations of migration, but also served a protective function, albeit misguided, to keep their mother angry rather than sad.

At the end of the session, I asked them all to bring items to the next session that would represent El Salvador and The Bronx, in order to begin a process that would affirm the connection of all three members to both places. In the second session, time was spent with each member sharing their items. The mother was surprised that both children brought items from El Salvador that represented very tender memories, including photographs and toys. She said that she had no idea that they had kept anything. Their items from The Bronx were a rock-and-roll tape and a poster from a concert. The son expressed surprise that this did not upset his mother, since at home they frequently fought about the music the children wanted to hear. The mother brought Salvadoran food she had made. She also brought a small pizza that she had bought to represent The Bronx, and said that lately the children were always eating pizza instead of the food she prepared. We sat and ate both the Salvadoran food and the pizza together.

At the end of this session in which both cultures were affirmed by all family members, I asked them to pick a time once a week for storytelling, when the

(continued)

Box 13.3
(continued)

children would listen to their mother's stories about El Salvador, followed by the mother's listening to the children's stories about The Bronx. This storytelling ritual was designed to interdict the previous pattern of distance and struggle, to affirm both cultures, to connect mother and adolescent children, and to allow for continuity of past and present. The family continued this storytelling ritual beyond the three weeks I had asked them to try it, and it became a part of their family life. Over time, the stories allowed for the expression of all of the members' loss and sadness and fear involved in their forced migration, while at the same time anchoring them in a new life that could include many elements of their heritage. Also, stories the children told about The Bronx enabled the son to begin to discuss his school problems, which he had been afraid to raise with his mother earlier.

This two-part ritual began with the family members' bringing the items that represented El Salvador and The Bronx to the session. During this in-session portion, the mother was able to discern that her children were still connected to El Salvador and the children were able to realize that their mother was not closed to their new experiences in The Bronx. A small dose of symmetry was able to interdict the previously escalating complementary pattern. The at-home storytelling ritual continued this pattern shift, while allowing for the healing process needed in a family that had been forced to flee their own home. (Case history from Imber-Black et al., 1988, pp. 59–61)

Form

We do not know whether it is wise to focus on the form or the content first. They seem to both gradually evolve in a "chicken and egg" manner as ideas about what to do influence ideas about how to do it and vice versa. Eventually, however, it is helpful to think through the form of the ritual. Whiting calls this process choosing the design *elements*. It refers to issues such as how much the rituals will be open vs. closed, how time and space will be used, and how much repetition will occur.

The open vs. closed aspect of rituals refers to how much the ritual is rigid or flexible. In rituals that are quite closed, there is little room for innovation or variation and there are understandings that define fairly clearly what is to be done. There must, of course, be some closed or structured aspects. In rituals that are more open, there are fewer rules and more flexibility for innovation, creativity, and individual differences. Apparently there can be wide variation in how closed or open rituals are, and they should be tailored to different situations and to the family's personal preferences, values, and lifestyle.

> Time simply refers to when the ritual is to be done—in the morning, every other day, on the weekend, 30 minutes in the evening. At home, in the woods, in the living room are phrases marking the space where it is to be done. How the elements of time and space are emphasized is often related to the previous elements of open and closed aspects. For example, in a ritual where the closed aspects are emphasized, the time and space ingredients are generally prescribed in specific ways. (Whiting, 1988, p. 89)

A third aspect of the form of rituals that must be dealt with is the amount of repetition. Many rituals are repeated frequently in families. For example, a prayer or period of silence before eating a meal, or kissing each other hello and goodbye, are two rituals that are performed daily in many families. Other rituals, however, are just performed only once for the people involved. Giving a person a name and having a funeral for them are two examples. Also, a family may want to create a ritual that will occur just once to help them deal with a unique situation.

An example of this type of ritual is a healing ritual that could be designed to help a family find a way to let go of a former relationship. These one-time rituals could be created for many situations such as finding ways to accept a family member back after the person has been excluded, or finding ways to cope with a personal or financial failure.

Content

In many ways content is the most important aspect to consider when designing or modifying rituals, because it gets to the heart of what rituals are about. The content is important in at least three different parts of rituals: (1) the behaviors that are performed, (2) the symbolism in what is done, and (3) the emotional aspects of the ritual.

Behaviors. Whiting (1988) has identified several ritual techniques or symbolic actions that help us understand the kinds of behavior that can be used in designing rituals. One of the categories he has identified is *letting go.*

> The symbolic actions described within the letting go category are commonly, yet not exclusively, utilized in healing and identity rituals. The letting go actions facilitate a cleansing and healing process. Over the years we have asked people to burn, freeze, bury, flush, or send up in balloons a variety of symbolic items such as photographs, rings, letters, written memories, psychiatric records, and clothes. Such ritual actions have assisted people in moving beyond traumatic events and meanings that have interfered with their living in the present.
>
> Often in healing rituals, especially if there has been a lengthy period of suffering and agonizing, these actions may be used as part of several rituals. Years ago, in working with a couple where the husband had an affair, they were asked to experiment with this painful issue from their past. On different occasions they were to bury, burn, freeze, and flush a variety of symbols that represented this painful past. Symbols included photographs of this couple during the time of the affair, a Christmas card, and angry feelings the wife had written on file cards. After each ritual action, they were to discuss how it felt to do that activity and to rank the effectiveness of each action. This couple decided that flushing was the most appropriate and effective ritualized action. Having some symbols submerged in their septic system provided the couple, especially the wife, with a new sense of pleasure and relief.
>
> In some instances the letting go ritualized activity needs to be combined with some form of holding on action. A college student recorded several traumatic childhood life experiences on separate pieces of paper. She placed them all in a helium-filled balloon and attached the balloon to a string. On prescribed occasions, she experimented with letting the balloon go and pulling it back in again. As she grew more comfortable with the idea of letting go of her past, she found that she was able to

> let out more and more string. Eventually, she was able to let the balloon fly away. This ritualized action combined the need to let go and the need to hold on in a manner that respected her pace and decision-making. (Whiting, 1988, pp. 93–94)

A second category of behaviors Whiting has identified is *giving and receiving.* Many traditional family rituals are marked by the exchanging of food, gifts, verbal expressions, and cards. These same processes can be used in designing and modifying rituals.

For example, when a teenager is ready to begin driving, the parents could give the teen a set of keys to the family automobile to symbolize the new status in an important step toward adulthood. When young adults are ready to leave home to attend college, families can use giving and receiving behaviors in rituals to help them accomplish this transition. The parents could give the student something like a Franklin Planner to symbolize "You're in charge of your life, and you can do it." The young adult who is leaving home could give to his parents an apron to use on family barbeques, and have an extra string sewn on that is broken. This could symbolize many things, such as the recognition that family life will go on even though there is a separation and that the apron strings are being broken.

A third category of behavior in Whiting's model is *documenting.* This is the process of writing something in an "official" way to document something such as an event, a change, or a transition. Sending thank-you cards is a simple example. Getting a marriage license and writing a will are other documenting processes that have enormous symbolism in them and can be used as rituals.

Love letters document commitment, care, concern, and interest. Many families have a ritual of sending notes of appreciation and love. Even something as subtle and minor as knowing that family members will place a long-distance telephone call to let others know they have arrived at a destination is a form of documentation, and when it is ritualized in a family it can have many positive effects.

Documenting rituals can be used to help family members remember pleasant experiences. For example, putting the pictures from a family vacation into a special album and making a place for it among other precious belongings, documents and confirms the positive aspects of the experience. Having a picture blown up so a larger copy can be framed and hung in a special place in the home documents membership, importance, unity, and special events.

During times when a family is having conflict, it can sometimes be helpful to write agreements on paper, have the family members involved sign them, and put them on a bulletin board. This can serve as a reminder and focus attention on the areas of agreement.

Symbolism. The second part of the content is the symbolism, and it is one of the most important parts of rituals. As Turner argued, "the symbol is the smallest unit of ritual" (Turner, 1967, p. 19).

Symbols are tangible or observable things that represent something else. Many different things can be symbols. For example, a symbol can be a tangible object, emblem, token, word, phrase, image, figure, or sign. The symbol derives its meaning from the object, idea, or other part of reality that it represents.

> *Symbols hold a density of meaning* that words alone cannot capture, but that can be held in the right brain. For example, residents of Dixie Valley, Nevada, when forced to leave their homes and land because it was taken over by the military for a target practice site, had a symbolic burial of "things that have been important to their lives in Dixie Valley and are being lost because of what happened" (*Valley Advocate*, September 14, 1987, p. 12). Among the items that they buried were "two articles of the Constitution, water from the artisan wells that kept the valley green, and a hip flask symbolic of the last drink one man (sic) will ever take in Dixie Valley." These items succinctly hold layers of possibility for interpretation that would take many words to explain. (J. Roberts, 1988, pp. 20–21)

Families and individuals differ in the kinds of symbols that can be important to them. Some families find symbols of the past, both of the current generation and of previous generations, are important. Other families studiously avoid symbols of the past. Some families find religious symbols meaningful, and others find them empty and uncomfortable.

One way to try to understand the symbolism in a family is to try to identify the paradigms that guide the family's thinking, images, and beliefs about what is important. Since family paradigms are highly abstract ideas, it is sometimes helpful to look at more concrete expressions of families to get clues about their paradigmatic beliefs. An examination of a family's main goals can provide clues about these abstract ideals and beliefs. Clues can also be acquired by observing the tangible objects families put on their walls, the way they dress, and the way they relate to their community.

Another way to get at what is symbolized in a family is to identify what evokes strong emotion. We find that when the parts of life that bring out strong emotions can be identified, an understanding of the family's symbols is close.

Emotion. There are few ideas that all family scientists can agree on, but there is widespread agreement that the emotional aspects of the family realm are extremely important. As a result, family theorists, family researchers, family therapists, and family life educators all pay great attention to the emotional processes as they try to understand and help families. This makes it doubly ironic that the literature about rituals almost ignores the emotional aspects. Scholars who have studied rituals highlight the cognitive aspects—the symbolism, the meanings, the metaphors, the perceptions. They also pay a great deal of attention to the repetition, the staging, the functions, and the therapeutic and developmental value of rituals.

Therapists and educators who use rituals to help families include the emotional aspects, but when they write books and papers to describe what they are doing and what rituals are, the emotional aspects are hardly ever mentioned. We believe this is an unfortunate omission, and that it is the combination of symbolism and emotionality that makes rituals such a rich part of the family realm.

We suggest that it is important to think about the emotional aspects whenever we help families develop or change rituals. We also suggest that when families want to change or invent rituals on their own, they pay as much attention to the emotional as any of the other aspects of rituals.

How do people feel during rituals? Are they attracted or repulsed? Do they experience feelings such as warmth, closeness, integrity, peace, or fulfillment? Or are the feelings generally negative? Is a graduation experience an inconvenience or a fulfillment? Is a wedding reception viewed as a charade or a celebration? Are family holidays an ordeal or a fulfilling emotional experience?

Most family rituals involve some degree of emotional involvement, and some are extremely intense. One of the issues either overtly or covertly dealt with when designing and changing rituals is the type of emotion that is expected and tolerated. How much intensity is desirable? At funerals, for example, the individuals in the immediate family often exhibit crying, wailing, and other forms of emotional distress. At weddings there are almost always tears as well as smiles.

The analog messages and the relationship messages that are sent with rituals help define what is appropriate emotionally, and occasionally it may be wise to turn these nonverbal communication processes into verbal messages. For example, when a family is designing a healing ritual to cope with a loss, it may be acceptable, even desirable, to verbalize some deeply felt emotions.

The neglect of the emotional aspect of rituals by family scholars means that we still have few ideas about how or when to deal with them. We hope this deficiency will be corrected in the coming years.

In summary, there are three main areas to deal with when we try to design or modify family rituals: the goals, form, and content. The Korner family situation described in Box 13.4 illustrates a creative way these concerns were dealt with in one situation. The goals were relatively clear. The form was helpful, and the symbolism helped the family accomplish a number of Level II changes as they worked through several serious problems.

Box 13.4
The Korner Family

A man, Mr. Korner, called requesting therapy for himself. He stated that he was separated from his wife and children and had just lost his job. He said he felt very depressed and wasn't sure that life was worth living. I asked whether he thought his separation was permanent, and since he was unsure, I asked him to invite his wife to the first session. During this first session, Mrs. Korner said she had tried for many years to get her husband to work on their problems, which included conflicts between them and between Mr. Korner and his 12-year-old son, Billy, but that Mr. Korner had always refused. They were now separated and had been for a year and a half, during which time Mrs. Korner had moved into a new house with Billy and their daughter, Sally, 10. Mrs. Korner had gone back to school and had just been hired for a good job. During this time, Mr. Korner had lost his job and was continuing to have very problematic relations with his son. She said she had tried to get him to go to therapy earlier, when their marriage was collapsing, but that he had refused, and she had gone by herself. Mrs. Korner said she did not want to come to therapy with her husband at this time, but that she might be willing to come in "from time to time."

Work commenced with Mr. Korner, focusing on his generally troubled relationships with his wife, his son, and his fellow workers. He allowed that he had been a very critical person and that he saw himself as very hard to live with, as he always put his wife down, often in front of other people. He said that during recent years his wife just refused to have company, and even family dinners had dwindled. He described himself as an unimaginative and uncreative person. Exploration of his own family of origin revealed that both of his parents drank alcohol to excess and that they were extremely critical of him and had often humiliated him in front of others. During therapy which focused on intergenerational patterns and Mr. Korner's place in those patterns, both as a child and now as an adult, Mr. Korner began to change his behavior, especially towards his wife. He was able to get a new job. He and his wife began to date, and she returned to the therapy, as they decided to reconcile. Here the therapy began to work on "new wedding vows," a ritualized process that allowed the couple to air past differences and set a tone for their future relationship. The couple's first wedding had been marred by the death of the wife's adored father two days after the wedding. Mr. Korner said he had felt he could never measure up to the memory of his wife's father. Their current effort was framed as a "new beginning, a fresh start."

While Mr. and Mrs. Korner were working on their new vows, they appeared for a therapy session looking very upset. They began to describe the children's, especially Billy's, unhappiness with the prospect of father's rejoining the family. Mr. Korner said that when he went to the house, Billy would say, "Who wants you here—go away!" Most recently, both children refused to go on a family outing that the parents had planned. Mr. and Mrs. Korner, who had set a date for Mr. Korner to move back home in three weeks, now felt uncertain. I asked them to bring the children to a session the following night.

Billy and Sally were very articulate and in our conversation they were able to state that, while they loved their father and really liked this "new" man who was coming over all the time, they were also very frightened that the changes would not last. Billy said, "We've become used to living just with our mother. It took a long time. What if we have to go through this again?" At this point, both children appeared more frightened than angry. Billy also described old fights between him and his father, which used to lead to fights between husband and wife, and expressed worry that these would occur again. He also described that in these fights Sally would side with their father, and that only recently were he and Sally able to get along. During the session, Mr. Korner apologized to Billy for all the old hurts, and both parents promised the children that the old way would not return. They described their new wedding vows to the children. They spoke about the sort of parents they planned to be for both children, and as they did so, the children visibly relaxed.

At the end of the session, I requested that Billy and Sally get together without their parents and plan a surprise for their parents on the occasion of their father rejoining the family. I then asked Mr. and Mrs. Korner to get together to plan a surprise for Billy and Sally on the occasion of Mr. Korner rejoining the family. All agreed to my request.

When I next saw the family a month later, Mr. Korner had, indeed, moved home. I asked about the surprises and heard the following:

Billy: We made a wedding cake! We baked four angel food cakes and stacked them up. It took us all day!
Therapist: Were your parents surprised?
Sally: Yeah!!! And we got frosting all over ourselves!
Mr. Korner (laughing): And all over the kitchen!

Mrs. Korner said she couldn't fathom how they had done it, since they told her they hadn't greased the pans between each baking! She also said they had put a piece in the freezer for next year's anniversary, as the date of the father's rejoining the family

(continued)

Box 13.4

(continued)

was now their "new anniversary." Billy, previously labeled "unimaginative, like his father," proudly told me that the cake had been his idea.

I then asked about the parents' surprise for the children. Mr. and Mrs. Korner had rented two adjoining hotel rooms and had taken the children out for a special night. When they arrived at the rooms the children found small gold-colored glasses with each one's name on a glass and the date. The parents split a large bottle of champagne and the children split a tiny bottle of champagne. While both parents had worked on most of the ideas for the surprise, the glasses were Mr. Korner's idea and he had made all of the arrangements, something which he would not have done previously. Before dinner, the parents had planned to exchange new wedding rings. At the last moment, they decided to include the children in this ring ceremony. Mr. Korner gave Sally the ring to hand to her mother, and Mrs. Korner gave Billy the ring to hand to his father, in a ceremony that metaphorically expressed the new relationship options available in the family.

I saw the family again in six months. They were doing well, and were able to articulate many differences from their prior interfactional patterns. Mr. and Mrs. Korner were able to discuss issues between them. Mr. Korner no longer criticized his wife or his son. Father and son were going out and doing things together, which they had never done before. They told me that they used the little gold glasses on special family occasions. At this session, I asked about whether they had always been a family that planned such nice celebrations as they had described to me and where they had learned to do such things. Mrs. Korner said she came from a family that always had lovely family events. Mr. Korner said that on holidays in his family, his parents would drink and fight and be verbally abusive to him. He had decided that, when he had his own family, they would not have family celebrations and would thereby avoid a lot of problems. For 14 years, the family followed Mr. Korner's plan, and remained under-ritualized, with no markers for family events or developmental change. Only when the family reunited with many new assumptions were they able to celebrate themselves with rituals.

The rituals designed by the family in response to my instructions to "make a surprise" functioned to reincorporate the husband and father as a member of the family, effectively mark the healing process between husband and wife and between father and son, highlight the father's new identity as caring, rather than critical, establish a new identity for the family as a family able to have special family events together in which all participated, punctuate the belief negotiation process involved in the new wedding vows, and serve as a celebration of their many personal and interpersonal changes. They chose symbols that defined them as being both like other families, e.g., a wedding cake and wedding rings, and as unique, e.g., special glasses with their names and new anniversary date on them. The symbols and symbolic actions highlighted each individual member (e.g., four cakes, four glasses), dyadic relationships (e.g., the large champagne bottle for the parents and the small one for the children), the shift in available alliances (e.g., the ring ceremony), and the family as a whole. Finally, the entire ritual connected past, present, and future for the family via a process that did not deny the hurts of the past, that marked the new relationships in the present, and that involved symbols to be used by the family in the future. (Case history quoted from Imber-Black et al., 1988, pp. 49–50)

SUMMARY

Family rituals and routines are valuable resources, and when they are wisely used they can help families attain important goals such as unity, closeness, intimacy, meaning, membership changes, and so forth. Seven family goals that rituals and routines can help with are: creating healthy emotional ties, making changes in family membership, healing, forming and redefining the identities of individuals and families, providing rites of passage that help families and individuals make developmental transitions, helping families create a sense of meaning and purpose, and creating an adequate sense of order and predictability.

Rituals and routines can be enabling or disabling in family systems. Therefore, families should be wise in how they create and enact them. Four ideas that can help families be wise are moderate ritualization, distinctiveness (when there are problems a family does not want to pass on to future generations), a balance of stability and change, and avoiding use of rituals in inappropriate ways.

KEY TERMS

Rituals
Routines
Form vs. content
Symbolism
Metaphor
Three stages of rituals: Preparation, Enactment, Return to normal behavior
Rite of passage
Distinctiveness of rituals

STUDY QUESTIONS

1. Explain what is meant by the idea that there is morphostasis and morphogenesis in family rituals.
2. How do rituals differ from routines?
3. List each of the phases of a ritual, using a family ritual you are familiar with to explain each.
4. How are rituals created?
5. How would you go about changing a ritual, or creating a new one?
6. How can a family ritual help us acquire a goal?

Work

14

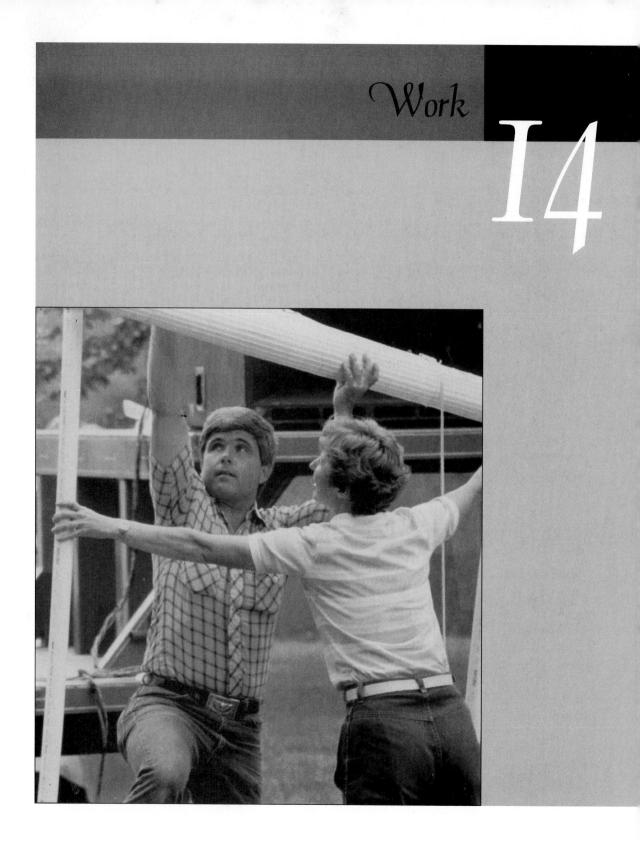

Main Ideas

1 // The change in our society from a family-centered to a market-centered economy has impacted the family realm in many ways, including the separation of work life and family life, the separation of work spheres for men and women, and the application of an economic model to household work.

2 // Living in modern families requires two kinds of work, family work and paid work. Family work includes parenting and personal and household maintenance activities; paid work includes jobs and careers.

3 // The industrialization of our society has created strong pressures to pattern family work after industrial models. In the process, the developmental, integrative, and spiritual dimensions of household work have been eclipsed.

4 // Family scientists apply an ecosystemic orientation to family work, highlighting the many potentials that shared participation in work in the home has for family life.

5 // Employment outside the home, paid work, is also an essential dimension of the family ecosystem. It creates demands on family resources—both personal and interactive—that need to be wisely managed.

I

n this chapter we consider two kinds of work that are necessary for the healthy functioning of the family system: first, the production by family members of goods and services meant for their own direct use, and second, the earning of income needed to purchase goods and services.

Work is an important link in the family ecosystem. Household work connects family members in goal-oriented interaction within the home environment, and employment links the family with other families, organizations, and institutions in the wider society.

Work and family are interdependent systems. The way work is conceived and structured, both within and outside the home, influences the quality of family life. In turn, the structure and quality of family life influence the quality of work life and worker productivity.

> *"[Work is] instrumental human activity, whose aim, at minimum, is the provision of goods and services for supporting human life."*
>
> —Piotrkowski, Rapoport & Rapoport, 1987

Industrialization and the Family

In the following section, we will examine the impact of industrialization on family life. In doing so, we are constrained by the limited historical information available, and the impossibility of recreating a "whole" picture of the past. Only limited historical information is available, particularly on the history of family work. A history of paid work is much easier to come by, for it pertains to the external, public spheres of life.

We will focus our attention on family and work in American history, and because of the nature of the available data, pay more attention to the middle class than to the poor or the wealthy. We begin with a review of the transition from a family to a market economy, and then consider the impact this transition had on the family roles of women, men, and children. We shall pay attention to trends and tendencies, recognizing that the families of bygone times, like those of today, were very diverse and that exceptions to the patterns observed can always be cited.

Transition from Family to Market Economy

Throughout history, families have been the primary human work group. People's associates in productive activity have been their kindred, and work has been the chief activity by which families sustained themselves and ensured their survival. Work has not been something separable from life; it has been the primary activity of life. Other essential processes, like education and recreation, took place, but they were not sharply distinguished from each other or from work. Family life incorporated all of these processes, along with other essential functions.

Not only was work the primary activity of life, but for most families, it was the primary activity of *all* family members. Although most societies have had small elites supported by the productive activity of others, typically these priestly or royal classes have been small. For most families, most of the time, it has been expected that all who were capable of productive work—old and young, male and female—would do their part.

The Industrial Revolution, which began in England in the 1700s, was accompanied by dramatic changes in the dynamics of work and family. Over the next three centuries, life in general, and family life in particular, became compartmentalized. Families had to accommodate their schedules to the structure of business and industry. Work, education, and recreation, which had been indistinguishable in the family context, became clearly delineated, separate activities. And where all family members had once shared the same workplace—the household—now each was designated a separate place: men in the factory or business, women in the home, and children in the playroom or in school.

Industrialism related to a market economy, not a family economy. It sacrificed family values to market values. As it became the dominant productive system, its values came to dominate other systems, including families. Industrialization worked, in that it produced products more efficiently than previous systems, and some analysts argued that its methods would improve the "products" of other social institutions, like schools and families. By the early decades of the present century, the priorities of the rational, market-oriented industrial world were being offered as models for restructuring family life.

Industrial experts in "scientific management" and home economics professionals urged that families adopt efficiency, as applied in industrial settings, as a criterion for assessing the utility of traditional ways of doing work (Gilbreth, 1913; Brown, 1984). If modern equipment was available to do the work, the market-oriented experts advised, the machines should be used so that family members could save their time and energy for "better things." What was once family work—or work that was an integral part of family life—was transformed into "housework," the household equivalent of work done in a business or factory.

Similarly, traditional parenting was said to involve many outmoded practices. The modern parent was supposed to learn from the example of the schools, which had already been rationally organized in line with market priorities. Child care and training in the home were to be "improved" with the aid of external "experts" (Gruenberg, 1940). Family recreation and physical activity were to be similarly "organized," made rational and efficient and performed under the direction of experts who, better than ordinary mothers and fathers, knew what was best.

Physical labor was to be avoided, either by the use of labor-saving devices, or by "human resource development," which made it possible to hire other people (or organizations) to do much of the work associated with family life and childrearing. Whatever families were, they were no longer to be centers of work activity.

This separation of work and family life has become so complete that today it is largely taken for granted. The successful "housewife" learns to hurry through "her" housework so she can have time to "enjoy life" with her family. The "breadwinner," at work in office or factory, trades the shortest possible work week for the highest possible wage in order to maximize time and money available for "living" away from the workplace.

Contrasting Realms of Work and Family

Today work life and family life are commonly viewed not only as separate but as contrasting spheres of life, two realms each with its distinct goals and values.

The study of the interplay of work and family life brings into sharp focus the differences between the family realm and the market realm. The ways we have structured both paid work and housework are often at odds with familial values, the one (markets) being governed by an individualistic and utilitarian economic paradigm and the other by an altruistic and familial paradigm (see Chapter 4). That these paradigms must often—perhaps usually—be at odds is readily apparent when the basic "drives" underlying each are compared. The family paradigm emphasizes personal relationships, continuity, and the maintenance of the group. As for the other, according to one of its most eminent analysts, "the only moving forces which political economy recognizes are the *lust for gain* and the *war between seekers after gain, competition*" (Karl Marx, 1844, as translated in Bottomore, 1956, p. 167).

The workplace, then, is based on exchange, an ethic of maximization of self-interest, and a stress on external rewards for individual effort. One is rewarded for what one can produce or accumulate, not what one is. In contrast, home life is fostered by benevolently motivated grants, an ethic of service to others, and a stress on internal rewards and communal effort. One is evaluated on the basis of who one is (belonging) rather than what one has (possessing).

Impact of Industrialization

Women's Family Roles

In colonial America, the work required for sustaining a household was demanding. Homes were small and families large; meals were mostly the one-pot variety cooked over an open hearth, generally consisting of stewed meat seasoned with herbs and vegetables, and a cornmeal bread.

The work processes of cooking required the labor of men, women, and children. There was a division of labor—men and women were responsible for different tasks—but there was also a "mutual dependence of one sex on the other" (Cowan, 1983, p. 29). Cooking itself was women's work, but much of the prior preparation of tools and foodstuffs was men's work: planting and harvesting the grain (women often grew the herbs and vegetables), grinding the grain into meal or flour, and whittling the wooden spoon used to stir the stew.

The interdependence of men and women did not necessarily foster egalitarian relationships. Families tended to be patriarchal, and "Although the wife might supervise the day-by-day performance of domestic chores, the weight of authority in the household clearly rested with the husband, who was seen as a moral arbiter as well as the ultimate decision-maker in the marriage" (Matthews, 1987, p. 4).

The status of women and "women's work" improved some in the 1800s. Increased population and industrial growth meant that many products formerly made in the home were now available for purchase. Families no longer had to produce their own cloth and soap, or grind their own flour. The open hearth gave way to stove-top cooking, making it possible to prepare meals with more than one dish. The availability of finer flours and ovens meant that the enterprising cook could now make homemade cakes and pastries of high quality. Some kinds of household production came to be considered "domestic art," and skill at these crafts was a mark of status. Necessary activities not designated as craft could sometimes be delegated. The practice of hiring domestic servants to assist with the more mundane household chores helped free the middle-class wife and mother to practice the domestic arts.

There was also more emphasis on the importance of good mothering in rearing and educating children, and a variety of social and public responsibilities came to be associated with home and hearth. Women were expected to take part in community life, to be represented in various political, religious, charitable, and neighborhood activities. By mid-century, a "golden age of domesticity" would arrive, at least for middle-class women.

In colonial times the father had been deemed the morally superior parent. In the nineteenth century, he was superseded by the mother (Demos, 1986). Motherhood took on greater political and religious significance. The literature of the day—magazines, advice books, and novels—glorified domesticity, motherhood, and housewifery. Educational opportunities for women increased, particularly opportunities for training in the domestic arts. Thrift and resourcefulness were extolled.

It was not enough for women to create home as a haven for their families. The sensitivities and insights they brought to the home might improve the wider society as well. Public-spirited mothers worked to repair the schism between the private world of family and the public world of paid work by extending the influence of home values into the public sphere.

> When the cult of domesticity reached its height, middle-class women began to organize for exerting influence in the world as never before and in such a way that public and private values were genuinely intermingled rather than being dichotomized. (Matthews, 1987, p. 35)

The combination of time to cultivate creative arts at home, the increased emotional investment in family, and the opportunity to make a difference in the world outside the home served to elevate the status of housewives to an unprecedented level.

By the late 1800s, the "golden age of domesticity" was in decline. The skilled homemaker no longer was accorded the high status of former decades. In part, the decline reflected a growing public spiritedness among women drawn to causes where they felt they could extend the influence of good homes to public life. And participation in causes like the temperance movement and women's suffrage meant less time available for home and family.

The decline in the status of women and "women's work" was also influenced by industrialization and the ideology that accompanied it. Industrialization cut into domesticity on several fronts. For one thing, the growing availability of factory jobs precipitated a "servant crisis." Young women formerly available as maids and servants could now find better-paid employment in the mills and factories. Husbands, children, maiden aunts—all the hands that had formerly been available to share in the home production processes—were drawn either to employment in factories and businesses or to public education. The care of home and family changed from a cooperative effort to a "one-woman job." Tasks previously bearable, if not pleasant, because of the social and relational benefits of working beside other family members, now became lonely and burdensome.

Industrialization promised to relieve some of the drudgery of housework. There were new, ready-made products from soaps to canned soups, and innovations like electricity, running water, refrigeration, washing machines, vacuum cleaners, and new gas ranges that replaced the old labor-intensive wood or coal stoves. However, all these had a much greater effect upon the jobs previously assigned to maids, husbands and children—fetching water, scrubbing clothes, cutting firewood, beating carpets—than on the work personally performed by the wife and mother. In fact, despite "labor-saving" trends, women's home tasks increased. Potential gains per task-unit were erased by an increase in household

Our perceptions of men's and women's roles have changed considerably in recent decades.

scale: meals became more complicated, there were more clothes per family member and they were to be washed more often, homes became larger, and the distance to "shopping centers" increased (Cowan, 1983).

At the same time, standards for housekeeping and child care increased, spurred by the discovery of the "household germ" and the hard sell in the mass media of corporate America's new household products. A growing, increasingly scientific marketing industry took aim at the American housewife. It was no longer enough to have clean clothes; now they had to be "sparkling clean."

To be sure, the improvements in health and standard of living made possible by these technological innovations were welcome ones. But where "housewives" were concerned they were not without a cost, as illustrated in anthropologist Dorothy Lee's (1964) depiction of the suburban housewife of the 1950s.

> We are living in a time when many women suddenly feel that they are replaceable. The automated stove and washing equipment, the mouth-watering frozen meals, the school activities and after-school groupings, the organized life for the weekend, all these can take over her special functions and she won't be missed, except that her husband may have to hire a driver to take the children to their endless distant appointments. And beyond this, many homemakers, with their good husbands and their dream house, their garden and their four children and their two shiny cars, are sick of their lives which they find empty of meaning.

Yet another change in the status of women's family work was its economic devaluation. Before industrialization, goods and services produced in the household were not only used by the family but might also be exchanged for other goods and services. An enterprising woman might trade surplus eggs for cloth at the dry goods store. With the expansion of the industrial market economy, the production of goods and services that had exchange value moved out of the home into the factory and marketplace. The home continued producing goods and services, of course, but only for the direct consumption of the family. Household production still has *use value*—it is necessary for the well-being of the family—but it no longer has *exchange value.* Whatever economic value one might assign to household labor, it cannot be translated into the cash needed to buy cars or television sets.

In today's society, the value of work is determined by its exchange value, or what it will bring in the marketplace. Since work in the home has only use value, it is outside the market economy. A society that evaluates works of art, athletes, or public works by the dollars they command (or cost) undervalues efforts to which no monetary value is customarily given.

Thus Margaret Benston (1969) contends that the "material basis for the inferior status of women" is in the cultural definition of "work" as commodity production in the marketplace, its value measured in dollars. Under this definition, housework is not "real work," and women who are "just housewives" are not taken seriously.

> In a society in which money determines value, women are a group who work outside the money economy. Their work is not worth money, is therefore valueless, is therefore not even real work. And women themselves, who do this valueless work, can hardly be expected to be worth as much as men, who work for money. In structural terms, the closest thing to the condition of women is the condition of others who are or were also outside of commodity production, i.e., serfs and peasants. (p. 367)

In an effort to increase the visibility and status of housework, some writers have assigned a dollar value to housework by estimating what it would cost to purchase similar products or services in the marketplace. One is surprised to learn, for example, that if housework is converted into purchasable goods and services and a dollar value assigned to it, it may account for somewhere between one-third and one-half of the total national product (GNP); or that time spent doing household work may be worth about twice the minimum wage. However, when we compare what a person might earn doing housework with what that same person can earn at a more prestigious job in the marketplace, housework fares quite poorly.

A more serious problem, from a family science perspective, is that efforts to assign an economic value to housework can make us overlook the most important, and priceless, aspects of family work. To illustrate: Make a list of a mother's main household activities during a typical day. What activities have you included? Preparing meals? Washing dishes? Laundering clothes? Straightening things and cleaning up? Such activities are the most observable and are the ones generally reported by families as primary work activities. They are the things that get counted in estimating the economic value of women's work in the home.

What isn't included? Does anything else happen *at the same time* that dishes are being washed, beds made, and meals prepared? Anything like helping a teen decide how to arrange transportation to a dance? Arbitrating a quarrel? Enacting a therapeutic role with a spouse? Singing to a small child? These, of course, are the most important activities of the household—the relational activities, the "while" activities—but they go uncounted and unnoticed. In fact, we call them "interruptions"; they get in the way of efficient dishwashing and bedmaking!

Focusing on the economic value of housework ignores the fact that housework is unique—different from work in other settings—because it is so closely woven into the fabric of family life. Reducing the value of housework to market terms pays attention to the products of the labor (the washed dish, the vacuumed house, the bathed child) but not the context of caring and personal attention, the individually oriented multilayered service that takes into account the past, present, and future of the individual served as well as the family unit. Focusing on the economic value of the primary activity teaches people to seek the most efficient, economical way to get the task done. It overlooks the fact that in most family interaction the task products are secondary to family process. The more important value of family work is its social value—the meaning associated with doing the work and the interaction experienced while doing the task.

Given the devaluation of "women's work" in families, perhaps it is no surprise that, by the last decades of this century, a majority of married women had joined the employed labor force. Family work, homework, housework, "women's work"—whatever it was—for most of the nation's women fell from primary work to the status of moonlighting, to what one did after work in one's "spare" time. Today women's roles, unlike those of men and children, still define home as a workplace rather than a place to relax. Those tasks traditionally labeled as housework continue to be attached more to female than to male roles.

Men's Family Roles

Industrialization increased women's family responsibilities and, initially, sharply limited their opportunities for participation in market work. It had an opposite influence on men's family roles. Their economic responsibilities increased and their participation in family processes declined.

Historians have paid attention to men's participation in public, and especially political, life, but not to their family involvement. As a result, there is limited historical information on men's family activities. Recently, however, family historians have begun to remedy this deficit, searching old letters and diaries, newspapers, business records, and government documents in an attempt to put together a picture of historical fatherhood (Bell, 1981; Demos, 1986). Using these sources it is possible to identify what people thought a good father should be, and even patterns of actual behavior can sometimes be identified.

Demos's description of early American family life includes a view of male involvement in family life. Mothers were more directly responsible than fathers for the everyday care of children, he says, but the fathers were the family leaders, the models of virtue, strength, and wisdom who were to be emulated. Demos studied admonitions to fathers by ministers and other moral entrepreneurs of the time in an attempt to uncover the primary characteristics of the ideal father. He reports that instructions to fathers "covered a broad range of tasks and responsibilities" while the "mother's part . . . was rarely, and barely, mentioned." Demos (1986) gives examples of the emotional investment of fathers in their children:

> An occasional diarist or correspondent can be glimpsed in postures of extreme parental concern: for example, a prominent New England merchant who sat up and "watched" overnight whenever one of his children became seriously ill. The depositional records of local courts afford scattered impressions of the same phenomenon: thus a village craftsman remembered that "when his child was sick, and like to die, he ran barefoot and barelegged, and with tears" through the night to find assistance. (p. 48)

Whether these represent isolated examples or typical patterns of fathering is difficult to assess at this point. Certainly there were also fathers who were uncaring and abusive, with or without social sanction (see Shorter's [1975] discussion of the apparent lack of feeling among many parents of this period, especially in Europe).

Bell's (1981) analysis of patterns of patriarchy in the preindustrial era are consistent with Demos's, and suggest that one reason for father involvement with children was the fact that fathers, mothers, and children all worked in the same sphere—the household. Sharing space and time facilitates intimate knowing of each other, and heightens opportunities for caring or conflict, as the case may be.

> While preindustrial society was theoretically organized in a patriarchal fashion, in practice there was much sharing of work, of emotional roles, and of childrearing by men and women. Work and family life were not separate spheres, but continually overlapped; and roles, though sometimes formally segregated along sexual lines, were often shared by members of both sexes. (Bell, 1981, p. 310)

The separation of work and home life that accompanied the transition to a market economy had drastic, far-reaching consequences for fathers. In the early days of industrialization men were gone long hours each day, often six days a week. "Now, being a father meant being separated from one's children for a considerable part of every working day" (Demos, 1986, p. 52). Fathers became strangers to the everyday goings-on of the family. In a similar vein, other family members had little knowledge about what the fathers actually did while "at work" or "at the office."

In the cash economy father's family role was redefined. His provisioning became indirect. He was now the provider, the "breadwinner," but no longer a participant in the "breadmaking" at home.

ARLO AND JANIS ® by Jimmy Johnson

ARLO 'N' JANICE by Johnson reprinted by permission of NEA, Inc.

Initially the effects of the changes in father's provider role seemed mostly positive.

> Providing could be seen and felt, on both sides, as an enlargement of paternal nurturance. The father who "brought home" the bacon, no less than the mother who cooked it and put it on the table, was supplying the vital needs of his children. . . . His work seemed mysterious and wonderful. . . . Father's intrinsic connection to all that lay outside home gave him a special status within it. . . . The sacrifices he had made, the risks he had run, the experience he had accumulated, the recognition he had achieved: all this made his opinions especially worthy to be heard (and accepted), his orders to be followed. (Demos, 1986, p. 52)

But the aura attached to this "larger-than-life" father was relatively short-lived. It gave way in the twentieth century to an image of men as ambitious, cool-headed, dispassionate, profit-maximizing individuals who were incompetent when it came to domestic activities. Men were no longer defined as nurturers, and nurturing even came to be seen as unmanly and unnatural.

Not only did the movement of men's work out of the home separate him from most family processes, but it also, perversely, led to a cultural, male-supported notion that his external position was superior. Instead of nurturers, men were managers, delegators, authoritarians who "'knew best,' 'ran the show' and exacted deference from their mates" (DeMott, 1985, p. 9).

Today efforts are being made on various fronts to reintroduce fathers into families, but the transition is not an easy one. As is often the case, ideology changes more easily than practice. Today in middle-class America the cultural expectation is that men will do at least "their share" of the housework and assume more responsibility for parenting than their fathers did. But as LaRossa (1988) points out, there is a gap between the culture and the conduct of fatherhood, between the way we believe things ought to be and the way they are. In fact, regardless of whether a wife works outside the home, she continues to do most of the housework and child care. Men with employed wives do only a little more housework than men whose wives are full-time homemakers.

Children's Family and Work Roles

Another important consequence of the disappearance of the family economy was a changed view of children and their place in families. In preindustrial societies, children lived, worked and learned in family settings. They worked because their families needed their help. And it was expected that, as they worked, they also would learn. Many of the things children learned while working were learned informally. Acquiring certain skills and attitudes was part of growing up, accepted as naturally as physical development.

In preindustrial and early industrial societies, children were viewed as potential economic assets. Not that they were viewed *only* in economic terms, but it was understood that investments made in them were returnable, in theory at least, to the kinship group and the community. In industrial and post-industrial economies, this is no longer true. In terms of economic cost and benefit, children have become consumption items. They represent a very substantial outlay of family resources (more so in countries like the United States, where much of the cost of higher education continues to be borne by individual families, than in countries where it is generally state supported), and families do not expect the economic return to kinship group or local community to be in any way commensurate to the outlay. Kenneth Kenniston (1977) aptly summarizes this modern reality:

> In our time, the family economy has disappeared almost completely. While once almost all American family members worked together at a common enterprise on whose success they collectively depended, today most American adult family members work for pay, while children rarely work at all. . . . The economic "value" of children to families has changed as a result. If weighed in crass economic terms, children were once a boon to the family economy; now they have become an enormous economic liability. (p. 14)

Several factors contributed to the deflation of children's economic value to families. One was the laws prohibiting child labor. With the industrial economy had come factory jobs for women and children, and many families, especially immigrant families without land and therefore without farm responsibilities for their children, found income from their children's work a useful supplement. This practice did not violate the traditional use of child labor in the service of family welfare.

Another element was the trend to compulsory formal education. The definition of childhood that emerged in the social legislation of the late nineteenth and early twentieth centuries dictated that children were to learn, not earn. By 1930, most American children were out of the labor market and in schools (Zelizer, 1985). It was no longer expected that children would make a contribution to the family economy. There were few exceptions: children were permitted to work in unpaid family enterprises, to deliver newspapers, and to work in motion pictures and the theater. Zelizer (1985) observes that "As twentieth-century children became defined by their sentimental, noneconomic value, child work could no longer remain 'real' work; it was only justifiable as a form of education or as a sort of game" (p. 98). In the nineteenth century, "child labor" had served the household economy; in the twentieth, "child work" was designed primarily to benefit the child.

While "work" was increasingly optional for children, "play" was enthroned as an essential part of their education. Like most every other activity in American life, play was rationalized, dissected, and analyzed. This included efforts by experts to redefine play and recreation in "more positive" ways, and a "heightened interest in the potentialities of the social processes involved in play" (Pangburn, 1940, p. 122). Play was supposed to be a "satisfying, skillful, and if possible creative recreational experience . . . important to well-developed personality" (Pangburn, 1940, p. 121).

If play had to be rationalized, so did work. Parents who had grown up in the old order clung to some notions that work was good for children. Here again, rational economic analysis prevailed: If work could be justified, it must enjoyable as well as economically useful, "playlike" as well as productive. Parents were told that work for children must be fun. Only if it promised a sizable component of enjoyment was a work activity appropriate for children. Drudgery was out; the experience had to be "worthwhile." Advertisements aimed at recruiting children as newspaper or magazine carriers reflected this definition, touting the work as "an enjoyable pastime." Attempts to sign up child actors justified the work as "a joyful child's game" (Zelizer, 1985, p. 98). In a similar vein:

> As child work shifted from instrumental to instructional, special consideration was given to domestic chores. When an article appearing in *Home Progress* advised parents, "Let your children work," the work referred to "some little household task," not too difficult of course, "for their tender bodies." (Zelizer, 1985, p. 98)

Studies show that most parents expect their children to do some work, but the total amount of family work they do is very limited. Children typically perform small tasks like fixing their own snacks, making their beds, and caring for pets. One of the most time-consuming "family" tasks done by teenage children is shopping, which includes "recreational" shopping (O'Neill, 1979).

One reason children spend so little time at family work is that, while their parents believe chores are good for children, they are unsure about why doing chores is beneficial, or just what the "good" to be derived really is. Research on this issue includes Wallinga and Sweaney (1985) who report that "involving children in household tasks that are appropriate for their level of development" encourages the development of independence, self-reliance and a healthy self-concept. Children who do housework can also learn to be "more coordinated, . . . to organize people and procedures, and develop a better understanding of interpersonal relations" (pp. 3–4).

Parents who assign children chores also have an opportunity to teach fairness, justice, and responsibility. Children learn that all family members can make a meaningful contribution to "family work," and that the tasks essential to orderly and harmonious living are not the exclusive obligation of one person or gender but rather are work generated *by* the processes of living, to be done in the normal course of daily life.

If family chores are to have positive developmental outcomes, parents must do more than merely assure that a child does the work. If assigned tasks are beyond a child's capabilities, or if parents constantly criticize the child's work, parental efforts to assure performance may generate negative outcomes. At least three variables affect the developmental outcomes of participation in family work. One is its perceived value, whether it is seen as something to be avoided or endured, or as having intrinsic merit, at least as a relational activity. Another is the way the family organizes the work, whether one works alone or with others, whether one has the main responsibility for tasks or merely helps, and whether the main priority is on doing or learning. The final and perhaps most important variable is the quality of interaction attending task performance. Positive developmental outcomes in children are more likely when parents are supportive, encouraging, and affectionate than when they are consistently demeaning, coercive, or punitive (Slaugh, 1982).

Box 14.1

How do we value work?

As far as the status of different kinds of work is concerned, there is an interesting hierarchy in our culture. Work with the lowest status tends to be that work which is most "entropic," i.e., where the tangible evidence of the effort is most easily destroyed. This is work that has to be done over and over again without leaving a lasting impact—cooking meals which are immediately eaten, sweeping factory floors which will soon be dirty again, cutting hedges and lawns which keep growing. In our society, as in all industrial cultures, jobs that involve highly entropic work—housework, services, agriculture—are given the lowest value and receive the lowest pay, although they are essential to our daily existence. These jobs are generally delegated to minority groups and to women. High-status jobs involve work that creates something lasting—skyscrapers, supersonic planes, space rockets . . . and all the other products of high technology. High status is also granted to all administrative work connected with high technology, however dull it may be.

This hierarchy of work is exactly opposite in spiritual traditions. There high-entropy work is highly valued and plays a significant role in the daily ritual of spiritual practice. Buddhist monks consider cooking, gardening or housecleaning part of their meditative activities, and Christian monks and nuns have a long tradition of agriculture, nursing, and other services. It seems that the high spiritual value accorded to entropic work in those traditions comes from a profound ecological awareness. Doing work that has to be done over and over again helps us recognize the natural cycles of growth and decay, of birth and death, and thus become aware of the dynamic order of the universe. "Ordinary" work, as the root meaning of the term indicates, is work that is in harmony with the order we perceive in the natural environment. (Capra, 1983, p. 12)

Recommendations for a Family Science Perspective

Many people see housework as low status work because it, like almost everything else, is defined in the framework of corporate America, as transmitted by the ubiquitous corporate-dominated media. Seen through the blinders of the economic perspective, the love, stewardship, service, and sacrifice components of personal care and nurturance are filtered out. What is left has no more meaning than the repetitive acts of the assembly line worker; it represents production for pay, piecework activity organized for efficiency and evaluated in terms of the income it produces. Only by adding the correction of an alternative orientation, like the family science perspective, are the essential human components of family work—developmental, integrative, and spiritual—brought into clear view.

It is important to remember that these characteristics, the positive outcomes of working together on necessary tasks, have sustained families throughout history. The devaluation of these essential activities in the context of unpaid family service (they are not as devalued if one is paid to do them) is the product of a particular way of seeing. In Box 14.1, Capra (1983) illustrates how work that is devalued by some may be valued highly by others, depending on their way of seeing.

Managing Paid Work and Family Roles

In the following section we consider some of the ways paid work affects family life, using an ecosystems view of family work. Recall that the assumptions of this perspective include the notion that families are open systems engaged in complex transactions with their environments, that the environments include the institutions and structures of work, and that these transactions are multiply reciprocal, in that each system influences, and is influenced by, the others (Piotrkowski et al., 1987, p. 252).

A well-recognized change in the work–family connection of recent years is that increasing numbers of women, particularly mothers of young children, have entered the paid work force. In 1940, one-fourth of U.S. women were in the labor force, and most of these were single, widowed, and divorced. A decade later, a majority of employed women were married, but only one-eighth of married women with young children were employed outside the home. Over the next three decades, married women with young children joined the labor force in record numbers. By 1988, mothers with children under age six had a labor-force participation rate of 57 percent, higher than that for American women generally. (This does *not* mean that 57 percent of mothers work full-time; this figure includes both part- and full-time workers, as well as farm women, women who work for pay at home, and those with seasonal jobs. In the 1980s, about 70 percent of employed women worked full-time.) (Caplow et al., 1990, pp. 123–25)

These figures suggest that the challenges for families created by the separation of work and family life are perhaps greater today than ever before. It is no longer only the husbands and fathers who spend most of their waking hours away from home and family. In ever-increasing numbers, wives and mothers, too, face the need to balance the competing demands of employment and family responsibility.

Competing Demands for Time and Energy

An obvious structural characteristic of paid work is that it takes time away from the family. While family research has looked at the implications of diminished family time for parent–child and husband–wife relations, the studies are inconclusive and can only provide clues as to the impact of work time on family relations.

More is known about the *amount* of time parents spend with children than about the *influence* of time spent in various activities on family development.

> Whatever the effects for child or parental development, . . . the parental allocation of time to children vividly and concretely underscores the nature of family life. Time is a scarce and valued resource; how it is allocated among competing roles is a significant indicator of what a family is about. Childrearing, of course, is a central function of the family; but without a commitment of time to the related activities, parents themselves cannot be the childrearers or at least they cannot invest themselves as fully in that role. Any lesser direct involvement of parents in childcare because of the time demands of a job does not necessarily imply any lesser emotional attachment to children, but it does indicate that the childrearing function has a lesser place in the life activities of parents and hence in the family as an institution. (Nock & Kingston, 1988, p. 62)

Nock and Kingston (1988) analyzed data from a 1981 national sample of 226 married couples to compare the time involvement of parents with children in single- and dual-earner families. They found that full-time homemakers with preschool children spend more than twice as much time in some contact with their preschool children as do employed mothers (525 vs. 251 minutes per day). The differences were less dramatic for time with school-age children, 355 vs. 230 minutes per day for at-home and employed mothers, respectively.

Fathers spend considerably less time in contact with their children than do mothers, regardless of the employment status of the mother. The amount of time fathers spend depends both on the age of the children and whether the family is single- or dual-earner. Fathers in single-earner families spend significantly more time with preschool children than do fathers in dual-earner families (194 vs. 144 minutes per day). However, fathers in single-earner families spend slightly less time with their school-age children than do fathers in dual-earner families (307 vs. 345 minutes per day).

About one-third of workers living in families experience "moderate" or "severe" conflict between work and family life (Pleck, Staines & Lang, 1980). The most common conflicts concern excessive work time, work schedules, and physically or psychologically demanding work that results in fatigue and irritability. In particular, high levels of work/family conflict are associated with frequent overtime, little control over overtime, shift work (especially afternoon shifts), irregular or unpredictable starting times, and little flexibility in work schedule. Working afternoon or evening shifts may mean never being home when most family members are present. Obviously, this limits the opportunity of the out-of-sync family member to interact with and therefore know about other family members. White and Keith (1990) report that shift work reduces marital quality and increases the probability of divorce.

The more hours worked, and the more those hours are out of synchronization with the normal demands of family life, the higher the probability of family conflict. As might be expected, the potential for family conflict is compounded when more than one person in the family is employed and when work schedules differ.

Parents report more work/family conflicts than nonparents, and parents of preschool children report more conflict than parents of school-age children (Pleck et al., 1980). Employed husbands report almost as much conflict as employed wives (37 percent vs. 34 percent), but husbands experience the conflicts differently.

> Men more often reported excessive work time, at least in part because they worked more hours than women. Women more often reported schedule conflicts, presumably because women more often have to see that family responsibilities are met and have to arrange their work schedule accordingly. Women's greater family responsibilities may also be the reason for their more frequent reports that physical and psychological consequences of work caused family problems. Fatigue and irritability brought home from work may make it more difficult for a woman to perform her family tasks, and thus, may cause a problem for her family. These same feelings may not have this effect for the husband because he generally has fewer home tasks to perform. (Pleck et al., 1980)

The challenges of balancing work and family time are compounded in single-parent and two-earner families. Paid work time demands are often greatest when families are young and family needs are greatest. This is particularly true for careers that demand "fast track" action. Parents face difficult decisions over whether to personally care for their infants and young children or to hire it done in order to devote time to careers.

In recent years some innovative companies have tried various forms of flexible scheduling in order to minimize the negative impacts of employment on family life. These include flextime (flexible starting and quitting times), four 12-hour days per week with three days off, a shorter work week than the 40-hour norm (including part-time work and job sharing), work-at-home ("telecommuting"), and providing time off. However, none of these innovations has solved the family–employment conflict. For example, studies show that flextime just isn't flexible enough, particularly for workers with primary child-care responsibilities (Bohen & Viveros-Long, 1981; Christensen & Staines, 1990).

Regardless of the time of day one works, work still takes energy, and a long day's work generates fatigue. This means that family time is often not a parent or partner's "best" time, but only what is "left over." Weick (1971) concluded that family interaction was often stressful and family decision making impaired because much of it occurred when members had low energy levels, such as at the beginning and the end of the day.

Some have argued that the demands work makes on parental time may be mitigated by a conscious effort to see that the time remaining for family activities is used in "high-quality" interaction. Certainly the importance of effort aimed at creating quality time should not be minimized, and activities that build family communication and solidarity should be encouraged. Turning housework into "family work" is one way to do this, although this kind of cooperative effort is not easy to orchestrate.

Unfortunately, the quantity/quality time argument is sometimes used to justify devoting little time to the family. It asks the question "What is the least amount of time I must spend with my family?" From a familial perspective, a wiser question would be "How much parental time is necessary to develop quality family relationships?" If enough "quantity time" is not provided, it may be impossible to create "quality time," for the latter necessarily grows out of the former. An IBM executive who took a six-month paternity leave when his seventh child was born illustrates this principle:

> I couldn't believe the children's energy when they got home from school each afternoon, bursting with the experiences of the day. I came to understand I must have missed 95 percent of their school lives by not being there when they got home. (Hill, 1991)

Foa's model of interpersonal and economic resource exchange (Chapter 12) helps us see why time is needed for developing interpersonal relationships in families. Economic resources, like money, can be exchanged quickly, and require no interpersonal contact. Interpersonal resources, like love, feelings of belonging, and trust, on the other hand, cannot be developed or exchanged in isolation. Their exchange (development) requires both interpersonal contact and time. Rewards come slowly, and usually require a long-term commitment to the relationship. There probably is no simple formula for computing how much time is required to develop and maintain loving family relationships, but we do know that it requires both quality and quantity time.

This point has been emphasized by Etzioni (1983):

> As part of the ideology that tries to legitimate absent parenting it has been argued that "quality" counts; that if you cannot spend much time with your child, you make up for it by making the minutes you do provide "count."
>
> Pop psychologists who promote this notion do not cite any data to show that one can make minutes into quality time on order. Indeed, it is more plausible that quality time occurs when you have longer stretches of "quantity" time, at moments that are neither predictable nor controllable. Most important, there is no evidence that quality time can make up for long stretches of no time, of parental absence. (p. 21)

ARLO & JANIS® by Jimmy Johnson

ARLO 'N' JANICE by Johnson reprinted by permission of NEA, Inc.

Most of us can identify with this idea in a personal way. Examples are abundant in popular songs and stories. Think of the parent you feel closest to, or people you trust the most. Did they only spend "quality" time, or did they spend a great deal of time of all kinds, good and bad, boring and exciting, high and low quality? The cost of work time is particularly observable where a parent must be gone for extended periods. If quality episodes are a function of duration and availability, then the child with a frequently absent parent is disadvantaged.

Grants, Exchanges, and Paid Work

Bivens (1976) suggests that the separation of work and home, and the resulting decrease in time parents and children spend together, has contributed to "misfiring" in the giving and receiving of interpersonal "grants." The less time parents and children spend with each other, the less well known they are to each other, and, therefore, the greater the chance that the grants they do give each other will not be what the recipient needs.

> Lessened communication between parents and children makes it difficult to identify the areas in which grants may be needed; because of such difficulties in cross-generation communications, the possibility of grants being made in either direction (children—parents) that really best meet the needs of the recipients is reduced.
>
> Young people seem not to know their parents at the point of perceiving what is terribly important to the parents—that is, what matters enough to have salient effects on their behavior. This may be due, in part at least, to the separation of the home and work, which deprives young people of the opportunity to know their parents by observing them in their work and seeing what it is that is important to them in that major life activity. (Bivens, 1976, p. 74)

Several researchers have reported that there is a tendency for employed parents to give their children monetized grants rather than personal grants. This has been the case for some time with the fathers and grandfathers, so much so that in the popular lore, children go to their mother when they need to talk, and to their father when they need money. Similarly, grandpa gives his grandkids a dollar but grandma bakes them cookies. When mothers have full-time employment, there is a greater likelihood that children will be cared for by a paid caretaker, that more prepared foods will be used and more meals eaten out, and that purchased goods and services will replace home-produced equivalents. In this regard, Bivens (1976) asks:

> What is likely to result in the monetizing of certain types of grants? For example, if more meals are eaten out—partly necessitated by, as well as made possible by, the mother working—what positive or negative effects on the integrative structure of the family are likely to result? (p. 75)

Children may enjoy at least an occasional meal at a fast food chain more than they enjoy one prepared and served at home. It is also possible, however, that less personal service between family members may result in lower interpersonal commitment and less understanding of each other.

Parents who recognize the potential pitfalls created by the time demands of paid work can learn to compensate. One mother of teenage sons who began full-time employment after years as a homemaker was frustrated by the demands of doing two jobs—paid work combined with no significant reduction in the expectations for performance of family work. She marshalled the support of her husband and sons: "I can't do all this alone. What will you do to help ease my load?" Her husband and sons agreed to take over the entire meal-preparation effort: They planned, shopped, cooked, served and cleaned up after all family meals. The result of their cooperative effort was increased closeness among the father and sons, and also an increased closeness to their mother that grew from a knowledge they had served her in a personal way.

Location of Paid Work

This characteristic of paid work highlights one of the differences between preindustrial and industrial occupations. Men, women, and children in preindustrial societies worked, but for the most part they worked in close proximity to each other, often in their own household. Industrialization first pulled men's work out of the family, and then, for a majority of U.S. families, women's work also. Most paid jobs are located out of the home, and many, such as trucking, business-related travel, and military duty, involve long separations. Thus paid work not only competes with family members for time and attention, but it also physically separates workers from their families.

Even people who do their paid work at home experience conflicts between the time demands of work and the needs of family life. Consider a mother teaching a piano lesson in her home. The piano lesson is taught after school—at the same time her 4-year-old son returns from nursery school. The mother is torn between giving her child the attention he wants and giving her pupil the lesson she is paying for. The 4-year-old makes several attempts to get his mother's attention; each time she replies "I'm busy." Both mother and child become increasingly frustrated. Whether the home-based occupation is piano teaching, telecommuting, tax consulting, or typing, paid work competes with family for time and attention and influences the way family life is structured.

Competing Demands for Commitment and Loyalty

In addition to the worker's time and energy, paid work requires some degree of commitment from the worker and may also involve commitment of the worker's family. Suppose your mother is an executive for a large company, and the company asks her to move to a new city to help open a new branch. The company assumes that the family of this executive (you, your brother, and your Dad) will change whatever other commitments they may have in order to support mother's occupational commitment. Or perhaps your father is expected to entertain clients at home. Your mother, and you, may be expected to get the house and a meal ready for the occasion. In other words, the occupation dictates not only the life of the employee, but also to some degree that of the employee's family. Jobs and careers vary in the amount of commitment they require. Kanter (1977) labels this occupational characteristic *absorption.*

> By *absorptive,* I mean occupational pursuits that not only demand the maximum commitment of the worker and define the context of family life; but also implicate other family members and command their direct participation in the work system in either its formal or informal aspects. (p. 26)

Some highly absorptive occupations have clear job-related tasks for wives: upper-status executives, foreign service officers, high-status politicians, clergy, and military officers are examples. Kanter (p. 29) notes that rarely is there a counterpart role for the husband if it is the wife who is the executive or minister. Occupations like farming and small family businesses also can be highly absorptive of all family members. Wage work like waitressing, mining, and low-skill factory work are among the least absorptive of occupations.

A study of military families illustrates the challenges involved in balancing the demands for commitment and loyalty between family and career. Both the military and the family are "greedy institutions" that seek to dominate their members' time (Coser, 1974; Segal, 1988).

Rewards and Resources

Employment produces income, prestige, and other benefits that have a pervasive influence on family life. A family's economic power, usually linked to employment, may influence the general level of tension or integration and the relative power of family members. Family income impacts marital satisfaction, and the individual access of a husband or wife to financial resources directly affects their options in family conflicts. There is a well-documented positive correlation between family income and family opportunity. Parents may justify giving priority to employment on the grounds that the income it provides improves the overall quality of family life. In absolute economic terms, that may be true. In terms of other paradigms, it often is not. The application of criteria other than economic may change the overall equation such that the net consequence of a decision to increase family income, perhaps by increasing hours at work, changing jobs, or a second family member taking outside employment, results in a reduction in the family's quality of life.

Occupational Cultures and Worldview

There is a relationship between types of occupations and childrearing styles. *The Sound of Music* illustrated this in an exaggerated way. Von Trapp, the military father, tried to govern his family as if the children were military recruits under his command. There is some evidence that parents parrot the administrative style of their jobs in their parenting. For example, people who work in highly regulated settings may discourage innovation and encourage obedience over creativity in their children (Kanter, 1977).

There are other ways the structure of work influences family life. There is the obvious influence of bureaucratic procedures in family governance, such as the formal scheduling of parent–child communication at set-aside times—"interviews" patterned after the ways of the workplace rather than an intimate knowing of each other that historically has been the essence of "family." Or family recreation may be patterned after occupational recreation, as something separate from the "work" of the family rather than integrated with it.

Emotional Climate

A famous magazine cover by Norman Rockwell showed a boss yelling at his employee, who goes home and yells at his wife, who yells at the child, who kicks the dog, who barks at the cat, who pounces on a mouse. Emotions and frustration from work spill over into families, and the reverse is also true: Family difficulties influence work performance. A person who feels good about the contribution she makes at work and gets along well with co-workers will have more energy for family interaction than the worker who has spent her emotional reserves coping with crises at work. People who work in stressful contexts tend to reflect that stress in their home lives.

Gender Differences in Experienced Conflicts

Characteristics associated with high achievement in the paid work sphere are not the same as those needed for good parenting. The more parents are committed to achievement in both realms, the more challenge and conflict they are apt to experience in trying to balance work and family demands. Carrilio and Eisenberg (1987) report that:

> Both men and women are attempting to balance tasks which are polar opposites: work requires competition, striving, rules, authority, hierarchical power relations and extremes of autonomy, while home life focuses upon the needs of others, mutuality, cooperation and embeddedness.
>
> Men and women are faced with the difficult task of somehow maintaining a sense of identity while permitting themselves to nurture and merge both with a spouse and with children. The demands of work pull them away from embeddedness while the demands of family pull them into it. Overbalancing on either extreme can be problematic both for the individual and for his/her intimate relationships. In particular, themes of envy and exploitation can interfere with the maintenance of mutually satisfying interpersonal relations. (p. 3)

Men and women may experience these conflicts differently, for men are socialized for participation in the paid work sphere and women are socialized for family life.

SUMMARY

The combination of outside employment and family responsibility creates many challenges to parents. Families that develop cooperative interaction patterns may find ways of coping that strengthen family ties. Others will struggle in competitive, divisive interaction.

It should be emphasized that the idea of the "traditional" family—the notion that man's place is on the outside breadwinning and woman's place is in the home caring for children—is largely a creation of industrialization. In other words, it is a *recent* idea, and not in fact very traditional. Historically, most families—men, women and children—worked together in family enterprises. While family members often had different role assignments, their tasks belonged to the same overall enterprise rather than to distinct and separate institutions.

A heightened awareness of the ways that the economic order impacts and challenges families should make it possible for people in families to devise ways to strengthen their families and assure that, despite outside employment of one or both parents, the irreplaceable benefits of family processes are not denied them.

Some suggestions include:

1. Be a transitional character. Changing intergenerational patterns in a positive way will make a difference in your family's future. If your father cooked meals and cleaned the bathroom, chances are you will do the same. If he did not, you can decide to change the pattern. For many, becoming an involved family member requires making a break from the patterns in which they were reared.
2. Cooperation. Both women and men must adopt cooperative as compared to competitive interaction styles. Analyze your contributions to the work that is done in your household. If the arrangement this accounting reveals is not fair, design a more equitable arrangement and try to make it work.
3. Adaptability. For both men and women, cultivate a willingness to continue learning, and to learn from each other.

KEY TERMS

Industrialization
Paid work
Housework
Family work
Family roles
Use value
Exchange value
Timing of work
Quality time
Quantity time

STUDY QUESTIONS

1. How did the relationship between work and the rest of life change for families as societies changed from preindustrial to industrial modes of production?
2. How do market values affect the ways people structure work in families?
3. How did industrialization change the kind and amount of work done by men and women in families? How permanent was the change?
4. What influence did industrialization have on the status of housework and on the status of women? Why was women's status affected in this way?
5. How have efforts to measure the economic value of housework contributed to the devaluing of its social value?
6. Were fathers in Colonial America more or less involved in the lives of their children than fathers today? Why?
7. What social processes contributed to the transition from children as economic assets to economic liabilities? How did industrialization influence children's participation in family work?
8. Under what conditions is children's participation in family work likely to have positive developmental

outcomes? When are negative outcomes likely to occur?

9. How do the time demands and timing of paid work influence familiy life? What can family members do to minimize the stresses created by the competing demands of work and family life?
10. How can Foa's model of economic and interpersonal resource exchange be applied in considering competing time demands of work and family?
11. Why do family members need both quantity and quality time with each other? What can they do to maximize the probability of at least some quality time?
12. How can the principles of reciprocal altruism be applied to ease the potential stresses created by conflicting demands of paid work and family life, both in single-earner and dual-earner families?
13. Considering the ways paid work influences family life, what can families do to minimize the stresses and increase the potential benefits of participation in both spheres of life?
14. Which is more important to familiy viability, paid work or family work? What is wrong with framing the question in this way? How might it better be stated to reflect the relationship between these activities?

15 Stress

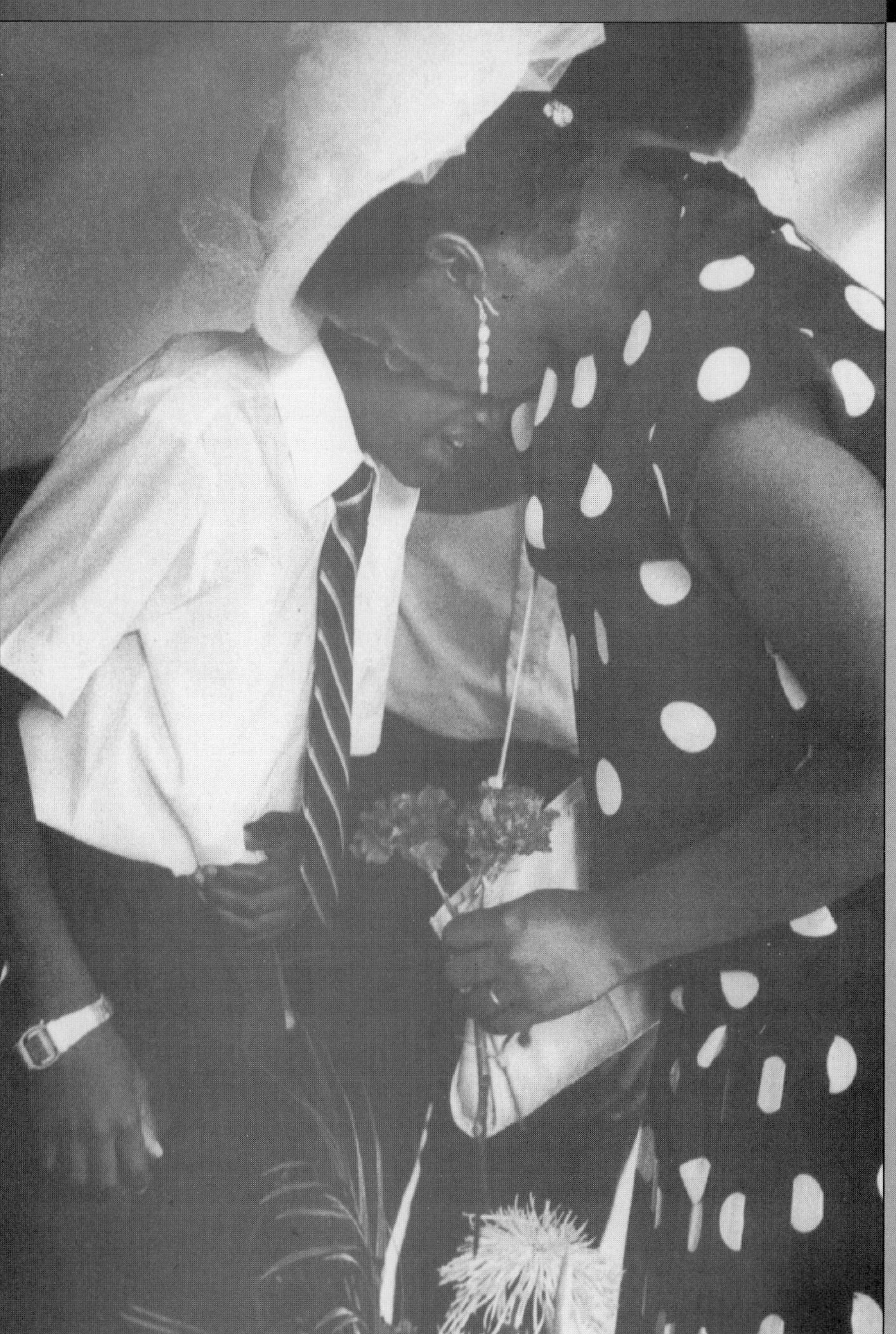

Main Ideas

1 // Stressor events cause varying degrees of disruption in family processes, and demand that the family find ways to cope effectively with new sets of inputs.

2 // Stressor events can come from within, or from outside, the family realm, and they often come while family members are still trying to cope with earlier such events.

3 // There are developmental processes and predictable patterns in the way family stress is managed, and recently research has identified at least five different ways in which families respond to stress.

4 // Researchers in family science have identified a number of Level I coping strategies that seem to be helpful—and several that seem to be harmful—in a wide variety of stressful situations.

5 // Recent research has begun to identify some coping strategies that deal with Level II and Level III changes in family systems.

6 // Family scientists are beginning to identify a few coping strategies that are helpful with certain types of stressor events—such as death or economic loss—but not helpful with others.

Imagine a couple in their mid-thirties. They are experiencing the long-awaited birth of their first child. The baby is born, and there seem to be no complications. It is a wonderful moment for both of them. As the husband is looking through the window at his child, he is approached by the doctor.

The doctor explains that there is something wrong and would like to speak to him in his office. The new father's heart is pounding as they sit down to talk. The doctor explains that the child is retarded. The father is somewhat panicky and defensive. He wants to know how the doctor can tell, since the child is just hours old. The doctor explains that the classical signs of Down's Syndrome are there: the slanted eyes, the simian crease in the palm, the floppy muscle tone. There can be no doubt.

The doctor goes on to suggest that raising a Down's child can be a very difficult task, even for the parents with the best of resources. He suggests that they

> ***"Success in family life comes not from avoiding stressful events and problems, but from coping with them effectively."***

begin thinking about institutionalizing the child, immediately, before becoming attached to the child.

The father is resistive and assures the doctor that this child has been in their dreams and thoughts for years. The doctor counters with logic, explaining that the child will be a burden on the family and that it would be better to just start over. He wants them to make a clean break and not emotionally invest.

Now the father and mother have a difficult choice to make. How do they wish to approach this unexpected event for which they have had little training and preparation? How would you respond?

Challenges such as this create *stress* in individuals and also in family systems.

Our thanks to Robert Burr, who contributed so much to this chapter.

In some situations, such as dealing with a mentally retarded infant, the stress can be severe, disabling, and enormously difficult. In other situations, the stress is more temporary, fleeting, and easy to cope with. Sometimes, such as in the above example, the behavior of professionals increases the family stress.

Most families find themselves coping with stressful situations many times and many different ways, and it is not uncommon for a number of them to occur at the same time. This chapter describes the various types of stressor events that families experience, and it describes the effects they have on family systems. It also summarizes what is known about enabling and disabling strategies that families tend to use.

Types of Stressor Events

A **stressor event** is something that happens to a family that cannot be managed effectively with the family's normal ways of doing things. In ecosystems terminology, they are inputs that come from the environment or from inside the family that cannot be managed comfortably with the normal transformation processes. They cannot be managed comfortably because the family system does not have the requisite variety of rules to deal with the new inputs.

Some stressor events cause more disruption in family processes than others. Holmes and Rahe (1967) developed a method of ranking the relative magnitude of various stressor events, and their ranking is shown in Table 15.1. The method they used was to ask 394 people to rate the seriousness of various changes people encounter. They gave marriage an arbitrary value, and asked them to compare other changes with this number. Their instructions said:

> As you complete each of the remaining events think to yourself, "is this event indicative of more or less readjustment than marriage?" "Would the readjustment take longer or shorter to accomplish?" If you decide the readjustment is more intense and protracted, then choose a *proportionately larger* number. . . . If you decide the event represents less and shorter readjustment than marriage then indicate how much less by placing a *proportionately smaller* number in the opposite blank. (If an event requires intense readjustment over a short time span, it may approximate in value an event requiring a less intense readjustment over a long period of time.) If the event is equal in social readjustment to marriage, record the number 50 opposite the event. (Holmes and Rahe, 1967, p. 213)

One of the interesting aspects of the Holmes and Rahe study is that 11 of the top 14 stressor events they studied occur in the family realm. This suggests that the

---

"In our view family stress is often greatest at transition points from one stage to another of the family developmental process, and symptoms are most likely to appear when there is an interruption or dislocation in the unfolding family life cycle."

—Carter & McGoldrick, 1989, pp. 4–5

TABLE 15.1 ***Social readjustment rating scale***

Rank	*Life event*	*Mean value*
1	Death of spouse	100
2	Divorce	73
3	Marital separation	65
4	Jail term	63
5	Death of close family member	63
6	Personal injury or illness	53
7	Marriage	50
8	Fired at work	47
9	Marital reconciliation	45
10	Retirement	45
11	Change in health of family member	44
12	Pregnancy	40
13	Sex difficulties	39
14	Gain of new family member	39
15	Business readjustment	39
16	Change in financial state	38
17	Death of close friend	37
18	Change to different line of work	36
19	Change in number of arguments with spouse	35
20	Mortgage over $10,000	31
21	Foreclosure of mortgage or loan	30
22	Change in responsibilities at work	29
23	Son or daughter leaving home	29
24	Trouble with in-laws	29
25	Outstanding personal achievement	28
26	Wife begin or stop work	26
27	Begin or end school	26
28	Change in living conditions	25
29	Revision of personal habits	24
30	Trouble with boss	23
31	Change in work hours or conditions	20
32	Change in residence	20
33	Change in schools	20
34	Change in recreation	19
35	Change in church activities	19
36	Change in social activities	18
37	Mortgage or loan less than $10,000	17
38	Change in sleeping habits	16
39	Change in number of family get-togethers	15
40	Change in eating habits	15
41	Vacation	13
42	Christmas	12
43	Minor violations of the law	11

Source: Holmes and Rahe, 1967.

familial part of life is the place where a large number of the more challenging and important life processes occur.

The Holmes and Rahe table demonstrates there are a large number of stressor events families encounter, and they occur in many different parts of life. There are many more stressor events in life that are not included in the Holmes and Rahe list, and it is helpful to be aware of this. For example, the following stressor events aren't in the Holmes and Rahe list.

Stressor events originating outside the family realm

War separation or reunion
Social discrimination
Economic depression
Natural disasters (floods, tornadoes, hurricanes)
Home being robbed or ransacked
Banks going bankrupt and losing savings
Family member in an airplane crash
Political revolution
Member of family being sued or arrested

Stressor events originating inside the family realm

Alcoholism of a family member
Senility of a family member
Family member becoming mentally ill
Serious illnesses (cancer, heart attack, stroke)
Rape of a member of the family
Family member in trouble with the law
Increased tasks and time commitments
Automobile accidents
Child running away
Family member contracting AIDS
Problems with schools
Desertion or return of a deserter
Unwanted pregnancy
Inability to bear children
Adolescent in family prematurely pregnant
Family member committing suicide
An affair or emotional triangle
Strained family relationships
Infidelity
Nonsupport
Physical abuse of a family member
Family member being sexually abused
Prolonged or serious depression
Child being born illegitimately
Relative coming to live with family
House burning
Mid-life crisis

When stressor events come one at a time, it is relatively easy for families to cope with them. However, it is common for several stressor events to happen at the same time, and for new ones to occur while the family is still dealing with previous stressor events. When this happens, it increases the difficulty families have in coping effectively with the new inputs. McCubbin and Patterson (1982) used the term *stress pile-up* to refer to the stress that families experience from several changes occurring simultaneously, or several occurring in a short period of time.

Systemic Process and Developmental Patterns

Systems theory has a number of concepts that help us understand how families are different when they are experiencing stress. To understand what happens when stressor events occur, it is helpful to review what happens in a system when families are not in stressful situations.

When things are "normal," a family system is in a process of transforming inputs into outputs with relative ease. It transforms inputs such as energy, time, space, and behavior into love, attention, discipline, growth, development, satisfaction, bonds, heritage, closeness, learning, and security. To carry out these transformation processes, each family develops a large number of rules of transformation that govern the hourly, daily, and weekly routines and cycles of life. Some of the rules are explicit, but most of them are implicit understandings about how to do things. Each family is continually monitoring the negative and positive feedback to see if the outputs are within the agreed-upon standards or limits in attaining the family goals.

Development and other changes are always creating morphogenesis in a family, but during "normal" periods the morphogenetic tendencies are moderated by morphostatic tendencies. The result is a dynamic balancing of change and order, innovation and constancy, and creativity and predictability. There also is a continual balancing and rebalancing of the needs people have for togetherness and separateness, and the system is always responding to generational, emotional, affective, economic, social, and ecological factors outside and inside the family. The family system is an evolving and dynamic flow of energy, resources, activity, tension, agreements, diversity, consensus, love, anger, new information, and old and new traditions. And, there is a changing composition of age, gender, and involvement. As families evolve through time they develop what systems theorists call a requisite variety of rules of transformation. This means they develop enough rules about how things should be done that they are able to transform the inputs into outputs that meet minimal standards in attaining goals.

Stress occurs when the feedback indicates that some new inputs in a family system might not have acceptable outputs. For example, if a new infant is born and the family has the requisite variety of rules to cope with this new input, there is no stress. If the new infant is born with a serious handicap, such as being mentally retarded, the retardation threatens the ability to create desirable outputs—such as to have healthy, normal children—and that creates stress.

All inputs cause some kind of change in a family system, but inputs that the family does not know how to handle with its available rules of transformation create changes that are stressful. For example, if a family has not had any experience dealing with the juvenile courts, and the family is sitting in front of the house when a police car drives up, they don't experience much stress. However, if the officer gets out, comes toward the family, and informs them he is there to arrest the 17-year-old daughter, they may not have the requisite variety of rules to know how to deal with the situation, and stress begins. If the officer informs the daughter that because of a ticket she did not pay there is a warrant for her arrest and he needs to handcuff her and have her come with him to the police station, the family is probably dealing with an unusual event that is a stressor for them. The parents may follow the police car to the station, help the child post bail and go home, but the family will never be the same, and they will remain in a stressful condition until they resolve the situation by adding some new understandings to their requisite variety of rules.

There is an analogy that is helpful in understanding family stress. Living in a family is like flying a complicated airplane that has thousands of gauges, red lights, warning lights, and buzzers. When things are normal the plane flies with no warning lights and the attention of the family can be on the scenery. However, when some part of the system is not operating satisfactorily, attention needs to be diverted to that part; if it is serious, it can disrupt the flight, necessitate an emergency landing, and cause a delay that prevents other goals from being attained. These diversions, where the family needs to "fix" the system, involve stress.

When a stressor event occurs in a family, it begins a number of processes that evolve in a developmental way. If the family is able to cope relatively quickly and easily, the transformation processes in the family are only slightly disrupted, and the family is able to resume its day-to-day routines. However, if the stressor event is serious enough that the family is not able to adjust quickly and easily, the stressor event initiates a number of fairly predictable developmental patterns.

Part of the developmental pattern in family stress is that stress has

> two phases: an acute phase in which energy is directed toward minimizing the impact of the stress, and a reorganization phase in which the new reality is faced and accepted. (McCubbin & Dahl, 1985, p. 154)

The **acute stage of family stress** is usually a fairly short period of time, when families are doing such things as defining the problem, "trying to get their feet back on the ground," trying to break the situation into manageable parts, getting their emotions under control, and trying to get information about the problem. During the **reorganization stage** they are creating new rules, changing the ways they relate, gradually coming to terms with their emotions, getting help from others if they need it, trying to be adaptable, and learning how to accept the new realities.

When family scientists first began to study family stress in the 1930s and 1940s,

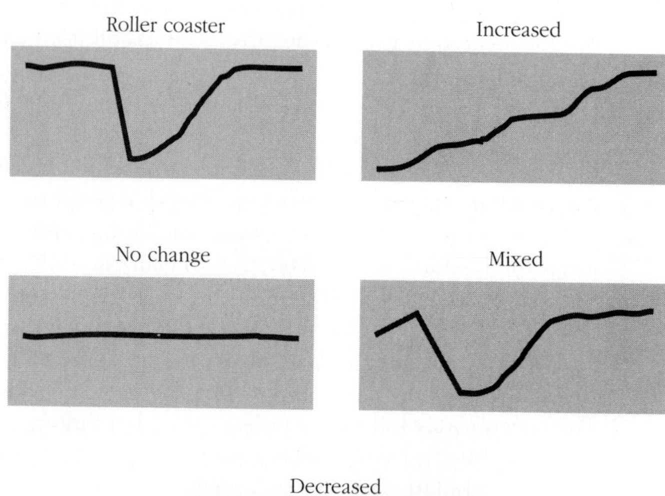

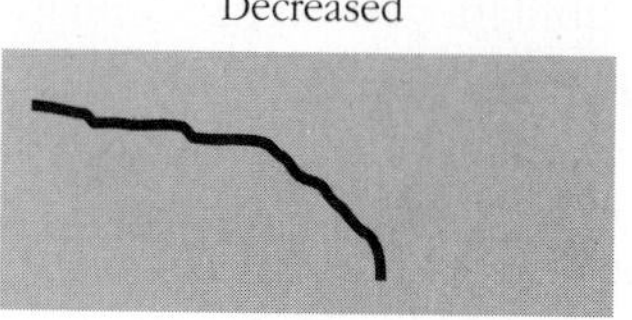

FIGURE 15.1 Five ways families respond to stress

they assumed that all families went through the "roller-coaster" pattern of adjustment that was first described by Koos (1946). Koos's roller-coaster pattern is shown in the upper left corner of Figure 15.1. In this response pattern, the horizontal line at the left shows the "normal" level of organization of a family before a stressor event occurs. After the stressor event occurs, a family moves into a period of disorganization (the acute stage). During this period, some normal transformation processes are disrupted as the family's attention is diverted to dealing with the stress. If the family is able to make adjustments that cope effectively with the stressor event, they move into a period of recovery.

During the reorganization phase, families rearrange their rules and transformation processes so they gradually recover. In some situations they are eventually better off than they were before the stressor event. For example, it may be stressful to move, but if the economic condition of the family improves after the move, the "normal" level of organization the family may have after the stressful period may be higher, as shown with the top line on the right of the diagram. In other situations, a family may never recover fully from a stressor event, and the new "normal" level may be lower than before the crisis. This may occur with problems such as a child running away, conflict that can't be resolved, loss of trust in a relationship, alcoholism and other forms of substance abuse, and economic losses.

There is some recent research that suggests Koos's roller-coaster pattern is an accurate description of the developmental pattern for some but not all families. Harker and Taylor (1993) interviewed families who had experienced six different types of stress, and they found the roller-coaster pattern was the response pattern only about half the time. They found the five different developmental patterns that are shown in Figure 15.1. About 18 percent of their families experienced a pattern they called *increased* effectiveness. In these families their family life became better as a result of the stressful situation, and the families didn't experience a period of disorganization. In 10 percent of the families the response pattern was *no change*; the family life didn't improve or get worse. About 5 percent of the families experienced *decreased* effectiveness, and 11 percent had a *mixed* pattern where they initially were better off and then experienced the roller-coaster pattern. The Harker and Taylor research helps us realize there are several different developmental patterns in the way families respond to stress.

There is a paradox in these insights. We usually don't think about stressful situations being desirable. We assume they bring pain, discomfort, anxiety, frustration, and anguish. Therefore, we usually assume it is better if we can avoid problems. While it is true that life without problems would be simpler and less painful, it is also apparently true that stressful situations can have beneficial aspects. And, ironically, when we look at the total lifespan and its experiences, we realize that some stress and problems are actually desirable.

One reason it may be "desirable" to encounter difficulties is that, in some ways, it is only as we experience pain, frustration, disappointment, and other adversities that we are able to experience the deepest and most satisfying joy, happiness, and sense of accomplishment and fulfillment. For example, the challenge of caring for a handicapped child can bring bonds of closeness, learning about the richness of sacrificing, abilities to be patient and loving, and insights about the subtle beauties of the human spirit that can be deeply rewarding.

Coping Strategies

One of the goals of the scientists who have studied family stress has been to identify the coping strategies families find helpful in dealing with stressful situations. This research began in the 1930s (Angell, 1936), and there are now a large number of studies that have discovered many helpful strategies (McCubbin et al., 1980b; Boss, 1987).

Coping strategies are processes, behaviors, or patterns of behaviors that families go through to adapt to stress (McCubbin & Dahl, 1985). According to Pearlin and Schooler (1982), having a large repertoire of coping strategies is more important than using one or two strategies well. They stated that:

> . . . it is apparent from the foregoing analyses that the kinds of responses and resources people are able to bring to bear in coping with life-strains make a difference to their emotional well-being. And it is equally apparent that there is no single coping mechanism so outstandingly effective that its possession alone would insure our ability to fend off the stressful consequences of strains. The magical wand does not appear in our results, and this suggests that having a particular weapon in one's arsenal is less important than having a variety of weapons. (Pearlin & Schooler, 1982, p. 127)

Level I Strategies

Research has been conducted on a large number of stressor events, and there are several strategies that seem to be helpful in dealing with all of them, in all of the developmental stages of family stress. These strategies all deal with Level I processes in family systems. Martin and Burr (1992) have suggested that the best way to think about these coping strategies is to group them according to the seven different aspects of family systems shown in Table 15.2.

The research that discovered these coping strategies has focused on a wide range of stressor events. It includes research about such stressor events as coping with a severe economic depression (Angell, 1936; Cavan & Ranck, 1938; Komarovsky, 1940), the trauma of fathers being drafted for military service, and the adjustments that are necessary when they return after a long period of time (Hill, 1949), alcoholism (Steinglass et al., 1987), divorce (Goode, 1956), famine, having a retarded child, disasters such as floods and tornados, and mental illness (Vogel & Bell, 1961). This list could go on and on because hundreds of studies have now been published.

Cognitive strategies. These strategies are things families can do intellectually (mentally) to help them cope with stress. Many researchers have found that having an optimistic or positive attitude when faced with problems is an effective coping strategy (Caplan, 1964; McCubbin, 1979). Practical methods of keeping a positive attitude include focusing on the positive aspects of life, visualizing a good outcome, and finding ways to help feel in control of the situation.

Part of the reason this strategy is helpful is because the attitude families have about stressful situations tends to be a self-fulfilling prophecy. W. I. Thomas developed a principle in the early decades of the twentieth century that summarizes this idea (Thomas & Thomas, 1928, p. 572). This idea is sometimes called the **definition of the situation principle**, and it is:

Principle *If people define situations as real, they are real in their consequences.*

Therefore, when the members of a family develop a positive attitude and believe they can cope effectively, they tend to cope effectively. When they believe a situation is too difficult to cope with, it actually becomes more difficult than it would be if they had different beliefs.

One of the reasons this process occurs is because when people have confidence in their ability to cope with a situation they tend to have different striving behaviors than when they believe they are defeated. They invest more energy and try harder. They focus on solutions rather than the overwhelming aspects of the problem, and this makes them more effective in finding and implementing solutions. Also, these attitudes often are contagious, and others often work harder and more effectively when a positive attitude prevails.

TABLE 15.2 ***Level I coping strategies that tend to be helpful in a wide variety of stressful situations***

General areas of coping	*Coping strategies*
1. Cognitive	1. Be accepting of the situation and others. 2. Gain useful knowledge. 3. Change how the situation is viewed or defined (reframe the situation).
2. Communication	4. Improve listening. 5. Have more openness and honesty. 6. Be more sensitive to nonverbal communication.
3. Emotional	7. Express feelings and affection more. 8. Deal with negative feelings. 9. Be more sensitive around emotional processes. 10. Control disabling expression of emotion.
4. Relationships	11. Increase cohesion (togetherness). 12. Increase cooperation. 13. Increase adaptability. 14. Develop increased trust. 15. Develop autonomy, independence, self-sufficiency. 16. Increase tolerance of each other.
5. Spiritual	17. Increase faith or seek help from God. 18. Become more involved in religious activities.
6. Environment	19. Seek help from others. 20. Fulfill expectations in organizations.
7. Individual development	21. Develop hobbies. 22. Increase self-sufficiency. 23. Cultivate individual resourcefulness.

Source: Burr & Klein, 1992.

This principle does not mean that families should be unrealistic in their attitudes, and it doesn't mean that merely having a positive attitude will do everything that needs to be done to cope with stressor events. A positive attitude can simultaneously exist with a good knowledge of the realities of situations, and efforts toward solving problems. The "definition of the situation" tends to have a predictable influence on how seriously stressor events influence families and on how families cope.

Another of the cognitive strategies is getting accurate information. Kaplan and others (1973) found in their research about how families cope with serious illnesses such as leukemia that it helps families if they get *accurate information* as soon as possible. It seems this would be an obvious thing to do, but research about how families actually operate in stressful situations indicates a large number of families do not do this well.

> Of the families studied, 87 percent failed to resolve successfully even the initial task of coping—that is, the tasks associated with confirmation of the diagnosis. Parents' reactions vary but fall into certain recognizable classes. Their most common reaction is to deny the reality of the diagnosis in as many ways as possible. Such parents avoid those who refer to the illness as leukemia. They themselves use euphemisms (for example, virus, anemia, blood disease) in speaking of the child's illness. They may even be fearful that the child will hear the news from someone outside the family. (Kaplan et al., 1973, p. 65)

In addition, the Kaplan research team found that it is helpful if all of the family members who are mature enough to understand are informed about the nature of the problem and the seriousness of it. All of the family's having accurate and prompt information allows them to mourn properly if necessary, to face up to future consequences, to make plans, and to take realistic action (Kaplan et al., 1973).

Without knowledge about details of the stressor event and how it might effect the family, none of these things can be done. Without information at the outset, it is difficult to engage in short-term or long-term coping strategies (such as finding ways to acquire social and emotional support and construct a realistic but positive definition of the situation). In addition, people who do not receive information promptly tend to become anxious and angered when a stressful situation is occurring. Often they concentrate on the worst possible alternatives, invent unrealistic expectations and explanations, and jump to false conclusions. Thus, the lack of information tends usually to make situations worse than they should be.

Another aspect of cognitive strategies is that when stressor events are precipitated by events outside the family, families seem to be able to deal with them more easily and effectively (Angell, 1936; Hill, 1949). This finding has several implications for the acute stage of coping. One implication is to try to externalize blame if possible. Another is to realize that, when it is not possible to attribute the blame outside the family, it is an important issue for the family that needs to be dealt with carefully. If someone in the family is blamed for the stressor event, the blaming itself tends to be another stressor event that can create a number of emotional, interpersonal, and perceptual reactions.

Communication strategies. There are a number of communication-oriented strategies that families seem to find helpful. Just having someone listen and try to understand can be enormously helpful. Trying to be honest and open in communication is helpful in most families. Two other communication strategies that tend to be helpful are to be empathetic and to be sensitive to nonverbal messages (McCubbin & Figley, 1983).

Emotional strategies. Research about family stress documents that stressor events tend to create strong emotional reactions. For example, when disasters strike, people become frantic in their attempts to locate members of their family. When couples discover they are not able to bear children, it usually takes years to adjust to the deeply felt emotional reactions (Snowden & Snowden, 1984).

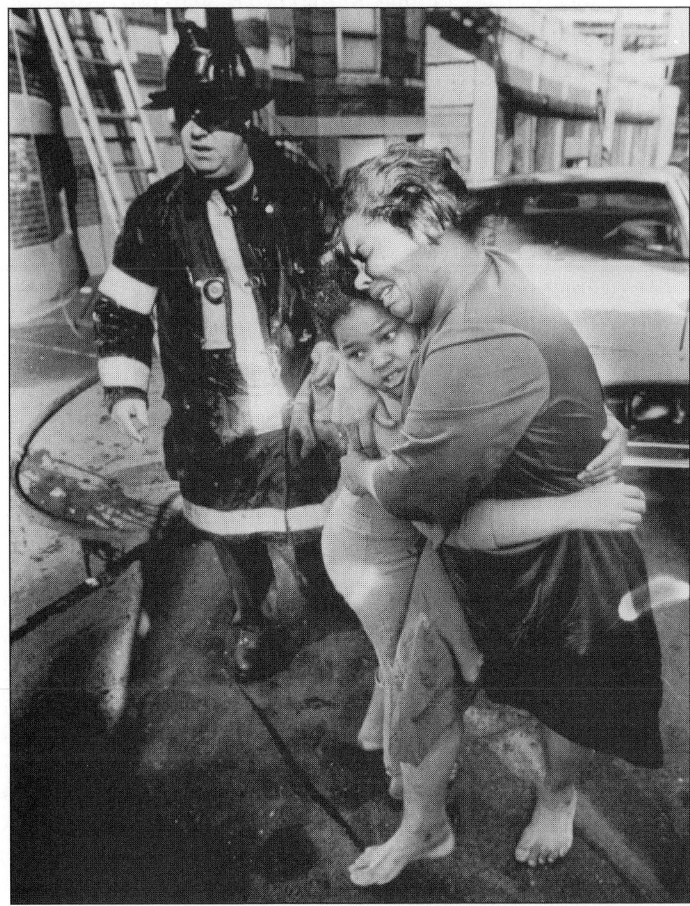

Stress can evoke strong emotional reactions. Some events are so stressful that they change our very definition of who we are.

Another aspect of managing emotions is that, with some stressor events such as chronic illness, families find themselves dealing with painful emotions over and over again. They get their feelings resolved at one stage of the illness, but as the illness moves to a new stage or new experiences occur, the emotional reactions resurface, and people need to deal again and again with feelings such as helplessness, loss, and "Why does this happen?"

According to Caplan (1964) and McCubbin (1979), the management of emotions involves two fairly different processes: (1) being aware of the emotions and fatigue, and (2) finding constructive ways to release or come to terms with the emotions.

The fusion principle that was described in Chapter 5 helps us realize that when emotions become intense they tend to take over. They tend to obscure other things that may be attempted. When emotions get intense, they can incapacitate a family and interfere with the process of coping with the stressful event. Families who are effective at coping with stress gradually learn that when emotions become intense, the attempts to "be sensible" and "reasonable" and "get things done" need to be set aside temporarily while the emotional reactions are dealt with.

To ignore the emotions, to pretend they don't exist, or to tell people they "shouldn't feel that way" doesn't eliminate them. It just forces the emotions into the part of the family "iceberg" that is below the surface, where family members are not aware of what is going on. Usually what happens in these situations is the emotions surface in other ways. Some examples of other ways emotions can surface are: people get angry at minor incidents, they often lose their temper, they develop physical illnesses such as having an upset stomach or always being tired or depressed, they turn to excesses with alcohol or sex, and so on. Therefore, emotions that are involved in a stressful experience need to be dealt with so they do not make coping more difficult. This can be facilitated by using the family as a collective support group, hugging, talking with others, being close, crying, reassuring, listening, getting feelings out, and being around loved ones.

Relationship strategies. The first generalization that was developed in the research about family stress is the idea that being flexible, pliable, or willing to change is helpful. Usually family scientists use the term *adaptability* to describe this. One of the first studies was by Robert Angell (1936), and this idea was the main conclusion his book contributed to the field. Since then, this idea has been found again and again to be an important coping strategy (Caplan, 1964; McCubbin et al., 1988; Boss, 1987).

Adaptability is the ability to be flexible and try something new. Families with this ability tend to be more accepting of change and roll with the punches. Families that are relatively adaptable are willing to try further coping strategies at all levels of change. This willingness to try more coping strategies teaches the family to be more proficient at the use of a wider variety of coping strategies, which increases their requisite variety.

The various parts of family systems tend to be intertwined. Therefore, changes in one part of the system influence other parts of the system. Kaplan and colleagues (1973) recognized this interdependence and suggested that it is helpful if the individuals in families can cope and mourn together when serious stressor events occur. A family can offer its individual members the potential of mutual support and access to its collective coping experience. According to Hill (1958), when helping an individual cope or handle stress, the individual should be treated as a family member—not as an independent individual.

Again the idea emerges that the family realm has more impact than most people realize. Families who can lean on each other emotionally have an advantage when dealing with life's problems. As McCubbin (1979) observed, maintaining family togetherness, even by taking the time to do simple things with the children and plan family outings, is an effective coping strategy for dealing with family stress.

Spiritual strategies. Many families find it helpful to turn to spiritual sources for strength, meaning, and assistance when they are experiencing family stress. These strategies include such things as praying, developing more faith, or becoming more involved in religious activities.

Environmental strategies. Families can call on many things in their environment to help them cope with stress. Support can come from family members, friends, work, clubs, police, churches, and so on. In addition to varying in source, social support also can vary in type. It can be emotional, financial, physical, or mental, for instance.

Many studies indicate that social support makes individuals and families less vulnerable when they experience such stressor events as losing a job or participating in a difficult line of work (Cobb, 1982), or are raising a chronically ill child, recovering from a natural disaster, or adjusting to war-induced separations (McCubbin & Dahl, 1985, p. 156).

Cobb (1976) stated that social support was an exchange of information between the family and environment that provided families with: (1) emotional support, leading the recipients to believe they are cared for and loved, (2) self-esteem, leading them to believe they are valued, and (3) network support, which gives them a sense of belonging.

Bronfenbrenner's (1979) review of the research in this area added an important new insight to the role of supportiveness inside families and to the amount of support families receive from environmental systems. When individuals and families are not coping with stressful events, it is growth producing to have considerable independence and autonomy and to have relatively little overt help, assistance, or support. However, when things are not going well, it then is helpful to have more supportiveness inside the family and in the interaction of the family system with the systems in its immediate environment. Another way of saying Bronfenbrenner's idea is that high supportiveness tends to be enabling when dealing with serious stressor events, but it can actually be disabling when things are going well.

Developmental strategies. There is a little research that suggests it can be useful to focus on some aspects of individual development. Some of these strategies include trying to promote self-sufficiency (without overdoing it), working out to keep physically fit, and being sure to keep up obligations to other organizations (such as employment, for instance).

Disabling strategies. Research has identified a number of ways of responding to stressor events that seem usually to have disabling or destructive effects. One of these is to react with violence. A number of research studies have found people tend to be more violent when experiencing stressful situations such as undesirable behavior by a child, unemployment, unhappiness in their marriage or in their employment, or illnesses (Gelles, 1974; Gil, 1970). The violence, however, tends to make situations worse. It destroys positive emotional feelings toward the violent individuals and creates a number of negative emotions such as mistrust, anger, confusion, shame, and hate.

Other strategies that usually are disabling are denial, avoidance, rejection, increased use of alcohol, hostility, producing garbled and dishonest communication about the problem, preventing communication, prohibiting and interrupting individual and collective grieving within the family, and weakening family relationships precisely when they most need to be strengthened (Kaplan et al., 1973; McCubbin et al., 1980b). These strategies usually aggravate the original problem and create other problems, such as less ability to plan solutions for the original problem (Kaplan et al., 1973).

Strategies at Higher Levels of Abstraction

Chapter 6 described three different levels of abstraction in family systems. Level I refers to the fairly observable and obvious transformation processes that people are aware of in their daily interaction. Level II refers to meta-level processes, or the rules about the rules. Level III refers to the family paradigms, which are the abstract beliefs and assumptions that make up a family's philosophy of life.

These three levels are helpful in understanding how stressor events influence families and how families try to cope with stress, because families seem to do different things when they are focusing on Level I processes than when they are forced to deal with Level II processes or the paradigmatic beliefs and assumptions of Level III.

According to Robert Burr's (1989) theory of family stress, families tend to focus on Level I processes when they start into the recovery stage of family stress. If the Level I changes are enough, families don't bother to disrupt the more complicated and fundamental parts of their family system at Level II. However, if their Level I attempts to cope are not effective, they eventually find it necessary to deal with Level II phenomena such as their meta-rules, their way of governing the family, and the hierarchies of power. If families are then able to deal effectively with their stressful situations at Level II, they rarely go further. However, if their attempts to cope at Level II are ineffective, they eventually find themselves reexamining their basic assumptions and philosophy of life.

Level II coping. When families are able to deal effectively with stressor events by using Level I processes, they return to a "normal" level of functioning. Using the airplane analogy, warning lights go off, buzzers stop buzzing, and gauges return to normal. Attention is again turned to other things. Many times, however, the Level I coping strategies aren't successful, and families find themselves deeper and deeper in crisis. In these situations, merely rearranging rules or changing the superficial or obvious aspects of the family is not enough. The family needs to make more fundamental changes.

Several examples of this process help illustrate what is involved with Level II crises. If a child is misbehaving in a fairly serious way, a family will usually try Level I strategies. They will do such things as grounding the child more, restricting privileges, withholding resources, or changing rules. If this does not solve the problem, the parents may need to reevaluate their whole approach toward discipline, and this is a Level II process. For example, they may need to realize they have been using methods of discipline that are appropriate for a young child, but their child is old enough that they need to use a set of more "adult" methods of relating to the child.

Another example is what happens in some marriages when one spouse wants to change the relationship. For example, a couple may have grown up in fairly traditional families where the males were dominant and females submissive, but one spouse gradually decides she or he does not like that type of relationship. This type of change is usually a stressor event, and merely changing Level I rules may not be enough. For example, letting her have her own checking account, letting her get a job, or letting her take classes at the university may not be enough. The couple may need to rearrange fundamental aspects of their relationship. For example, they may need to change the idea that the husband is supposed to "let" the wife do things, and move to an equalitarian relationship where neither of them is responsible for what the other does. Changes such as these are more complicated, abstract, and fundamental than Level I changes because they deal with the rules about the rules.

Another example of the difference between Level I and Level II coping is the way a family might respond to a child starting to use illegal drugs. A Level I strategy that deals with family boundaries would be to restrict the child's friends. This would change the family boundaries so they are less open. However, the change would just be in one area of the family boundaries, so it would only be a Level I change. However, if this did not work, the family may decide the family boundaries in general are too open, and they may decide to become more closed overall. This would be a Level II change because it would change a more fundamental aspect of the system.

Many families use Level II methods, but most of them probably are not aware of the differences in abstraction involved. It is likely that most families would need to study these concepts in a family science course or get professional help to understand these differences.

Some of the coping strategies involved in Level II change are getting professional help, making implicit rules explicit, reviewing basic methods of coping, discussing the rules about how rules are made and changed in the family, and discussing the methods that are used in decision making.

Pauline Boss (1975) introduced another concept into the field that seems to us to deal with Level II coping strategies. The concept is **boundary ambiguity**, and it occurs when families are uncertain in their perception of who is in or out of the family or who is performing what roles and tasks within the family system. Her initial research was with military families, who cope frequently with the father moving in and out of the family. Military families find this problem especially severe when the father is listed as missing-in-action (MIA). The problem also occurs with families experiencing divorce, joint custody, desertion, and some chronic illnesses.

When families, or professionals working with families, understand this concept, they can use it to help families cope because they can try to get the ambiguity within tolerable limits. Some strategies for helping families deal with their boundary ambiguity are to talk about who is in and out of the family, whether family members will be in or out for an identifiable period of time, and what the boundaries inside the family ought to be. Other strategies are to avoid keeping a physically absent family member psychologically present when it is disruptive for the family. The latest research suggests it may be disruptive for some family members and not others and in some situations and not others (Boss, 1987, p. 712).

Level III coping. When families are able to deal effectively with stressor events by using Level I or Level II processes, they return to a "normal" state. However, in some situations, families are not able to manage the new system inputs with these strategies. When this occurs, the family gradually slips into a more serious crisis situation. When this happens, the very fabric of the family is in trouble, and the paradigmatic assumptions are called into question. The family's basic philosophy and orientations to life are examined, and these basic beliefs may evolve, change, be discarded, or reconstructed. Examples of this include changes in the way a family relates to its environment, changes in beliefs about who the family can count on when the chips are down, changes in beliefs about God and the role of the spiritual part of life, changes in beliefs about whether people are inherently good or bad, and differentiation from kin.

The following example illustrates the differences that are involved in a Level III crisis. If a family that did not approve of drug use found that their teenage son was taking drugs, this would be a stressor event. The first strategies this family would use are likely to be Level I changes. The parents could talk to the son about how dangerous drugs are or express disapproval. If these particular Level I methods do not work, the family might try other Level I changes such as making him come in earlier, grounding him, and taking away his access to money.

There is no limit to the specific Level I changes that families can try. However, if they do not work, the family would eventually resort to more fundamental changes, Level II changes. They may try to change their basic parenting methods, try to get professional assistance to make other changes, change where the child lives, or change the basic structure of the family.

If these Level II methods do not work, the family will tend eventually to question some of their basic beliefs. For example, they may adopt a more fatalistic view of life and conclude that things will happen as they will, and they have less control over their world than they thought they had. They may rearrange their priorities in life and become more or less involved in trying to change their community values and structure. They may reevaluate their beliefs about the appropriateness of drug laws and decide to oppose the legal system or crusade for more stringent laws. They may even decide to join their child in exploring the use of drugs.

Strategies Relevant for Specific Situations

Some stressor events are relatively different from other stressor events, and some of the strategies that are helpful in one context are not helpful in others. Family scientists have only begun to discover what is unique about different types of stressors, but a few ideas have been developed. This section of the chapter reviews some of the strategies for coping with specific types of stressful processes.

Coping with death. Death is a very important part of family systems. As Friedman (1985) has observed:

> Death is the single most important event in family life. From an individual point of view it marks the end; from a family point of view it is often a beginning that initiates processes in the family that can continue for generations. (p. 168)

According to Kübler-Ross (1969), people go through five stages when they encounter the death of someone who is close to them. The stages are: (1) denial and isolation, (2) anger, (3) bargaining, (4) depression, and (5) acceptance. These

---

Box 15.1

Coping with a serious illness

The following example illustrates many of the coping strategies that have been discussed, and the benefit that can come out of stress if it is handled well.

> John D. was the eldest of seven children, an active 12-year-old boy involved in many activities. The family was close, and Mr. D.'s job provided them with a reasonably good financial situation. The parents were understandably shocked when told that John had leukemia. Their initial reactions were typical of those of other parents, but they expressed their shock and grief openly and together. They understood that leukemia is a fatal illness for which there is no cure, respected and trusted the physicians, and made no attempt to seek corroborative or contradictory diagnoses from other physicians. The parents did not try to hide their feelings from each other but found strength and encouragement in grieving together.
>
> From the start, Mr. and Mrs. D. knew they must talk to their son about the diagnosis. They told him he had a serious illness that most children did not survive and encouraged him to trust the physicians, who would do everything within their power to keep him as well as possible for as long as they could. John and his parents were able to cry together over the implications of the illness. Mr. and Mrs. D. also talked with John's 10-year-old sister about the situation, since the two children were especially close.
>
> The parents clearly wanted to be as honest as possible with John. The limited time remaining was doubly precious and was not to be wasted playing games or jeopardizing relationships. The pain of accepting their child's impending death would be even more unbearable if he turned away from them and no longer trusted them. They had never lied to him and were sure their frankness allowed them to trust, respect, and love each other.
>
> At times, the family had to express feelings of sadness by crying and mourning and no one tried to inhibit this. Mr. and Mrs. D. allowed John time to himself, but he was always free to go back to one or both of them with questions that were bothering him. He was a remarkable child whom everyone enjoyed. He was a bright, sensitive boy who wrote a science paper on leukemia for which he received an "A." (Kaplan et al., 1973, p. 64)

---

same stages do not appear when most stressor events occur in families, and it is likely that they occur with death because death creates a wider range of emotional feelings, and the feelings are associated with some of the most fundamental parts of life.

With most stressor events, families benefit by eliminating the stress process as quickly as possible. For example, if someone loses their job, it is usually best if another job is acquired quickly. If families acquire a new member, lose a member, have an accident, or have an illness, the family system is less disrupted if the crisis is resolved quickly.

Death is an exception to this general rule. When a member of a family dies it creates such a wide range of emotional reactions, and the emotions are so deep and fundamental, that it takes a long time to work through them. As Walsh and McGoldrick (1988) observed, "The process of mourning is likely to take at least 1 to 2 years, with each new season, holiday, and anniversary reevoking the loss" (p. 311).

One way family scientists think about this principle is in terms of the "angle of recovery" in the bottom of the roller-coaster diagram. A number of research studies have found that, with most stressor events, the smaller the angle of recovery the better for the family (Hill, 1949; Waller & Hill, 1951). With death, however, a larger angle is more effective because it allows the family time to experience the mourning and bereavement that is necessary.

Another activity that is helpful in coping with death is for family members to choose a time when they can work through unresolved concerns and begin the process of reorganizing the family system. As Friedman (1985) has observed:

> When families can be encouraged to come together openly with the dying member, pernicious emotional processes that otherwise might have survived undeterred for generations can be thrown off track. (p. 170)

Interpersonal and occupational stressors. Foa's model (discussed in Chapter 11) and some other research suggest that the strategies that are helpful in situations where the main concerns are emotional and interpersonal tend to be different from the strategies that are helpful with less personal stressors such as occupational and economic stress. Pearlin and Schooler (1982) found that with relatively impersonal stressor events, such as those stemming from economic or occupational experiences, the most effective forms of coping involved the manipulation of goals and values in a way that increases the emotional distance of the individual from the problem. On the other hand, problems arising from the relatively close interpersonal relations in the family realm are best handled by coping mechanisms in which the individual remains committed to, and engaged with, the relevant others (p. 134). In other words, when dealing with stress in the family, it is better to maintain close relationships and not avoid the individuals, the relationships, or the stress.

Because people can move in and out of the business world relatively easily, it is possible in the public realms to make changes that will distance stressful situations. However, because the family realm is unique, in that there is a certain permanence to family relationships, it is more difficult and even unhealthy to avoid or distance oneself from most problems inside the family realm.

SUMMARY

Many events can create stress in families, and some stressor events are more serious than others. Also, some of them come from the environment, and others come from inside family systems. The process of family stress has developmental stages, and there seem to be five different patterns in the way families respond to stress: a roller-coaster pattern where some families experience disorganization followed by reorganization, a descending pattern where some families become disorganized and stay there, an ascending pattern where some families get better off in a stressful situation and stay there, a no change pattern and a mixed pattern where some families are better off and then have the roller-coaster experience. Research about families has begun to identify coping strategies that families can use to deal effectively with stressful situations, and seven different types of coping strategies were discussed. During the recovery stage of family stress, families use Level I, Level II, and Level III coping strategies.

KEY TERMS

Stress
Family stress
Stressor events
Requisite variety
Stress pile-up
Developmental processes in stress: Acute stage, Reorganization stage
Response patterns to stress: Roller coaster, Increased effectiveness, Decreased effectiveness, No change, Mixed pattern
Coping strategies
Boundary ambiguity

STUDY QUESTIONS

1. Define *stressor event.*
2. List 10 stressor events that have happened to you or someone you know in the past year.
3. What are the characteristics of the acute stage of stress?
4. Choose one of the stressor events in question 2 and tell what coping strategies were used to resolve it.
5. Describe how the use of emotions in stress can be a coping strategy.
6. Give three examples of a disabling strategy.
7. Contrast the difference between Level II coping and Level III coping.

16 Abuse

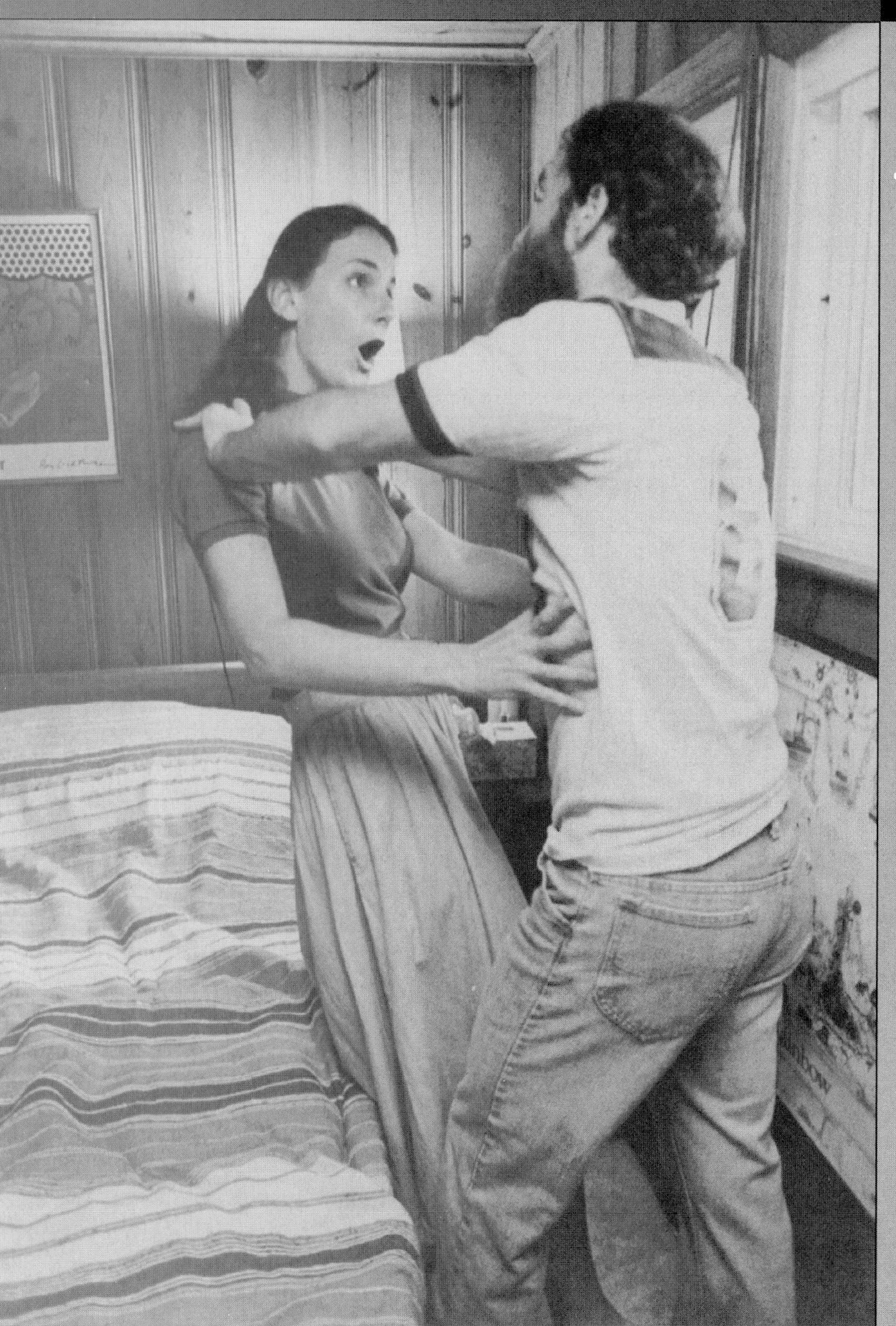

Main Ideas

1 // Abuse—physical, sexual, and substance—is a pervasive and dangerous problem in our society.

2 // The principle of fusion helps us understand the cycle of violence in the family realm, which is often learned through generational transmission. Families can be taught to avoid violent behaviors by learning appropriate levels of differentiation and anger-control techniques.

3 // Research has discovered that the venting of verbal aggression (once encouraged) is an inappropriate outlet for stress.

4 // Coping with the effects of sexual abuse is a long-term process and involves people's deepest emotional levels.

5 // We are just beginning to understand that substance abuse is a symptom of emotional, spiritual, and physical family dysfunction.

6 // Strategies for dealing with abuse include changing levels of fusion, reestablishing the emotionally cut off family, de-triangling children, and creating greater understanding of intergenerational processes.

In the classic novel *Oliver Twist*, one of the central characters, Nancy, is married by common law to Sikes. The violence depicted in their relationship is graphic and severe:

> "Get up . . . Bill," said Nancy in the low voice of alarm, "why do you look like that at me?" Sikes sat regarding her, for a few seconds, with dilated nostrils and heaving breast; and then, grasping her by the head and throat, dragged her into the middle of the room, and looking once towards the door, placed his heavy hand upon her mouth. "Bill, Bill! . . ." gasped Nancy. . . . Sikes freed an arm, and grasped his pistol. The certainty of immediate detection if he fired, flashed across his mind even in the midst of his fury; and he beat it twice with all the force he could summon, upon Nancy's upturned face.
>
> . . . She staggered and fell, nearly blinded with the blood that rained down from a deep gash in her forehead. [As Nancy struggles to free herself, Sikes again], shutting out the sight [of her] with his hand, seized a heavy club and struck her down. (Dickens, 1894, pp. 383–84)

> ***"The group to which most people look for love and gentleness is also the most violent civilian group in our society."***
>
> —Murray Straus, 1980

Interpersonal violence is a common theme in literature. For decades, novels, movies, and short stories have portrayed family violence. Surprisingly, family scientists have only recently discovered this topic. In fact, the systematic study of family violence is barely 15 years old (Gelles, 1980). For years, our society did not see family violence as a problem even though thousands of abusive incidents were reported every year (Bybee, 1979; Gelles, 1980; Gelles & Straus, 1979; Scott, 1977; Star, 1980). It has been suggested that the family is the most violent institution in our culture except, perhaps, for the police force and the military (Gelles & Straus, 1979).

The terms *violence* and *abuse* are used frequently in this chapter. Although certain acts are obviously abusive (breaking a spouse's arm), other acts are less clearly defined as such. For example, some think spanking a child is abusive, while others consider it an effective discipline strategy. Those who have conducted the most research on the general topic of abuse have defined **abuse** "as an act carried out with the intention of, or an act perceived as having the intention of, physically hurting another person" (Gelles & Straus, 1979).

Physical Abuse

The first family researchers to document the extent of marital violence found that about 16 percent of a national probability sample (2143 couples) had engaged in a violent act during the year prior to the 1975 study (Straus et al., 1980). At that time, it was estimated that in the United States about one of every six couples experienced yearly a situation in which one spouse committed a violent act against the other. When the total time a couple had been married or together was considered, the number rose to 28 percent. In other words, by the mid-1970s about one in four American couples had experienced at least one episode of violence during their marriage.

The same researchers more recently surveyed 6002 couples selected as a national probability sample (Straus & Gelles, 1986). In the second follow-up survey, a drop in the frequency of marital violence was found. Straus and Gelles (1986) were unsure why the drop occurred. Yet even when the more conservative estimates of the second study are considered the rates are quite alarming. The family is, often, a dangerous place to be.

There is a variety of types of abuse in families and family-like relationships. Among them are dating violence, physical abuse (including sexual abuse), emotional abuse, substance abuse (alcohol and drug), and abuse of the elderly. While there is an abundance of research literature on each of these types, this chapter focuses on those areas of abuse in which research has been done from a family-process, systemic approach. The overall purpose of this chapter is to show how abuse in families emerges and is maintained as a process of systems.

Also, it is important to note that abuse in families is sometimes reciprocal. In other words, there is abuse from teenager to parent, wife to husband, and husband to wife. In this chapter, however, the focus is on the more prevalent issue of abuse from parent to child and husband to wife.

Dating, and Cohabitation Relationships

The media have recently given considerable attention to violence in dating relationships, including incidence of hitting, rape, and even murder. The popular ideal is that during a dating relationship, partners have a romantic and enjoyable interaction and are on their best behavior. Unfortunately, for many that may not be the case. In a recent study of 5786 dating couples, it was found that about 20 percent had experienced a physical assault during the previous year (Stets & Straus, 1989). In another study, McKinney (1986) found that among college students, 48 percent reported at least one kind of physical violence or threat during a dating situation. Regardless of background, race, religion, or status, "violence in dating situations is a universal problem on campuses" (Kierman & Taylor, 1990). Makepeace (1989) found that violence was most intense on first dates. He discovered that physical injury, emotional trauma, and forced sex were more likely to occur on a first date than with someone whom the person had been seeing more regularly. It was also noted that most of the violence occurred within the context of sexual activity and when alcohol was present.

Additionally, cohabiting couples report more violence than do married couples (Stets & Straus, 1989). The incidence of violence is not only higher among cohabiting couples (about 35 percent reported physical assault during the year before the study) but the severity is also greater. Again, the precipitating disagreement is likely to concern sex and jealousy (Makepeace, 1989). Other possible contributing factors are high levels of alcohol use and a tendency to be more insecure (those living together might have more difficulty with relationship commitment) (Lane & Gwarney-Gibbs, 1985).

Children

The abuse of children has a slightly longer history as an issue for scientific concern, but not much longer. About 25 years ago, researchers (Kempe et al., 1962) suggested that violence against children was a significant and important topic. Since that time there have been many attempts to determine just how severe a problem child abuse really is. Child abuse may not be a problem that is "becoming," since it has always occurred. In 1973, for example, it was estimated that between 2.5 and 4 million children in the United States were abused each year (Gil, 1973). Other researchers have reported 2 to 3 million cases of abuse in a typical year (Light, 1973; Nagi, 1975; Cohen & Sussman, 1975).

Gelles (1978) reported that 63 percent of families with children reported they had exercised some type of violence against the children in their homes during the preceding year. Gelles concluded that violence in the home was a *pattern* of parent–child relationships, not just an isolated event. Many parents saw some abusive activities as "normal" parenting tactics (spanking and slapping), but Gelles estimated that if his figures were extrapolated to the entire nation, there might have been as many as 2 million young people who were "kicked, bitten, or punched in 1975" (Gelles, 1978, p. 587). As many as one-half million children were "beaten up" (not just spanked) and perhaps 46,000 were threatened by parents who had used a knife or firearm against the child. These statistics, while only estimates, were powerful enough to elicit a national response that included changes in most state laws mandating that school teachers, police, and other public service workers must report suspected child abuse.

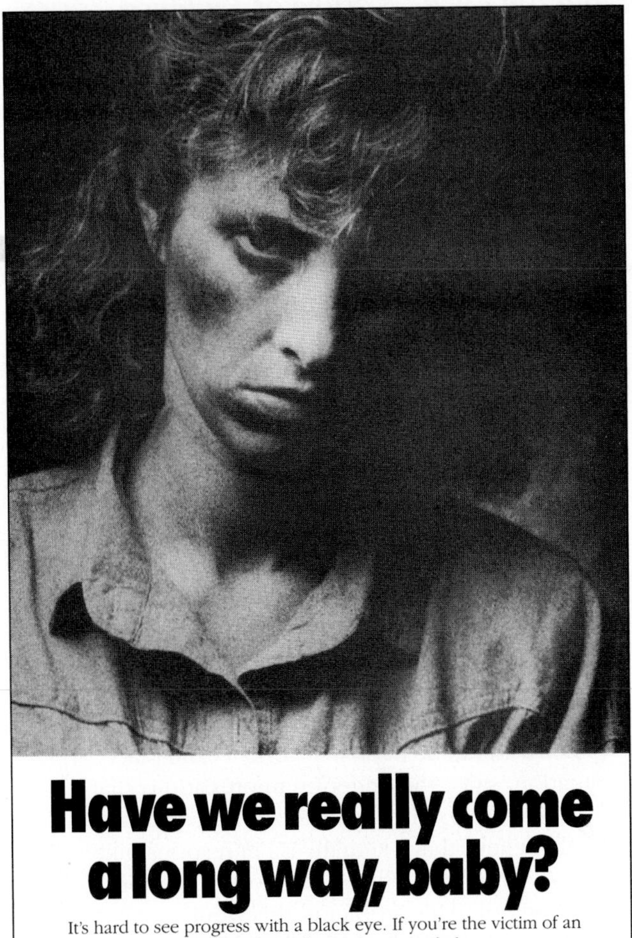

Have we really come a long way, baby?
It's hard to see progress with a black eye. If you're the victim of an abusive relationship, you can get help.

Although public awareness is on the rise, domestic violence continues to be a major national problem.

Understanding Physical Violence

There are three important aspects of violence that we must particularly study, since they provide insight into how family science helps us to understand the destructive nature of abuse. First, violence and abuse are transmitted from one generation to another. Second, high emotionality within a family tends to increase the likelihood that violence will occur. Third, there is a paradox in many violent families in that women tend to stay in the relationship even when they are in great danger. The following section addresses each of these ideas.

Emotional Fusion and the Cyclic Nature of Violence

In Chapter 9, the idea of rule sequences was discussed. Rule sequences of family behavior seem to be repetitive in nature and can be either enabling or disabling. A particularly disabling rule sequence might occur when part of the cyclical pattern in a family involves acts of violence to another family member. Some researchers have suggested that there is an identifiable cycle in abusive families (Walker, 1984). The first phase of this cycle is called the **tension building phase**.

An important element of the tension building phase is the role played by emotions. In Chapter 5, the idea of emotional fusion was discussed. The fusion principle stated that when fusion is high in families, the emotional system dominates what happens. When fusion is low, family members under high stress are able to use their intellectual systems more effectively. The inability to differentiate between emotion and reason creates a situation in which emotions will govern. This is especially problematic for men who have been socialized to be more violent, aggressive, and powerful. They often report that they were "out of control" and did not really mean to abuse. They relate a sense of being swept away by their feelings. For such men and women, anger control workshops, counseling, and individual help are essential.

During this phase there are also many incidents of frustration and tension that build within the relationship. The usual battlegrounds are finances, sex, and issues of power or control. In many cases, the wife will attempt to control the frequency and severity of these incidents by trying to please the batterer and barter with him to keep his world a calm place. She seems to be in control of the situation, since the lingering impression is that it is her job to keep him happy (Walker, 1979). The unfortunate outcome is that she (and others around her) might believe that it actually is her responsibility to prevent the abuse. She might say to herself and others, "If I were just more skillful at reading his moods and understanding his problems, this would never happen." In fact, the only element of this process over which she might have some influence is the *timing* of the next battering (phase two). Some researchers have noted that occasionally women appear to speed up the process by "misbehaving." They apparently do this to minimize the abuse. They might believe that it is better to have more frequent, less intense violence than to allow it build up (Walker, 1988; Orton, 1989).

During the **explosion/crisis phase**, the worst injuries occur. The tension in the marriage has risen to levels deemed intolerable. Generally, he sets out to "teach her a lesson." He may want to put her in her place, he may want to put an end to the tension, or he may unwittingly take out the tension in his own life (from work, for example) on her as a scapegoat for his troubles. This phase is usually short, but quite intense. It can last for two or three days, but usually for only a few hours. In many cases, there are repeated incidents of hitting, often from both spouses (Walker, 1988).

The final phase of this rule sequence is called the **aftermath**. Now that the tension is released, the batterer is contrite, and begs forgiveness. He might sincerely promise never to do it again. In too many cases, she believes this episode will be the last time, or that she caused it and she has indeed "learned her lesson." The most difficult element of this disabling rule sequence is that it creates a symbiotic relationship, an almost unalterable interdependence. Both believe that the sequence they have created is merely a part of their relationship. This makes intervention a difficult task, especially during the aftermath phase.

Many times battered women report that they were surprised by what touched off the battering. She might have been unaware of job pressures or he might have come home unexpectedly drunk. It is important to note that alcohol is implicated in most battering (Edelson, Miller, Stone & Chapman, 1985). In fact, some researchers estimate the battering–alcohol association at about 74 percent. Another fact about abuse is that it is much more likely to begin during a first pregnancy. As a result, miscarriages are five times more common among battered women than among the nonbattered (McGrath, 1979).

Whatever the reason, and whatever the outcome, spouse battering is destructive and dysfunctional. It creates a "web of terror" (Edelson et al., 1985) and perpetuates a most unhealthy way of working out the problems of life.

Intergenerational Transmission of Violence

One of the most tragic consequences of family violence is that it is often transmitted from one generation to another. Research on violence has consistently found that families serve as training grounds for children, with each generation passing on its patterns and rules about violence. Children raised with violence are more likely to approve of violence as an acceptable way of solving problems and to use violence both within and outside of the family (Steinmetz et al., 1987; Steinmetz, 1977; Straus et al., 1980). There is an abundance of research which shows that when a person has been brutalized as a child, his or her chances of being involved in violent acts as an adult are much greater. These future exploits can include murder (Bender & Grugett, 1951), rape (Brownmiller, 1975) assault (Wilt & Bannon, 1976), and spouse abuse (Straus et al., 1980).

Most likely, the intergenerational nature of violence occurs because a child has been exposed to only limited and specific discipline methods and responses to situations of stress. There are significant gender differences, however, in our responses to harsh parenting tactics. For example, Feshback (1970) has shown that boys respond to physical punishment by becoming more aggressive; girls, on the other hand, become more passive.

A family background of violence also predicts such things as courtship violence (Bernard & Bernard, 1983; Makepeace, 1983). Studies clearly show that the type of violence used by a parent, either in anger or as a discipline strategy, can be mirrored and used by the child later when he or she becomes a parent. However, this transfer of violence does not always happen. A child will often become a transitional character (see Chapter 3), or one who vows never to treat his children the way he was treated. Those who have been abused as children do not always feel that they can never be different. They can, in fact, change.

Why Do Abused Women Stay?

There are several myths that need to be put to rest with regard to women who are abused. For example, abused women *do not* secretly enjoy the pain. Nor do they look forward to abuse; they do not provoke men to fulfill some inner need to be abused. They often try to leave, but many times are unsuccessful. Most do eventually divorce, but only after a long history of battering (Bell & Harper, 1977, p. 22). There are a number of reasons why women do not move more quickly toward this option.

Fear. First, a battered woman's lack of power in her relationship is rooted in fear (Gelles, 1977). She may believe, and in some cases rightly so, that if she calls the police she will be beaten worse or even killed. The family is the most common milieu for homicide (Gelles, 1977).

The response by our legal system to family abuse has a long and varied history. For many years, the system condoned and even encouraged family violence. For example, English common law asserted that family matters were essentially matters of property. In England, and consequently also in America, such issues were considered the domain of the Civil Code, the code that covered property. Women and children were considered property, and the man was the master of his home. Therefore, the husband had a right to chastise his wife and children physically. As time went on, moderation was proposed and restrictions were enacted: The man could correct his wife or child only with a stick smaller in diameter than his thumb (hence the term, "rule of thumb"). This ruling provided a great boon for importers of cane, a durable and virtually unbreakable length of wood. Every father and school teacher had his cane handy as a constant threat. The net result was years of socialization which suggested that a man had the right to punish and control his property (wife, children, servants, cattle). A woman without access to power, therefore, was left with fear. She dared not contradict or disobey. Most importantly, she dared not speak against his "right" to punish her.

While these legal issues have long since been resolved, our cultural heritage is slow to die and continues to influence us. Until very recently, there has been little protection for battered women. Even today police response to abuse is not always consistent. Most police officers dread making calls involving domestic violence. When they do make arrests, it appears that the arrest, as opposed to giving advice or making the offender leave the premises, is a significant deterrence to future abuse (Berk & Newton, 1985).

The economics of leaving. Another barrier that keeps battered women from leaving is situational economics. It can be very difficult financially for her simply to leave a relationship, especially when children are involved. The literature on women in poverty sends a strong message about the difficulties faced by single women with children following separation and divorce. One study found that an abused wife was less likely to leave a relationship if she had never finished high school (Blumberg & Coleman, 1989). However, as her income rises, and her work opportunities increase, abuse decreases.

Religious pressures. Religious pressure should not be overlooked as a significant hurdle for women who wish to leave an abusive situation (Horton & Williamson, 1988). There is considerable pressure put on those in battering situations to stay in the relationship, especially when the religious organization has strong, inflexible attitudes concerning the sacredness of marriage and its obligations. To leave may mean disenfranchisement from the church and fellow believers.

Continuing love. While the battered wife does not enjoy being beaten, she might still love her husband and therefore not leave. She might continue to believe that change is possible, and that he will reform.

A woman's "responsibility." Finally, women continue to accept the cultural mandate that it is their responsibility to keep a marriage together. "Women are trained to stay. They are responsible for the marriage. If they leave, it's their fault" (Gelles, 1977). The wife may see it as her duty to give aid and comfort to her struggling husband. She stays with the violent mate from a sense of duty and loyalty.

Regardless of the reason, staying is often a fatal decision. During recent years, in response to an increased awareness of this problem, every state in the United States has developed a network of abuse shelters for battered wives. These shelters provide a safe place for women and children. They assist with the economic and emotional problems associated with abuse. Family service workers in these shelters provide support, counseling, and even job hunting and educational assistance.

One of the great ironies of the shelter network is that once a women has taken refuge, she could be at even greater risk. Women who take other measures (seek a restraining order, seek counseling, or call the police) have greater success in decreasing abuse over the long term (Berk, Newton & Berk, 1986). By contrast, those who simply escape to the shelter, and then return when emotions have subsided, risk increased violence and retribution for disobedience. The following sections deal more specifically with the types of interventions currently being used to respond to the abuse problem.

Crisis Intervention: Violence in the Family

When a battered woman calls a hot line, she is probably in a crisis situation that is dangerous to her or her children. Generally speaking, the crisis worker must know that such women have severe feelings of vulnerability, helplessness, intense fear, and anxiety (Roberts, 1988). As she contacts shelters, hot lines, and other community social service workers, she is reaching out at a particularly vulnerable time. The quality of the response from the worker is vital to the successful resolution of the situation.

Community response to violence. Usually, police are the first on the scene of a reported domestic violence situation. Many police forces now employ special officers who have had extensive training in family violence issues and who do nothing but respond to domestic calls. For example, in Hennipin County, Minnesota (Greater Minneapolis), response teams have been organized as a part of the county attorney's office. The teams patrol at night between 6 P.M. and 4 A.M. and are specially trained to deal with highly volatile situations. They have received instruction in self-defense and radio-backup procedures. They have learned to be specialists in defusing difficult situations.

Another community service that is a first provider for abuse situations is the local hospital. Many hospitals have trained emergency-room staff who can detect and assess battering. Often it is the hospital staff who is called on to testify and produce evidence in court.

The community hot line is another integral element of effective community response. When a battered women calls a hot line, she must receive an immediate response (Roberts, 1988). It is important that she not be placed on hold or have to interact with an answering machine. Of course, the primary goal of the worker is to assess the level of danger, but all situations must be taken seriously. Many hot lines work with or are connected directly to abuse shelters. In the shelter situation, the goal is to provide a safe haven from the immediate threat to women and children. A woman can usually stay for only a limited number of days. During this time, staff assist her in recovery and help her with the difficult decisions she must make. Child care is often available while the woman receives counseling help.

At the state level are the Child Protective Services (CPS) agencies. Funded by state and federal money, the purpose of these agencies is to intervene on behalf of a child for the child's protection. Community CPS agencies operate as an arm of the county or state departments of social service. These agencies protect children and rehabilitate families through assessment, treatment, and coordination of local services.

It has long been recognized that one person (for example, a counselor, acting alone) is ineffective in addressing the complexities of child abuse. One popular type of violence intervention involves the use of multidisciplinary, interagency teams. These teams work together to resolve abuse cases, bringing to each situation the training from their respective areas. In extreme cases, the child may be taken from its birth parents and placed by the agency if there is sufficient evidence of danger. Such children are placed first in emergency shelters, and possibly later in foster care if longer periods of separation are needed. Permanent placement of a child is an issue that courts must decide. In larger cities, special juvenile courts are established to deal exclusively with these issues.

Intervention in the family. A variety of suggestions have been made about reducing violence in the family. Statistically, it has been established that the only sure way to reduce violence in families is for parents to have one or no children, to alter their lifestyles so that there is little or no stress, and to develop a family situation where all decisions are made democratically (Straus et al., 1980). Since such situations are infrequent, it is obvious that most of us live in homes that are potentially dangerous. The next question is, since we do live in a stressful time in history, when violence exists all around us, what can be done? Straus, Gelles, and Steinmetz (1980) have made the following recommendations for our society:

- Reduce some of the sources of stress that create inequality, including unemployment, inadequate health care, and the overloading of parental responsibilities, such as those often experienced by single parents.
- Eliminate sexism. As long as gender imbalance exists there will be power struggles that can lead to violence.
- Develop better education for parents. Teach them alternative ways of dealing with the stresses of life.
- Eliminate norms that glorify violence. For example, encourage media to promote more nonviolent programming.

Another intervention that can be implemented at the familial level includes the training of abusive family members in anger management. Many counseling centers offer practical courses that teach people alternative responses to stressful situations. These courses can also include sessions that teach family members appropriate levels of differentiation (see Chapter 5). The ability to separate emotions from our thinking processes is critical in overcoming violent responses to volatile situations.

Strategies that don't work. In the ebb and flow of self-help fads aimed at personal and family issues, there are strategies that do not work but which are often presented as cure-alls for targeted problems. One such strategy, promoted for many years as a way to deal with anger and hostility in families, was introduced by Bach and Wyden in their widely read book *The Intimate Enemy* (1968), which promoted the idea that "couples who fight together are couples who stay together—provided they know how to fight properly." The general idea touted in this genre of literature is that aggression is therapeutic and necessary for healthy interpersonal development. In one "educational" session, women clients who were dating were told, "Don't be afraid to be a real shrew, a real bitch! Get rid of your pent-up hostilities! Tell them where you're really at! Let it be total vicious, exaggerated hyperbole!" (Straus, 1974). This theoretical idea was later extended, and marital counselors were encouraged to let clients battle each other in therapy sessions with plastic bats and punching pillows. As one researcher claimed, "Hurting is a necessary part of a [marriage] relationship."

These "ventilation" theories (Berkowitz, 1973) assume that all of us have a genetic propensity or natural tendency to be aggressive that cannot be controlled if bottled up. If we endeavor to suppress and restrain these feelings, they will only grow and fester until a destructive explosion occurs. Therefore, the appropriate strategy, according to this idea, is to let it all out.

Other theoretical positions assume the opposite to be true. That is, the more frequently an act is performed, the "greater likelihood that it will become a standard part of the behavior repertory of the individual and of the expectations of others for the behavior of that individual" (Straus, 1974, p. 14). Using this logic, one would assume that it would be better to learn the art of restraint and the use of rational problem-solving methods to deal effectively with stress.

While it is important for couples to develop appropriate emotional honesty, it is also inappropriate for anyone to believe they have the right to vent their personal feelings of aggression on another family member. In an important research study on this topic, Straus (1973) tested 385 couples to discover how effective venting strategies actually were in reducing family violence. The findings of this study clearly showed that increases in verbal aggression will lead to increases in physical aggression. The two seem to go hand-in-hand.

Interestingly, it was also found that the more an individual was able to call upon rational, thinking processes in times of stress, the fewer acts of violence were reported. In short, in times of stress, the strategy of venting aggressive feelings is counterproductive to the overall goal of dealing with and resolving the problem. The very thing one hopes to resolve will be pushed farther away, and even destroyed. A more appropriate response is to practice the difficult skill of separating high emotion from thoughts.

Sexual Abuse

The idea of using children as sex objects or of maritally raping someone is difficult to understand and could even be disturbing to some. Unfortunately, these are not uncommon practices. Such exploitation in family relationships represents "the worst of times" that families might experience. Of particular interest and concern to family scientists is the issue of incest. Its effects are especially long-term and negative.

Incest

Incest is defined as sexual relations between close relatives. This includes relations between father and daughter, mother and son, and brother and sister. Close relatives also include stepparents and step-siblings. The definition of sexual relations is not restricted to intercourse, but might also include fondling of genitals and breasts, and oral sex. Even though such sexual abuse is fairly widespread, most who are not employed in the family science arena are surprised to find out just how prevalent it is. In a recent research study, in which several thousand households were contacted nationwide, it was discovered that 27 percent of the women in the survey and 16 percent of the men reported they had been victims of sexual abuse as children (Finkelhor et al., 1990).

Worldwide, incest has been a nearly universal taboo. The only known exceptions were a few periods in ancient history wherein some royal families of Peru, Egypt, and Hawaii were exempt.

Valerie and Mohr (1979) have found that severe marital conflict had occurred in more than two-thirds of families reporting incest. It has also been noted that more than one-third of incestuous families have four or more children. Family scientists are still struggling to disentangle the dysfunctional dynamics that lead to these problems.

As scholars attempt to unravel the mysteries of incest, they have begun by noting several factors that could be labelled "predisposing conditions" (Justice & Justice, 1979). These conditions should not be construed as causal factors, but are rather conditions which seem to create a situation ripe for incest. Researchers have noted that a man who initiates incestuous behavior often has a kind of unreal fantasy about his mother. He may see her as an "all-loving" mother capable of solving any problem. Somehow the adult father transfers that fantasy to his daughter. He might have decided that his wife cannot fulfill that unrealistic role, but feels his daughter could. Additionally, many of these fathers are under high stress in the home. In Chapter 15, we mentioned several inappropriate ways used by adults to deal with the extreme pressures of life. For example, as stress increases, many people turn to alcohol as a form of escape.

Another indicator or predisposition for incest is that sexual relations between the mother and father have ceased or been severely limited. There is some evidence to suggest that mothers might actually collude in this process, as a form of unconscious withdrawal from the situation. They might not wish to upset the equilibrium of the situation by confronting what they may suspect.

The daughter might also appear hungry for affection. In undifferentiated families, where emotion and rational thinking are rarely separated (see Chapter 5), some children experience an extreme need for validation and emotional closeness. Another contributing factor in many reported incest cases is isolation. Isolated families lack the social support and network of friends that can prevent incest from occurring.

According to Justice and Justice (1979), incestuous fathers have "symbiotic personalities." They crave intimacy and might have had unusually close emotional ties with their mothers. They are likely to be introverts, may be tyrants to their families, and probably are rationalizers. In other words, they can justify any situation to attempt to fill their unsatisfied emotional needs.

The composition of abusing families also sheds some light on the problem. In one study of 60 sexually abusive families, it was found that 95 percent of the victims were female, and 65 percent were black. Additionally, 80 percent of these cases involved a male offender who was the male parent figure in the home. It is also important to note that stepchildren are much more likely to be sexually abused than are those living with their birth parents. In one study, about 1 in 6 young women living with a male parent who was a stepfather reported being abused before she reached age 14. In contrast, women whose primary male parent was a birth father reported sexual abuse at the rate of 1 in 43 (Russell, 1986).

The most devastating effects of sexual abuse stem from intercourse between father and daughter (Morrow & Sorell, 1989). Among the effects that have been noted in young women who were victimized are decreases in feelings of self-worth, higher levels of depression, and increases in self-destructive behavior such as running away, attempted suicide, and drug abuse. Both men and women who suffered incest as children have reported that the experience lives on in them (Edwards & Donalson, 1989).

The high number of runaways among abused young women may have little to do with self-destructive behavior. Recent research shows that about half of all adolescent runaways are fleeing sexual abuse at home (Graham, 1984). Thus they are quitting an intolerable situation and feel they have no place to go. Such behavior can hardly be termed self-destructive.

One of the most devastating aspects of sexual abuse is how long its effects last. Much like the post-traumatic stress experienced by a soldier in war, incest victims also report that they have recurrent thoughts and emotions about events that took place years before. They experience feelings of detachment and numbness, and seek to avoid situations that remind them of their childhood trauma. Throughout this text, a major recurring theme has been how important emotions are to the family realm. Although little research has been done to directly substantiate how familial emotions are affected by incest, it is certain that the impact is intense and ubiquitous. Obviously, unresolved past experiences will affect the future family of the young victim. Incest might also lead to a general lack of trust, fear of intimate relationships, and marital sexual dysfunction. Childhood molestation is often reported by women who seek counseling for sexual dysfunction problems in marriage (McGuire & Wagner, 1978). Many report they do not like the touching and foreplay elements of sex and often feel a disgust during intercourse. The intensity of such feelings is strongly related to the duration and frequency of the original incident (Courtois, 1979). Feelings about sex among these victims are also related to whether or not they have sought counseling and disclosed and dealt with these issues.

The incest victim often learns to adopt the role of victim. This pattern might follow her into other relationships, and she often finds herself attracting and being attracted to marriage partners who will perpetuate that role. There is some evidence to suggest that sexual abusers, both male and female, were abused themselves. In one study, it was found that about 80 percent of child molesters were themselves abused as children (Graham, 1984).

Crisis Intervention: The Sexually Abusive Family

The intervention of incestuous situations is usually very difficult. One of the most significant problems is that adults are reluctant to believe the child. Additionally,

Box 16.1
If you were abused

If you were abused as a child and have not received counseling help with this issue, you should do so. There is no point in waiting, and anyone who had such an experience should at least spend one session with a trained and licensed counselor to ascertain how this affected you. If you are reading this book as part of a course in family studies, your teacher should be able to find such a person. However, with this and other serious personal issues, you should not expect your teacher to also be your counselor. Seek out those who are specifically trained in helping victims deal with these issues.

the child might sense that to reveal the situation could mean a great deal of embarrassment and crisis for all family members. This high degree of despair and fear causes them to attempt to ignore the problem. Unfortunately, it is the child who often bears the greatest burden of fear and isolation. He or she is often racked by feelings of shame and humiliation and might feel unfit to ever be loved or to marry someone.

The first step in dealing with this process is disclosure. Secrecy is vital for an offender to continue the insidious actions, but once the secret is disclosed, the power of the offender is greatly reduced. Methods of disclosure vary. In only one-third of the cases does the child actually tell someone (Burgess & Conger, 1977). Discovery more often comes as a result of blood on the child's pants, dramatic changes in the child's behavior, or the discovery of unaccountable money or other gifts.

The dilemma following discovery is difficult. If the offender is removed from the family, more trauma might occur. The child may be seen as a traitor. As was discussed in Chapter 9, family rules, whether good or bad, are difficult to change, and it can be dangerous to the person who breaks them. The nonparticipant often reports feelings of conflicting loyalties (Burgess & Conger, 1977). There are several competing expectations that must be dealt with. Should the mother, for example, be loyal to her husband, who she probably cares for and loves? Should she be a good citizen and follow her "duty" to the laws of the land, seeing that he is prosecuted for serious offense? Or should her primary loyalty be to the child? Clearly, not all of these expectations can be honored (Burgess & Conger, 1977).

Most counselors recognize that intervention in these situations is difficult and demanding. Many treat the problem with a family systems approach, assuming that at least part of the solution is to strengthen the relationship of husband and wife (Giarretto, 1976). Of course, the inappropriate intergenerational tie between abuser and child is one of the primary targets of therapy. For most children, long hours of counseling are required to ease the guilt and shame associated with this problem.

Substance Abuse

Substance abuse in families is a significant and difficult problem in our culture. In the following sections, only one of many types of substance abuse is described: alcohol abuse. It is perhaps the most significant and deadly form of abuse occurring in families.

Alcohol

As far as historians can tell, humans have always made and consumed beverages that intoxicate. Even biblical accounts reveal widespread use and abuse of wine and other fermented drinks. The writings of the ancient Greeks often speak of "mead," an intoxicating drink made from fermented honey.

In the United States since 1850, the yearly alcohol consumption has averaged about two gallons per man, women, and child. Recently, this figure has begun to approach the three-gallon mark (DeLuca, 1981). About 49 percent of the alcohol consumed is beer, 39 percent is distilled spirits (whiskey, vodka) and the rest (12 percent) is wine.

The National Institute of Alcohol and Alcoholism (NIAAA) reports that there are specific periods in the life cycle when consumption is greater. The peak time for males to be "heavy" drinkers (at least once a week consuming 60 ounces of beer, 20 ounces of wine, or 5 ounces of distilled spirits at one sitting) is between ages 21 and 34. Females tend to be heavy drinkers later in life, between ages 35 and 49. There are also significant differences in alcohol consumption by race and ethnic background. Hispanics of both sexes have been found to have higher levels of alcohol consumption than whites. Blacks and whites have about the same consumption levels (DeLuca, 1981).

It has been well documented that alcohol consumption is directly related to a variety of medical problems. In 1981 the director of NIAAA reported to Congress that a multiplicity of problems are created by excessive alcohol consumption, including heart-muscle disease, high blood pressure, brain atrophy and dysfunction, increases in mouth, pharynx, larynx, and esophagus cancers. Overall, alcohol abusers have about a 10- to 12-year decrease in life expectancy (DeLuca, 1981). Additionally, alcohol use by pregnant women can cause **fetal alcohol syndrome**. Children born with this problem often have mental retardation, deformities, and growth defects.

Unfortunately, the alcohol abuser does not hurt only the self. As many as two-thirds of fatal motor vehicle accidents involve alcohol. More than half of the deaths to adults in fires and drowning entail alcohol use (DeLuca, 1981). Overall it is estimated that as many as 7 percent of American adults and 19 percent of American adolescents (3.3 million) have an alcohol problem. The cost to taxpayers is enormous: close to $90 billion yearly, including lost production, insurance costs, accidents, and fire. Recent estimates indicate that about 10 million Americans are addicted to alcohol (National Institute of Mental Health Study, cited in Leo, 1984). According to the National Institute of Mental Health, alcohol addiction is the fourth highest cause of death in the United States.

Even social drinking, when alcohol is not a chronic problem, might pose a significant danger to family and community. In the past few decades, social drinking has become a significant element in family rituals (Gross, 1983). As will be recalled, rituals can work for either good or ill in a family (see Chapter 13). It has also been found that women have increased their levels of participation in family alcohol consumption. In fact, family scientists have long noted that alcoholism is likely to be a "family disease" (Steinglass et al., 1987). It is familial in nature because it often involves all members of the family in a complex series of interactions.

Importantly, the abuse of alcohol in families has a significant and potentially damaging effect on children. The destructive dynamics of alcoholism have been noted in several places (for example, Black, 1981). In short, a child observes severe conflict between his parents and takes note of the dysfunctional nature of

During periods of alcohol abuse, a parent may not consider the needs of other family members.

one or both parents (Eells, 1986). The nonalcoholic parent is either emotionally out of control or is emotionally smothering the child. There are repetitive cycles of conflict, short-lived truces, and returns to drinking, hostility, and inappropriate distance regulation. These cycles will be discussed later in this chapter. The net result is that progress toward family goals is constantly interrupted, which creates a feeling of hopelessness and despair (Eells, 1986). Another significant effect of alcohol abuse on children is that the parent is not "there" during important critical periods of development and growth. This is doubly important, since many alcoholic families also construct extremely impermeable family boundaries which disallow outsiders from fulfilling the child's needs. The child in an alcoholic family "cannot be a child in the normal sense and successfully negotiate the usual age-appropriate developmental tasks. . . . Without a supportive network, the child and his family must rely on their own meager resources, the family dynamics become even more intense, and more dysfunction occurs" (Eells, 1986, p. 499).

A child is thus forced to adopt survival strategies such as the frequent use of fantasy and exaggerated hopes for a more perfect world. Unfortunately, fantasies and unrealistic hopes cannot fulfill the needs of adolescents. One researcher asserts that when fantasies fail, a child will turn to a variety of other behaviors like acting-out, withdrawal, expressions of suicide, over- or underachievement, or hyperactivity. As they get older, these children also frequently turn to alcohol use as a way to solve problems (Eells, 1986). These kinds of dynamics lead to family systems marked by high levels of anxiety and fusion (Bowen, 1978). The child is often very vulnerable to stress and fusion-producing behaviors.

The process of morphogenesis is apt to be at work in these situations. As was discussed in Chapter 2, morphogenesis "refers to those processes in complex system-environment exchanges that tend to preserve or maintain a system's given form, organization, or state" (Buckley, 1967, pp. 58–59). In other words, the family establishes behavior patterns and rule sequences that strengthen their resistance to change. One researcher has suggested that alcoholic families do not pass through normal developmental stages (see Chapter 7). Instead, they seem trapped within the cycles created by the alcohol abuse. They tend to remain fixated in a destructive cycle, vacillating between "sober and intoxicated" interactional states (Steinglass, Weinger & Mendelson, 1971; Steinglass et al., 1987). Although violence, divorce, and economic problems are frequently mentioned as correlates to alcohol use, "these visible evidences of the potentially destructive effect of drinking on family life tend to obscure the fact that the more usual long-range impact of alcoholism on the family is probably far more subtle" (Steinglass, 1981, p. 578).

The subtle aspects of alcoholic family interaction are an example of complex rule sequences, discussed in Chapter 8. Rule sequences are often described as being cyclical in nature. One thing triggers another, and the rather predictable cycle repeats, over and over. In an alcoholic family during the intoxication stage, the family can be characterized as more adaptive (Steinglass et al., 1987). A family might seem more energized, interaction rates increase, family members seem more animated, and sexual activity increases. However, the second part of this rule sequence is the return to a sober stage. The member who has been absent (physically, emotionally, or both) "returns" to the family and resumes the roles held before the intoxicated state. The complex rule sequence lets other family members know what they need to do to help the family maintain its balance. This tendency to cycle between intoxicated and sober phases allows the family to survive in spite of the grip this pernicious and destructive disease has on them (Steinglass et al., 1987). Steinglass showed in one study (Steinglass, 1981) that being "wet" or "dry" was a significant predictor of such interactional dynamics as distance regulation. Families in a "wet" cycle were much less flexible in distance regulation with other family members. (A flexible pattern in this research was one in which family members spent periods of time in the same rooms together but also had times of independent activity.) When families entered a "dry" cycle, the complex rule sequence demanded less rigidity, and permitted family members to come and go with more self-determination.

Another aspect of this disease is that its perpetuation is reinforced by a significant and overriding paradigm held by the family. Chapter 6 introduced the term *paradigm*. These pervasive and contextual themes that direct family behavior can take on many forms. Unfortunately, alcohol abuse can become a dominant paradigmatic theme. Steinglass (1981) says that when the alcoholic paradigmatic theme dominates, it "plays such a central role in the life of the families that it has become an organizing principle for interactional behavior. At a microscopic level this notion suggests that important aspects of interactional behavior are intimately tied to the presence or absence of alcohol at the moment the behavior is occurring; at a more macroscopic level, it suggests that overall patterns of interaction within the family take on unique characteristics dependent on the alcohol-related life phase the family is currently experiencing" (Steinglass, 1981, p. 578).

The theme of alcohol abuse becomes so pervasive that many aspects of family functioning, such as the simple rules, rituals, boundaries, and emotional regulations, are tied to the phases of intoxication and sobriety. Many families move through these phases and transitions while trying to maintain the integrity of the unit. The pattern of change is one of switching between two ways of life: Everyone knows the rules and sequences of each, and for the most part, both are rather stable, but ultimately destructive. The stability results from each family member's knowing what to do and how to change back and forth. The destruction, of course, comes as the problems associated with the behavior render the alcoholic increasingly dysfunctional and dependent.

Crisis Intervention: The Alcoholic Family

As counselors and family crisis workers deal with the alcoholic family, they have found specific interventions that work well. The following ideas come from an article written by Mary Ann Walsh Eells (1986), who has summarized some of the major intervention strategies used when the problem is approached from a family process perspective.

Differentiating the self. One of the most effective ways of dealing with an alcohol situation is to confront problems of differentiation and fusion within the family. For example, the counselor will often find that the wife of an alcoholic husband has fused into the undifferentiated family ego mass (see Chapter 5). The coaching and intervention strategy is aimed at getting the wife to attend to her true feelings, and begin to use a more rational approach to the problem. If she is in a fused state, she is apt to be caught up in the high emotional drama of the family, without considering her individual assessments of the situation. Therefore, the counselor coaches her to define herself more by taking "I" positions, and calmly figuring out and stating her observations about the family situation, regardless of the emotional reaction those observations might bring from other family members. Other family members are taught to identify "triggers" that prompt emotional reactions in her and in themselves. Through this identification process, all can begin to learn the process of differentiation and emotional control. As the wife (in this case) begins to distance herself from the family emotions, she experiences a sense of relief and release from the anxiety caused by high levels of emotional fusion. As the treatment proceeds, family members experience a gradual reduction in the level of anxiety and obsessive thoughts that controlled them prior to the change.

Pursuers and distancers. Spouses of alcoholics often function in a role called the "pursuer." A pursuer is continually chasing the "distancer" alcoholic spouse (Forgerty, 1988). The more she pursues, nags, and cajoles him to moderate his drinking, the more he resists and distances himself from the family. Her pursuing has the opposite of its intended effect. Instead of bringing the spouse closer, it pushes him away. The role of the counselor, therefore, is to interrupt this dysfunctional complex rule sequence and build a relationship that reflects a balance of power.

Emotional cutoff. It is usually apparent that both the alcoholic and spouse have cut off all potential intruders who might have the power to interrupt the complex sequences that perpetuate the alcoholic system. The greater the cutoff of family and friends, the greater the intensity of emotion "and fusion in the . . . family, and the more severe the dysfunction of all family members" (Eells, 1986, p. 501). The family members should be taught that cutting off causes more distance and pain. They must be helped to reestablish those critical familial and friendship ties, which can in turn be a significant resource to them.

Triangling. Children are often the victims of dysfunctional emotional triangles in alcoholic families. Frequently there is conflict between the alcoholic and spouse. The spouse might even form an inappropriate intergenerational tie with a child. As the spouse moves emotionally toward the target child, the relationship takes on destructive qualities. For example, the parent can become too protective and close, confiding and overburdening the child with issues meant more for adults. The child often sides with the nonalcoholic parent, creating conflict and hostility with the alcoholic parent. Some have suggested that the child has an unspoken hope of being able to make up for some of the disappointment caused by the disintegrating marital relationship. Yet this only makes the emotional tension greater and the dysfunction more intense.

The counselor's job is to demonstrate to the family how such triangles work. Next, a key task is to help de-triangulation occur. This rebalancing is difficult and requires a realignment of intense generational alliances. By structuring more distance between the child and the over-close parent, the anxiety and emotional fusion can recede.

Using the genogram. Counselors are turning more and more to the use of the genogram as a way to illustrate the dynamics and processes which are adopted by families in crisis. As children are "triangled in by their parents, lower levels of differentiation and alcoholic behaviors are transmitted to the next generation" (Eells, 1986, p. 502). One type of strategy is to have family members confront a three- or four-generational chart showing alliances, other triangles, and emotional cutoffs. By confronting them with the past, issues of generational transmission and genetic predispositions can be approached. Recognizing genetic and familial vulnerability can be very useful in helping family members understand how to prevent the transmission from reoccurring.

Summary

The quote at the beginning of this chapter sums up the intensity of the dilemma we face in our families. On the one hand we seek, and most of the time get, support, love, and warmth from our families. But occasionally, things go wrong and families become the tempest in our lives. They become the never-ending storm of stress, pain, and disappointment. The family microsystem has an enormous impact on the individual. That impact can be for good or ill. It has become quite clear, in recent years, that the home as idealized sanctuary is inaccurate for many people. For a growing segment of society, the family is not a haven but a hostile and even dangerous environment. The challenge, of course, is to turn that trend around.

Key Terms

Abuse
Incidence of abuse
Dating violence
Child abuse
The cycle of violence
Intergenerational transmission of violence
Women in violence
Abuse intervention strategies
Sexual abuse
Incest
Substance abuse
Intervention in alcohol-dependent families

Study Questions

1. Give your own definition of abuse, then consider the way it was defined in the chapter, and compare the two.
2. Why do women stay in abusive situations? Based on what was said in the text, describe several reasons why women stay, according to researchers.
3. Why is venting of emotion an inappropriate outlet for stress?
4. Briefly describe how fusion is an integral element in understanding abuse in families.
5. What can a person do to change abusive family behavior?

Sexuality and Reproduction

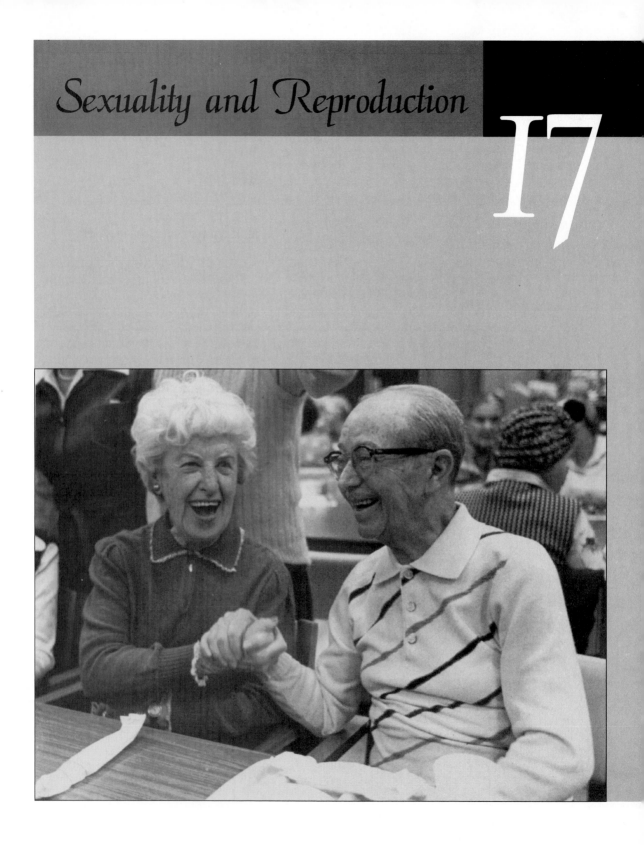

17

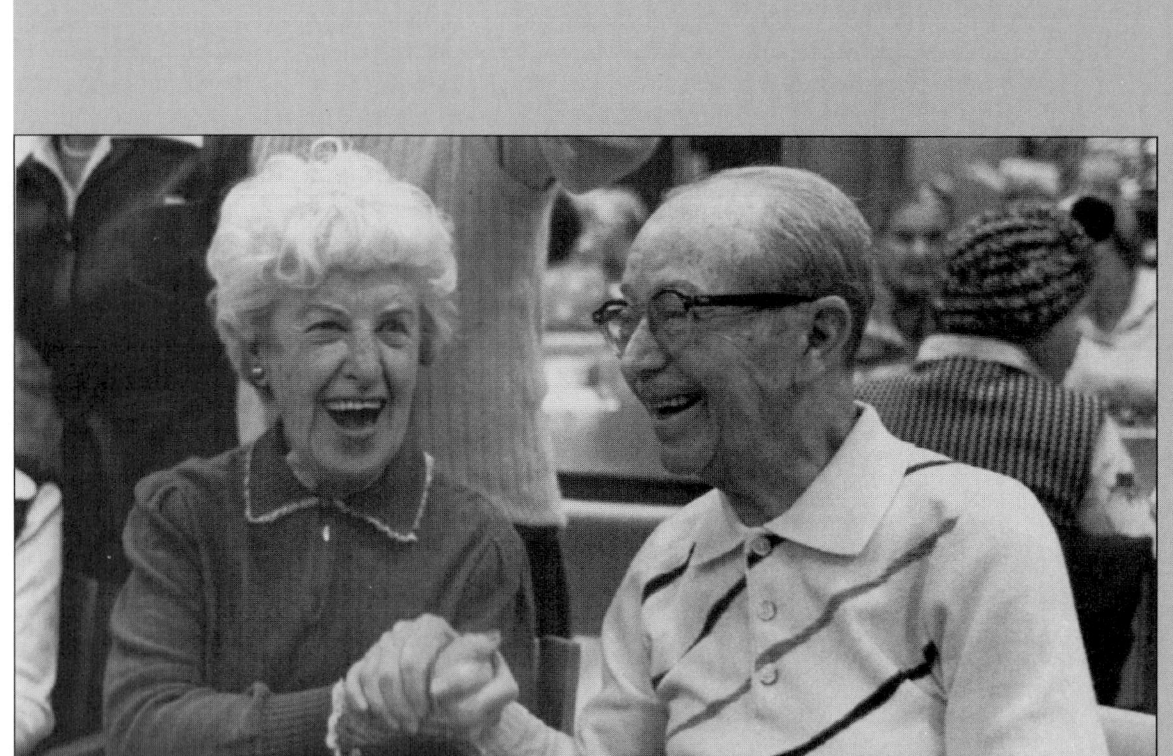

Main Ideas

1 // While sex has differing connotations from one person to another, there are few who would deny that sexuality in marriage is a critical and vital element.

2 // Competition between partners or demanding things from one another may cause the loss of joy in a sexual relationship, while a spirit of mutuality and support allows a profound and pleasing level of intimacy.

3 // It is useful for sexual partners to understand Masters and Johnson's four stages of sexual response, because the differing physiological responses of males and females can cause problems for the uninformed.

4 // There are a number of sexual dysfunctions that can be ameliorated by consulting with professionals.

5 // The principle of least interest helps explain the imbalance of power in some sexual relationships, and it is related to the ability to rewrite sexual scripts.

6 // The problems of infertility are widespread, and have led to several new methods to assist couples to conceive. These include artificial insemination, the technology for which has created many as yet unresolved ethical issues.

The term *sexuality* has different meanings for all of us. For example, it can recall the physical pleasure that comes with sexual activity. It can be an expression of emotional attachment to someone we care about intensely. Many couples comment that they feel a sense of bondedness when they experience the sexual responsiveness of their partner. To others, sexuality might mean a duty that must be fulfilled to please a partner or to maintain peace. *Sex* might simply connote the act of procreation, or it might signify the ultimate in closeness and intimacy—the sharing of that center of the universe in a special and private moment.

According to one report, those who rate sexual intimacy as "fulfilling" are more likely to be young, male, and in the higher income and educational levels (Connecticut Mutual Life Report, 1981). As we will discuss, feelings about sexual intimacy change over time and with circumstances. Few, however, would say that sexuality in marriage is not a critical and vital element.

"For human beings, the more powerful need is not for sex per se, but for relationship, intimacy, and affirmation."

—Rollo May, 1969

Issues in Marital Sexuality

Obviously there are important sexual issues within a variety of relationships, but this chapter will focus on sexual intercourse in the marital relationship. In keeping with the theme of this book, we will examine only those aspects of sexuality that deal directly with family processes. In other contexts, of course, it would be crucial to discuss such issues as sexuality before marriage, and sexuality among gay and cohabiting couples. We contend, however, that marital sexual intimacy has a different texture to it than does sexuality in other realms.

Importance of Sex in Marriage

The question is often asked "Can one have a good marriage and a poor sexual relationship?" Certainly there are ample cases where sex has minor importance in a marital situation, but most couples who have reported their marriage as either "excellent" or "very good" have also reported that physical affection and sexual passion were key elements in their relationship (Schwartz & Jackson, 1989). It is important to note that these results were obtained from 9000 readers of a magazine who chose to respond to a questionnaire. Additionally, no attempt was made to establish a causal relationship between good sex and a good marriage. That connection remains unsubstantiated.

Sexual fulfillment. When therapists work with couples having sexual problems, they often start with the relationship itself before turning their attention to sexual issues. Sexual fulfillment is a natural response to a close relationship. A couple's out-of-bed relationship and attitudes about sex are the elements which determine the quality of their sexual relationship. Many aspects of life can alter our attitudes about sex. For example, in a study of dual-career marriages, researchers found that when a wife becomes employed outside the home, she is likely to become more sexually demanding and assertive (Johnson, Kaplan & Tusel, 1979). These researchers attributed this to a change in attitude about life in general that carried over to the sexual relationship. In particular, working wives were less likely to accept the blame if their sexual life was unsatisfactory or boring. In a related study, other researchers found that newlywed couples had diverse views of their sexual activity. Those who found the relationship more satisfying and interesting were couples in which there was a greater balance of power and equity (Hatfield, Greenberger, Traupmann & Lambert, 1982).

Effective communication about sex. Another important key to understanding sexuality within a family is to consider how family members communicate about it. For example, has sexuality become an arena for power struggles, or has a couple learned to cooperate and nurture each other's self-concept? A family must have open channels of communication and the ability to resolve conflict in noncompetitive ways.

Chapter 12 presented the cooperation principle, which says that cooperation will facilitate the attainment of family goals, while competition will disrupt that attainment. The principle can also be extrapolated to the area of marital sex. When partners struggle over sexual issues, the attainment of sexual intimacy is greatly disrupted. Unresolved hostile feelings and conflict about sex hinder the primary goal of marital sexuality, which is the building of a bonded, sensual, and caring relationship. Therapists often note that sex can be a battleground for feelings and anxieties about other issues. Sex can become a means of expressing power differences and communicating more subtle analogic messages in the relationship.

As was illustrated in Chapter 12, when competition is high in relationships, honesty decreases, while the amount of misinformation increases. Open communication and the subsequent waning of a competitive spirit regarding sex are vital to resolving conflicts and sharing doubts and anxieties about sex. For most people, being open about the issue of sexuality is especially difficult, and misunderstandings and silent power struggles about sex can cause genuine stress in a relationship.

Since some of the more important values in family relationships are love, intimacy, and positive affect, it is important that couples learn the delicate art of managing conflict and competition, especially in areas like sex. Here are several suggestions for decreasing the competition and stress in a marital relationship.

First, partners can avoid the pitfalls of competitive sexual relationships by not passing judgment on the expressed fantasies and needs of the other partner. Nor is it helpful to demand information from one's partner about private thoughts or feelings that occur during sexual activity. Chapter 9, on communication, discussed the idea of over-disclosure when too much is revealed in a relationship. Of course, there are times when discussion of sexual activity is appropriate, and in a cooperative relationship each partner will accept what the other says about feelings and preferences. However, over-discussion and continual exploration of sexual activity can be just as problematic as too little sharing of desires and feelings (Masters & Johnson, 1976).

Masters and Johnson (1976) have suggested that instead of verbal over-disclosure and prying for information about sexual desires and feelings, a couple should consider the principle of mutuality. Mutuality means that "all sexual messages between two people, whether conveyed by words or actions, by tone of voice or touch of fingers, be exchanged in the spirit of having a common cause. . . . [This means that] two people are united in an effort to discover what is best for both" (Masters & Johnson, 1976, p. 53). Discovery is the key element here. The process of discovering is so intimate and so personal that even talking about it can be uncomfortable and destructive. A couple must learn and explore together what is mutually enhancing. This discovery process builds closeness and self-worth among married partners. By contrast, the competitive strategy focuses on performance, asking questions which are meant to solicit validation, like "How was it for you?" If you have to ask, you have missed the point of the experience!

The Four Stages of Human Sexual Response

When sexual response is initiated, the entire body responds. Among the physical changes that occur are increases in blood pressure and pulse rate. The sexual response cycle has been extensively studied by Masters and Johnson (1966), who alerted us to the four distinct phases of the sexual cycle.

The beginning of the *excitement phase* is marked by a dramatic change in body metabolism. Through stimulation the blood pressure and heart rate climb noticeably. The genital areas engorge with blood, making them sensitive to touch. For some (75 percent of women and 25 percent of men), areas of the skin turn reddish, like a strong blush. This phenomenon is called sexual flush.

The *plateau phase* of sexual response is simply an intensification of the excitement phase. The penis is now fully erect. The vagina is well lubricated and the inner and outer labia (lips of the vagina) are engorged with blood. This enlarges the vaginal opening, allowing the penis easy entry. Intercourse often begins during this phase. Physical tension increases rapidly, as do the involuntary impulses for thrusting. Heart rates also increase dramatically, and sexual flush might now cover much of the woman's body. The woman's clitoris pulls deeply beneath the clitoral hood. Since the vagina is not overly supplied with nerve endings, stimulation of the clitoral area is more likely to continue the arousal sequence in a woman than intercourse itself.

Orgasm, or climax, is the third phase, and consists of a pulsing, involuntary release of sexual tension. It is extremely pleasurable, lasting only a few seconds and accompanied by dramatic physical changes. The female orgasm ordinarily consists of several involuntary contractions of the sphincter muscle near the front of the vagina. Masters and Johnson noted that these usually occur about one second apart and range from 5 to 12 in number. The intensity, number, and duration of each contraction seem to correlate with the intensity of the total experience. Some have noted that the experience is so intense that other senses can actually be blocked.

For adult men, orgasm is somewhat localized and focuses on ejaculation, the rhythmic discharge of seminal fluid that contains sperm. At some point, ejaculatory inevitability is reached; this means that the process of ejaculation and subsequent resolution cannot be stopped.

Men normally experience a single orgasm that concludes with ejaculation. Women, on the other hand, can and often do experience multiple orgasms. Researchers estimate that about 15 percent of women regularly have multiple orgasms (McCary, 1979).

Resolution means completion, return, or conclusion. For men, the *resolution phase* is involuntary and dramatic. Within a few minutes after ejaculation, the blood is involuntarily released from the penis, and the erection is lost. No amount of stimulation can alter the speed of recovery for the male or produce another orgasm. The length of time that must pass before he can re-enter the excitement phase varies with each person. Typically, young men have quicker recovery periods.

The time for recovery is called the *refractory period*. During this time the penis and labia return to normal size and shape, heart rates and blood pressures decrease, and respiration returns to normal. Women can actually continue the sexual response without a refractory period. When a female becomes exhausted or wishes to enter resolution, she simply decreases or ends the stimulation.

Sexual Dysfunctions

It is not uncommon for couples who are very happy with other aspects of their marital relationship to find they have problems with sexual response. In fact, given the complex nature of the physical response and the intense emotional backgrounds brought to each sexual encounter, it is remarkable that more people do not report problems. The following section covers a few of the common difficulties couples sometimes have to confront.

Premature ejaculation. Premature ejaculation results from a man's inability to control his ejaculatory reflex. Men who have this problem report that when aroused they go rapidly from excitement directly to orgasm. Whether this response occurs "too soon" is a matter of cultural and personal preference. However, as will be pointed out later in this chapter, gaining some control over the speed of the sexual process can be important. One useful definition of a premature ejaculator is that he moves so quickly through the sexual response cycle that the plateau phase is virtually nonexistent.

There are many reasons why a man might develop this type of response. Most therapists say that inexperience and lack of understanding the sexual response cycle are primary contributors. Additionally, he might be very anxious and thus become oversensitive to the process. Whatever the cause, the outcome can cause severe problems where both partners become frustrated and even angry.

There are several ways for couples to deal with this issue. In fact, of all the problems confronting marriage therapists, premature ejaculation is probably the easiest to manage. There are a variety of specific steps and strategies that can be taught to both partners. In addition, there are a number of self-help books that address the topic. The basic concept in these therapeutic approaches is to teach couples that the important part of sexual response is not necessarily the male's ejaculation. Instead, couples are taught the delicate art of being responsive and sensitive to their partner's sexual cycle and to their own particular needs. Specific techniques are also taught that show a couple how to extend the plateau phase.

Overstimulation. As with most bodily functions, there are a variety of physiological differences in how we respond during arousal. One type of arousal in women can result in the retraction of the clitoris into its sheath. Perhaps it is so sensitive that stimulation causes discomfort. When the sexual script of the male (see Sexual Scripts later on) calls for stimulating the clitoris, as if it were a "magic button," this sensitive organ can essentially disappear. Frustrated, the man ceases his stimulation, and the clitoris reappears. Again he begins to stimulate, but again it disappears. Both partners can become annoyed and might experience a sense of embarrassment and inadequacy. The solution involves a direct sharing, either verbally or nonverbally, of what is pleasurable and what is not.

Vaginismus. One of the more difficult sexual problems to solve is vaginismus. Following the excitement phase, the vaginal opening and outer third of the canal involuntarily constrict. When this sphincter muscle closes, the mouth of the vagina involuntarily constricts, prohibiting penis entry. If intercourse continues when the muscle is in full spasm, the experience will be painful for both man and woman. Researchers have identified that this problem can be either primary or secondary in nature. Primary vaginismus occurs when the muscle constricts so tightly that no object can penetrate, even tampons. With secondary vaginismus, constriction during intercourse is present, but vaginal penetration has been previously possible (Shortle & Jewelewicz, 1986).

Vaginismus is most often reported by two groups of women. The first are those who as children received extreme religious training that portrayed sex as evil or shameful. The second category of women who report this problem are those who have been sexually abused. Rape, incest, and childhood molestation are all commonly linked to this problem.

The common therapy for vaginismus involves relaxation exercises and an examination of "performance-oriented" sexual scripts. Along with redefining these sexual scripts, the therapist can show the clients how to introduce systematic dilation. This is a technique in which the female inserts larger and larger objects (such as fingers) into the vaginal area. When both strategies are combined, the results are usually positive.

Impotence. Impotence, or erectile dysfunction, is the loss of or the lack of ability to maintain an erect penis sufficient to perform the act of sexual intercourse. There are a variety of reasons why this occurs. Among the most prominent are illness, injury, drugs, and physical exhaustion. In fact, one of the most common contraindications of prescribed drugs is the possibility of impotence. For example, most medications for hypertension (problems with blood pressure) can increase the possibility of an impotent reaction.

Anxiety is probably the next most common cause of impotence. In young men, especially, the fear of not "performing well" for a woman can often be linked to an impotent reaction. She might have made it clear that she expects a certain high level of performance, and in his attempt to meet that expectation, his fear blocks any response at all.

The therapies for impotence vary. For those with organic problems or with physical injury, it might be necessary to implant an artificial device in the penis that allows mechanical erection. A man with anxiety problems must be taught to break the dysfunctional cycle of anxiety-performance-failure. His partner must be taught to be patient, caring, and nondemanding. Again, a competent sex therapist has many strategies that can remedy these problems.

Unstable plateau. Many women report a two-stage sexual cycle, instead of the usual four (Masters & Johnson, 1966; Hite, 1976). In this situation, the plateau and orgasm phases never occur. Instead, she moves from the excitement phase directly to a long resolution phase, skipping the plateau phase. When the plateau phase is not reached, the subsequent leap to orgasm is also impossible, since her sexual tension is not strong enough for her body to respond at the higher level. Some women learn to adjust to this type of sexual response and are not bothered by having few, if any, orgasmic responses. Others report frustration and feelings of being cheated. Such feelings can contribute to the intense dynamics discussed below in the section on the principle of least interest.

Sexual Scripts

Ira Reiss (1986) has indicated that human sexual behavior is governed by **sexual scripts**. These are essentially complex rule sequences (see Chapter 8) that provide the basis for directing how partners sexually interact with one another: He does X, she then does Y, he responds with Q. As Reiss says, "Human sexuality in all societies consists of those scripts shared by a group that are supposed to lead to erotic arousal and in turn produce genital response" (Reiss, 1986, p. 20). These rule sequences prescribe who will be the initiator, how long a sexual session should last, and how much value is placed on orgasm. Sexual scripts also dictate what can and cannot be talked about, and what can and cannot be touched (Gagnon & Simon, 1973).

As couples begin to share their sexual scripts and expectations, they learn that every sexual encounter is not going to be ideal. While life tends to be less than perfect, there are steps that can be taken to even out the imbalances. The following is an application of how sexual scripts can work for either good or ill in building a relationship.

The principle of least interest. Family researchers have long noted that the person who is in a position of "least interest" has the greatest power in a given situation (Waller & Hill, 1951). For example, the partner who cares the least about a relationship has the greatest power. By contrast, if you care the most, and are in a position of greatest interest, you will do more to ensure that the relationship continues; you will be more likely to adapt and conform for the sake of the relationship. The person who cares the least about the relationship, or some aspect of the relationship, will have more power because he or she can do without the relationship if it does not produce what is wanted. For example, a man who finds himself deeply committed to a woman who is unsure whether she desires the relationship will be in a poor bargaining position.

This principle has several applications in family relationships. In any arena of marital decision making, it is likely that one partner (or other person in the family system) will care more about the outcome of a decision than the other. For example, if children care little about school and achievement, they will have greater power in that situation than the parents who are trying everything they can think of to encourage study. Power and control are much better balanced in any situation when there is a relatively equal amount of vested interest by both people. Imagine a young man who is more interested in a potential spouse than she is interested in him. She has the power to control the situation, simply because she has nothing to lose if the relationship ends.

The least-interest principle has significant applications in the arena of sexual scripts. Suppose that a man does not understand the issue of premature ejaculation; in his sexual script he sees himself as the initiator and believes that women have a lower sexual drive and that orgasm for women is rarely important. On the other hand, his female partner believes that sexuality is an equally shared event, and that either person can be the initiator. In their initial sexual encounters, he is highly excitable and quickly passes to the resolution phase while she is still in the excitement phase. Since he does not understand the difference between men's and women's sexual cycles, he mistakenly believes that she has had a good experience, merely because he did. Let's further compound this problem and assume that the two different sexual scripts both dictate that it is inappropriate to share openly about the process. The pattern is repeated over and over, and she is left unfulfilled, possibly angry, and usually frustrated. He is left somewhat satisfied, but probably mystified, wondering why she is not enjoying his sexual pleasure.

In this case, who is in the position of least interest? Of course, the answer is the woman. If night after night, month after month, she is merely a facilitator for his sexual pleasure, she will not value the experience as he does. When she becomes the person of least interest, she controls the frequency of sexual expression. If he enjoys sex, she now has a powerful leverage to use in other aspects of the relationship: "If you don't do such and such, I won't allow our nightly adventure." Since the experience is less rewarding for her, she controls it.

The answer to this dilemma is simple. Sex has to be a mutually shared and enjoyed process. The skillful sex therapist can easily help ameliorate this problem by teaching the man about the sexual response cycle, and teaching both partners about achieving orgasm for her. When the process is pleasurable for both, neither partner will be in the position of greatest or least interest.

Planning Time for Intimacy

As couples build and change their sexual scripts, it is important for them to learn to arrange busy schedules so that sexual activity is included. Here, one of the most significant barriers occurs when a couple's rule sequence includes an unspoken belief that sexual activity should be spontaneous.

Therapists usually counsel busy married couples to make planning choices about sexual activity. When sex is left to spontaneity and chance, it decreases in frequency and the relationship suffers. Scheduling time together does not have to mean that intercourse is expected or demanded. It can also mean just being in one place together without interruption. It may mean hiring a babysitter who will take children away for a few hours or overnight, or planning a getaway. In our pragmatic world of chores and duties, just being alone might be hard to justify. The wellness of a relationship, however, is vital. Couples must provide the necessary resources to see that it flourishes.

One therapy team advises couples to spend 30 minutes each night for a quiet talk, "with clothes off and defenses down," if possible (Koch and Koch, 1976, p. 35). Whatever the strategy, the principle is that a couple's sexual script should be examined and thought through; a script that "just emerges" might be one that needs some adjustment.

Sexual intimacy is an important element in healthy relationships.

Artificial Reproduction

Another issue closely related to the issue of sexuality is that of **artificial reproduction**. A primary issue in this topic is infertility, which is the inability to bear children. As we enter the twenty-first century and relevant biotechnology flourishes, this topic will take on great importance.

The reproductive process usually proceeds without incident and is so private that most of us take it for granted. We assume that anyone who wants to, *can* become a parent, but unfortunately, the reality is very different. Consider the following figures:

- About 1 in 10 couples are infertile (DHSS, 1988, p. 17).
- In America there are over 1 million marriages of young couples each year. This means that over 100,000 new couples each year are infertile.

- It is estimated that less than half of these couples are able to conceive after they seek help. This means that over 50 percent, or 50,000, new couples every year terminate treatment unsuccessfully.

Although these are only statistics, their impact on the families involved is important for students of family science to understand. Infertility can affect generational ties, emotional reactions, and the private side of a family. To understand these effects, we must discover what is happening within the private lives of infertile couples. Some glimpses come from comments made during a study conducted in England (Snowden et al., 1983, pp. 15–17).

"Anyone who's never actually been told, you can't tell them the feeling that you get. It's like being hit with a sledge hammer. I never felt so ill in my life. It took me a long while to get over it."

"If you tell most people you are sterile, they think you are not virile and you can be jibed about it and people just don't understand."

"My major hangup was based on this rather metaphysical notion of genetic immortality. What depressed me most of all, and overwhelmed me mentally, was the idea that at this point my genetic channel stops. That's the end. And that was the most chilling thing I had to take on board."

"I must be frank and say that I still wish that I could father a child; this is still a faint note of sadness to me. But it doesn't intrude into my relationship with these two children, because I can put my hand on my heart and say I wouldn't really change them. But if somebody suddenly discovered that my fertility had come back, I would want to try most vigorously to have a child. I think that's a very primeval and natural response."

"When I was holding someone's baby, or even looking after little children, I'd play with them and do all sorts of things and it was lovely. But when I went home, I could have climbed up the wall because there was so much love inside of me that I couldn't give."

These glimpses into the inner lives of people struggling with the problem of infertility are very revealing. If we are sensitive to the power and depth of these expressions, we can begin to understand the impact this problem has on a family. Infertility is usually a devastating and serious crisis for many couples. In this section, we will explore some of the issues surrounding this problem.

Terminology and Techniques

Fortunately for many infertile couples, new methods have been found to help them cope with their infertility. The first method developed was artificial insemination using the husband's sperm. It was first used in the 1770s (Snowden et al., 1983, p. 8), but wasn't widely implemented until the twentieth century (Snowden & Mitchell, 1981, pp. 13–15). Since then it has helped many couples to conceive.

Other developments have been made in this century, and there is now a wide range of techniques for artificial reproduction. The beneficial result is that many

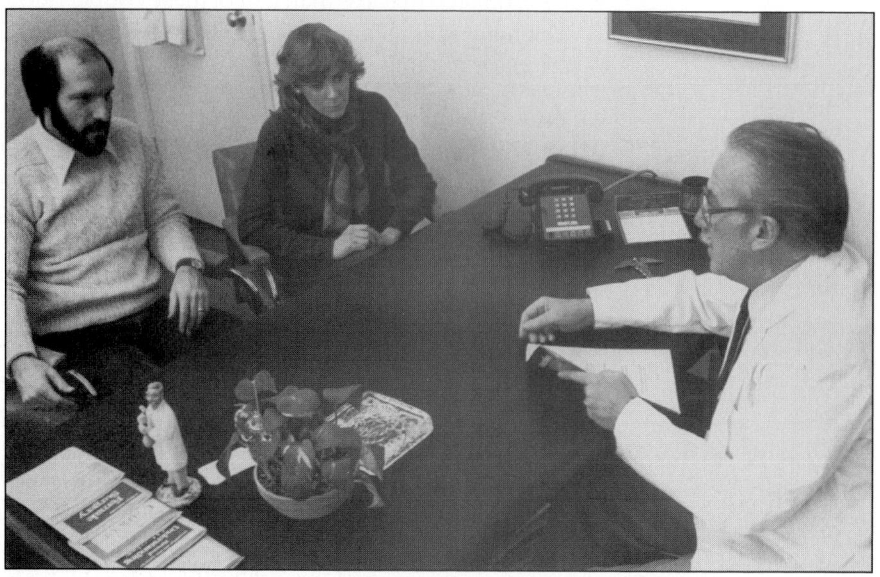

A variety of new methods are available to help couples cope with infertility.

couples who want children are able to bear them. These new developments, however, have a more complicated side. They raise a number of important new issues, concerns, and questions that are, in Clifford Grobstein's words, "epic in human history" (1981, p. 61), and we also need to address them here.

Artificial insemination is the process of placing sperm inside a woman's vagina by means other than sexual intercourse. In artificial insemination by husband (AIH), the husband's or partner's sperm is used. In artificial insemination by donor (AID), the sperm from a man who is not the woman's husband is used.

Oocyte donation is the process of securing an ovum from the ovary of one woman and using it to create a pregnancy in another woman. It is thus the opposite of artificial insemination. It is sometimes called "egg donation."

External fertilization is a very different technique. It is also called *in vitro fertilization* (IVF) and the "test tube" method. External fertilization is used mainly when a woman has no fallopian tubes or if the tubes are blocked. It is also used in cases where the partner's semen contains an insufficient number of spermatozoa, since sperm are often better able to fertilize an egg cell under laboratory conditions than under the conditions of sexual intercourse. IVF might also be adopted in the case of couples who appear entirely normal in their reproductive capacity but cannot achieve conception (Council for Science and Society, 1984, p. 15).

Surrogacy is a very different method of artificial reproduction. A surrogate is a person who acts for, or takes the place of, another. In reproduction, surrogacy is when a couple arranges to use the husband's sperm to artificially inseminate a woman other than his wife. The surrogate mother agrees that after the child is born it will be given to the couple.[1]

New methods of artificial reproduction are being developed on a regular basis. Some of the techniques that have recently become feasible are known as GIFT, POST, and VISPER. GIFT is Gamete Intra-Fallopian Transfer. POST is Peritoneal Oocyte and Sperm Transfer. Both of these involve collecting eggs from a woman and sperm from a man (the husband when possible) and putting them directly into the woman's fallopian tubes (GIFT) or peritoneum (POST). VISPER is Vaginal Intra-peritoneal SPerm TransfER. This technique involves placing the sperm directly into the woman's peritoneal cavity. None of these methods are possible if a woman's fallopian tubes are missing or blocked; instead, IVF must be used.

The new developments in reproductive technology have made it necessary to develop new concepts about family roles. Snowden and colleagues (1983) have clarified family terminology by differentiating between the genetic mother, carrying mother, nurturing mother, genetic father, and nurturing father. These differences are important for two reasons. First, these roles are intricately tied to some of our most deeply experienced feelings (affective states), and that makes them important for families and family scientists. Second, they help us understand some unusual situations that now exist in families, and this can lead to the establishment of strategies to help those families cope.

Issues About Artificial Reproduction

Many new issues have been raised by the emerging reproductive technologies. Some of the issues are so general that there is widespread concern about them as well as a large literature devoted to them, which includes writings from philosophical, theological, legal, medical, social work, political science, sociological, and psychological points of view.

Some of the general issues on artificial reproduction are of peripheral interest to family scientists, but many of them are relevant. If family scholars do not help families cope with these issues, they will be dealt with by others. If that were to occur, some of the insights and recommendations that could be acquired from a family science perspective might go unrecognized.

Those who study these issues generally agree about many aspects of artificial reproduction. For example, there seems to be unanimity that "the human embryo is entitled to profound respect" (DHEW, 1979). It is also agreed that the goal of policies, research, and practitioners should be to answer questions like:

> What will lead to the kind of society in which the greatest possible number are able to satisfy their most important needs and desires? What will most reduce misery and suffering? These are basic moral principles that all of us can accept, at least as an important part of morality. (Singer & Wells, 1984, p. 202)

Ethics of gamete transplants. One issue at the heart of many controversies over artificial reproduction is whether gamete transplants compromise sexual ethics. Some individuals, as well as some very influential organizations including several large Christian churches, believe transplants are unethical, but many others believe they are morally justifiable. The main question in this issue is whether sperm and ova transplants violate certain beliefs, including the biblical injunction against adultery (Exodus 20:14). Our review of the literature revealed three different opinions.

One opinion is based on the premise that sexual intercourse outside marriage is morally acceptable. Those who begin from this premise logically conclude that no ethical impropriety stems from the use of artificial methods such as AID and egg donation. We do not know what percentage of today's population subscribes to this belief, but we suspect it is a small minority.

The other two opinions grow out of a different premise, that sexual intercourse outside marriage is not acceptable. The difference between these two opinions lies in the various behaviors permitted within a marriage. One group believes that everything about the reproductive process should be confined to the marital relationship. This leads to the most cautious of the three conclusions, that artificial methods which transfer sperm and ova are ethically inappropriate.

The third possibility is to view sexual intercourse and the medical process of gamete transplants as fundamentally different processes. According to this view, the physical intimacies, emotions, and behaviors associated with sexual intercourse should be confined to the marital relationship. The transplanting of gametes, on the other hand, should be viewed as a form of medical treatment for the health problem of infertility. As such, it should be guided by the same ethical guidelines used for other medical treatments involving the transfer of body parts. Gamete transfer is thus in the same category as blood transfusions and organ transplants. It logically follows that even though sexual intercourse should be confined to marriage, there is nothing unethical about AID and oocyte donation.

Since those who originally canonized current religious beliefs and codes of conduct did not need to deal with these questions, the new technologies have created ambiguity in most groups advancing religious reasons for restrictive sexual beliefs. Some of this ambiguity is being dissipated as religious leaders come to terms with the questions. Not surprisingly, however, different religious groups are coming to different conclusions. The Archbishop of Canterbury declared in 1948 that AID was immoral and should be made a criminal offense (Snowden & Snowden, 1984, p. 26). The position of the Catholic church was clarified in Pope Paul VI's *Humanae Vitae* (1968). He declared that "Never is it permitted to separate" the various parts of the reproductive process, and thus gamete transfer is unethical. Other religious groups seem to be taking a position that does not oppose the new technologies.

Current insights cannot resolve the issue of gamete transplanting because it is basically a matter of religious and subcultural beliefs. Occasionally, however, family experts find themselves in situations where the issue is a concern. When they do, there are several ways they can be helpful. First, they can help people understand the issue and assist them in attaining their goals. They can also use the methods of "value reasoning" developed by Margaret Arcus (1980) and her colleagues to help individuals and groups reason as effectively as possible about the issue.

Family scientists should be sensitive to the importance people place on their beliefs in this area, and should always respond in ways that communicate this sensitivity.

Another of the important issues associated with the new technologies is the age-old concern about the role of government and law. Simply stated, the question is, How much and in what ways should government be involved in an area that is as private as reproduction?

One of the main differences between the private and public realms is that most of what happens in the private realm lies outside law. This reasoning is the basis for beliefs such as the separation of church and state and many of the privileges that are granted in the Bill of Rights. The parts of the family realm that do come under the law are parts that are fairly public. For example, there is consensus in modern societies that things such as weddings, wills, property, and property ownership should be governed by law. Also, when behavior in the family realm goes beyond certain limits, it comes under the regulation of legal systems. Some examples of these excesses are physical abuse, assault, and child neglect.

The parts of the family realm that are regulated by law, however, are only a minuscule piece of what happens within a family. This separation between the private and public is important for the effective functioning of a family, because the family realm deals mostly with things that would be legally unenforceable.[2] The concept of unenforceability is important to political and family science theory. Our whole view of civilization and government-by-law depends on a sophisticated infrastructure of unenforceable rules that are managed in the private part of society by organizations such as the family.

When we understand the importance of unenforceable rules and the private sphere in the human condition, the main question becomes, How possible or desirable is it to transform the reproductive processes (which are primarily familial and therefore private phenomena) into processes that can be governed by public-realm mentalities or by enforcement systems? A simple version of the answer is that some dimensions of our reproductive technologies should be given the protection of law, but other parts should be left in the private sphere. A more complicated version is that, thus far, we have not examined this issue enough to determine what the most desirable balance should be. The dilemma comes from the probability that if we do not develop legal control over such things as the artificial creation, storing, and manipulation of embryos and fetuses, we might allow some grossly undesirable and inhumane practices to occur.

On the other hand, if we tried to legislate the unenforceable aspects of what couples can and cannot do, we would be trying to legalize an area that should, because of the nature of some familial phenomena, be outside the law. Such an undertaking would not be successful. Inevitably, we would need to modify our attempts after they proved futile.

Applications in Family Science

When we think about artificial reproduction from a family science perspective, we focus on aspects different from those of other scholarly perspectives. Familial perspectives tend to embrace generational, developmental, affective, and ecosystemic aspects more than do other points of view.

One helpful aspect of a familial approach is to think of artificial reproduction techniques as a set of strategies used to deal with a less-than-ideal situation.[3] When we take this approach, it influences how we view some of the issues, and how we think about and use some of the alternatives.

Exploring Issues About Surrogacy

Family science teachers and researchers need to explore issues such as what surrogacy means for the surrogate mother, what it means for the child as he or she matures, whether it should be legally regulated, its effects on the other individuals involved, the morality involved, the commercialization of surrogacy, and strategies for dealing with it as effectively as possible.

There are many issues within the surrogacy question that have not been explored enough to reach even tentative conclusions. These include the rights of the surrogate mother, the rights of the child to have access to information about surrogacy, the influence of deliberate choices about these matters on the family relations and individuals involved, and the implications of these practices for those who have an orthodox Christian view of sexual chastity.

There have been some attempts to identify public opinion about surrogacy. Surveys in 1982 in Australia and Britain found that only a minority approved of it: 32 percent in Australia and 20 percent in Britain. In Australia 44 percent thought surrogacy should not be approved, and in Britain 55 percent were against it. On the legal side, most authorities agree that children should ultimately know what happened and how they were genetically linked to their parents.

Another issue has to do with recordkeeping. For example, should the birth certificate of children born through artificial reproduction methods contain any information about the details of their conception? Should records be kept so that donors can be identified later, and if so, how much information should be kept? Such information should also be essential if offspring want to ascertain that there is no prohibited relationship with an intended spouse (a possibility that can cause anxiety, although it is statistically very unlikely) (DHSS, 1988, p. 14).

Effects on Family Process

Family scientists necessarily wonder whether there are any overall effects of artificial reproduction on family processes. Do the couples who experience artificial reproduction have many problems or regrets, or is it generally a satisfactory experience? The interviews from the previously cited Snowden study (1983) are the best data we have. In this study, couples were eager to express their gratitude for the technology. Most claimed to have no regrets (Snowden, 1983, p. 81). Additionally, there seemed to be no problems in accepting the child or the new situation.

We have very little real data about whether artificial reproduction has harmful or beneficial effects on marriages. However, there "is no evidence that couples who have had a child by AID are any more likely to divorce than other couples. Indeed, it is sometimes claimed that the divorce rate among AID couples is lower than among other couples" (Snowden & Snowden, 1984, p. 65).

Developmental changes. A developmental change apparently occurs in couples who use artificial reproduction. The Snowden research found that almost all of the participating couples initially planned to hide from the child the fact that she or he was conceived by AID (Snowden & Snowden, 1984, p. 97). Later, however, as new situations arose that had not been anticipated, the majority changed their minds and decided to tell the child after all.

The situations prompting this turnaround were often simple things such as a child being assigned in school to examine genetic characteristics like eye color in the family. Other reasons couples eventually decided to tell their children were more important. For example, some couples wanted to maintain an atmosphere of openness, honesty, and lack of deception in their home, and they gradually realized that not telling their child the truth about the birth would be inconsistent with their own standards.

Developmental changes like this might eventually become unnecessary. As attitudes about artificial reproduction change, there might be no hesitation to tell the truth from the very start.

Genealogical bewilderment. The concept of **genealogical bewilderment** was developed by Wellisch (1952) and later expanded by Sants (1964). "A genealogically bewildered child is one who either has no knowledge of their natural parents or only uncertain knowledge of them. The ensuing state of confusion and uncertainty fundamentally undermines his security and thus affects his mental health" (Sants, 1964, p. 24). According to Sants, this is usually not a problem until children become adolescents, when they may begin to search for clues to the past.

At the same time, McWhinnie (1984) has suggested that genealogically bewildered children have fears about what they might discover (p. 20). The concept of genealogical bewilderment is also helpful in understanding some of the adjustments that parents face. For example, family therapists have demonstrated that emotional health in a family is facilitated when family members have relatively clear generational boundaries. Lidz (1958) was the first to summarize these ideas into a general principle, which we discussed in Chapter 3 as the generational alliance principle. His principle demonstrates that clear generational boundaries and alliances facilitate mental health in children while confusion in these areas is disruptive. Later, Minuchin (1974) and Haley (1976) demonstrated that generational boundaries can impact many aspects of health in families.

One particular type of artificial reproduction probably aggravates genealogical bewilderment and confusion of roles. This is when the donors of eggs or sperm are personal acquaintances, or even relatives, of the nurturing parents. We humans are so adaptable and resourceful that some families probably can work out satisfactory arrangements even in this situation, but there are more complications, greater confusion, and more difficulties than when donors remain anonymous.

According to Snowden's (1984) data, most families seem able to cope effectively with the challenges of genealogical bewilderment, but some probably have more difficulty than others. The advantage in academically identifying this type of problem is that it documents an actual challenge faced by some families; hopefully, this will lead to the development and sharing of strategies to help families facing this difficulty.

Emotional response. There is considerable evidence that infertility and the use of artificial reproduction tend to create a number of affective problems for families. One of these is a feeling of inadequacy that is almost universally experienced. This leads to different responses in different people. In the Snowden study, several husbands had offered their wives a "divorce because they could not give her children; they had somehow not fulfilled their part in an often unspoken and poorly understood assumption. The husband feels he has 'let the side down' and cannot fulfill the role he thinks his partner expects of him. Perhaps the offer of a divorce is more of a cry for help at a time of stress and anguish when there is a feeling of isolation and of being incomplete" (Snowden & Snowden, 1984, p. 18). Nonverbal communication detected in the Snowden interviews suggested that some of the participating families were continuing to experience important challenges resulting from these feelings. The Snowden study also found that artificial reproduction creates an "unnatural" set of beliefs and feelings about secrecy: "The most significant feature of the 66 interviews was the couples' perceived need for secrecy about their AID experiences. It was the topic of secrecy which dominated all other issues and which affected family relationships in a variety of ways" (Snowden, 1984, p. 320). The Snowden research team found that couples were not effective in making decisions about artificial reproduction until they had dealt with their feelings about their infertility by effective communication (Snowden & Snowden, 1984, pp. 63–64).

Apparently, coping with infertility and making decisions about artificial reproduction are different. These challenges can awaken some deeply felt emotions and disturb a person's very sense of identity. They also force people to think about the most important purposes of life, and they affect the ways in which people relate to each other in their most important relationships. Therefore, these challenges often require a great deal of time, attention, and concern. Dealing with them in the self can involve a lot of tears, pain, soul searching, and unexplainable emotions. Support and acceptance have to be assured and reassured many times, and sometimes the same feelings need to be talked about and ventilated over and over again.

There has been a great deal of research about the strategies that help families cope with crises. One key emotional situation is how and when to tell the child about being the product of an artificial reproduction process. This situation is fairly similar to that of adoption, and many of the guidelines that have been discovered about adoption probably also apply to artificial reproduction. This suggests that it would be helpful for parents first to "think through" how they want to talk with their children about their birth circumstances. Parents ought to decide beforehand what their children will be able to understand at different ages, what will be important for them to know, and how they will share it with them.

The abilities to understand each other and reach consensus in decisions are also helpful strategies in coping with infertility and artificial reproduction. Most couples studied by Snowden had to come to full agreement about the decision to employ AID. If only one partner wanted to use the process, the chances of successfully conceiving would probably have been dramatically altered.

Summary

The cornerstone of the family realm is the process of humans reproducing themselves. Before our modern era, reproduction occurred only through the natural methods of sexual intercourse, pregnancy, and childrearing. Recent developments have changed this. A sophisticated technology for artificial reproduction is now in use, and further developments are expected. There has been a great deal of discussion and debate about the implications of this emerging technology for humanity, but until very recently the dialogue occurred only among scholars with nonfamilial perspectives such as theology, biology, and philosophy. Recently, however, family scholars have begun to identify the familial dimensions of reproductive technology. They have added new issues and ideas to the dialogue. For example, there are now discussions on whether the stages of human development that occur after the birth of an artificially conceived child are the same as for a natural child. These issues were not discussed until family scholars introduced them.

In this chapter we have attempted to select from the voluminous literature on reproduction a manageable amount of basic information that is essential for family scholars to understand. We have introduced some basic terminology, issues, and ideas about the familial aspects of sexuality and artificial reproduction. We have also suggested that much progress can still be made in learning about and dealing with these issues.

Key Terms

Sexual fulfillment
Sexual communication
Principle of mutuality
Four stages of sexual response
Premature ejaculation
Overstimulation
Vaginismus
Impotence
Sexual scripts
Principle of least interest
Artificial reproduction
AID (artificial insemination by donor)
AIH (artificial insemination by husband)
Oocyte donation
External fertilization (often called in vitro fertilization, IVF, or test-tube method)
Surrogate mother
GIFT
POST
VISPER
Genetic mother
Unenforceables
Genealogical bewilderment

Study Questions

1. Explain how competition can influence the sexual aspects of one's relationship.
2. What is the principle of mutuality? How does it help us understand sexual issues in relationships?
3. What are the four stages of human sexual response?
4. Describe the problem of a premature ejaculator.
5. What is meant by unstable plateau?
6. How can the principle of least interest be useful in explaining sexual problems that can occur in relationships.
7. What is the current fertility rate in the United States?
8. Define the following: oocyte donation, external fertilization, artificial insemination.
9. What are the technical and emotional issues that surround the issue of surrogacy?
10. Describe what is meant by genealogical bewilderment.

Notes

1. In some ways this concept is misleading. A woman who is called a surrogate mother is actually the genetic and physical mother of the child. It would probably be more accurate to describe the rearing mother as the surrogate. In spite of these inconsistencies, the term has become so common that we will continue to use it in this sense.
2. This insight is another of the many that we owe to the team of scholars at the University of Exeter. The group who were the most helpful to this chapter were Robert Snowden, Elizabeth Snowden, and Kurt Back. Many of the ideas in this chapter were improved through our consultation with them.

3. There has been a great deal of debate about the role of artificial methods, and there are many extreme positions (Grobstein, 1981, pp. 62–64). For example, Kass (1972) has argued that artificial methods are so degrading they cannot be considered human reproduction, while Fletcher (1974) argued against the "meiotic roulette" of natural methods. It may be that future technologies will utilize some artificial methods that are superior to natural methods, but for practical purposes, for the present and for the foreseeable future, reproductive alternatives remain therapeutic devices for unfortunate conditions.

Additional Resources

Singer, Peter, and Deane Wells, 1984. *The Reproductive Revolution: New Ways of Making Babies.* Oxford: Oxford University Press.

Snowden, Robert, and Elizabeth Snowden, 1984. *The Gift of a Child.* London: George Allen and Unwin.

Technical Books:

Grobstein, Clifford, 1981. *From Chance to Purpose.* Reading, Mass.: Addison-Wesley.

Lasker, Judith N., and Susan Borg, 1987. *In Search of Parenthood.* Boston: Beacon Press.

Snowden, Robert, and G. D. Mitchell, 1981. *The Artificial Family: A Consideration of Artificial Insemination by Donor.* London: George Allen and Unwin.

Snowden, Robert R., G. D. Mitchell, and E. M. Snowden, 1983. *Artificial Reproduction: A Social Investigation.* London: George Allen and Unwin.

Divorce

18

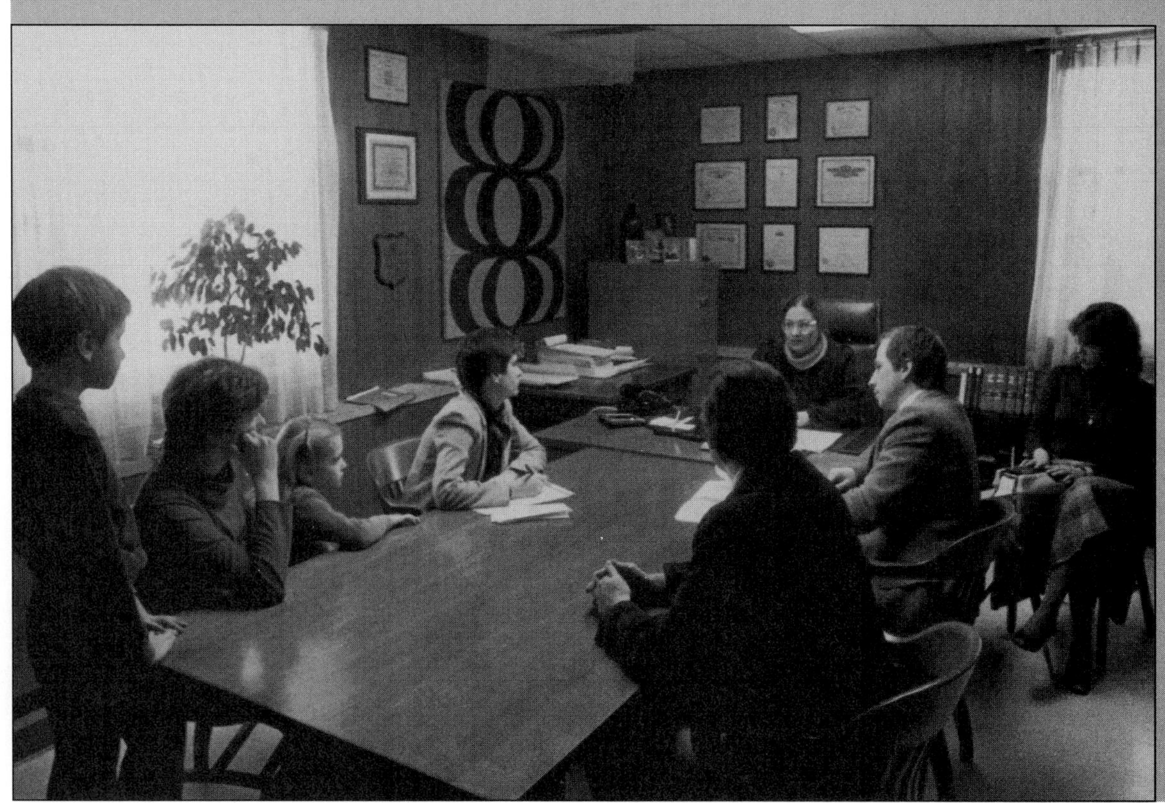

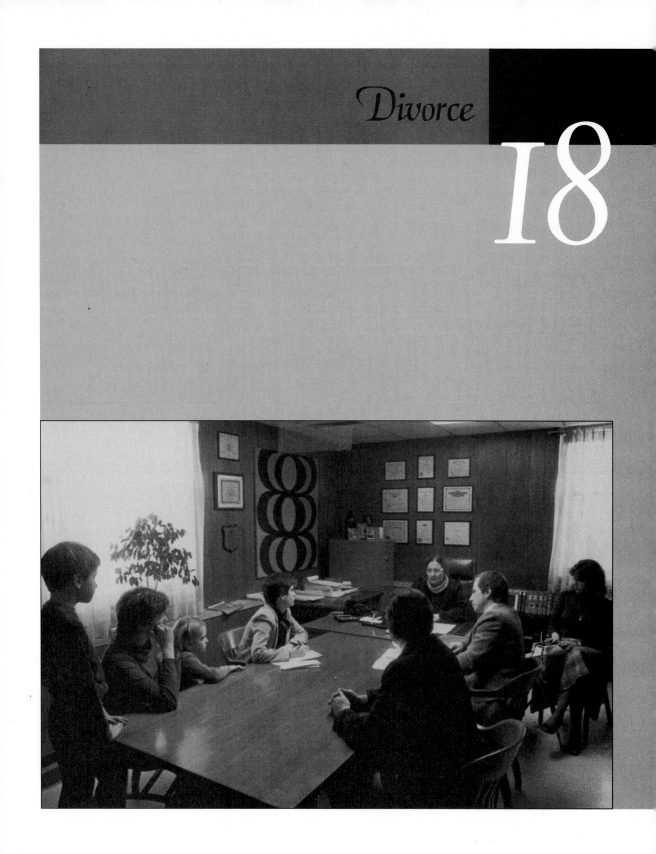

Main Ideas

1 // Historically, the nature of divorce has changed over time from an individual, religious, and state perspective. Sociologically, divorce rates change dramatically, responding to social changes.

2 // The "causes" of divorce are very difficult to identify and it is not a "normal" stage in the family life cycle.

3 // The disengaging family experiences changes in valence, increases in paradigmatic intensity, boundary changes, and alterations in public versus private activities.

4 // The family in separation may experience "emotional closeout" and changes in family rules and patterns.

5 // Among the issues facing those who divorce are dramatic shifts in levels of stress, problems with the executive subsystem, generational alliances, and role strain.

6 // Divorce has significant and, many times, negative influences on children.

Divorce is the most common procedure for ending marital relationships. The purpose of this chapter is to describe the process of divorce as it occurs in the family system. This topic is particularly relevant since many marriages end in the divorce court. In fact, very few U.S. marriages (about 20 percent) are composed of the "ideal" type: birth mother and birth father and children. Therefore, it is critical for serious students of family science to become familiar with the divorce processes. Those working with families will encounter this ubiquitous social phenomena. Additionally, some who read this book will eventually divorce and possibly remarry. Studying divorce now can provide valuable professional and personal insights.

"Love, the quest; marriage, the conquest; divorce, the inquest."

—Helen Rowland

The Nature of Divorce

According to the National Center for Health Statistics (1989), there has been an annual doubling of the divorce rates between 1962 and 1982. Every year there is in excess of 1 million divorces in the United States. The rate vacillates but has remained relatively stable for several years. This high rate means that large numbers of children become involved. In the early 1960s only about 7 out of every 1000 children in the United States experienced a divorce in a given year. By the 1990s, about 18 of every 1000 children experienced a divorce by their parents.

It was once supposed that only the wealthy and famous divorce; now divorce happens at all socioeconomic levels. Also, the average age of divorce for men

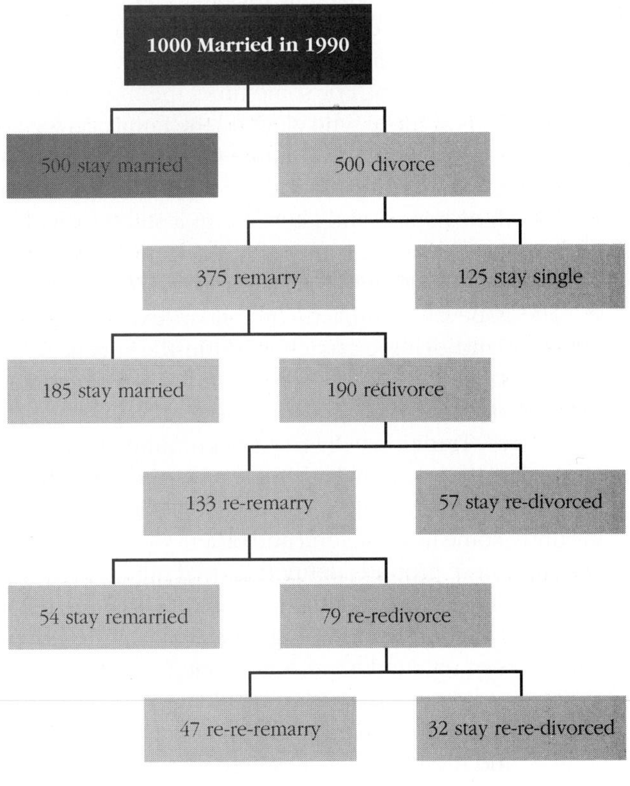

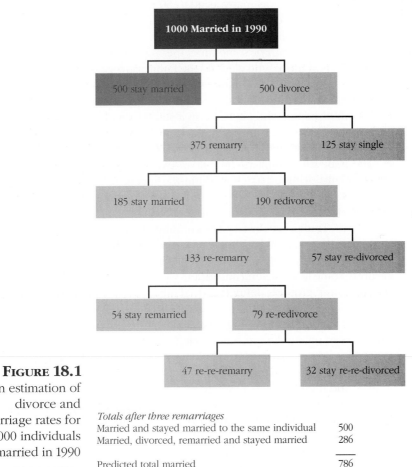

FIGURE 18.1 An estimation of divorce and remarriage rates for 1000 individuals married in 1990

Totals after three remarriages	
Married and stayed married to the same individual	500
Married, divorced, remarried and stayed married	286
Predicted total married	786

and women is about 30 years old. Most of the men remarry, fewer of the women do, especially if they have more than one child and if they are over age 30.

Figure 18.1 presents each of the divorce possibilities. As can be seen, among the divorce possibilities most people do end up marrying again. That, however, does not mean that divorce is easy for those who go through it. Sociologists have learned that women who go through a divorce experience some type of transitory poverty (Ross & Sawhill, 1978; Day & Bahr, 1980). Sociologists have also noted that, while general public attitudes toward divorce became more accepting, it is still abundantly clear that many women are severely affected economically (Weitzman, 1985).

Sociologists have tried to give us an explanation as to why the divorce rate may have shot up during the 1970s and 1980s. Among the reasons suggested for these dramatic changes are changes in social attitudes about women working outside the home, the "me-first" attitudes of the 1970s, and the decrease in divorce stigmatization (Kaslow & Schwartz, 1988).

It is estimated that as many as 40 to 50 percent of marriages performed this year will eventually end in divorce. A very high percentage of those individuals will remarry, and stay remarried (Bumpass, 1990). Even if they divorce again, many will re-remarry. For some time, the high divorce rate was used as literary ammunition for those who claimed the family, as we know it, was unravelling at the seams. Most would now agree that there has been a change in how marriage is viewed, but there has not been a substantial retreat from it. Marriage has been redefined, reshaped, and altered. But it still remains a fact that most of us marry and stay married to the same individual, and those who divorce still participate in a family.

The issue of no-fault divorce is an excellent example of how our view of marriage and divorce has changed in the recent past. Before the 1970s, when people wanted to divorce, they had to provide some type of evidence that an erring partner had wronged the marriage contract. Each state had a list of grounds for divorce. Traditional divorce laws required that the plaintiff in a divorce action show that the plaintiff had been wronged—by the partner's adultery, cruelty, felon status, or sexual impotence, for example. Each state had its own list of grounds; some listed several and others were very restrictive, listing only a few. In essence, these grounds defined marital minimums; when these minimums were not met, there was a justifiable cause for wanting to separate.

These divorce proceedings were by nature adversarial (Weitzman, 1985). Each person retained an attorney, one to prove fault, the other to defend if the fault was contested. An important element of this procedure was that the "guilty" party was punished. In most cases, the husband was found guilty of some marital "crime" and therefore was required to compensate the victim, namely the wife. He would be remanded to pay support or alimony, and many times the amount would be based not only on need but also on the severity of the crime. The underlying theme was that we should punish those who destroy the sanctity of the home. The message was also sent that women, in our society, were to be supported by men. Provisions for payment of alimony and support reflected the idea that women could and should be compensated for "domestic labor" (Weitzman, 1985).

It was believed that by eliminating the adversarial nature of this process, the rights of women would be better served, and the sting and trauma of divorce would be lessened. Starting in 1970, the states gradually accepted new divorce laws that allowed individuals to say to the judge, "We do not get along, we do not like each other. We don't want to be married any longer." The implication was that no one person had to be at fault for individuals to want a divorce. Advocates of no-fault divorce believed that these types of laws would make the divorce more fair, painless, and realistic.

Unfortunately, there were some unexpected results of that movement. Since no-fault laws do not assign guilt (*cannot* assign guilt), the penalty for such wrongs was also lifted in many cases. The end result has been economically disadvantageous for many women. While couples may now divorce more easily, with lessened conflict, women are now getting less court-awarded support as a result (Weitzman, 1985). The current law offers little recourse for those who feel they may have been wronged or treated unfairly. The divorce prerogative has moved from a state or religious issue to a more individual choice, with society as anxious onlooker. Women and children seem to be at a disadvantage in our no-fault system.

The Myth of the Romantic Divorce

Along with the trend of making divorce easier to obtain, there arose what has been called the "myth of the romantic divorce," in which divorcing couples expect the divorce to be relatively easy, liberating, and an event that creates self-discovery (Heatherington, Cox & Cox, 1977). Several popular books in the field of family relationships encouraged couples to have a "creative" divorce (Kranzler, 1975). Other advice peddlers suggested that divorce was merely a type of "rite of passage" for older adults (Sheehy, 1974). Two marriage therapists write about this idea in the following way:

> We feel depressed about divorce. We feel discouraged about the cavalier attitude that people take toward divorce. Our attitude is in part shaped by the anesthetizing effect that it has on personhood and by the impact that it has on children as they try to rationalize their parents' behavior, usually to protect the parents. It is very rare in our clinical practice to see a divorce that works. Divorces are too much like psychological amputations with all the sequelae of phantom limb pain, altered ways of functioning, changes in self-image, and the crazy sense of being a cultural object instead of a self. The reason for doing therapy with a dissolving marriage is simply to make it into an elective surgical procedure so that functioning is better post-surgically.
>
> The craziest thing about marriages is that one cannot get divorced. We just do not seem to make it out of intimate relationships. It is obviously possible to divide up the property and to decide not live together any more, but it is impossible to go back to being single. Marriage is like a stew that has irreversible and irrevocable characteristics that the parts cannot be rid of. Divorce is leaving part of the self behind, like the rabbit who escapes the trap by gnawing one leg off. (Whitaker & Keith, 1977, p. 71)

Searching for the "Causes" of Divorce

A common research strategy in the field of sociology is to search for "the causes" of divorce. Sociologists, for example, have shown that low age at marriage correlates highly with early and frequent divorce (Glenn & Supancic, 1984; Glick & Norton, 1979). Teens may have low resources, unrealistic expectations, and poorer coping skills to deal with the stress of married life.

There are several other notable correlates to the occurrence of divorce. Among them are premarital pregnancy (Bumpass & Sweet, 1972), race difference (Carter & Glick, 1976; Galligan & Bahr, 1978), and religion (Catholics have fewer divorces than Protestants) (Kitson, Babri & Roach, 1985).

When professionals have tried to find out what couples' perceptions are about why they are divorcing, they get such disparate versions from each spouse that it would appear that the individuals were talking about two different marriages (Raschke, 1987). The only common theme reported in the research is that both partners agreed that there was a "lack of communication/understanding."

Interestingly, the second most popular cause listed by men in the above study was "not sure what happened" (Kitson & Sussman, 1982). Other types of "causes" have been studied with varying results. Among them are: drinking, extramarital sex, immaturity, and "being out with the boys."

Taking an indeterministic approach, one of the most important things to discover about divorce is to identify elements of the process. In this way, families can become more sensitized and know when they are approaching situations that may lead to divorce. Also, an awareness of these issues will assist family members and community helpers to know better what to do in response to the process.

The Family Science Perspective

One of the many ways to approach the issue of divorce is to examine it from a family science perspective. The topics that follow attempt to apply principles and concepts presented in earlier chapters to the process of divorce.

Equifinality and Causes of Divorce

An important concept from the family science perspective is equifinality. As part of the previous discussion of determinism, the principle of equifinality (Chapter 2) was introduced. This principle states that a particular outcome can have many different beginnings. The divorce process is an excellent example of this idea. When looking for the "causes" of divorce, we need to remember the principle of equifinality, which suggests that there are probably as many different events leading to divorce as there are divorces. When a couple files for divorce, there will be a variety of stories and histories stated as reasons. It is often the case that the husband's "story" is quite different from that of the wife (Levinger, 1966). Therefore, it is clear that searching for the "true" story may be difficult if not impossible.

Divorce and Family Development

In Chapter 7, on family development, the idea of life-cycle patterns was discussed: The study of family development is about how general life-cycle patterns occur in family systems. When we approach divorce as a life-cycle issue, there are several important ideas to consider. One idea that has received attention in recent years is that divorce may be so prevalent that it has become a normal and expected element of the family life cycle.

Even though the divorce rates are high, it does not necessarily follow that those increases generate a "normalized" expectation. In other words, the divorce event is really quite prevalent in our society today, but it is not a necessary aspect of family development. When it does occur, those headed for estrangement usually pass through very similar developmental processes. These processes are activated by the divorce. Divorce itself, however, should probably not be viewed as a "normal" phase of family development.

However, just because divorce is not a normal element of the family life cycle does not imply that it is necessarily pathological. For many years divorce was regarded as the result of some psychological pathology of the individuals involved. This was very detrimental to those experiencing family trauma, and in addition it was an ineffective approach for those attempting to administer to families in need.

In other words, because divorce is a highly visible event does not qualify it for a place in the family life cycle along with such events as childbearing. However, once divorce does occur, there are certain aspects that remind us of the cycles or patterns found in the other family development issues.

The Stages of Divorce

Another very useful family science concept in understanding the nature of the divorce process is the idea of *stages* (or stations) *of divorce.* These ideas have been developed by researchers to help describe the divorce/remarriage process. The following is an overview of those stages and some of the issues inherent in each.

Several authors have suggested a number of stages that can be used to conceptualize divorce patterns and processes, once a family has entered into that pathway (Ahrons & Rogers, 1987; Bohannan, 1979). There are two sets of stages highlighted in the following section. One describes families passing through divorce. The other set of stages is about the effects of divorce on children.

As we consider these stages, it is important to remember two ideas. First, the very concept of stage is a difficult one at best. It is difficult to tell when one stage ends and another begins. Also, most stages are frail attempts to bring order to very complex processes. Often the suggested stages do not capture the complexity of the family system. Still, they can be used as a conceptual framework to organize what is known about the nature of divorce.

Second, one might consider the nature of each of these changes. In Chapter 9 it was suggested that life events and changes reflect levels of analysis. These levels were referred to as transformation processes, meta-processes, and family paradigms. As the person passes through the divorce process, it is probably useful to consider what level of change (see Chapter 15, on stress) that particular family system was experiencing. As each stage of this process is presented, we suggest the levels of analysis that pertain to the experienced changes.

The diagram in Figure 18.2 shows the bonds and connections in an intact family. This diagram represents a situation wherein the mother and father report that they are closely bonded and enjoy each other's company. For the sake of the example, assume their relationship is as reported and they are relatively "happy" in their family situation. Each child is loved and cared for, there is a sense of goal completion, and appropriate boundaries exist between family members and between the family and community. They meet crisis and stress with some degree of success. This means they have appropriate levels of adaptability, cohesion,

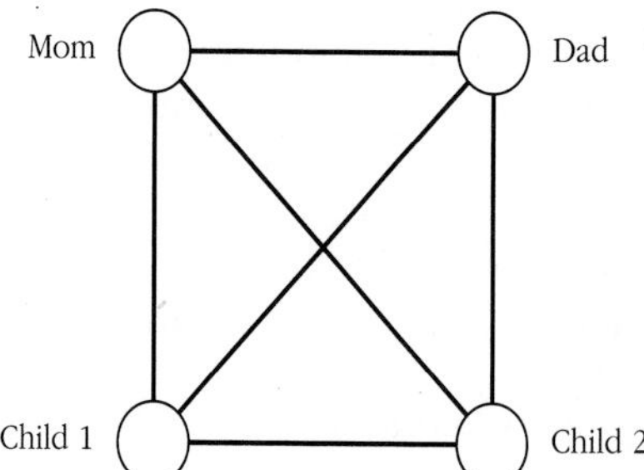

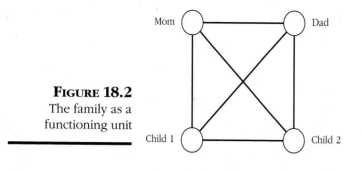

FIGURE 18.2
The family as a functioning unit

adequate resources, and probably good problem-solving ability. Such a family is assumed to be functioning, or in other words, "intact." The process of dissolution takes place when the system makes a transformation from being intact to being disengaged or dissolved.

The intact family rarely experiences paradigmatic shifts, and infrequently engages in meta-level process. For the most part, their interaction is about transformational processes. They may spend the bulk of their interactive time in repetitive sequential patterns of behavior focusing on daily routines and tasks. Occasionally, they may need to tune up those routines by switching to meta-level processes in which the routines and assignments are discussed.

The Disengaging Family

As can be seen from Figure 18.3, this stage of the divorce process represents disengagement. The characteristics of this stage are highlighted by many drastic changes in the lives of the individuals involved. For example, this may be the first time system members have admitted that the system is going to change. Ahrons refers to this as "individual and family metacognition" (Ahrons, 1980). During this time family members may, for the first time, really admit all is not well. Additionally, in the pre-separation stage there may be continuing, gradual emotional separation (Ahrons & Rogers, 1987).

Possibly family members in this stage spend much more time in the meta-processing mode. That means they may spend hours at a time asking questions like "What is it we do in our routines of life that have brought us to this point?" Or they may ask "Do I really love Alex?" This can be very devitalizing and emotionally draining. The preoccupation with meta-level analysis by family members can also mean a decreased effectiveness in getting the transformational business done. The daily routines become victim to the barrage of meta-level reflections.

The stress and dissatisfaction may become so intense at this point that family members begin to feel hopeless about getting the system to operate as it once did, or as they would like to. The following are some of the possible changes that can occur during this stage.

Emotional changes. Central to the idea of separation is the notion that somewhere along the line there is a **shift in valence**. *Valence* is a scientific term

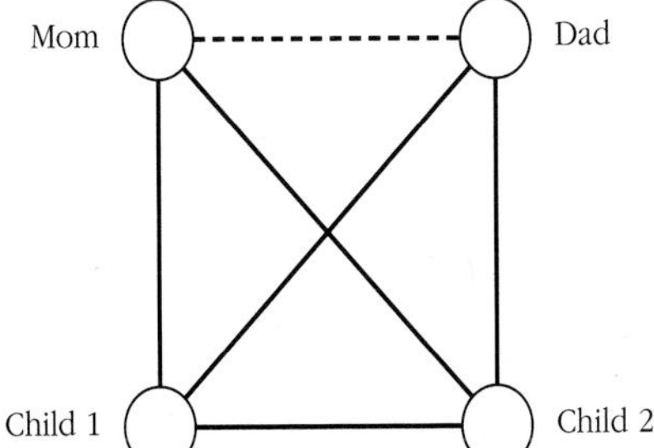

FIGURE 18.3
The family begins to disengage

which usually refers to the charge of an electron found within an atom. Within the family system we assume that, most of the time, functioning families maintain a positive valence. That is, there is a sense of closeness, bonding, and they feel attracted to each other.

There are at least two mile markers along the road to disengagement. Before the relationship begins to dissolve there is a sense of emotional closeness; the relationship is working and the partners care about one another. The first marker can be described as a sense of growing hostility and anger about mismatched expectations. The second marker could be called an emotional divorce, in which a person discovers that he or she does not care. There may be a residual of anger and hostility from feelings of betrayal, or deep sadness about the loss of a significant relationship. Many who have gone through the process report a feeling of lost emotion. This is shown in the case study of Barbara and Marvin.

The opposite of intense emotional affect, or love, is not anger, but emptiness and distance. Another word for the feelings of emotional divorce is disenchantment. Disenchantment means that there is a strong sense of loss of emotional attachment. The term *disenchantment* is very similar to the idea of emotional distance explored in Chapter 5. It is the rejection or violation of deep and meaningful emotional attachments.

Box 18.1
Disengaging

Barbara and Marvin were both very successful in their community. Marvin was a physician and Barbara operated a thriving dress shop. As the years passed, Marvin was consumed by his job. He spent an enormous amount of time keeping himself on top of its many demanding problems. He expected Barbara to entertain guests, and to be there for him when he was gone weekends and nights. She was expected to be the "model wife." At another level, Barbara perceived her husband as rejecting, cold, and insensitive to the changes that were occurring in her life. Each time there was an insensitivity, or indiscretion, Barbara would say to herself, "Oh, well. It doesn't matter." She reports arising one morning and realizing that in fact it did not matter. She would sit in the counseling session, staring blankly into space, searching for words to describe the emptiness.

There are many possible coping responses family members may have to the stress of disengagement. For example, there may be increases in pseudo-mutuality, as a type of denial and running away from the reality of the situation. Another coping strategy sometimes used is ritual maintenance. Through the maintenance of certain family rituals, an attempt can be made to show that things are not spiralling out of orbit (Ahrons & Rogers, 1987, p. 58). For example, they may hold hands and joke in public as they play the role of the happy couple. They may seek out other intimate relationships, invoking the power of emotional triangles as a way to examine their relationship with the spouse (Ahrons & Rogers, 1987).

Increases in paradigmatic intensity. As mentioned in Chapter 6, when families are under stress they attempt to exaggerate the family paradigm as a strategy to solve the problem. Families threatened with dissolution may try to intensify the strategies, patterns, and ways of solving problems they know best. If they are an open family, for example, they may try harder to be more open and sharing. It is very frustrating for the family when being more open does little to relieve the stress of impending dissolution.

Changes in boundaries. Sometimes family members respond to the disengagement process by redefining boundaries. For example, some researchers (including Ahrons & Rogers, 1987, p. 61) have suggested that in this phase a distressed partner may, for the first time, go against a family rule and confide very private marital information to a sister, mother, or friend. The husband or wife, while behaving "normally" to others, might begin preparing close friends for the changes that may be imminent.

There may also be more overt changes in family boundaries. For example, there may be changes in traditions (like not kissing before leaving home), informal rules (like not sitting next to the spouse watching TV), and routines (like ceasing regular couple activities).

Public versus private activities. As the family system begins to unravel, some boundaries may be crossed with regard to the private realm. It has been suggested that one coping strategy common in this situation is when one of the partners (or both) start making the deteriorating situation more public (Ahrons & Rogers, 1987). For example, one of the partners may be frequently seen in public places, noticeably without the spouse (Ahrons & Rogers, 1987, p. 60). This message is the beginning of the public announcement that the couple may be experimenting with relationship changes. Further, there may be a significant increase in the number of comments about partner inadequacies and other marital problems. Part of the process of disenchantment and emotional divorce is the delicate redefinition of a relationship to one's "public" world (friends, coworkers, extended family).

The period of disengagement is highlighted by a period of role readjustment for all family members. When families are functioning effectively members usually become closer through shared experiences of emotional intimacy, mutual nurturance, cooperation in goal attainment, and consensus about values and

"Well, against the odds, here we are—Fran, her ex; me, my ex, Dick, my ex's new, Phil, Fran's ex's new, Pearl, Fran's ex's ex, David, Fran's ex's ex's new—CHEERS!"

Reprinted by permission of Wm. Hamilton.

beliefs (Keshet, 1980, p. 519). The process of disengagement usually requires a major paradigmatic shift where the shared goals, feelings, and nurturance are reduced to fewer and fewer roles. The roles which remain intact to the very last are usually those associated with the tasks of parenting (Keshet, 1980, p. 519).

For some, this stage of disillusionment may mean more than just a shift to meta-level analysis. It may mean an actual paradigmatic shift, which comes about when they begin to make the process public. The message to those outside the family is that there is now a new and significantly different family systemic process under construction. The foundations of the old one have been shaken, and the new one is emerging—for better or worse.

In summary, as disenchantment increases so do hostility, anger, and distrust. Eventually one or more family members experiences a time of emotional divorce and distance. While there may be successful attempts to revitalize the system, often this does not succeed. Along the way there may be other coping strategies by the system in response to its increasing disintegration. As the distance increases, there are fewer shared thoughts, infrequent resolutions of problems, and decreased attempts to "fix" what is wrong. Many times the sense of haplessness is really a reflection of the struggle to find out what to fix.

The Family in Separation

One of the primary characteristics of this stage of the divorce process is when one of the parents actually moves out. This dramatic change in systems has many far-

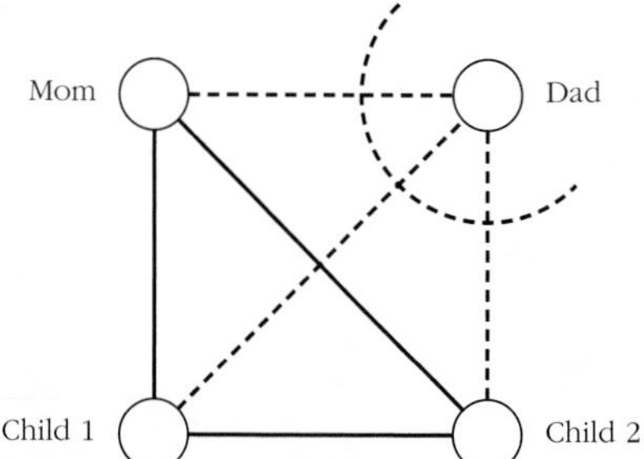

FIGURE 18.4 Separation is complete

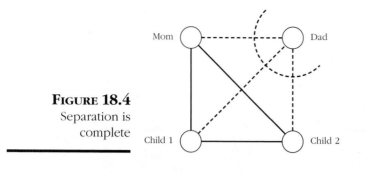

reaching effects. Among them is the time when the departing parent is characterized by the system as outside of the system.

Emotions. In Chapter 5 the emotionality principle stated that when there were intense emotions in a family system the emotions would dominate what happened in the system. A key problem for many going through the divorce process is that, while one of the partners may have experienced an emotional divorce, loss of emotion, or disenchantment, the other may not. Many times the result is increased emotional intensity. When feelings are so intense they have a way of dominating all other aspects of life. They dominate what we think and how we respond to the other roles we are trying to perform. One possible response to this increased emotion is what some authors have called a time of "freezing out" (Farber, 1964), "closing ranks" (Hill, 1949), or "closing out" (Boss, 1977). During this time some families may choose as a coping strategy to close out the departing member. Family members may believe that closing out the individual who has left will speed up the rebuilding process, but this is not necessarily so.

While most researchers suggest that healthy adjustment to divorce is associated with termination of relationships (Kressel & Deutsch, 1977), better coping is also associated with less emotional close-out of the noncustodial parent. Those who leave and are emotionally closed out may experience more depression (Grief, 1979), increased dissatisfaction with parent–child relationships (Ahrons, 1979), and increases in stress resulting from loss of the parenting/spouse role (Keshet & Rosenthat, 1978). Those who remain with the children, usually mothers, report dramatic increases in depression, probably resulting from the increased burdens of the parenting role (Brandwein, Brown & Fox, 1974). Additionally, children who lose their father out of the home and experience little contact with him are reported to have much greater developmental and emotional distress (Heatherington, 1979; Wallerstein & Kelly, 1980).

Divorce as a non-institution. In most of the major life transitions there is some type of cultural marker that tells those observing when we have passed from one stage to another. When we get married, for example, there are many well-recognized steps to follow: announcements, showers, bachelor parties, wedding ceremonies. With divorce, the absence of these institutionalized procedures makes the process much more difficult. In Chapter 7 the idea of anticipatory socialization was mentioned. This principle suggests that the ease of transition from one role to another depends in some measure on prior knowledge and what to expect during the transition and after. When the procedure is non-institutionalized, as is the case with divorce (Cherlin, 1978), it makes for awkwardness during role transition. Additionally, people go through this process with little support from friends or other family members. When this lack of support is combined with little knowledge of what to do, individuals may feel overwhelmed.

In addition to a shortage of clear transition procedures, the process also lacks necessary ritual. In Chapter 13 it was suggested that family ritual provides stability in times of stress. During divorce, neither the community nor the family involved is sure just what to do. Should they be happy that unhappy people are making a change? Or should they be sad that things could not be worked through?

Changes in rules. Chapter 8 demonstrated that simple and complex rules have the ability to regulate and define our relationships with one another. When divorce proceeds, many of those rules must be reexamined, some discarded, and many rewritten. This process alone, without all of the other problems associated with divorce, can be very debilitating.

Levels of analysis. Both Level II and Level III changes can take place during divorce. At the very least, divorcing family members experience Level II changes in their families. They must rethink the way they do the everyday routines of life and probably spend a great deal of time reflecting on what is happening to them.

For others, it is a wider and more disruptive processes. Some families experience the paradigmatic shifts of Level III. Their whole world may be dumped upside down. For example, they may have believed that their family was "forever." They may have had a paradigmatic theme that said "Our family can survive anything" or " Family loyalty is everything to us." When the decision to divorce is finally announced, it may shake the very beliefs that make up the family paradigm.

The pain of dissolution. The decision to divorce is rarely a mutual one (Kelly, 1980), which means that generally one person wants out of the relationship and the other does not. The result is that the impact of the divorce is different for those who are the "leavers" and those who are "left." Typically more women than men initiate divorce (Kelly, 1980; Kaslow & Schwartz, 1987). But more men actually leave the home than women.

In any event, most researchers and clinicians agree that the time of actual physical separation is very painful. Living alone means facing the world without a partner. For many it means starting over to search for a companion. Additionally, it means facing the unknown, which can be a frightening experience (Weiss, 1975). It also means the dismantling of that special kin world which is the source of family-based emotions, creation of children, and the perpetuation of generational ties.

The emotional climate in a family system following the loss of one of the parents can be very disruptive. Chiriboga and Cutler (1977) found that disengaged spouses needed time to "shift gears." This means that they need time to adjust to the new, and sometimes overwhelming, role of single parent. The transition from couplehood to singlehood is usually stressful and requires relearning how to cope effectively in the unmarried world. Trafford (1984) goes further and suggests that living single can be like an emotional earthquake. She describes this earthquake in the following way: "The post-separation period is similar to the pain and confusion of adolescence. . . . Separating from a spouse is analogous to leaving home" (p. 40).

There are a variety of ways family members may respond as one of the parents leave. Some may increase the intensity of household or work-related tasks. Others may spend most of their time engrossed in the replay of what went wrong; their bitterness and anger can permeate the family and is probably ineffective in helping the system to regain a functioning equilibrium. Still others may increase the level of enmeshment with children. This effort to engulf and become overly invested in the children may be a "lifeline . . . so that they won't also 'abandon' the deserted parent" (Kaslow & Schwartz, 1987, p. 59). Among the feelings reported by those who are left (as opposed to the leavers) is anger turned into energy. They may be heard to say "I'll show you, you so-and-so." Most report the feelings of being overwhelmed, and even depressed (Kaslow & Schwartz, 1987). Regardless of the response, the system is dramatically changed, and in addition, the system responds to the needs of those within by seeking some form of balance and equilibration. Probably the major task for the system is regeneration and renewal. Since a primary goal of any system is to maintain balance, disrupted systems have the enormous task of trying to recover to the point where the tasks of life can be done in a planned and orderly way.

Epigenesis principle. The epigenesis principle states that how well we do in solving the stresses and problems of earlier stages influences our ability to perform in later ones. This is particularly true of the divorce process. The level of success in making this difficult transition will depend on how well system members solved problems, made decisions, effectively communicated, and resolved crises before the divorce began to unfold. One implication of this is in regard to assessment. Those working with families who may be facing divorce could spend valuable time assessing family processes like how well the family deals with crisis, how they make decisions, the level of emotional fusion, and the amount of competitive communication. According to this principle, history is a good predictor of future performance.

The Divorce Becomes Final

The decision actually to divorce is difficult for most. A primary question many ask is "Would I (and my spouse) be happier if I were to divorce?" Interestingly, a national study revealed that divorced and separated individuals reported lower levels of life satisfaction and generally had a more negative attitude about life

Even older children can be deeply affected by divorce.

than either married or never-married women (Campbell, Converse & Rogers, 1976). Divorced persons also report poorer health (Lynch, 1977) and more depression (Vega, Warheit & Meinhardt, 1984). The great dilemma for the individual is in choosing among undesirable options: staying married to someone for whom there is little affection, versus divorcing and facing the world alone.

In any event, there are many consequences for the family, but among the most dramatic are the effects on the children.

Children's Responses to Divorce

The effects of divorce on children has been of major concern to social scientists for several decades (Coddington, 1973; Fine, Moreland & Schwebel, 1983; Goode,

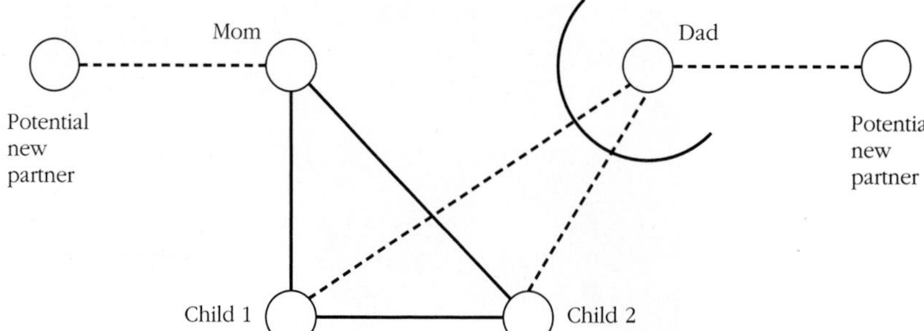

FIGURE 18.5 The divorce is finalized

1956; Kalter & Rembar, 1981; Lamb, 1977; Wallerstein & Kelly, 1980). Overall, divorce has its greatest impact on children when their "families contained a distant, uninvolved, unsupportive, or angry noncustodial father and/or a chronically embittered, angry, vengeful custodial mother" (Jacobs, 1982, p. 1235).

There are several tasks children must attend to as they pass through the pain of divorce (Wallerstein, 1983). The first is acknowledgment. Children (especially younger children, not infants) need to accept the reality of the situation. This may be very difficult for them, since many children fear they will either lose the remaining parent, or that they themselves will have to leave.

Task number two is really a parental responsibility. Children must not become part of hostility being expressed by the parents. They must be allowed to function independently of the battle within the parental subsystem. Adequate resolution of this task means that the child does not become or remain triangulated (Bowen, 1978).

A triangulated child may become the "football" in the parents' contest. On the other hand, older children may see themselves as needing to promote change in the relationship between the two parents. Remember that the third person in an emotional triangle generally cannot bring about change in the relationship of the other two. In fact, attempts to change the relationship by a child may have the opposite of the desired effect. The child may feel increased guilt and hostility toward both parents when that happens. Also recall that if the third person in an emotional triangle is unsuccessful in change attempts, the stress of the situation may fall squarely on the third person. That would be not only unfortunate for the child but also extremely disruptive, and could affect psychological well-being.

The third task involves the resolution and alteration of family traditions. This process should take at least one full year (including birthdays, holidays, vacation time, and school time). There are so many traditions and family rules that have to be renegotiated for the remaining family members that this process is probably one of the more difficult and time-consuming of all.

A fourth task children must face is the resolution of anger and self-blame. Often school-age children will carry ideas that if they had been more obedient, more helpful, not such a bother, then the family would not have dissolved. According to Wallerstein, "divorce gives rise to anger at the parent who sought the divorce or both parents for their perceived self-centeredness or unresponsiveness to the wishes of the child to maintain the intact family" (Wallerstein, 1983, p. 239).

The fifth task of the child is to accept the permanence of divorce. This tends to be easier for younger children. Older children may suffer from "Let's Get Together" syndrome. In the early 1960s there was a very popular Walt Disney movie called *The Parent Trap*. In this movie, twin sisters meet each other for the first time at a summer camp, and realize they are sisters. The plot unfolds as they act out a common childhood fantasy, that they can scheme and manipulate the situation, sabotage the father's upcoming marriage to an "evil" stepmother, and get the original mother and father back together. Of course the plan works in the movie, but rarely in real life.

Wallerstein has suggested that young adults who have been through a divorce in their family of origin may also experience a sense of dread about future relationships. The pain of family dissolution, particularly when the above task remains unresolved, may constrain a person's willingness to risk a potentially serious relationship.

As the custodial parent struggles with the weight of being alone it is common for her or him to look for those who can help with the burden. One of the resources individuals turn to is their children. For better or worse, custodial parents may find themselves asking a child for advice, help with child care, help with daily decisions, and even using a child as a "dumping ground" for the feelings and thoughts both about everyday life crises and those brought on by the divorce. The child may take on the role of "fill-in parent." This role may even be formalized by the exiting parent, who says "Now son, while I'm gone you are the man around here." As Minuchin (1974) notes, clear boundaries between the emerging new subsystem elements is critical for a functional transition. Paradoxically, the clarification of the new boundaries may actually be a source of stress (Ahrons & Rogers, 1987). In theory, when a marriage is intact, there is an executive subsystem that has at least two primary jobs when children are present. The first is to be spouse and companion to the other person in the executive subsystem. The second is to extend that energy to children. When the executive subsystem is disintegrating, the boundaries and duties associated with that subsystem can become very confused. One primary task, therefore, during the living-alone phase is the redefinition of those boundaries. One measure of success in this process is those parents who are able to unravel this intricate tapestry, maintain a viable relationship with the children, and yet realign the spousal element of the subsystem.

There is little research to tell us the outcome of a parent's recruiting a child into the vacancy left by the absent parent. It may be expedient and convenient, but in the extreme can lead to problems. One of the most obvious problems crops up when a remarriage occurs and the child is demoted from executive subsystem back to "buck private." By that reasoning, it would seem wise for parents to try to avoid any formalized or extensive transfer of power to the child.

Another issue that arises in generational alliances is inappropriate disclosure. If the parent chooses to bring a child into the executive subsystem during this stressful time, what is disclosed to the child may inadvertently be unfair or burdensome. The child may feel over-responsible, overburdened, and overwhelmed with adult-level problems and little experience to know how to help.

Summary

The divorce process is difficult for most families. For some it is a shift in their entire worldview and way of life. For others it is less dramatic, but few escape without the process having a long-lasting and significant impact. Divorce has changed from a state- and religion-controlled event to one of personal choice. This has been formalized by wide acceptance of no-fault divorce laws. As a family goes through divorce they experience several important stages of dissolution. In each stage they must redefine and re-examine the boundaries, rules, and processes of interaction of each family member. The greatest problems of divorce come when children are involved. Separation and disillusionment have long-lasting effects for many. While divorce is no longer considered to be a sign of mental illness or personal dysfunction, it still is a traumatic and discouraging process for most.

Key Terms

No-fault divorce
Divorce rates
Myth of the romantic divorce
Causes of divorce
Equifinality
Stages of divorce
The disengaging family
Valence shift
Disenchantment
Paradigmatic intensity
Boundary change
Emotional divorce
Non-institution of divorce
Epigenesis and divorce
Children and divorce

Study Questions

1. How has the nature of divorce (how it is done, or if it can be done) changed historically?
2. Why is it so difficult to identify the "causes" of divorce? List as many reasons as you can that you have heard from other people. How do those reasons fit with the explanations given in the text?

3. What is meant by a "change in 'valence" in a relationship?
4. Describe, as best you can, what it would mean to a person to be emotionally divorced, or to experience emotional close-out.
5. In a short essay, make the case that divorce is traumatic for children.

Alternative Family Forms

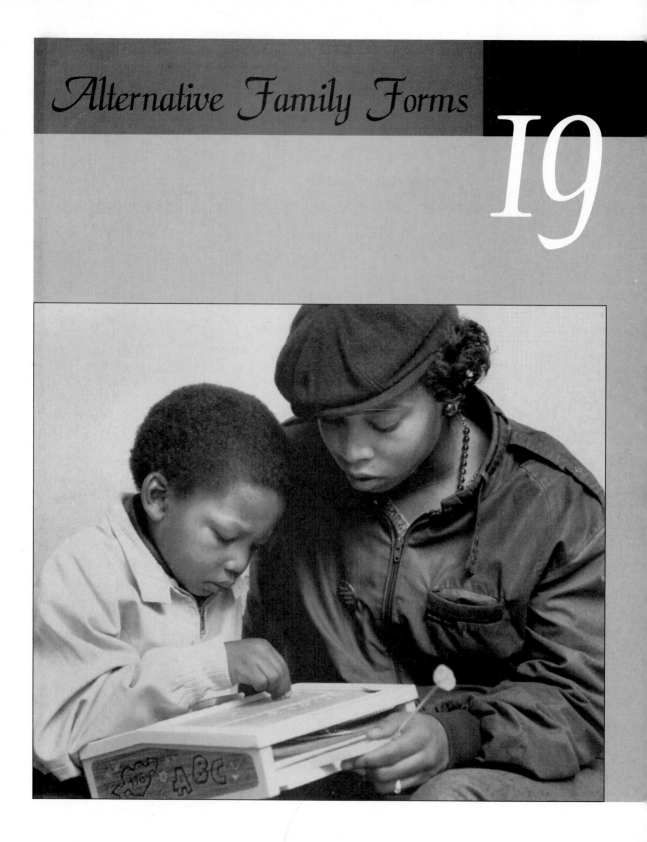

19